CONSTRUCTION CHANGE ORDER CLAIMS

Second Edition

Michael T. Callahan

Editor

Published by Wolters Kluwer in New York.

Wolters Kluwer serves customers worldwide with CCH, Aspen Publishers and Kluwer Law International products.

Printed in the United States of America

8 9 0

Library of Congress Cataloging-in-Publication Data

Construction change order claims/Michael T. Callahan.—2nd ed.
     p. cm.
   Includes index.
   ISBN 978-0-7355-5237-1
1. Construction contracts—United States. 2. Construction industry—Law and legislation—United States. 3. Liability (Law)—United States. I. Callahan, Michael T.

   KF902.C5929 2005
   343.73'078624—dc22

                                                                              2005022405

About Wolters Kluwer Law & Business

Wolters Kluwer Law & Business is a leading global provider of intelligent information and digital solutions for legal and business professionals in key specialty areas, and respected educational resources for professors and law students. Wolters Kluwer Law & Business connects legal and business professionals as well as those in the education market with timely, specialized authoritative content and information-enabled solutions to support success through productivity, accuracy and mobility.

Serving customers worldwide, Wolters Kluwer Law & Business products include those under the Aspen Publishers, CCH, Kluwer Law International, Loislaw, ftwilliam.com and MediRegs family of products.

CCH products have been a trusted resource since 1913, and are highly regarded resources for legal, securities, antitrust and trade regulation, government contracting, banking, pension, payroll, employment and labor, and healthcare reimbursement and compliance professionals.

Aspen Publishers products provide essential information to attorneys, business professionals and law students. Written by preeminent authorities, the product line offers analytical and practical information in a range of specialty practice areas from securities law and intellectual property to mergers and acquisitions and pension/benefits. Aspen's trusted legal education resources provide professors and students with high-quality, up-to-date and effective resources for successful instruction and study in all areas of the law.

Kluwer Law International products provide the global business community with reliable international legal information in English. Legal practitioners, corporate counsel and business executives around the world rely on Kluwer Law journals, looseleafs, books, and electronic products for comprehensive information in many areas of international legal practice.

Loislaw is a comprehensive online legal research product providing legal content to law firm practitioners of various specializations. Loislaw provides attorneys with the ability to quickly and efficiently find the necessary legal information they need, when and where they need it, by facilitating access to primary law as well as state-specific law, records, forms and treatises.

ftwilliam.com offers employee benefits professionals the highest quality plan documents (retirement, welfare and non-qualified) and government forms (5500/PBGC, 1099 and IRS) software at highly competitive prices.

MediRegs products provide integrated health care compliance content and software solutions for professionals in healthcare, higher education and life sciences, including professionals in accounting, law and consulting.

Wolters Kluwer Law & Business, a division of Wolters Kluwer, is headquartered in New York. Wolters Kluwer is a market-leading global information services company focused on professionals.

WOLTERS KLUWER SUPPLEMENT NOTICE

This product is updated on a periodic basis with supplements and/or new editions to reflect important changes in the subject matter.

If you would like information about enrolling this product in the update service, or wish to receive updates billed separately with a 30-day examination review, please contact our Customer Service Department at 1-800-234-1660 or email us at: *customer.service@wolterskluwer.com*. You can also contact us at:

Wolters Kluwer
Distribution Center
7201 McKinney Circle
Frederick, MD 21704

Important Contact Information

- To order any title, go to *www.wklawbusiness.com* or call 1-800-638-8437.

- To reinstate your manual update service, call 1-800-638-8437.

- To contact Customer Service, e-mail *customer.service@wolterskluwer.com*, call 1-800-234-1660, fax 1-800-901-9075, or mail correspondence to: Order Department—Wolters Kluwer, PO Box 990, Frederick, MD 21705.

- To review your account history or pay an invoice online, visit *www.aspenpublishers.com/payinvoices*.

ABOUT THE EDITOR

Michael T. Callahan is president of CCL Construction Consultants, Inc. He maintains an active consulting practice in the measurement and responsibility of delay, along with the quantification of additional performance costs and other construction- and design-related matters. He earned a B.A. from the University of Kansas and both a J.D. and L.L.M. from the University of Missouri-Kansas City. Mr. Callahan is the author of *Procurement of Construction and Design Contracts* (Aspen Publishers 2005) and co-author of other Aspen publications *Construction Delay Claims* and *Construction Defect Claims and Litigation*; is the author of other books for other publishers; and writes and publishes a monthly newsletter summarizing current design and construction literature, *CCL Summaries*. He was an adjunct professor at the University of Kansas and has lectured throughout the United States, Europe, the Middle East, and Far East on design- and construction-related topics. He is a member of the Kansas, New Jersey, and Missouri bars by examination. Mr. Callahan is also a frequent arbitrator, negotiator, and mediator, and is a regional advisor to the American Arbitration Association. Author queries are invited at CCL's Web site, *cclcon.com*.

ABOUT THE CONTRIBUTORS

Jason B. Adkisson is an associate in the Construction Law & Public Contracts Group of Kilpatrick Stockton, LLP. Mr. Adkisson attended Purdue University and graduated with a B.A. in political science in 1997. He earned his J.D. from Tulane University School of Law in 2000. While in law school, he was a Notes and Comments Editor for the *Tulane Maritime Law Journal*. Mr. Adkisson is admitted to both the State Bar of Georgia and the U.S. Court of Federal Claims.

Jon T. Anderson is a partner with Thelen Reid & Priest, LLP, San Francisco, California. Mr. Anderson's professional experience includes prosecution and defense of claims arising out of and relating to design-construction projects and federal and state government contracts, including development and analysis and litigation, arbitration, mediation, and negotiation of claims on behalf of contractors, consultants, and owners. He is a graduate of Harvard Law School and is a member of the American Law Institute and ABA Forum Committee on Construction Law. He is admitted to practice in California and before the U.S. Claims Court and Court of Appeal for the Federal Circuit.

Peter V. Badala is a Vice President with the San Francisco, California, office of The Barrington Consulting Group, Inc. Mr. Badala frequently advises companies and counsel on the accounting, financial, and economic aspects of commercial construction and public contract disputes. This consultation has included the review and evaluation of costs associated with labor and material cost escalation, labor productivity, extended field and home office overhead and interest costs arising from formal and constructive changes, differing site conditions, delay, suspension, constructive acceleration, and other issues. Mr. Badala graduated from Georgetown University in Washington, D.C., with a B.S. in business administration with an emphasis in accounting.

Christopher B. Butler is an associate with Oles, Morrison, Rinker & Baker and a member of the firm's Construction and public Contract Law practice group. His practice focuses on complex litigation. He has also advised clients on copyright and trademark matters. Chris graduated *cum laude* from Seattle University School of Law in 1997 and received his bachelor's degree in French Language in 1991 from Saint John's University in Minnesota. He is a member of the Washington State and American Bar Associations and is admitted to practice in the Western District of Washington.

Randall L. Erickson is a partner in the Orange County, California, office of Crowell & Moring LLP. He has over 30 years' experience in the construction industry, specializing in construction claims and construction defect disputes, public contracts and bid disputes, labor law issues, real estate development, and related environment concerns. He has served as an arbitrator, mediator, and expert witness, and is on the Large and Complex Case panel at the American Arbitration Association. Mr. Erickson is a graduate of the University of Wisconsin at Madison, and Duke University School of Law, where he served as research editor of the *Duke Law Journal*. He served as law clerk to The Honorable O.D. Hamlin on the United States Court of Appeal, Ninth Circuit. Mr. Erickson was the 1995 Chairman of Legal Advisory Committee for the Associated General Contractors (AGC) of California, and a member of the Legislative Committee of the AGC, former Vice-Chairman of the Construction Claims Division of the Public Contract Law Section of the American Bar Association. He has lectured and written numerous articles on construction claims contracting and related environmental remediation issues.

James L. Ferro is a partner in the law firm of Gibbs, Giden, Locher & Turner LLP in Los Angeles, California. He specializes in construction law and practices in the representation of owners, contractors, subcontractors, and design professionals in construction industry matters and disputes. He obtained his B.S. in business administration at California State University, Northridge, and his J.D. from Loyola Law School, Los Angeles, California. Mr. Ferro is a member of the Public Contract Law and Litigation Sections, and the Forum Committee on the Construction Industry of the American Bar Association. He has conducted various seminars for construction trade groups and professional associations and is a co-author of the first edition of this book.

Scott Robert Fradin is a partner with the Chicago firm of Stein, Ray & Harris LLP. His practice focuses on all aspects of the construction process. Mr. Fradin is extensively involved in the drafting and negotiating of contracts for architects, engineers, and general contractors on both national and international projects. Mr. Fradin has extensive experience before federal and state courts and the American Arbitration Association, as well as other alternative dispute resolution forums. Mr. Fradin has spoken before design professional organizations regarding various construction law topics and has been involved in lobbying efforts concerning the use of the design-build delivery system by public entities in Illinois. Mr. Fradin has also lectured on construction law at Chicago-Kent College of Law—IIT. Mr. Fradin received his J.D. from Chicago-Kent College of Law—IIT in 1996 where he graduated Order of the Coif, with high honors, and was a Member and Senior Associate of the Chicago-Kent Law Review. He received his B.S in architectural studies in 1986 and his master's degree in architecture in 1988 from the University of Illinois. Mr. Fradin is a member of the Chicago and American Bar Associations. He is admitted to practice in Illinois and the U.S. District Court for the Northern District of Illinois. Mr. Fradin has been a licensed architect in Illinois since 1990 and is an active member of the American Institute of Architects.

Kenneth C. Gibbs is a senior partner of Gibbs, Giden, Locher & Turner LLP, a firm practicing exclusively in the representation of owners, contractors, subcontractors, material suppliers, and design professionals in construction industry matters and disputes. Mr. Gibbs has written many books and articles on construction industry-related topics, including "California Construction Law," now in its 16th edition. He has also conducted many seminars for construction trade groups and professional associations nationwide and has been a principal speaker on several occasions at the Construction Law SuperConference. Mr. Gibbs is a member of the Public Contract Law Section and the Forum Committee on the Construction Industry of the American Bar Association. He is also a member of the Large and Complex Case Panel of the American Arbitration Association and an arbitrator on the State of California Public Works Arbitration Panel. Mr. Gibbs often serves as mediator of construction industry disputes in both the public and private sectors and has mediated more than 500 construction matters.

Christopher D. Hawkins is an officer of Nelson, Kinder, Mosseau & Saturley, PC. He is a member of the firm's Construction Industry Practice Group. Mr. Hawkins has represented contractors and subcontractors in a variety of construction claims matters before arbitration panels and state and federal courts. Prior to joining NKMS, Mr. Hawkins practiced business litigation and criminal defense. Mr. Hawkins earned his B.A. from Middlebury College and his J.D. from the University of Connecticut School of Law.

Andrea A. Hight graduated from Texas A&M University *magna cum laude* in 2001 and went on to the Baylor School of Law where she received her J.D. in 2004. Upon graduation from Baylor, Andrea joined the firm of Canterbury, Stuber, Elder, Gooch and Surratt, P.C. in Dallas, Texas. Andrea is a member of the Dallas Young Lawyers Association and the Construction Law Section of the Dallas Bar.

Nicholas K. Holmes is an officer in the law firm of Nelson, Kinder, Mosseau & Saturley, PC, located in Boston, Massachusetts, and Manchester, New Hampshire. He is a member of the firm's Construction Industry Practice Group. His practice is devoted primarily to construction litigation, representing owners, architects, engineers, and contractors before arbitration panels, and in state and federal courts throughout the United States. Mr. Holmes received a B.A. in history from Cornell University, and a J.D. from the University of Wisconsin.

Edward B. Keidan is a partner at Conway & Mrowiec, specializing in construction law. Mr. Keidan has represented prime contractors, design/builders, owners, architects, and trade contractors in payment disputes, delay damages claims, defective work claim's and many other disputes. Mr. Keidan has addressed construction industry seminars on new developments in construction law, scheduling issues, design/build issues, contractual language, quantification of delay, mechanic's lien and payment bond claims, and public contracting issues. He is a member of the Illinois bar, and is licensed to practice before the Northern District of Illinois (including admission to the Trial Bar), the Seventh Circuit Court of Appeals, and the Northern District of Indiana, and has appeared pro hac vice in other jurisdictions. He received his B.A. (*with distinction*) and his J.D. (*cum laude*) from the University of Michigan.

Kimberly Brant King has practiced with the Kansas City, Misouri, law firm Lathrop & Gage L.C. since 2001. Ms. King's litigation practice primarily involves the representation of architects, engineers, property owners, and contractors in resolving complex multi-party construction disputes. Prior to joining the firm in 2001, Ms. King practiced in Northern California where she handled a variety of civil litigation matters, including asbestos, real estate, construction, personal injury, wrongful death, and products liability. She received her B.A. from Rockhurst University, and her J.D. from Santa Clara University School of Law.

Val S. McWhorter is a founding partner at the law firm of Smith, Pachter, McWhorter & Allen, where he has focused his practice in the area of construction law for 30 years. He holds a J.D. from Washington & Lee University. His practice has included representing contractors in large, complex claims arising under federal, state, and local government contracts, as well as contracts between private parties. Mr. McWhorter has engaged in substantial litigation before various federal Boards of Contract Appeals, federal courts, and state courts. He has also served as an advocate in the mediation of construction contract disputes before numerous mediators involving a wide variety of projects. Mr. McWhorter's success in resolving construction contract disputes earned him a nomination as *Construction Man of the Year* with *Engineering News Record* in 1991. He is a frequent speaker at the National Construction SuperConference, and Industry and Bar Association meetings.

John S. Mrowiec is a founding partner in the firm of Conway & Mrowiec concentrating on construction and public contracts law. Mr. Mrowiec represents project participants in arbitration, litigation, mediation, contract drafting, and claim preparation. He has tried, arbitrated, or mediated several complex cases throughout the United States. Mr. Mrowiec also represents contractors in bid protests on public projects and in bankruptcies of subcontractors and owners. He prosecutes and defends mechanic's liens and bond claims and assists project management. Mr. Mrowiec is a faculty member at DePaul University's Real Estate Center, Construction

Management Certificate Program, the law columnist for the McGraw-Hill monthly *Midwest Construction*, and a frequent contributor to several publications on construction law. In 2002, Mr. Mrowiec was selected by his peers as one of the top 1 percent of lawyers in Illinois in conjunction with Leading Lawyers Network and is listed by them as one of the top construction lawyers in Illinois.

James F. Nagle is a partner with Oles, Morrison, Rinker & Baker and a member of the firm's Construction and Public Contract Law practice group. His practice focuses on government contracts and construction law. Jim's extensive experience includes work with supply, services, international, major systems, and construction contracts. He has represented owners, contractors, subcontractors, sureties, architects, engineers, and all parties in the contracting process. His reputation is such that both the government and contractors have used him as a consultant, expert witness, or arbitrator/mediator. In addition to his client work, Jim has written numerous books and articles on federal contracting, and is a frequent lecturer on government procurement. Jim received his law degree from Rutgers University in 1973 and an LLM and SJD in government contracts from the National Law Center at George Washington University in 1986. He also holds a bachelor's degree from the Georgetown University School of Foreign Service. Jim is a member of the Washington State, District of Columbia, and American Bar Associations. He is also the past president of the Boards of Contract Appeals Bar Association and former director of publications for professional associations.

Ryan D. O'Dell is an attorney with Lathrop & Gage L.C. in Kansas City, Missouri. He is an honors graduate of the University of Arizona and the University of Missouri–Columbia School of Law, where he served as Editor and Chief of the Journal of Dispute Resolution. His experience includes all phases of state and federal litigation and alternative dispute resolution. His litigation practice emphasizes public and private construction matters in which he represents architects, engineers, owners, contractors, and municipalities in resolving complex, multi-party construction disputes.

Michael L. Orndahl is currently the Assistant General Counsel with MYR Group Inc., a holding company of specialty electrical contractors, including The L.E. Myers Co., Sturgeon Electric Company, Inc., Harlan Electric Company, Hawkeye Construction, Inc., and Great Southwestern Construction, Inc. These companies operate 35 offices across the United States. In addition to his corporate duties, he is responsible for construction claims management, contract preparation and negotiation, risk management, and claims avoidance. Previously, Mr. Orndahl practiced construction law with the firm of Militello, Zanck & Coen in Crystal Lake, Illinois, where his practice was focused on construction law, including construction litigation, construction arbitration, contract preparation and negotiation, and mechanics' lien litigation. His clients included owners, general contractors, subcontractors, and lenders. He is a graduate of Loyola University School of Law and a member of the American Bar Association (Forum on the Construction Industry), the American Corporate Counsel Association, the American Subcontractor's Association, and is a Certified McHenry County Arbitrator for Court Mandated Arbitrations.

Hugh E. Reynolds, Jr., is a senior attorney at Locke Reynolds LLP in Indianapolis, Indiana. He received a B.S. from the University of Notre Dame and a J.D. from the University of Michigan Law School. He is a past Chair of the Tort and Insurance Practice Section of the American Bar Association, a member of its Council and one of its delegates to the ABA House of Delegates, and a past Chair of its Fidelity and Surety Law and Appellate Advocacy Committees. He was on the Governing Committee of the Forum on the Construction Industry of the American Bar Association (1984-90), was the Chair for one year and editor of the *Construction Lawyer* for two years. Mr. Reynolds is a past president of the Federation of Insurance & Corporate Counsel, a past member of the Board of Directors of the Defense Research Institute, a founding Fellow of the American College of Construction Lawyers, and a member of the American College of Trial Lawyers. He is a member of the American Law Institute and was an advisor to the committee that revised the Restatement of the Law of Suretyship. Mr. Reynolds was also the ABA advisor to the Commissioners on Uniform Laws, revising the Uniform Statutory Construction Act, and to the Drafting Committee that provided a Model Act on Punitive Damages. Mr. Reynolds is certified by the National Board of Trial Advocacy.

Joel J. Rhiner is a partner in the law firm of Stein, Ray & Harris LLP, where he practices primarily in the area of construction law. After graduating *summa cum laude* from the University of Iowa in 1987, Mr. Rhiner received his law degree in 1990 from the University of California in Los Angeles, where he served as editor of the UCLA Law Review. He is a member of the Federal Trial Bar, Illinois and Iowa Bars, and American Bar Association (Forum on the Construction Industry of the American Bar Association). He is a lecturer of Construction Law at the IIT Chicago-Kent College of Law and has addressed a number of different contractors, and subcontractors concerning construction law and litigation issues. He has also made several contributions to construction law literature. Mr. Rhiner has successfully tried or arbitrated over a dozen claims on behalf of engineers, architects, contractors, and subcontractors involving a variety of projects, including highways and roadways, electical power plants, wastewater treatment facilities, commercial buildings, and commercial rail.

Richard D. Rhyne is a member in the Construction Law Group of Lathrop & Gage, L.C. Mr. Rhyne has over 30 years of experience in successfully representing construction contractors, owners, insurance and surety bond companies, and other corporate clients in multi-million dollar construction cases, as well as in general litigation and commercial law matters. Mr. Rhyne has also participated in over 100 arbitrations as either counsel or arbitrator, including several international disputes. Mr. Rhyne earned a B.S. in business administration from the University of Missouri in 1969 and a J.D. with Distinction in 1974 at the University of Missouri, Kansas City. He is a member of a number of professional organizations, including the ABA Forum on the Construction Industry and the Construction Law Committee of the Missouri Bar and is a Past Chair of the KCMBA Construction Law Committee. Mr. Rhyne is admitted to practice in the State of Missouri, in the United States District Courts for the Western and Eastern District of Missouri, the United States District Court of Kansas, and the United States Court of Appeals for the Eighth and Tenth Circuits.

G. Steven Ruprecht is a shareholder in Brown & Dunn, P.C. in Kansas City, Missouri. He graduated from the University of Missouri, Columbia, in 1970 with a B.S. in geology and from the University of Missouri, Kansas City School of Law in 1973. Mr. Ruprecht is a member of the ABA Fidelity & Surety Committee, where he served as a Vice-Chair from 1989 through 1994; the ABA Forum Committee on the Construction Industry; and the International Association of Defense Counsel Fidelity & Surety Committee, where he served as a Vice-Chair for a number of years and Chairman in 1988. Mr. Ruprecht has authored numerous articles for the fidelity, surety, and construction industry and has served as a speaker for numerous Continuing Legal Education programs for the American Bar Association, the International Association of Defense Counsel, Missouri Bar Association, the National Business Institute, Lorman Seminars, and Seminars International.

Mark O. Simundson is a Contracts Administration Manager with The Bechtel Group Inc. in San Francisco, California. Mr. Simundson has extensive experience in all aspects of the preparation and defense of claims involving domestic and international construction and insurance disputes. He works on both government contract and commercial matters specializing in the measurement of lost productivity due to delays or disruptions. Prior to joining Bechtel, Mr. Simundson worked for a national public accounting firm and private consulting firm representing both owners and contractors on construction matters. Mr. Simundson is a graduate of Augustana College with a B.A. in accounting and business administration.

Mark A. Smith is National Director of Ernst & Young's Construction Consulting and Litigation Services in San Francisco, California. He assists in overseeing and coordinating the professional services that the firm provides to over 1,000 construction clients. In addition, he is called upon to provide expert testimony on a variety of complex claims and litigation cases. Mr. Smith received his B.S. and M.S. in civil engineering from Oklahoma State University and a Ph.D. in civil engineering, with specialization in construction engineering and project management, from the University of Texas at Austin. He is also a licensed professional engineer. Prior to joining Ernst & Young, Mr. Smith served on the Graduate Engineering Faculty of the University of Maryland, where he established an academic program in Construction Engineering and Project Management.

David G. Surratt is a partner in the Dallas law firm of Canterbury, Stuber, Elder, Gooch & Surratt, P.C., practicing primarily in construction law and mechanic's liens, including litigation and arbitration of construction disputes. Mr. Surratt is a member of the Dallas and American Bar (Forum on the Construction Industry, Litigation Section) Associations, and the State Bar of Texas (District 6-A Grievance Committee). He is a frequent speaker on construction and lien laws to professionals and trade associations, including the Associated General Contractors of America and the Construction Law Section of the Dallas Bar Association.

Neal J. Sweeney is a partner in the Construction and Public Contracts Group of Kilpatrick Stockton, LLP. For over 20 years, he has practiced exclusively in the area of construction law and public contracts, with further concentration in large public works projects. He has extensive experience in various forms of construction Alternative Dispute Resolution techniques, including dispute review boards, mediation, and structured negotiation. Much of Mr. Sweeney's work has involved wastewater treatment facilities and conveyance systems. Mr. Sweeney has written extensively on construction law, government contracts, and related topics. He has contributed as a co-author to numerous books, including the Aspen publications *Design-Build Contracting Handbook* (2d ed. 2001) and *Proving and Pricing Construction Claims* (2d ed. 1996). Mr. Sweeney has also edited 13 books on construction law, including *Common Sense Contracting* (Wiley 1997) and the annual *Construction Law Update* (Aspen) since 1992. He also regularly contributes articles to periodicals including *Development, Constructor, the ASCE Management Journal,* and *Water Environment and Technology* magazines. Mr. Sweeney is a regular lecturer on construction law for a variety of trade and bar organizations and educational institutions, including Water Environment Federation, the Design-Build Institute of America, American Society of Professional Engineers, Risk and Insurance Management Society, Stanford University, and Georgia Tech. Mr. Sweeney graduated from Rutgers University, with high honors 1979, Rutgers Scholar and received his J.D. from George Washington University, with honors, 1982.

Robert B. Thum is a partner with Thelen Reid & Priest, LLP. He has specialized in engineering and construction law since 1974, providing contract advice and dispute resolution services for owners (public and private), engineers, general contractors, and major trade subcontractors.

He has litigated and arbitrated a wide variety of cases involving major infrastructure projects, as well as refineries, industrial plants, hospitals, schools, and high-rise buildings. Mr. Thum serves as Construction Arbitrator on the State of California's Public Works Arbitration Program and is a member of the American Arbitration Association's National Panel of Construction Arbitrators. For over 20 years he has participated in Alternative Dispute Resolution of engineering and construction disputes, and has mediated many cases to settlement. Mr. Thum has been published widely on construction law topics and has been invited to speak to numerous industry groups throughout the nation on subjects related to construction law and ADR.

Sarah-Nell H. Walsh is an associate in the Construction Law & Public Contracts Group of Kilpatrick Stockton, LLP. Her practice is primarily devoted to the representation of clients in the construction field, including owners, contractors, sureties, and subcontractors. Ms. Walsh graduated from the University of Virginia in 2001 with her B.A. in religious studies and earned her J.D. from William & Mary School of Law in 2004.

SUMMARY OF CONTENTS

CONTENTS

Chapter 6
CONTRACTOR CERTIFICATIONS AND FALSE CLAIMS   141

G. Steven Ruprecht

Chapter 7
CHANGES RESULTING FROM BREACH OF IMPLIED
WARRANTIES, MISREPRESENTATION, AND
NONDISCLOSURE OF SUPERIOR KNOWLEDGE

167

Nicholas K. Holmes
Christopher D. Hawkins

Chapter 8
CHANGES RESULTING FROM AMBIGUOUS
SPECIFICATIONS   205

Randall L. Erickson

Chapter 9
CHANGES THAT RESULT FROM DELAYS AND
INTERFERENCES   225

John S. Mrowiec
Edward B. Keidan

Chapter 10
CHANGES RESULTING FROM IMPOSSIBILITY OR
IMPRACTICABILITY OF PERFORMANCE   255

Jon T. Anderson

Chapter 11
THE CARDINAL CHANGE   285

Kenneth C. Gibbs
James L. Ferro

Chapter 15
PREPARING AND DEFENDING A CLAIM FOR DAMAGES: A PRACTICAL GUIDE   435

David G. Surratt
Andrea A. Hight

Chapter 16
SURETY ISSUES PERTAINING TO CHANGES 479

Hugh E. Reynolds, Jr.

Chapter 17
ACCOUNTING FOR CHANGE ORDERS: HOW AND WHEN TO RECOGNIZE REVENUE FROM CHANGE ORDERS 501

Peter V. Badala
Mark O. Simundson

Chapter 18
PROVING AND PRICING DAMAGES   521

Val S. McWhorter
Mark A. Smith

PREFACE

When I began supplementing the First Edition in 1996, I learned quickly that there was always more new case law and industry comment than space in one annual supplement. Changes and change orders, along with the mysteries of constructive changes, pre-existing duties, and authority, remained firmly at the head of the list as reasons for construction and design disputes. New case law concerning changes and change orders came from our judicial systems every month; and the facts necessary to understand to apply that case law were many and complex. I am honored to prepare the second edition that includes such challenges.

Just as *Construction Change Order Claims* focuses on changes, there have been many changes for the Second Edition. Principal among them are the three new chapters that have been added:

- Chapter 5, "Challenging the Finality of an Executed Change Order," is a logical expansion to the breadth of the book. The new authors Joel Rhiner and Scott Fradin close the circle with an important part missing from the first edition.

- Chapter 6, "Contractor Certifications and False Claims," was written by G. Steven Ruprecht from Brown & Dunn in Kansas City. When the First Edition was printed, the construction and design industry was just beginning to understand the significance of the False Claims Act. False claims accusations have found their way into many change order disputes; and liability for false claims has been recognized in all sorts of certifications that many contractors so commonly encounter that the certfications may not be seriously considered. This chapter was necessary to complete the treatise.

- Chapter 12, "Changes Resulting from Termination," resulted in large part from the Supreme Court's 1997 denial of the Federal Circuit's decision in *Krygoski Construction v. United States* (restraining the government's use of termination for convenience to reduce the cost of an executed contract if not pleased with the contract amount).

Several new authors also were responsible for revising existing chapters, including Christopher Butler at Oles, Morrison, Rinker & Baker in Seattle; Nicholas Holmes and Christopher Hawkins at Nelson, Kinder, Mosseau & Saturley in Manchester; John Mrowiec and Ed Keidan from Conway & Mrowiec in Chicago; Michael Orndahl from the MYR Group in Chicago; Ryan O'Dell and Kimberly King at Lathrop & Gage in

Kansas City; and David Surratt at Canterbury, Stuber, Elder, Gooch & Surratt in Dallas.

Existing chapters have been expanded and updated with appropriate case law through 2004. Dick Rhyne and his group have rewritten and expanded the sections on differing site conditions and the pre-existing duty rule in Chapter 2. Jon Anderson's impressive original chapter on "Changes Resulting from Impossibility or Impracticability of Performance" is even more scholarly and comprehensive in this Second Edition. Ken Gibbs and James Ferro provide a cutting-edge survey of the status of "The Cardinal Change" in both state and federal jurisdictions, along with their newly revised Chapter 11. Neal Sweeney and his team have turned an impressive chapter in the First Edition into a stunningly updated Chapter 14 on "Prelitigation Advice," which includes a significant new section on liquidating agreements.

This Second Edition maintains and expands the high standards set in the first edition for both material and authors. It remains the most useful, complete, and definitive work on changes and change orders available in the construction and design industry today.

June 2005   MICHAEL T. CALLAHAN
CCL Construction Consultants, Inc.
Chicago, IL
cclcon@ix.netcom.com

CHAPTER 1

THE OWNER'S RIGHT TO MAKE CHANGES AND THE CONTRACTOR'S RIGHT TO BE PAID

Michael T. Callahan

§ 1.01   CONSTRUCTION CHANGES: AN EXCEPTION TO ORDINARY CONTRACT PRINCIPLES

The construction contract defines, among other things, the scope of the contractor's work and how the contractor gets paid. Although often detailed, complex, and hard to read, construction contracts are never complete at the time they are signed. The one certainty that exists on a construction project is that during its performance external events will require that the contractor's work be changed in one respect or another. It is for this reason that construction contracts typically give the owner the right to order unilateral changes in the work during the course of construction. This right to make unilateral changes, typically contained in the changes clause of the contract, runs counter to the practice in most business contracts in which express written agreement of all parties to an amendment is required before there can be any change in the contract. The changes process is one of the unique characteristics that make the construction process so different from any other business endeavor.

§ 1.02   REASONS CHANGE CLAUSE IS NEEDED

There are many reasons why a construction contract requires that changes be recognized and the contract modified during performance instead of terminated and a new contract negotiated. Designs are never perfect; the owner wants the flexibility to revise its plan to take advantage of better ideas or technological advances; or the owner wants the contractor to take the risk of the unexpected to obtain a lower price and promises to increase the contract price if the unexpected occurs;[1] or anticipated events have an unexpected effect.

A "change" in the context of a construction contract means that some aspect of the contractor's performance is different from what had been anticipated originally. A change may take the form of a disruption; a physical condition discovered during performance that differs from the announced conditions; or an unexpected event. Once a change is recognized, the contractor may initiate the administrative process that may culminate in the owner's issuance of a "change order," also often called a "modification." Change order claims deal with the events and administrative process between recognition of the change and the issuance of (or failure to issue) a change order.

[A]   Impossibility of Perfect Drawings and Specifications

No design is ever perfect. No set of drawings and specifications has ever achieved perfection, and none ever will. This results from a number of factors. Every building is unique, "one of a kind," never before designed or built. A project is designed and built specially to the owner's order. A drawing is merely a small-scale

---

[1] See, for example, § 7.02[F][1].

representation of what is expected to be constructed. As such, it cannot reflect the full detail of the completed work. Architecture and engineering are not exact sciences. A set of contract documents may contain literally hundreds of thousands of design decisions and details, spread out over dozens or perhaps hundreds of separate drawing sheets and detailed schedules, and hundreds of pages of specifications, all of which need to be coordinated with each other. During the course of drafting and design, the alteration of merely one detail may affect countless other details. Therefore, designs, drawings, and specifications can be *expected* to contain ambiguities, gaps, discrepancies, and conflicts, which, when identified, need to be corrected through some kind of change process.[2]

Although most design defects may be remedied by modifications in the work, some detailed design may be impossible to perform. Distinguishing among the impractical design, a design that is simply more expensive to construct than the contractor expected, and a design that is impossible to complete is a difficult task often left to judicial interpretation.

[B] Process Exposes Imperfect Designs as Soon as Possible

The construction process has been organized, through long tradition and practice, in ways that encourage and enable the participants to identify as early as possible the inevitable imperfections in the design documents. It is important that these imperfections be identified and corrected early, when changes cost little or nothing, before the project moves into the high-spending procurement and construction phases. This process of exposing and correcting mistakes or discrepancies in the design starts when contractors and subcontractors review the solicitation for bids or proposals in order to develop their proposals. These contractors, when doing takeoffs, may discover many of the more obvious discrepancies in the documents. The smooth functioning of the construction process requires that when subcontractors and contractors discover these imperfections, they make them known to the designer, who then clarifies them in an addendum to the bidding documents. Pre-bid conferences are typically held between prospective bidders, the designer, and the owner, at which time bidders' questions about the documents can also be asked and answered. Questions in pre-bid conferences may also result in the issuance of a clarifying addendum.

Revisions to the bidding documents before the bid date are of course not "changes" because at the bidding stage there is no contract in existence. However, after the contract has been executed, any modification to the contract constitutes a change. The contract documents typically provide a process whereby the contractor informs the designer of discrepancies and asks questions, and the designer issues interpretations of the documents, supplying clarifying details. For example, discrepancies are often noted during the course of ordering and procuring materials and equipment. During the preparation of shop drawings and other submittals, contractors and subcontractors are required to focus on the details of the design

---

[2] See **Chapters 7** and **8** on changes resulting from defective or ambiguous drawings and specifications.

and to illustrate how they intend to construct a particular portion of the project. These, too, must be interpreted and clarified, and they may result in a change. The process of preparing coordination drawings to coordinate the work of the various trades gives the general contractor a further opportunity to discover conflicts and discrepancies, which are likewise reported to the architect for clarification or change.

[C] Unexpected Events

It is impossible to foresee all of the events that can affect the work and schedule of a construction project. Unexpected events and surprises are often discovered, such as the existence of subsurface rock, underground obstacles, or unusual soil conditions; unusual weather; actions of regulatory authorities; unexpected field conditions; or the unavailability or anticipated delay in delivery of materials and equipment. When such events occur, they can result in changes in the scope of the work and in schedule delays that need to be dealt with as changes.[3]

Often, the possibility of an event may be anticipated, but the effect or size cannot be. Although expected, the occurrences often involve unexpected consequences that justify a modification. For example, in *Reliance Insurance Co. v. County of Monroe*,[4] the contract anticipated that contaminated soil might be encountered and provided for the containment of contaminants. During the construction, the contractor proposed a design modification at no additional cost to deal with the discovery of anticipated contaminants. A field change order was issued. While performing this work, the contractor encountered toxic hazardous wastes. The county approved certain costs associated with the wastes, but denied other claims brought by the contractor involving work stoppages. The county argued that the contractor had assumed the risks accompanying its proposed change order and therefore had waived its right to recover for additional costs. The court held that the county was liable for the costs associated with its claim. The contractor was not aware of the presence of the hazardous substances; it could not have anticipated the condition from its experience or from an inspection of the site; and the condition varied from normal conditions present in performing similar work.

In *S.A. Healy Co. v. Milwaukee Metropolitan Sewerage District*,[5] applying Wisconsin law, the contractor sued to recover an adjustment for differing site conditions. The parties contracted for the construction of a vertical shaft 300-feet deep and 13 feet in diameter to carry liquid wastes to storage and treatment facilities. The inflow of groundwater was recognized from the beginning as a potentially serious impediment to the project, and consolidation grouting and test wells were anticipated. After this was performed and tests were concluded, the engineer approved excavation. But the contractor nevertheless experienced difficulties in constructing the shaft due to a heavy flow of groundwater into the underground

---

[3] See **Chapter 9**.
[4] 604 N.Y.S.2d 439, 198 A.D.2d 871 (1993).
[5] 50 F.3d 476 (7th Cir. 1995).

work that exceeded inflows discovered in tests. This increased the cost of construction. The contractor claimed that the contract indicated the maximum inflow that would be expected; anything significantly above that level would support an adjustment. The court affirmed the judgment for the contractor, construing the contract against the defendant drafter consistent with the statements from the defendant's engineer that the contractor's claim had merit.

[D]   Impractical Risk Allocations

The contract documents allocate the various contract risks among the different participants in the project. The ideal method of allocating risks is to assign each risk to the party who is best able to control, manage, or absorb that risk. In this way maximum efficiency and economy are achieved. However, many owners attempt to shift to the contractors risks that cannot effectively be controlled, managed, or absorbed by the persons to whom the risks are assigned. In turn, general contractors try to shift these risks to subcontractors, and so on down the line. Although these unrealistic shiftings of risk may be reflected in higher bid prices to take care of the gamble that the risk might occur, the process of evaluating such risks is uncertain and unscientific. There is no way accurately to determine in advance the cost of handling a risk that is beyond the capability of the contractor and that might or might not occur. Newton's Third Law of Motion—every action creates an equal and opposite reaction—applies to human conduct as well as to physics. Accordingly, as a natural response, when risks materialize that the contractor or subcontractor has not covered in its bid and these events cost the contractor or subcontractor money or delay, the contractor or subcontractor will probably find a basis to request a change. This will occur no matter how clearly the contract language assigning the unforeseen risk might be.

[E]   Contractor-Suggested Changes

Contractors often suggest design changes in order to facilitate construction, save time, or save money. On many projects "value engineering" proposals from the contractor for changes are encouraged and rewarded.[6] The value engineering process encourages contractors to reduce their costs in exchange for a share of the savings. Although in federal construction the value engineering process is defined in detail, value engineering in state and local or private construction is treated more informally. The federal VECP clause provides in pertinent part:

(b)   ... "Value engineering change proposal (VECP)" ... shall include the following:

    (1)   A description of the difference between the existing contract requirement and that proposed, the comparative advantages and disadvantages of

---

[6] FAR 52.248-3.

each, a justification when an item's function or characteristics are being altered, and the effect of the change on the end item's performance.

(2) A list and analysis of the contract requirements that must be changed if the VECP is accepted, including any suggested specification revisions.

(3) A separate, detailed cost estimate for (i) the affected portions of the existing contract requirement and (ii) the VECP. The cost reduction associated with the VECP shall take into account the Contractor's allowable development and implementation costs, including any amount attributable to subcontracts under paragraph (h) of this clause.

(4) A description and estimate of costs the Government may incur in implementing the VECP, such as test and evaluation and operating and support costs.

(5) A prediction of any effects the proposed change would have on collateral costs to the agency.

(6) A statement of the time by which a contract modification accepting the VECP must be issued in order to achieve the maximum cost reduction, noting any effect on the contract completion time or delivery schedule.

(7) Identification of any previous submissions of the VECP, including the dates submitted, the agencies and contract numbers involved, and previous Government actions, if known.

Without the required elements, no VECP exists. In *C.A. Rasmussen, Inc. v. United States*,[7] for example, the court concluded that the contractor-provided information was insufficient to meet the seven compliance requirements for a valid VECP. The contractor provided no list and analysis of contract requirements that must be changed if the alleged VECP was accepted. The contractor failed to include a separate and detailed cost estimate for the affected portions of the existing contract requirements as well as the alleged VECP, but instead merely provided the amount of increase of the contract. Further, the contractor failed to describe and estimate the costs that the federal agency might incur in implementing the alleged VECP or predict any effects that the proposed change might have on collateral costs to the agency.

A contractor's VECP shifts the risk of design deficiencies related to that change proposal to the contractor. In *Guy F. Atkinson Construction Co.*,[8] the contract specified that construction of a segment of the Washington, D.C., subway system's tunnel lining could be built using one of two methods. After award of the contract, Atkinson submitted a VECP for a revised concrete lining design that saved some $4 million. Problems with the tunnel alignment required portions of the tunnel lining to be installed with a thickness of less than 12 inches. While permitted to install lining that was less than 12 inches thick, Atkinson was required to

---

[7] 52 Fed. Cl. 345 (2002).
[8] ENGBCA No. 6145, 98-1 BCA (CCH) ¶ 29,582 (1997).

add additional reinforcing steel to achieve a 2.5 safety factor. Atkinson submitted a claim for the added reinforcing steel because its VECP was based on a lower safety factor.

The ENGBCA found that the owner had consistently required the VECP to be based on a safety factor of 2.5 in the event the tunnel lining was less than 12 inches. The ENGBCA rejected Atkinson's claim based on its finding that a 2.5 safety factor had been required consistently and that the accepted VECP did not reduce that factor. The board stated that VECPs place the risk on the proposing contractor that the proposal will be successful and match the original contract specifications.

However, a contractor-initiated change order does not impose a greater burden on the contractor than undertaken under the contract. If so, any releases in the contractor-initiated change order do not prevent the contractor from recovering additional costs permitted under the contract. In *Reliance Insurance Co. v. County of Monroe*,[9] the contractor proposed a design modification during the construction at no additional cost and a field change order was issued. While performing the changed work, the contractor encountered toxic hazardous wastes that had been anticipated under the contract. Although the owner approved certain costs associated with containing the toxic wastes, it denied other claims associated with discovery of the waste. The county argued that the contractor had assumed the risks accompanying its proposed change order and therefore had waived its right to recover for additional costs. The *Reliance Insurance* court held that the contractor did not assume the risk and that the county was liable for the costs associated with discovery of the toxic waste, because the contractor was not aware of the presence of the hazardous substance (despite provisions for containment in the contract documents); it could not have anticipated the conditions from its experience or from an inspection of the site; and the condition varied from normal conditions present in similar work.

Further, a contractor that initiates changes without consulting the owner may have volunteered the changed work. In *Combustion Engineering, Inc. v. Miller Hydro Group*,[10] applying Maine law, the contractor entered into an agreement with the utility to build a facility on a turnkey basis. The facility was to provide a certain level of power capacity. Subject to the utility's capacity specifications, the utility left it to the contractor to design and build the facility. The turnkey contract provided that the contractor would earn a sliding-scale bonus for efficiency to the extent that the facility produced power in excess of a specified level. There was a corresponding penalty that would reduce compensation if the facility were less efficient than a stated minimum output. The contract provided the means of determining output for purposes of the bonus or penalty clause and permitted the utility to demand a retest by a different tester if it was dissatisfied with the first test. If the contractor built a highly efficient plant of the size specified, it would be entitled to a bonus of up to $850,000 in addition to the fixed price of $24 million.

---

[9] 604 N.Y.S.2d 439, 198 A.D.2d 871 (1993).
[10] 13 F.3d 437 (1st Cir. 1993).

The contractor built a plant larger than that set forth in the specifications and with a greater capacity. The utility claimed that the increase in size was made to manipulate the bonus provisions and that it had not become aware of the increased size until it was too late to modify the plant. The contractor invested an additional $1 million to increase the size and a tester reported the capacity at a figure that would yield an $8 million bonus. The utility objected to the test and sought a retest. It refused to accept the facility or make the final construction payments. The contractor refused to agree to the retest and filed suit.

The contractor sought the final payment, amounts withheld from prior payments, an early completion bonus, and the incentive bonus in the amount of $8.16 million. The utility counterclaimed, asserting breach of contract, fraud, and racketeering claims. The utility claimed that it was potentially liable for penalties for building a facility larger than its license permitted and that it could be required to reconstruct fish-protection facilities that were keyed to the originally planned smaller plant. The court held that the contractor breached the contract by building the facility with larger capacity merely to earn the bonus. The contractor's intentional breach of contract barred its claims for unjust enrichment. The court also affirmed the dismissal of the racketeering counterclaim.

[F] Owner-Requested Changes

One of the most frequent sources of changes after construction has started is a decision by the owner to make a change for its own convenience. As long as the nature of the change is such that it does not exceed the original scope of the work to such a degree that it is a "cardinal change" and thus a breach of contract,[11] the owner is free to order such changes. This freedom often also permits the owner's choice to end the contractor's performance by terminating the contract. Termination may be either by default or "convenience" if so permitted in the contract.[12]

§1.03 THE CHANGES CLAUSE

A changes clause provides that an owner, without invalidating the contract, may order extra work or make changes to the existing work by altering, adding to, or deducting from the work, with the contract sum and contract time being adjusted accordingly.

Article 7 of the *General Conditions of the Contract for Construction* published by the American Institute of Architects describes a typical change procedure.[13] Under this procedure, changes to the work may be accomplished after

---

[11] See **Chapter 11**.
[12] See **Chapter 12**.
[13] AIA Doc. A201, General Conditions of the Contract for Construction (1997).

execution of the contract, "and without invalidating the Contract," by change order, construction change directive, or order for a minor change in the work:

A *change order* is a written agreement between the owner, contractor, and architect upon a change in the work and any appropriate adjustment in the contract sum or the contract time

A *construction change directive* is a written order signed by the owner and architect directing the contractor to make a change in the work and stating a proposed basis for any appropriate adjustment in the contract sum and the contract time. A construction change directive may result in a change order if agreement is reached between the contractor and the owner. But even in the absence of total agreement, the construction change directive by itself constitutes a change in the contract documents, with determination of any appropriate adjustment in contract sum or contract time being handled in accordance with specified detailed procedures.

A *minor change in the work* is a written order by the architect to make a change that does not involve adjustment in the contract sum or extension of the contract time and that is not inconsistent with the intent of the contract documents.

The contractor may agree to the proposed adjustment in the construction change directive by signing the directive, in which case the directive becomes a change order.[14] If the contractor disagrees with the proposed price adjustment, or is silent, it becomes the designer's responsibility to determine the adjustment based upon the contractor's cost records and reasonable allowance for overhead and project. Pending the designer's determination, amounts not in dispute may be included in Applications for Payment.[15] Since the contractor prepares the application, the contractor must take the initiative to assure issuance of the directive and inclusion of the value of the changes in the payment request.[16]

§ 1.04 CONTRACTOR'S RIGHT TO ADJUSTMENT IN CONTRACT SUM AND CONTRACT TIME

Although the owner may unilaterally order that changes be made, there is a commensurate duty on the part of the owner to pay and make appropriate adjustments to the schedule occasioned by the change. An owner that fails to pay for ordered changes may abandon the contract.[17] Before the owner is liable for payment, the changed work must meet certain qualifications. It must not be an existing obligation of the contractor.[18] There must be consideration for the contractor's changed performance.[19] The owner's representative must have the authority to

---

[14] AIA Doc. A201, ¶ 7.3.5.

[15] AIA Doc. A201, ¶ 7.3.6.

[16] Hinkle, *The Payment Process Under A201*, 16 Constr. Law. 26-27 (No. 1, Jan. 1996) (citing A201, ¶ 9.3.1.1).

[17] O'Brien & Gere Tech. Servs. v. Fru-Con, 2004 U.S. App. LEXIS 22519 (8th Cir. 2004).

[18] See § 2.03[A].

[19] See § 2.06[B].

order or acquiesce to the change.[20] Proper notice for the performance of the changed work must exist.[21]

Change order provisions typically define how to calculate the value for adjustments to contract sum and contract time. Despite these definitions, changes in contract sum and contract time are typically reached on the basis of negotiations. If unit prices for specific items of work have previously been agreed upon, those unit prices can be the basis for the mutual agreement. If recognized markups for contractor's work and subcontractor's work have previously been agreed upon, these also form the basis for negotiations.[22]

If the contract documents have provided for an escrow bid documents process,[23] the parties can refer to the contractor's original quantity takeoffs, calculations, quotations, and other information used in arriving at the bid price as a realistic yardstick for negotiating the cost of changes and establishing the legitimacy of cost factors used in calculations supporting the cost of changes.

In contrast, in a cost-plus contract the contractor essentially pre-negotiates its right to adjustment for any ordered extra work and avoids a negotiation when the contract is for a "not to exceed" price. For example, in *Vakili v. Hawkersmith*,[24] the court held that a writing requirement in the change order clause in a cost-plus contract does not prevent payment for all costs incorporated into the project. Vakili entered into a contract with Hawkersmith Construction to build a house. The contractor estimated $270,778.79 to build the house. The owner maintained that they informed the contractor that $270,000.00 would be a ceiling price. The contractor only agreed to build the house on a cost-plus basis. The parties entered into a contract provided by the contractor. The contract stated that the contractor was entitled to 10 percent above the costs of construction. The $270,778.89 amount was not referenced in the contract. The owner reserved the right to order work changes authorized by a written change order signed by the parties. There were a number of plan changes. The owner was not provided any revised estimates of what the total cost of the house would be. The contractor presented the owner with an itemized final statement of costs indicating that the owner owed $29,466.66 plus $1,088.56 for reimbursement of the premium for workers' compensation insurance coverage. The owner refused to pay, stating the cost had exceeded the maximum estimate amount. The contractor filed a lien. The owner filed a complaint. The trial court found that only bills submitted relating to a retaining wall and the cost for the "punch list" had not been approved by the owner and awarded the contractor $30,945.10 reduced by the cost of the retaining wall and the cost for repairs and finishing detail. The owner appealed. All changes during construction were made by order of or with the consent of the owner except for the costs of a retaining wall and "punch list" costs after completion. As to these two items, the trial

---

[20] See **Chapter 3**.

[21] See **Chapter 13**.

[22] *See, e.g.,* AIA Doc. A511, Guide for Supplementary Conditions, ¶ 7.3.10 (1987).

[23] American Society of Civil Eng'rs, Avoiding and Resolving Disputes During Construction 22-24 (1991).

[24] 2001 Tenn. App. LEXIS 742 (2001).

court did not allow recovery by the contractor. The evidence did not preponderate against the findings of the trial judge.

§ 1.05   DETERMINATION OF COST AND TIME IN ABSENCE OF AGREEMENT

[A]   According to the Contract

In the AIA changes procedure, various alternative methods are provided for determination of the adjustments if there is not total agreement on changes in contract sum or contract time. Adjustments in the contract sum are based on one of the following methods:

1. Mutual agreement on a lump sum

2. Mutual agreement on unit prices

3. Reimbursement of costs determined in a manner agreed upon by the parties, plus a mutually agreed-upon fixed or percentage fee; or, in the absence of agreement

4. Reimbursement of reasonable costs, as determined by the architect, plus, in case of an increase in the contract sum, a reasonable allowance for overhead and profit.[25]

This last cost-plus process is exemplified by General Conditions in which costs are broken down into the following categories:

1. Labor costs including fringe benefits and insurance

2. Supplies and equipment

3. Machinery and equipment rental costs

4. All bond and insurance premiums, permits, and taxes related to the work

5. Supervision and field office costs directly attributable to the change.[26]

If the parties agree with the determination made by the designer, the agreement is documented in a change order. If agreement is not reached, the designer's determination is subject to the dispute resolution procedures provided elsewhere in the contract. If the designer's determination of the cost is not reasonable, the contractor may successfully challenge it. For example, in *RaDec v. School District*,[27] a contractor was permitted to recover additional payment for earthwork because an architect's determination that the cost of the revised sitework plan reduced the contract amount was patently erroneous and equivalent to bad faith,

---

[25] *See* AIA Doc. A201, ¶ 7.3.3 (1997).

[26] AIA Doc. A201, ¶ 7.3.6.

[27] 248 Neb. 338, 535 N.W.2d 408 (1995).

according to the Supreme Court of Nebraska. The contract provided that the costs of changes were to be determined by the architect. The architect revised the earth-work plan so that no fill dirt would be needed at the site, rejected the contractor's proposed credits due to the change, and issued a unilateral change deducting $189,000 from the contract. The contractor sued, claiming $85,000 additional payment for the change. The trial court awarded $80,269.

The appellate court concluded that the architect's determination had no reasonable basis or was patently erroneous and constituted a gross mistake as would necessarily imply bad faith. As a result, the court concluded that the contractor provision authorizing the architect to resolve the cost of the change was not binding on the contractor.

The designer is often required to make cost determinations on behalf of both the owner and the contractor. In such situations, the designer acts as a third-party neutral protecting the interests of both parties. The designer wears two hats: one as the owner's agent and the other as a third-party neutral. If the designer ignores the interests of one party when acting as a neutral, the designer's decision may be challenged. The designer in *RaDec* ignored the interests of the contractor and so its decision was overturned by the court.

In *J.S. Sweet Co. v. White County Bridge Commission*,[28] J.S. Sweet Co. contracted with the White County Bridge Commission for repair work on a toll bridge. The contract called for Sweet to remove the top one-quarter inch of concrete and any bad concrete found on the deck. Sweet was then to patch any resulting holes and place an epoxy overlay and a wearing surface. Following a dispute with the commission overpayment, Sweet filed a mechanic's lien against the bridge and foreclosed the lien alleging unjust enrichment and breach of contract. The commission responded with a counterclaim against Sweet for breach of contract. The trial court awarded Sweet $78,868.64.

The commission asserted that the trial court erroneously employed Sweet's measurements rather than those offered by the commission in calculating the payment due to Sweet for patching. The trial court found Sweet's calculations of concrete removal and patching to be more probably correct than the commission's engineer. The commission contended that the trial court was bound by the engineer's calculations because the contract required that the engineer shall determine all questions in relation to the work subject only to review by the commission. The commission asserted that the provision prevented Sweet from obtaining judicial review of the commission's calculation of the amount of patching work completed by Sweet.

The appellate court found that whether the contract provided that the engineer will be the sole arbiter of disputes regarding the project, it was an established law that the estimates made by the engineer were not conclusive. They were only prima facie correct and may be attacked either for fraud, mistake, or gross negligence that implied bad faith or a failure to exercise honest judgment. Sweet directed the court to evidence that the engineer made his measurements for the final quantities prior to

---

[28] 714 N.E.2d 219 (Ind. App. Ct. 1999).

the completion of the construction activities that would determine the amount of patching that would be done. The appellate court concluded that such evidence reasonably supported a conclusion that the premature timing of the engineer's measurements constituted mistake, gross negligence, or failure to exercise honest judgment. The trial court's choice of Sweet's calculations with respect to patching rather than the Commission's was not clearly erroneous.

Contracts that require third-party neutral decisions should consider a true third party to make the determination instead of the designer. Partnering utilizes third-party neutrals as facilitators instead of designers; claims boards use third-party neutrals to resolve disputes on the jobsite instead of designers. Calculating the value of a change should also be accomplished by a realistically neutral party instead of the designer.

[B] Constructive Changes

Sometimes a court will recognize a change occurred even though the parties dispute whether the required performance has been changed. A court-recognized change is known as a "constructive change." Generally, this means that a court will treat an event or claim as a change even though the owner did not.[29]

§ 1.06 CONTRACTOR'S OBLIGATION TO CONTINUE CONSTRUCTION

Because of the inevitability of changes and the necessity of continuing the work despite the occurrence of changes, the contract typically requires that the contractor must continue with the work, including work that is being changed, pending any necessary adjustments in the contract sum or the contract time.[30] This protects the owner against possible work stoppages or delays that might result while negotiations are underway about contract sum or contract time.

§ 1.07 PAYMENT TO CONTRACTOR PENDING AGREEMENT ON CHANGE

[A] Contract's Payment System

Before final agreement is reached on a change in the contract sum resulting from a change, amounts not in dispute may be included in the periodic applications

---

[29] See § **4.06**.

[30] AIA Doc. A201, ¶ 4.3.4 (1987). Roy F. Weston, Inc. v. Halliburton NUS Envtl. Corp., 839 F. Supp. 1151 (E.D. Pa. 1993) (Subcontractor was to empty the contents of above-ground tanks. It had difficulty pumping out the contents of those tanks because they included solid matter that could not be pumped. This dispute ultimately resulted in termination of the subcontractor. The court granted the defendant's motion for summary judgment, finding that the mere fact that the tanks contained solid matter did not constitute a differing site condition. The plaintiff's failure to perform without an adjustment supported the termination.).

for payment.[31] Releasing lien rights in exchange for progress payments does not release the contractor's rights for disputed changes. For example, in *Amelco Electric v. City of Thousand Oaks*,[32] each month during its work on the project, Amelco received a progress payment from the city. In connection with each progress payment, Amelco gave an "Unconditional Waiver and Release Upon Progress Payment." The language of the release was mandated by the California Code and stated that Amelco had received a progress payment "for labor, services, equipment or material furnished to The City of Thousand Oaks on the job of Civic Arts Plaza ... and does hereby release pro tanto any mechanic's lien, stop notice or bond right that the undersigned has on the above referenced job ..." through the date of the release. The city contended that Amelco released its claim for damages by executing these releases. The appellate court stated that the releases were expressly limited to Amelco's mechanic's lien, stop notice, or payment bond rights. An action to foreclose a lien under the mechanics' lien statutes did not preclude a personal action against the purchaser of materials. Amelco's release of one available remedy did not, without more, release its right to pursue other remedies.

[B] Recovery for Payment for False Claims

Under both federal and state acts, owners may recover any payments made to contractors that submit false payment requests for changes or claims.[33] Just what acts may be considered a false request for payment are broader than a progress payment or change order payment request. If a claim for payment is determined to be false, the owner may recovery not only the amount of the false payment, but also penalties from the contractor. Most false claim acts also permit third parties that expose the false payment to both bring the action and share in any recovery.

§ 1.08 DISPUTES

Most contracts include a disputes clause that defines the administrative procedure for the submission and resolution of change order disputes. Sometimes the dispute concerns a modification that has been executed, but that one party claims does not reflect the true intent of the parties.[34]

Although the disputes clause does not preclude the dispute resolution process mandated by the contract during performance of the project, many change order disputes are postponed until the work is completed. Disputed extensions of time, for example, may be determined at the conclusion of the project.[35]

---

[31] AIA Doc. A201, ¶ 7.3.7 (1987).
[32] 82 Cal. App. 4th 373, 98 Cal. Rptr. 2d 159 (2000).
[33] See **Chapter 6**.
[34] See **Chapter 5**.
[35] For example, *see* Idaho Power Co. v. Cogeneration, Inc., 9 P.3d 1204 (Idaho 2000).

CHAPTER 2

SCOPE OF TYPICAL CLAUSES

Richard D. Rhyne
Ryan D. O'Dell
Kimberly Brant King

§2.01   INTRODUCTION

The need to make changes on a construction project is a matter of practical reality. Even the most thoughtfully planned project may necessitate changes due to inadequate design; differing site conditions; specified methods of construction that have become obsolete, unfeasible, or even illegal; or materials that have become too expensive or unavailable. Obviously, because changes usually become much more expensive once construction has begun, it is crucial for the owner of the project to select a competent design professional.

However, even the best design professional does not have the foresight to provide for all contingencies, and owners constantly change their minds and their requirements. Therefore, it is essential that the contract documents provide for a clear and concise procedure under which the project can be changed. This chapter analyzes various change order clauses to determine whether the owner is required to compensate the contractor for the change or extra, or whether the work is within the scope of the basic contract price. Stated simply, in order to recover for extra work, the contractor must prove the work was truly "extra." In addition, the chapter addresses the narrow issue of changes versus convenience terminations regarding pricing changes on government contracts.

§2.02   CHANGE ORDER CLAUSES

The "typical" change order clause[1] provides: "Changes in the Work may be accomplished after execution of the Contract, and without invalidating the Contract, by Change Order, Construction Change Directive or order for a minor change in the Work, subject to the limitations stated in this Article 7 and elsewhere in the Contract Documents."[2] Similarly, the typical construction change directives clause provides: "The Owner may by Construction Change Directive, without invalidating the Contract, order changes in the Work within the general scope of the Contract consisting of additions, deletions or other revisions, the Contract Sum and Contract Time being adjusted accordingly."[3]

The federal government standard form contract provides for changes in the contract work as follows:

3. CHANGES

(a) The Contracting Officer may, at any time, without notice to the sureties, by written order, make any change in the work within the general scope of the contract, including but not limited to changes:

(1) In the specifications (including drawings and designs);

(2) In the method or manner of performance of the work;

---

[1] The clause is "typical" because between 300,000 and 400,000 copies of AIA Document A201 are sold each year.

[2] AIA Doc. A201, General Conditions of the Contract for Construction, ¶ 7.1.1 (1987).

[3] AIA Doc. A201, ¶ 7.3.1.

(3) In the Government furnished facilities, equipment, materials, services or site; or

(4) Directing acceleration in the performance of the work. . . .

(c) Except as provided in this clause, no order, statement, or conduct of the Contracting Officer shall be treated as a change under this clause or entitle the Contractor to an equitable adjustment.[4]

The function of a change order or construction change directive clause is clear. Without it, the owner could not make changes without breaching the contract as there is no inherent implied right of the owner to make changes in the contract.[5] The right to make changes is a contractual right. The primary purpose of the changes clause is to give the owner the right to unilaterally alter the contract work. The clause thus gives the owner the freedom to control the work to be done, allowing him to respond to unexpected events without invalidating or re-negotiating the contract. In addition, if there were no procedure to change the contract, the contractor would be forced to bid the contract at a higher price to avoid bearing the risk of changed or differing site conditions.[6] In other words, the clause serves to facilitate the implementation of changes desired by the owner, as well as to establish a procedure under which the contractor can receive additional compensation for extra work.

Although simple in concept, the changes clause is a frequent source of disputes between the owner and contractor. Issues commonly arise such as whether the extra work is truly "extra" as opposed to simply something the contractor was already obligated to do under the original contract; who has the authority to issue or consent to a change order; whether the authorizing change order must be in writing; whether appropriate notices have been provided as set forth in the contract; and what appropriate adjustment in contract price or completion time should be made to accommodate the change work.

Even if a change order or construction change directive is executed, however, recovery for the purported extra work may be barred unless the contractor can show that he performed work over and above what he was required to do under the original contract. In general, the contractor must establish the following elements in order to obtain additional compensation for extra work:

1. That the work was outside the scope of the original contract between the parties

2. That the extra items or changes were ordered at the direction of the owner

3. That the owner either expressly or impliedly agreed to pay extra

---

[4] Federal Government Standard Form 23A. The changes clause for use in federal contracts can be found at 48 C.F.R. § 52.219 (1987).

[5] J.D. Lambert & L. White, Handbook of Modern Construction Law 89 (1982).

[6] Lambert & White, Handbook of Modern Construction Law 89.

4. That the extra items were not furnished voluntarily by the contractor

5. That the extra items were not rendered necessary by any fault of the contractor.[7]

In any case, when the contractor is seeking to recover for extra work, it should be kept in mind that the contractor has the burden of establishing each and every element. In fact, some courts have held that this showing must be by clear and convincing evidence.[8]

This chapter focuses primarily on the first element—whether the work was within or outside the scope of the contract—but includes a brief discussion on all of the required elements.

§ 2.03   PRE-EXISTING DUTY RULE

[A]   In General

Any discussion of whether work falls within, as opposed to outside, the parties' contract begins with an analysis of the contract itself and contract law. In order for any contract to be enforceable, it must be supported by consideration. Simply put, each party to the contract must receive something of value in exchange for his performance of the contract. Courts have long held that a promise to perform work that a party is already obligated to perform under the existing contract is not sufficient consideration and, thus, is unenforceable. This principle is commonly referred to as the pre existing duty rule.

The following is a simple example of the pre-existing duty rule. Employer hires Worker for a one year term to commence in January at $500 per week. In February the parties agree to modify the agreement by increasing the compensation for the same term to $600 per week. Employer's promise to pay the additional $100 per week is unenforceable because Worker has suffered no additional detriment; he is merely performing what he is already required to do.[9] Even though Employer and Worker "agreed" to the additional compensation, Employer is under no obligation to pay Worker anything more than $500 per week.

In the construction setting, Farnsworth states the issue as follows:

> Suppose that a contractor agrees to contract a building and, after the work has begun, threatens to walk off the job unless the owner promises to pay an additional sum. The owner, in urgent need of the building and despairing of finding another contractor quickly, promises to pay the sum in return for the contractor's finishing the work. On completion of the building, the owner refuses to pay more than the original contract price. Is the modification enforceable, so

---

[7] Duncan v. Cannon, 561 N.E.2d 1147 (Ill. App. Ct. 1990).

[8] *Duncan,* 561 N.E.2d 1147.

[9] *See* J. Calamari & J. Perillo, Handbook on the Law of Contracts § 61 (1970).

that the contractor can recover the additional sum from the owner? Today a natural response would be to analyze the problem in terms of duress. It is only relatively recently, however, that the common law doctrine of duress has been broadened to encompass such situations of "economic duress." The traditional analysis of the problem proceeds, instead, in terms of the doctrine of consideration. Under that doctrine the owner would prevail on the ground that there was no consideration for his promise. All that the contractor did in return for the new promise was to perform a duty that he owed under an existing contract, and under the pre existing duty rule, performance of a pre existing duty is not consideration.[10]

The *Restatement (Second) of Contracts* § 73 states the rule as follows: "Performance of a legal duty owed to a promisor which is neither doubtful nor the subject of honest dispute is not consideration; but a similar performance is consideration if it differs from what was required by the duty in a way which reflects more than a pretense of bargain."[11] The comment to the Restatement makes it clear that in cases when the pre-existing duty rule may be applicable, there is often a suspicion that the promise seeking to be enforced was gratuitous, mistaken, or unconscionable, or that the promise was made due to duress, misrepresentation, or undue influence.[12] Whatever the case, the Restatement renders unnecessary any inquiry into why the promise was made and denies enforcement to all such promises.[13]

The origin of the rule and the reasons that led courts to adopt it in the first place are less than clear. Clearly, the rule is based in part on avoiding promises entered into on the basis of economic duress. As Corbin notes:

> [i]t is certainly possible that a contractor may purposely bid low in order to get the contract, and then refuse to perform, after it is too late to obtain another contractor without loss and inconvenience, in order to induce a promise of more pay. The strict enforcement of the supposed general rule would tend to remove this temptation from bidders, since they would know that a promise so induced would not be legally enforceable.[14]

---

[10] E.A. Farnsworth, Contracts § 4.21, at 271 (1982).

[11] Restatement (Second) of Contracts § 73 (1979).

[12] The comment to Restatement (Second) of Contracts § 73 provides in part:

> a. Rationale. A claim that the performance of a legal duty furnished consideration for a promise often raises a suspicion that the transaction was gratuitous or mistaken or unconscionable. . . . Mistake, misrepresentation, duress, undue influence, or public policy may invalidate the transaction even though there is consideration. But the rule of this Section renders unnecessary any inquiry into the existence of such an invalidating clause, and denies enforcement to some promises which would otherwise be valid. Because of the likelihood that the promise was obtained by an express or implied threat to withhold performance of a legal duty, the promise does not have the presumptive social utility normally found in a bargain. Enforcement must therefore rest on some substantive or formal basis other than the mere fact of bargain.

[13] *Id.*

[14] Corbin on Contracts § 171, at 106 (1963).

Therefore, if a contractor and owner agree to relocate a door, and if the contractor could perform the "change" with no additional cost under the contract, an agreement by the owner to pay an additional amount for the change might be unenforceable under the pre existing duty rule. If the contractor is expecting additional compensation for the change, he should be prepared to present evidence of additional costs incurred associated with the change, along with other evidence supporting the five factor test set out in § 2.02.

[B] Case Law

In the following cases, the courts denied the contractor recovery for extra work based on the pre existing duty rule.

[1] *Morning Star Enterprises v. R.H. Grover*

Morning Star (the subcontractor) brought an action against Grover (the contractor) to recover amounts allegedly due from construction of a sludge stabilization and dewatering facility.[15] Grover counterclaimed, alleging that Morning Star owed the contractor additional sums arising from the project.

One of the issues in the case was whether Morning Star was required by the contract to seal certain windows installed by Grover. Morning Star asserted that due to Grover's mistake, a two inch gap existed between the side of the window frame and the panels, which Morning Star was not obligated to cure. It further asserted that it only contracted to "caulk," not "seal" the windows. The court found otherwise, holding that the contract obligated Morning Star to completely install and seal the windows.

[2] *Argeros & Co. v. Commonwealth*

The contractor entered into an agreement with the Pennsylvania Department of Transportation to paint several bridges.[16] While painting one of the bridges, the contractor determined that the weight of the bridge was 260 tons, as opposed to the "approximately 180 tons" listed in the bid proposal and in the contract. The contractor painted the entire bridge and then made a claim against the owner for the "extra" work. The court, in denying the contractor recovery, noted:

> An instruction to complete work that it was already obliged to perform does not constitute a modification of a contract nor does it constitute economic duress. [The contractor] knew the bridge contained a steel deck, that the bid listed the steel deck and that all metal surfaces had to be painted under the contract and, having signed the contract, it is bound by it.[17]

---

[15] Morning Star Enters. v. R.H. Grover, 805 P.2d 553 (Mont. 1991).
[16] Argeros & Co. v. Commonwealth, 477 A.2d 1065 (Pa. Commw. Ct. 1982).
[17] 477 A.2d 1065, 1068.

§ 2.04   THE CONTRACT

Whether the pre-existing duty rule bars the contractor's claim for additional compensation depends on the facts of each case as well as an interpretation of the documents constituting the agreement between the parties. A determination of what documents constitute the parties' agreement is the first step in deciding whether the contractor is entitled to recover additional payment from an owner for extra work.[18] Very often, the contract documents make it clear who bears the risk under the particular set of circumstances.

The contract documents almost always include inter alia the owner contractor agreement, the general conditions, the design plans and specifications, and the local building code. Courts have held that if the language of the documents is clear and unambiguous, the language alone will control and there is nothing for the courts to construe or interpret.[19] In other words, if the contract clearly states that the contractor cannot recover for extra work in a certain situation, the court will deny recovery and refuse to look at the circumstances surrounding the extra work.

In addition, the contract may include by reference certain published standards such as military or testing standards. For example, a bridge contract with the state of Kansas will automatically include by reference the Kansas Department of Transportation Standard Specifications for State Road and Bridge Construction, all 2,500 pages.[20] All documents included by reference in the contract must be reviewed by the contractor to adequately determine the scope of his undertaking.

The language used in the documents will be given its plain and ordinary meaning.[21] Simply stated, the court will not look outside the four corners of the contract documents unless an ambiguity exists when the contract documents taken as a whole are reasonably subject to two different interpretations. Only then will the court resort to the usual rules of construction to ascertain what the parties[22] intended by the language they used.

If, however, an ambiguity exists, a court will consider evidence of what the parties intended to accomplish by the contract. Very often, this is a simple analysis, as illustrated by *Watson Lumber Co. v. Guennewig.*[23] In *Watson,* the contractor made a claim for numerous extras arising under a home construction contract. One of the "extras" asserted was for the kitchen and bathroom ceilings, which had been lowered to cover the duct work. In denying the builder's claim, the court noted that

---

[18] *See* AIA Doc. A201, ¶ 1.1.1 (1987).

[19] *See* 17A Am. Jur. 2d Contracts § 337 (1991).

[20] Kansas Dep't of Transp., Standard Specifications for State Road and Bridge Construction (1990).

[21] *See* 17A Am. Jur. 2d Contracts § 337 (1991) and cases cited therein.

[22] 17A Am. Jur. 2d Contracts § 337 (1991).

[23] 226 N.E.2d 270 (Ill. App. Ct. 1967).

"[w]e consider it unlikely that the parties intended to build a house without duct work or with duct work exposed."[24]

[A] Work Clause

The typical work clause provides:

> The term "Work" means the construction and services required by the Contract Documents, whether completed or partially completed, and includes all other labor, materials, equipment and services provided or to be provided by the Contractor to fulfill the Contractor's obligations. The Work may constitute the whole or a part of the project.[25]

The work clause stands as a bar to recovery for extra work, unless the contractor can prove that the work performed was outside the contractor's obligations, as defined by the relevant contract documents.

[B] Scope-of-Work Clause

The typical scope-of-work clause allows the owner and contractor to be as broad or as narrow as they wish in defining what will constitute "the work." It is critical, however, that both the contractor and owner understand the importance of the scope of work clause and that each party understand as precisely as possible the work to be done for the agreed payment. As one authority notes:

> The need for this clause is obvious: The owner wants as much work as possible for the payment, whereas the contractor wants to do as little as possible. Therefore the owner tries to define the scope as broadly as possible ("all labor materials, services, and other work necessary to erect the building"); in contrast, the contractor seeks to define specific tasks ("install roof trusses, plywood and asphalt shingles"), with everything else being an "extra."[26]

The drafter of the scope-of-work clause should carefully examine all the documents related to the project. Among these are the plans and specifications, the instructions provided to bidders on the project, the bid and bid estimates submitted by the contractor awarded the job, correspondence, shop drawings, and all other provisions of the agreement (even though these documents may not be a part of the contract documents).[27] In addition, the contractor should always visit the site prior to drafting the clause. Under most standard form contracts, execution of the

---

[24] Watson Lumber Co. v. Guennewig, 226 N.E.2d 270 (Ill. App. Ct. 1967).
[25] *See, e.g.*, AIA Doc. A201, ¶ 1.1.3 (1987).
[26] S.M. Siegfried, Introduction to Construction Law 21 (1987).
[27] Siegfried, Introduction to Construction Law 21.

contract represents that the contractor has visited the site and become familiar with local conditions under which the work is to be performed.[28] Lastly, the contractor should take field measurements at the site and compare the information with the contract documents.[29] Because the scope-of-work clause will determine what each party's obligations are under the contract, it should be the last provision drafted and should not be done in haste.

[C] Building Codes

In a well-drafted contract, the issue of which party will be responsible for complying with local ordinances and building codes will rarely arise. For example, AIA Document A201 specifically provides that the contractor is not responsible for determining whether or not the contract documents comply with the various laws, statutes, codes, and regulations that might be applicable, but the contractor must notify the owner and architect in writing if he believes the contract or any portion thereof is in violation of any law or code.[30] Under the AIA documents, the contractor will almost always be able to recover for extra work associated with complying with local ordinances and building codes. However, if the contractor performs work knowing it to be in violation of any law, ordinance, or building code, and the contractor fails to notify the architect and owner, under the AIA documents the contractor must assume full responsibility for the work and bear any costs that result.[31]

If AIA documents are not used, special attention must be paid as to which party is responsible for complying with the local ordinances and building codes. When the building code is incorporated into the contract but the specifications require a lesser grade of material, which will control? Will the contractor be able to recover the extra costs associated with complying with the building code even though he originally complied with the specifications?

The answer appears to be no. In *Howard J. White, Inc. v. Varian Associates*,[32] the contractor attempted to recover $2,080.40 for "extra" work in installing cast-iron sewer pipe instead of the clay pipe called for in the specifications. The city building code, which was incorporated into the contract, required cast-iron pipe. In determining that the contractor could not recover for the work and materials, the court held that the building code, not the specifications, controlled.

[D] Differing or Changed Site Conditions

Differing Site Conditions (DSC) are unforeseen physical conditions that are encountered at the construction site that make the job more difficult, time-consuming,

---

[28] *See, e.g.*, AIA Doc. A201, ¶ 1.2.2 (1987).
[29] *See, e.g.*, AIA Doc. A201, ¶ 3.2.1.
[30] AIA Doc. A201, ¶ 3.7.3.
[31] AIA Doc. A201, ¶ 3.7.4.
[32] 2 Cal. Rptr. 871 (Ct. App. 1960).

or expensive than anticipated at the time of contracting. The most common example of a differing site condition involves subsurface conditions at the construction site.[33] DSC may also involve latent conditions of any kind, such as quantities of materials and substances that differ from those stated in the contract. Differing Site Conditions usually result in increased expense and time. In the absence of a DSC Clause, a contractor who agrees to perform a project for a fixed sum will generally absorb any losses resulting from unforeseen conditions on the construction site.[34]

[1]   Differing Site Conditions Clauses/Changed Conditions Clauses

A contract should include a clause that covers the contractor's right to recover additional compensation in the event the contractor encounters unforeseen conditions on the project. These clauses are known by a number of different names including "Changed Conditions Clauses," "Changed Site Conditions Clauses," or "Differing Site Conditions Clauses." The purpose of the DSC clause is "to allow contractors to submit more accurate bids by eliminating the need for contractors to inflate their bids to account for contingencies that may not occur."[35] The DSC clause shifts the expense and burden of the unexpected site conditions to the owner of the site.[36]

DSC, or Changed Conditions, Clauses are found in federal, state, and most private contracts. For instance, DSC clauses are found in the construction contract forms of the Federal Acquisition Regulations,[37] the American Institute of Architects' (AIA) *General Conditions of the Contract for Construction,*[38] the

---

[33] Sherman Botts & Eric Ablin, Unforeseen Conditions on the Project (2003) (unpublished article, Lathrop & Gage L.C.) (on file with authors).

[34] Green Constr. Co. v. Kansas Power & Light Co., 1 F.3d 1005, 1009 (10th Cir. 1993) (citing Reese Constr. Co. v. State Highway Comm'n, 627 P.2d 361, 364 (1981)); *see also* Botts & Ablin, Unforeseen Conditions on the Project (citing Justin Sweet, Legal Aspects of Architecture, Engineering, and the Construction Process 478 (6th ed. 2000)).

[35] H.B. Mac, Inc. v. United States, 153 F.3d 1338, 1343 (Fed. Cir. 1998).

[36] *See, e.g.,* Fru-Con Constr. Corp. v. United States, 43 Fed. Cl. 306, 318 (1999).

[37] *See* FAR 36.236-2, 48 C.F.R. § 52.236-2(a), which provides as follows:

DIFFERING SITE CONDITIONS (APR 1984)
(a) The Contractor shall promptly, and before the conditions are disturbed, give a written notice to the Contracting Officer of (1) subsurface or latent physical conditions at the site which differ materially from those indicated in this contract, or (2) unknown physical conditions at the site, of an unusual nature, which differ materially from those ordinarily encountered and generally recognized as inhering in work of the character provided for in the contract.

[38] *See* AIA Doc. A201, General Conditions of the Contract for Construction, ¶ 4.3.4 (1997), which provides as follows:

4.3.4 Claims for Concealed or Unknown Conditions. If conditions are encountered at the site which are (1) subsurface or otherwise concealed physical conditions which differ materially from those indicated in the Contract Documents or (2) unknown physical conditions of an unusual nature, which differ materially from those ordinarily found to exist and generally recognized as inherent in construction activities of the

Engineering Joint Contract Documents Committee (EJCDC) Conditions of Contract,[39] and the Design Build Institute of America (DBIA) Standard Form of General Conditions of Contract Between Owner and Design-Builder,[40] and are

---

character provided for in the Contract Documents, then notice by the observing party shall be given to the other party promptly before conditions are disturbed and in no event later than 21 days after first observance of the conditions. The Architect will promptly investigate such conditions and, if they differ materially and cause an increase or decrease in the Contractor's cost of, or time required for, performance of any part of the Work, will recommend an equitable adjustment in the Contract Sum or Contract Time, or both. If the Architect determines that the conditions at the site are not materially different from those indicated in the Contract Documents and that no change in the terms of the Contract is justified, the Architect shall so notify the Owner and Contractor in writing, stating the reasons. Claims by either party in opposition to such determination must be made within 21 days after the Architect has given notice of the decision. If the conditions encountered are materially different, the Contract Sum and Contract Time shall be equitably adjusted, but if the Owner and Contractor cannot agree on an adjustment in the Contract Sum or Contract Time, the adjustment shall be referred to the Architect for initial determination, subject to further proceedings pursuant to Paragraph 4.4.

[39] *See* EJCDC Doc. No. C-700, Standard General Conditions of the Construction Contract, ¶ 4.03(A)(1)-(4) (2002), which provides as follows:

4.03 *Differing Subsurface or Physical Conditions*
    A. *Notice:* If Contractor believes that any subsurface or physical condition at or contiguous to the Site that is uncovered or revealed either:
        1. is of such a nature as to establish that any "technical data" on which Contractor is entitled to rely as provided in Paragraph 4.02 is materially inaccurate; or
        2. is of such a nature as to require a change in the Contract Documents; or
        3. differs materially from that shown or indicated in the Contract Documents; or
        4. is of an unusual nature, and differs materially from conditions ordinarily encountered and generally recognized as inherent in work of the character provided for in the Contract Documents; then Contract shall, promptly after becoming aware thereof and before further disturbing the subsurface or physical conditions or performing any Work in connection therewith (except in an emergency as required by Paragraph 6.16.A), notify Owner and Engineer in writing about such condition. Contractor shall not further disturb such condition or perform any Work in connection therewith (except as aforesaid) until receipt of written order to do so. . . .

[40] DBIA Doc. No. 535, Standard Form of General Conditions of Contract Between Owner and Design-Builder, ¶ 4.2.1 (1st ed. 1998), which provides as follows:

4.2 Differing Site Conditions
    4.2.1 Concealed or latent physical conditions or subsurface conditions at the Site that (i) materially differ from the conditions indicated in the Contract Documents or (ii) are of an unusual nature, differing materially from the conditions ordinarily encountered and generally recognized as inherent in the Work are collectively referred to herein as "Differing Site Conditions." If Design-Builder encounters a Differing Site Condition, Design-Builder will be entitled to an adjustment in the Contract Price and/or Contract Time(s) to the extent Design-Builder's cost and/or time of performance are adversely impacted by the Differing Site Condition.

required in certain federal highway construction contracts.[41] Additionally, many states include DSC clauses in their public works contracts.[42]

A DSC clause typically identifies two types of differing site conditions for which the contractor is entitled to an equitable adjustment of the contract price or time for performance. Type I conditions are those actual conditions at the site that differ materially from what is _represented in the contract documents_.[43] Type II conditions are those actual conditions that differ materially from those that would _normally be expected in a construction project of that kind_.[44] Thus, in accordance with the DSC clause, the contractor may recover additional compensation if he can demonstrate that a Type I or a Type II condition exists.

There are many similarities among the DSC clauses in the key standard construction contracts mentioned above. For instance, the AIA clause refers to "concealed physical conditions," the Federal Acquisition Regulations (FAR) refer to "latent physical conditions," and the DBIA clause refers to both "concealed and latent physical conditions." Likewise, in the second prong of the DSC clause, the AIA, EJCDC, the FAR, and DBIA have almost identical language concerning unusual conditions that are covered under the DSC clause. For example, the AIA clause covers unusual conditions that "differ materially from those ordinarily found to exist and generally recognized as inherent in construction activities of the

---

[41] _See_ 69 FR 72133; 23 C.F.R. § 635.109(a)(1), Standardized changed condition clauses, which provides in pertinent part as follows:

(a) Except as provided in paragraph (b) of this section, the following changed conditions contract clauses shall be made part of, and incorporated in, each highway construction project approved under 23 U.S.C. 106.

(1) Differing site conditions.

(i) During the progress of the work, if subsurface or latent physical conditions are encountered at the site differing materially from those indicated in the contract or if unknown physical conditions of an unusual nature, differing materially from those ordinarily encountered and generally recognized as inherent in the work provided for in the contract, are encountered at the site, the party discovering such conditions shall promptly notify the other party in writing of the specific differing conditions before the site is disturbed and before the affected work is performed.

(ii) Upon written notification, the engineer will investigate the conditions, and if it is determined that the conditions materially differ and cause an increase or decrease in the cost or time required for the performance of any work under the contract, an adjustment, excluding anticipated profits, will be made and the contract modified in writing accordingly. The engineer will notify the contractor of the determination whether or not an adjustment of the contract is warranted.

(iii) No contract adjustment which results in a benefit to the contractor will be allowed unless the contractor has provided the required written notice.

(iv) No contract adjustment will be allowed under this clause for any effects caused on unchanged work. (This provision may be omitted by the STD's at their option.)

[42] _See, e.g.,_ Cal. Public Contracts Code § 1704 (2004).

[43] _See, e.g.,_ Comtrol, Inc. v. United States, 294 F.3d 1357 (Fed. Cir. 2002); H.B. Mac, Inc. v. United States, 153 F.3d 1338 (Fed. Cir. 1998).

[44] _See, e.g., H.B. Mac,_ 153 F.3d 1338, 1343.

character provided,"[45] the EJCDC provision covers unusual conditions that differ "materially from conditions ordinarily encountered and generally recognized as inherent in work of the character provided,"[46] the FAR provide relief for unusual conditions that differ "materially from those ordinarily encountered and generally recognized as inhering in work of the character provided," and DBIA covers unusual conditions that differ "materially from the conditions ordinarily encountered and generally recognized as inherent in the Work."[47] tered and generally recognized as inherent in the Work."[47]

From a risk allocation approach, the standard construction contract forms can differ by the inclusion of exculpatory provisions stating one or more of the following: 1) the owner and architect do not assume any responsibility for any subsurface conditions; 2) the information concerning site conditions was obtained by the owner for its own use in designing the project; 3) a requirement that the bidders investigate the site and determine the site conditions themselves; 4) anything discovered by the contractor after execution of the contract is the sole responsibility of the contractor; 5) the owner and architect do not warrant the sufficiency or accuracy of the information provided; and 6) the contractor is responsible for completing all excavation work regardless of what formations are encountered.[48]

The DSC clauses in the various standard construction contracts also contain different requirements regarding the notice that needs to be provided to the owner upon encountering a DSC.[49]

[2]   Site Inspection Clauses

Even if a contract contains a DSC, it will likely also contain a site inspection clause imposing on contractors the responsibility for all conditions that can be observed by reasonable inspection of the site. For example, site investigation clauses are found in the construction contract forms of the FAR[50] and AIA *General Conditions of the Contract for Construction.*[51] A contractor that fails to make a reasonable site inspection generally will not be allowed to recover later for conditions that would have been observed by the contractor during a reasonable site inspection.[52]

---

[45] AIA Doc. A201, General Conditions of the Contract for Construction (1997).

[46] EJCDC Doc. No. C-700, Standard General Conditions of the Construction Contract (2002).

[47] FAR 36.236-2, 48 C.F.R. § 52.236-2(a); DBIA Doc. No. 535, Standard Form of General Conditions of Contract Between Owner and Design-Builder (1st ed. 1998); *see also* Jeffrey M. Chu, *Differing Site Conditions: Whose Risk Are They?*, Constr. Law. 2 (Apr. 2000).

[48] *See* Philip L. Bruner & Patrick J. O'Connor, Jr., Bruner & O'Connor on Construction Law, Vol. 2, § 5:108, pp. 161-63 (2002).

[49] See discussion in § 2.04[D][5].

[50] *See* 48 C.F.R. § 52.236-3, Site Investigation and Conditions Affecting the Work (Apr. 1984).

[51] *See* AIA Doc. A201, ¶1.5.2, providing that "[e]xecution of the Contract by the Contractor is a representation that the Contractor has visited the site, become generally familiar with local conditions under which the Work is to be performed and correlated personal observations with requirements of the Contract Documents."

[52] T.L. James & Co. v. Traylor Bros., 294 F.3d 743 (5th Cir. 2002).

In *T.L. James*, the municipal port authority contracted with a contractor to perform dredging work for the project. The contractor entered into a contract with a subcontractor to perform the dredging work. Shortly after construction commenced, the contractor began to encounter significant obstructions that, according to the contractor, were not identified in the plans and specifications. These obstructions, discovered during the dredging work, caused a "ripple effect" and created serious delays that impacted the entire project. The project was eventually finished over a year after the expected completion date. The subcontractor sued the general contractor for additional work performed in connection with the project and the general contractor brought a third-party claim against the port authority for indemnity.[53]

The bidding documents advised the bidders that there were "unknown infrastructures" at the site and that there were "numerous steel and timber piles removed to the approximate existing mud line in the area of the required dredging." The documents also provided that any costs incurred due to cutting off piles were to be the responsibility of the bidder.[54] The general contractor alleged that the Port Authority had information on the latent obstructions in the site area that it failed to produce during the bidding process.[55] The court found that because the contractor failed to conduct an adequate investigation of the site, it cannot now complain of the character and amount of work it had to perform under the contract.[56] The court further found that the contract sufficiently put the contractor on notice of both known and unknown obstructions on the site, referring the contractor to the Port's maps and archives room for a more detailed map of the site. The court also found that it was reasonably foreseeable for a prudent bidder to anticipate encountering varying river currents and accompanying siltation problems in wharf and bridge work on the river. Additionally, the court found that the conditions of the soil and the change in pile driving criteria were not substantial deviations from that described in the bid package. Based on all of these factors, especially the contractor's duty to investigate for possible obstructions not included in the plans, the court held that the contractor was not entitled to additional compensation from the Port Authority.[57]

[3] Type I Differing Site Conditions

To prevail on a claim for Type I Differing Site Conditions, a contractor must prove by a preponderance of the evidence that: (a) the contract documents *affirmatively* indicate latent or subsurface physical conditions at the site; (b) the actual conditions encountered at the site *materially differ* from the conditions indicated in the contract; (c) the actual conditions were reasonably unforeseeable based on

---

[53] *T.L. James*, 294 F.3d 743, 745.
[54] *T.L. James*, 294 F.3d 743, 745.
[55] *T.L. James*, 294 F.3d 743, 745-46.
[56] *T.L. James*, 294 F.3d 743, 751.
[57] *T.L. James*, 294 F.3d 743, 751-53.

the information available to the contractor during bidding; (d) it must have reasonably relied upon the contract and contract-related documents; and (e) it was damaged as a result of the material variation between the expected and the encountered conditions.[58]

The determination of what documents are included as part of the "contract documents" is a critical inquiry in analyzing a Type I DSC claim. For example, an owner may seek to exclude geotechnical information from the "contract documents." The exclusion of geotechnical information from the "contract documents" can create problems because "geotechnical information is usually the most descriptive as to subsurface conditions at a site."[59]

The various standard construction contract forms have different definitions of what are included in the "contract documents." Under the AIA conditions, the "Contract Documents" consist of the agreement between the owner and contractor; the conditions of the contract (general, supplementary, and other conditions); drawings, specifications, and addenda issued prior to the execution of the contract; and other documents listed in the agreement and modifications issued after execution of the contract.[60] The AIA conditions do not expressly include geotechnical information as part of the contract documents.[61]

On the other hand, the EJCDC conditions provide that "contract documents" include those items designated in the agreement and expressly state that "approved Shop Drawings, other Contractor's submittals, and the reports and drawings of subsurface and physical conditions are not Contract Documents."[62] The EJCDC conditions further state that, although they are not contract documents, the contractor may rely upon the general accuracy of the "technical data" contained in such reports and drawings concerning subsurface or physical conditions.[63] A number of cases involving federal contracts offer a contradictory approach, interpreting the term "contract documents" broadly to include bidding documents, such as Invitations to Bid, drawings, and specifications, as well as documents and materials mentioned in the bidding documents, such as geotechnical reports.[64]

[a] Affirmative Indications of Latent or Subsurface Physical Conditions

A contractor is not eligible for an equitable adjustment for a Type I DSC unless the contract documents indicated what the latent or subsurface physical conditions would be.[65] A Type I claim may be based on either an express or

---

[58] See Manuel Bros. v. United States, 55 Fed. Cl. 8, 42 (2002) (citing H.B. Mac, 153 F.3d 1338, 1345); see also Comtrol, 294 F.3d 1357, 1362.

[59] See Bruner & O'Connor on Construction Law, Vol. 2, § 5:108, at pp. 168-69.

[60] See AIA Doc. A201, ¶ 1.1.1.

[61] Bruner & O'Connor on Construction Law, Vol. 2, § 5:108, at p. 169.

[62] EJCDC Doc. No. C-700, Standard General Conditions of the Construction Contract ¶ 1.01(12) (2002).

[63] EJCDC Doc. No. C-700, Standard General Conditions of the Construction Contract ¶ 4.02.

[64] See, e.g., Fru-Con Constr., 43 Fed. Cl. 306, 317-18.

[65] See, e.g., H.B. Mac, 153 F.3d 1338, 1345; Comtrol, 294 F.3d 1357, 1363.

implied indication in the contract documents.[66] The analysis of a Type I DSC is relatively straightforward when an express indication of the subsurface conditions exists.[67] The analysis of a Type I DSC becomes more difficult when the contract documents by implication indicate the subsurface physical conditions.[68]

D.F.K. Enterprises provides a useful example of a recent case where the court found that the contract documents affirmatively represented the site conditions. In *D.F.K. Enterprises,* the contractor received a contract to paint water storage tanks at the White Sands Missile Range. The contract included the construction of a containment system around the tanks.[69] The containment system specified in the solicitation consisted of large nylon reinforced tarps tied together and anchored with ropes and/or cables, which is particularly susceptible to tears during high winds.[70] Prior to awarding the contract, the Army Corps of Engineers (the Corps) issued a formal response to a question raised about the normal wind speed at the job by directing the bidders to the U.S. Weather Service. The contractor failed to contact the U.S. Weather Service prior to bidding on the project. When the contractor first visited the jobsite, it was very hot with very little wind.[71]

The Solicitation issued by the Corps contained certain time adjustments to the contract for delays caused by unusually severe weather. The Corps' internal guidance directed that wind be considered a potential source of adverse weather delay, but the Corps did not include wind conditions on the anticipated adverse weather chart for the project. After receiving the contract, the contractor began to experience a series of high wind days that began to rip the tarps. These conditions forced the contractor to temporarily cease its paint removal operations until the winds subsided.[72] The contractor requested a contract modification for the additional costs incurred due to the wind conditions at the base, stating that the Corps personnel had advised it that high winds often appeared from February through May or later. The Corps responded that the differing site conditions clause does not apply to "acts of God," i.e., weather. The contractor returned to the jobsite in late June and received a contract modification extending its completion date for 82 days due to weather-related delays.[73] The contractor then submitted a claim for additional direct and indirect costs resulting from alleged defective plans and specifications, alleging that the Corps inaccurately disclosed the anticipated weather delays.[74]

The court held that the weather chart issued by the Corps made an affirmative representation of past weather conditions at the jobsite and reasonably could be

---

[66] *See, e.g.,* Foster Constr. C.A. & Williams Bros. Co. v. United States, 193 Ct. Cl. 587, 435 F.2d 873, 881 (1970).

[67] *See, e.g.,* D.F.K. Enters., Inc. v. United States, 45 Fed. Cl. 280 (1999).

[68] *See Foster Constr.*, 435 F.2d 873, 881.

[69] *D.F.K. Enters.,* 45 Fed. Cl. 280, 281-82.

[70] *D.F.K. Enters.,* 45 Fed. Cl. 282.

[71] *D.F.K. Enters.,* 45 Fed. Cl. 282.

[72] *D.F.K. Enters.,* 45 Fed. Cl. 282, 283.

[73] *D.F.K. Enters.,* 45 Fed. Cl. 282, 283-84.

[74] *D.F.K. Enters.,* 45 Fed. Cl. 282, 284.

relied on by the contractor. Because the chart failed to consider the potential for delays caused by wind, therefore, it was misleading.[75] The court concluded, however, that fact questions about the contractor's actual reliance and the reasonableness of its site inspection precluded summary judgment for the contractor.[76]

On the other hand, *Kiewit Construction Co. v. United States*[77] presents a case where an affirmative representation of site conditions was not found. In *Kiewit*, the U.S. Court of Federal Claims held that the contractor was not entitled to an equitable adjustment based upon a Type I DSC at the work site because the contract did not contain representations regarding subsurface conditions.[78] Kiewit entered into a contract with the Huntington District of the Army Corps of Engineers regarding the construction of the Winfield Locks and the Dam on the Kanawha River in West Virginia. Kiewit was hired to dewater the work site by excavating a designated area to form a new cofferdam and build and implement a dewatering system consisting of a groundwater and surface water control to lower the water table within the excavation area.[79] Although Kiewit installed and operated the dewatering system within the minimum required system guidelines in the contract, it did not sufficiently lower the groundwater level.[80] Kiewit claimed that the Contract specifications represented a number of conditions that differed from the actual work site conditions, resulting in excess, unforeseeable costs.[81] For instance, the contract specifications contained Predrainage Design Assumptions, which made statements that "the bottom of the cofferdam cells and the downstream guide wall and landside lock wall form a tight contact with the bedrock, that the sheet pile cutoff walls and slurry trench cutoff wall will prevent any significant seepage into the work area, and that the bedrock at the sight is tight."[82]

In rejecting Kiewit's claim, the court held that the identified contract provisions did not constitute representations concerning subsurface conditions, but rather "list[ed] baseline assumptions incorporated into the design of the minimum prescribed dewatering system."[83] Additionally, the contract contained a disclaimer clause stating that "[t]hese assumptions may or may not be completely valid." The court held that because the assumptions did not constitute representations and the contract gave no indication of the subsurface conditions at the work site, the risk for all unknown or unanticipated subsurface conditions remains with Kiewit.[84]

[b]   Actual Conditions Must Differ Materially

See discussion on Type II Differing Site Conditions in **§ 2.04[D][4][b].**

---

[75] *D.F.K. Enters.*, 45 Fed. Cl. 282, 287.
[76] *D.F.K. Enters.*, 45 Fed. Cl. 282, 288-90.
[77] 56 Fed. Cl. 414 (2003).
[78] 56 Fed. Cl. 414, 423.
[79] 56 Fed. Cl. 414, 416.
[80] 56 Fed. Cl. 414, 417.
[81] 56 Fed. Cl. 414, 423.
[82] 56 Fed. Cl. 414, 417.
[83] 56 Fed. Cl. 414, 423.
[84] 56 Fed. Cl. 414, 423-24.

[c] Foreseeability

In order for a contractor to prevail on a Type I DSC claim, it must establish that the conditions actually encountered were "reasonably unforeseeable based on all the information available to the contractor at the time of bidding."[85] Conditions that are discoverable by a reasonable site visit and diligent review of the contract documents will be chargeable to the contractor.[86]

In *H.B. Mac*,[87] the contractor sought an equitable adjustment for differing site conditions. The contractor received a contract for construction of a reinforced concrete motor vehicle maintenance facility and motor vehicle wash rack facility. The military base on which the work was to be performed contained a variety of sedimentary soils. The site was within 700 yards of the ocean and a lagoon. Bidders were provided with contract specifications and drawings, including eight soil borings. The boring logs showed the presence of a layer of limestone as well as soils that consisted primarily of sands and gravels. Three of the borings showed that the water table was located approximately 12 feet below the surface. The other five borings did not reach down to the water table.[88] The government did not provide any other subsurface information to the bidders, such as geologic data or soils reports.[89] The contract between the government and the contractor contained the standard Site Investigation and Conditions Affecting the Work Clause, set forth in FAR 52.236-2, that required the contractor to satisfy itself as to any subsurface materials or obstacles to be encountered from a reasonable inspection of the site.[90] The contractor submitted its bid without conducting a pre-bid site visit.[91]

During excavation, the contractor encountered soil saturated with ground water and the walls of the excavation began collapsing. In spite of efforts to install temporary safety shoring, the shorings failed and the sides of the excavation collapsed.[92] During the excavation for the oil/water separator tank, the contractor never encountered a thick layer of limestone similar to what was indicated in the borings.[93] The contractor requested an equitable adjustment under the contract for costs associated with installing the sheet pile shoring at the site for the oil/water separator tank. The contractor claimed that the thick layer of unstable black silty clay material that it encountered, combined with the total absence of a thick layer of limestone, constituted a Type I DSC.[94]

The court stated that "[i]t is well-settled that a contractor is charged with knowledge of the conditions that a pre-bid site visit would have revealed."[95] The

---

[85] *H.B. Mac*, 153 F.3d 1338, 1347.
[86] Hardwick Bros. Co., II v. United States, 36 Fed. Cl. 347, 406 (1996).
[87] 153 F.3d 1338 (Fed. Cir. 1998).
[88] 153 F.3d 1338, 1341.
[89] 153 F.3d 1338, 1341.
[90] 153 F.3d 1338, 1343.
[91] 153 F.3d 1338, 1346.
[92] 153 F.3d 1338, 1341-42.
[93] 153 F.3d 1338, 1342.
[94] 153 F.3d 1338, 1342-43.
[95] 153 F.3d 1338, 1346 (citing Hardwick Bros. Co., II v. United States, 36 Fed. Cl. 347, 406 (1996)).

court held that the contractor's pre-bid failure to determine the potential need for sheet piling was not reasonable and therefore no equitable adjustment was appropriate.[96] The court found that "a reasonable and prudent contractor, who was to perform excavation to a depth significantly below the water table at a site within 700 yards of the ocean that was intersected with streams, and who was not given boring logs indicating subsurface conditions at the site, would have foreseen the need for sheet piling."[97]

[d] Reliance

In order to prevail on a Type I DSC claim, the contractor must also show that it reasonably relied upon its interpretation of the contract and contract-related documents.[98] A contractor is presumed to know that which a reasonable bidder would have known from reading the contract and other documentation. "Reasonable reliance cannot exist where the contractor bids without having reviewed the contract documents on which it seeks to rely."[99]

Additionally, a contractor will not be able to recover for a differing site condition when a patent ambiguity exists in the contract documents. A "patent" ambiguity is one that is "glaring, substantial, or patently obvious."[100] Rather, such an ambiguity would create a duty on the part of the contractor to inquire. A contractor's failure to satisfy this duty will preclude it from proffering its interpretation of the contract documents after the fact.[101]

In *Comtrol*,[102] the Federal Circuit Court of Appeals affirmed the trial court's decision denying the contractor's claims for differing site conditions and defective specifications. Comtrol had a contract with the Federal Aviation Administration (FAA) for construction work at the Salt Lake City International Airport. Comtrol sought equitable adjustments for two site conditions: 1) the presence of quick sand and 2) the placement of a fuel pipeline.[103] For both conditions, Comtrol claimed differing site conditions and defective specifications.[104]

As to the soil conditions, the solicitation stated that "Hard material . . . may be encountered," and defined "hard material" as "weathered rock, dense consolidated deposits or conglomerate materials which are not included in the definition of 'rock' but which usually require the use of heavy excavation equipment with ripper teeth or the use of jack hammers for removal."[105] Bidders were advised to

---

[96] 153 F.3d 1338, 1347-48.

[97] 153 F.3d 1338, 1347-48.

[98] *Fru-Con Constr.*, 43 Fed. Cl. 306, 317-18.

[99] *Comtrol*, 294 F.3d 1357, 1364.

[100] *Comtrol*, 294 F.3d 1357, 1365.

[101] *See Comtrol*, 294 F.3d 1357, 1365; W.M. Schlosser, Inc. v. United States, 50 Fed. Cl. 147, 154 (Fed. Cl. 2001).

[102] 294 F.3d 1357 (Fed. Cir. 2002).

[103] 294 F.3d 1357, 1359.

[104] 294 F.3d 1357, 1359.

[105] 294 F.3d 1357, 1360.

include in their bids the cost of collecting and disposing of surface and subsurface water encountered during construction. The solicitation encouraged a site visit and incorporated by reference an engineering report and contract drawings. Despite these urgings, Comtrol did not review the engineering report before submitting its bid. The report disclosed that the subsurface material was clay and that "all of the subsurface materials are natural deposits."[106] The report also stated that the soils had recently been saturated with water and that groundwater was encountered at approximately seven feet for one test hole and two feet for the remaining test holes.[107] The contractor proceeded with excavating by driving a sheet pile wall around the perimeter of the excavation to contain groundwater and during that work encountered loose sand, water, and quick sand.[108]

The court noted that the specifications did not affirmatively represent that only hard material would be encountered. The court held that, because the contract documents did not specifically mention the type of soil to be encountered, Comtrol could not be said to have encountered conditions differing materially from those indicated in the specifications.[109] Additionally, the court stated that "[r]easonable reliance cannot exist where the contractor bid without having reviewed the contract documents on which it seeks to rely." The court reasoned that the contractor, having failed to review the engineering report and all contract documents concerning subsurface conditions, cannot show that it reasonably relied on the engineering report's description of soil and water conditions.[110] Thus, the court held that Comtrol could not use the engineering report that it did not review prior to bidding as the basis for a Type I DSC claim.[111]

As to the pipeline condition, the solicitation stated that "No pipes ... except those indicated, will be encountered." However, one of the drawings referenced in the Solicitation noted that an existing pipeline was to be relocated by others.[112] These drawings were maintained at the FAA offices, but Comtrol did not request or obtain these drawings until after the failure of the sheet pile wall.[113]

The court found a patent ambiguity in the documents because they did not indicate when the pipeline would be relocated or whether the contractor would encounter the old, new, or neither pipeline. The court held that the contractor could not recover because the patent ambiguity in the contract documents put the contractor on notice that a fuel pipeline may exist at or near the construction site, creating a duty for the contractor to seek clarification of this ambiguity.[114] Therefore, the court held that Comtrol could not establish a differing site conditions claim or defective specifications claim relating to the pipeline "because it

---

[106] 294 F.3d 1357, 1360.
[107] 294 F.3d 1357, 1360.
[108] 294 F.3d 1357, 1360.
[109] 294 F.3d 1357, 1363.
[110] 294 F.3d 1357, 1360.
[111] 294 F.3d 1357, 1360-61.
[112] 294 F.3d 1357, 1365.
[113] 294 F.3d 1357, 1361.
[114] 294 F.3d 1357, 1365.

cannot establish that it acted as a reasonably prudent contractor in interpreting the contract documents."[115]

On the other hand, a contractor that discovers during the construction that the site conditions are not as represented in the contract documents will normally be entitled to recover the extra costs it incurs as a result of the inaccuracies.[116] In *T. Brown Constructors,* the contractor received a contract to perform grading, drainage, and asphaltic surfacing for a highway. The contractor sought additional compensation for extra work related to a differing site condition, among other items.[117] The contract required the contractor to produce aggregates for the pavement structure, which were formed by a process of crushing raw material taken from a quarry and sifting the crushed material through an appropriate size sieve.[118] Before crushing the raw material, the processor must remove the clay. The government provided two test results to the contractors for bidding. One of these was a wash sieve test that identified the amount of material in the quarry. However, the washed sieve test was not performed according to the government standards because the sample comprised of weathered rock taken from the face of the pit. The government prepared a note to the bidders specifically alerting them to the problem with the test results, but it failed to transmit the note to the bidders.[119]

The contractor based its bid on the government's test results of the clay content in the quarry. However, the contractor encountered a significantly higher amount of clay than indicated in the test results. The court found that the government misrepresented the composition of the quarry by omitting the note indicating that the washed sieve test results were performed on a weathered sample. The court also held that the contractor reasonably relied on the washed sieve analysis results, thus supporting a recovery for extra work based on the unit price set forth in the contract.[120]

[4] Type II Differing Site Conditions

To prevail on a claim for Type II DSC, a party must prove by a preponderance of the evidence that (a) the physical condition at the site was unknown; or (b) said condition was unusual and could not be reasonably anticipated by the contractor from his study of the contract documents, his inspection of the site, and his general experience, if any, in the contract area; and (c) the condition encountered was materially different from those ordinarily encountered and generally recognized as inhering in the work of this character.[121] In order for a contractor to

---

[115] 294 F.3d 1357, 1365.

[116] *See* T. Brown Constructors, Inc. v. Pena, 132 F.3d 724 (Fed. Cir. 1998).

[117] 132 F.3d 724, 726.

[118] 132 F.3d 724, 727.

[119] 132 F.3d 724, 728-29.

[120] 132 F.3d 724, 729.

[121] Youngdale & Sons Constr. Co. v. United States, 27 Fed. Cl. 516, 537 (1993); Randa/Madison Joint Venture III v. Dahlberg, 239 F.3d 1264, 1276 (Fed. Cir. 2001).

recover for a Type II DSC, the condition must have existed during the contract's execution.[122] A Type II DSC is generally more difficult to prove than a Type I DSC and usually arises when the contract documents do not indicate sufficiently the particular conditions.[123]

[a]   Unknown or Unusual Physical Conditions

One of the most significant Type II DSC cases is *Servidone Construction Corp.*[124] In *Servidone*, a public contractor brought suit against the government seeking extra compensation for differing site conditions. The contractor received a bid in the sum of $25.8 million for construction of a dam in Dallas, Texas. After completing the project, the contractor submitted a DSC claim, seeking a total of $41.9 million in additional compensation. The contractor claimed that it encountered tough soils that were too difficult to excavate, unload, compact and process. The contractor claimed that the toughness of the soils arose in part from the poorly crystallized or non-crystalline montmoril-lonite and calcium carbonate in the soils, which, when wet, formed a highly unusual inorganic jelly-like substance. One expert described the fill material as behaving like paraffin or grease.[125]

The court held that the contractor encountered soils that "were unusual and differed materially from the soils generally encountered in the Dallas/Ft. Worth area." In determining whether the contractor reasonably could have anticipated the soil conditions, the court found that the contractor had acted unreasonably in preparing its bid in that it conducted only a one-day site visit and should have anticipated some of the difficulty of the soils. However, the court reasoned that a reasonable contractor, having done an adequate site inspection, would not have anticipated the conditions actually found. Accordingly, the court held that the contractor was entitled to recover damages to the extent that it could not have reasonably anticipated the condition.[126]

[b]   Actual Conditions Must Differ Materially

Most standard DSC clauses require that a contractor prove that the actual conditions at the site "differ materially" from those conditions: 1) indicated in the contract for a Type I DSC claim, and 2) encountered and generally recognized as inherent in the work for a Type II DSC claim.

For example, in *Foundation International, Inc. v. E.T. Ige Construction, Inc.,*[127] the court held that an alleged cost increase in drilling through basalt layer

---

[122] Manuel Bros. v. United States, 55 Fed. Cl. 8, 44 (2002).

[123] *See, e.g., Manuel Bros.,* 55 Fed. Cl. 8, 45; *see also* Servidone Constr. Co. v. United States, 19 Cl. Ct. 346, 360 (1990).

[124] 19 Cl. Ct. 346 (1990).

[125] 19 Cl. Ct. 346, 360.

[126] 19 Cl. Ct. 346, 367-75.

[127] 102 Hawaii 487 (2003).

was not a "material difference" justifying application of the differing site condition clause. The excavation subcontractor, Foundation International, brought an action against the general contractor and engineering firm for alleged extra costs incurred in a bridge construction project. The general contractor brought a third-party claim, seeking to pass on any extra cost to the state.[128]

This project in part involved the construction of 71 drill shafts extending, according to the plans, a minimum of 4 feet into basalt. The plans further stated that the pile tip elevations shown on the longitudinal section are estimated elevations and the actual pile tip elevations will be determined by the engineer.[129] Before submitting its bid for the whole project, the general contractor received an unsolicited proposal from Foundation to do the drilled shaft work. Foundation quoted a lump sum amount for both the excavation and the concrete work. Relying on the prices quoted in Foundation's proposal, the general contractor submitted a bid to the State.[130] The general contractor received the contract for the project and subcontracted the work to Foundation.[131]

Upon drilling, Foundation reached the basalt layer at abutment one a few feet below the bottom footing elevation. Foundation drove the shaft four feet into the basalt and announced its intention to drill no further. The state protested stating that the plans and specifications indicated that the shaft must be excavated to the approximate tip elevation. The state argued that this would require Foundation to drill at least 15 feet and only if at that point 4 feet of basalt had been excavated, could Foundation stop drilling. Foundation argued that this would require it to do more expensive digging than it had anticipated in its estimate and price proposal and notified the state in writing of its intention to claim extra compensation for the additional excavation.[132]

At the state engineer's request, another engineer reviewed the design and determined that the four-foot embedment requirement was sufficient. For unknown reasons, the head engineer disagreed and informed the state engineer that a minimum pile length of 12 feet and a minimum embedment requirement of 4 feet was required. Accordingly, the state told Foundation that all shafts must be at least 12 feet in length, even if this required the excavation of more than 4 feet of basalt. Foundation did not learn of the other engineer's findings until it received them in discovery.[133]

Foundation took the position that any excavation beyond the four-foot embedment was "extra work" or a differing site condition for which it was entitled extra compensation.[134] The court disagreed, finding that the plain language of the contract did not limit excavation to four feet of embedment.[135] The court found

---

[128] 102 Hawaii 487, 490-91.
[129] 102 Hawaii 487, 491-92.
[130] 102 Hawaii 487, 491-92.
[131] 102 Hawaii 487, 491-92.
[132] 102 Hawaii 487, 492-43.
[133] 102 Hawaii 487, 493.
[134] 102 Hawaii 487, 493.
[135] 102 Hawaii 487, 495.

unpersuasive the subcontractor's argument that a substantial change occurred by the requirement to excavate beyond four feet of basalt, reasoning that the contract documents were plain that the work would entail all shaft excavation, whether the material was "soil rock, weathered rock, stone, natural or man-made obstructions, or materials of other descriptions."[136] Additionally, the boring information provided by the state demonstrated that the basalt layer was found at varying elevations. The court noted that the uncontested findings also demonstrated that the Foundation's president knew before bidding that the basalt layer could emerge at higher then expected levels. Accordingly, the court held that the alleged increase in drilling through the basalt layer did not constitute a material difference justifying the application of the DSC clause.[137]

[5] Notice Requirements

Most federal, state and private contracts require the contractor to immediately notify the owner of the differing site condition and obtain his written authorization before proceeding with the work.[138] The notice requirements are placed in contracts to provide the owner the opportunity to investigate the site and to minimize the costs resulting from the DSC. The standard construction contracts mentioned above include different notice requirements for compliance by the contractor.

For example, the Federal Acquisition Regulations require the contractor to "promptly, and before the conditions are disturbed, give a written notice to the Contracting Officer of the condition."[139] Similarly, the AIA Document A201 mandates that a contractor give notice of the condition to the other party before conditions are disturbed and in no event later than 21 days after first observance of the conditions.[140] However, the AIA contract does not expressly require the contractor to provide written notice of the condition. The DBIA contract requires that, upon encountering the DSC, the contractor provides prompt written notice to the owner of the condition, which shall be no later than 14 days after the condition has been encountered and to the extent reasonably possible, the contractor is to provide such notice before the DSC has been substantially disturbed or altered.[141] In contrast, the EJCDC contract requires the contractor to notify the owner and engineer in writing about such condition and forbids the contractor from further disturbing such condition or performing any additional work (except in case of an emergency as defined by the contract) until receipt of written order to do so.[142] Also, in certain

---

[136] 102 Hawaii 487, 502.

[137] 102 Hawaii 487, 502.

[138] See also **Chapter 13**, which deals exclusively with notice requirements.

[139] *See* 48 C.F.R. § 52.236-2(a).

[140] *See* AIA Doc. A201, ¶ 4.3.4.

[141] DBIA Standard Form of General Conditions Between Owner and Design-Builder, ¶ 4.2.2 (1st ed. 1998).

[142] EJCDC Doc. No. C-700, Standard General Conditions of the Construction Contract, ¶ 4.03A (2002).

federal highway construction contracts, the party discovering such conditions must "promptly notify the other party in writing of the specific differing site conditions before the site is disturbed and before the affected work is performed."[143]

A failure by the contractor to comply with the notice requirements may preclude a claim for relief for a DSC.[144] However, a contractor may be permitted to recover in the absence of notice, if the owner cannot prove that it was prejudiced or disadvantaged due to the lack of notice.[145]

In *Fru-Con*, the contractor brought suit against the government claiming that it encountered a DSC in repairing the walls of a lock and dam project. The repair work included the installation of new floating mooring bitts (FMBs), which required that the contractor remove concrete from the lock chamber wall. The contractor began blasting the concrete, but overbreak occurred at all FMB sites. The contractor did not provide notice to the government of this DSC until after completion of the project. The contracting officer's representative on site testified that if he had received notice he could have considered the possibility of eliminating the work entirely because it was not a necessary function of the lock and other FMBs already existed at the lock sites.[146] The court stated that, while the contractor did not know the cause of the overbreak, its consequences were evident. Inexplicably, the contractor pressed ahead. Under these circumstances, the court held that the contractor's failure to notify the government of the DSC prejudiced the government, especially when considered in light of the potential remedial alternatives.[147] Thus, the court held that the contractor could not prevail on its DSC claim regarding the concrete because it did not provide the requisite notice to the government.[148]

§ 2.05   VOLUNTEER WORK OR MISTAKES BY CONTRACTOR

In order to recover for extra work, not only must the contractor prove that the extra work was outside the scope of the parties' original contract, the contractor must also prove that the extra work was not performed voluntarily and that the extra work was not caused by any mistake by the contractor.

As to work performed voluntarily, this is usually a simple analysis that requires a fact intensive review. If there is no evidence that the owner requested the work or that the work was necessary to fulfill the contractor's obligations under the relevant contract documents, the court will deny recovery.[149]

Regarding defective work, the general rule is that a contractor who has failed to perform his contract cannot recover either by way of contract or on a quantum

---

[143] *See* 69 FR 72133; 23 C.F.R. § 635.109(a)(1).

[144] *See, e.g.*, Fru-Con Constr. v. United States, 43 Fed. Cl. 306 (1999).

[145] 43 Fed. Cl. 306, 328.

[146] 43 Fed. Cl. 306, 326.

[147] 43 Fed. Cl. 306, 327.

[148] 43 Fed. Cl. 306, 327-28.

[149] *See, e.g.*, Dusenka v. Dusenka, 21 N.W.2d 528 (Minn. 1946).

meruit basis.[150] In some jurisdictions however, recovery is allowed on a quantum meruit theory. In *Bouterie v. Carre*,[151] the plaintiff brought an action to recover for painting work that had not been properly performed. The defendant refused to pay for the work on the ground that the work was defective. The court in *Bouterie* noted:

> The defendant has mistaken his remedy. He has no right to refuse absolutely to pay for the work he has received and was enjoying. The jurisprudence of this state is that a contractor who has delivered his work to the owner may sue him when he has received it and is in the enjoyment of it; and that the contractor may recover the value of the work which has inured to the benefit of the owner, although the work be defective or unfinished; if a price has been agreed upon the remedy of the owner is a reduction thereof to an amount necessary to perfect or to complete the work according to contract.[152]

The court went on to note that "[t]he amount recoverable depends upon the extent of the benefit conferred having reference to the contract for the entire work, and this is usually the contract price, less the damages caused by not complying with the exact terms of the contract."[153]

§2.06 AVOIDING THE PRE-EXISTING DUTY RULE

In many jurisdictions, the pre-existing duty rule has fallen out of favor as a means to resolve scope of work, contract modification, and payment disputes in construction cases. The pre-existing duty rule has been criticized as "an artificial obstacle to good faith contract changes" and, in some jurisdictions, it has been abolished in favor of other, less stringent rules of contract modification and theories of contract damage recovery.[154] If the rule is considered, most courts will

---

[150] L.V. Werbin, Legal Guide for Contractors, Architects and Engineers 75 (1961).

[151] 6 So. 2d 218 (La. Ct. App. 1942).

[152] 6 So. 2d 218, 220.

[153] 6 So. 2d 218, 220.

[154] *See* Angel v. Murray, 322 A.2d 630 (R.I. 1974); Standard Alliance Indus., Inc. v. Black Clawson Co., 587 F.2d 813, 829 n.35 (6th Cir. 1978). Indeed, the Uniform Commercial Code (U.C.C.) has abolished the pre-existing duty rule. *See* U.C.C. § 2-209. In *Angel*, the court stated:

> ... the courts have been reluctant to apply the preexisting duty rule when a party to a contract encounters unanticipated difficulties and the other party, not influenced by coercion or duress, voluntarily agrees to pay additional compensation for work already required to be performed under the contract. ... Although the preexisting duty rule has served a useful purpose insofar as it deters parties from using coercion and duress to obtain additional compensation, it has been widely criticize as a general rule of law.

With regard to the pre-existing duty rule, one legal scholar has stated:

> There has been growing doubt as to the soundness of this doctrine as a matter of social policy. ... In certain classes of cases, this doubt has influenced courts to refuse to apply the rule, or to ignore it, in their actual decisions. Like other legal rules, this rule is in process of growth and change, the process being more active here than in most

endeavor to find the required consideration where the parties have negotiated for a contract modification voluntarily and in good faith.[155] However, modern contract provisions and legal and equitable theories employed to resolve construction disputes do utilize and build upon the concepts underlying the pre-existing duty rule.

Construction contracts usually contain "work" and "scope of work" clauses, and may contain plans and specifications, which, to varying degrees, define the duties the contractor is to perform in exchange for the compensation stated in the contract.[156] On many projects, each act to be performed by the contractor cannot be described in detail in the contract documents. The terms of the contract must generalize, at least to some extent, the contractor's obligations. And, in some cases, the work and/or scope of work is deliberately stated in broad terms.[157] As a consequence, the parties to the contract may interpret the contractor's responsibilities differently, leading to disputes related to the work to be performed and the compensation to be paid.

When the contractor's work exceeds or deviates from the scope of the work the contractor anticipated at the time of contracting, the contractor will seek additional payment for the extra work performed or promised. The contractor will rely on the limits of the contract's scope of work to claim additional payment for extra work falling outside that scope. Conversely, the owner will claim the contract's scope of work includes all work performed or promised to be performed by the contractor for the agreed contract price. According to the owner, the contractor's pre-existing duties under the existing contract require the contractor to perform the work for which the contractor seeks additional compensation.

---

instances. The result of this is that a court should no longer accept this rule as fully established. It should never use it as the major premise of a decision, at least without giving careful thought to the circumstances of the particular case, to the moral deserts of the parties, and to the social feelings and interest that are involved. It is certain that the rule, stated in general and all-inclusive terms, is no longer so well-settled that a court must apply it though the heavens fall. 1A Corbin on Contracts § 171. *See also* Calamari & Perillo, Contracts § 61.

322 A.2d 630, 635-36.

[155] *See Standard Alliance*, 587 F.2d 813, 829 n.35 (6th Cir. 1978). *See also* Restatement (Second) of Contracts § 89, Modification of Executory Contract, which provides:

A promise modifying a duty under a contract not fully performed on either side is binding
    (a) if the modification is fair and equitable in view of circumstances not anticipated by the parties when the contract was made; or
    (b) to the extent provided by statute; or
    (c) to the extent that justice requires enforcement in view of material change of position in reliance on the promise.

[156] See §§ **2.05** and **2.06**.

[157] For example, the American Institute of Architect's (AIA) Standard Form of Agreement Between Owner and Contractor, Article 2—The Work of this Contract (1997), provides: "The Contactor shall fully execute the Work described in the Contract Documents, except to the extent specifically indicated in the Contract Documents to be the responsibility of others." AIA Doc. A111, Standard Form of Agreement Between Owner and Contractor (1997).

Thus, the threshold questions become: (1) what is the "duty" (i.e., "scope of work") the contractor agreed to perform under the terms of the existing contract, and (2) what is the contractor fairly entitled to be paid for the work actually performed? To answer these questions requires an assessment of the parties' expectations of the work contemplated under the contract at the time of contracting. In complex construction cases, the strictures of the pre-existing duty rule's premise—a well-defined scope of work—do not provide courts a sufficient legal framework to resolve disputes. While the governing principle of the pre-existing duty rule still applies in most cases, courts turn to other legal doctrines to resolve these questions in modern construction disputes.

Contracting parties usually include specific contract provisions, which permit changes in the contractor's work and its compensation, including changed conditions clauses and equitable adjustment clauses.[158] In construing these provisions and resolving construction contract disputes, courts have employed legal and equitable doctrines, including contract modification, contract rescission or abandonment, the cardinal change doctrine, and quantum meruit.

These contract provisions and legal theories implicate the pre-existing duty rule's basic principle: a promise to perform work that a party is already obligated to perform under the existing contract is not sufficient consideration to enforce the promise. Thus, regardless of the theory of recovery employed, the contractor must show that due to changed conditions or other factors not contemplated by the parties at the time of contracting, it is equitable to award the contractor additional compensation. The legal theories discussed herein exemplify the tension between owners and contractors relating to the scope of the contractor's work, the application of the pre-existing duty rule, and the use of other legal and equitable doctrines to fairly compensate the contractor for work performed and from which the owner derives benefit.

[A] Traditional Exceptions to the Pre-existing Duty Rule— Additional Compensation and Rescission

Under traditional common law, two exceptions to the pre-existing duty rule permit modification of an existing contract.[159] The first is for the promisee to

---

[158] *See* AIA Doc. A201, ARTICLE 7 CHANGES IN THE WORK, which provides in part:

§ 7.1 GENERAL

§ 7.1.1 Changes in the Work may be accomplished after execution of the Contract, and without invalidating the Contract, by Change Order, Construction Change Directive or order for a minor change in the Work, subject to the limitations stated in this Article 7 and elsewhere in the Contract Documents.

§ 7.1.2 A Change Order shall be based upon agreement among the Owner, Contractor and Architect; a Construction Change Directive requires agreement by the Owner and Architect and may or may not be agreed to by the Contractor; an order for a minor change in the Work may be issued by the Architect alone.

§ 7.1.3 Changes in the Work shall be performed under applicable provisions of the Contract Documents, and the Contractor shall proceed promptly, unless otherwise provided in the Change Order, Construction Change Directive or order for a minor change in the Work.

[159] Contempo Design, Inc. v. Chicago & Northeast Illinois Dist. Council of Carpenters, 226 F.3d 535, 550 (7th Cir. 2000).

undertake to do something in addition to what she already is obligated to do under her pre-existing duty.[160] If additional consideration is given, then the contract modification is valid.

The second exception requires the parties to agree to rescind the original contract, which allows them to create a different contract on entirely new terms, without providing additional consideration[161] "In theory, this must leave both parties with at least an instant of freedom, during which they are no longer bound by the old contract or under no duty to make a new one."[162] While it appears straightforward, the rescission exception to the pre-existing duty rule is not without its pitfalls.[163]

Great care should be taken when distinguishing between a purported contract modification and the rescission of an existing contract followed by consummation of a new contract. Indeed, some courts recognize that "where an alleged rescission is coupled with a simultaneous reentry into a new contract and the terms of that new contract are more favorable to only one of the parties, doubt is created as to the mutuality of the agreement to rescind the original contract."[164]

In *McCallum Highlands, Ltd. v. Washington Capital DUS, Inc.*, the court, in nullifying a modification, distinguished between the modification of a contract and the rescission of an existing contract.[165] The court questioned the logic of the rescission exception, finding that the exception "is based on circular logic because the validity of the new agreement depends upon the rescission and the validity of the rescission depends upon the new agreement."[166] Thus, in that case, the court refused to find that the parties had rescinded the original agreement and provided adequate consideration for a subsequent agreement because the rescission of the original commitment occurred simultaneously with the creation of the amended agreement, and because the terms were more favorable to one party.[167]

To avoid this result, the Restatement (Second) of Contracts § 89 extinguishes the additional consideration requirement to modify a contract. Section 89 provides in pertinent part:

> A promise modifying a duty under a contract not fully performed on either side is binding: (a) if the modification is fair and equitable in view of circumstances not anticipated by the parties when the contract was made.

---

[160] *Contempo*, 226 F.3d 535, 550.

[161] *Contempo*, 226 F.3d 535, 550.

[162] *Contempo*, 226 F.3d 535, 550.

[163] The validity of this exception to the pre-existing duty rule has been questioned by a number of authorities. *See, e.g.*, 3 Williston on Contracts § 7:37; 1A Corbin on Contracts § 186 (1963); Restatement (Second) of Contracts § 89 cmt. B (1981); John D. Calamari & Joseph M. Perillo, Contracts 206 (3d ed. 1987).

[164] McCallum Highlands, Ltd. v. Washington Capital DUS, Inc., 66 F.3d 89, 93-94 (5th Cir. 1995).

[165] 66 F.3d 89, 93.

[166] 66 F.3d 89, 93.

[167] 66 F.3d 89, 93.

The basis for the Restatement's treatment of contract modification rests upon whether a modification is fair and equitable, requiring an objectively demonstrable reason for seeking a modification.[168] No additional consideration is required. However, the reason for modification must rest in circumstances not anticipated when the contract was made.[169] When such a reason exists, the relative financial strength of the parties, the formality with which the modification is made, the extent to which it is performed or relied on, and other circumstances may be relevant to show or negate imposition or unfair surprise.[170]

Thus, in order to avoid the sometimes harsh effects of the pre-existing duty rule, contractors should be careful to address the issue of extra work at the time it first arises. Moreover, contractors should be ready to demonstrate that the compensation sought for extra work was not contemplated at the time the parties entered the contract. If the contractor secures the owner's agreement that the extra or additional work is outside the scope of the party's contract, then the contractor stands a better chance of ultimately recovering for the work based on additional consideration or changed conditions. Very often, this can be accomplished by changing the specifications for the project or extending the time for completion of the work. Although this may sound simple, courts will generally not weigh consideration for a contract and will allow the contractor to recover for the extra work.[171]

[B] Contract Abandonment and the Cardinal Change Doctrine

Both contract abandonment and the cardinal change doctrine may be utilized to establish a basis for recovery outside the original contract and avoid the pre-existing duty rule.[172] Either or both theories may apply in cases where the contractual obligations of the contractor vary materially from the original expectations of the parties regarding the scope and manner of the work.[173] Where a contractor claims that a contract has been mutually abandoned or cardinally changed, courts will consider whether the contractor's overall undertaking "so far exceeded the general scope of his anticipated obligations that the only equitable remedy is a recovery in quantum meruit."[174]

[1] Contract Abandonment

A contract may be abandoned expressly or implicitly by the parties acting inconsistently with its terms.[175] "The proof must be clear and convincing to sustain

---

[168] Restatement (Second) of Contracts § 89 cmt. B.

[169] Restatement (Second) of Contracts § 89 cmt. B.

[170] Restatement (Second) of Contracts § 89 cmt. B.

[171] *See* Bouterie v. Carre, 6 So. 2d 218 (La. Ct. App. 1942).

[172] L.K. Comstock & Co. v. Becon Constr. Co., 932 F. Supp. 906, 931 (E.D. Ky. 1993). **Chapter 11** provides a more detailed discussion of the cardinal change.

[173] *L.K. Comstock*, 932 F. Supp. 906.

[174] *L.K. Comstock*, 932 F. Supp. 906. *See also* J.A. Jones Constr. Co. v. Lehrer McGovern Bovis, Inc., 89 P.3d 1009, 1019 n.25 (Nev. 2004).

[175] *L.K. Comstock*, 932 F. Supp. 906, 931.

a finding that the contract has been abandoned"[176] to avoid the pre-existing duty rule.

Courts recognize abandonment as a valid principle in construction disputes. Parties to a construction contract may manifest their intent to abandon the contract by their conduct, and abandonment may be implicit from the circumstances surrounding the performance of the work.[177] When determining whether a contract has been abandoned, courts have considered, among other factors, "the number of changes, the effect of the changes on the original and change work in terms of extra costs and the number of workers needed, and whether the parties observed the contract terms, including the contract procedure for changes."[178] One court applied the principle of abandonment even though the contractor continued with construction, finding that "[a]lthough the contract [was] ... abandoned, the work [was] ... not."[179] "Abandonment can be shown by acts and conduct consistent with the intent to abandon, and the district court may discount contrary testimony that no abandonment existed."[180] "Proof of abandonment must be made by clear, unequivocal, and decisive evidence, and must manifest the parties' actual intent to abandon contract rights."[181]

In *Schwartz v. Shelby Construction Co.*,[182] the Supreme Court of Missouri applied the principle of abandonment to a construction contract in which the general contractor failed to provide the plumbing subcontractor with a complete set of plans. The court found that the subcontractor was left "to his own devices," which evidenced a "substantial lack of cooperation."[183]

The *Schwartz* court also found the defendant had repeatedly represented the job as one for mass production prefabrication when, in fact, progress of the work resulted in frequent obstacles and the need for constant adaptation by the subcontractor.[184] The work could not be planned because the exact dimensions of each building varied from one to the next.[185] The court found that all parties were aware that the subcontractor could not complete the work within the contract price. The subcontractor insisted that the job they were performing was totally different from the work called for under the contract, and that the project should be paid for on a "time and materials" basis.[186]

The court concluded that the parties had abandoned the contract due to the day-to-day changes made from the beginning to the completion of the job.[187] The court stated that:

---

[176] *L.K. Comstock,* 932 F. Supp. 906, 933.

[177] *L.K. Comstock,* 932 F. Supp. 906, 933.

[178] *L.K. Comstock,* 932 F. Supp. 906, 933.

[179] Norman Peterson Co. v. Container Corp. of Am., 172 Cal. App. 3d 628, 218 Cal. Rptr. 592, 598 (1985).

[180] O'Brien & Gere Tech. Servs. Inc. v. Fru-Con/Fluor Daniel Joint Venture, 380 F.3d 447, 455 (8th Cir. 2004). *Accord* Land Improvement, Inc. v. Ferguson, 800 S.W.2d 460, 464 (Mo. Ct. App. 1990).

[181] *Id. Accord* McBee v. Gustaaf Vadecnocke Revocable Trust, 986 S.W.2d 170, 173 (Mo. 1999).

[182] 338 S.W.2d 781 (Mo. 1960).

[183] Schwartz v. Shelby Constr. Co., 338 S.W.2d 781, 790 (Mo. 1960).

[184] *Schwartz,* 338 S.W.2d 781, 790.

[185] *Schwartz,* 338 S.W.2d 781, 784-86.

[186] *Schwartz,* 338 S.W.2d 781, 790.

[187] *Schwartz,* 338 S.W.2d 781, 790.

An abandonment may be accomplished by express mutual consent or by implied consent through the actions of the parties ... Plaintiff cannot be guilty of a breach of the contract if it has been mutually abandoned. ... Where acts and conduct are relied on to constitute an abandonment, they "must be positive, unequivocal and inconsistent with an intent to be further bound by the contract."[188]

Once a court determines that a contract has been abandoned, the court will employ equitable theories, like quantum meruit, to compensate the contractor for work performed.

In *O'Brien & Gere Technical Services Inc. v. Fru-Con/Fluor Daniel Joint Venture*,[189] the Eighth Circuit affirmed an award of additional compensation to a subcontractor for the reasonable value of its services, which exceeded the contract price. The subcontractor sued in quantum meruit for the reasonable value of the work performed. In support of its claimed damages, the subcontractor presented the following evidence: (1) an extremely tight construction schedule that the parties could not meet; (2) the actual work became substantially different from work contemplated under the contract; (3) the parties disagreed about what documents defined the basic scope of the work and design stage from which work changes should be measured; and (4) the parties re-negotiated advance payments in exchange for new subcontract milestones in lieu of issuing subcontract modifications.[190]

The court found that quantum meruit, under Missouri law, permits the reasonable value of services as measured by the price usually and customarily paid for such or like services at the time and in the location where services are rendered.[191] "Recovery in quantum meruit is generally limited to the agreed-upon price for the goods and services; the contract price does not limit recovery, however, where the parties abandon the contract."[192]

Because the subcontractor was already paid in excess of the contract price, the court found that the subcontractor could recover additional compensation under quantum meruit only if the parties had abandoned the existing contract.[193] Under Missouri law, "[a]n abandonment may be accomplished by express mutual consent or by an implied consent through the actions of the parties."[194]

The court concluded that the subcontractor did present clear and convincing evidence that the parties manifested an intent to abandon their rights under the contract. In reaching this conclusion, the court found it most important that the

---

[188] *Schwartz,* 338 S.W.2d 781, 788, citing Sauder v. Dittmar, 118 F.2d 524, 530 (10th Cir. 1941).

[189] 380 F.3d 447 (8th Cir. 2004).

[190] 380 F.3d 447, 454.

[191] 380 F.3d 447, 454.

[192] 380 F.3d 447, 454. *See* Holland v. Tandem Computers, Inc., 49 F.3d 1287, 1288-89 (8th Cir. 1995).

[193] 380 F.3d 447, 454.

[194] Schwartz v. Shelby Constr. Co., 338 S.W.2d 781, 788 (Mo. 1960).

parties could not keep up with the "extremely tight construction schedule they set for themselves."[195] The court stated:

> Contrary to their expectations in reaching an agreement, the kickoff meeting, subcontract execution, and first modification were each delayed by several precious weeks or more. Later, defective designs and performance by both parties caused further delays, which in turn had a detrimental domino effect in two ways: They set back the cumulative work schedule, and they exacerbated [the subcontractor's] precarious cash-flow position, which in turn forced [the subcontractor] again to postpone work. In short, the project progressed at a different pace from that contemplated by the subcontract; the parties departed from the contract milestones, even after they were amended.[196]

Moreover, the court found that the actual job became substantially different from the contract job.[197] The scope, quantity, and frequency of changes are factors the court considered in finding the parties had abandoned the contract as a result of the substantial changes that affected the work during construction.

The subcontractor was awarded "the reasonable value of its services" in excess of the contract price because the parties had abandoned the existing terms of the contract. Thus, the pre-existing duty rule did not preclude the subcontractor's recovery, on an equitable basis, for work that arguably fell within the ambit of the scope of the contractor's work under the existing contract. Instead, the court permitted the subcontractor to avoid the terms of the existing contract by abandonment of that contract, in order to recover in equity for the reasonable value of its services.

By contrast, in *McMillion Dozer Service,. v. JOH Construction Co.,*[198] the court determined that the parties were bound by their contract and that the subcontractor could not recover for changed conditions.

The subcontractor sued to recover additional payment from the landowner and the contractor as a result of delays caused by a break in an electrical line, late work permits, plant shutdowns, and excess rainfall.[199] The subcontractor agreed to construct drainage ditches under a fixed-price contract. Prior to construction, the subcontractor was provided with plans, which located subsurface structures. During construction, the subcontractor encountered a structure in an area not identified in the project plans. While removing the structure, an electrical line beneath the structure was damaged, causing the plant and the project to shut down. As a

---

[195] O'Brien & Gere Tech. Servs. Inc. v. Fru-Con/Fluor Daniel Joint Venture, 380 F.3d 447, 454 (8th Cir. 2004).

[196] *O'Brien,* 380 F.3d 447, 454.

[197] The subcontract contained a change order provision that required the subcontractor to make changes to its scope of work whenever it received written instructions for changes from the contractor. Although the subcontractor was required to "promptly proceed in compliance with such written instructions," it could not collect on any increase in costs from the change until the parties had agreed to the price in writing. The subcontract also contained a merger clause, which required that modification to the subcontract be in writing or otherwise be unenforceable.

[198] 720 So. 2d 1239 (La. App. 5th Cir. 1998).

[199] 720 So. 2d 1239, 1241.

consequence, the subcontractor's work was delayed by several weeks. In addition, the project was shut down for maintenance, which caused routine delays in issuance of daily safety permits, without which the subcontractor was strictly forbidden to begin work. Finally, the subcontractor claimed that extreme rain caused additional loss of time.[200]

Under the equitable adjustment clause of its subcontract, the subcontractor sought an equitable adjustment of its payment due to the delays caused by these factors. The contractor responded that most of the subcontractor's lack of progress was due to bad crews and lack of continuity in field supervision. The trial court denied the subcontractor's claim for additional payment, finding no basis for the imposition of an equitable adjustment of the fixed-price contract.[201]

The Court of Appeals of Louisiana affirmed the trial court's judgment. The court denied the subcontractor's claims under the subcontract's "equitable adjustment" clause for additional payments due to alleged changes in the scope of work. The court found that the evidence adduced provided a reasonable factual basis in the record to support the conclusion that none of these factors constituted a change in the scope of the work sufficient to trigger the "equitable adjustment" clause of the contract.[202] Essentially, the court determined that the delay factors did not alter the scope of work the subcontractor agreed to perform and, therefore, the subcontractor was not entitled to additional compensation under the subcontract.[203]

[2] Cardinal Change Doctrine

The cardinal change doctrine serves "to provide a breach remedy for contractors who are directed . . . to perform work which is not within the general scope of the contract and which is therefore not redressable under the contract."[204] The cardinal change doctrine developed as a means to respond to unilateral changes imposed by the party for whom the work is being performed, and concerns about misuse or overuse of that unilateral authority.[205] As one court put it, "the power of

---

[200] 720 So. 2d 1239, 1241.

[201] 720 So. 2d 1239, 1242.

[202] 720 So. 2d 1239, 1243.

[203] *See also* Pellerin Constr., Inc. v. Witco Corp., 169 F. Supp. 2d 568 (E.D. La. 2001) (changes in project's scope were insufficient to trigger doctrine of cardinal change and recovery under theory of quantum meruit or unjust enrichment was not available given the existence of a contract); L.K. Comstock & Co. v. Becon Constr. Co., 932 F. Supp. 906 (E.D. Ky. 1993). *Cf.* A.C.E.S., Inc., ASBCA No. 21,417, 79-1 BCA (CCH) ¶ 12,809, 1979 WL 2350 (1979) (contractor was "entitled to an equitable adjustment based on the underabsorption of fixed overhead" during shut down days attributable to the owner); Worsham Constr. Co., ASBCA No. 25,907, 85-2 BCA (CCH) ¶ 18,018 at 90370, 1985 WL 16693 (1985) (awarding damages for unabsorbed overhead costs resulting from the delay and ultimate termination of contract); Adam Barr's Son, ASBCA No. 15,178, 71-1 BCA (CCH) ¶ 8917 at 41428, 1971 WL 1664 (1971) (awarding an overhead allowance for a 67-day period of work suspension).

[204] J.A. Jones Constr. Co. v. Lehrer McGovern Bovis, Inc., 89 P.3d 1009, 1020 (Nev. 2004). *See also L.K. Comstock,* 932 F. Supp. 906 (E.D. Ky. 1993).

[205] *L.K. Comstock,* 932 F. Supp. 906, 937.

the owner, be it a federal agency or a private developer, to order changes is subject to abuse."[206] "The theory of cardinal change allows a contractor in a losing contract, where the owner has abused its power, to bring an action for material breach of contract, alleging that the changes ordered exceed the reasonable expectations of the parties."[207] Thus, the changes clause found in most public[208] and private[209] construction contracts are the central focus of the cardinal change doctrine.[210]

In *J.A. Jones Construction Co. v. Lehrer McGovern Bovis, Inc.,*[211] a subcontractor brought claims against the contractor for breach of contract and quantum meruit. In support of its quantum meruit claim, the subcontractor asserted that delays and changes in the scope and sequence of its work created substantial additional work for which the contractor refused to compensate the subcontractor.

The trial court refused to recognize the cardinal change doctrine, and determined that even if the doctrine were available, it would not apply.[212] Reversing the trial court, the Supreme Court of Nevada found that a claim of cardinal change did lie and should be analyzed thusly:

> Whether a change is cardinal is principally a question of fact, requiring that each case be analyzed individually in light of the totality of the circumstances. "Each case must be analyzed on its own facts and in light of its own circumstances,

---

[206] *L.K. Comstock,* 932 F. Supp. 906, 937. *See also* Housing Auth. of Texarkana v. E.W. Johnson Constr. Co., 573 S.W.2d 316 (1978) (award based upon breach of warranty of plans and specifications and project for remodeling public housing resulting in cardinal changes to contract upheld; changes were not within scope of original contract and forced contractor into different undertaking than original contract); Rudd v. Anderson, 285 N.E.2d 836, 840 (1972) (outlining development of Indian law standing for the proposition that where there is a lump sum construction contract, if "cumulative changes no longer appear to be an appendage of the original ... contract, reasonable value is the only feasible test of total value for the total construction."); *cf.* Hensel Phelps Constr. Co. v. King County, 787 P.2d 58 (1990) (rejecting cardinal change claim by contractor for construction of county jail because magnitude of changes was insufficient to measure up to damages found to be cardinal in court of claims cases, and because plaintiff failed to exhaust contracts remedial provisions); Watt Plumbing, Air Conditioning & Elec., Inc. v. Tulsa Rig, Reel & Mfg. Co., 533 P.2d 980, 982 (Okla. 1975) (trial court affirmed in determination that "cardinal change doctrine was not applicable where the subcontractor agrees to perform for an agreed price the changes alleged to constitute a cardinal change").

[207] *J.A. Jones,* 89 P.3d 1009, 1020.

[208] In the public contract setting, the limits under the cardinal change doctrine to the nature and magnitude of changes the government can order under the contract "prevents government agencies from circumventing the competitive procurement process by adopting drastic modifications beyond the original scope of a contract." *L.K. Comstock,* 932 F. Supp. 906, 937. *Accord* Cray Research, Inc. v. Department of Navy, 556 F. Supp. 201, 203 (D.D.C. 1982).

[209] "Although the cardinal change doctrine was created as a check on the government's ability to circumvent the competitive-bidding process by ordering drastic changes beyond those contemplated in the contract, and has been predominantly discussed in disputes based on government contracts, its underlying premise—that compensation for costs resulting from an abuse of authority under the changes clause should not be limited by the terms of that clause—applies to private contracts that include changes clauses." *J.A. Jones,* 89 P.3d 1009, 1020.

[210] *See L.K. Comstock,* 932 F. Supp. 906, 937.

[211] *J.A. Jones,* 89 P.3d 1009, 1020.

[212] *J.A. Jones,* 89 P.3d 1009, 1019-20.

giving just consideration to the magnitude and quality of the changes ordered and their cumulative effect upon the project as a whole." Further, [a] determination of the scope and nature of alleged changes requires a fact-intensive inquiry into the events that led to the excess work and their effect on the parties. The court must investigate the contract as a whole to determine whether [the owner or construction manager] is responsible for the contractor's difficulty.

The court recognized that other courts consider, *inter alia*, the following factors when determining whether a cardinal change has occurred: (i) whether there is a significant change in the magnitude of work to be performed; (ii) whether the change is designed to procure a totally different item or drastically alter the quality, character, nature, or type of work contemplated by the original contract; and (iii) whether the cost of the work ordered greatly exceeds the original contract cost.[213]

Applying these factors, the court found that there were material changes to the subcontractor's scope of work caused by resequencing and delay and substantial additional monetary costs associated with change orders.[214] As a consequence, the court held that the trial court erred in dismissing the subcontractor's cardinal change claim.[215] Other courts, however, have not applied the cardinal change doctrine in similar circumstances.

The court in *L.K. Comstock* undertakes an extensive discussion of the cardinal change doctrine, ultimately concluding that the contractor was not entitled to additional restitution on a theory of cardinal change.[216]

The court found that "the central consideration should be the effect [of the changes] on the contractor's anticipated work."[217] Indeed, the court cited with approval another court's finding that "[t]he fact that a party may have sought, released, or otherwise compromised a claim under a contract's equitable adjustment clause or other remedial clauses will not necessarily operate as a bar to claims for relief outside the contract."[218] Contract limitations on claims for extra costs may not limit the contractor's claim for work performed that is "fundamentally outside of the scope of the contract."[219]

---

[213] *J.A. Jones*, 89 P.3d 1009, 1020-21.

[214] *J.A. Jones*, 89 P.3d 1009, 1020-21.

[215] *J.A. Jones*, 89 P.3d 1009, 1020-21. However, the court also noted that recovery of a party's total costs of performance in quantum meruit, as claimed by the subcontractor, may not be an appropriate measure of recovery where a cardinal change has been found. *Id.* at n.41, citing Amelco Elec. v. City of Thousand Oaks, 27 Cal. 4th 228, 115 Cal. Rptr. 2d 900, 38 P.3d 1120, 1126 (2002) (the total cost method is disfavored as a measure of damages).

[216] 932 F. Supp. 906, 936-46.

[217] 932 F. Supp. 906, 940.

[218] 932 F. Supp. 906, 941, citing Allied Materials & Equip. Co. v. United States, 569 F.2d 562 (Ct. Cl. 1978).

[219] 932 F. Supp. 906, 941. *Cf.* Pellerin Constr., Inc. v. Witco Corp., 169 F. Supp. 2d 568 (E.D. La. 2001) (changes in project's scope were insufficient to trigger doctrine of cardinal change and recovery under theory of quantum meruit or unjust enrichment was not available given the existence of a contract).

Nevertheless, the court held that the subcontractor's continued performance of the construction project, its adherence to the contractual change order process, and the reaffirmation of the contract after its work was 90 percent complete, militated against recovery under the cardinal change doctrine.[220] Instead, the contractor was bound to recover under the contract—"[subcontractor's] action is appropriately one for breach of the changes clauses based on [the owner's] alleged failure to make a proper 'equitably adjustment' to the contract price."[221]

Thus, whether the cardinal change doctrine is applied depends upon the court and the facts of each case. In any case, however, a contractor seeking to recover under the cardinal change doctrine (or contract abandonment) should be prepared to show that the work it performed was fundamentally different from the scope of work it anticipated under the contract. Otherwise, the contractor may be limited to recovery under a breach of the change order or equitable adjustment clauses of the contract.

[C] Constructive Changes

Courts sometimes avoid the pre-existing duty rule by reasoning that the owner's conduct (or lack of conduct) gives rise to what is known as a "constructive change."[222] This type of change arises from informal acts or omissions of the owner or the owner's agent that change the requirements of the contract. These actions or omissions cause the contractor to perform work not required by the contract, thus increasing the contractor's cost of performance. They entitle the contractor to additional compensation. Any oral or written act or omission by the owner that requires the contractor to perform work outside the scope of the original contract obligations may constitute a constructive change. A constructive change order may be implied when additional or changed work is done with the owner's knowledge or approval, even though the contractor receives no explicit direction to perform the work by the owner.

The most common types of constructive changes involve ambiguous specifications, a direction to change the method of performance, rejection of "or equal" substitutions, defective materials, over-inspection, and rejection of conforming work. The topic of constructive changes is discussed in more detail in **Chapter 4**.

[D] Defective Plans and Specifications

The specifications are virtually always a part of the contract. AIA Document A201 (1987) defines the specifications as the portion of the contract documents

---

[220] 932 F. Supp. 906, 946.

[221] 932 F. Supp. 906, 946.

[222] For an excellent discussion of this topic with regard to government contracts, *see* C.L. Vacketta & K.P. Mullen, Constructive Change Orders, in Briefing Papers, No. 92-13, 2d Series (3d ed. Dec. 1992).

that consists of the written requirements for materials, equipment, labor, and services and the standards that apply.[223]

One issue that frequently arises when a contractor attempts to recover extra work involves ambiguous or defective specifications.[224] Numerous courts have held that an owner that furnishes plans and specifications to a contractor impliedly warrants that the work will meet the requirements of the contract if the plans and specifications are followed.[225] The contractor is generally allowed to recover its extra costs incurred in attempting to perform the contract in reliance on the specifications, based on a breach of implied warranty theory.[226] As one court notes:

> A project owner which furnishes plans and specifications to a contractor impliedly warrants their sufficiency. When the contractor incurs additional expenses attempting to perform a contract pursuant to defective specifications, the contractor is entitled to recover its extra costs thereafter incurred by reason of the breach of the implied warranty.[227]

However, the contractor's reliance on the plans or specifications must be reasonable in light of all the circumstances. In cases of ambiguous or defective plans or specifications, courts will generally apply the rule of *contra proferentum,* which requires that a contract be construed against the party who wrote it.[228] As previously discussed, in most cases this will allow the contractor to recover. However, the *contra proferentum* rule does not apply in the case of a patent ambiguity, which is defined as an ambiguity existing on the face of the document.[229]

In *Newson v. United States,*[230] the court held that several provisions of a contract for hospital improvements were patently ambiguous with regard to whether the contractor should have included in his bid certain costs associated with renovating a portion of a building that was included in the specifications but not in the drawings. The court affirmed the board of contract appeals in holding that the contractor was barred from recovering for work done beyond that required under the contractor's interpretation of the contract. The holding was based primarily on the fact that given the obvious nature of the ambiguity, the contractor had a duty to inquire about the ambiguity and could not take advantage of the government by failing to inquire of the contracting officer the true meaning of the contract.[231]

---

[223] AIA Doc. A201, ¶ 1.1.6 (1987).

[224] For an excellent discussion of this issue, *see* L.V. Werbin, Legal Guide for Contractors, Architects and Engineers 74 (1961).

[225] *See, e.g.,* CIG Contractors v. State Bldg. Comm'n, 510 So. 2d 510 (Miss. 1987), and cases cited therein.

[226] Fairbanks N. Star Borough v. Kandik Constr., 795 P.2d 793 (Alaska 1990).

[227] 795 P.2d 793.

[228] United States v. Heckinger, 397 U.S. 203 (1970).

[229] Max Drill, Inc. v. United States, 427 F.2d 1233 (Ct. Cl. 1970).

[230] 676 F.2d 647 (Ct. Cl. 1982).

[231] 676 F.2d 647. *See also* Beacon Constr. Co. v. United States, 314 F.2d 501 (Ct. Cl. 1963).

Similarly, in *Wickham v. United States,*[232] the contract drawings required the doors of a factory to open inward, which was contrary to the applicable building code. The contractor admitted that he realized it was an error, but had nevertheless continued work on the doors without notifying the engineer. The contractor was held responsible for the costs of reversing the doors.

[E]   Rescission and New Contract

One way courts have found to avoid the pre-existing duty rule is to find an agreement of rescission, followed by a new contract, thus allowing the court to ignore the issue of consideration altogether.[233] In other words, if the parties agree to terminate their original contract, they are free to "make a new deal" that encompasses the proposed extra or additional work. Because the original contract was terminated, the contractor does not owe any "pre-existing duty" to the owner.[234]

Some courts, however, have on occasion become somewhat creative in their attempts to circumvent the pre-existing duty rule based on rescission.[235] For example, in *Martiniellow v. Bamel,*[236] the plaintiff entered into a contract under which he was to excavate a cellar so that a series of shops could be constructed. The contract required the work to be done in accordance with the Boston building code. After work began, it was discovered that the land was filled and that substantial additional excavation would be required in order to comply with the code. The parties discussed the matter and agreed to discuss the issue further upon completion of the work. After the work was finished, the parties met and agreed upon the plaintiff's compensation. Thereafter, the defendant refused to pay the plaintiff for the extra work incurred, based upon the pre-existing duty rule.

The court, while addressing the issue of mutual mistake, held that the parties had rescinded the old contract and entered into a new contract. The court noted:

> [R]escission of the old contract ... affords consideration for the contract on which the second count of the declaration on an account annexed is founded. This conclusion in no way conflicts with the settled general principle that a promise to make additional payment to one for doing that which he was under a prior legal obligation to do is not binding for want of a valid consideration.[237]

---

[232] 546 F.2d 395 (Ct. Cl. 1976).

[233] *See, e.g.,* Schwartzreich v. Bauman-Basch, 131 N.E. 887 (N.Y. 1921).

[234] *See* J. Calamari & J. Perillo, Handbook on the Law of Contracts § 61 (1970).

[235] Calamari & Perillo, Handbook on the Law of Contracts § 61. In fact, according to Professors Calamari and Perillo, "[s]ome courts have found, on tenuous grounds, that the preexisting contract has been rescinded by mutual agreement even where the rescission and the new agreement are simultaneous" (citation omitted).

[236] 150 N.E. 838 (Mass. 1926).

[237] 150 N.E. 838, 839.

[F] Legislative Reforms

Some states' hostilities to the pre-existing duty rule have led the legislature to abolish the rule by statute. In those states, a signed writing is a sufficient substitute for consideration and will support a modification of a contract.[238] In other words, an executed change order will allow the contractor to recover despite the owner's assertions that the work performed by the contractor was within the scope of the contractor's original obligations. However, there is also a duty of good faith implied in every contract, and if the owner can establish that the contractor acted in bad faith under an economic duress theory, recovery may be denied.

§ 2.07 RESULT ORIENTED COURTS

Corbin notes that "[i]t has become clear that the moral and economic elements in any case that involves the [pre-existing duty] rule should be weighed by the court, and that the fact of pre-existing legal duty should not be in itself decisive."[239]

Many courts have become increasingly hostile to the rule and have crafted numerous ways to avoid the rule such as those previously described. In many instances, courts look at the facts of the particular case and focus on the motive of the contractor seeking to recover for extra work. If the contractor's demand for more money is motivated by greed and opportunism, such as when the contractor knows the owner is under pressure to reach a particular completion deadline, the court may rely on the pre-existing duty rule to deny recovery.[240] As one authority notes:

> In determining whether recovery for extra work is justified, courts must be on guard against opportunistic behavior, as it is both contrary to the concept of a relationship and frequently at the heart of extra work cases. To police opportunism, the courts must look for contract clauses that give one or the other party undue power in the face of unforeseen events. They must carefully scrutinize structures of the contract that govern the relationship, their potentiality for abuse by one or both sides, and the compensation scheme that the contract create.[241]

[238] *See, e.g.,* Mich. Comp. Laws Ann. § 566.1 (West); N.Y. Gen. Oblig. L. § 5-1103 (McKinney, 1963). N.Y. Gen. Oblig. L. § 5-1103 provides:

> An agreement, promise or undertaking to change or modify, or to discharge in whole or in part, any contract, obligation, or lease, or any mortgage or other security interest in personal or real property, shall not be invalid because of the absence of consideration, provided that the agreement, promise or undertaking changing, modifying, or discharging such contract, obligation, lease, mortgage or security interest, shall be in writing and signed by the party against whom it is sought to enforce the change, modification or discharge, or by his agent.

[239] A. Corbin, Corbin on Contracts § 106 (1963).

[240] T.C. Galligan, Jr., *Extra Work in Construction Cases: Restitution, Relationship, and Revision,* 63 Tul. L. Rev. 799 (1989).

[241] Galligan, *Extra Work in Construction Cases: Restitution, Relationship, and Revision,* 63 Tul. L. Rev. 799, 861.

However, if the demand is based on a discovery of circumstances or the occurrence of events that makes the contractor's performance much more difficult or expensive, the court may labor to bring the case within some exception to the rule, such as those noted. Many authorities have criticized these decisions because they are uncertain and unpredictable, thus destroying the parties' ability to plan for the future.[242] However, because the question of extra work is fact-intensive and requires the court to analyze the facts on a case-by-case basis, there does not appear to be any change in how courts will resolve these cases. Contractors and owners should assume that courts will remain result oriented.

§ 2.08 DEDUCTIVE CHANGES OR TERMINATION FOR CONVENIENCE

As discussed, change order clauses typically give the owner the right to unilaterally alter the contract work. The change order clause not only facilitates the performance of the extra work, it serves as a mechanism under which the contractor receives additional compensation. In the government contract setting, however, the owner (government) usually has the luxury of unilaterally reducing the amount of work without liability (deductive change orders), or ending the contract altogether (termination for convenience). Most government contracts (and, increasingly, private contracts) contain both of these provisions. The termination-for-convenience provision allows the government the flexibility of removing the contractor without being required to show cause. For example, the Department of Energy suggests that the following language be used in all management and operating contracts: "The performance of work under this contract may be terminated by the government in whole, or from time to time, in part, ... whenever, for any reason, the contracting officer shall determine any such termination is in the best interest of the Government."[243]

The question of whether to terminate for convenience or issue a deductive change order often arises when the government decides to delete work from a contract. The contracting officer has two options. He can either issue a partial termination for the convenience of the government[244] or issue a deductive change order, thereby reducing the quantity of the work as well as the price.[245] The contractor's compensation may differ dramatically, depending on which course of action the contracting officer follows. The language will control, and both the termination-for-convenience and changes provisions should be reviewed. As one author notes:

---

[242] Galligan, *Extra Work in Construction Cases: Restitution, Relationship, and Revision*, 63 Tul. L. Rev. 799, 861.

[243] Defense Acquisition Reg. 7-103.21, 48 C.F.R. § 970.5204-45 (1984).

[244] J.C. McBride, Government Contracts, Cyclopedic Guide to Law, Administration, Procedure § 28.280 (1990).

[245] McBride, Government Contracts, Cyclopedic Guide to Law, Administration, Procedure § 28.280 (1990).

When the contract is for a lump sum, this rule [that the Contracting Officer can choose between the termination clause and a deductive change order] can lead to significantly different amounts of equitable adjustment because of the differences in pricing between the two clauses. Such differences will be minimal when the deleted work can be done by the contractor for an amount approximating the amount he included in the contract for the work. However, if the deleted work will cost more than originally anticipated, an equitable adjustment under the changes clause will be greater than the amount recovered by the Government under the Termination for Convenience Clause. Conversely, if the deleted work will cost less than originally anticipated, the Government will normally recover a greater amount under the Termination clause than under the Changes clause.[246]

These discrepancies in recovery result because the standard termination clause contained in fixed price supply contracts states that on termination, the total amount to be received by the contractor shall not exceed the total contract price as reduced by the amount of payments otherwise made and as further reduced by the contract price of work not terminated. In other words, the clause imposes a ceiling on the amount of a termination settlement. The changes clause does not impose such a limitation.[247]

Similarly, if the contract is partially terminated and the nonterminated portion was performed at a loss, the governing regulation requires a loss adjustment. The same is not true when a change is involved. Thus, one can see the importance of the contracting officer's decision on whether to delete the work by means of a change order or to effect a partial termination.

Some courts have resolved this issue by holding that the changes clause may be used by the government if the deductive change meets the general requirements of the changes clause. Thus, it has been held that the changes clause could not be used if the change reduced the quantity of items to be delivered under the contract but did not alter the contract specifications, as a change in specifications is one of the requirements for a changes clause.

This logic has been criticized, however, because it allows the contracting officer the choice of using the changes clause to delete any amount of work originally required by the specifications and to circumvent entirely the termination-for-convenience clause. Some courts have recognized this issue and instead have questioned whether the deletion has a major or minor effect on the work. As the court noted in *J.W. Bateson Co. v. United States*:[248]

> It is obvious that there can be no hard and fast line between a "termination" and "change" in the sense of these contracts. By a shift of circumstances, the two words may be made to verge on each other, or, on the other hand, may be made to stand far apart. Anybody would readily agree that when a contract for

---

[246] R.C. Nash, Jr., Government Contract Changes (1975).
[247] J.C. McBride, Government Contracts, Cyclopedic Guide to Law, Administration, Procedure § 28.280[2] (1987).
[248] 308 F.2d 510 (5th Cir. 1962).

430 buildings is cut down to 81 buildings, there has been a partial termination, and there would be the same unanimity in saying that the use of a shingle roof in place of a composition roof on a house would be a change rather than a termination, yet if a contract for a dwelling and basement has the basement eliminated, there would be a borderline picture, and that fairly could be called a change as readily as a partial termination. The long and short of it is that the proper yardstick in judging between a change and a termination in projects of this magnitude would best be found by thinking in terms of major and minor variations in the plans.[249]

The application of these tests has led to inconsistent results in the cases that have been litigated. One commentator concludes that use of the changes clause should be restricted to those cases when the deletion is connected with additions or other alterations to the contract work, not when the "change" is merely reducing the quantity of items to be delivered under the contract.[250]

The types of damages recoverable in a termination-for-convenience case vary greatly depending on the circumstances and the contract provisions, and they are beyond the scope of this chapter.[251] The measure of damages will depend on any applicable regulations and the scope of the termination-for-convenience and changes clauses.[252]

---

[249] 308 F.2d 510, 513.

[250] Nash, Government Contract Changes 65.

[251] For a general discussion of this issue, see McBride, Government Contracts, Cyclopedic Guide to Law, Administration, Procedure § 28.280[2] (1987); P.J. Martell & D.G. Featherstun, Convenience Termination: More Selected Problems, in Briefing Papers, No. 91-13 (Dec. 1991).

[252] For an excellent analysis of the differences in pricing between a termination for convenience and a change, see Nash, Government Contract Changes 430.

CHAPTER 3

AUTHORITY TO ORDER CHANGES
Robert B. Thum

§3.01   INTRODUCTION

Fundamental to the success of any construction project is the ability to change the work. The limitations inherent in even the best design are such that some modification is likely to be necessary before or during performance to correct errors and omissions or to allow for newly recognized functions or features. So important is the need for flexibility that virtually every construction contract contains a changes clause, pursuant to which the work (or the way in which it is to be accomplished) may be added to, deleted, or in some other manner adjusted according to its terms. No matter how universal the need to adapt the design to meet evolving project demands, however, only one party, the owner, is granted the right to order a change in the work under the standard changes clause. The contractor, itself powerless to alter the plans and specifications, is obliged to execute the change as ordered and seek to recover from the owner appropriate additional compensation and time.

Many issues are presented when the contractor is ordered to change the work. The contractor must address questions of scope, compensation, extension of contract completion date, impact on other activities, and resource allocation, among others. One crucial matter, however, is often overlooked or given insufficient attention at the time, that is, whether the individual issuing the order is in fact authorized to do so under the changes clause or otherwise.

A contractor ignores the matter of authority at its peril. Not only does the obligation to perform the change depend in the first instance on the authorization for the order, but so does the right to be compensated. As a general rule, a contractor is under no duty to execute an unsanctioned change order. By the same token, the owner has no duty to pay for work changed without proper authorization and, indeed, may reject it as not conforming to the plans and specifications. Contractor claims for compensation and time associated with unauthorized changes will generally fail. Such serious consequences illustrate the importance of a thorough analysis of authority before undertaking to perform changed work on a construction project.

This chapter addresses various facets of the authority issue, including the source of the authority to order changes; the different kinds of authority; the consequences of performing unauthorized changes on public (federal and state) and private construction projects; and the owner's ratification of unsanctioned changes. The related matters of noncompliance with the procedures prescribed in the changes clause (such as the requirement for a written change order prior to performance) and those acts of otherwise unauthorized persons that give rise to "constructive changes" are addressed in **Chapter 4.**

§3.02   SOURCE OF AUTHORITY

The source of the authority to order changes is the changes clause itself. In addition to a statement of rights, duties, and limitations that arise when a modification is proposed for the contract work, standard clauses clearly specify who has the authority to make changes in the first instance. Under the federal changes clause, it is the contracting officer (the government employee vested with legal authority to bind the United States to a contractual agreement). The Federal Acquisition Regulations (FAR) provide in pertinent part:

(a) *The Contracting Officer* may, at any time, without notice to the sureties, if any, by written order designated or indicated to be a change order, make changes within the general scope of the contract, including changes
(1) In the specifications (including drawings and designs);
(2) In the method or manner of performance of the work;
(3) In the Government-furnished facilities, equipment, materials, services, or site; or
(4) Directing acceleration in the performance of the work.
(b) Any other written or oral order (which as used in this paragraph (b), includes direction, instruction, interpretation, or determination) from *the Contracting Officer* that causes a change shall be treated as a change order under this clause. . . .
(c) Except as provided in this clause, no order, statement, or conduct of *the Contracting Officer* shall be treated as a change under this clause or entitle the Contractor to an equitable adjustment.[1]

Other widely used changes clauses for state and local construction clearly specify that the public body, through its designated representative, may make changes to the work. For example, California's Standard Specifications provide:

Changes.—The *Department* reserves the right to make such alterations, deviations, additions to or deletions from the plans and specifications, including the right to increase or decrease the quantity of any item or portions of the work or to delete any item or portion of the work, as may be deemed by *the Engineer* to be necessary or advisable and to require such extra work as may be determined by the Engineer to be required for proper completion or construction of the whole work contemplated.

Those changes will be set forth in a contract change order which will specify, in addition to the work to be done in connection with the change made, adjustment of the contract time, if any, and the basis of compensations for that work. A contract change order will not become effective until approved by *the Engineer*.[2]

---

[1] FAR 52.243-4, Changes (Aug. 1987) (emphasis added), used on fixed-price construction contracts. A comparable shortform clause, addressing both changes and differing site conditions, FAR 52.243-5, is used on contracts of $25,000 or less. The FAR is found at Title 48 of the Code of Federal Regulations.

[2] State of California, Standard Specifications § 4-1.03 (2002) (emphasis added) prepared and issued by the Department of Transportation. Similar language may be found in clauses for local public projects. For instance, the Standard Specifications for Public Works Construction (drafted by the Joint Cooperative Committee of the Southern California Chapter of the American Public Works Association and the Southern California Districts of the Associated General Contractors of California and used by the City of Los Angeles and numerous other local public agencies in the

The standard changes clauses used on private construction projects are to similar effect. The *Standard General Conditions of the Construction Contract*, issued by the Engineers Joint Contract Documents Committee (EJCDC) and endorsed by the Associated General Contractors of America (AGC), sets forth the owner's right to change the work in Article 10, as follows:

> Without invalidating the Contract and without notice to any surety, *OWNER* may, at any time or from time to time, order additions, deletions or revisions in the Work by a Change Order, or a Work Change Directive. Upon receipt of any such document, CONTRACTOR shall promptly proceed with the Work involved which will be performed under the applicable conditions of the Contract Documents (except as otherwise specifically provided).[3]

Likewise, the American Institute of Architects' (AIA) *General Conditions of the Contract for Construction* provides the source of authority to order changes to the work. Paragraph 7.3, Construction Change Directives, provides in pertinent part:

> A Construction Change Directive is a written order prepared by the Architect and signed by *the Owner* and Architect, directing a change in the Work prior to agreement on adjustment, if any, in the Contract Sum or Contract Time, or both. *The Owner* may by Construction Change Directive, without invalidating the Contract, order changes in the Work within the general scope of the Contract consisting of additions, deletions or other revisions, the Contract Sum and Contract Time being adjusted accordingly.[4]

Given these standard clauses, it is rarely disputed which party—owner or contractor—has the right to make changes in the work. The real issue is which

---

California area) vest the owner with the right to order changes, subject to stated limitations [hereinafter Standard Specifications for Public Works]. Section 3-2.1 (2003) states:

> The Agency may change the Plans, Specifications, character of the work, or quantity of work provided the total arithmetic dollar value of all such changes, both additive and deductive, does not exceed 25 percent of the Contract Price. Should it be necessary to exceed this limitation, the change shall be by written Supplemental Agreement between the Contractor and Agency, unless both parties agree to proceed with the change by Change Order.

[3] EJCDC Doc. No. C-700 (2002) (emphasis added). *See also* Associated General Contractors of California, Standard Form Prime Contract, AGCC-1 (2005), General Conditions, art. 15.1 ("The Work shall be subject to change by additions, deletions or revisions by Owner").

[4] AIA Doc. A201, General Conditions of the Contract for Construction, ¶ 7.3 (1997) (emphasis added). The "change directive" was introduced by the 1987 revision, providing an explicit basis for the owner's unilateral change when the contractor's agreement cannot be reached. The change order, provided for in ¶ 7.2, is now a formal trilateral written modification to the work, signed by the owner, architect, and contractor upon agreement to all terms. *See* AIA California Council, A201 Commentary at 36-39 (Professional Liability Papers, Dec. 1989). The former version of A201 employed language comparable to the "change directive" for change orders: "The Owner, without invalidating the contract, may order changes in the work within the general scope of the Contract, consisting of additions, deletions or other revisions." *Id.* ¶ 12.1, Change Orders (1976).

individual purporting to act on behalf of the owner in the exercise of this right has the warrant to order the contractor to execute a change. To address this matter, which is of crucial importance to the contractor, it is necessary to examine the different kinds of authority with which an owner's representative can be vested on a construction project.

§ 3.03 TYPES OF AUTHORITY

Except when it is a natural person, the owner must act through agents or representatives to discharge responsibilities and receive entitlements under a construction contract. An agency relationship is created when the owner appoints another (that is, an employee, contracting officer, resident officer/engineer in charge of construction, or architect/engineer) to act on its behalf in certain respects with regard to a project, and the appointment is accepted.[5] The appointment may be in writing or oral and may prescribe generally or specifically the powers and authority vested in the agent.[6] Thereafter, the acts and omissions of that representative within the scope of its authority will bind the owner and render it liable to the contractor, just as though they had been the acts or omissions of the owner itself.[7] The responsibilities of the owner and the rights of the contractor regarding ordered changes thus depend upon the scope and extent of the agent's authority.

[A] Actual Authority

There are two types of authority with which the owner's representative may be vested: actual and apparent. Actual authority is the grant of power in fact made by the owner. The grant itself may be either express or implied. For construction projects of any complexity, actual authority is usually expressed in written form. For example, the architect's authority to act on behalf of the owner (as well as limitations thereon) during the construction phase is set forth in detail not only in the Owner-Architect Agreement (AIA Doc. B141) but also in the General Conditions (AIA Doc. A201).[8] Such specificity serves well to confirm for the

---

[5] Restatement (Second) of Agency § 1 (1958). *See* J. Sweet, Legal Aspects of Architecture, Engineering and the Construction Process §§ 4.01-4.07 (4th ed. 1989).

[6] *See, e.g.,* FAR 1.603-3, the Contracting Officer's Certificate of Appointment, Standard Form 1402; the specification of the architect's rights and responsibilities in AIA Doc. B141, Terms and Conditions of Agreement between Owner and Architect, arts. 1-3 (1997); AIA Doc. A201, art. 4 (1997).

[7] Restatement (Second) of Agency § 140 (1958). *See* J. Acret, Architects and Engineers §§ 8.01-8.06 (3d ed. 1993).

[8] *See, e.g.,* AIA Doc. B141, ¶¶ 2.6.1-2.6.19 (1997); AIA Doc. A201, ¶¶ 4.1-4.6 (1997). To avoid conflict and confusion, given the AIA's trilateral orientation to construction projects, the description of the architect's authority is carefully correlated between the two documents.

owner and architect the agreed scope of authority and to define its limits for the contractor.[9]

Beyond that expressly conferred, however, the owner's representative possesses the implied authority to undertake those incidental tasks that are appurtenant or necessary to the fulfillment of its identified duties. An engineer authorized to accept or reject the work has the implied authority to dictate the number and type of tests required for acceptance (even if this constitutes a change).[10] Similarly, in some circumstances an engineer has the implied authority to waive specification requirements in the course of pre-acceptance inspection.[11] However, there are limits on the implication of actual authority. Contract clauses may, and frequently do, negate implied authority in a given area.[12] In addition, the acts in question may not relate closely enough to the agent's express duties to warrant implication of authority. An architect given broad responsibility for supervision of the work, interpretation of the design documents, and acceptance of the completed project, for instance, does not necessarily have the implied authority to extend the agreed contract completion date and waive liquidated damages.[13]

[B]   Apparent Authority

While actual authority is defined by the terms of appointment from owner to representative, apparent authority derives from the relationship among the owner, representative, and contractor. There is apparent authority when the owner leads the contractor to believe that the architect, engineer, construction manager, inspector, or any other representative has been granted the authority to perform a particular task or function. The owner will be bound even by its agent's otherwise

---

[9] *See generally* K.D. Carey, *Assessing Liability of Architects and Engineers for Construction Supervision,* 1979 Ins. L.J. 147 (1979).

[10] Switlik Parachute Co., ASBCA No. 17,920, 74-2 BCA (CCH) ¶ 10,970 (1974); *see also* Warren Painting Co., ASBCA No. 6511, 61-2 BCA (CCH) ¶ 3199 (1961); Cameo Curtains, Inc., ASBCA No. 3574, 58-2 BCA (CCH) ¶ 2051 (1958).

[11] Gresham & Co. v. United States, 470 F.2d 542 (Ct. Cl. 1972); K&M Constr., ENGBCA No. 3115, 73-2 BCA (CCH) ¶ 10,034 (1973). *See also* Diamond B. Constr. Co. v. City of Plaquemine, 673 So. 2d 636 (La. Ct. App. 1996) (Engineer, as named representative for city, had contractual authority to make final inspection of project and issue certificate of substantial completion and certificate for payment if engineer determined that the work was acceptable under the contract. City could not make later inspection and withhold payment for incomplete and defective work not in accordance with specifications. Contractor entitled to entire amount of retainage.); Ferman Co., ASBCA No. 8102, 1962 BCA (CCH) ¶ 3566 (1962) (procurement agent had authority to answer pre-bid questions); Gillet & Assoc., ASBCA No. 14,696, 73-1 BCA (CCH) ¶ 10,016 (1973).

[12] *See, e.g.,* EJCDC Doc. No. C-700, Standard General Conditions of the Construction Contract, ¶¶ 6.05, 6.17, 9.01, 9.03 (2002); AIA Doc. A201, ¶¶ 4.2.1-4.2.3, 4.2.7 (1997).

[13] Town of Bono v. Universal Tank & Iron Works, Inc., 239 Ark. 924, 395 S.W.2d 330 (1965); Randall & Blake, Inc. v. Metro Wastewater Reclamation Dist., 77 P.3d 804 (Colo. Ct. App. 2003) (owner's representative does not have the actual authority to impose on the contractor a reduced contract price on a lump-sum contract if the work was easier than anticipated). *See generally* 6 C.J.S. Architects § 7 (1975); 5 Am. Jur. 2d Architects § 6 (1962).

unsanctioned acts that the contractor reasonably believes are within that individual's scope of authority.[14]

Apparent authority plays an important part in change order claims because the contractor cannot always know precisely the amount and extent of power granted by the owner to its project representatives. Without the protection the doctrine affords, a contractor executing a change in the genuinely mistaken belief that the representative had authority to order it, would be denied compensation or other relief. Conversely, a contractor that declined to perform an ordered change, reasonably—but incorrectly—assuming that the representative had no warrant, could be defaulted. The doctrine of apparent authority has even been applied to a representative's execution of an entire construction contract and agreement to terms of its compensation.[15]

The law does not saddle the ignorant contractor with the risk of error when the owner has held its resident engineer or architect out as empowered to act in a given capacity.[16] If, however, the contractor knew or should have known that the owner's representative had no authority to sign a change order, it will be denied relief.[17] Contract clauses that limit the duties and responsibilities of the architect or engineer serve to put the contractor on notice that the owner has not empowered its representative in certain areas and that the representative's unauthorized acts will not bind the owner.[18] Apparent authority will not permit the contractor to escape the consequences of its error when reliance has not been reasonable or justified under the circumstances.

§ 3.04 FEDERAL PROJECTS

One of the primary rules affecting federal projects is that the government can be bound only by employees or agents with actual authority. Unlike private construction (and much other state and local public work), the normal principles of apparent authority do not apply. In *Federal Crop Insurance Corp. v. Merrill*,[19] the Supreme Court held that a contractor cannot rely on mere appearances—no matter

---

[14] Restatement (Second) of Agency §§ 27, 140 (1958); J. Sweet, Legal Aspects of Architecture, Engineering and the Construction Process § 4.06 (4th ed. 1989). *See also* Diamond B. Constr. Co. v. City of Plaquemine, 673 So. 2d 636 (La. Ct. App. 1996) (Engineer, as named representative for city, had contractual authority to make final inspection of project and issue certificate of substantial completion and certificate for payment if engineer determined that the work was acceptable under the contract. City could not make later inspection and withhold payment for incomplete and defective work not in accordance with specifications. Contractor entitled to entire amount of retainage.).

[15] Frank Sullivan Co. v. Midwest Sheet Metal Works, 335 F.2d 33 (8th Cir. 1964); E. Paul Kovacs & Co. v. Alpert, 180 Conn. 120, 429 A.2d 829 (1980).

[16] Menard & Co. v. Marshall Bldg. Sys., 539 A.2d 523 (R.I. 1988); Klepp Wood Flooring Corp. v. Butterfield, 176 Conn. 528, 409 A.2d 1017 (1979).

[17] Delta Constr. Co. v. City of Jackson, 198 So. 2d 592 (Miss. 1967).

[18] *Delta Constr.*, 198 So. 2d 592; CCC Builders, Inc. v. City Council, 237 Ga. 589, 229 S.E.2d 349 (1976); *see* limiting contract clauses in AIA Doc. A201, ¶¶ 4.2.1-4.2.3, 4.2.7 (1997); EJCDC Doc. No. C-700, ¶¶ 6.05, 6.17, 9.01, 9.03 (2002).

[19] 332 U.S. 380 (1947).

how reasonable it might be to do so under the circumstances—but must instead shoulder the task of ascertaining whether the individual purporting to act for the government is properly authorized to do so:

> Whatever the form in which the Government functions, anyone entering into an arrangement with the Government takes the risk of having accurately ascertained that he who purports to act for the Government stays within the bounds of his authority. The scope of this authority may be explicitly defined by Congress or be limited by delegated legislation, properly exercised through the rule-making power. And this is so even though, as here, the agent himself may have been unaware of the limitations upon his authority.[20]

Because the standard federal changes clause for federal projects provides that only the contracting officer may make changes,[21] the contractor must assure itself that the individual ordering a change is the designated contracting officer or has been delegated the contracting officer's authority. If there is no actual authority to order the change, the government will not be bound and the contractor cannot recover on its change claims.[22]

[A] Contracting Officer

Federal Acquisition Regulation 2.101 defines the *contracting officer* as that person "with the authority to enter into, administer, and/or terminate contracts and make related findings" and specifically includes "authorized representatives of the contracting officer acting within the limits of their authority as delegated by the contracting officer."[23] Upon appointment, the contracting officer is issued a certificate that must show authority restrictions, if any.[24] The Certificate of Appointment is often displayed in the contracting officer's work area, allowing contractors and the general public to determine the extent of authority granted.[25]

The task of determining the contracting officer's actual authority can be a daunting one. Beyond ascertaining any limitations in the certificate itself, a contractor may be required to consult relevant statutes and regulations. On a very broad level, the contracting officer is empowered to enter into, administer, and terminate contracts and make related findings and is responsible for ensuring

---

[20] 332 U.S. 380, 383.

[21] FAR 52.243-4 (1987). See § 3.02.

[22] *See, e.g.*, Southwest Marine of S.F. Inc., ASBCA No. 29,953, 87-3 BCA (CCH) ¶ 2003 (1987); Strick Corp., ASBCA No. 15,921, 73-2 BCA (CCH) ¶ 10,077 (1973).

[23] This definition is incorporated into federal construction contracts through the definitions clause required by FAR 52.202-1.

[24] FAR 1.603-3. The Certificate of Appointment (or warrant) is issued on Standard Form 1402, which provides a space to be filled in after the words "Subject to the limitations contained in the Federal Acquisition Regulation and to the following."

[25] Agency regulations requiring public display include General Services Administration, GSAR 501.603-3, and Veterans Administration, VAAR 801.690-8. *See also* FAR 1.602-1, -2, -3; 53.301-1402.

contract compliance and safeguarding the interests of the government.[26] More specifically, the contracting officer is authorized to evaluate proposals, negotiate price adjustments, determine the allowability of costs, approve progress payments, review engineering changes, accept or reject waivers, resolve disputes, settle terminations for convenience, and negotiate and agree to contract modifications among many other powers and responsibilities set forth in the FAR.[27]

Although it may be assumed generally that the designated contracting officer enjoys absolute power to order changes and execute modifications reflecting those changes, there may be limitations on authority of which the contractor is unaware. Certain agencies, for example, employ tiers of contracting officers with differing dollar level authority to execute contracts, sign change orders, and settle claims.[28] In addition, the FAR establishes specialized "subsidiary" contracting officers with official titles but with powers carefully circumscribed and limited to given spheres of government procurement.[29] Further, judicial decisions impact on the powers that may be exercised by contracting officers. One board, for example, found that a contracting officer exceeded its authority by agreeing to a contract modification in exchange for the contractor's performance of a pre-existing duty under the contract.[30] Another refused to enforce a termination settlement when the contracting officer had failed to seek approval of a settlement review board, as required by published regulations.[31]

Under the circumstances, therefore, the prudent contractor will investigate and carefully consider all available information (including appointment documentation and any pertinent regulations) that might disclose limitations on the actual authority of the contracting officer to order changes in the work. Under the *Federal Crop Insurance* rule, the risk of error falls on the contractor.

[B] Authorized Representatives

Specifically included in the definition of contracting officer in FAR 2.101 are "authorized representatives" of the contracting officer "acting within the limits of

---

[26] FAR 1.602-1, -2.

[27] *See generally* FAR Subpt. 42.3; Peters v. United States, 694 F.2d 687 (Fed. Cir. 1982).

[28] The GSA, for example, has established five tiers of contracting officer authority: up to $2,500; up to $25,000; up to $10,000; up to $100,000; and unlimited. GSAR 501.603(g).

[29] In addition to contracting officers, the FAR provides for administrative contracting officers, termination contracting officers, and corporate administrative contracting officers. *See* FAR 2.101; FAR Subpts. 42.1, 42.6. Subsidiary contracting officers are infrequently used on construction projects. Occasionally, the contracting officer will delegate certain administrative responsibilities to a construction manager or architect/engineer. *See* Stephenson Assocs., Inc., GSBCA No. 6573, 86-3 BCA (CCH) ¶ 19,071 (1986) (construction manager delegated full administrative contracting officer authority).

[30] Beavers Constr. Co., AGBCA No. 83-125-1, 84-1 BCA (CCH) ¶ 17,067 (1984); *see also* Edward Hines Lumber Co., AGBCA No. 75-125, 76-1 BCA (CCH) ¶ 11,854 (1976).

[31] Atlantic, Gulf & Pac. Co., ASBCA No. 13,533, 72-1 BCA (CCH) ¶ 9415 (1972) (even though both the contracting officer and government counsel had assured the contractor that board approval was unnecessary).

their authority as delegated by the contracting officer." The exact status and warrant of such contracting officer's representatives can create confusion for the contractor attempting to determine whether the individual ordering a change has the necessary actual authority. While the FAR is silent as to the scope of authority, agency regulations usually provide that the grant of power to the representatives is narrow and confined to an identified functional area.[32] Agencies typically furnish a letter or other formal document describing in detail a given representative's authority and setting any limitations. That letter is to be provided to contractors dealing with the representative.[33]

While some contracting officer representatives are prohibited from ordering and executing change orders, some agencies allow the contracting officer the power to authorize the representative to issue change orders.[34] If allowed, this authorization must be in writing.[35] Contractors should proceed on the assumption, then, that representatives do not have authority to order changes, unless specifically demonstrated to the contrary by authorization letter, regulation, or otherwise. If a change is ordered by such a representative, the contractor should direct all communications, including compliance with any contractual notice or submissions requirements, directly to the contracting officer, unless instructed otherwise by the contracting officer.

[C] Federal Employees

On a construction project a number of federal employees assist the contracting officer in discharging its overall responsibilities on behalf of the government. Procurement and contract specialists, construction managers, engineers, inspectors, QA/QC personnel, and auditors are among the representatives of the government who may have substantial contact with the contractor during a *project* regarding matters within their respective areas of expertise. In some instances that

---

[32] *See, e.g.*, GSA Acquisition Reg. 542.202, 542.302.

[33] The Departments of Energy, General Services, Interior, and Labor; NASA; and the Veterans Administration furnish letters of authority. The Department of Justice and the U.S. Information Agency require incorporation of contract clauses specifying the representative's scope of authority.

[34] One agency previously (this provision no longer exists in agency regs) required incorporation of a contract clause warning contractors as follows:

> The [authorized representative] shall not have the authority to make changes in the scope or terms and conditions of the contract; only the Contracting Officer has such authority. THE RESULTANT CONTRACTOR IS HEREBY FOREWARNED THAT IT MAY BE HELD FULLY RESPONSIBLE FOR ANY CHANGES NOT AUTHORIZED IN ADVANCE, IN WRITING, BY THE CONTRACTING OFFICER, AND MAY BE DENIED COMPENSATION FOR ANY ADDITIONAL WORK PERFORMED WHICH IS NOT SO AUTHORIZED.

U.S. Information Agency Acquisition Reg. 1952.247-70.

[35] GSA Acquisition Reg. 543.202.

contact may lead to an instruction, direction, or suggestion that the contractor execute a change to the work. Unlike the contracting officer (or contracting officer's representatives), however, these employees have received no warrant or designation to bind the government and in most instances have no authority whatever to order a change.[36] The contractor that proceeds on the basis of such an order does so at its risk. As with the contracting officer's representatives, the prudent contractor should presume that such employees act without authority in the matter of changes and should address all necessary notices and communications directly to the contracting officer.

Notwithstanding the absence of warrant or designation, boards of contract appeals have sometimes found that these federal employees may be authorized representatives of the contracting officer. In one case, the Armed Services Board held that a project manager was the proper official to respond to technical questions and, thus, the "contracting officer's representative."[37] In another, the Board found that the contracting officer's statement that a particular employee was "the man to satisfy," together with deferral to him on equipment matters, constituted the contracting officer's appointment of an authorized representative.[38]

In response to cases of this sort, some agencies have prepared contract clauses that highlight limitations on the authority of federal employees to put contractors on actual notice, particularly in change situations. The General Services Administration's authorities and limitations clause provides in part:[39]

> The Contractor shall perform the contract in accordance with any order (including but not limited to instruction, direction, interpretation or determination) issued by an authorized representative in accordance with his authority to act for the Contracting Officer; but the Contractor assumes all the risk and consequences of performing the contract in accordance with any order (including but not limited to instruction, direction, interpretation or determination) of anyone not authorized to issue such order.

[D]   Constructive Changes

In the case of constructive changes,[40] the contractor is almost always acting in response to the initiative of a government representative who lacks actual authority to order a change. Strict application of the *Federal Crop Insurance* rule[41]

---

[36] *See, e.g.*, Construction Equip. Lease Co. v. United States, 26 Cl. Ct. 341 (1992).

[37] Walter Straga, ASBCA No. 26,134, 83-2 BCA (CCH) ¶ 16,611 (1983). *See also* WRB Corp. v. United States, 183 Ct. Cl. 409 (1968); Randall H. Sharpe, ASBCA No. 22,800, 79-1 BCA (CCH) ¶ 13,869 (1979).

[38] Contractors Equip. Rental Co., ASBCA No. 13,052, 70-1 BCA (CCH) ¶ 8183 (1970). *See also* Centre Mfg. Co. v. United States, 392 F.2d 229 (Ct. Cl. 1968).

[39] GSA Acquisition Reg. 552.236-71.

[40] FAR 52.243-4(b); see discussion of constructive changes in **Chapter 4**.

[41] 332 U.S. 380 (1947) (rejecting "apparent" authority and requiring actual authority to bind the government).

would mean that no one but the contracting officer could act in such a way as to give rise to a constructive change because no one else has actual authority to do so. This would preclude the contractor from recovering its additional costs or time in situations when it had little choice but to follow the direction or interpretation of the representative. Rigid enforcement of the rule could lead to serious inequities.

Recognizing this, the courts and boards have tried to harmonize the rigid rule with the everyday realities of government construction and procurement. Because the doctrine of apparent authority cannot be employed, the cases look to find whether there has been an implied delegation of actual authority. The courts and boards have focused on the details of the representative's job duties, how they were performed, and how the representative interacted with the contractor. In general, the more technical the task, the more frequently authority has been found. Particularly in situations when the representative is interpreting the technical specifications, the cases uphold an implied delegation of the contracting officer's actual authority. For example, when a technical engineer misinterpreted the specification and improperly required the contractor to remove and replace conforming work, the contractor was permitted to recover on the basis of a constructive change.[42] Rejecting the argument that an inspector's mistake was unauthorized, the Armed Services Board reasoned that any delegation to interpret the specifications must include the authority not only to make correct interpretations, but also to make incorrect ones.[43]

Most of the constructive change cases when authority has been found have involved elements of specification interpretation or performance inspection. Improper rejection of work, excessive testing or inspection, requiring additional work, as well as deletion of testing and waiving of specification requirements all have been determined to be within the representative's implied authority.[44] In doing so, the courts and boards have focused on the actual responsibilities discharged, as opposed to the formal title carried by the representative. Illustrative is the Court of Claims' rejection of labels in overturning an Armed Services Board decision on appeal:

> The Board has found that Rossi was a mere "technical" representative acting in a "non-contractual capacity." This characterization of Rossi's function is not supported by substantial evidence on the whole record. The plain undisputed fact is that Rossi was sent to [the] plant in Alabama by the contracting officer for the whole purpose of settling the problem involving the surplus material and hydrostatic test failures. An integral part of this function is that of giving

---

[42] *See, e.g.*, Warren Painting Co., ASBCA No. 6511, 61-2 BCA (CCH) ¶ 3199 (1961); Cameo Curtains, Inc., ASBCA No. 3574, 58-2 BCA (CCH) ¶ 2051 (1958).

[43] Davis Decorating Serv., ASBCA No. 17,342, 73-2 BCA (CCH) ¶ 10,107 (1973).

[44] *See, e.g.*, J.B.L. Constr. Co., VABCA No. 1799, 86-1 BCA (CCH) ¶ 18,529 (1986); Switlik Parachute Co., ASBCA No. 17,920, 74-2 BCA (CCH) ¶ 10,970 (1974); Bregman Constr. Co., ASBCA No. 9000, 1964 BCA (CCH) ¶ 4426 (1964); Lillard's, ASBCA No. 6630, 61-1 BCA (CCH) ¶ 3053 (1961); Swinerton & Walberg Co., ASBCA No. 3144, 56-2 BCA (CCH) ¶ 1038 (1956).

guidance and any necessary instructions to the contractor. If Rossi were not sent to Alabama for this purpose, then his visit loses all significance. In fact, Rossi was successful, and did find the solution to the problem, and instructed the contractor to adopt the solution. Liability for the actions of a Government agent, who carried out exactly what he was ordered to do, cannot be avoided by pointing to labels. The appellation, "technical adviser," does not detract from Rossi's actual function. It is to the actuality that we look.[45]

On the other hand, a number of decisions have declined to find implied authority when the government placed limitations on the representative's authority, of which the contractor was actually aware or could have been aware had it acted with reasonable diligence. For example, the Court of Claims denied a constructive change claim predicated upon incorrect interpretations of a "technical advisory group" because the contractor had been informed that the group had no authority to issue changes (which instead had to be brought directly to the contracting officer).[46] Boards also have ruled against contractors who were expressly advised by letter of limitations to the authority of project managers and other government personnel.[47] Finally, a number of decisions[48] have enforced the standard inspection clause, which currently states: "the inspector [is not] authorized to change any term or condition of the specification without the Contracting Officer's written authorization."[49]

It is not always easy to square the decisions that find an implied delegation of authority with the decisions that deny recovery. The latter depend heavily on the extent of contractor knowledge and reliance, factors related more to the doctrine of apparent authority (made obsolete by *Federal Crop Insurance*) than to actual authority. Outcome prediction can be difficult with shifting legal underpinnings. For instance, in *Max Drill, Inc. v. United States*,[50] notwithstanding an IFB clause explicitly warning that "[o]ral explanations or instructions given before the award of the contract will not be binding," the contractor relied on technical explanations provided by the government representative. In finding that the representative in fact had authority to explain the specifications, that the contractor's reliance was

---

[45] Centre Mfg. Co. v. United States, 329 F.2d 229, 236 (Ct. Cl. 1968).

[46] Singer Co. v. United States, 215 Ct. Cl. 281, 568 F.2d 695 (1977). *See also* Flinchbaugh Prod. Corp., ASBCA No. 19,851, 78-2 BCA (CCH) ¶ 13,375 (1978).

[47] Woodcraft Corp. v. United States, 173 F. Supp. 613 (Ct. Cl. 1959); International Hardwood Co., ASBCA No. 17,486, 74-2 BCA (CCH) ¶ 10,794 (1974); Antrim Constr. Co., IBCA No. 882-12-70, 71-2 BCA (CCH) ¶ 8983 (1971) and IBCA No. 914-6-71, 73-1 BCA (CCH) ¶ 10,017 (1973). See **§ 3.04[B]**.

[48] *See, e.g.*, Varo, Inc., DOTBCA No. 1695, 87-3 BCA (CCH) ¶ 20,199 (1987); AAAA Enter., ASBCA No. 28,555, 85-1 BCA (CCH) ¶ 17,828 (1985); Arizona Mach. & Welding Works, Inc., IBCA No. 480-2-65, 65-2 BCA (CCH) ¶ 5281 (1965); Barton & Sons Co., ASBCA No. 9477, 65-2 BCA (CCH) ¶ 4874 (1965); Luxaire Sunbeam Heating & Elec. Co., ASBCA No. 10,300, 65-2 BCA (CCH) ¶ 4971 (1965).

[49] FAR 52.246-12 (1987) (Inspection of Construction).

[50] 427 F.2d 1233 (Ct. Cl. 1970).

reasonable, and that the disclamatory clause did not control, the court noted that "it would be inane to believe that the [government representative] was at the site for no real purpose."[51]

The consequences of mistaking authority can be severe. A contractor should proceed cautiously when dealing with government representatives other than the contracting officer, especially if there are limiting clauses in the contract or applicable regulations or the contracting officer has issued letters describing limitations on the representative's authority. Communications, as well as required notice and submissions relating to constructive changes, should be addressed directly to the contracting officer. If feasible, confirmation of the representative's authority may also be sought from the contracting officer prior to performing any work fairly considered as changed.

§ 3.05   OTHER PUBLIC PROJECTS

Many of the policy considerations that underpin the federal rule requiring actual authority are echoed in decisions regarding state and local projects. Courts, faced with actions by public employees that exceed their authorization or run afoul of legislative prescriptions, frequently find that the contractor must shoulder the consequences. Although the doctrine of apparent authority has not been rejected in its entirety as in federal construction, it is sparingly applied. Thus, in the arena of public contracts, it is again the contractor that bears the risk of unauthorized changes.

[A]   Engineer

Analysis of the contract documents and specifications is necessary to reveal the responsibilities and authority of the public owner's agents. Although these will differ from project to project depending on the jurisdiction, the clauses in the Standard Specifications for Public Works Construction, utilized by the City of Los Angeles, are typical:

> Engineer [definition].—The Chief Engineer of the Agency, or other person designated by the Board, acting either directly or through authorized agents.
> AUTHORITY OF BOARD AND ENGINEER. The Board has the final authority in all matters affecting the Work. Within the scope of the Contract, the Engineer has the authority to enforce compliance with the Plans and Specifications. The Contractor shall promptly comply with instructions from the Engineer or an authorized person.
> The decision of the Engineer is final and binding on all questions relating to: quantities; the acceptability of material; equipment or work; the execution, progress or sequence of work; and the interpretation of the Plans,

---

[51] 427 F.2d 1233, 1243.

Specifications, or other drawings. This shall be precedent to any payment under the Contract, unless otherwise ordered by Board.[52]

The grant of authority to the engineer in these provisions is broad, but not plenary or unqualified. Although matters of specification interpretation, inspection, and performance evaluation fall within its authority, the engineer does not appear to have the power to order changes, that being reserved for the agency board itself.[53]

As with federal projects, the contractor must carefully analyze the specifications, public laws, official appointments, and any other pertinent documents to determine if the owner's agent (whether the engineer or designated representative of the engineer) has the warrant to issue a particular change. This may be quite difficult, due to the organizational informality of many public bodies. Nonetheless, the courts generally have refused to allow a contractor to recover when the agent lacked actual authority to change the work. For example, when a contract provided that no payment would be made for changes without approval by the city's board of trustees, the court denied the contractor's claim, even though the engineer specifically directed the contractor to perform the extra work and promised the contractor that the city would pay for it.[54] The court found that the direction was illegal (ultra vires) and the promise unenforceable:

> It is well settled that an implied contract does not arise for work done for a municipality under an ultra vires contract. That would have the effect of putting the power to contract where none existed, and would in effect change the charter of the city. As the engineers here were not permitted to contract on behalf of the city under the terms of the contract defining and limiting their powers, to hold that they could by their conduct give rise to an implied contract would in effect change the express contract and brush away the

---

[52] Standard Specifications for Public Works §§ 1-2, 2-10 (2003). *See also* Dep't of Transportation, State of California, Standard Specifications §§ 1-1.18, 5-1.01 (2002), which provide:

> Engineer [definition].—The Chief Engineer, Department of Transportation, acting either directly or through properly authorized agents, the agents acting within the scope of the particular duties delegated to them.
> Authority of Engineer.—The Engineer shall decide all questions which may arise as to the quality or acceptability of materials furnished and work performed and as to the manner of performance and rate of progress of the work; all questions which may arise as to the interpretation of the plans and specifications; all questions as to the acceptable fulfillment of the contract on the part of the Contractor; and all questions as to compensation. The Engineer's decision shall be final, and the Engineer shall have authority to enforce and make effective those decisions and orders which the Contractor fails to carry out promptly.

[53] *See* text of the changes clause, Standard Specifications for Public Works § 3-2.1. *Cf.* State of California's Standard Specifications in which the engineer is granted authority to order and approve changes. Jeffrey B. Peterson & Assocs. v. Dayton Metro. Hous. Auth., 2000 Ohio App. LEXIS 3259 (2000) (an Ohio contracting officer did not abuse its discretion when it relied on information provided by others to terminate a contractor for default).

[54] Contra Costa Constr. Co. v. City of Daly City, 48 Cal. App. 622, 192 P. 178 (1920).

safeguards the city had placed in the contract for its protection. The city cannot be held liable for the acts of the engineers in ordering this work, unless the engineers in fact had the power to do so. One dealing with a municipal corporation is chargeable with knowledge of the limitations of power of its agents and officers.[55]

Other decisions, when the specifications required advance approval of changes by boards or agency heads, have similarly rejected contractors' claims for changes ordered by unsanctioned field personnel.[56]

[B] Limiting Legislation

The contractor must be acutely aware of any statute or ordinance that places restrictions on the ability of the agent, or the owner itself, to alter or increase the quantity of work. For example, the controlling legislation of many public entities requires that work exceeding a certain threshold amount must have either agency board approval or competitive bidding.[57] Often the dollar threshold is small, calling into question whether what might otherwise be a straightforward change can be issued on even a modest public job. In one case involving a large project,[58] an ordinance required that all work in excess of $3,500 must be publicly bid. The contractor constructing a $12,500,000 wastewater treatment plant was directed by the engineer to install a $10,225 diesel fuel tank and, after completion of the work, sought compensation for the change. The court held that the tank installation was something more than "those ordinary and comparatively unimportant departures from the plans and specifications" normally treated under the changes clause, and thus required public bidding. In denying recovery, the court stated:

> To hold otherwise would turn every public improvement contract into an open-ended agreement for additions from time to time that were not within the contemplation of the parties at the time the underlying contract was entered into.
>
> Although it is a harsh rule, and we can sympathize with [the contractor's] predicament, we are compelled to adhere to statutory and case law directives. Contractors who do business with public entities do so at their peril. They are

---

[55] *Contra Costa Constr.*, 48 Cal. App. 622, 624, 192 P. 178, 179 (citations omitted).

[56] *See, e.g.*, Dick Corp. v. State Pub. Sch. Bldg. Auth., 365 A.2d 663 (Pa. Commw. Ct. 1976); Bares v. City of Portola, 124 Cal. App. 2d 813, 269 P.2d 239 (1954); Burke v. Allegheny County, 336 Pa. 411, 9 A.2d 396 (1939); Thomas Kelly & Sons, Inc. v. City of L.A., 6 Cal. App. 2d 539, 45 P.2d 223 (1935). *See also* Acoustics, Inc. v. Trepte, 14 Cal. App. 3d 887, 92 Cal. Rptr. 723 (1971).

[57] Cal. Pub. Cont. Code § 20142 (West) provides that a county board of supervisors may authorize an official to order changes not to exceed: $5,000 on contracts up to $50,000; 10 percent of the original contract on contracts from $50,000 to $250,000; and $25,000 plus 5 percent of original contract on contracts over $250,000. No change can exceed $150,000 under any circumstances.

[58] Robert L. Carr Co. v. City of Sioux Falls, 416 N.W.2d 602 (S.D. 1987).

charged with the duty to be familiar with the statutory requirements and to adhere to them.[59]

Although most courts adhere to the policy arguments expressed in the foregoing cases, an occasional decision has invoked equitable principles, including those of apparent authority, to resolve change order disputes on public projects. For instance, when a subcontractor received directions from the state's field representative to move and place dirt surcharge and was assured by the representative that he had authority to order the change, the subcontractor was permitted to recover based upon apparent authority and equitable estoppel:

Estoppel, being in derogation of normal rights, is applied sparingly by the courts. To rely on equitable estoppel, a party must prove not only that he relied upon a representation or other conduct, but also that he was justified in doing so. . . .

The record establishes beyond doubt that [the contractor] did not vary the construction sequence until verbally assured that it would be paid a specified amount for changing the procedure and until Paving's [the subcontractor] agent witnessed a notation to that effect made by the Department's employee, Luno, on the contract plans and specifications. It is significant that the notation was made immediately following Graves' [the engineer] approval of the change in a telephone conversation with Luno. That Graves did not hold the position of assistant chief construction engineer is of no moment under the circumstances. So far as [Paving] was concerned, Graves was possessed of authority to approve the change. The record also establishes that it was customary between the parties, in matters involving contract changes, for the [subcontractor] to proceed on verbal authority upon being assured of approval and upon also being assured the required written authority would follow. In this case, that same procedure was followed with respect to the change order issued in connection with extra work performed to correct the slope failure hereinbefore mentioned. In case of the slope failure, the written approval ensued; in regard to the work sequence change, the promised approval did not materialize. Paving had a right to expect the approval would be granted in writing and relied thereon.

Where an employee, agent or representative is clothed with apparent authority and acts pursuant thereto, his employer is estopped to deny such authority.[60]

---

[59] *Robert L. Carr Co.*, 416 N.W.2d 602, 604. One justice, concurring specially, upheld the policy but worried about the equities: "Public policy, essentially, forbids the enforcement of this contract. The entire purpose of the statute . . . is to protect the public. This takes us to a gnawing, aching question of conscience. Should the City of Sioux Falls reap an equipment windfall?" *Id.* (citations omitted). *But see* Shea-Kaiser-Lockheed-Healy v. Department of Water & Power, 75 Cal. App. 3d 679, 140 Cal. Rptr. 884 (1977) (holding on rehearing (over a vigorous dissent) that competitive bidding statutes apply only to the procedure by which the price of goods purchased by a public entity are set, not to the determination of damages against the public body for breach of a purchase contract).

[60] Louisiana Paving Co. v. State Dep't of Highways, 372 So. 2d 245, 249-50 (La. Ct. App. 1979) (citations omitted). *See also* D'Onofrio Bros. Constr. Corp. v. New York City Bd. of Educ., 421 N.Y.S.2d 377 (App. Div. 1979); Savin Bros. v. State, 405 N.Y.S.2d 516 (App. Div. 1978), *aff'd*, 419 N.Y.S.2d 969 (N.Y. 1979); Westenberger v. State Dep't of Educ., 333 So. 2d 264 (La. Ct. App. 1976); Stahelin v. Board of Educ., 230 N.E.2d 465 (Ill. App. Ct. 1967); Rogers v. First Sewerage Dist., 171 So. 2d 820 (La. Ct. App. 1965).

In this decision, the subcontractor had consistently acted with great prudence in receiving and acting upon field directions from the owner to change the work. An unusually strong showing of apparent authority and estoppel was made. In other cases when the contractor has taken few, if any, steps to assure actual authority or protect its interests, the courts have been less inclined to allow purely equitable principles to influence the outcome of change claims.[61]

§ 3.06   PRIVATE PROJECTS

A major distinction between public projects and private projects is that, with respect to the latter, the courts have been more willing to embrace the doctrines of apparent authority and equitable estoppel in ruling on change order issues. Policy considerations offered to justify the rigid requirement for actual authority on federal and other public jobs simply do not come into play when the owner is a private entity. In evaluating authority issues, the cases have focused more on the language of the specifications (both granting a warrant and limiting it) and the nature of the relationship between the owner, architect/engineer, and contractor. Although the contractual language continues to be given great weight, it has been tempered as appropriate by the concurrent interpretation of the parties and the underlying fairness of their dealings with one another.

[A]   Architect/Engineer

The first step for the contractor faced with an ordered change on a private project is to determine exactly what authority has been accorded the architect/engineer under the specifications, its agreement with the owner, or in any other manner. The risk of mistake is no less serious for the contractor on private jobs than public projects. The investigation has the same objectives and is undertaken in essentially the same fashion.

Although formal designations or certificates are used only rarely in the private sector, there is de facto industry standardization in contract terms because of the influence of the AIA General Conditions, EJCDC Standard General Conditions, and similar forms.[62] It is typical for the owner to grant sweeping responsibilities to the architect/engineer to act as its agent to interpret the plans and specifications, inspect the work, and generally oversee the efficient progress of construction.[63]

---

[61] *Cf.* Wiggins Constr. Co. v. Joint Sch. Dist. No. 3, 35 Wis. 2d 632, 151 N.W.2d 642 (1967) (contractor held liable to public owner in damages for following the architect's unauthorized order to change the pitch of the roof).

[62] AIA Doc. A201, ¶¶ 4.2.1-4.2.3, 4.2.7, 7.2, 7.3 (1997); EJCDC Doc. No. C-700, ¶¶ 6.05, 6.17, 9.01, 9.03 (2002).

[63] *See generally* AIA Doc. A201, ¶¶ 4.2.1, 4.2.4, 4.2.6, 4.2.7, 4.2.11 (1997); AIA Doc. B141, ¶¶ 2.6.1-2.6.19 (1997). In ¶ 4.1.1, the architect is defined as "the person lawfully licensed to practice architecture . . . [including] the Architect's authorized representative." Comparable provisions appear in the EJCDC Doc. No. C-700 (2002).

While these and similar provisions expressly vest the architect/engineer with great authority, they do not of themselves confer any authorization to effect changes in the contract. In fact, the AIA General Conditions provide that except when the owner, architect/engineer, and contractor all agree on the terms of and execute a formal change order,[64] only the owner has the right unilaterally to order a change.[65] By strong negative implication, then, the AIA General Conditions and other industry standard construction contract clauses provide no independent authority for the architect/engineer to alter the work or its manner of performance without the owner's express warrant.[66]

That is the conclusion drawn by a number of courts that have examined the general relationship between the owner and the architect/engineer. For the contractor to recover, it must overcome any limiting language in the contract and affirmatively demonstrate that the architect/engineer ordering the change indeed had authority. Typical is *Cape Fear Electric Co. v. Star News Newspapers, Inc.,*[67] in which a contractor installed a more expensive conduit at the direction of an engineer, even though there was no evidence the owner had appointed it an agent or delegated any authority to alter the contract work. The court denied the contractor's change claim on the basis of the engineer's lack of authority, even though the contractor had done the work under protest. The court explained its decision as follows:

> For example, had Engineers insisted that the specifications required Contractor to install conduit made of gold and had Contractor done so even though under protest, we suppose no one would contend that Owner should be bound to pay Contractor for its increased cost absent a Change Order issued in the manner and as authorized in the contract between Owner and Contractor. While the present case *is* not so extreme, the same principle applied. We conclude that the order directing verdict dismissing Contractor's claim against Owner was properly entered.[68]

This is a rule of general application. It has been held that "in the absence of express authority, an architect, as such, has no power to waive or modify a stipulation requiring a written order for alterations or extras."[69] The architect/engineer with responsibility "for general supervision of the work" has no authority to alter the plans or to bind the owner regarding changes.[70] Even if an architect assures the

---

[64] AIA Doc. A201, ¶¶ 7.1.2, 7.2.1 (1997) (architect prepares and signs); *see also* EJCDC Doc. No. C-700 (2002) (engineer recommends); § **3.02**.

[65] *See* AIA Doc. A201, ¶¶ 7.3.1-7.3.2 (1997) (construction change directive procedure).

[66] It should be noted that both the AIA Doc. A201 (¶ 7.4.1) and EJCDC Doc. No. C-700 (¶ 9.04) do authorize the architect/engineer to make "minor" changes to the work not involving any adjustment in contract sum or time. The presence of the minor changes clauses highlights the absence of any similar authority to order changes that affect the contractor's cost and schedule.

[67] 22 N.C. App. 519, 207 S.E.2d 323, *cert. denied*, 385 N.C. 757, 209 S.E.2d 280 (1974).

[68] 207 S.E.2d 323, 328. *See also* Kirk Reid Co. v. Fine, 205 Va. 778, 139 S.E.2d 829 (1965).

[69] Whitfield Constr. Co. v. Commercial Dev. Corp., 392 F. Supp. 982 (D.V.I. 1975).

[70] Kirk Reid Co. v. Fine, 205 Va. 778, 139 S.E.2d 829 (1965).

contractor that a change order will be approved, the contractor cannot recover from the owner who refuses to sign, unless there is proof the architect had proper changes authority.[71] The same holds true for supervisory and consulting personnel, insurance adjusters, even the owner's spouse.[72]

Illustrative is *Missouri Portland Cement Co. v. J.A. Jones Construction Co.*[73] The contractor complied with the directions of the owner's representative to caulk, rather than weld, connections between steel cement storage silos and their supporting columns. The representative was not a registered engineer and had no actual or implied authority to interpret the plans or order changes. His only authorized function was to act as a liaison between the owner and contractor. When the silos later collapsed due to the absence of welding, the owner sued the contractor to recover damages. There being no authority vested in the representative, the court rejected the contractor's defense that the owner was bound by and responsible for the change and awarded damages against the contractor.

[B] Apparent Authority

Although the consequences of the contractor's mistaking the authority of the architect/engineer or another of the owner's representatives are as severe on a private job as a public project, the risk is ameliorated to some extent by the doctrine of apparent authority. Apparent authority is created when the owner acts in such a way that the contractor reasonably concludes the owner's agent has the authority to undertake a certain task for and on behalf of the owner.[74] As demonstrated in the previous cases, the mere fact that the architect/engineer claims to have authority is not sufficient to create an apparent authority; the impetus must come from the owner, not the agent. If, however, a contractor reasonably believes the agent has authority, based upon the acts of the owner, then the owner will be bound as though the agent had actual authority (even if it had no authority at all).[75]

The reasonableness of the contractor's reliance is judged on the basis of a variety of factors, including the information of which it is actually aware (from any source), the diligence of its efforts in attempting to ascertain the extent of authority (reading specifications, inquiry of the architect, confirmation by the owner), and any pattern of conduct on the project that confirms the contractor's

---

[71] Citizens Nat'l Bank v. L.L. Glascock, Inc., 243 So. 2d 67 (Miss. 1971).

[72] Wisinger v. Casten, 550 So. 2d 685 (La. Ct. App. 1989) (insurance adjuster); Able Constr. Co. v. School Dist., 188 Neb. 166, 195 N.W.2d 744 (1972) (engineer); Guenther v. Moffet, 71 A. 153 (N.J. 1908), and Walber v. Jacobson, 143 Minn. 210, 173 N.W. 409 (1919) (spouses); Wagner v. Graziano Constr. Co., 390 Pa. 445, 136 A.2d 82 (1957).

[73] 323 F. Supp. 242 (M.D. Tenn. 1970). *See also* Dehnert v. Arrow Sprinklers, Inc., 705 P.2d 846 (Wyo. 1985); Alexander v. Gerald E. Morrisey, Inc., 137 Vt. 20, 399 A.2d 503 (1979).

[74] See § 3.03[B].

[75] Frank Sullivan Co. v. Midwest Sheet Metal Works, 335 F.2d 33 (8th Cir. 1964).

belief.[76] If, for example, the contractor knew from reading the specifications (or would have known if it had read them with this question in mind) that the architect/engineer had been granted only limited authority by the owner to interpret the plans and no authority to alter them, its reliance on an assertion of authority in ordering a change would not be reasonable.

On the other hand, if, as in *Fletcher v. Laguna Vista Corp.*,[77] the owner had consistently and without objection paid the contractor compensation for change orders executed only by the architect (despite a clause clearly requiring their execution by the owner), the contractor might reasonably conclude that the owner had invested the architect with the authority to change the work. Reaching just that result, the court stated:

> [T]he manner in which the parties themselves have interpreted the contract through their course of dealings is of utmost importance. The record in this case is filled with testimony to the accord that both [owners] and [contractor] had relied on architect Frye to make adjustments in the contract sum and had abided by his decision. [Owners] knew that there would be at least a slight overage in the sums spent by [contractor] for overhead but had never objected. [Owners] accepted decreases in the cost of the millwork which were incorporated into a change order signed only by architect Frye and the contractor. The parties themselves have interpreted the contract to allow an increase and a decrease in the contract sum with only the written signature of architect Frye. Even if the contract does not grant this authority to architect Frye, the parties through their course of dealings have interpreted and modified the document so as to place in the hands of architect Frye the final authority to authorize increases and decreases in the contract sum.[78]

In the final analysis, whether apparent authority will be found or not depends on a variety of specific facts demonstrating, or disproving, the reasonableness of the contractor's reliance. With industry standard clauses that make it clear that the architect/engineer does not act with the owner's authority in the matter of changes, it may be difficult in most situations for contractors to justify reliance on manifestations of authority without a clear pattern of conduct similar to that found in *Fletcher.*

§ 3.07 RATIFICATION

Ratification is the owner's adoption of the otherwise unauthorized act of its agent, thereby retroactively sanctioning it and making it binding on the owner.[79]

---

[76] *See, e.g.*, Gymo Constr. Co. v. Architectural Glass & Windows, Inc., 884 F.2d 1362 (11th Cir. 1989); McDevitt & Street Co. v. Marriott Corp., 713 F. Supp. 906 (E.D. Va. 1989), *aff'd in part and rev'd in part without op.*, 948 F.2d 1281 (4th Cir. 1991); Design & Prods., Inc. v. United States, 18 Cl. Ct. 168 (1989), *reconsideration denied*, 21 Cl. Ct. 145 (1990); Apex Control Sys., Inc. v. Alaska Mech., Inc., 776 P.2d 310 (Alaska 1989); Cloud Constr. v. Schneider, Inc., 491 So. 2d 32 (La. Ct. App. 1986).

[77] 275 So. 2d 579 (Fla. Dist. Ct. App. 1973).

[78] 275 So. 2d 579, 580-81.

[79] Audit Servs., Inc. v. Francis Tindall Constr., 600 P.2d 811 (Mont. 1979); Sawyer v. Pierce, 580 S.W.2d 117 (Tex. Civ. App. 1979).

Even if a contractor had improvidently proceeded with changed work knowing that the architect/engineer had no authority to order it, the owner's later ratification would validate the contractor's claim for its additional costs.[80]

Ratification may assume different forms. It can be express, that is, the owner, learning the architect has improperly ordered a modification to the roof pitch, states that the change was authorized.[81] Similarly, if the owner executes a change order confirming the extra work, demonstrating its ex post facto acceptance of the unauthorized act, there has been an express ratification. In either case, the owner explicitly has adopted the previously unsanctioned act and agreed to be bound by it.

Ratification may also be implied from the actions of the owner. Implied ratification is based on the expectation that the owner, upon learning of the unauthorized act, would ordinarily disavow it.[82] Thus, when the owner knowingly accepts extra work, or fails to reject the contractor's compensation request when it had the opportunity to do so, the courts view such behavior as evidence of the owner's willingness to adopt the unsanctioned act of the agent as its own.[83] Among the situations when ratification has been found are these: the owner's acquiescence in change orders signed only by the architect[84] or the engineer;[85] making payment on unapproved change orders;[86] remaining silent upon learning of the changed work.[87] In one case,[88] a field agreement was reached for the contractor (as opposed to the owner's engineers) to measure the quantities of unanticipated rock encountered during excavation. The contractor made the measurements, submitted invoices based on those measurements, and was paid. The court found that even though the owner's field representative lacked authority to transfer measurement

---

[80] *See, e.g.*, Mateyka v. Schroeder, 152 Ill. App. 3d 854, 504 N.E.2d 1289 (1987); Reavy Grady & Crouch Realtors v. Hall, 110 Ill. App. 3d 325, 442 N.E.2d 307 (1982); Wing v. Lederer, 77 Ill. App. 3d 413, 22 N.E.2d 535 (1966).

[81] Jenco v. Jefferson Ins. Co., 575 F. Supp. 980 (E.D.N.Y. 1983). For federal projects, FAR 1.602-3(c) (1988) has severely restricted the availability of express ratification, putting it beyond the authority of most contracting officers. *See also* Timberland Paving & Constr. Co. v. United States, 8 Cl. Ct. 653 (1985).

[82] Security Ins. Co. v. Mato, 13 Ill. App. 3d 11, 298 N.E.2d 725 (1973).

[83] Olsen & Sons, Inc., GSBCA No. 2094, 1964 BCA (CCH) ¶ 4146 (1964); Norwood Precision Prods., ASBCA No. 24,083, 80-1 BCA (CCH) ¶ 14,405 (1980); Chicago Lumber & Coal Co. v. Garmer, 132 Iowa 282, 109 N.W. 780 (1906).

[84] Massachusetts Bonding & Ins. Co. v. Lenz, 40 Ariz. 46, 9 P.2d 408 (1932).

[85] Olsen & Sons, Inc., GSBCA No. 2094, 1964 BCA (CCH) ¶ 4146 (1964); Norwood Precision Prods., ASBCA No. 24,083, 80-1 BCA (CCH) ¶ 14,405 (1980); Vaughn Constr. Co. v. Virginia Ry. Co., 80 W. Va. 440, 103 S.E. 293 (1920).

[86] Allied Contractors, Inc., IBCA No. 322, 1964 BCA (CCH) ¶ 4379 (1964); INTASA, Inc., Comp. Gen. Dec. No. B180876, 74-1 CPD 1 148 (1974); Son-Shine Grading, Inc. v. ADM Constr. Co., 315 S.E.2d 346 (N.C. Ct. App. 1984).

[87] McDevitt & Street Co. v. Marriott Corp., 713 F. Supp. 906 (E.D. Va. 1989), *aff'd in part and rev'd in part without op.*, 948 F.2d 1281 (4th Cir. 1991); Bruce Tile Co. v. Copelan, 185 Ga. App. 469, 364 S.E.2d 603 (1988); Wehr Constructors, Inc. v. Steel Fabricators, Inc., 769 S.W.2d 51 (Ky. Ct. App. 1988); Kantoff v. Sedlak Motor Sales, 8 Ill. App. 2d 8, 130 N.E.2d 289 (1966).

[88] Son-Shine Grading, Inc. v. ADM Constr. Co., 315 S.E.2d 346 (N.C. Ct. App. 1984).

responsibilities to the contractor, the owner knew of the arrangement and made payments to the contractor without objection. This constituted a ratification of the unauthorized contract modification and bound the owner to make payment in accordance with that modification.

The fundamental bases for implied ratification are actual knowledge and inaction in the face of that knowledge. In *Williams v. United States*,[89] an agreement was reached with an unauthorized government agent to swap use of government equipment for the contractor's seal coating of certain roads. The Court of Claims ruled that the government ratified its agent's arrangement:

> The roads that were seal coated were wholly within the base where the contracting officer was located. It seems incredible that he did not know all about the agreement and by his inaction ratify it. Certainly he did not repudiate the agreement, and he did not appear as a witness. The [contractors] carried out their part of the agreement for which the Government received the benefit. We feel that there then arose an implied contract.[90]

As with the doctrine of apparent authority, ratification depends in large measure upon the specific facts of the situation, the degree of knowledge the owner possesses, and the importance of the changed work in the context of the overall project. To the extent the owner has knowingly accepted the benefit of the unauthorized changed work or paid for it in whole or part, there is a strong case for ratification.

---

[89] 127 F. Supp. 617 (Ct. Cl. 1955).
[90] 127 F. Supp. 617, 623.

CHAPTER 4

FORMAL CHANGE ORDERS AND CONSTRUCTIVE CHANGES

James F. Nagle
Christopher B. Butler

§4.01 INTRODUCTION

Most construction contracts contain a changes clause that allows the owner to change the contract unilaterally within certain limits, normally the general scope of the contract.[1] If an owner changes the essential or main purpose of the contract, a cardinal change has occurred and the owner has breached the contract.[2]

Changes clauses are essential because they give the parties the flexibility to alter the contract to accommodate unexpected circumstances and to adopt new technology. The contractor is protected because the change must be within scope and the contract must be adjusted equitably in price, schedule, or other requirements. Even if such a clause is not in the contract, the parties can agree to alter the contract,[3] but absent a changes clause, modification of a contract must be agreed to by both parties and cannot be done unilaterally.[4] Such a modification must be supported by adequate consideration because it is essentially a separate contract.

Changes are not always additions or extras. The elimination of work originally included in the contract can be a change, typically called *credit*.[5] Delays caused by change orders, architects' interpretations, and stop orders may be processed under the changes provisions.[6] Besides providing that the owner has the right to make changes in the work, a typical changes clause requires that the contractor perform owner-ordered changes, that the change order be written and signed, and that a particular process be followed on how the change is priced.

§4.02 FEDERAL CLAUSES

The Federal Acquisition Regulation (FAR) has a dedicated Web page that can be found at *www.arnet.gov/far/.* The site contains not only the current and archived FARs, but also information regarding proposed changes to the regulations, and

---

[1] *See, e.g.,* Aragona Constr. Co. v. United States, 165 Ct. Cl. 382 (1964); McMaster v. State, 108 N.Y. 542, 15 N.E. 417 (1888).

[2] See **Chapter 11**.

[3] McDonald Constr. Co. v. Murray, 5 Wash. App. 68, 485 P.2d 626 (1971).

[4] Dondevold v. Blaine Sch. Dist. No. 503, 91 Wash. 2d 632, 590 P.2d 1268 (1979).

[5] *See* AIA Doc. A201, General Conditions of the Contract for Construction, ¶ 7.3.1 (1997); Trimpoli v. State, 249 N.Y.S.2d 154, 20 A.D.2d 933 (1964); Reliance Ins. Co. v. County of Monroe, 604 N.Y.S.2d 439, 198 A.D.2d 871 (1993) (Contract anticipated that contaminated soil might be encountered and provided for the containment of contaminants. During the construction, the contractor proposed a design modification at no additional cost. A field change order was issued. While performing this work, the contractor encountered the toxic hazardous wastes. The county approved certain costs associated with the wastes, but denied other claims brought by the contractor involving work stoppages. The county argued that the contractor had assumed the risks accompanying its proposed change order and therefore had waived its right to recover for additional costs. The court held that the contractor did not assume the risk and that the county was liable for the costs associated with this Type II differing site conditions claim. The contractor was not aware of the presence of the hazardous substances, it could not have anticipated the condition from its experience or from an inspection of the site, and the condition varied from normal conditions present in performing similar work.).

[6] Nelse Mortensen & Co. v. Group Health Coop., 17 Wash. App. 703, 566 P.2d 560 (1977).

copies of the Federal Acquisition Circulars, or FACs. The standard changes clause for fixed-price construction contracts is at FAR 52.243-4:

CHANGES (AUG 1987)

   (a) The Contracting Officer may, at any time, without notice to the sureties, if any, by written order designated or indicated to be a change order, make changes in the work within the general scope of the contract, including changes—
      (1) In the specifications (including drawings and designs);
      (2) In the method or manner of performance of the work;
      (3) In the Government-furnished facilities, equipment, materials, services, or site; or
      (4) Directing acceleration in the performance of the work.
   (b) Any other written or oral order (which, as used in this paragraph (b), includes direction, instruction, interpretation, or determination) from the Contracting Officer that causes a change shall be treated as a change order under this clause; provided, that the Contractor gives the Contracting Officer written notice stating—
      (1) The date, circumstances, and source of the order; and
      (2) That the Contractor regards the order as a change order.
   (c) Except as provided in this clause, no order, statement, or conduct of the Contracting Officer shall be treated as a change under this clause or entitle the Contractor to an equitable adjustment.
   (d) If any change under this clause causes an increase or decrease in the Contractor's cost of, or the time required for, the performance of any part of the work under this contract, whether or not changed by any such order, the Contracting Officer shall make an equitable adjustment and modify the contract in writing. However, except for an adjustment based on defective specifications, no adjustment for any change under paragraph (b) of this clause shall be made for any costs incurred more than 20 days before the Contractor gives written notice as required. In the case of defective specifications for which the Government is responsible, the equitable adjustment shall include any increased cost reasonably incurred by the Contractor in attempting to comply with the defective specifications.
   (e) The Contractor must assert its right to an adjustment under this clause within 30 days after (1) receipt of a written change order under paragraph (a) of this clause, or (2) the furnishing of a written notice under paragraph (b) of this clause, by submitting to the Contracting Officer a written statement describing the general nature and amount of the proposal, unless this period is extended by the Government. The statement of proposal for adjustment may be included in the notice under paragraph (b) of this clause.
   (f) No proposal by the Contractor for an equitable adjustment shall be allowed if asserted after final payment under this contract.

The clause explicitly recognizes changes other than formal written change orders.[7] It allows an equitable adjustment for any oral or written direction, instruction, or interpretation from the contracting officer that causes a change, provided the contractor gives the contracting officer written notice stating the date, circumstances, and source of the change and that the contractor considers the government's action a change. The clause then provides that no other order, statement, or conduct of the contracting officer will be considered a change. The clause also requires the contractor to assert its right to an adjustment setting forth the general nature and monetary extent of the claim within 30 days after (1) receipt of a written change order, or (2) furnishing the appraisal notice of conduct constituting a change.

The changes clause for cost-reimbursement construction contracts is at FAR 52.243-2 (Alt. III) and allows changes only "in the plans and specifications or instructions incorporated" in the contract:

CHANGES-COST-REIMBURSEMENT (AUG 1987)

(a) The Contracting Officer may at any time, by written order, and without notice to the sureties, if any, make changes within the general scope of this contract in the plans and specifications or instructions incorporated in the contract.

(b) If any such change causes an increase or decrease in the estimated cost of, or the time required for, performance of any part of the work under this contract, whether or not changed by the order, or otherwise affects any other terms and conditions of this contract, the Contracting Officer shall make an equitable adjustment in the—

(1) estimated cost, delivery or completion schedule, or both;

(2) amount of any fixed fee; and

(3) other affected terms and shall modify the contract accordingly.

(c) The Contractor must assert its right to an adjustment under this clause within 30 days from the date of receipt of the written order. However, if the Contracting Officer decides that the facts justify it, the Contracting Officer may receive and act upon a proposal submitted before final payment of the contract.

(d) Failure to agree to any adjustment shall be a dispute under the Disputes clause. However, nothing in this clause shall excuse the Contractor from proceeding with the contract as changed.

(e) Notwithstanding the terms and conditions of paragraphs (a) and (b) of this clause, the estimated cost of this contract and, if this contract is incrementally funded, the funds allotted for the performance of this contract, shall

---

[7] *Administrative change* means a unilateral contract change in writing that does not affect the substantive rights of the parties (e.g., a change in the paying office or the appropriation data) (FAR 43.101).

Change order means a written order signed by the contracting officer directing the contractor to make a change that the changes clause authorizes the contracting officer to order without the contractor's consent (FAR 43.101).

not be increased or considered to be increased except by specific written modification of the contract indicating the new contract estimated cost and, if this contract is incrementally funded, the new amount allotted to the contract. Until this modification is made, the Contractor shall not be obligated to continue performance or incur costs beyond the point established in the Limitation of Cost or Limitation of Funds clause of this contract.

The FAR includes several other standard clauses governing changes to the work or change procedures of which to be aware: 52.243-1 Changes-Fixed-Price; 52.243-3 Changes-Time-and-Materials or Labor-Hours; 52.243-5 Changes and Changed Conditions; 52.243-6 Change Order Accounting; and 52.243-7 Notification of Changes. Not all of these clauses are applicable in a construction contract, however, depending on the nature of the work being performed on behalf of the Federal Government, contractors must be aware of and follow the applicable procedures.

§ 4.03   OTHER STANDARD CLAUSES

The AIA publishes what it terms "families" of construction documents. Additional information regarding these documents is available on the AIA Web site at *http://www.aia.org/docs_default*. Series "A" documents govern the owner/contractor relationship, and the general terms and conditions are found in the various permutations of A201. The most current version is A201, *General Conditions of the Contract for Construction* (1997).

Under the 1976 version of AIA Document A201, the changes clause was at Article 12. Under Subparagraph 12.1.2, the owner could order changes defined as editions, deletions, or other revisions within the general scope of the work.[8] A change order under Subparagraph 12.1.1 had to be signed by both the owner and the architect and had to be in writing. Only the owner could order changes and the architect could order minor changes, which would not change the contract price or schedule, under Subparagraph 12.1.4.

The 1987 AIA Document A201, *General Conditions of the Contract for Construction,* moved its changes clause to Article 7 and added a third mechanism involving change: a construction change directive. So three vehicles exist under A201: a change order (¶ 7.2), a construction change directive (¶ 7.3),[9] or a minor change (¶ 7.4).[10]

In the 1997 update of A201, the AIA further modified the changes process. This revision included new language that prevents the contractor from making substitutions without consent from the owner (¶ 3.4.2), clarifies the change

---

[8] *See* J. Sweet, Sweet on Construction Industry Contracts: Major AIA Documents § 11.03 (Aspen Publishers, Inc., 4th ed. 2002) [hereinafter Sweet, Construction Industry Contracts].

[9] In 1979, the AIA published G713, the Construction Change Authorization, which led to the CCD mechanism.

[10] *See* Sweet, Construction Industry Contracts § 11.04.

order/Construction Change Directive (CCD)/minor change system, and includes new language regarding payment for disputed changes (¶ 7.3.8). These changes are discussed fully in Sweet, *Construction Industry Contracts* §§ 11.02-11.06.

Other organizations that publish commonly used standard form contracts include the National Society of Professional Engineers (NSPE) and the Associated General Contractors (AGC). The NSPE committee, which publishes its contract documents, is the Engineers Joint Contract Documents Committee (EJCDC), whose documents can be found on their Web site at *http://www.nspe.org/ejcdc/home.asp*. The differences between these standard form contracts are best understood if one realizes the perspective from which each was drafted. So, for example, while the AGC standard form 200 contract incorporates some of the same language as AIA document A201, the fact that the AGC document eliminates the architect from the equation explains why the change order provisions may be perceived as being more contractor friendly.[11]

[A] Change Orders

Under the AIA document, a change order must be signed by the owner, architect, and the contractor to reflect their agreement upon a change in the work, the amount to be paid for it, and the extent of any contract time adjustment. Under the scheme envisioned by the AIA, a CCD would normally precede a change order, wherein the change would be performed under the CCD and be formalized in a change order.[12] Under the AGC scheme, this is the only method by which the scope of work may be changed. The change must be mutually agreed-upon between the owner and the contractor, and be in writing.

In federal contracts, this is termed a supplemental agreement or a bilateral modification signed by the contractor and the contracting officer. A *supplemental agreement* is a contract modification that is accomplished by the mutual action of the parties.[13] It is a new agreement, dependent upon the consent of the contractor, modifying the terms of the old agreement. It need not be based on any authority existing in the contract.

[B] Construction Change Directive

The AIA Document A201 creates a second type of change.[14] A construction change directive (CCD) should be used when there is not complete agreement on the terms of the change order. The AGC has rejected the concept of the CCD in

---

[11] *See generally* Steven G.M. Stein, 1 Construction Law § 3.06[4][b][vii] (Lexis 2004), for a more detailed discussion of the AGC contract change provisions.

[12] *See* Sweet, Construction Industry Contracts § 11.05[C].

[13] FAR 43.101.

[14] Construction change directives are covered in Sweet, Construction Industry Contracts § 11.05[D].

favor of the agreed-upon change order. The EJCDC, however, incorporates the same language as the AIA. While a change order under Subparagraph 7.1.2 requires agreement of the owner, contractor, and architect, Subparagraph 7.1.2 states that a CCD requires agreement from the owner and the architect "and may or may not be agreed to by the contractor." Paragraph 7.3 states that the CCD is prepared by the architect and signed by the owner and the architect. Under Subparagraph 7.3.1 it can but need not state a proposed adjustment in price and time. This is what would traditionally have been known as a change order. Under Subparagraph 7.3.1, a CCD must be "within the general scope of the contract." The AIA replaced the language of Subparagraph 7.3.8 governing payment for changes under the CCD. In the event of a dispute over the cost of a change, the amounts not in dispute shall be submitted to the owner and the parties shall indicate which portion of the work and costs upon which the parties agree and disagree. The architect is charged with determining the amounts of the disputed changes for payment. The architect's determination of the disputed amount is then open to challenge under the dispute provision in Article 4 of the contract.

[C] Minor Changes

Paragraph 7.4 of AIA Document A201 allows the architect to order minor changes in the work that do not involve adjustment in the contract sum or extension of the contract time and are not inconsistent with the intent of the contract documents. Such changes must be effected by written order.[15]

For the protection of all parties, minor changes should be rare, particularly when the owner is available. Otherwise disputes inevitably arise over whether a change is truly minor. In *Whitfield Construction Co. v. Commercial Development Corp.,*[16] the court interpreted an earlier AIA document and concluded that the strength of walls was not minor and therefore could not be subject to a minor change. Accordingly, any contractor who at the direction of the architect performs changed work that is likely to result in increased cost or time does so at its peril. In *J.M. Humphries Construction Co. v. City of Memphis,*[17] compensation was denied when the contractor failed to obtain a change order from the owner after the architect had agreed to "minor changes." Consequently, if the contractor does not agree that the change ordered by the architect does not involve change in price or time, it should object immediately.

EJCDC No. 1910-8 uses different terminology. What the AIA calls a change order, the EJCDC calls a "written amendment" at Paragraph 1.45. The AIA construction change directive is the EJCDC's work change directive at Paragraph 1.44. What the AIA calls a minor change, the EJCDC calls a field order at Paragraph 1.19. The EJCDC gives the engineer authority to order by field order

---

[15] *See* Sweet, Construction Industry Contracts § 11.05[E].

[16] 392 F. Supp. 982 (D.V.I. 1975).

[17] 623 S.W.2d 276 (Tenn. Ct. App. 1981).

a minor deviation that must be "compatible with the design and concept of the completed project as a functioning whole as indicated by the contract documents" at Paragraph 9.5.[18] Commentators and association groups have criticized this new terminology and pointed out that practitioners will continue to say "change orders" and "modifications," but if the terminology is in the contract, it should be referenced.[19]

The Associated General Contractors of America (AGC) use Paragraph 18 in their Form 3 as the changes clause. Individual states and large owners will also use their own versions and changes terminology.[20] Whichever the form, changes must be issued only by someone with authority to do so.[21] Most changes clauses specify who has the authority to order changes. It may be the owner's architect, engineer, or husband;[22] the owner and architect jointly; or simply the owner. In public construction, it may be the town engineer; the public agency, board, or commission that contracted for the work; the controller; specified city officials; or any other person or officer designated in the contract. The contractor's right to rely on changes directed by an owner's representative is limited by the actual authority of the agent. In *Odell v. 704 Broadway Condominiums,* the court held that the power of attorney granted by the condominium owners to the condominium board did not give the board's president the authority to modify the construction contract.[23]

The federal government has come out with a new changes clause for contracts for commercial items: FAR 52.212-4, "Contract Terms and Conditions— Commercial Items." This clause states, in Subparagraph (c): "Changes. Changes in the terms and conditions of this contract may be made only by written agreement of the parties." For contracts in which this clause is used, the owner may not change the contract unilaterally. The change must be by bilateral agreement of the parties. Although this clause is used only in contracts for commercial items, and does not overrule the traditional changes clause the federal government puts in its construction contract, it can be involved in construction contracting if the general contractor is buying commercial items from vendors or subcontractors.[24]

§4.04 ORAL CHANGES

Changes clauses usually require that all orders for changes or extra work be in writing and signed by the owner and architect or other designated persons. Such provisions protect the owner from unexpected costs or unjustified claims for additional compensation[25] when the contractor changes the work making it more

---

[18] EJCDC No. 1910-8 (1983).
[19] *See* Sweet, Construction Industry Contracts § 11.01.
[20] *See* R. Postner & R. Rubin, New York Construction Law Manual 146 (1992) (dealing with common changes clauses in New York State).
[21] *See, e.g.,* AIA Doc. A201, ¶ 12.1; EJCDC Doc. 1910-8, art. 10.1.
[22] Walter v. Horwitz, 60 N.Y.S.2d 327 (Sup. Ct.), *aff'd,* 65 N.Y.S.2d 672, 271 A.D. 802 (1946).
[23] 728 N.Y.S.2d 464, 284 A.D.2d 52 (2001).
[24] *See* FAR Subpt. 44.4.
[25] Langly v. Rouss, 185 N.Y. 201, 77 N.E. 1168 (1906).

expensive without the owner's consent. This protects an owner from overreaching and protects both parties by ensuring an accurate record of the change.

Owners who orally direct or accept changes sometimes argue that they owe no payment for charged work because the contractor failed to insist on a written change order as specified by the contract. This defense is often rejected, especially if the owner has suffered no harm from lack of the written order. This result is a commonsense solution to prevent unjust enrichment. If an owner or the owner's authorized agent asks the contractor to perform work and agrees to pay for it, and the contractor does so to the benefit of the owner, the proposition that the owner should be bound by the agreement to pay for the work is obvious.[26] In other words, if the change was needed, the owner knew that the change was being made, and the owner failed to stop the contractor, courts will not normally allow the owner to escape payment.

When some harm may result from enforcing an oral modification or unjust enrichment may occur, an oral modification may not be enforced. For example, the value of oral modifications that had been paid by the owner directly to a supplier were not permitted to be added to the subcontract amount used by a general contractor to calculate subcontractor's overpayment when the subcontract required written change orders in *Farina Building Co. v. General Lumber & Supply Co.*[27] In *Farina Building*, Farina Building Co. contracted to build a home. The building contract stated a fixed price of $167,971, of which $12,600 was designated and escrowed for custom windows. Subsequently, the owner decided to switch the brand of windows. Farina requested a quote for the new windows from General Lumber & Supply (General). General requested and received an estimate from Radford, its supplier. Radford erred in providing a quote of $11,686, including sales tax, for 30 rather than the required 32 windows. General provided the erroneous quote to Farina. Based on General's quote Farina had an agreed, enforceable contract price of $11,686 for the Andersen windows. Farina told the owner that the window change created a price increase, characterized the verbal window upgrade as a "change order," and told the owner that she would have to deposit an additional $2,954 with General before General would order the Andersen windows.

The building contract stated that "no changes in the plan and specifications are to be made except upon written order . . . signed by Buyer and Builder setting forth a detailed description of the changes . . . and the cost, or credit, therefor." There was no written change order to the building contract concerning windows. The owner paid the additional $2,954 deposit directly to General. General credited the deposit to the owner. All 32 windows were delivered to the construction site, and the Andersen windows invoice reflected the corrected price for 32 windows, rather than 30, at $14,711.90. General drew $12,000 from the building contract escrow of $12,600 and retained the $2,954 deposited by the owner for the change

---

[26] *See* Traylor v. Henkels & McCoy, Inc., 99 Idaho 56, 585 P.2d 970 (1978); Restaurants Sierra, Inc. v. Ramos, 97 Cal. App. 3d 482, 158 Cal. Rptr. 733 (1979). *See also* J. Acret, Construction Litigation Handbook (1986).

[27] 263 Wis. 2d 431, 662 N.W.2d 678 (Wis. Ct. App. 2003).

to Andersen windows, for a total of $14,954, or $242.10 over the billed amount for the Andersen windows. Farina sued the supplier to recover the overpayment. The trial court held that Farina was entitled to the difference between $11,686, the contract price between Farina and General based on the mistaken quote on the Andersen windows, and the $14,954 amount paid to General, or $3,268 in damages.

The appellate court explained that under the building contract, Farina would have been entitled to draw an amount of $12,600 for windows. General withdrew $12,000 from the escrow, $314 more than it was entitled to withdraw under the existing subcontract with Farina. Farina was entitled to $314 damages from General. No written change to the building contract existed. Therefore, the trial court's conclusion that Farina was entitled to an amount in excess of the $12,600 contract amount was in error. The difference between the $12,600 window costs allowed in the building contract and available in the $11,686 escrow was $914, the maximum amount that Farina could claim under the original building contract without a required written change order. Farina's directive to the owner to pay the additional amount to General was made extraneous to the building contract and to the escrowed amount that Farina was entitled to for the window costs. To the extent that the trial court entered judgment inconsistent with the building contract, and with Farina's entitlements under the building contract for windows, the judgment damages awarded to Farina were set aside.

Courts have used a variety of theories to reach this equitable result and probably most often have used a waiver theory.[28] So, for example, in a case where a contractor receives oral approval for its changes, and the owner accepts the changes, the owner is deemed to have waived the written change order requirement of the contract.[29] Like any contract requirement, the requirement for written orders may be waived by a party or a party's agent if the agent has the authority to do so.[30] Rarely would an agent have the authority to waive a contract requirement, and an owner is not bound by its agent's unauthorized waiver.

For example, in *F. Garofalo Electric Co. v. New York University*,[31] Garofalo Electric Co. was the electrical contractor for a building at NYU. Garofalo claimed that NYU and the Construction Manager (CM) directed it to perform extra work, agreed to pay for such extra work, and that it performed the additional work and furnished additional materials. Garofalo filed suit against NYU and the CM for breach of contract seeking damages for delays and extra work. On summary, NYU argued that Garofalo failed to provide the contractually required written notice and

---

[28] Regarding the avoidance of the requirement for written changes, *see* 13 Am. Jur. 2d Building and Construction Contracts § 24; *see also* Annotation, *Effect of Stipulation, in Private Building or Construction Contracts, that Alterations or Extras Must Be Ordered in Writing*, 2 A.L.R.3d 620 (1965); Annotation, *Effect of Stipulation, in Public Building or Construction Contracts, that Alterations or Extras Must Be Ordered in Writing*, 1 A.L.R.3d 1273 (1965).

[29] Flooring Sys. v. Staat Constr. Co., 100 S.W.3d 835 (Mo. 2003); Wisch & Vaughan Constr. Co. v. Melrose Properties Corp., 21 S.W.3d 36 (Ohio 2000).

[30] Consolidated Elec. Distrib., Inc. v. Gier, 24 Wash. App. 671, 602 P.2d 1206 (1979).

[31] 705 N.Y.S.2d 327, 270 A.D.2d 76, (2000).

documentation of its claims and that the Statute of Frauds barred the claims because Garofalo failed to demonstrate partial performance of the oral modification. The CM argued that the electrical contractor had waived its claim for extra work by failing to comply with the notice requirements in the contract.

Garofalo did not claim that it complied with the notice requirements or that the contract was modified by a signed writing, but argued, based upon deposition testimony, that NYU or the CM either abandoned, waived, or modified those requirements. Garofalo asserted that although the contract required that documentation be sent to both NYU and the CM, the CM directed it to deal exclusively with the CM and not to correspond with NYU, and to proceed without the required paperwork. Denying NYU's motion, the court found that genuine issues of fact existed whether electrical contractor contemporaneously advised the CM of all work it considered to be extra; whether the CM was apprised of all delays imposed; and whether there was a departure from the notice requirements by both parties.

The reviewing court reversed, stating that the contract's notice and documentation requirements for extra work and delay damages were conditions precedent to recovery and the failure to strictly comply is a waiver of such claims. Because Garofalo conceded that it did not strictly comply with the contract's mandates, it clearly waived its claims and NYU's motion should be granted. The court's rationale was that where a written contract provides that it can be modified only by a signed writing, an oral modification is not enforceable unless it is fully executed or there has been a partial performance "unequivocally referable" to the oral modification. The reviewing court found nothing in the record that unequivocally referred to an intent to modify the notice provisions. In any event, any reliance on the purported waiver and/or modification on the part of the electrical contractor, a sophisticated contractor, which would result in nearly $2 million in extra work and delay damages, was unreasonable.

However, a waiver may be inferred from an owner's oral order to do extra work when the owner promises to pay the contractor for the work.[32] For example, in *V.L. Nicholson & Co. v. Transcon Investment & Finance, Ltd.,*[33] the developer orally asked the contractor to proceed after approval of certain changes to the scope of the work. The Tennessee Supreme Court ruled the developer was bound on an implied-in-fact contract because it approved changes in the scope of the work, approved progress payments, and did not order the contractor to stop the extra work in progress.

Sometimes the owner may be held to have acquiesced to the oral change if he is present during changes or alterations.[34] For example, after a contractor and owner discussed construction of a pond, the contractor installed the pond. The owner knew of its installation but "expressed no dissatisfaction." The owner could

---

[32] Louis N. Picciano & Son v. Olympic Constr. Co., 492 N.Y.S.2d 476, 112 A.D.2d 604, *appeal dismissed*, 66 N.Y.2d 854, 498 N.Y.S.2d 366, 489 N.E.2d 253 (1985).

[33] 595 S.W.2d 474 (Tenn. 1980).

[34] Perry v. Levenson, 81 N.Y.S. 586, 82 A.D. 94 (1903).

not avoid paying for the pond by relying on the contractor's failure to obtain written authorization.[35]

The more involved the owner is with the project, the more likely it is that a court will find that the owner waived the strict terms of the contract. In *Brinich v. Jencka*, the homeowners and the contractor signed an agreement, which provided that any modifications must be in writing, signed by the parties.[36] During the course of construction, the homeowners continually left notes for the contractor and his subcontractors regarding changes or modifications to the work in progress. Only one addition, an extension to the garage, was covered by a written agreement signed by the parties. The contractor failed to invoice the homeowners for these modifications at the time they were completed. Once the homeowners obtained an occupancy permit and moved into the house they refused to allow the contractor onto the property, and refused to authorize disbursement of the final draw. The contractor sued, alleging breach of written and oral contracts, unjust enrichment, tortious interference with contractual relations, and defamation. The jury returned a verdict in favor of the contractor for $87,635.21.

The appellate court agreed with the trial court that there was sufficient evidence to conclude that the homeowners requested and approved oral modifications to the original contract, noting that the homeowner visited the jobsite almost every day and was aware of the many modifications to the original plans. The appellate court held that because the contract was silent as to the actual pricing of contract modifications, the contractor's parol evidence regarding the terms was not improper despite the existence of an integration clause.

Likewise, in *C.L. Maddox, Inc. v. Coalfield Services, Inc.*,[37] the contractor sued its subcontractor for breach of an oral contract for demolition and reinstallation of a mining facility. The contractor subcontracted all of the job except for the fabrication of the new facility. The subcontractor did not go underground and inspect the facility because it had previously done this type of work. The subcontractor started work and encountered problems resulting in slow progress. The subcontractor then made repeated requests for the contractor to sign a prior proposed contract, but the contractor refused and the subcontractor stopped work. The subcontractor presented an invoice, which the contractor agreed to pay less the 10-percent retention conditioned on the subcontractor signing an acceptance letter. The letter extended the deadline for the completion of the work but carried a liquidated damage clause. The subcontractor argued that this was insufficient time to complete the work due to the differing conditions. The subcontractor never resumed work, and the contractor filed this suit for damages caused by the subcontractor's abandonment of the work after completing 45 percent of the work. The court held that the subcontractor's work stoppage was not a legitimate self-help response to the contractor's failure to make promised progress payments where the subcontractor had not transmitted the invoice to the contractor prior to stopping

---

[35] Miller v. McMahon, 523 N.Y.S.2d 185, 135 A.D.2d 1030 (1987).

[36] 757 A.2d 388 (Pa. Super. Ct. 2000).

[37] 51 F.3d 76 (7th Cir. 1995).

work. The court held that the stoppage constituted a breach of contract unless it could be found that this was excused by the contractor's actions. The court also found that the contractor's refusal to sign the subcontractor's proposal constituted an anticipatory breach that supported the stoppage. The court affirmed the judgment for the subcontractor in part, reversed in part, and remanded the case for further proceedings.

Similarly, courts often enforce oral modifications, when acquiesced to by the parties in their course of dealing, despite the existence of explicit contract terms requiring a writing. This is true even in cost-plus contracts. In *T.W. Morton Builders v. von Buedingen*,[38] the plaintiff home improvement contractor brought suit to foreclose on its mechanic's lien after the homeowners failed to pay in full for the work. The homeowners counterclaimed for breach of contract and unfair trade practices. The homeowners sought the addition of a master bedroom/bathroom wing, a barn, and other significant improvements. They received bids, including one from the plaintiff for $540,000. Following negotiations during which the scope of the work was scaled down, they accepted the plaintiff's bid of $370,000. The parties used an AIA form providing that the payment for the work would be on a cost-plus-fee basis. The contract recited that the negotiated price was only an estimate, with the actual amount adjusted for changes in the work. The contract provided that costs attributable to the negligence of the contractor would not be reimbursed, and any changes resulting in additional costs would only be effective when a change order was signed by the homeowners. During the work, the parties failed to follow the change order procedure, since changes were frequently made. The final cost for the bid plus written authorized change orders totaled $654,000. The court held that this indeed was a cost-plus contract and not a fixed fee. There was no evidence to support the claim of unfair or deceptive trade practices. The court affirmed the judgment for the contractor and awarded the contractor attorneys' fees pursuant to the mechanic's lien statute.

In most cases, when public work is ordered orally, courts hold that the state or local government has waived the requirement for a written order.[39] In one case, the court found that the city had waived its right to have a written change order as a condition precedent to payment when it was undisputed that the city had requested the authorizations in question. The court even stated that the denial of the city's engineer to certify payment for them was bad faith.[40]

However, where public works contracts are concerned, some courts appear to be less willing to find waiver. A possible explanation for this phenomenon is that in the era of tighter public budgets, courts are more willing to impose additional burdens upon contractors in order to protect the commonweal. In *Bartlett Construction Co. v. St. Bernard Parish Council*,[41] a Louisiana appellate court held

---

[38] 450 S.E.2d 87 (S.C. Ct. App. 1994).

[39] Heiskell v. H.C. Enters., Inc., 429 S.W.2d 71 (Ark. 1968); State Highway Dep't v. Wright Contracting Co., 131 S.E.2d 808 (Ga. Ct. App. 1963).

[40] City of Mound Bayon v. Ray Collins Constr. Co., 499 So. 2d 1354 (Miss. 1986).

[41] 763 So. 2d 94, 99-1186 (La. App. 4th Cir. 2000).

that a contractor cannot rely on the oral statement of the public owner's engineer that conflicts with the express terms of the contract. According to the Louisiana court, the only exception to the rule that public works contracts must be in writing was limited to the performance of additional work that unjustly enriched the owner.

The contractor in that case did not fall within the exception, as the contractor did not expend any extra money in completing the work stipulated in the contract. Moreover, the contractor's claim that it relied on the owner's engineer's statement conflicted with the express language of the contract. If the contractor indeed relied on that statement, it should have articulated its concerns before it signed a contract contrary to the engineer's statement and insisted that any discrepancies be addressed in writing at that time. The appellate court held that the contractor was paid in accordance with the contract and there was no breach of the contract by the owner.[42]

Similarly, in *A. Beecher Greenman Construction Corp. v. Village of Northport*,[43] the contractor was awarded the contract to rehabilitate a sanitary pumping station. There were provisions for the assessment of liquidated damages for untimely completion. The contractor also was required to pay engineer inspection costs even for work performed after the completion date. The work was completed 12 days late, and the village withheld money as liquidated damages and for the inspection expense. The contractor filed this suit seeking to recover for extra work performed. It argued that it was entitled to an extension of time for completion. Where the contractor failed to provide written notice to the village in the form of a request for an extension of time and for an adjustment for extra work, it was not entitled to recover for the work or for the liquidated damages. Clearly, the result would have been different had the contractor followed the change order process set forth in the contract.[44]

The Washington State Supreme Court took an even more restrictive view regarding an owner's waiver of contractual change order provisions and a contractor's need to follow the change order process in its contract in *Mike M. Johnson, Inc. v. Spokane County*.[45] In that case the contractor on a county sewer project was ordered to stop work after the county discovered that a previously re-designed section of the project had failed to take into account other existing utilities. The county shut down the contractor during this second re-design for six weeks. The parties' contract contained very specific notice and claim procedures, which stated that the contractor's failure to follow said procedures constituted a waiver, and that full compliance with the contract was a condition precedent to the contractor's

---

[42] *But see* Empire Asphalt Paving v. Town of Kent, 625 N.Y.S.2d 241, 214 A.D.2d 533 (1995), where the court held that in their prior course of dealing the plaintiff contractor and the town waived contract provisions requiring that modifications be in writing because the parties waived the writing requirement on every occasion that either party made a change request.

[43] 619 N.Y.S.2d 293, 209 A.D.2d 565 (1994).

[44] *See also* Seneca Valley, Inc. v. Village of Caldwell, 156 Ohio App. 3d 628, 808 N.E.2d 422 (2004); Cas Constr. Co. v. Town of East Hartford, 82 Conn. App. 543, 845 A.2d 466 (2004).

[45] 150 Wash. 2d 375, 78 P.3d 161 (2003).

right to seek judicial relief. The contractor submitted a notice of claim, and was directed to submit a formal claim under the contract. Because it was on standby, the contractor could not provide the information required under the formal process, but did so after work had resumed, in specific detail. The county attorney replied to this claim and specifically stated that the response was not a formal recognition of the contractor's claims and that the county was not waiving any future claims or defenses it might have in the dispute. The project ultimately was completed a month behind schedule, during which time the contractor and the county's field engineer were in constant communication regarding both the delays and costs associated with the delays. When the contractor presented its claim to the county, the county rejected it based upon the contractor's failure to follow the strict change notice process in the contract. The contractor sued, and the county won at summary judgment arguing that the contractor's failure to strictly comply with its contractual obligations was a waiver.

The court of appeals reversed, taking a "common sense approach."[46] The court found that the contractor did provide written notice and that the county had actual notice of the contractor's claims due to its involvement in the day-to-day activities of the contractor at the jobsite and as such, strict compliance with the technical claims procedure had been implicitly waived by the county. The owner's actual notice of the changed conditions and subsequent work directed and required by the owner because of those conditions excused the contractor from having to comply with the formal contractual provisions.

On appeal to the state supreme court, the court of appeals was reversed. The court held that actual notice is not an exception to compliance with explicit and formal contractual provisions. In its decision, the supreme court focused more on the county attorney's statements over the actual involvement of the county engineers at the jobsite. The court left open the possibility that an owner can be found to have waived contractual claim procedures where the owner directs, authorizes, gives permits for, and/or requests the changed work. Why, then, the supreme court did not find waiver under the facts of this case remains a mystery. This case may, however, be an "outlier," dependent upon the particular facts of that case and not a harbinger of a new trend. The court's decision has recently been challenged by the very same appellate court that the supreme court overturned in *Mike M. Johnson.*[47]

The appellate panel in *Weber Construction, Inc. v. Spokane County* was asked to reconsider its prior ruling in the case in light of *Mike M. Johnson.* The panel did, and specifically held that the county waived strict compliance with the very same contractual protest and claim provisions in the contract as were at issue in *Mike M. Johnson.*

The writing provision may also be waived by conduct if, for example, the parties consistently do not follow contract procedures for review and approval of change orders and extra work.[48] In one case, the contract required that alterations

---

[46] 112 Wash. App. 462, 49 P.3d 916 (2002).

[47] Weber Constr., Inc. v. Spokane County, 98 P.3d 60 (Wash. App. 2004).

[48] Joseph F. Egan, Inc. v. City of New York, 17 N.Y.2d 90, 268 N.Y.S. 301, 215 N.E.2d 490 (1966).

be made by written memorandum agreed to by the owner and the general contractor.[49] During the course of the work, alterations were made without the owner's written approval, but the owner made progress payments without protest. Later in litigation, the owner tried to allege the unauthorized variations as the basis of a counterclaim. The court held, however, that the owner had waived the requirement. The owner was a former general contractor and carpenter who was present on the job virtually every day and acquiesced to the explanation of matters about which he complained. Furthermore, he made payments on the buildings without objection, and he indicated approval of the general contractor's work on certain occasions.

So, the party's practice of ignoring the written change order requirements modifies that part of the contract and removes it as a bar to recovery if the contractor fails to obtain the writing.[50] Other courts have gone so far as to treat a continuing course of conduct between the parties involving extensive nonwritten change orders to be an abandonment of the contractual, written change order requirement.[51] And of course, oral direction from the owner, which merely directs the contractor to make repairs necessary to make the project comply with the plans and specifications, is not a change at all.[52] However, where the inadequacy of the plans and specifications is the cause of the nonconformity, an owner may still have liability for the changes.

Estoppel is another legal theory used by courts to avoid the enforceability of the covenant against oral modifications. In these cases where the owner has acted or represented something that is relied upon by the other party, the owner is then prohibited from denying its representation. In *Harrington v. McCarthy*,[53] the contract required that changes be ordered in writing before the work was performed. During construction, however, the owner asked the contractor to perform extra work without putting the changes in writing. The Idaho Supreme Court ruled that the owner was estopped to rely on contract provisions that required written change orders. Other courts have determined that the parties in fact have novated the contract by their course of conduct.[54]

Contractors must recognize that because the writing requirement serves legitimate purposes, it can be enforced strictly. If the contractor fails to establish a waiver by "clear and unmistakable evidence," courts will bar the contractor's recovery.[55] A similar failure would occur if the contractor fails to prove a "definite agreement to pay" by the owner.[56] In such cases, the owner typically demonstrates

---

[49] Swenson v. Lowe, 5 Wash. App. 186, 486 P.2d 1120 (1971).

[50] *See* D.K. Meyer Corp. v. Breveo, 206 Neb. 318, 292 N.W.2d 773 (1980).

[51] H.T.C. Corp. v. Olds, 486 P.2d 463 (Colo. Ct. App. 1971); *see* L. Pepe & G. Haese, *Changes in Scope Claims*, Proving & Pricing Construction Claims 252 (R. Cushman & D. Carpenter eds., 1990).

[52] Town of Palm Beach v. Ryan Inc. E., 786 So. 2d 665, 26 Fla. L. Weekly D1502 (2001).

[53] 91 Idaho 307, 420 P.2d 790 (1966).

[54] *See* J. Acret, Construction Litigation Handbook § 6.08 (1986).

[55] Service Steel Erectors Co. v. SCE, Inc., 573 F. Supp. 177 (W.D. Va. 1983); Hall Contracting Corp. v. Entergy Servs., Inc., 309 F.3d 468 (8th Cir. 2002).

[56] Linneman Constr., Inc. v. Montana-Dakota Utils. Co., 504 F.2d 1365 (8th Cir. 1974).

that the work was done pursuant to the directives of unauthorized agents,[57] or even without its knowledge,[58] thus making the contractor a volunteer.[59] In *J.M. Humphries Construction Co. v. City of Memphis*,[60] the contractor failed to obtain a change order before going ahead with extra work and was not allowed to collect extra costs because written approval was required in the city contract. The contractor's right to rely on changes directed by an owners' representative is limited by the actual authority of the agent. In *Odell v. 704 Broadway Condominiums*,[61] the court held that the power of attorney granted by the condominium owners to the condominium board did not give the president of the board the authority to modify the construction contract. Similarly, if a contractor performs work that is not required by the contract documents, the approval of the architect is not necessarily binding on the owner. Often the architect is viewed as an independent contractor as opposed to the general agent of the owner.[62]

§4.05 PROCESSING THE CHANGE

How a change order is processed will vary from owner to owner. Typically the changes clause of a contract establishes a procedure that results in a written modification to the contract, describing the precise nature of the new and different work to be performed and the compensation to be paid. This process if often triggered by a "bulletin" or similar communication from the architect, notifying the contractor of the requirement for a change to the design, defining detail, explaining the new and different work to be performed, and requesting a cost proposal for performing that work.[63]

---

[57] Hartline-Thomas, Inc. v. H.W. Ivey Constr. Co., 161 Ga. App. 91, 289 S.E.2d 196 (1982).

[58] J.A. Tobin Constr. Co. v. Kemp, 239 Kan. 240, 718 P.2d 302 (1986).

[59] Post Constr. Co., HUDBCA No. 82-722-C25, 84-1 BCA (CCH) ¶ 16,959 (1983).

[60] 623 S.W.2d 276 (Tenn. Ct. App. 1981).

[61] 728 N.Y.S.2d 464, 284 A.D.2d 52 (2001).

[62] *See* Reid v. Fine, 205 Va. 778, 139 S.E.2d 829 (1965).

[63] *See* L. Pepe, Pricing and Proving Construction Claims for Changes in Scope in Unforeseen Conditions, Presentation at the Construction & Litigation Superconference (Nov. 1991). Reliance Ins. Co. v. County of Monroe, 604 N.Y.S.2d 439, 198 A.D.2d 871 (1993) (Contract anticipated that contaminated soil might be encountered and provided for the containment of contaminants. During the construction, the contractor proposed a design modification at no additional cost. A field change order was issued. While performing this work, the contractor encountered the toxic hazardous wastes. The county approved certain costs associated with the wastes, but denied other claims brought by the contractor involving work stoppages. The county argued that the contractor had assumed the risks accompanying its proposed change order and therefore had waived its right to recover for additional costs. The court held that the contractor did not assume the risk and that the county was liable for the costs associated with this Type II differing site conditions claim. The contractor was not aware of the presence of the hazardous substances, it could not have anticipated the condition from its experience or from an inspection of the site, and the condition varied from normal conditions present in performing similar work.).

Often, before initiating the formal process, the owner will ask the contractor for an estimate of the cost and time impact. Once that is provided, the owner can then more intelligently decide whether to order the change. Normally, the expense of putting together such a proposal is not reimbursable if the owner does not order the change. It is viewed as a bid and proposal cost that is not reimbursable if the contract is not awarded. Exceptions occur, however, if the owner uses the proposal in any other way.[64]

Depending on the contract, there may be several steps for processing a change order. For example, the contractor on a municipal contract may submit a claim for extra work to the project architect who then recommends approval of the claim to the municipal board. If the board approves the claim, it passes a resolution. The contractor is then notified of the resolution and may submit a requisition for the extra the following month. In a private contract the same steps may be involved, with the architect submitting the claim to the owner for approval rather than to a board. For example, AIA Document A201 provides that the contractor must submit a written claim for additional cost or time to the architect and that the architect will review the claim within ten days. If the architect approves the claim, he recommends approval by the owner. The owner then either agrees or disagrees with the architect.[65]

[A]   When the Change Can Be Ordered

The owner may order a change any time during the performance of the contract, provided the change is ordered prior to final payment. In *J.D. Hedin Construction Co. v. United States,* the Court of Claims held:

> We know of no contract requirement or any obligation imposed by law which restricts the government's power to order changes within a specific period . . . .
> The contracting officer can order changes as long as the finished product was substantially the same as originally contracted for. However, changes may not be ordered after final payment.[66]

[B]   Without Notice to the Sureties

The clauses often state that the change can be made "without notice to the sureties." This is designed to avoid the possibility that an obligation of the surety's performance might be diluted (under the general law of suretyship) in the event of a change in the contract without notice to the surety. Because the contract containing this changes clause is approved by the surety, such notice is no longer necessary.

---

[64] *See* Campos Constr. Co., VABCA No. 3019, 90-3 BCA (CCH) ¶ 23,235 (1990).

[65] General Conditions of the Contract for Construction, ¶¶ 4.3.7, 4.3.8, 4.4.1 (1987).

[66] 347 F.2d 235 (1965).

§ 4.06   CONSTRUCTIVE CHANGES

"Constructive change" is an all-encompassing phrase that can include any action or inaction on the part of the owner or its agents that changes or interferes with a contractor's permitted method of performing the contract but that is not formally implemented through a change order. *Constructive changes* are changes caused by the owner but not acknowledged by it as a change. Common examples are improper inspection, improper rejections of work, defective specifications, failure to disclose superior knowledge, and acceleration. Such actions are commonly grouped as constructive changes, a term that developed in federal contracting.[67]

Probably most changes are not express change orders but constructive changes. As the Court of Claims stated:

> We, as well as the Armed Services Board of Contract Appeals, have held that, if a contracting officer compels the contractor to perform work not required under the terms of the contract, his order to perform, albeit oral, constitutes an authorized but unilateral change in the work called for by the contract and entitles the contractor to an equitable adjustment in accordance with the changes provision. The court has considered it to be idle for the contractor to demand a written order from the contracting officer for an extra when the contracting officer was insisting that the work required was not additional . . . and, therefore, has often dispensed, on these occasions, with the formality of issuing a written change order under the standard clause.[68]

The constructive change order doctrine requires a "change" element and the "order" element. To determine the "change" element, the judge must determine whether performance went beyond the minimum performance required by the contract. This includes changes in the method or manner of performance in which the contractor legitimately had planned to perform the contract. The specifications may have remained the same, but the contractor's operation has been altered somehow. For example, in one case, excessive noise at a government facility adjacent to the contractor's construction site interfered with the contractor's performance.[69] And in *American Construction Co.,*[70] the board held that requiring the contractor to obtain insurance for government furnished property for which it was already responsible was a compensable contract change.

In *S. Hanson Lumber Co. v. DeMoss,*[71] the owner improperly required the contractor to use a more expensive type of material than required by the contract. The court held that the owner was liable for the contractor's extra cost. Similarly, in *Charles Meads & Co. v. City of New York,*[72] a bridge contractor was entitled to

---

[67] *See* J.F. Nagle, Federal Construction Contracting § 22.4 (1992).

[68] Len Co. & Assocs. v. United States, 181 Ct. Cl. 29, 385 F.2d 438 (1967).

[69] Nichols Dynamics, Inc., ASBCA No. 17,949, 75-2 BCA (CCH) ¶ 11,556 (1975).

[70] ENGBCA No. 5485, 88-2 BCA (CCH) ¶ 20,628 (1988).

[71] 253 Iowa 204, 111 N.W.2d 681 (1961).

[72] 181 N.Y.S. 704, 191 A.D. 365 (1920).

additional compensation when the architect refused to allow the contractor to follow the method of construction permitted in the contract and, instead, required the contractor to use a more complicated and expensive method.

The judge must also determine whether the "order" element exists. To be compensable, a constructive change must have been made as the result of an order, that is, the owner's representative, "by his words or his deeds, must require the contractor to perform work which is not a necessary part of his contract."[73] In *Al Johnson Construction Co. v. United States*,[74] the Claims Court granted the constructive change claim of a contractor on a Mississippi River control structure project. The contractor was told by the Army Corps of Engineers to install additional wells because its dewatering plan was inadequate. Although there was no explicit government directive to install a specific number of wells, the court concluded that the Corps' conduct surrounding its review of the contractor's dewatering plan constituted a constructive change order to install additional wells.

In *Fox v. Mountain West Electric, Inc.*,[75] the Idaho Supreme Court held that an implied-in-fact contract exists when the parties do not agree about change order pricing, but still continue to work under the contract. Lockheed Martin Idaho Technologies Co. requested bids for a comprehensive fire alarm system. Mountain West Electric installed electrical wiring, conduit, and related attachments. Fox provided services in designing, drafting, testing, and assisting in the installation of fire alarm systems. At a pre-bid meeting, the contractors concluded that it would be advantageous to work together on the project. They agreed that Fox would work under Mountain West Electric. Fox prepared a bid for its materials and services, which was incorporated into Mountain West Electric's bid to the owner. Mountain West Electric was awarded the owner's fixed-price contract. Many changes and modifications to the owner's contract were made. A dispute between the contractors arose over the procedure for the compensation of the change orders. Mountain West Electric proposed a flow-down procedure, whereby Fox would receive whatever compensation the owner agreed to pay Mountain West Electric. Fox suggested a bidding procedure. No compensation arrangement was agreed upon. Fox left the project after delivering the remaining equipment and materials. Fox contracted with another contractor to complete the project. Fox filed suit and Mountain West Electric counterclaimed. The district court found that because the parties never agreed about the procedures for change orders, but continued to work under the owner's contract, they had an implied-in-fact contract. The court found in favor of Mountain West Electric and awarded fees. Fox appealed.

Fox argued there was no meeting of the minds on the change order compensation procedure, and that the standard in the fire alarm industry was a bidding process rather than a flow-down method. Mountain West Electric contended that Fox understood that it would receive a fixed price under the owner's contract and

---

[73] Industrial Research Assocs., Inc., DCAB No. WB-5, 68-1 BCA (CCH) ¶ 7069 at 32,686 (1968).
[74] 20 Cl. Ct. 184 (1990).
[75] 137 Idaho 703, 52 P.3d 848 (2002).

that it would receive the change order amounts allowed by the owner. Although the procedure was the same for each change order, each party treated the pricing submitted by Fox for the change orders in a different manner. The treatment was not sufficient to establish a meeting of the minds or to establish a course of dealing when there was no "common basis of understanding for interpreting the parties' expressions." There was an implied-in-fact contract using the industry standard's flow-down method of compensation for the change orders rather than a series of fixed-price contracts between the contractors. An implied-in-fact contract allowed for the reasonable compensation of Fox.

Judges have applied the constructive changes doctrine in situations when:

1. The owner has erroneously interpreted the contract.[76]

2. The owner has directed a particular manner of performance not specified in the contract.[77]

3. The owner has furnished defective specifications.[78]

4. The owner has required higher inspection standards than called for in the contract.[79]

5. The owner has failed to disclose technical information to the contractor.[80]

6. The owner has accelerated performance constructively.[81]

For a constructive change order to bind the owner, it must be issued by an authorized representative who has the actual authority to modify the contract. Contractors who have actual or constructive notice of any limitations on a representative's authority cannot bind the owner when these agents act beyond their actual authority. So, contractors must ascertain whether the agents with whom they deal are acting within the scope of their authority.

Virtually any action of the owner can constitute a constructive change. Indeed, the same act can be and often is the basis of a delay claim and a claim for

---

[76] Chris Berg, Inc. v. United States, 197 Ct. Cl. 503 (1972). Sergent Mech. Sys., Inc. v. United States, 34 Fed. Cl. 505 (1995) (Series of directives triggered by presence of a plant that was not legally protected resulted in constructive changes in the contract. Before contractor started excavation, government prohibited any disturbance of any areas where shagbark manzanita was growing, because government was under mistaken impression that plant was on the endangered species list. Contractor claimed for delay and increased costs because it was forced to excavate smaller pits with steeper sides. Court of Federal Claims said even if plant had been legally protected, government would have been required to alert contractor to its presence; resulting restrictions on construction activities should have been stipulated in the contract, and general contract provisions that required contractor to adhere to environmental and safety regulations were insufficient.).

[77] Big 4 Mech. Contractors, Inc., ASBCA No. 20,897, 77-2 BCA (CCH) ¶ 12,716 (1977).

[78] Hol-Gar Mfg. Corp. v. United States, 175 Ct. Cl. 518, 360 F.2d 634 (1966).

[79] Comspace Corp., ASBCA No. 11,474, 69-2 BCA (CCH) ¶ 7855 (1969).

[80] Hempstead Maint. Serv., GSBCA No. 3127, 71-1 BCA (CCH) ¶ 8809 (1971).

[81] Fischbach & Moore Int'l Corp., ASBCA No. 18,146, 77-1 BCA (CCH) ¶ 12,300 (1977).

increased work. Most constructive changes are the subject of scrutiny in other chapters, but two should be discussed briefly here.

[A]   Disagreements over Contract Interpretation

Many constructive changes originate in a difference of opinion as to the proper interpretation of the contract. For example, the owner refuses to issue a formal change order for the work in question because he believes that the work is already required by the contract and that, therefore, a change is unnecessary.[82]

In *Brasfield & Gorrie, Inc.*,[83] the misinterpretation involved the price of the change. The government had awarded a contract for construction of a courthouse. The work included the drilling of foundation caissons, with payment based on the linear foot. The government then ordered the contractor to drill two adjacent caissons of a larger diameter using a different drilling technique. The contractor negotiated higher unit prices based on the increased costs, but the urgency of the schedule caused the government to order the contractor to proceed before this agreement could be formalized. The government later reneged on the increased unit prices and said the contractor was adequately compensated for the additional work under the unit prices provided in the original contract. The board disagreed. The two additional caissons involved work of a different and more difficult nature that the original caissons. Brasfield was not bound by the contractual unit price and was entitled under the changes caused to recover the increased costs of performance.

The contractor is entitled to an equitable adjustment if the owner interferes with the contractor's performance by unreasonably dictating the method of performance (and rejecting methods that were permitted under a proper interpretation of the contract).[84] When the contract directs the work to be done by one of the several specified methods as approved, the words "as approved" do not divest the contractor of the choice of methods. In *Albert C. Rondinelli*,[85] the contractor chose one of the methods, but was directed to use another method that was prohibited by the specifications. The owner contended that the words "as approved" gave it the right to reject the contractor's choice of one of the specified methods. To accept this position, the board ruled, would place the contractor in the owner's unrestrained power "contrary to the tenets of mutuality of obligation." Owners cannot use the approval power to substitute their judgment for that of a contractor merely because they think their method is superior to the proposed one.[86]

Chris Berg, Inc. & Associates[87] involved a contract for the construction of a building in Alaska where the contractor was required to thaw permafrost. The

---

[82] Dawson Constr. Co., GSBCA No. 3820, 75-1 BCA (CCH) ¶ 11,339 (1975).

[83] GSBCA No. 8605, 89-2 BCA (CCH) ¶ 21,673 (1989).

[84] Murdock Constr. Co., IBCA No. 1050-12-74, 77-2 BCA (CCH) ¶ 12,728 (1977) (prohibiting removal of concrete curb forms until 24 hours after concrete had been poured).

[85] ASBCA No. 9900, 65-1 BCA (CCH) ¶ 4674 (1965).

[86] Hensel Phelps Constr. Co., ENGBCA No. 3674, 77-1 BCA (CCH) ¶ 12,475 (1977).

[87] ASBCA No. 3466, 58-1 BCA (CCH) ¶ 1792 (1958).

method of doing so was left to the skill, judgment, and technical knowledge of the contractor. When the contractor submitted for approval its plan for thawing permafrost, the owner rejected the plan and directed that another method be used. The board ruled that when a contract specifies the objective to be achieved, but not the methods for doing so, and the owner rejects a proposed method reasonably designed to accomplish the intended result without a clear showing that the proposed method will not work, the contractor is entitled to an equitable adjustment. Furthermore, a reserved right of approval does not permit the owner to direct a different sequence of work than the contractor had planned.[88] Nor does a right to direct removal of an employee carry with it the right to require submission of names of individuals proposed for various positions for advance approval.[89]

[B] Accelerations

Acceleration occurs when a contractor is forced to perform work faster than required under the original contract.[90] In *Siefford v. Housing Authority of Humboldt*,[91] the court recognized that owners often cause delays that force contractors to speed up their work in order to finish at or before the contract completion date. Such "acceleration" is an acceptable basis for an action for damages.

Acceleration can be either express or constructive. *Express acceleration* occurs when the owner directs the contractor to speed up performance to beat the contract delivery schedule. The federal changes clause, for example, expressly recognizes the right of the contracting officer to accelerate performance. There is no dispute that the contractor is contractually entitled to more time, but because of changing government needs, acceleration is necessary. In other cases, a contractor effectively is compelled to speed up progress to overcome previous excusable delays and meet a fixed completion date. The latter situation is termed *constructive acceleration* and is treated as a constructive change.

Certain elements are necessary for constructive acceleration:

1. The contractor encountered an excusable delay for which it was entitled to an owner time extension;

2. Notice by the contractor to the owner of such delay;

3. An order by the owner to accelerate in spite of the excusable delay; and

4. Additional costs incurred due to the acceleration order.

Contractors rely on being able to perform work in a logical sequence at a measured pace. When the rate or sequence of work is disrupted through acceleration, it is not unusual to see major increases in costs of performance. Acceleration often takes

---

[88] S. Rosenthal & Son, Inc., ASBCA No. 6684, 1963 BCA (CCH) ¶ 3791 (1963).

[89] A.L. Dougherty Overseas, Inc., ASBCA No. 11,683, 68-2 BCA (CCH) ¶ 6571 (1968); Martin Marietta Cos., ASBCA No. 12,143, 69-1 BCA (CCH) ¶ 7660 (1969).

[90] *See* J.F. Nagle, Federal Construction Contracting § 22.13 (1992).

[91] 192 Neb. 643, 223 N.W.2d 816 (1974).

the form of added crews or equipment, and labor costs may be increased through greater use of overtime. In such cases the contract price will be increased, not to cover the costs of the original excusable delay but to cover only the costs of acceleration, extra personnel or equipment, and overtime.

The Construction Industry Institute Changes Impact Task Force investigated 106 projects to determine the factors impacting cost and schedule growth. The data were sorted according to fixed-price and cost-reimbursable contracts. On cost-reimbursable projects, three driving factors were studied: cost, schedule, and quality. Cost overruns were more acute when the primary driving factor was schedule. Schedule overruns were more frequent when the driving factor of cost was most dominant. Quality driving was not a major factor in either type of overrun.[92]

The first element of an acceleration claim requires an excusable delay in completing performance, entitling the contractor to an extension of performance time.[93] In *Titan Pacific Construction Corp. v. United States*,[94] the claims court rejected the claim of a contractor that it was entitled to compensation for an acceleration effort resulting from the Navy's failure to grant appropriate time extensions for excusable delays. The court found that the contractor had not been required to accelerate because of the Navy's failure to grant time extensions for excusable delays, but rather to correct the poor performance of one of its subcontractors that had resulted in nonexcusable delays.

The second element of an acceleration claim requires that the contractor preserve its claim by (1) notifying the owner of its excusable delay, and (2) requesting an extension of time, with supporting information "sufficient to allow the [owner] to make a reasonable determination" regarding the request. If the contractor fails to comply with these requirements and then accelerates, it may be treated as a "volunteer" and the claim will be denied. Failure to notify the owner of the delay and request a time extension (with supporting information) may be excused in certain situations. For example, if the owner makes it clear that it will not even consider a claim for a time extension, the contractor need not comply with the notice and request requirements.[95]

The third element of a claim for acceleration is an express or implied owner order to take steps to overcome the excusable delay, complete the work at the earliest possible date, or complete the work earlier than the date the contractor is entitled to because of the excusable delay. An express order (oral or written) to maintain the original contract schedule is called an actual or directed acceleration order. An implied order to maintain the original contract schedule is called a constructive acceleration order. Thus, when the owner demands that the contractor perform within the original or adjusted schedule, even though the contractor is

---

[92] Thomas & Napolitan, *The Effects of Changes on Labor Productivity: Why and How Much*, 10 Construction Industry Institute, Source Document 99 (Aug. 1994).

[93] Carney Gen. Contractors, Inc., NASA No. 375-4, 79-1 BCA (CCH) ¶ 13,855 (1979).

[94] 17 Cl. Ct. 630 (1989).

[95] Carney Gen. Contractors, Inc., NASA No. 375-4, 79-1 BCA (CCH) ¶ 13,855 (1979); Corabetta Constr. Co., PSBCA No. 299, 77-2 BCA (CCH) ¶ 12,699 (1977).

entitled to a time extension, judges have held that the contractor is "constructively accelerated."[96]

Whether there has been a constructive acceleration order depends upon the statements, actions, or inactions in each particular case. A constructive order to accelerate will be found if the owner takes some action "equivalent of an order" directing the contractor to meet the original completion date regardless of excusable delays.[97] The contractor must show that the owner expressly or impliedly ordered the contractor to perform in a shorter period of time than that to which it was entitled. In *Pathman Construction Co.*,[98] the government impressed on the contractor that the building was urgently needed before winter. By virtue of the contract's liquidated-damages provisions (which were read to the contractor in one instance), the government indicated that it intended to assess liquidated damages against the contractor if it did not complete earlier than was contractually required. The board concluded that the contractor was accelerated.

Such an order may be implied then if the owner expresses urgency, especially if the owner threatens default or assessment of liquidated damages, or actually assesses liquidated damages for not meeting the schedule;[99] requests any measures necessary to finish the work within the original contract time;[100] or pressures the contractor to employ additional labor to increase production.[101] A mere request to submit a plan showing how to regain lost time is not a constructive acceleration order.[102] Similarly, suggestions to use more workers in response to an inquiry seeking advice[103] or expressions of concern that the contractor is falling behind schedule[104] probably do not constitute constructive orders to accelerate. The failure to grant an adequate time extension in a timely manner may amount to an acceleration order.[105]

To provide the last element of an acceleration claim, the contractor must prove that it actually accelerated, or at least made an effort to accelerate, and that it incurred additional costs as a result. It is not necessary that the acceleration efforts succeed. A reasonable attempt to meet the completion date is all that is required.

In an acceleration claim, the contractor cannot recover all of its costs. It can recover only those costs that exceed the costs it would have incurred if it had not been accelerated. In such cases, the contract price will be increased, not to cover the costs of the original excusable delay but to cover only the costs of acceleration— extra personnel, equipment, or overtime. Thus, the contractor must be able to show

---

[96] *See* Norair Eng'g Corp. v. United States, 229 Ct. Cl. 160, 666 F.2d 546 (1981); American Mach. & Foundry Co., ASBCA No. 10,173, 67-2 BCA (CCH) ¶ 6540 (1967).

[97] Constructors-Pamco, ENGBCA No. 3468, 76-2 BCA (CCH) ¶ 11,950 (1976).

[98] ASBCA No. 14,285, 71-1 BCA (CCH) ¶ 8905 (1971).

[99] Fischbach & Moore Int'l Corp., ASBCA No. 18,146, 77-1 BCA (CCH) ¶ 12,300 (1977).

[100] Raymond Int'l, Inc., ASBCA No. 13,121, 70-1 BCA (CCH) ¶ 8341 (1970).

[101] M.S.I. Corp., GSBCA No. 2429, 68-2 BCA (CCH) ¶ 7377 (1968).

[102] A. Teichert & Sons, Inc., ASBCA No. 10,265, 68-2 BCA (CCH) ¶ 7175 (1968).

[103] Iversen Constr. Co., IBCA No. 981-1-73, 76-1 BCA (CCH) ¶ 11,644 (1976).

[104] Superior Asphalt & Concrete Co., AGBCA No. 75-142, 77-2 BCA (CCH) ¶ 12,851 (1977).

[105] *See* M.S.I. Corp., GSBCA No. 2429, 68-2 BCA (CCH) ¶ 7377 (1968).

the difference between its costs before and after acceleration. The costs of acceleration can include those that arise from inefficiency.

[C] Matters Not Considered Constructive Changes

In order to prove a constructive change, the contractor must prove that the change was caused by the owner. Actions by foreign governments, unless they are embargoes or other delays listed in the contract as an excusable delay, do not affect contract price or performance.[106] In *RPM Construction Co.*,[107] the contractor was not entitled to recover the costs of installing groundwater monitoring wells under the contract for the installation of an underground fuel tank because the installation work was not directed by the government. Instead, it was directed by the issuance of a site citation by the state environmental agency that required the contractor to install the monitoring wells as a remedial measure.

Contractors cannot receive relief merely because costs have risen to the point that assures a financial loss.[108] This occurs even if the contractor is blameless and the problem came from war,[109] fire,[110] increased transportation charges,[111] or strikes.[112] Often, prices have not risen at all; the contractor simply bid too low on material;[113] miscalculated overhead;[114] assumed a certain amount of other business that failed to appear;[115] or tried to protect a competitive advantage.[116]

---

[106] Planned Sys. Int'l, Inc., GSBCA No. 4976, 78-2 BCA (CCH) ¶ 13,264 (1978); Anglobel Trading, ASBCA No. 8250, 1962 BCA (CCH) ¶ 3558 (1962).

[107] ASBCA No. 36,965, 90-3 BCA (CCH) ¶ 23,051 (1990).

[108] Minneapolis Scientific Controls Corp., ASBCA No. 9113, 65-1 BCA (CCH) ¶ 4541 (1965).

[109] Minnesota Chippewa Tribe, IBCA No. 1025-3-74, 75-1 BCA (CCH) ¶ 11,264 (1975) (1973 Arab-Israeli War). The board distinguished Automated Extruding & Packaging, Inc., GSBCA No. 4036, 74-2 BCA (CCH) ¶ 10,949 (1974), *reh'g denied*, 75-1 BCA (CCH) ¶ 11,067 (1975), in which an embargo caused by that war made certain material unavailable and thereby caused an excusable delay. *See also* Zoda v. United States, 148 Ct. Cl. 49, 180 F. Supp. 419 (1960); Johnson Automatic Arms, Inc., ASBCA No. 758 (1951); *but see* Dougherty Overseas, Inc., ENGBCA No. 2625, 68-2 BCA (CCH) ¶ 7165 (1968).

[110] Petrofuels Ref. Co., ASBCA No. 9986, 1964 BCA (CCH) ¶ 4341 (1964).

[111] Browne & Bryan Lumber Co., B-172531, 75-1 CPD ¶ 39 (1975); Heinfield Enters., ASBCA Nos. 11,838, 11,839, 67-1 BCA (CCH) ¶ 6102 (1967); *but see* James F. Richards Constr. Co., ENGBCA No. 2652, 66-2 BCA (CCH) ¶ 5809 (1966). Materials became unavailable in contractor's locale but were available far away, which would have required large cost increases, primarily due to increased transportation costs. Rather than pay higher costs, the appellant continued to search for a closer source. The Board held the contractor was entitled to an excusable delay. *See also* Dillon v. United States, 140 Ct. Cl. 508, 156 F. Supp. 719 (1957).

[112] Ertel Mfg. Corp., ASBCA No. 697 (1951); Southern Steel Corp., ASBCA No. 6579, 61-1 BCA (CCH) ¶ 2965 (1961).

[113] Minneapolis Scientific Controls Corp., ASBCA No. 9113, 65-1 BCA (CCH) ¶ 4541 (1965).

[114] Drillmation Co., ASBCA No. 12,501, 69-1 BCA (CCH) ¶ 7632 (1969).

[115] Astronautics Publ'g Co., ASBCA Nos. 12,006, 12,667, 67-2 BCA (CCH) ¶ 6609 (1967).

[116] *See* Firestone Indus. Rubber Prod. Co., ASBCA Nos. 16,650, 17,938, 74-1 BCA (CCH) ¶ 10,516 at 49,828, *aff'd sub nom.* Firestone Tire & Rubber Co. v. United States, 214 Ct. Cl. 457, 558 F.2d 577 (1977); Gallatin & Virden, *Buying-In: The Downside of Competition*, Constr. Mgmt., Nov. 1984 at 5.

Another prime reason for rising prices is a shortage of an item, for example, oil[117] and oil-based products such as asphalt,[118] or plastic[119] and lumber.[120] In *Essential Construction Co. & Himount Constructors, Ltd.,*[121] although Canadian lumber was cheap and plentiful, the contract required more expensive domestic lumber. The board determined that this higher price was no excuse. The contractor should have arranged for firm commitments or advised the owner of the need for Canadian lumber prior to award.[122] A similar result occurred in *CCC Construction Co.*[123] The contractor claimed increased cost because of the unavailability of steel. The board found that steel was available if the contractor had properly used the defense priority system.

§ 4.07   DUTY TO PROCEED

Most contracts give the owner or its architect and engineer the right to direct the contractor to proceed with disputed work.[124] Under such a clause, the contractor must proceed unless the work in question is so far beyond the scope of the contract as to be a cardinal change. The contractor may give notice that it is working under protest, thus reserving its right to make a claim for payment of the work. But if the contractor refuses to proceed, it can be held in default and its contract terminated.[125] Even if the contractor is later found to have been correct, that is, the work is found to have been extra work and to have entitled the contractor to extra compensation, its failure to proceed under protest can result in a loss of its claim for lost profits.[126]

---

[117] H&S Oil Co., ASBCA No. 16,321, 72-2 BCA (CCH) ¶ 9520 (1972); Air-Speed, Inc., PSBCA No. 96, 75-1 BCA (CCH) ¶ 11,113 (1975).

[118] So Ros Sahakij Ltd., P'ship, ASBCA No. 19,238, 75-1 BCA (CCH) ¶ 11,028 (1975).

[119] All Molded Plastics Co., ASBCA No. 20,012, 76-2 BCA (CCH) ¶ 12,119 (1976).

[120] Brazier Lumber Co., ASBCA No. 18,601, 76-2 BCA (CCH) ¶ 2207 (1976); Essential Constr. Co. & Himount Constructors, Ltd., ASBCA Nos. 18,463, 18,509, 75-2 BCA (CCH) ¶ 11,469 (1975).

[121] ASBCA Nos. 18,463, 18,509, 75-2 BCA (CCH) ¶ 11,469 (1975).

[122] *See* MPT Enters., ASBCA No. 25,483, 84-3 BCA (CCH) ¶ 17,625 (1984); Pinel Tool Co., GSBCA Nos. 4380 et al., 762 BCA (CCH) ¶ 12,009 (1976); Szemco, Inc., ASBCA No. 9892, 1964 BCA (CCH) ¶ 4503 (1964).

[123] ASBCA No. 20,586, 77-1 BCA (CCH) ¶ 12,272 (1977).

[124] *See* FAR 52.243-4. Other provisions that give the owner the right to direct the contractor to proceed and give notice that he is working under protest and reserving his right to claim include AIA General Conditions of the Contract for Construction (A201), ¶¶ 7.9.3, 12.3; *see* R. Postner & R. Rubin, New York Construction Law Manual 157 (1992) for a copy of New York City's standard contract clause giving a similar right.

[125] Ferguson Contracting Co. v. State, 195 N.Y.S. 901, 202 A.D.2d 97 (1922), *aff'd*, 237 N.Y. 186, 142 N.E. 580 (1923). Chamberlain v. Puckett Constr., 921 P.2d 1237 (Mont. 1996) (subcontractor breached agreement by insisting that changes in subcontract be signed by prime contractor's owner rather than authorized representative and refusing to begin work absent performance of an act not required by subcontract; when party threatens not to perform unless it receives some additional consideration or assurance not called for in the contract, that party has repudiated the contract and is in breach); *see also* George F. Marshall & Gordon F. Blackwell, ENGBCA 6066, 00-1 BCA ¶ 30,730.

[126] John W. Johnson, Inc. v. Basic Constr. Co., 292 F. Supp. 300 (D.D.C. 1968), *aff'd*, 429 F.2d 764 (D.D.C. 1970); C.W. Schmid Plumbing & Heating Co., ASBCA No. 7738, 62 BCA (CCH) ¶ 3458 (1962).

This dilemma is illustrated by *Yukon Services, Inc.,*[127] which involved a contract for the construction of a road in Alaska. When the road could not be constructed in accordance with the specifications, the government changed the specifications by requiring that the roadbed be excavated to a lower grade in a rocky area so as to provide fill material for the troublesome swampy area. The contractor refused to proceed as directed under the changed specifications, alleging that the government had breached the contract. The government then terminated the contract for default. On appeal, the board upheld the default termination, finding that performance under the changed specifications was possible and that the change in specifications was not a cardinal change.

A contractor that refuses to proceed without resolving a dispute concerning additional performance costs repudiates its contract. In *Anderson Excavating & Wrecking Co. v. Sanitary Improvement District No. 177,*[128] Sanitary Improvement District No. 177 (SID) sought bids for a seawall construction and dredging project. The project involved erecting seawalls around three islands in a boating lake and dredging the lake to make it more uniform in depth. An engineering firm, Lamp, Rynearson & Associates, Inc., designed the plans for the project. The plans called for the dredged material to be disposed of on the three islands. After receiving bids, the SID split the project into two contracts and phases of work. Phase I of the project involved the construction of the seawalls and was awarded to Big River Construction. Anderson Excavating & Wrecking Company (Anderson) was awarded phase II of the project, which involved the dredging of the lake. Anderson was concerned before the contract was signed that the seawalls would not be able to hold the weight of the dredged material. There were delays in the progress of Big River Construction's work. Lamp issued a change order that extended the contract completion date. A dispute arose between Anderson and the SID about Anderson's ability to place the dredged material on the islands. According to Anderson's project manager, the islands were rounded on top and any material placed there would run off into the lake. Because the contract would hold Anderson liable for excess material surcharging the seawalls and for damage to the seawalls, Anderson was concerned about liability. A meeting was held to discuss the problem. Three options were discussed at the meeting: (1) issuance of a change order to allow additional payment to Anderson, (2) termination of the contract without financial liability to either party, and (3) execution of the work by Anderson according to Anderson's interpretation of the contract. Anderson wrote to Lamp stating:

> To prepare the islands for placement of dredged materials will cost approximately $27,000.00. If the S.I.D. is prepared to issue a Change Order to that effect Anderson will begin as agreed. However, if the S.I.D. is unwilling to issue the Change Order, then there appears to be only two other alternatives.
>
> First, they could rebid the dredging portion of the contract, and include the areas left unaddressed such as the island preparation. In this case Anderson

---

[127] AGBCA No. 213, 69-2 BCA (CCH) ¶ 7843 (1969).
[128] 265 Neb. 61, 654 N.W.2d 376 (2002).

> would be willing to relinquish all rights under this contract without any further expense to the S.I.D., provided that the performance and payment bonds are returned . . . .

The second alternative required all parties to prepare for litigation and rely upon the judicial system for determination. Should this become necessary, Anderson also prepared to exercise this alternative. After receiving the letter, Bard recommended that the SID accept the proposal to terminate the contract "in view of the above disagreements and your desire to review the amount of dredging and possible alternate disposal sites . . . ." The SID did not terminate the contract. Lamp and the SID behaved as if there was a contract still in place. Anderson never commenced work on the dredging project, and neither Lamp nor the SID demanded that work be commenced. Anderson brought suit against the SID alleging that: (1) the SID refused to go forward with the contract or to sign a proposed change order to the contract about the responsibility for the preparation of the islands; (2) the SID abandoned and breached the contract; and (3) Anderson incurred expenses in preparing to begin work on the contract, including costs incurred for insurance and performance bonds. Anderson's petition alleged a breach of contract cause of action seeking lost profits and expenses for preparation for work on the project. The SID denied the allegations and alleged that Anderson had breached and abandoned the contract.

The SID moved for summary judgment. The district court granted the motion and dismissed Anderson's petition, and Anderson appealed. The Nebraska Court of Appeals determined that there were genuine issues of material fact preventing summary judgment on the issue of Anderson's reliance on the contract and reversed, and remanded. On remand, the SID moved for partial summary judgment on the breach of contract cause of action, arguing that the court of appeals' decision determined that there were issues of fact only on the "detrimental reliance" cause of action. The district court granted the motion. After a bench trial, the court determined that Anderson had repudiated the contract when it demanded a change order or that the project be rebid and threatening litigation. The court determined that the unilateral repudiation of the contract precluded any equitable claims for recovery or for breach of contract. The court dismissed the petition. Anderson appealed.

The Nebraska Supreme Court found that Anderson would not perform the contract as originally agreed. Thus, it was not clearly erroneous for the court to find that the letter was a repudiation of the contract. Anderson argued that the court wrongly focused on only the letter and should have considered events that happened before and after the letter was sent. For example, Anderson contended that the SID continued to behave as if a contract existed after the letter was sent and that there was evidence that the parties were still attempting to find a solution to the problem. Anderson's arguments failed because Anderson never specifically retracted its repudiation. Further, any additional attempts by the SID to change the location for the placement of the dredged material did not change the fact that a repudiation occurred. Thus, the court was not clearly wrong when it determined that Anderson had repudiated the contract and could not recover reliance damages.

A federal government contractor who receives direction from an owner must perform in accordance with that direction and submit its claims as required under the contract.[129] Where the owner rejects the contractor's claims, the aggrieved contractor is not without options, however. As in *Alliant Techsystems,* a disappointed contractor may pursue a declaratory judgment on the disputed contractual claim once the contracting officer issues a final determination. It is important to note that the subject contract in *Alliant Techsystems* was subject to the Contract Disputes Act (CDA), and the same option may not be available to the contractor whose contract does not incorporate the provisions of the Act. The contractor in *Alliant,* despite having sought and received instruction from the court, nevertheless refused to perform and, as noted above, was judged to be in default of its contractual obligations.[130]

An exception exists if the work in question is outside the scope of the contract and therefore constitutes a cardinal change.[131] Courts have also found other exceptions. In *Dick Corp. v. State Public School Building Authority,*[132] the court found no duty to proceed when the agency refused to issue a written order and the contract required written orders. In *Northern Corp. v. Chugach Electrical Ass'n,*[133] the court found no duty to proceed when the owner ordered a "highly hazardous" method of performance that the court characterized as "impossible." Similarly, in *R.G. Pope Construction Co. v. Guardrail of Roanoke, Inc.,*[134] the court found no duty to proceed when the site was not made available until seven months after the original completion date and material costs had tripled. *Metropolitan Sewerage Commission v. R.W. Construction, Inc.*[135] explains that a contractor may be justified in not proceeding with performance when:

1. The changed condition causes a substantial increase in the contractor's costs;

2. The contractor cannot continue funding the work without an immediate increase in the contract price;

3. The owner refuses to negotiate such an adjustment.

So, for example, in *Bielecki v. Painting Plus, Inc.,*[136] the purchasers sought to buy a lot for $100,000 and have the contractor build a luxury home. The contract provided for the payment of $360,000 for the construction work, and payment to the contractor based upon $90 per square foot. The purchasers then requested an additional 680 square feet prior to the completion of the plans and specifications and other extras totaling $38,500 for which they agreed to pay. The contractor then

---

[129] Alliant Techsystems v. United States, 178 F.3d 1260, 1277 (Fed. Cir. 1999).

[130] 178 F.3d 1260, 1272.

[131] Rathburn Eng'g Corp., ASBCA No. 5187, 59-2 BCA (CCH) ¶ 2289 (1959); Hensler v. City of L.A., 124 Cal. App. 2d 71, 268 P.2d 12 (1954).

[132] 365 A.2d 663 (Pa. Commw. Ct. 1976).

[133] 518 P.2d 76 (Alaska), *vacated on other grounds and remanded,* 523 P.2d 1243 (Alaska 1974).

[134] 244 S.E.2d 774 (Va. 1978).

[135] 241 N.W.2d 371, 383 (Wis. 1976).

[136] 264 Ill. App. 3d 344, 637 N.E.2d 1054 (1994).

demanded that the purchasers execute an addendum that would increase the price by $191,800 over the original price. The purchasers argued that the additional costs demanded were grossly excessive and unwarranted by the changes in the scope of the work. The purchasers repeatedly demanded that the contractor honor the original contract and start work pursuant to the time limitations contained in the contract, but the contractor refused. The contractor argued that no final contract had been executed, therefore there was no agreement as to the terms of the contract. It alleged that the purchasers breached the contract and obtained the plans for the house through misrepresentation.

The purchasers sued the contractor seeking specific performance and damages. The court found that there was an enforceable contract, and the contract was not ambiguous. Judgment was affirmed for the purchasers. They were entitled to increase the size of the house and add the extras where the contract provided that the plans could be so altered.

In *Clark-Fitzpatrick, Inc./Franki Foundation Co. v. Gill*,[137] the subcontractor sued the general contractor, whereupon the general filed a third-party action against the Department of Transportation, which counterclaimed against the general. The general contractor was awarded the contract to replace a bridge. Upon commencement of the work, problems arose leading to various disputes, the most important being the unexpected behavior of the soils at the bottom of the bay. The department changed the pile-design concept from a friction-pile to a more expensive composite-pile design, but disagreed with the general contractor on the additional cost. The department ordered the contractor to continue working under a force account, and the contractor filed suit seeking injunctive relief, termination of the contract, and damages. The parties entered into a termination agreement, whereupon the subcontractor filed this action seeking damages relating to the termination.

The court held that the contractor's failure to give formal notice to the department of extra remedial work was not a waiver of such claims. It was entitled to recover delay damages caused by the department's holding preconstruction meetings and delaying the award of the contract. The subcontractor was entitled to recover its additional overhead costs attributable to the department's breach, but was not entitled to recover for lost profits.

---

[137] 652 A.2d 440 (R.I. 1994).

CHAPTER 5

CHALLENGING THE FINALITY OF AN EXECUTED CHANGE ORDER

Joel J. Rhiner
Scott Robert Fradin

§ 5.01   INTRODUCTION

You would have a hard time finding a construction contract that does not give the owner the right to order changes in the work. This contractual right gives the owner the ability to increase (or, in some instances, decrease) the scope of the work and at the same time, gives the contractor the ability to earn additional compensation for the performance of this additional work. However, the contractor's ability to earn additional compensation for change orders is not without risk. Unless the contractor has been given the luxury of performing the work on a time and material basis, the contractor must estimate what the cost of the work will be, whether the changed work will have any impact on the schedule, and whether the changed work will delay, disrupt, or otherwise hinder the contractor's performance of the original scope of work.

While a typical change order contains language providing that the contractor acknowledges 1) the amount of the change agreed to by the parties, and 2) that no additional compensation will be provided, more often than not, the change order will also contain general release language. This release language typically provides that: "in consideration of $[amount] and other good and valuable consideration, the receipt of which is hereby acknowledged, [name] does hereby waive, release and relinquish any and all claims, demands and right of lien for work, labor and/or materials furnished on the above described project."[1]

However, circumstances often arise after the change order has been executed that increase the costs associated with the performance of the changed work. Usually the contractor or subcontractor performing the changed work discovers that it did not correctly anticipate some part of the performance that affects its costs, the cost of the changed work, or how performance of the changed work would be impeded or restricted by other circumstances, or that it did not understand all the work involved in performing the change. Despite having released its right to recover its additional performance costs, the contractor often requests additional compensation from the owner to cover these increased costs. Just as often, however, the owner resists the request and relies upon the release language contained in the change order. Critically, and much to the dismay of contractors and subcontractors, courts and contracting boards will generally enforce release type language contained in a change order.

This chapter discusses the finality of an executed change order and how courts interpret the type of release language typically found in change orders to either deny the contractor additional compensation or to allow the contractor to avoid the effect of that language. The chapter then analyzes the legal defenses that a party can assert to avoid being bound by a release contained in an executed change order. Finally, the chapter discusses some suggested modifications to the language of the change order that may allow the contractor to seek recovery for increased costs associated with the performance of the changed work.

---

[1] Vulcan Painters, Inc. v. MCI Constructors, Inc., 41 F.3d 1457 (11th Cir. 1995).

§ 5.02   THE EXECUTED CHANGE ORDER AS AN ACCORD AND SATISFACTION

A change order that simply provides the contractor with payment for the performance of extra work is nothing more than a modification. However, when a change order combines payment for the performance of the extra work with a release of claims by the contractor arising from the performance of the changed work, the change order is then considered to be an accord and satisfaction.

[A]   Basic Legal Principals

[1]   The Accord and Satisfaction

At bottom, an accord and satisfaction is a bilateral contract. In fact, it has been described by one court as "a type of executed, substituted contract."[2] Accordingly, an accord and satisfaction requires the same, basic elements of contract formation:[3] (1) proper subject matter; (2) competent parties; (3) a meeting of the minds; (4) consideration; and (5) performance.[4] Further, courts interpreting an accord and satisfaction apply the same, basic principals of contract construction when analyzing an accord and satisfaction. Critically, to have an accord and satisfaction, substantial performance must not only be agreed upon, but it must be accomplished.[5] For example, if an owner settled a disputed change order with the condition that payment must be received within ten days, but does not pay within the required ten days or only makes a partial payment, no accord and satisfaction may have occurred.

But, how then does an accord and satisfaction differ from a basic contract? The answer can be found in the definition of accord and satisfaction found in the *Restatement (Second) of Contracts*. According to the Restatement:

(1) An accord is a contract under which an obligee promises to accept a stated performance in satisfaction of the obligor's existing duty. Performance of the accord discharges the original duty.

(2) Until performance of the accord, the original duty is suspended unless there is such a breach of the accord by the obligor as discharges the new duty of the obligee to accept the performance in satisfaction. If there is such a breach, the obligee may enforce either the original duty or any duty under the accord.

(3) Breach of the accord by the obligee does not discharge the original duty, but the obligor may maintain a suit for specific performance of the accord, in addition to any claim for damages for partial breach.[6]

---

[2] Cipriano v. Triad Mech., Inc., 925 P.2d 918, 921 n.6 (Or. Ct. App. 1996).

[3] Majestic Bldg. Material v. Gateway Plumbing, 694 S.W.2d 762, 764 (Mo. Ct. App. 1985); Ayers Plastics Co. v. Packaging Prods., 597 S.W.2d 177, 181 (Mo. Ct. App. 1979).

[4] C.A. Rasmussen, Inc. v. United States, 52 Fed. Cl. 345 (2002).

[5] Gitre v. Kessler Prods. Co., 387 Mich. 619, 198 N.W.2d 405, 408 (1972).

[6] Restatement (Second) of Contracts § 281 (1981).

From this definition, it becomes clear that the key difference between a simple contract and an accord and satisfaction is that to have an accord and satisfaction there must be a "pre-existing duty."

[2] The Release

The term "release" is defined in *Black's Law Dictionary* as the "relinquishment, concession or giving up of a right, claim or privilege, by the person in whom it exists or to whom it accrues, to the person against whom it might have been demanded or enforced."[7] The *Restatement (Second) of Contracts* similarly provides that "a release is a writing providing that a duty owed to the maker of the release is discharged immediately upon the occurrence of a condition."[8]

[B] Binding Nature—Case Law Examined

Courts have often determined that, because of an accord and satisfaction, the agreed amount of the change order may not be re-negotiated. For example, in *Gainesville-Alachua County Regional Airport Authority v. R. Hyden Construction, Inc.*,[9] the parties contracted for improvements at a regional airport. The Airport Authority challenged a judgment that awarded the contractor damages, with attorney's fees and costs, following a jury finding that the Airport Authority breached the construction contract by failing to approve an additional payment for expenses in connection with changes to the project. The parties' construction contract contained provisions for change orders that addressed adjustments of the contract price. The parties executed a change order for work on the project identifying several items that had been incorporated into the project. The change order established a new contract sum with explicit provisions indicating that the change order reflected the "final agreement" to "all adjustments" in the contract sum, and that the increased payment "represents the total amount due . . . for any and all items pertaining to the work" under the change order. After executing the change order, the contractor submitted another change order request, seeking an additional payment for general conditions and other costs associated with the work. The Airport Authority declined to pay the additional amount. Notwithstanding the language contained in the change order, the trial court allowed the contractor to seek certain "overhead type items" as "direct costs associated" with the change order.

The Airport Authority moved for a directed verdict at trial, and after the jury returned a verdict in favor of the contractor, the court denied the Airport Authority's motion and entered a judgment for the contractor. The Airport Authority appealed and the appellate court concluded that the change order, which the parties had previously executed, fully established the total amount due for the

---

[7] Black's Law Dictionary (5th ed. 1979).
[8] Restatement (Second) of Contracts, § 284 (1981).
[9] 766 So. 2d 1238 (Fla. Dist. Ct. App. 2000).

changes, and that contractor's claim for an additional payment should not have been submitted to the jury as it was precluded by the change order agreement.

Similarly, an agreement as to additional time for the performance of the additional work contained in an executed change order is generally upheld. In *Pete Vicari, General Contractor, Inc. v. United States*,[10] Pete Vicari, General Contractor, Inc. entered into a fixed-price contract with the U.S. Coast Guard. During the course of performance, adverse weather conditions at the site delayed the project's completion. The contractor requested time extensions due to weather, which the contracting officer independently evaluated, granting sometimes more and sometimes less than requested by the contractor. The contractor also claimed additional reimbursement for delays in architect approval and design deficiencies. The negotiated settlement both compensated the contractor and granted an additional time extension. The settlement recited that it was in full satisfaction of the contractor's claims for both "delays" and "design deficiencies." In consideration for plaintiff's release of its claims regarding the design deficiencies, the government gave up its right to assess liquidated damages for delay in completion of the project. The change orders for each extension that were executed included the following release:

> In consideration of the modification agreed to herein as complete equitable adjustment, the contractor hereby releases the Government from any and all liability under this contract for further equitable adjustments attributable to such facts or circumstances giving rise to the proposal for adjustment including all claims for impacts, delays, and disruptions.

After completion, the contractor filed a claim, which the contracting officer denied, then sued the government. In its complaint, the contractor requested an additional $86,564.42 for 58 weather delays. The contractor also sought $116,729.01 for an additional 82 days of delay due to design deficiencies. The government contended that recovery for delays should be barred because the change orders constituted accords and satisfactions and there was no reservation of rights. The claims court held that the modifications granting the time extensions were bilateral contract modifications and, therefore, the contractor's claims for additional time and costs were barred.[11]

Further, courts have held that language in a change order providing that the amount of the individual change is in full satisfactions of the changed work waives and releases any claim for further compensation for cumulative impact costs unless the contractor expressly reserves that right.[12] For example, in *Vanlar*

---

[10] 47 Fed. Cl. 353 (2000).

[11] Columbia Constr. Co., ENGBCA No. 6182, 96-1 BCA (CCH) ¶ 27,980 (1995) (contractor could not assert delay claim on behalf of subcontractor because contract modification stated that no time extension would be granted, because work was not on critical path; because issue of delay had been considered, contractor had waived right to time extensions).

[12] *The Cumulative Impact of Multiple Changes*, 18 Construction Claims Monthly 1 (No. 5, May 1996).

Construction, Inc. v. County of Los Angeles,[13] a public owner issued 81 change orders. Each change order contained general waiver and release language and was signed by the contractor. The California Court of Appeals acknowledged that the large number of changes may have had a cumulative impact on the contractor's performance costs, but the court said that any right to such a claim had been waived. The court felt that if the contractor contemplated a future claim for impact costs, it was obligated to request that a suitable reservation clause be included before signing the change order.

A similar result was reached by the Board of Contract Appeals in *In re Appeal of Central Mechanical Construction.*[14] In that case, the contractor realized the cumulative cost impact of the multiple changes only after signing a negotiated settlement of the changes that included a waiver and release, without reserving its right to a cumulative impact claim. The board determined that the waiver and releases barred any subsequent claim.[15] Federal courts also have concluded that a general waiver and release typically bars subsequent cumulative impact claims. In *Atlantic Dry Dock Corp. v. United States,*[16] the District Court for the Middle District of Florida held that releases in the change orders were unambiguous and intended to resolve all claims for damages caused by the delay and disruption, whether cumulative or otherwise.[17] This result has also been reached by state courts. For example, in *Uhle v. Tarlton Corp.,*[18] a subcontractor executed 23 written change orders with the general contractor. None of the change orders included any language that preserved any claim for indirect, impact, or delay costs. In the trial court, the subcontractor claimed that the cumulative impact of the multiple change orders created an exception to the rule of accord and satisfaction and, therefore, permitted recovery of additional performance costs relating to the executed change orders. The subcontractor admitted, however, that the labor and materials it had supplied to the general contractor were within the scope of its subcontract. The Missouri court held that the subcontractor could not recover its impact costs because they did not constitute extra work, or work not contemplated by the parties, and not controlled by the subcontract. The court ruled that all costs associated with the change orders were costs controlled by the contract. The court also determined that because the subcontractor had not added any language to the change orders that specifically preserved its rights to seek impact costs, the subcontractor had waived them.

Lastly, an accord and satisfaction may be expressed by an invoice and contractor's affidavit that no additional money is owed. A good example is found in

---

[13] 217 Cal. Rptr. 53 (Ct. App. 1985).

[14] ASBCA No. 29,434 (1986).

[15] *See also* John Massman Contracting Co. v. United States, 23 Cl. Ct. 24 (1991) (general waiver and release applied to claim for cumulative impact despite contractor's characterization of language as boilerplate that was never intended to include impact costs).

[16] 773 F. Supp. 335 (M.D. Fla. 1991).

[17] Baltz & Morrissey, *Contractor's Claims for Cumulative Impact: Valid but Difficult to Recover,* 32 Procurement Law. 19 (No. 1, Fall 1996).

[18] 938 S.W.2d 594 (Mo. Ct. App. 1997).

the case of *Vintson v. Lichtenberg*.[19] Vintson, a general contractor, contracted with the Lichtenbergs to build a new house for $686,200. The parties agreed that when the contractor substantially completed the house, the buyers would pay the remaining unpaid amount of the contract price together with all amounts due on change orders. The parties agreed that as a condition precedent to final payment, the contractor was to submit to the owners an affidavit stating that all labor, materials and equipment, and other indebtedness connected with the work for which the property might be responsible or encumbered by lien had been paid in full. The owners moved into the house, and the contractor gave them an invoice for additional construction costs not covered by the contract price. The contractor stated that the additional charges were for overages and excess costs it incurred in the construction. The owners paid the balance of the invoice and the contractor executed a contractor's affidavit, affirming that the improvements or repairs were fully completed according to the terms of the contract, and that the agreed price or the reasonable value of the labor, services, and materials had been paid. Notwithstanding the affidavit, the contractor filed suit against the owners claiming that they owed an additional $55,832.72 for change orders and extra items. The owners moved for partial summary judgment on the ground that the contractor's affidavit barred a claim for payment of extra costs. The contractor asserted that the buyers were indebted to it and that, at the time it executed the affidavit, the parties knew that the buyers still owed money for extra work. The contractor testified that he had executed the affidavit to "accommodate" the owners in closing their loan, and its "sole purpose was to dissolve all lien rights, not to acknowledge payment." The trial court held that the contractor's affidavit barred a claim for additional charges and on appeal, the Georgia Court of Appeals, noting the contractor's unequivocal averments in the affidavit, held that it was unreasonable that the contractor would have remained quiet about the $54,000 claim merely as an accommodation to the buyers, when both its invoice and contractor's affidavit clearly reflected that no such money was owed. The contractor was an experienced builder who had executed contractor's affidavits in the past. Accordingly, when the contractor executed the affidavit, it was an agreement that the owners did not owe any money under the contract.

§ 5.03   CHALLENGING THE EXECUTED CHANGE ORDER

[A]   Challenging the Scope of an Executed Change Order

It is not unusual during the course of performance of changed work that a dispute arises between the owner and the contractor concerning the scope of the work to be performed under the change order. In those instances when the contractor requests additional compensation for out-of-scope work, the owner will, in all likelihood, assert that the scope as set forth in the executed change order covers the disputed work and, therefore, deny the contractor's claim for additional

---

[19] 245 Ga. App. 250, 537 S.E.2d 703 (2002).

compensation. Accordingly, in order for the contractor to recover, the contractor must seek to modify the terms of the change order setting forth the scope of work. However, because the change order is, at bottom, a contract, there are very limited circumstances that will allow the contractor to modify its terms. Courts that have considered the issue have held that a change order may be modified only under very limited circumstances. Generally, a contractor must show either a mutual mistake of fact or that the change order was not a completely integrated agreement.

[1] Mistake as to Scope

[a] *Mutual Mistake*

A mutual mistake occurs when both parties, at the time of contracting, share a misconception about a basic assumption or vital fact upon which they based their bargain. A contract that is based on a mutual mistake of fact is voidable and may be rescinded or reformed. The *Restatement (Second) of Contracts* § 155 provides:

> Where a writing that evidences or embodies an agreement in whole or in part fails to express the agreement because of a mistake of both parties as to the contents or effect of the writing, the court may at the request of a party reform the writing to express the agreement. . . .[20]

The Restatement further explains that "[t]he error in expressing the agreement [which may be reformed under Section 155] may consist in the omission or erroneous reduction to writing of a term agreed upon or the inclusion of a term not agreed upon."[21]

To modify an executed change order as to scope due to mutual mistake of fact, a contractor must generally show that:

- in negotiating the modification, the owner and contractor were mistaken in their belief regarding a fact;

- the mistaken belief constituted a basic assumption underlying the modification;

- the mistake had a material effect on the bargain; and

- the change order did not put the risk of that mistake on the contractor.[22]

However, courts may review other factors when examining whether a mistake is sufficient to modify an executed change order. In this regard, courts may look to the degree of carelessness (the more careless the party alleging mistake the less likely mistake will be found), the values exchanged (has the party seeking to

---

[20] Restatement (Second) of Contracts § 155 (1979).
[21] Restatement (Second) of Contracts § 155 cmt. a.
[22] Peterson Builders, Inc. v. United States, 34 Fed. Cl. 182, 183 (1995).

enforce the change order as written received a large benefit for little consideration), when the mistake was recognized (has the party asserting mistake acted
before the other party detrimentally relied on the mistake), and, lastly, who
assumed the risk of the mistake.[23]

The case of *Peterson Builders, Inc. v. United States*[24] is instructive. In this
case, Peterson Builders, Inc., a shipbuilder, attempted to set aside a change order
to an agreement with the Navy for the construction of minesweepers, alleging
mutual mistake of fact. The original agreement provided that the contractor was to
be paid its costs plus an incentive fee for designing and building the ship. The original contract was "capped" at $99 million but, after change orders, the cost cap
was increased to $104 million. Typically, however, the contractor's final costs
were $113 million. The contractor requested an adjustment to the cost cap, which
the Navy rejected. In the lawsuit the contractor filed, the contractor alleged mutual
mistake arguing that both parties had believed that the detailed design of the ship
was substantially complete at the time that the parties had entered into a modification capping the allowable cost under the contract. The contractor further alleged
that the design underwent numerous, unanticipated changes after the cap was
imposed that caused the cap to be exceeded by $8 million.

In discussing the first element necessary to prove mistake of fact, i.e., both
parties were mistaken in their belief regarding a fact, the court held that the evidence proved that the Navy did not share the contractor's mistaken assumption
that the design detail of ship was substantially complete. According to the court,
the Navy's belief regarding the completeness of design did not constitute a basic
assumption underlying modification; rather, the evidence indicated that the modification was motivated by the Navy's desire to limit its liability and, therefore, the
change order placed risk of mistake on the contractor. According to the court, "[a]
mistake on the part of one party will not provide a basis for rescission, particularly
where the mistake is based on an unwarranted assumption of the party who should
have known better in light of its experience."[25] The court further held that "[t]o
support reformation, a mistaken assumption of fact must be with regard to something that can be contemporaneously verified, i.e., a fact that can be independently
and objectively established at the time the contract is entered into."[26] In the instant
case, the fact, i.e., no more design changes, by its very nature, was no more than a
prediction.

As to the fourth element, i.e., the change order did not put the risk of that
mistake on the contractor, the *Peterson Builders* court found that the contractor
was an experienced shipbuilder; based on the history and tumultuousness of the
evolution of the detailed design, the contractor should have kept the possibility of

---

[23] Sweet, Legal Aspects of Architecture, Engineering and the Construction Process 49 (5th ed. 1994).

[24] 34 Fed. Cl. 182 (1995).

[25] 34 Fed. Cl. 182, 183, citing McNamara Constr. of Manitoba, Ltd. v. United States, 206 Ct. Cl. 1, 10, 509 F.2d 1166, 1171 (1975).

[26] 34 Fed. Cl. 182, 184.

future changes to the detail design in mind when negotiating the modification. By failing to take such a possibility into account, the contractor assumed the risk that the costs would exceed the cap. Accordingly, the court held that the contractor had failed to establish that the change order fixing the cost cap should be set aside based on mutual mistake.

[b] Unilateral Mistake

As with avoidance of a contract on the basis of unilateral mistake, the requirements for avoidance of a change order based on unilateral mistake are: (1) the mistake is related to a material feature of the change order; (2) it occurred notwithstanding the exercise of reasonable care; (3) it is of such grave consequence that enforcement of the change order would be unconscionable; and (4) the other party can be placed in status quo.[27] Evidence of such conditions must be clear and positive. However, if the parties to a change order make assumptions as to the cost to be incurred for performance of the changed work, mistakes in those assumptions will not be cause for rescinding the contract because each party assumes the risk that their assumption as to the cost of performance was wrong. A change order fairly entered into cannot be avoided or disregarded by one of the parties because he discovers that the change order is less profitable to him than he anticipated when he entered into it.[28] Further, the unilateral mistake of one party to a change order may not be relied upon to relieve that party from the obligations under the change order where the party's own negligence and lack of prudence resulted in the mistake.

The case of *Guyler v. United States*[29] is informative. In *Guyler*, a contractor contracted with the government for the construction of 12 buildings. The central issue raised in the case centers around whether the contract required the contractor to paint the interior masonry walls. The original drawings did not indicate that the interior masonry walls were to be painted; rather, the specifications provided that "interior exposed masonry surfaces, *indicated on the drawings to be painted*, shall be painted in accordance with the attached Figure." During the course of the work, the government issued a change in the painting specification for the project which, among other things, deleted the words "*indicated on the drawings to be painted*." The contractor submitted a price quote for the changed work requested by the government. When it came time to paint the interior masonry walls, the painting subcontractor refused stating that the contract did not require the painting of any interior masonry walls. The government demanded that the walls be painted and the contractor painted the walls under protest. The contractor submitted a claim for the additional painting work and the claim was denied. Accordingly, the contractor appealed the decision to the Court of Claims. In awarding the contractor damages

---

[27] Wil-Fred's, Inc. v. Metropolitan Sanitary Dist. of Greater Chicago, 372 N.E.2d 946, 951 (Ill. Ct. App. 1978).

[28] Diedrich v. Northern Illinois Publ'g Co., 350 N.E.2d 857, 864 (Ill. Ct. App. 1976).

[29] 314 F.2d 506 (1963).

for the additional painting work, the court found that there was a unilateral mistake that allowed for reformation of the change order. According to the court,

> When the plaintiff submitted his price quotations for the changes covered by modification No. 3, he sent a detailed breakdown for each item of work but he included nothing for interior masonry painting. This omission must have been clear to the contracting officer, who examined the breakdown submitted before he approved the plaintiff's bid for the additional work. In spite of this, plaintiff's attention was not called to the matter by the contracting officer. . . .[30]

The dissent in *Guyler* took strong exception to the majority's holding and focused on the issue of whether the contractor had exercised "reasonable care." According to the dissent,

> Plaintiff does not deny that he knew these words had been deleted, but he says he did not understand the significance of this. Why he did not understand it, I am at a loss to understand. All he had to do was to read this provision of the specifications with these words stricken. Anybody—certainly a contractor of the experience of this plaintiff—reading this provision of the specifications with these words deleted, would know that the contract required that all interior masonry surfaces should be painted. The long and short of the matter is plaintiff was careless. We cannot reform a contract because a party did not exercise due care in reading it.[31]

[2] Lack of Integration

A contractor may also challenge the scope of an executed change order by claiming that, at the time of the execution of the change order, both parties orally agreed that additional costs relating to the modification would be included in a later change order. Obviously, in order to succeed, the contractor must provide evidence of the oral agreement. However, as a basic rule of contract interpretation, a court will not allow a party to introduce parol evidence, i.e., evidence of a prior oral agreement, to contradict the unambiguous terms of a change order. In order to avoid this rule, the contractor may attempt to argue that the change order is not an integrated agreement. As a matter of basic contract law, in order for a contract to be considered a completely integrated agreement, a court must determine whether the parties intended the writing to be a final expression of the terms it contains. The nature of the writing itself is often considered to be convincing evidence of the intention of the parties. While some courts have held that if the terms of a writing are thorough and specific, the agreement is to be taken conclusively as an integrated one with respect to those terms, the *Restatement (Second) of Contracts* reflects the prevailing view that other evidence, including evidence of prior negotiations, is still admissible to show that the writing was not intended as the

---

[30] 314 F.2d 506, 510.
[31] 314 F.2d 506, 512.

final expression of the terms it contains.[32] However, only prior consistent additional terms not evidenced by the writing may be considered. In other words, if the asserted parol evidence is inconsistent with an express term of the writing, the evidence will not be considered.

The case of *State v. Triad Mechanical, Inc.*[33] is instructive. In that case, the contractor and the Oregon Department of Fish and Wildlife (ODFW) entered into a contract for improvements to a fish hatchery. The contract provided for the removal of a specified amount of rock and that any excavation in excess of this amount would be compensated by change order. During construction, the contractor encountered rock in excess of the amount set forth in the contract and, accordingly, requested a change order. A change order was executed and upon completion of the project, the contractor presented a claim to ODFW for delay and impact costs associated with excavating the extra rock. According to the contractor, before executing the change order, and at the meeting where the change order was discussed, the parties agreed to postpone consideration of delay and impact costs. ODFW, however, contended that the terms of the parties' agreement on the extra excavation were contained in the change order. Critically, there was no mention in the change order of an agreement that another claim would be submitted for the delay and impact costs associated with the additional excavation. After completing the contract, the contractor submitted its claims for delay and impact costs associated with excavating extra rock. ODFW refused to pay the claims, contending that the contractor had waived further claims for costs incurred as a result of the extra rock when it signed the change orders.

The contractor filed a lawsuit against ODFW and ODFW moved for summary judgment. In granting ODFW's motion, the trial court found that the change order was a completely integrated agreement and that the contractor was barred from offering parol evidence to contradict its express terms. The contractor appealed and the court affirmed holding that the contractor's assertion of an alleged oral agreement that delay and impact claims were to be postponed was inconsistent with terms of the executed change order and, therefore, inadmissible. According to the court, the alleged oral agreement was so closely connected to the subject matter in the change order that it would not be natural to fail to address it in the change order particularly in light of the fact that the contract at issue was a sophisticated business transaction.

[B] Challenging the Release Contained in an Executed Change Order

There are special and limited situations when a claim for additional costs arising out of the performance of changed work can be prosecuted notwithstanding

---

[32] Restatement (Second) of Contracts § 209(3) (". . .where the parties reduce an agreement to a writing which in view of its completeness and specificity reasonably appears to be a complete agreement, it is taken to be an integrated agreement unless it is established by other evidence that the writing did not constitute the final expression.").

[33] 144 Or. App. 106, 925 P.2d 918 (1996).

the fact that the contractor has executed a release that appears to bar the claim. For example, courts will reform a release where it can be shown that, by reason of mutual mistake, neither party intended for the release to cover the claim for additional costs. Similarly, if a contractor can show that the release was procured through fraud or duress, a court may hold that the release will not bar prosecution of the claim. Additionally, if it can be shown that there was no meeting of the minds as to the scope of the release, courts may also reform the release. Lastly, if the contractor can prove that the parties considered the claim subsequent to the execution of the change order, the contractor may be able to argue waiver.

[1] Mistake

The elements of proof of mutual mistake that allow for relief are: (1) the parties to the contract were mistaken in their belief regarding an existing fact; (2) that mistaken belief constituted a basic assumption underlying the contract; (3) the mistake had a material effect on the bargain; and (4) the contract did not put the risk of the mistake on the party seeking reformation.[34] The underlying basis for such an action is the existence of a mutual understanding between the parties that the parties agreed to reduce to a writing, but through mutual mistake a material provision was omitted.[35] Critically, however, avoidance of a contract is allowed only when clear and convincing evidence compels the conclusion that the instrument as it stands does not properly reflect the true intention of the parties and that there has been either a mutual mistake or a mistake by one party and fraud by the other.[36]

The case of *T.L. Roof & Associates Construction Co. v. United States*[37] is informative. T.L. Roof & Associates Construction Co. contracted with the United States Army Corps of Engineers for the construction of a telecommunications facility. During the course of the project, the government issued 48 change orders. As a result of these changes and other delays, project completion was delayed six months. The contractor filed a claim with the contracting officer seeking costs related to the delay. The contracting officer failed to respond to the claim and the contractor filed a suit against the government in the Court of Claims seeking over $1 million. The government filed a motion for summary judgment arguing the defense of accord and satisfaction. Each of the change orders at issue contained the following release language:

> It is further understood and agreed that this adjustment constitutes compensation in full on behalf of the contractor and its subcontractors and suppliers for

---

[34] John T. Jones Constr. Co., ASBCA Nos. 48,303, 48,593 (Nov. 12, 1997); Black's Law Dictionary 1001 (6th ed. 1990) ("Mutual mistake is where the parties have a common intention, but it is induced by a common or mutual mistake.").

[35] Briarcliffe Lakeside Townhouse Owners Ass'n v. City of Wheaton, 524 N.E.2d 230 (Ill. Ct. App. 1988).

[36] 319 South La Salle Corp. v. Lopin, 311 N.E.2d 288 (Ill. Ct. App. 1974).

[37] 28 Fed. Cl. 572 (1993).

all costs and markup directly or indirectly attributable to the change ordered, for all delays related thereto, and for performance of the change within the time frame stated.

According to the government, this language barred the contractor from presenting any claim based on delay in completing the project. The contractor responded that during the negotiations concerning the modifications and during discussions concerning contract completion, the parties specifically discussed delay and impact claims and had agreed to defer consideration of these claims until such time as the contractor could more accurately assess its damages. Accordingly, the contractor argued that its execution of these change orders was based on a mutual mistake.

After reviewing the evidence, the court concluded that the change orders may have been the product of a mutual mistake. The court stated that the evidence presented indicated that (1) the contractor believed it had an agreement with the government that its delay claim would be preserved for future consideration; (2) the government was aware of the contractor's understanding and that the government had the same understanding; and (3) the contractor may not have signed the change orders if it had believed that the release language would bar its delay and impact claim.[38] Accordingly, the court denied the government's motion holding that there was a fact issue concerning whether the release provision in the change order was the result of mistake.

[2] Fraud

In order for a contractor to avoid the general release contained in an executed change order on the basis of common law fraud, courts require that a contractor plead and prove the following five elements: (1) a false statement of material fact; (2) known or believed to be false by the party making it; (3) intent to induce the other party to act; (4) action by the other party in reliance on the truth of the statement; and (5) damage to the other party resulting from such reliance.[39] Most courts and boards require that a party's reliance on false statement of material fact must be justified. In order to be justified, such reliance must be reasonable in light of the circumstances.[40]

In *C&H Commercial Contractors, Inc. v. United States*,[41] the court considered whether certain change orders constituted an accord and satisfaction between the parties. C&H sought additional compensation from the government due to certain delays and impacts associated with the changed work. The government argued

---

[38] 28 Fed. Cl. 572, 578.

[39] People ex rel. Peters v. Murphy-Knight, 618 N.E.2d 459, 463 (Ill. Ct. App. 1993).

[40] *See* Bank of Chicago v. Park Nat'l Bank, 640 N.E.2d 1288 (Ill. Ct. App. 1994) (holding that participants in commercial transactions are held to marketplace standards of vigilance and independent inspection).

[41] 35 Fed. Cl. 246 (1996).

that C&H's claims for damages were barred by the doctrine of accord and satisfaction because the change orders at issue included waivers releasing the government from liability for further equitable adjustments. Moreover, none of the change orders contained any reservation to seek further damages. As expected, C&H contended that the parties had agreed that the delay and impact claims could be submitted later. C&H's officers, in earlier depositions, explained that before signing each of the change orders, they expressed concern that the release language would prevent them from bringing additional claims for delay and impact costs; that the government had assured them that they would be entitled to submit subsequent claims for delay and impact costs despite the express release language; and that they had signed the modifications in reliance on those government assurances. The contracting officer, in a related trial, testified that C&H repeatedly expressed concern over the release language when the modifications were executed; the contracting officer had told C&H then that the modifications represented adjustments for the direct cost for the work but not for delay; and that the government would not require C&H to give up any right it might have. The same contracting officer also wrote an internal memo confirming that C&H's vice president did not want to sign any document that could waive its right to file a claim when the contract was completed. The memo stated that the government had repeatedly explained that if the contractor felt either the government actions or the total number of change orders collectively caused additional impact, the contractor could file a claim at the end of the contract. Based on this evidence, the court concluded that there was sufficient evidence to prove misrepresentation by the government. Accordingly, the court held that the change orders did not constitute an accord and satisfaction, and, therefore, the contractor was allowed to prosecute its delay and impact claims.

[3] Economic Duress

A further basis on which a contractor may seek to avoid the release contained in a change order is to assert economic duress or business compulsion.[42] Economic duress occurs if one party exerts excessive pressure beyond permissible bargaining and the other party consents because it has no real choice. The rationale underlying the principle of economic duress is the imposition of certain minimal standards of business ethics in the marketplace.

> Hard bargaining, efficient breaches, and reasonable settlements of good faith disputes are acceptable, even desirable, in our economic system. However, the minimum standards are not limited to precepts of rationality and self-interest — they include equitable notions of fairness and propriety which preclude the

---

[42] The doctrine of business compulsion is a category of duress recognized in some states that reduces the standard of coercion and duress required to prove common law duress. As with economic duress, to show business compulsion, the claimant must establish wrongful conduct that prevented it from exercising its free will in agreeing to an accord. Fizzell v. Meeker, 339 F. Supp. 624 (W.D. Mo. 1970).

wrongful exploitation of business exigencies to obtain disproportionate exchanges of value which, in turn, undermine the freedom of contract and the proper functioning of the system. The doctrine of economic duress comes into play *only* when conventional alternatives and remedies are unavailable to correct aberrational abuse of these norms. It is available to prevent injustice, not to create injustice.[43]

To establish duress, it must be shown that the act or threat left the individual bereft of the quality of mind essential to the making of a contract.[44] The acts or threats complained of must be wrongful; however, the term "wrongful" is not limited to acts that are criminal, tortious, or in violation of a contractual duty, but extends to acts that are wrongful in a moral sense as well.[45] However, it is well settled that, where consent to an agreement is secured merely through hard bargaining positions or financial pressures, economic duress does not exist.[46] This has been explained on a court's belief that if the economic duress concept were used too frequently, many contracts could be upset.[47] "Rather, the conduct of the party obtaining the advantage must be shown to be tainted with some degree of fraud or wrongdoing in order to have an agreement invalidated on the basis of duress."[48]

"Ordinarily, a threat to break a contract does not constitute duress, and to infer duress, there must be some probable consequences of the threat for which the remedy for the breach afforded by the courts is inadequate. If there is no full and adequate remedy from the courts for the breach, the coercive effect of the threatened action may be inferred."[49] Furthermore, a finding of duress is less likely if the party has the assistance of counsel and adequate time to consider the proposed contractual terms.[50]

In *Pete Vicari, General Contractor, Inc. v. United States*,[51] the contractor requested time extensions due to delays in architect approval and design deficiencies. The negotiated settlement both compensated the contractor and granted an additional time extension. The settlement recited that it was in full satisfaction of the contractor's claims for both delays and design deficiencies. After completion, the contractor filed a claim then sued the government for an additional 82 days that resulted from the design deficiencies for $116,729.01. The contractor claimed that the settlement agreement it executed was void because it was executed under duress. The contractor argued that it was subjected to severe economic distress

[43] Centric Corp. v. Morrison-Knudsen Co., 731 P.2d 411 (Okla. 1986).
[44] 731 P.2d 411.
[45] Hurd v. Wildman, Harrold, Allen & Dixon, 707 N.E.2d 609, 614-15 (Ill. Ct. App. 1999).
[46] 707 N.E.2d 609, 614-15.
[47] Sweet, Legal Aspects of Architecture, Engineering and the Construction Process 49 (5th ed. 1994), citing Centric Corp. v. Morrison-Knudsen Co., 731 P.2d 411 (Okla. 1986).
[48] Alexander v. Standard Oil Co., 423 N.E.2d 578, 582-83 (Ill. Ct. App. 1981).
[49] Kaplan v. Keith, 377 N.E.2d 279, 281 (Ill. Ct. App. 1978).
[50] Pete Vicari, General Contractor, Inc. v. United States, 47 Fed. Cl. 353 (2000) (recognizing that when a party has ample time for inquiry, examination, and reflection, it is less likely that the party's will would be overborne by economic duress).
[51] 47 Fed. Cl. 353.

caused by the government withholding liquidated damages in addition to financial losses caused by design deficiencies on the project. Additionally, the contractor charged that the government intentionally denied its claims for equitable adjustment shortly before the settlement negotiations were to take place to add pressure to settle its claims.

The claims court stated that the facts and circumstances surrounding the execution of the settlement agreement did not indicate that the contractor had involuntarily entered into the agreement. According to the court, the requirements to establish economic duress are "exacting." The court stated that the contractor "must show that Government coercion was the cause of the contractor's financial distress and that the Government employed extra-contractual means to effect this distress."[52] Critically, " 'the Government is not precluded from using influence that is within the bounds of the contract to effect its goals. In other words, the Government may freely exercise its legitimate powers to enforce the provisions of the contract.' "[53] According to the court, the intervening time between negotiations and plaintiff's signing of the contract, approximately eight days, provided plaintiff with ample time to independently review the agreement and explore alternative courses of action. Furthermore, the contractor had not claimed that the government exercised any influence that was beyond the rights under the original contract. Therefore, the court concluded that there had been no government coercion.

[4]   Lack of Assent — No Meeting of the Minds

As discussed above, one of the fundamental requirements for the creation of a binding accord and satisfaction is a meeting of the minds. Without mutual assent, there cannot be a valid accord. This principal is exemplified in *M.J. Daly & Sons, Inc. v. City of West Haven*.[54] In that case, M.J. Daly & Sons, a general contractor, agreed to make improvements to the City of West Haven's sewage disposal system. The contractor discovered an underground structure, which was not shown on the plans, which delayed the start of excavation. Later, the contractor discovered that the force main pipe running from the pumping station to the water pollution control plant was made of asbestos cement and a parallel force main pipe needed to be installed. The parties prepared a change order to allow the contractor to construct a new force main, and work on the project stopped while the engineers prepared the plans and specifications. Later, an existing pump failed, requiring the contractor to perform emergency bypass pumping. Construction of the new force main delayed work on the rest of the project. Later, under a separate change order, the city compensated the contractor for delay on the project. In its action against the city, the contractor claimed damages for extended home office overhead and

---

[52] 47 Fed. Cl. 353, 360, citing Liebherr Crane Corp. v. United States, 810 F.2d 1153, 1158 (Fed. Cir. 1987).

[53] 47 Fed. Cl. 353, 360, citing Niko Contracting Co. v. United States, 39 Fed. Cl. 795, 802 (1997), *aff'd*, 173 F.3d 437 (Fed. Cir. 1998).

[54] 783 A.2d 1138 (Conn. Ct. App. 2001).

damages for down time incurred while one of its subcontractors installed the new force main. The city claimed that the change order compensating the contractor for delay constituted an accord and satisfaction of the contractor's claims. However, because the parties were aware of a number of potential claims by the contractor and, further, since the delay change order was silent with respect to those claims, the trial court found that the delay change order did not constitute an accord and satisfaction because there was no meeting of the minds between the contractor and the city that the payments tendered by the city were in full satisfaction of the contractor's claim.

The case of *Westerhold v. United States*[55] is also illustrative. In that case, the government had contracted for the construction of steel walkways. Due to an omission in the design of a steel bridge, the contractor requested a change order for the additional work made necessary because of the omission. Although the contractor had requested both time and money, the government only granted an adjustment in the contract sum. The contractor brought a claim against the government seeking compensation for the costs of delay due to the defective bridge design. The government asserted, in its defense, the general rule that "entitlement is barred by an accord and satisfaction when a comprehensive contract modification is executed without reserving the right to bring additional claims."[56] The modification read "[t]he undersigned contractor agrees to perform any or all of the above changes for the amount indicated. No work on any of the above changes shall be started until this proposal is accepted by the contracting officer." The contracting officer on the project accepted the proposal and hand wrote on the proposal "price accepted — Requested time extension is rejected due to insufficient justification." The court observed that there was neither language to the effect that this was in full satisfaction of all claims arising out of the need to include more camber, nor was there any language on the part of the contractor reserving the right to seek further compensation. In fact, there was no reference to delay costs anywhere in the contract modification. The court then observed that even though the change order was executed in August, the issue of time extensions was not resolved until three months later. On these facts, it was clear to the court that the change order did not settle all issues concerning the omission because negotiations for time extensions continued after the signing of the change order. According to the court, "[t]his continued negotiation evidences the fact that a meeting of the minds did not exist so as to treat the contract modification as a release of further claims pertaining to the camber."[57] Thus, the court found that there was not an

---

[55] 28 Fed. Cl. 172 (1993).

[56] 28 Fed. Cl. 172, 174, citing De Barros v. United States, 5 Cl. Ct. 391 (1984); B.D. Click Co. v. United States, 222 Ct. Cl. 290, 295, 614 F.2d 748 (1980); Merritt-Chapman & Scott Corp. v. United States, 198 Ct. Cl. 223, 458 F.2d 42 (1972); Brock & Blevins Co. v. United States, 170 Ct. Cl. 52, 59, 343 F.2d 951 (1965).

[57] 28 Fed. Cl. 172, 175 ("[P]ast administrative boards have held that the Government's consideration of the merits of a claim, following the execution of a release, indicates that the parties did not intend the release to extinguish the claim, and hence did not bar the contractor's earlier claim." A&K Plumbing & Mech., Inc. v. United States, 1 Cl. Ct. 716, 723 (1983).).

accord and satisfaction since there was no evidence of a meeting of the minds and some evidence that there was, in fact, no meeting of the minds.

In *Safeco Credit v. United States*,[58] a contractor sought to avoid the effect of a general release contained in change orders issued by the Navy on a project for the construction of berthing improvements to a naval dock. The Navy added or changed work on the project by 53 change orders. Many of the change orders extended the time period for completion of the work. The parties disagreed about the effect of these change orders on the contract completion dates and, in turn, on the contractor's possible liability for failure to complete the project on time. However, all the change orders contained release language that purported to release the Navy from liability on any related claims for equitable adjustment. After completion of the project, the contractor filed a claim with the contracting officer seeking over $600,000 in home office overhead. The contracting officer denied the claim and the contractor appealed to the Court of Claims.

In the Court of Claims, the contractor asserted that its home office overhead claim was not barred by the release language because there was no meeting of the minds between the contractor and the Navy. The contractor contended that "sev eral named government officials, with required authority, assured [the contractor] that [the contractor] could later seek an equitable adjustment of home office over-head despite the accord and satisfaction language."[59] The Navy moved for summary judgment asserting that each change order was clear and comprehensive. In analyzing the contractor's argument, the court stated that the intent of the parties controls in determining if there was a meeting of the minds. According to the court, "'the contract modification represents the best source of evidence regarding intent.'"[60] The release in each change order stated:

> Acceptance of this modification by the contractor constitutes an accord and satisfaction and represents payment in full (for both time and money) for any and all costs, impact effect, and/or delays arising out of, or incidental to, the work as herein revised and the extension of the contract completion time.

The court further recognized that it was precluded from considering parol evidence of the parties' prior dealings when "put forth for the purpose of varying the meaning of clear, unambiguous language."[61] According to the court, the contractor had to show something more than a "subjective intent" to preclude summary judgment for the Navy on its defense of accord and satisfaction. Accordingly, the court held that the contractor's allegation of its intent not to waive a claim at the time it executed change orders was insufficient to raise a genuine issue of material fact so as to preclude summary judgment for the government.

---

[58] 44 Fed. Cl. 406 (1999).

[59] 44 Fed. Cl. 406, 420.

[60] 44 Fed. Cl. 406, 419, quoting McLain Plumbing & Elec. Serv. Inc. v. United States, 30 Fed. Cl. 70, 81 (1993).

[61] 44 Fed. Cl. 406, 419.

[5]   Consideration of Release Claims Subsequent to Execution of the Change Order

A waiver is defined as the "intentional or voluntary relinquishment of a know right, or such conduct as warrants an inference of the relinquishment of such right. . . ."[62] In the context of a fully executed change order, a waiver of the benefits of a release contained in that change order may occur when the owner considers a contractor's claim for time and money arising out of the performance of changed work subsequent to the execution of the change order.[63] It has been stated that the execution of a general release will not bar a contractor from bringing claims inconsistent with the release where the parties' actions subsequent to the execution of the release evidences a waiver of the release.[64] However, the mere consideration of a contractor's claim is not sufficient to affect a forfeiture of the owner's rights under the release.[65]

For example, in *John T. Jones Construction Co.*,[66] the Board of Contract Appeals found that an unqualified release in a change order did not result in an accord and satisfaction because, after execution of the change order, the parties continued to consider the contractor's standby power claim associated with the change order. The board indicated that the government's continued consideration of the contractor's claim for compensation due to delay arising out of the standby power change order evidenced a waiver of the effect of the release. In support of this finding, the board noted that the government later issued a unilateral change order providing the contractor with compensation for other delays associated with the standby power change.

§ 5.04   AVOIDING THE GENERAL RELEASE—MODIFYING THE TERMS OF THE CHANGE ORDER

Section 5.03 of this chapter discusses the legal defenses that a contractor can assert to overcome the finality of an executed change order. Unfortunately, contractors who seek to challenge the finality of a change order, through the assertion of affirmative defenses such as mistake, fraud, or duress, often face an uphill battle. Courts generally enforce the release language found in change orders and place the burden on the contractor to prove how that release is ineffective or nonbinding. Consequently, the best opportunity that the contractor may have to avoid

---

[62] Black's Law Dictionary 1580 (6th ed. 1990).

[63] Winn-Senter Constr. Co. v. United States, 110 Ct. Cl. 34, 65-66 (1948).

[64] Robert E. McKee, Inc. v. City of Atlanta, 431 F. Supp. 1198, 1200 (N.D. Ga. 1977); *see also* A&K Plumbing & Mech., Inc. v. United States, 1 Cl. Ct. 716, 723 (1983) (recognizing that "past administrative boards have held that the Government's consideration of the merits of a claim, following execution of a release, indicates parties did not intend the release to extinguish the claim, and hence did not bar the contractor's earlier claim").

[65] *Cf.* Associated Mech. Contractors, Inc. v. Martin K. Eby Constr. Co., 964 F. Supp. 1576 (M.D. Ga. 1997).

[66] ASBCA Nos. 48,303, 48,593 (Nov. 12, 1997).

waiving unanticipated claims for additional time or compensation due to changed work is during the negotiation of that change order.

One way of avoiding the effect of a general release is to carefully choose the terms used in the release. For example, in *C.A. Rasmussen, Inc. v. United States*,[67] the United States Army Corps of Engineers awarded a fixed-price contract for the construction of channel improvements. The work required the construction of, among other things, a stone protection channel. The specification required the use of stone from the site but, in the event that the stone on site was insufficient, the contractor was to provide stone from another source. Additionally, the contract contained a provision that allowed for the contractor to share in savings that resulted from contractor-suggested value engineering. During construction, it became apparent that the on-site stone would not be sufficient and, therefore, the contractor recommended a different source. The government accepted the contractor's substitution and a change order was executed. Upon completion, the contractor requested over $1 million for alleged value engineering services since the cost of the substituted stone was substantially less than that of the on-site stone. The government argued that the change order contained release language that provided that the contract adjustment was full compensation for "all costs and markups directly or indirectly attributable for the change ordered, for all delays related thereto, for all extended overhead costs, and for performance of the change within the time frame stated."[68] According to the government, this language precluded the contractor from additional compensation based on the work. The court, in analyzing the express language of the change order, held that the change order was only to compensate the contractor for *costs* associated with a change and not from recovering *savings* associated with the contractor's suggested value engineering. Accordingly, the court held that the change order was not, by the terms used, an accord and satisfaction and, therefore, the contractor was entitled to seek compensation associated with the value engineering savings.

Perhaps the best way to avoid waiving unanticipated claims when executing a change order is to include an "exception" to the release stating that certain claims are excluded from the change order. Such an "exception" must be sufficiently detailed to inform the owner of the source, substance, or scope of the "exception." For example, a contractor who is uncertain about the impact that a change order might have on the schedule should make it clear that the change order does not compensate, nor does the contractor waive, the right to seek additional time or costs from delays because of the changed work. Additionally, the contractor should attempt to limit the scope of the change order by defining the base line against which the change order was priced. For example:

> The time and cost adjustments hereby accepted for Change Order _____ cover the direct cost of the change order and the impact of the change order on the scope of work as defined by the original contract scope of work and those

---

[67] 52 Fed. Cl. 345 (2002).
[68] 52 Fed. Cl. 345, 351.

change orders formally implemented on or before ____, but excluding Change Order ____.[69]

Critically, however, while the contractor does not need to include a "certified claim" for all the acts it intends to except, merely referring to claims in general will not be sufficient to enforce an exception against subsequent challenges to enforce a release.[70] Thus, it has been held that simply reserving claims for "all costs" in a change order is insufficient for a contractor to recover overhead costs resulting from delay because of the change order. The case of *Linda Newman Construction v. United States*[71] is instructive. In that case, Linda Newman Construction contracted with the Veterans Administration to build an addition to a medical center. The contract expressly limited overhead recovery arising from a change order to a percentage of the cost of the change. During the course of construction, the government issued 244 change orders pursuant to which the parties calculated the direct cost of the change and provided overhead on that amount. Each change order reserved to the contractor the right to seek an equitable adjustment for "all costs arising from the impact of the change orders on unchanged work," but also incorporated the overhead recovery limitation contained in the original contract. After execution of the change orders, the contractor sought an equitable adjustment, which included additional overhead costs arising from the impact of the change order on unchanged work. The government, however, rejected the claim for additional overhead costs. The contractor filed suit, arguing that the exception language contained in the change orders allowed for recovery of all costs resulting from the impact of the changed work on unchanged work. The government argued that the exception did not modify the language limiting overhead recovery contained in the contract. The government moved for summary judgment and, on granting the motion, the claims court concluded that the change order covered all overhead costs, and that the "costs arising from the impact on unchanged work" referred only to direct costs that were attributable to some impact on the unchanged portion of the work.

In sum, contractors who seek to limit the scope of release language in change orders should be plain and direct in drafting their "exceptions" to that release. Courts generally seem unwilling to consider "exceptions" to releases that are not sufficiently detailed and that might prevent the owner from understanding that the contractor is still reserving the right to later seek additional time or compensation. Thus, the contractor who attempts to "pull one over" on the owner by failing to specify which claims are specifically excepted from the release runs the risk of having the "exception" be found insufficient.

---

[69] Michael R. Finke, *A Better Way to Estimate and Mitigate Disruption,* 124 J. Constr. Eng'g & Mgmt. 490 (No. 6, Nov./Dec. 1998) at 337.

[70] Sweet, Legal Aspects of Architecture, Engineering and the Construction Process 475 (5th ed. 1994), citing Mingus Constructors, Inc. v. United States, 812 F.2d 1387 (Fed. Cir. 1987) (blunderbuss exception for any claims against government not sufficiently specific to avoid general release).

[71] 48 Fed. Cl. 231 (2000).

CHAPTER 6

CONTRACTOR CERTIFICATIONS AND FALSE CLAIMS

G. Steven Ruprecht

§ 6.01 CONTRACTOR CERTIFICATIONS

[A] Federal Contracts: The Obligation to Certify

[1] Progress of the Work and Payments

The Federal Acquisition Regulations (FAR) provide for the making of contract payments on federal projects.[1] The payment process is replete with certification obligations imposed upon the contractor. For example, under the regulation providing for "Payments Under Fixed Price Contracts"[2] the government makes payments monthly as the work proceeds, or more often as determined by the contracting officer, on estimates of the work accomplished that meets the standards of quality established under the contract.[3] Progress payments are limited to the value of the work in place, less retainage.[4] Therefore, many government contracts contain a provision that a schedule of contract values shall be provided to the government for payment purposes:

> The Contractor shall furnish a breakdown of the total contract price showing the amount included therein for each principal category of the work which shall substantiate the payment amount requested, in order to provide a basis for determining progress payments, in such detail as requested by the Contracting Officer.[5]

By law, a government contracting officer cannot make "advance payments" to a contractor.[6] Payments must be proportional to the work accomplished, or services and goods delivered or provided. A payment on a construction contract can be made only if measured within the reasonable discretion of the contracting officer against the actual progress of the work.

Thus, contractor certifications are required. In order to be paid, the contractor must certify that to the best of the contractor's knowledge and belief the amounts requested to be paid by the government are only for contract work in accordance with the specifications; that payments to subcontractors and suppliers of the contractor have been made from previous payments received on the contract; that timely payments will be made from the proceeds of the payment covered by the certification; and, finally, that the request for progress payment does not include any amounts that the prime contractor intends to withhold or retain from payment to a subcontractor or a supplier in accordance with the terms and conditions of the subcontract.[7]

---

[1] 48 C.F.R. §§ 52.232-1 *et seq.*
[2] FAR 52.232-5; 48 C.F.R. § 32.111(a)(5).
[3] 39 U.S.C. §§ 3901 *et seq.*
[4] 48 C.F.R. §§ 32.501 *et seq.*
[5] FAR 52.232-5(b).
[6] FAR 52.232-12.
[7] 32 U.S.C. § 3903(b).

The standard government contract requirement for progress payment certification is found in form 1443, which states:

> I certify that the above statement (with attachments) has been prepared from the books and records of the above-named contractor in accordance with the contract and the instructions hereon and to the best of my knowledge and belief that it is correct, that all the costs of contract performance (except as herewith reported in writing) have been paid to the extent shown herein, or where not shown as paid, have been paid, or will be paid currently by the contractor, when due, in the ordinary course of business, that the work reflected above has been performed, that the quantities and amounts involved are consistent with the requirements of the contract.

Along with this certification, the contractor is obligated to submit supporting information to corroborate and justify the certified request. This includes an itemization of the work and summary of payment requests for subcontractors and suppliers together with a breakdown in the amounts of work shown under principal categories.

[2] Changes and Claims for Equitable Adjustment of Contract Price

Federal Acquisition Regulations also govern changes to be made to the contract.[8] Contracting officers, and others to whom authority has been delegated, are given authority to make unilateral changes that are within the scope of the original contract.[9] Changes are issued in writing, generally on standard forms, like government Form 30. A changes clause, pursuant to which changes are made, is found in most fixed-price contracts,[10] cost-reimbursement contracts,[11] and time-and-material contracts.[12]

When a contractor believes a change has been made in the contract by the government, the contractor must request issuance of a written change order by the contracting officer. The contractor should, within the time limit specified in the changes clause, send to the contracting officer a written statement of claim or notice that a claim will be submitted at a later date. Failure to do so may result in the change or claim being barred.[13] If the government accepts the contractor's request, then a contract modification is issued. However, if the government does not accept the request from the contractor, other procedures are warranted and a claim must be made.

---

[8] FAR 43.000, Subpt. 43.2.
[9] FAR 43.201.
[10] FAR 52.243-1.
[11] FAR 52.243-2.
[12] FAR 52.243-3.
[13] Irwin & Leighton v. United States, 104 Ct. Cl. 84 (1945).

[a] Contract Disputes Act Certification

Under the Federal Contract Disputes Act,[14] all claims by a contractor against the government relating to a contract shall be made in writing and submitted to the contracting officer for decision. The contracting officer's decision also shall be in writing and state the reasons for the decision.[15] The decision is final unless appealed.[16] If the claim is for greater than $100,000 in amount, then it must be certified by the contractor.

A contractor is defined as ". . . a party to a government contract other than the government."[17] This does not include a subcontractor to the prime contractor. Only the prime contractor can submit a claim to the government. Therefore, the prime contractor must sponsor any claim belonging to a subcontractor.

A claim is defined as ". . . a non routine request for payment." Examples are a request for a change in the contract scope of the work, an equitable adjustment in contract price, or a modification of some other contract term or condition found in the documents. Routine requests for payment to the government, such as a progress payment, a voucher, or an invoice are not claims for purposes of the Contract Disputes Act. However, if a dispute exists between the contractor and the government as to the quantum of an invoice or a voucher, then the dispute is treated as a claim under the Act.[18]

As to a surety company that takes over a government contract upon the default of the principal contractor, the Contract Disputes Act provides no specific guidance as to procedure and certification of surety claims. However, case law provides that a surety, in privity of contract with the government under a Takeover Agreement, is subject to the requirements of the CDA.[19] Certification of a claim under the CDA is jurisdictional for purposes of the Act.[20]

[b] Specific Requirements

The specific requirements regarding the certification and submission of a CDA claim are set forth in the Act.[21] If a claim is for an amount in excess of $100,000, then the contractor must certify that:

---

[14] 41 U.S.C. § 605; 48 C.F.R., Subpt. 33.2, "Disputes and Appeals."

[15] 41 U.S.C. § 605(a)(c)(1).

[16] 41 U.S.C. § 605(b).

[17] 41 U.S.C. § 601(4).

[18] Reflectone, Inc. v. Dalton, 60 F.3d 1572 (Fed. Cir. 1995), resolving issues raised by DAWCO v. United States, 930 F.2d 872 (Fed. Cir. 1991), and its progeny. Note that a claim does not include government claims against a contractor under the Civil False Claims Act. There claims are excluded from coverage under the CDA; United States ex rel. O'Keefe v. McDonnell Douglas Corp., 918 F. Supp. 1338 (E.D. Mo. 1996).

[19] Travelers Indem. Co. v. United States, 16 Ct. Cl. 142 (1988).

[20] Universal Sur. Co. v. United States, 10 Ct. Cl. 794 (1986).

[21] 41 U.S.C. § 605; Boards of Contract Appeals now have concurrent jurisdiction with the U.S. Court of Federal Claims (f/k/a U.S. Claims Court); see Court of Federal Claims Technical and Procedural Improvements Act 1992, 41 U.S.C. §§ 607(d), 609(a)(1).

1. The claim is made in good faith.

2. The supporting data are accurate to the best of the contractor's knowledge and belief.

3. The amount requested accurately reflects the adjustment for which the contractor believes the government is liable.

4. The party certifying the claim is duly authorized to certify the claim on behalf of the contractor.

5. The claim is certified by someone authorized to bind the contract.[22]

[c]   Who Can Certify the Claim

The CDA originally did not define persons qualified to or capable of certifying a CDA claim. The Federal Acquisition Regulations, however, provide that:

> If the contractor is not an individual, the certification shall be executed by (i) a senior company official in charge of the contractor's plant; or (ii) an officer or general partner of the contractor having overall responsibility for the contractor's affairs.[23]

The 1992 Federal Courts Administration Act supplemented the CDA stating that a certification required by 41 U.S.C. § 605(c)(1):

> . . . may be executed by any person duly authorized to bind the contractor with respect to the claim.[24]

The 1992 Amendment further required the certifier to state that he/she is:

> . . . duly authorized to certify the claim on behalf of the contractor.

The 1992 Amendment also provides that a defective certification can be corrected any time before entry of final judgment without the need for the contractor to restart the process of claim.[25]

[d]   Certification of a Subcontractor Claim

Because a subcontractor has no privity of contract with the government, it must rely on the prime contractor to submit (or pass through) any subcontractor claim.[26] If the subcontractor's claim exceeds the dollar threshold for certification

---

[22] 41 U.S.C. § 605(c)(7); 48 C.F.R. § 33.207(c) (3/10/94).
[23] 48 C.F.R. § 33.207(c)(2).
[24] 41 U.S.C. § 605(c)(7).
[25] 41 U.S.C. § 605(c)(2)(A)(B).
[26] Ericson Air Crane Co. v. United States, 731 F.2d 810 (Fed. Cir. 1984).

under the CDA, the prime contractor must certify the subcontractor's claim prior to submission to the government.[27] The prime contractor cannot exclusively rely on the subcontractor's certification for purposes of the CDA.[28]

Since the prime contractor merely acts as a conduit for the subcontractor's claim, the law does not impose upon the prime contractor the same rigid certification standard as if the prime contractor were submitting its own claim. This is due to the prime contractor's limited control over the subcontractor. The prime contractor may not have access to the subcontractor's supporting data, may not know if it is accurate, whether the claim reflects an amount to which the subcontractor is truly entitled, or even whether the subcontractor has made the claim to the prime contractor in good faith. In the extreme, the prime contractor may dispute the subcontractor's entitlement to the claim made, but, nevertheless, must certify it and pass it through to the government. Therefore, the prime contractor need not certify that it agrees with the subcontractor's claim, but merely that there are good grounds for it.[29]

In *Transamerica Insurance Corp., f/u/o Stroup Sheet Metal Works v. United States,*[30] the prime contractor certified the subcontractor's claim using the CDA certification language but qualified it in a cover letter stating that the contractor did not have access to the subcontractor's books and records and, therefore, could not make any affirmative statement as to the amount of the claim. The prime contractor also stated, however, that it had no reason to believe that the cost figures and estimate were inaccurate. The court found that even with the qualifying language, the certificate "substantially complied" with the CDA requirements because the prime contractor believed that the subcontractor had good grounds for the claim.[31] In another case, *United States v. Turner Construction Co.,*[32] Turner recommended that the government reject the subcontractor's claim. Later, however, Turner certified the claim and passed it through. Over the objections of the government that Turner's prior rejection of the claim conflicted with Turner's later certification, the court said that it was not relevant to the certification process how the prime contractor would resolve the dispute on the merits (since the prime contractor was not a substitute for the contracting officer in determining the merits); but, rather, it was only relevant that the prime contractor believed there were good grounds for the claim.[33]

In contrast to the *Transamerica* and *Turner* cases, improper CDA certifications were found where the prime contractor stated that the amount of the claim

---

[27] Thermodyn Contractors, Inc. v. General Servs. Admin., GSBCA No. 11,911, 93-1 BCA (CCH) ¶ 25,408 (1992).

[28] Appeal of Webb Mech. Ent. Inc., ASBCA No. 39,838, 90-2 BCA (CCH) ¶ 22,928 (1990).

[29] Matter of Commonwealth Elec. Co., 118 B.R. 720 (Bankr. Neb. 1990) (prime's certification of subcontractor's claim not admission that amount is due).

[30] 973 F.2d 1572 (Fed. Cir. 1992).

[31] *See also* Appeal of Cox Constr. Co. & Hoehn Mgmt. Co., ASBCA No. 31,072, 85-3 BCA (CCH) ¶ 18,507 (1985).

[32] 827 F.2d 1554 (Fed. Cir. 1987).

[33] *See also* Dillingham NA, Inc. v. United States, 33 Fed. Cl. 495 (1995); and Arnold M. Diamond, Inc. v. Dalton, 25 F.3d 1006 (Fed. Cir. 1994) (prime contractor did not consider good faith existed to certify claim but was ordered by bankruptcy court to certify the claim).

accurately reflected the amount for which the subcontractor (not the prime contractor) believed the government was liable;[34] where the prime contractor had not reviewed the subcontractor's claim but instead would advise the government of the prime contractor's position at a later date;[35] and where the prime contractor failed to assert the accuracy and completeness of the subcontractor's supporting data [36] Generally, courts and Boards of Contract Appeals will not look to whether statements contained in the certification are accurate but to whether the certification language is present.[37]

The ultimate test for propriety of compliance of the certification with the requirements of the CDA relative to a subcontractor's claim is set out in *Blake Construction Co. v. United States*:[38]

> It is not required that the certifier have personal knowledge that the data supporting the claim is accurate and complete; it is sufficient that a certifier have "indirect" knowledge. . . . [T]he primary requisite is that it must be worded so the contractor assumes liability for fraud.[39]

In sum, the prime contractor must sponsor the subcontractor's claim and certify it in accordance with the CDA language; but, substantial compliance with the certification requirements will suffice so long as there are good grounds for the subcontractor's claim and the claim is not fraudulent. Acceptance of liability by the prime for subcontractor fraud appears to be the dominant factor.

In that regard, a prime contractor should consider requiring a subcontractor to enter into a liquidating agreement requiring the subcontractor to certify its claim to the prime contractor in the same manner as the prime contractor must certify the claim to the government; and requiring that the subcontractor defend and indemnify the prime contractor from any adverse ramifications of the prime contractor's certification of the claim.[40]

[3] Other Types of Certifications

In addition to the primary certification requirements above for payment and claims under the contract, other miscellaneous certification requirements exist under federal law. Some examples are discussed in the following subsections.

---

[34] Century Constr. Co. v. United States, 22 Ct. Cl. 63 (1990); *see also* Appeal of Siena Bianca, Inc., ASBCA No. 30,910, 85-3 BCA (CCH) ¶ 18,440 (1985).

[35] Alvarado Constr. Co. v. United States, 32 Fed. Cl. 184 (1994).

[36] Appeal of Raymond Kaiser Eng'r Inc./Kaiser Steel Corp., ASBCA No. 34,133, 87-3 BCA (CCH) ¶ 20,140 (1987).

[37] Ocoto Elec., Inc., ASBCA No. 45,856, 94-3 BCA (CCH) ¶ 26,958, *recon. denied*, 94 BCA (CCH) ¶ 27,106 (1994).

[38] 28 Fed. Cl. 672 (1993).

[39] 28 Fed. Cl. 672, 681, 682.

[40] *See generally* Herman M. Braude, *Pass-Through Claims and Liquidation Agreements*, 89-7 Constr. Briefings (Federal Publications), June 1989; *see also* Pierce Ass'n v. Nemours Found., 865 F.2d 530 (3d Cir. 1988).

[a] Certification by Bidder

The qualified products clause found in 48 C.F.R. § 2.209-1(c)(e) requires a bidder to identify the item name and number of the qualified product and the test number, if known, and to submit evidence of the qualification if tests have been conducted and the product is not listed at the time of bidding. This is a certification of the bidder of qualification. Failure to make the certification, however, is not fatal, since the government can verify facts at a later date; and erroneous certification may be corrected.[41]

[b] Buy American Act

When procurement is for the acquisition of supplies, bidders are required to provide a Buy American Certificate.[42] This certificate relates to the articles actually delivered. The statutory requirements are not met by a certificate stating that the contractor intends to comply. The form of certificate is found in the Federal Acquisition Regulations.[43]

[c] Certificate of Current Cost and Pricing Data

A contractor may be required to execute a Current Cost and Pricing Data Certificate,[44] when required under the Federal Acquisition Regulations.[45] This certificate states that the cost or pricing data are accurate, complete, and current as of the date of the agreement. The government requirements may extend to submission of certifications from subcontractors as well.[46] The duty to provide the data cannot be waived and, therefore, a certificate will be required initially[47] and for modifications.[48]

[d] Identity of Interest Forms

In order to avoid conflicts of interest, these forms may require a contractor to disclose any identity of interest among owners, contractors, subcontractors, and architects, including financial interests in projects and directorships, family relationships, and side deals.[49]

---

[41] Master Power, Inc., 90-2 CPD 434 (1990).

[42] 48 C.F.R. § 25.1101.

[43] 48 C.F.R. § 52.225-2; *see also* 48 C.F.R. § 52.225-4 (NAFTA and Israel Trade Certificates) and 48 C.F.R. § 52.225-6 (Trade Agreements Act Certificates).

[44] FAR 15.406-2.

[45] FAR 15.403-3.

[46] FAR 15.404-3 and 52.215-12.

[47] M-R-S Mfg. Co. v. United States, 492 F.2d 835 (Ct. Cl. 1974).

[48] Universal Restoration, Inc. v. United States, 8 Ct. Cl. 5101 (1985).

[49] HUD Form 3305 (8/97) re: Handbook 4470.1 re: Mortgagor/Mortgagee and HUD Commission Form 3/15/02 and 18 U.S.C. § 1001.

[e] Owner/Contractor Cost Breakdown Forms

These forms may require a contractor to certify as follows:

I certify that all the information stated herein, as well as any information provided in the accompaniment herewith, is true and accurate. Warning HUD will
prosecute false claims and statements. Conviction may result in criminal or
civil penalties.[50]

[f] Labor Standards and Prevailing Wage Requirements

This form may require the contractor to certify that the contractor is an eligible
contractor under the Federal Labor Regulations[51] and under the Davis-Bacon Act;[52]
and further that the contractor will not subcontract to an ineligible subcontractor.[53]

[g] Other Certifications

In addition to the above example certifications, contractors may be called
upon to certify, attest to, assert, or verify in one written form or another: bid documents; pricing information; cost estimates; contractor qualifications to enter into
contracts; prior business history; that no construction has been started prior to loan
documents being put in place; progress of the work; value of the work completed;
actual costs incurred; shipment of goods; compliance of work with contract documents, specifications or other industry standards; compliance of the work with
applicable laws, codes, and regulations; that work is subject to reimbursement by
the government; payment of subcontractors and suppliers; payment of prevailing
wages;[54] certifications under Copeland Anti-Kickback Act;[55] contract work hours
and Safety Standard Act compliance;[56] payroll reports; MBE participation;[57] the
labeling of goods; first article test reports or other quality control test reports;
progress of the work reports; and small business DBE status to name just a few.

[B] State and Local Contracts: The Obligation to Certify

A survey of local, state, county, and municipal certification requirements is
beyond the scope of this chapter. However, contractors who publicly bid state and
local work on a competitive basis also provide information both in advance of and

---

[50] OMB 2502, No. 044, exp. 2/31/03; 18 U.S.C. §§ 1001, 1010, 1012; 31 U.S.C. § 3729.

[51] 29 C.F.R., Pt. 5.

[52] 40 U.S.C. §§ 3141 *et seq.*

[53] FHA Form No. 2482, rev. 10/88.

[54] Davis-Bacon Act, 40 U.S.C. § 3144(b)(1).

[55] 40 U.S.C. § 3145.

[56] 40 U.S.C. § 3601.

[57] Affirmative Action/Equal Employment Opportunity, 48 C.F.R. § 22.810(f), FAR 52.222-27,
Equal Employment Opportunity Executive Order 11246.

after bid opening. They apply for payments as the work progresses, and make claims for extra work and extensions of time, in addition to a myriad of other written representations and statements along the way. All of these written statements may result in contractor liability for breach of contract, fraud, misrepresentation, or false claims under local law.

Most public entities and agencies have bidding requirements for construction contracts that involve the use of public money for public use improvements. The bidding rules are found in state statutes, state administrative regulations, county regulations and municipal ordinances. Anytime a contractor bids public work, it subjects itself to local laws and case precedent regarding false and fraudulent statements made to induce a public entity to act or pay money. This also is true for quasi-public bodies as well; such as turnpike authorities; school, road, levy, water, sewer, and drainage districts; and port authorities.

Often, public entities "pre-qualify" both bidders and vendors. Administrative regulations control the pre-qualification process.[58] Pre-qualification may require the contractor to submit specific information regarding financial background; bonding capacity; pending contracts; performance history; the existence of litigation and claims, references, licensing status, residency, MBE, WBE, and DBE status; and other related data to provide the public entity background information in order to determine whether the bidder is qualified to perform the work. The accuracy of this information is critical to the public entity's decision to permit the contractor to bid. This information may or may not be submitted under verification or certification procedures. Typically, contracts are awarded under statute to the lowest and best bidder or the lowest, responsible, responsive bidder. Any misstatements given in the pre-qualification process may mislead the public entity into awarding a contract under the designated contract award standards. Fraud in the inducement remains paramount.

In addition, many states have antitrust statutes prohibiting collusive bidding or bid rigging. Violators can be subject to criminal and civil penalties.[59] In Missouri, for example, both the state and private citizens may bring antitrust cases for contractor violations and violators are subject to treble damages, court costs, and attorneys' fees. Signed, sealed bids may carry with them implied certification that the contractor is not engaging in collusive bidding practices.[60] In addition to requirements for payment of money and for claims, state and local contractors may also be required to verify, certify, or report in writing facts regarding nondiscriminatory actions; local prompt payment statute requirements; subcontractor listing requirements; civil rights law requirements; ADA compliance; age discrimination requirements; state human rights act compliance;

---

[58] 41 U.S.C. § 253(c); 10 U.S.C. § 2319.

[59] Mo. Rev. Stat. § 416.031, Missouri Anti-Trust Law; *see also* 15 U.S.C. § 1, Sherman Anti-Trust Act.

[60] Collusive bidding can violate 31 U.S.C. § 3729, 18 U.S.C. § 1001, 18 U.S.C. § 1961 (RICO), 39 U.S.C. § 3005 (Federal Mail and Wire Fraud Acts).

and family and medical leave, fair labor standards, prevailing wage, ERISA, and NLRA requirements, particularly where Federal money may be involved in the state and local work.

[C] Private Contracts: The Obligation to Certify

[1] Progress of the Work and Payments

In the private setting, certification obligations, if any, are generally found in the contract, not in the local law. The variety of certification requirements to be found is limited only by the variety of contract forms that may be used by the owner and the contractor.

Oftentimes, a certification process is set forth in many standard form industry agreements for both progress of the work and payment when the work has been concluded. The most widely used forms of agreement are issued by the American Institute of Architects (AIA). Under the AIA documents, the construction payment process uses a form of affidavit by the contractor to certify that the work is done and that subcontractors and suppliers have been paid.[61]

AIA Document G702, Application and Certification for Payment (1992), provides:

> The undersigned Contractor certifies that to the best of the Contractor's knowledge, information and belief the work covered by this Application for Payment has been completed in accordance with the contract documents, that all amounts have been paid by the Contractor for work for which previous Certificates for Payment were issued and payments received from the Owner, and that the current payment shown hereunder is now due.[62]

A number of states provide penalties for false swearing of an affidavit such as in the AIA Payment Certificate.[63] And, similar to federal requirements, AIA Document A201 (1997), Paragraph 9.2 requires the contractor to submit a Schedule of Values allocating portions of the work applied for following the Schedule of Values.

[2] Final Payment

Under AIA Document A201 (1997), a specific affidavit also is required for final payment. Subparagraph 9.10.2 provides that:

---

[61] AIA Doc. A201, General Conditions of the Construction Contract, ¶ 9.3.1 (1997), and AIA Doc. G702, Application and Certification for Payment (1992); *see also* AGC Doc. No. 600, Subcontract for Building Construction, ¶ 5.1.2 (1987).

[62] *See* Myers & Chapman, Inc. v. Thomas G. Evans, Inc., 374 S.E.2d 385 (N.C. 1988) (subcontractor found to have certified application in grossly negligent but not fraudulent manner).

[63] *See, e.g.*, Fla. Stat. Ann. §§ 713.35, 713.34; Mich. Comp. Laws Ann. § 570.1110(10); Tex. Prop. Law Ann. § 53.026; Ill. Stat. ch. 82, § 21.01.

Neither final payment nor any remaining retained percentage shall become due until the contractor submits to the architect (1) an affidavit that payroll, bills for materials and equipment, and other indebtedness connected with the work . . . have been paid. . . .

While both the progress payment certification and final payment affidavit expose the contractor to claims of fraudulent statements by the owner, neither provides any level of protection to the owner regarding claims by downstream subcontractors. A contractor that refuses to pay bills downstream to subcontractors and suppliers may expose the owner to mechanic's lien claims under state law.[64]

[3] Mechanic's Lien Waiver/Affidavits of Claim

As noted, certifications and affidavits are meant to protect the owner from claims of lien exposing the owner to possible double payment. In order to effect this protection, the certificate and affidavit are often accompanied by lien waivers and waivers of claim affidavits signed by the contractor. The lien waiver formally relinquishes a contractor's or subcontractor's right to file a mechanic's lien upon the project in exchange for the payment made. The lien waiver can be prospective (*in futuro*) for all claims on a parcel, to the extent payment is made, or final and complete for all claims on the project at the end. The claim waiver accomplishes the same purpose for a claim whether for increased time or increased price.[65]

Most state mechanic's lien laws also require that claims filed as mechanic's liens be signed and sworn to under penalty of lien fraud.[66] For example, the State of Missouri requires that a mechanic's lien statement contain a verification of the lien statement by oath of the filer or some credible person on behalf of the filer.[67] Any original contractor, subcontractor, or supplier who fails or refuses to pay any subcontractor, materialman, supplier, or laborer for services or materials provided pursuant to any contract for which the original contractor, subcontractor, or supplier has been paid with intent to defraud, commits the crime of lien fraud.[68] Lien fraud is a Class C felony in Missouri if the lien is in excess of $500.00; otherwise, it is a misdemeanor.[69]

There are no requirements under the AIA documents for a contractor to certify a "claim" for change in price or schedule. Under the AIA documents (AIA Doc. A201, ¶ 4.3), a claim is defined as an assertion by a party seeking adjustment

---

[64] The federal government is protected from this type of claim by the Miller Act and the inability of a contractor to lien public projects used for public purposes.

[65] *See* Allgood Elec. Co. v. Martin K. Eby Constr. Co., 85 F.3d 1547 (11th Cir. 1996); *see also* AIA Doc. G70, Contractor Affidavit of Payment of Debts and Claims (1994); AIA Doc G706, Contractor Waiver and Lien Release (1994).

[66] *See* Cushman, Butler & Shor, 50 State Construction Lien and Bond Law (Aspen Publishers, 2d ed. 2000).

[67] Mo. Rev. Stat. § 429.080 (1992); *see also* Kan. Stat. Ann. §§ 60-1101 *et seq.*

[68] Mo. Rev. Stat. § 419.014(1) (1992).

[69] Mo. Rev. Stat. § 429.014.2 and .3 (1992).

or interpretation of a contract term, payment of money, extension of contract time, or other relief. The claim also includes other "disputes" arising from or out of the contract. Claims are to be made in writing, but under the AIA contract, forms need not be "certified" or "verified."

Like requests for progress payments or final payments, such representations made by the contractor to induce payment may subject the contractor to local laws for fraud and misrepresentation to the extent that any damage occurs to the other party.

[4]   Implied Certifications

An implied certification also has been found by some courts. In one instance the court found that a contractor's express certification of its payment vouchers extended beyond the voucher and the mere demand for payment of the amount of money certified. The court found that the certificate also extended to "all fraudulent attempts to cause the government to pay out sums of money." In that case, the contractor's payment vouchers were found impliedly to certify the contractor's continuing adherence to other contract requirements involving the contractor's relationships under an 8(a) set-aside program. The withholding of information regarding prohibited contract arrangements caused the government mistakenly to pay out funds; in essence, a false claim.[70]

Other examples of implied certifications might be a contractor's certification that it is not in violation of other contract terms and provisions; that it is not in violation of local, state, or federal law, or codes or regulations; or that it is eligible to receive funds subject to other collateral payment requirements.

Another example might be found under AIA Document A201 (1997), where the general contractor provides for "tests and inspections" to be arranged by the contractor. Certifications of testing, inspection, and approvals are required. If the contractor subcontracts this testing and inspection to a subcontractor and then submits the results to the architect or engineer, presumably the general contractor adopts and sponsors those results and, in theory, could be liable for implied certification when requesting payment of money for progress of the inspected and tested work.

Contrary to the above, other courts limit liability for implied certifications on the theory that services rendered in violation of a statute or regulation do not necessarily constitute a false claim for the payment of money under the False Claims Act. On the other hand, if the payment of money is conditioned upon the collateral certification, then argument for lack of application may fail.

---

[70] Abtech Constr., Inc. v. United States, 31 Fed. Cl. 429 (1994); *see also* R. Webber, *Exploring the Outer Boundaries of False Claims Act Liabilities: Implied Certification and Materiality*, 36 The Procurement Law. 14 (No. 2, Winter 2001).

§ 6.02   FRAUDLENT/FALSE CLAIMS

[A]   Federal Law

There are a number of federal statutes (as well as common law) that have application to the certification of progress payments, change orders, and claims. They are:

1. Criminal False Statements Act.[71]

2. Criminal False Claims Act.[72]

3. Civil False Claims Act.[73]

4. Common Law Fraud.

[1]   Criminal False Statements Act

The Criminal False Statements Act prohibits the knowing and willful falsification, concealment, or cover up of material facts; the making of a false, fictitious, or fraudulent statement or representation; or the use of a false writing or document knowing the same to be false, fictitious, or fraudulent.[74] The statement may be oral or written and does not have to be certified, verified, or made under oath.[75] There is no requirement of reliance on the writing on the part of the government in taking action but only that the activity could tend to influence government action.[76]

Of importance is how the law addresses the element of willful conduct or the requirement of intent or actual knowledge of the statement's falsity. Actual knowledge of falsity is not required, but specific intent to deceive is required. The law is willing to accept a showing of reckless disregard or reckless indifference for the truth in the use of a statement to create liability and demonstrate intent.[77] The potential liability is serious. Violations are felonies subjecting the wrongdoer to a $10,000 fine or imprisonment for not more than five years or both. At least one case found that a contractor was recklessly indifferent sufficient to satisfy the

---

[71] 18 U.S.C. § 1001.

[72] 18 U.S.C. § 287.

[73] 31 U.S.C. § 3729; *see also* Steven D. Gordon, *Suspension and Debarment from Federal Programs*, 23 Pub. Cont. L.J. 573 (1994).

[74] 18 U.S.C. § 1001.

[75] United States v. Massey, 550 F.2d 300 (5th Cir. 1977).

[76] United States v. Parsons, 967 F.2d 452 (10th Cir. 1992); United States v. Norris, 749 F.2d 1116 (4th Cir. 1984), *cert. denied,* 471 U.S. 1065 (1985); United States v. Langer, 962 F.2d 592 (7th Cir. 1992) (false statement regarding First Article Test Report); United States v. Anderson, 879 F.2d 369 (8th Cir. 1989) (false statement regarding participation in Section 8A Program); Hughes v. United States, 899 F.2d 1495 (6th Cir. 1990); United States v. Swain, 927 F.2d 15, 30 (11th Cir. 1984).

[77] United States v. Dothard, 666 F.2d 498 (11th Cir. 1982); United States v. Tamargo, 637 F.2d 346 (5th Cir.), *cert. denied,* 454 U.S. 824 (1981); United States v. White, 765 F.2d 1469 (11th Cir. 1985).

scienter requirement of the statute by failing to read a form signed in connection with a certificate prepared for a bid submitted on a government project.[78]

While there are no known cases where a takeover surety has been found guilty under this particular statute for making a false statement in connection with, for example, a schedule of values or a pay estimate submission predicated on that schedule when completing a job, there are cases where government contractors have been found liable for submitting false invoices.[79] In *United States v. Brack*,[80] a completing contractor submitted false and inflated bid documents to a surety to complete a defaulted and terminated contract and also submitted false statements regarding subcontract prices and costs of the work in order to obtain payment. The contractor was convicted of violating the Criminal False Statements Act even though the statements were not made directly to the government. The court considered the scheme to defraud to be within the jurisdiction of a government agency since the surety and the defaulted prime contractor participated in the SBA Bond Guaranty Program. Furthermore, causing another person to make a false statement also subjects the proponent to prosecution.[81] Therefore, prudence compels a reasonable inquiry to determine the accuracy and correctness of statements made to the government or for government consumption.

[2] Criminal False Claims Act

The Criminal False Claims Act is similar to the Criminal False Statements Act. The primary difference is that the falsity must be in conjunction with a claim rather than with a statement. The purpose of the Act is to ensure the integrity of claims and vouchers submitted to the government for payment.[82] A claim is defined as a request for money or property[83] which, of course, would encompass a pay estimate. Like the Criminal False Statements Act, which requires only an attempt to influence the government to act, this Act requires only an attempt to cause the government to part with money. The standard of proof for criminal liability under this Act is beyond a reasonable doubt like other criminal cases. And, only the Department of Justice may bring an action under the Criminal False Claims Act, whereas *qui tam* actions may be brought under the Federal Civil False Claims Act.

Again, a $10,000 fine, five years' imprisonment, or both are the possible end result. Debarment is also possible.[84] Knowledge of the falsity of the claim is

---

[78] United States v. Puente, 982 F.2d 156, 159 (5th Cir. 1993) (deliberately failed to read certification form signed).

[79] Holmer v. General Dynamics Corp., 17 Cal. App. 4th 1418, 22 Cal. Rptr. 2d 172 (1993); United States v. Gibson, 881 F.2d 318 (6th Cir. 1989); *White*, 765 F.2d 1469.

[80] 747 F.2d 1142 (7th Cir. 1984), *cert. denied*, 469 U.S. 1216 (1985).

[81] United States v. Kiefer, 799 F.2d 1115 (6th Cir. 1980).

[82] United States v. Maher, 582 F.2d 842 (4th Cir. 1978).

[83] 31 U.S.C. § 3729(c).

[84] FAR 9.406-2(a)(1); In re Debarment of Gassman, GSBCA No. D-3, 79-1 BCA (CCH) ¶ 13,771.

required to fulfill the scienter requirement.[85] While actual guilty knowledge generally is required, the scienter requirement can be fulfilled in rare instances by guilty avoidance of knowledge or a bona fide belief resulting from negligence.[86] A contractor may be found guilty under the Criminal False Claims Act by causing an intermediary (like a subcontractor) to submit a false claim as well.[87] Prudent inquiries should provide the necessary protections to avoid exposure for the intentional and improper type of conduct prohibited by this Act. There are no known cases where a surety has been found guilty of violating this Act after taking over the work from a defaulting contractor.

[3] Civil False Claims Act

The Civil False Claims Act is the civil counterpart to the Criminal False Claims Act. Like the Criminal False Claims Act, it extends to nonfraudulent conduct of a lesser quality, i.e., the knowing submission of a claim for money to the government containing false, fraudulent, or inaccurate information. It includes, among other things, the knowing presentation of a false claim for payment and/or the knowing use of a false statement to make a claim for payment.[88] The Civil False Claims Act does not limit claims to signed certifications.[89] Damages include a civil penalty of $5,000-$10,000 plus treble damages for the government's actual loss resulting from the false claim,[90] after setoffs to which the government may be entitled are applied.

The Civil False Claims Act was enacted in 1863 to counteract fraud by government contractors during the Civil War. It also was known as the Lincoln Law. It fell into disuse after the Civil War and was weakened significantly by subsequent amendments in 1872 and 1943, when the government prohibited *qui tam* claims based on information possessed by the federal government. The Act was amended significantly again in 1986,[91] increasing the amount of litigation under the Act in recent years. The law lists seven different acts for which a contractor might be liable,[92] including false payment claims, making false statements or making false records to support a false claim, engaging in a conspiracy to promote payment by the government of a false claim, or making a record to avoid a claim or obligation to the government (a reverse false claim).

---

[85] United States v. Gumbs, 283 F.3d 128 (3d Cir. 2002); United States v. Cotton, 89 F.3d 387 (7th Cir. 1996).

[86] United States v. Cooperative Grain & Supply Co., 476 F.2d 47, 59 (8th Cir. 1973) (extreme carelessness shown).

[87] *Gumbs*, 283 F.3d 128.

[88] 31 U.S.C. § 3729(a)(1)(2), "an invoice is a demand for payment of money, an invoice to the Government is a 'claim'"; German v. United States, 96 Ct. Cl. 540 (1943); United States v. Bornstein, 423 U.S. 303 (1976) (subcontractor invoice to contractor for falsely labeled goods).

[89] United States v. Neifert-White Co., 390 U.S. 228 (1968).

[90] 31 U.S.C. § 3729(a), recovery may be reduced to two times actual damages if defendant cooperates and if no consequential damages present.

[91] 31 U.S.C. § 3729-31.

[92] 31 U.S.C. § 3729(a)(1)-(4).

Subcontractors also may be liable under the Act for submitting a false claim[93] to a prime contractor that in turn submits the claim to the government.[94] And, where the prime contractor sponsors the subcontractor's claim, the prime contractor may be exposed to liability for conspiracy as well.[95]

A knowing submission or a knowing use is required. These would include submission or use with actual knowledge of the information, deliberate ignorance of the truth or falsity of the information, or other acts in reckless disregard of the truth or falsity of the information.[96] No proof of specific intent to defraud is necessary, but ignorance and recklessness will suffice.[97] Mere negligence or mistake will not.[98] A corporation may be liable for the acts of its employees as long as they are acting within the course and scope of their employment, even if no management personnel were aware of the false claim.[99] Although not specifically set forth in the Act, a false claim must be material. That is, the falsity must have been with respect to a fact likely to have affected the government's decision to pay.[100]

Like the two criminal acts, this Act is designed to ensure that the government only pays for what it receives. However, a contractor's demand or request may qualify as a claim regardless of whether or not the government pays for it.[101]

[4] Government Knowledge Defense

With respect to this Act, there is an often used defense known as the government knowledge defense.[102] This defense is based on simple logic. A construction

---

[93] 39 U.S.C. § 3729(a)(1).

[94] United States v. Bornstein, 423 U.S. 303 (1976).

[95] 31 U.S.C. § 3729(a)(3).

[96] 31 U.S.C. § 3729(b).

[97] *But see* Harrison v. United States, 101 Ct. Cl. 413 (1944) (misstatement in a substantially correct invoice is not in itself fraudulent without proof of intent to defraud); Miller v. United States, 550 F.2d 17 (Ct. Cl. 1979) (False Claims Act violation found but fraud not found where evidence indicated pattern of negligence, ineptitude, carelessness, slothfulness, and slipshod supervision, but no clear intent to cheat); *see also* United States v. Greenberg, 237 F. Supp. 439 (S.D.N.Y. 1965) (submission of false payroll reports to obtain payment of voucher). Also, actionable since 1986, "Reverse False Claim"—using false statements to avoid payment to the government; *see* United States v. American Heart Research Found., 996 F.2d 7 (1st Cir. 1993).

[98] United States ex rel. Rakow v. ProBuilders Corp., 37 F.3d 930 (9th Cir. 2002).

[99] United States ex rel. Bryant v. Williams Bldg. Corp., 158 F. Supp. 2d 1001 (S.D. 2001).

[100] United States v. Data Translation, Inc., 984 F.2d 1256 (1st Cir. 1992); United States ex rel. Lurkey v. Baxter Health Care Corp., 183 F.3d 730 (7th Cir. 1999); Harrison v. Westinghouse Savannah River Co., 176 F.3d 776 (4th Cir. 1999); United States v. Adler, 623 F.2d 1287 (8th Cir. 1980).

[101] United States v. Hillough, 848 F.2d 1253 (11th Cir. 1988).

[102] *See* Neal J. Wilson, *The Government Knowledge "Defense" to Civil False Claims Actions,* 24 Pub. Cont. L.J. 43 (Fall 1994); United States ex rel. Durcholz v. FKW, Inc., 189 F.3d 542 (7th Cir. 1999); United States ex rel. Haygood v. Sonoma County Water Agency, 929 F.2d 1416 (9th Cir. 1991); Tyger Constr. Co. v. United States, 28 Fed. Cl. 35 (1993). Other defenses include statute of limitations and statute of repose—six years after violation, or three years after government knows or should have known of material facts, but not later than ten years after the violation. 31 U.S.C. § 3731(b).

claim cannot be false for purposes of the Act if the government has knowledge of the material facts surrounding the claim at the time the claim is submitted. This is a fact-specific defense and there are many factors that bear on its viability in court.

[5] Common Law Fraud/Innocent Misrepresentation

A common law civil fraud action for false certificates or false representations made in a pay estimate, a change order request, or a claim comes with the special burdens of proof of fraud in local jurisdictions. Fraud is defined, generally, as a deceitful practice, or willful device, resorted to with intent to deprive another of his rights, or in some manner to do him injury.[103] Fraud has been defined further as a conscious wrongdoing, an act committed with an intention to cheat or be dishonest.[104] For there to be a fraud by a contractor or a surety there must be a false representation of a material fact, by word or conduct, without a positive belief by the maker in the truth of the representation and with an intent to mislead, resulting in detriment to the person to whom made. A contractor or surety that perpetrates a fraud on the government also can violate one or more of the statutes noted above.

The law does distinguish, however, between fraud and an innocent misrepresentation. An innocent misrepresentation is a material misstatement of fact not known to be false, or a failure to disclose a fact without intent to deceive.[105] Other possible theories of liability, in addition to the above statutes, might include negligence, coercion, deceit, and deceptive trade practices.

[6] Duty to Inquire

To what extent must a contractor or subcontractor go, and what means need it employ, prior to executing certifications and passing them to the government? For example, questions regarding the quality of work performed by a contractor are of equal importance to the question of quantity of work performed. Any quantity performed that does not meet contractual quality standards is work that will have to be done again or, at a minimum, equal value credited to the government.[106]

---

[103] Black's Law Dictionary (5th ed.).

[104] United States v. Wunderlich, 342 U.S. 98, 72 S. Ct. 154, 155 (1951); J.E.T.S., Inc. v. United States, 838 F.2d 1196 (Fed. Cir. 1988) (fraud in obtaining a contract through false certification of small business status).

[105] Green Constr. Co. v. Kansas Power & Light Co., 732 F. Supp. 1550 (D.C. Kan. 1990).

[106] 48 C.F.R. § 52.236-5(c), "[a]ll work under the contract shall be performed in a skillful and workmanlike manner"; 48 C.F.R. § 52.232-5(b), payment will be made on estimates of work only for work "... which meets the standards of quality under the contract"; 48 C.F.R. § 52.246-12 (required by 48 C.F.R. § 46.312) (requiring removal and replacement of defective work unless government accepts the work with an appropriate adjustment in contract price).

False statements regarding the quality of work are, therefore, actionable under the Criminal False Statements Act[107] and the Civil False Claims Act.[108] Billing for work that is potentially defective may easily result in actions under these Acts. But what about billing for work only suspected to be nonconforming? That is, where the contractor is unsure of whether the work meets the intent of the contract documents or not. This clearly raises a question of a contractor's duty to inquire regarding statements made to the government.

All of the penalty statutes, and the common law of fraud, prohibit a contractor (or a takeover surety) from treating the work in a way that is reckless, indifferent, or in deliberate avoidance of discovery of the truth regarding the conformity of the work to the contract documents or to other certifications made. Bona fide beliefs resulting from negligence do not suffice. Innocent intentions predicated upon ignorance, however, appear just as dangerous as evil intentions predicated on knowledge. Without a doubt, the federal statutes create a "duty of inquiry" as to the true facts before any action is taken by a contractor or a surety that might induce the government to act or to part with money.

But, what triggers the duty of inquiry? For example, how far must a contractor or a surety go to determine conformance or nonconformance of the work beyond that required in the contract documents before proceeding to bill the government? How much effort must be expended to discover unknown nonconforming work? How much effort must be expended to verify the accuracy of the certifications made? How much effort must be expended to discover unknown nonconforming work? Will suspected nonconforming work trigger a duty of further inquiry? How suspect must the work be? When will a contractor or surety be charged with knowledge that the existing work may not conform to contract requirements?

These questions are not easily answered. The certification for payment given to the government requires that the contractor state that:

> . . . To the best of [my] knowledge and belief . . . the amounts requested [for payment] are only for performance in accordance with the specifications, terms and conditions of the contract; . . . .[109]

Therefore, the inquiry concerns the contractor's representation that to the best of its knowledge and belief the work conforms. But what does a contractor's "best knowledge and belief" mean? And, particularly, what does it mean when attached to a particular statement of fact?

---

[107] United States v. Brittain, 931 F.2d 1413 (10th Cir. 1991) (water pollution discharge monitoring reports); United States v. Langer, 962 F.2d 592 (7th Cir. 1992) (first article test reports stating tests met or exceeded specification).

[108] United States v. Aerodex, Inc., 327 F. Supp. 1027 (S.D. Fla. 1970), *rev'd on other grounds*, 469 F.2d 1003 (5th Cir. 1972) (certification that items supplied met specifications, together with invoice, with knowledge that items did not conform); Faulk v. United States, 198 F.2d 169 (5th Cir. 1952) (certification that invoiced milk met specifications); United States v. Wertheimer, 434 F.2d 1004 (2d Cir. 1970); Fleming v. United States, 336 F.2d 475 (10th Cir. 1964) (certification to government that unshipped goods were in fact shipped).

[109] 48 C.F.R. § 52.232-5(c)(1); 31 U.S.C. § 3903(b)(1)(B)(i).

Arguably, what the certification means is that to the best of the contractor's knowledge the government has not been tendered, and will not receive from the contractor, something less than or different from that which is expected under the terms and conditions of the contract documents.[110] In other words, the government's expectations for the quality of work will be met by the work tendered by the contractor. This is nothing more than a simple "reasonable expectation" rule. Stated another way, the contract will not be breached and the contract requirements will be complied with substantially in all respects.

The expectations of the government likely will not be measured by any subjective criteria of what the contractor believes the government expects in exchange for payment. More likely, it will involve an objective test in the sense of what a reasonable contractor would believe is expected relative to the contract work, given the requirements of the contract documents. Therefore, if a reasonable contractor would not believe the work conforms to the contract documents, then the certifying contractor's subjective beliefs about conformance would appear to be irrelevant.

The question of what is reasonable for a contractor to believe under the circumstances or what a reasonable expectation of the government should be in any given situation is, of course, fact specific. No doubt questions regarding the nature of the suspected defective or nonconforming work is important, as is the extent of the nonconformity; the need for destructive or nondestructive testing to determine the nature and extent of the nonconformity; the ability of the contractor to remediate the work at a later date; the cost to remediate the work; the time frames involved both with the determination of the nonconformity and the determination of the nature and extent of remediation, if necessary; if testing occurred, a determination of the accuracy of the testing methods, the accuracy of the test results, and the margins of failure; whether the defect is of a dangerous nature to both person and property; whether the nonconformity is likely to manifest itself more clearly at a later date, if at all; whether, if not revealed immediately, the nonconformity will become a latent defect in the project not capable of ascertainment or remediation at a later date; and, whether it is the kind of nonconformity that ultimately might be acceptable to the government but at a reduced cost. These questions all play a role in the determination of what is reasonable under the circumstances.

In sum, there is no easy answer to a question that is predicated upon difficult facts. The Ninth Circuit Court of Appeals observed in *Wang v. FMC Corp.*,[111] a False Claims Act case, that:

> The False Claims Act is concerned with ferreting out wrongdoing not scientific errors. What is false as a matter of science is not, by that very fact, wrong as a matter of morals. The Act would not put either Ptolemy or Copernicus on trial.

---

[110] *See generally* Boisjoly v. Morton Thiokol, Inc., 706 F. Supp. 795 (D. Utah 1988).
[111] 975 F.2d 1412, 1421 (9th Cir. 1992).

Clearly, what the False Claims Act (and the other statutes) seeks to uncover are outright lies and fraudulent conduct of all kinds, not mere scientifically untrue statements. It is the knowing assertion of untrue statements of fact that violates the law. Some reasonable amount of gray, however, lies between assertion of an outright lie with a black heart and the simple statement of an untrue scientific fact with a white empty mind.

[B] Other False Certification Claims

The following is a sampling of other false certification claims:

1. False bid documents and pricing information;[112]

2. False certificates of work done or amount due;[113]

3. False certification that the work met contract requirements;[114]

4. False certification that the work was subject to reimbursement;[115]

---

[112] United States ex rel. Fallon v. Accudyn Corp., 880 F. Supp. 636 (W.D. Wis. 1995) (false pricing information stating that all costs associated with completion included environmental compliance); United States ex rel. Marcus v. Hess, 317 U.S. 537 (1943) (collusive bidding); United States v. White, 765 F.2d 1469 (11th Cir. 1985); United States v. Hartness, 845 F.2d 158 (8th Cir. 1987) (an estimate as a false statement despite being labeled as an estimate where based upon data or formulas known to be false); United States v. Poarch, 878 F.2d 1355 (11th Cir. 1989) (failure to disclose complete pricing data); United States v. Brown, 482 F.2d 1359 (9th Cir. 1973) (fictitious bid); United States v. Balk, 706 F.2d 1056 (9th Cir. 1983) (falsification of qualification by contractor); Harrison v. Westinghouse Savannah River Co., 176 F.3d 776 (4th Cir. 1999) (misrepresentation for need and cost of hiring a subcontractor); United States ex rel. Alexander v. Dyn Corp., 924 F. Supp. 292 (D.C. Cir. 1996) (false representation of prior business records); *but see* United States v. Farina, 153 F. Supp. 819 (D.N.J. 1957) (stating that a bid is not a claim).

[113] Al Munford, Inc. v. United States, 34 Fed. Cl. 62 (1995) (double billing for work previously billed and paid for); United States v. Board of Educ., 697 F. Supp. 167 (D.N.J. 1988) (billing for work of no value to government); Commercial Constr., Inc. v. United States, 154 F.3d 1357 (Fed. Cir. 1998) (billing for extra work not performed); United States v. Wertheimer, 434 F.2d 1004 (2d Cir. 1970) (certification that unshipped goods had been shipped).

[114] United States ex rel. Shaw v. AAA Eng'rs Drafting, Inc., 213 F.3d 519 (10th Cir. 2000); United States ex rel. Bryant v. Williams Bldg. Corp., 158 F. Supp. 2d 1001 (S.D. 2001); United States v. Advance Tool Co., 902 F. Supp. 1001 (W.D. Mo. 1995) (tool switch out without knowledge of government); City of Pomona v. Superior Court, 89 Cal. App. 4th 793 107 Cal. Rptr. 2d 710 (2001) (product failed to comply with industry standard); United States v. Aerodex, Inc., 327 F. Supp. 1027 (S.D. Fla. 1970), *rev'd on other grounds*, 469 F.2d 1003 (5th Cir. 1972) (false certification that items supplied met specifications); Faulk v. United States, 198 F.2d 169 (5th Cir. 1952) (certification that invoiced milk met specifications); *but see* United States ex rel. Pickens v. GLR Constructors, Inc., 196 FRD 69 (S.D. Ohio 2000) (judgment for contractor that violated environmental requirements despite certifying compliance).

[115] United States ex rel. Wilkens v. North Am. Constr. Corp., 101 F. Supp. 2d 500 (S.D. Tex. 2001) (certifying in a request for equitable adjustment that the contractor performed additional work due to differing site conditions contrary to facts).

5. False certification that the subcontractors were paid;[116]

6. False certification that the contractor paid prevailing wages;[117]

7. False certification (implied) regarding DBE participation in project;[118]

8. False information submitted by supplier to government distributor;[119]

9. False statement to the government regarding product testing and/or other reports;[120]

10. False progress reports;[121]

11. False certification of small business status;[122]

12. False certified payrolls;[123]

13. False progress payment applications;[124]

14. Altered invoices.[125]

[C] *Qui Tam* Actions Under the False Claims Act

[1] *Qui Tam* Provisions

The Civil False Claims Act contains a *qui tam* (whistleblower) provision that allows for a private citizen (also known as a relator) to institute a lawsuit against a contractor to enforce the Civil False Claims Act provisions on behalf of

---

[116] 31 U.S.C. § 3903(b)(1); FAR 52.232-5(c)(2), by prime contractor; 31 U.S.C. § 3905; FAR 52.232(5)(2)(01), by subcontractor; *see also* Lamb Eng'g & Constr. Co. v. United States, 58 Fed. Cl. 106 (2003).

[117] 40 U.S.C. § 276(a); United States ex rel. Plumbers & Steamfitters Local Union No. 38 v. C.W. Roen Constr. Co., 183 F.3d 1088 (9th Cir. 1999); United States v. Schimmeler, 127 F.3d 875 (9th Cir. 1997); United States ex rel. Burns v. A.D. Roe Co., 186 F.3d 717 (6th Cir. 1999); *see also* United States v. Greenberg, 237 F. Supp. 439 (S.D.N.Y. 1965) (submission of false payroll reports).

[118] Abtech Constr., Inc. v. United States, 31 Fed. Cl. 429 (1994); *see also* United States v. Anderson, 879 F.2d 369 (8th Cir. 1989) (false statement regarding participation in 8(a) program).

[119] City of Pomona v. James Jones Co., 89 Cal. App. 4th 793 (2001); *see also* United States v. Bornstein, 423 U.S. 303 (1976) (falsely labeled goods); United States v. Nat'l Wholesale, 236 F.2d 944 (9th Cir. 1956) (mislabeled goods).

[120] Varljen v. Cleveland Gear Co., 250 F.3d 426 (6th Cir. 2001); United States v. Langer, 962 F.2d 592 (7th Cir. 1992) (false statement in first article test report); United States v. Brittain, 931 F.2d 1413 (10th Cir. 1991) (false water pollution discharge monitoring reports).

[121] United States v. Planning Research Corp., 59 F.3d 196 (D.C. Cir. 1995).

[122] J.E.T.S., Inc. v. United States, 838 F.2d 1196 (Fed. Cir. 1988).

[123] United States v. J. Greenbaum & Sons, 123 F.2d 770 (2d Cir. 1941) (a Criminal False Statement Act case).

[124] United States v. Campbell, 848 F.2d 846 (8th Cir. 1988); United States v. Chenault, 844 F.2d 1124 (5th Cir. 1988); United States v. Elkin, 731 F.2d 1005 (2d Cir. 1984); Au Bon Pain Corp. v. Artect, Inc., 653 F.2d 61 (2d Cir. 1981).

[125] Young-Montenay, Inc. v. United States, 15 F.3d 1040 (Fed. Cir. 1994) (prosecution under FCA, 31 U.S.C. § 3729).

the government.[126] The relator need not show that he or she suffered any direct injury or damage as a result of the contractor's acts.[127]

The Department of Justice (DOJ) may elect to intervene in any *qui tam* lawsuit filed by a relator and proceed as the primary plaintiff with the relator continuing as a co-plaintiff with the DOJ.[128] If a lawsuit results in a recovery against the defendant contractor, the relator is entitled to a share of the recovery as an incentive for *qui tam* plaintiffs to file actions. The relator may be entitled to between 15 and 25 percent of the claim proceeds if the government elects to intervene in the case and between 25 and 30 percent of the proceeds if the government does not intervene.[129] The relator is entitled to recover for either a settlement or a judgment. The exact amount recovered by the relator, however, depends upon the relator's substantial "contributions" to the prosecution of the claim.[130]

Anyone may file a lawsuit as a *qui tam* relator/plaintiff. Often employees, competitors, subcontractors, or public interest groups file lawsuits as relators. And, so long as the relator's position does not require that the relator report the false claim violation, he or she may file the claim.[131] If the relator is otherwise required to report the claim, the lawsuit is subject to dismissal by the court.[132]

[2] Anti-Retaliation Provision

The Act also contains an anti-retaliation provision to militate against employers retaliating against employees who file *qui tam* lawsuits.[133] The provision provides that:

> [a]n employee who is discharged, demoted, suspended, threatened, harassed, or in any manner discriminated against in . . . employment . . . will be entitled to all relief necessary to make the employee whole, including reinstatement, double back pay, interest, special damages, litigation costs and attorneys' fees.[134]

This provision does not apply, however, to states (or other political subdivisions) that do not qualify as a "person" under the False Claims Act."[135]

---

[126] 31 U.S.C. § 3730(b)(1).

[127] *But see* Riley v. St. Luke's Hosp., 196 F.3d 514 (5th Cir. 1999) (where a court found relator lacked standing to sue because the government had not intervened and the relator had suffered no injury).

[128] 31 U.S.C. § 3730(b)(1).

[129] 31 U.S.C. §§ 3730(d)(1) & (2).

[130] 31 U.S.C. § 3730(d)(1).

[131] United States ex rel. Givelere v. Smith, 760 F. Supp. 72 (E.D. Pa. 1991).

[132] United States ex rel. LeBlanc v. Raytheon Corp., 913 F.2d 17 (1st Cir. 1990); United States ex rel. Fine v. Chevron USA, Inc., 72 F.3d 740 (9th Cir. 1995).

[133] 31 U.S.C. § 3730(h).

[134] 31 U.S.C. § 3730(h).

[135] *United States ex rel. Bhatmajor v. Kiewit Pac. Co.*, 2000 U.S. Dist. LEXIS 14400 (N.D. Cal. 2000).

[3]   Direct Knowledge Requirement

The 1986 Amendment to the Civil False Claims Act permits *qui tam* lawsuits by relators even if the government already has knowledge of the facts relevant to the violation, so long as the relator has "independent and direct knowledge" of the violation. Independent and direct knowledge must be alleged in the relator's complaint.[136]

[4]   Original Source/Public Disclosure Bar

A relator also must qualify as an original source of the information.[137] The relator must plead and prove that he or she obtained direct and independent knowledge of the violation through his or her own efforts and not through the labor of others or knowledge obtained by a relator from government reports, audits, hearings, investigations, public disclosures in criminal or civil or administrative hearings, or through the news media, all of which will not qualify as original source knowledge. This rule is commonly known as the public disclosure bar.[138]

The Civil False Claims Act creates a four-part test to determine whether the jurisdictional bar of public disclosure applies.[139] An original source must have direct and independent knowledge of the violation and must voluntarily provide that information to the government before filing suit.[140]

[D]   State False Claims Laws

Many states have adopted false claims statutes patterned after the Federal Civil False Claims Act. Local case law, however, is developing much more slowly than the Federal law. At least two states have criminal false claims laws as well as civil laws.[141]

A number of states—California, Delaware, the District of Columbia, Florida, Hawaii, Illinois, Massachusetts, Nevada, Tennessee, and Virginia—have adopted

---

[136] United States ex rel. Atkinson v. Pennsylvania Shipbuilding Co., 2000 U.S. Dist. LEXIS 12081 (E.D. Pa. 2000).

[137] 31 U.S.C. § 3730(e)(4)(B); United States ex rel. Stone v. Rockwell Int'l Corp., 282 F.3d 787 (10th Cir. 2002).

[138] 31 U.S.C. § 3730(e)(3) & (4)(A); United States ex rel. Mislick PBT v. Housing Auth., 186 F.3d 376 (3d Cir. 1999).

[139] United States ex rel. Lendenthal v. General Dynamics Corp., 61 F.3d 1402 (9th Cir. 1995); 31 U.S.C. § 3730(e)(4)(a).

[140] 31 U.S.C. § 3730(e)(4)(B); United States ex rel. Barth v. Ridgedale Elec., Inc., 44 F.3d 699 (8th Cir. 1995) (finding that public disclosure had occurred and relator had independent knowledge but not direct knowledge due to learning of the information through an intermediate source); *see also* Wang v. FMC Corp., 975 F.2d 1412 (9th Cir. 1992) (relator not an original source, information publicly disclosed); United States v. Darrel F. Young, Inc., 909 F. Supp. 1010 (E.D. Va. 1995) (relator not qualified).

[141] Cal. Penal Code § 72; N.J. Stat. Ann. § 2C: 21-34.

civil false claims statutes similar to the Federal Act.[142] The California law allows local authorities to prosecute.[143] Some states make a contractor liable if it discovers that it benefited from a false claim and fails to disclose the false claim within a reasonable time.[144] California also expresses that "claims" shall include requests for services, in addition to those for money or property.

Most states have anti-fraud statutes that would apply to false claims against public entities but do not contain *qui tam* provisions. For example, Arkansas, Louisiana, Michigan, New Mexico, North Carolina, Texas, Utah, and Washington all have false claims statutes limited to healthcare fraud, but those in Louisiana, New Mexico, and Texas do contain *qui tam* provisions. The states of Texas and Washington are considering proposed legislation to expand their statutes to other areas. There are many states, including Alabama, Alaska, Colorado, Connecticut, Kansas, Maryland, Mississippi, Missouri, Montana, New Jersey, New York, Oklahoma, and Pennsylvania, that have introduced bills in their legislatures for adoption of false claims statutes that are similar to the Federal Civil False Claims Act; although the bills introduced in Alaska, Connecticut, and Kansas lack whistleblower provisions. In any instance involving local violations, state statutes must be consulted for current application.

---

[142] Cal. Gov't Code § 12650; Fla. Stat. Ann. § 68.081-092 (1995); Haw. Code Ann. § 661-7; Whistleblower Reward & Protection Act, 740 Ill. Stat. Ann. § 175 (1995); Mass. Gen. Laws Ann. ch. 93 (1995).

[143] Cal. Code § 12652b(1)-2, (c)(5).

[144] Cal. Code § 12651(a)(8); D.C. Code Ann. § 2-308.14(a)(8); Tenn. Code Ann. § 4-18-103(a)(8).

CHAPTER 7

CHANGES RESULTING FROM BREACH OF IMPLIED WARRANTIES, MISREPRESENTATION, AND NONDISCLOSURE OF SUPERIOR KNOWLEDGE

Nicholas K. Holmes
Christopher D. Hawkins

Authors' Note: The authors gratefully acknowledge the contributions of Michael T. McInerny, Esq., and Paul B. Nolette, Esq.

§ 7.01   INTRODUCTION

This chapter focuses on the contract documents. The contract documents are intended to describe the results to be obtained, the work to be accomplished, and the allocation of risks between the parties. It is difficult to fully describe a complex construction project, and drawings and specifications are at best an imperfect way for the owner to express its intentions. Nonetheless, these documents typically form the basis for the contractor's fixed price and frame the parties' expectations for the project. When problems are encountered, the first step is to review the contract documents, and to understand the context in which they were formulated.

Disputes over delays and extra costs frequently arise when contract documents are incomplete or erroneous, when the documents contain omissions or internal conflicts, or when the completed project fails to perform as intended. Sometimes it is easy to identify an error in the plans. On other occasions, it is not so plain: the parties may argue over what the contract documents *should have* included, what terms were *implicit* in the contract, or what the parties *could reasonably have expected*. The doctrines and theories discussed in this chapter are often used to bridge the gap between what the contract actually says and what the parties understood it to mean.

[A]   Design Specifications

The legal theories discussed here are applicable to *design specifications*. Most fixed-price construction projects utilize design specifications (also known as *method* specifications), that detail the exact structure to be built. The contractor is required to build the structure in strict accordance with the plans and specifications. In contrast, *performance* specifications provide only the performance requirements of the finished structure, and the contractor is given discretion to achieve that goal. Contracts based upon performance specifications leave little room for dispute over implied owner warranties or defective drawings and specifications.[1]

In some instances, the contract may contain a mix of design and performance specifications. There, "the key inquiry is the extent of the discretion afforded the contractor. . . . The greater the discretion, the more the specifications are construed as performance measures."[2] As a general rule, a claim for implied owner warranty or defective contract documents only lies where the owner provides explicit direction by way of a design specification.

---

[1] Stuyvesant Dredging Co. v. United States, 834 F.2d 1576, 1582 (Fed. Cir. 1987); Blake Constr. Co. v. United States, 987 F.2d 743, 745 (Fed. Cir.), *cert. denied*, 510 U.S. 963 (1993).

[2] Turner Constr. Co. v. United States, 54 Fed. Cl. 388 (2002), *rev'd*, 367 F.3d 1319 (Fed. Cir. 2004), citing *Blake*, 987 F.2d 743, 746. *See also* PCL Constr. Servs., Inc. v. United States, 47 Fed. Cl. 745, 795-96 (2000); Fruin-Colnon Corp. v. Niagara Frontier Transp. Auth., 585 N.Y.S.2d 248, 180 A.D.2d 222, 230 (N.Y. App. Div. 1992).

[B]   Implied Warranties

Section 7.02 below discusses implied warranties relevant to construction contracts. These include the *Spearin* doctrine, a judicially created rule, which provides that when an owner issues design specifications to a contractor, the owner impliedly warrants the adequacy of those plans and specifications. Also discussed are warranties related to sole-source specifications and those arising out of the owner's designation of service subcontractors.

Other implied warranties, such as the implied covenant of good faith and fair dealing applicable to every contract,[3] apply to construction contracts but are not treated here in detail.

[C]   Misrepresentation

Section 7.03 discusses the circumstances under which misrepresentations may amount to a breach of the implied warranty of plans and specifications. An owner may be held liable for extra costs incurred as a result of misrepresentations in the plans or specifications, or misrepresentations related to differing site conditions. There is a split of authority regarding whether misrepresentation claims against government entities are barred by the doctrine of sovereign immunity. To prove a misrepresentation claim, the contractor must show that the owner (1) made a misrepresentation (2) of material fact (3) that induced the contractor to enter into the contract, that (4) the contractor reasonably relied upon the misrepresentation and (5) suffered damages as a result.

[D]   Superior Knowledge

Section 7.04 discusses the owner's liability for failure to disclose superior knowledge of material facts. The owner's implied warranty of plans and specifications, and the implied obligation of good faith and fair dealing, include an obligation to disclose information material to bidding or contract performance. The owner may be held liable for delays or additional costs caused by its failure to disclose material information. This obligation is limited, however, to information in the owner's sole possession or control. The owner is not obligated to disclose information reasonably available in public records or through other accessible sources.

The rationale for this rule is that the contractual allocation of risk may be effectively nullified and rendered less efficient if the owner withholds information material to the contractor's performance not otherwise reasonably accessible by the contractor.

Courts applying this rule carefully examine whether the owner possessed unique information regarding site conditions, whether the information was reasonably available to the contractor through other sources, the extent to which the

---

[3] Restatement (Second) of Contracts § 205 (1981).

contractor's losses were based upon erroneous inferences drawn of owner-supplied data, as opposed to errors in the data itself, and the contractor's diligence in pursuing information relevant to site conditions.

[E]   Disclaimers

Section 7.05 discusses contractual disclaimers. Owners utilize disclaimers in an attempt to reduce their risk in the event the project takes longer or costs more than anticipated. For example, owners commonly attempt to disclaim the contractor's ability to rely upon the accuracy or completeness of owner-supplied information, and transfer the risk of unknown site conditions to the contractor. In addition, some owners attempt to disclaim the implied warranty of plans and specifications. These disclaimers may also, however, result in higher bids as contractors attempt to hedge the risks posed by disclaimer provisions.

Site investigation clauses generally only protect owners from risks arising from site conditions that could have been discovered by the contractor upon reasonable investigation. What constitutes a "reasonable investigation" depends upon the particular facts and circumstances of each case, as well as upon whether the contract contains a differing site conditions clause. Courts generally will not interpret a site disclaimer clause so broadly as to effectively nullify contractual provisions regarding differing site conditions.

Similarly, clauses disclaiming reliance upon owner-supplied information are sometimes enforced, and sometimes not enforced. Their viability frequently depends upon whether the contractor relied upon the information, and whether its reliance was reasonable under the circumstances. Courts are sometimes reluctant to enforce a general disclaimer to nullify specific representations of information important to the contractor's performance.

There is no clear consensus on whether, and to what extent, owners may transfer or disclaim their implied warranty of plans and specifications. One court has held that an express contractual warranty that the work would be free from defects negated the implied warranty. Other courts have held that this express warranty was limited to those portions of the work under the contractor's control, and did not extend to the performance of components selected and specified by the owner. In addition, at least one court has suggested that attempts to disclaim the implied warranty of plans and specifications may be unconscionable and unenforceable.

§ 7.02   IMPLIED WARRANTIES

[A]   Plans and Specifications

[1]   The *Spearin* Doctrine

In 1918, the United States Supreme Court issued a landmark decision addressing allocation of risks of defective plans and specifications between the owner and contractor. This case forms the underpinning for much of the law underlying the relationship between owners and contractors.

In *United States v. Spearin*,[4] Spearin contracted with the government to build a dry dock at the Brooklyn Navy Yard. The government provided plans calling for the relocation of a six-foot storm sewer, and specified the dimensions, materials of construction, and location of the rebuilt sewer. Spearin fully complied with the government's specifications, and the relocated section was accepted as satisfactory. Unknown to Spearin and to the government,[5] a nearby seven-foot sewer line was partially blocked by a dam that prevented water from backing up into the seven-foot sewer. After Spearin had moved the sewer, but before the dry dock was complete, pressure in the sewer caused by a combination of high tides, heavy rains, and the dam, caused the sewer installed by Spearin to break and flood the site. An investigation revealed that the sewer failed because the design did not take into consideration the dam in the seven-foot sewer. The Secretary of the Navy refused to pay for the damages and annulled the contract. Spearin filed suit to recover the balance due on his work plus lost profits.

The Supreme Court held that where an owner provides plans and specifications to a contractor, the owner impliedly warrants the adequacy of the plans and specifications. "[I]f the contractor is bound to build according to plans and specifications prepared by the owner, the contractor will not be responsible for the consequences of defects in the plans and specifications."[6] The implied warranty is not overcome by contractual clauses requiring the contractor to visit the site, check the plans, assume responsibility for the work until completion and acceptance, or inform themselves of the requirements of the work.[7]

This principle—that a party that furnishes plans or specifications for a contractor to follow in a construction job impliedly warrants their adequacy and accuracy—has become known as the *Spearin* doctrine.

The warranty is implied in the contract, and does not depend upon the owner's negligence. An owner or a prime contractor that furnishes plans or specifications for a project is held to have impliedly warranted their adequacy and accuracy, even if the plans or specifications were prepared by another party, such as an architect or engineer, on the owner's behalf.[8] For example, in *APAC Carolina, Inc. v. Town of Allendale*,[9] the Fourth Circuit held that the general contractor could be liable to a subcontractor for breach of an implied warranty as to the sufficiency of plans for construction of a sewage treatment plant even though the general contractor neither participated in drafting the plans nor held itself out as having special knowledge.

---

[4] 248 U.S. 132 (1918).

[5] The government was aware, however, that the site had flooded in the past, but failed to disclose that fact to Spearin.

[6] *Spearin*, 248 U.S. 132, 136.

[7] *Spearin*, 248 U.S. 132, 137 (1918). There is a split of authority on whether the implied warranty of plans and specifications may be specifically disclaimed. See § 7.05[C].

[8] The owner may, of course, have recourse against the architect or engineer depending upon the terms of those contracts.

[9] 41 F.3d 157 (4th Cir. 1994).

A contractor may not claim damages for breach of an implied warranty if the contractor was negligent in constructing the work, if the contractor failed to faithfully follow the plans, *or* if the contractor was aware the plans were flawed. As one federal court noted, the implied warranty has a practical component:

> [C]ontractors are businessmen, and in the business of bidding on Government contracts they are usually pressed for time and are consciously seeking to underbid a number of competitors. Consequently, they estimate only on those costs which they feel the contract terms will permit the Government to insist upon in the way of performance. They are obligated to bring to the Government's attention major discrepancies or errors which they detect in the specifications or drawings, or else fail to do so at their peril. But they are not expected to exercise clairvoyance in spotting hidden ambiguities in the bid documents, and they are protected if they innocently construe in their own favor an ambiguity equally susceptible to another construction.[10]

Owners should understand this practical component and should not expect contractors to detect and correct all defects within the short and often hectic project bidding period. Conversely, contractors should not expect owners and courts to be as sympathetic as indicated by the preceding statement. This practical component will be affected by varying contractual or performance strategies, such as negotiated contracts or fast-track contracts.

[2] Rationale for the *Spearin* Doctrine

If a contractor is bound by a contract to construct a project according to plans and specifications provided by the owner, the risk that the plans and specifications are flawed should be borne by the party that provided them, not by the contractor. If the contractor follows the owner's plans and specifications, it should be compensated for its work when it turns out that the work done in accordance with the plans and specifications does not produce the intended results.[11]

The *Spearin* doctrine has a practical basis in certain attributes of competitive bidding, such as time pressure and the theory of providing the lowest price for only the requirements specified in the plans and specifications.[12] These attributes may be present in varying degrees in contracts awarded in ways other than through competitive bidding.

Most states have adopted the principle that every construction contract includes an implied warranty by the owner of the accuracy and adequacy of the plans and specifications. The basis for the implied warranty was clearly stated by one California court:

> It may be stated generally that where the plans and specifications induce a public contractor reasonably to believe that certain indicated conditions actually

---

[10] Blount Bros. Constr. Co. v. United States, 346 F.2d 962 (Ct. Cl. 1965).
[11] Dayton-Wright v. United States, 64 Ct. Cl. 544 (1928).
[12] Blount Bros. Constr. Co. v. United States, 346 F.2d 962 (Ct. Cl. 1965).

exist and may be relied upon in submitting a bid, he is entitled to recover the value of such extra work as was necessitated by the conditions being other than as represented.[13]

[B] Sole Source of Supply

A variation on the *Spearin* doctrine arises when the owner specifies a sole source of supply or subcontractor. In that situation, the owner may impliedly warrant that the item or subcontractor will perform adequately. This doctrine is sometimes referred to as the implied warranty of suitability or capability.

The policy underlying this implied warranty is that a contractor should not be liable for the performance of a component or vendor when it is not afforded an opportunity to evaluate the component's suitability or the subcontractor's capability to perform its specified work. If the contractor were compelled to bear this risk, bids would tend to be higher as contractors sought to hedge the risk that an owner-specified vendor might perform inadequately. In addition, a sole-specified subcontractor may have significantly more bargaining power against the prime contractor than a subcontractor selected through a competitive bidding process.

The implied warranty of suitability developed in cases where the government-specified vendor supplied a specific component critical to contract performance. In general, the implied warranty has been applied where a contractor failed to meet contractual specifications because of some deficiency associated with the component supplied by the sole specified vendor. In this sense, the implied warranty appears to be a relatively straightforward extension of the *Spearin* doctrine. In addition, some boards of appeal have extended this warranty to government-specified service providers, while others have declined to do so. As will be discussed in more detail below, this split of opinion may be based upon the prime contractor's ability to direct and control the work of service subcontractors.

[1] Implied Warranty of Suitability—*Franklin E. Penny* and Its Progeny

The leading implied warranty of suitability case is *Franklin E. Penny Co. v. United States*.[14] In *Franklin E. Penny*, the Navy solicited bids for the manufacture of shock mounts for missile containers. The shock mounts included a subassembly that called for the bonding of rubber blocks to metal plates. The bid specifications identified four approved manufacturers for the bonding process. Franklin submitted a bid based upon the first manufacturer's quoted price and was awarded the contract. Franklin later learned that the first vendor was not tooled to perform the job, and thus would not be competitive, two of the remaining suppliers were out of business, and that the fourth was unwilling to do the work.

---

[13] Gogo v. Los Angeles County Flood Control Dist., 45 Cal. App. 2d 334, 114 P.2d 65 (1941).
[14] 524 F.2d 668 (Ct. Cl. 1975).

Franklin obtained a time extension to locate and qualify another supplier. Franklin located another supplier within the extension period, which needed additional time to produce the components. Franklin requested and was granted a second extension, but the new supplier proved unable to produce the components within the extension period. Franklin requested a third extension, which the government denied.

The Court of Claims rejected Franklin's argument that the government's specification of suppliers constituted an implied warranty that the named sources were ready, willing, and able to perform the contract work. The court held that the government warranted only that the listed suppliers have the *ability* to do the work, but not the supplier's *willingness* to do the work. In light of Franklin's failures to meet the contractual delivery dates, the court held that the government was within its rights to terminate the contract.

In dicta, the Court of Claims suggested that under certain circumstances, the government will bear the risk of the subcontractor's defective performance:

> To be sure, the rule would be otherwise if the delay resulted from circumstances with respect to which the Government bore the risk. Thus, for example, if it had been the case here that the Government had *selected the subcontractor* or had *vouched for the competence of the one selected*, then delays attributable to that subcontractor's technical problems (in doing the work) would remain within the Government's sphere of responsibility.[15]

This dicta distinguishes between the listing of a number of acceptable subcontractors, in which the owner warrants no more than the subcontractors' ability to meet the contractual requirements, and the government's selection of or vouching for a particular subcontractor, where the owner may remain liable for delays caused by the subcontractor.

The *Franklin E. Penny* dicta was later extended to a situation where the government-specified vendor was late performing the contract. In *Appeal of Stephenson Associates, Inc.*,[16] the Government specified environmental control systems manufactured by a named vendor for use on a firing range. The vendor did not deliver the air-handling units on time, which delayed completion of Stephenson's work and caused it damages.

The board found that the vendor had been in direct contact with the government's architects before the air-handling units were installed. Accordingly, the court held that delivery of the air handling systems was affected "by the Government's influence." In dicta, the board suggested that:

> [e]ven in a situation where the Government has had no post-award involvement with a subcontractor it has directed the prime to use, we would have some difficulty (as did the Court of Claims in *Penny*) applying a rule that puts the prime contractor at the mercy of that subcontractor.

---

[15] 524 F.2d 668, 676 (emphasis added).
[16] GSBCA No. 6573, 86-3 BCA ¶ 19,071 (May 15, 1986).

In essence, the board held that it is unfair to compel prime contractors to bear the risk of a subcontractor's nonperformance when they are not afforded an opportunity to evaluate the subcontractor's ability to perform.

In *Appeal of Jacksonville Shipyards, Inc.*,[17] the Armed Services Board of Contract Appeals held that the government was liable for increased costs incurred based upon the fact that the government "vouched" for the performance of its specified vendor. The government specified a paint system manufactured by a specific vendor. The contractor utilized the specified paint and strictly complied with the manufacturer's recommendations. The paint began to peel shortly after the vessel was put back in service, and the vessel was returned for sandblasting and repainting. Shortly before reapplication was to commence, the paint manufacturer amended its application instructions. The contractor claimed damages against the government for the cost of sandblasting the hull and reapplying the paint. The board held that the government in effect vouched for the paint system when applied pursuant to the manufacturer's instructions, and that any defect in the paint system remained within the government's sphere of responsibility.

This case supports the general rule that where the government specifies a sole source of supply, and the contractor follows the supplier's instructions, the government remains liable for the risk that the supplier's performance does not serve its intended purpose.

[2] Limitations on the Implied Warranty of Suitability

The Armed Services Board of Contract Appeals articulated a limitation to the implied warranty of suitability in *Appeal of DeLaval Turbine, Inc.*[18] The board in that case held that the implied warranty of suitability does not extend to improperly manufactured components. In essence, the government warrants that the specified vendor is *capable* of meeting the specifications, not that its performance *will* comply with the specifications. The court held that the contractor should structure its subcontract to protect itself from the risks of the subcontractor's deficient performance.

More general limitations of the implied warranty were discussed in *Appeal of Modular Devices, Inc.*[19] The Armed Services Board of Contract Appeals held that the implied warranty attached to approved sources does not extend to areas beyond the government's control. The government warrants only that the specified component, "when timely delivered and flawlessly manufactured," will meet the contractual requirements. In essence, the board held the implied warranty that a sole source of supply does not extend the scope of the *Spearin* warranty.

The board's decisions in *DeLaval Turbine* and *Modular Devices* do not recognize the distinction between inadequate specifications and a sole-specified

---

[17] ASBCA No. 32,300 (July 11, 1986).
[18] ASBCA No. 21,797, 78-2 BCA (CCH) ¶ 13,521 (Oct. 27, 1978).
[19] ASBCA No. 33,708, 87-2 BCA (CCH) ¶ 19,798 (Apr. 14, 1987).

source of supply. A contractor responsible for performing work in accordance with owner-supplied specifications that prove to be defective ordinarily retains discretion over construction means and methods. The specification of a sole source of supply, however, significantly alters the ordinary balance of bargaining power between a prime contractor and its subcontractors. As pointed out in *Franklin E. Penny* and *Stephenson Associates*, a prime contractor may have significantly less leverage in dealing with a sole-specified vendor than it would have otherwise, and may not be able to transfer entirely the risk of the subcontractor's deficient performance to the subcontractor.

[C] Implied Warranty of Capability: Service Subcontractor Performance

There is a split of authority regarding whether the implied warranty of capability extends to the performance of a service subcontractor. This split may rest implicitly on the fact that, while the prime contractor has little or no control over the manufacture or fabrication of a specific component, the prime contractor may have greater ability to govern and manage the work of a service subcontractor. Courts and boards may recognize that prime contractors typically protect themselves from the poor performance of subcontractors through flow-down provisions and other contractual devices, and apparently see no reason to reallocate that risk where the contractor also has authority to direct and manage the subcontractor's work.

[1] Cases Holding Warranty Applies to Service Subcontractor Performance

Two cases suggest that the implied warranty might extend to the deficient performance of a sole-specified service subcontractor.

In *Appeal of Amos & Andrews Plumbing, Inc.*,[20] the contractor was hired to modify flare stacks and install piping for a fuel loading system at a Naval refueling station in California. The government required that the contractor utilize the services of the manufacturer of the flare stack in designing and performing the flare stack modifications. Certain parts and procedures specified by the manufacturer proved ineffective, and the contractor incurred additional costs rectifying the problems. The contractor sought to recover its additional costs from the government. The Armed Services Board of Contract Appeals held that, "since the Government designated the expert, it vouched for the expert's competence, and therefore, any costs attributable to technical problems that arose as a result of the expert's determination were 'within the government's sphere of responsibility.'" The board then remanded the case to the hearings officer for a determination of the contractor's damages in rendering the flare stack operational.

---

[20] ASBCA No. 29,142 (Apr. 23, 1986).

In *Appeal of Browne, Inc.*,[21] the government required that Browne utilize a specific subcontractor to upgrade three boilers at a submarine base. Browne alleged that it incurred additional costs because the government-specified subcontractor failed to perform adequately, and sought to recover those costs from the government. The government argued that it only warranted that the subcontractor was capable of doing the work, not that the subcontractor's performance would be flawless, and moved to strike Browne's claim. The board held that because the government specified a single source of supply, it was not clear whether the implied warranty of capability extended to the subcontractor's continued capability during performance. The board found an inconsistency between the narrow scope of the implied warranty of capability and the *Franklin E. Penny* dicta suggesting that the government might bear the risk of delay attributable to the shortcomings of its specified subcontractor's performance. In light of this uncertainty, the board denied the government's motion to strike Browne's claim based upon implied warranty of capability pending a hearing on disputed facts.

[2] Cases Holding Warranty Does Not Apply to Service Subcontractor Performance

Some courts have held that the implied warranty of suitability does not extend to the performance of sole specified service subcontractors.

In *General Ship Corp. v. United States*,[22] the Navy contracted with GSC to overhaul the U.S.S. Garcia. The Navy required that GSC subcontract with the Elliott Co. to overhaul the ship's superchargers. Elliott's subcontractor cleaned, repaired, and reassembled the superchargers. As GSC was reinstalling the superchargers, they found metal particles in the oil sump. The oil sump had to be drained and cleaned, at considerable expense. GSC filed a claim for equitable adjustment based upon this occurrence, and upon the incompetence of Elliott's designated site representative. The Navy denied the claim. GSC filed suit in the U.S. District Court for the District of Massachusetts, and the parties filed cross-motions for summary judgment.

The court found that the government's designation of a specific subcontractor does not shift the entire risk of the subcontractor's defective performance to the government. The prime contractor bids on the job fully aware and accepting of the subcontractor specification, and should provide whatever protection it thinks it needs in its subcontract. Citing *Franklin E. Penny*, the court noted that some decisions have found an implied warranty of capability when the subcontractor is required to manufacture a specific part, and declined to extend the implied warranty to cases where the government specifies a service contractor.

In *Appeal of Datametrics, Inc.*,[23] the government provided the contractor with a "composite" specification, which encompassed features of both design and

---

[21] ASBCA No. 24,434 (May 12, 1980).
[22] 634 F. Supp. 868 (D. Mass. 1986).
[23] ASBCA No. 16,086 (June 25, 1974).

purchase description specifications, for certain items. The government also specified that the contractor acquire certain electronic components from two specified man-ufacturers. The government-specified components, when tested in isolation from the entire system, generally proved adequate to meet the purchase description. When incorporated into the overall system, however, variances in the normal oper-ating range of the specified components caused the final product to fail compli-ance with the performance specification. To overcome this difficulty, the contractor had to hand-match components until each product met the performance criteria. This took substantially more time than the contractor anticipated.

The board found, however, that while the government was responsible for defects in its design, it was not responsible for defects in the components supplied by the specified vendors. The board found that the contractor should have drawn its subcontracts so as to protect itself from the risk of defective performance.

A further variation arose in *Edward M. Crough, Inc. v. Department of General Services of the District of Columbia.*[24] The court in that case articulated an implied warranty of commercial availability wherein the government implicitly warranted that items specified by brand name were in fact commercially available. The court further found that this warranty did not relieve the contractor of its usual risk of nonperformance stemming from its relationship with subcontractors. The court held that the government had created the implied warranty of availability, but that the contractor had not proven that the warranty had been breached. In sum, the contractor proved that the specified subcontractor *refused* to perform, not that it was *incapable* of performing. The court held that the subcontractor's refusal to perform the subcontract was an issue for the contractor to resolve, and entirely beyond the government's control.

[D]   Defects Encountered During Construction

When the contractor discovers design defects during construction, the issue is whether the contractor is entitled to the extra costs it incurs as a result of the defects. As a general rule, the answer is yes. The owner warrants the accuracy of the plans and specifications so that if the contractor incurs extra costs due to defects in the plans and specifications, the owner is liable for those extra costs.[25]

[1]   Differing Site Conditions

When the contractor encounters unexpected subsurface conditions, changes are usually necessary. Different excavation methods may be required by unfore-seen soil types, or additional dewatering efforts may be required when unexpect-edly heavy groundwater is encountered. Almost always, these changes lead to additional costs. Disputes over unforeseen subsurface conditions arise frequently because it is difficult to predict the exact nature of what lies beneath the ground.

---

[24] 572 A.2d 457 (D.C. Ct. App. 1987).
[25] United States v. Spearin, 248 U.S. 132 (1918); see § 7.02[A].

The owner may have dug test pits or made soil borings, but each of these samplings only shows conditions at one location. The test pits or borings are often hundreds or thousands of feet apart, leaving plenty of room for costly and time-consuming surprises.

Unexpected subsurface conditions do not necessarily justify additional compensation. If the contract documents made an explicit representation of subsurface conditions and that representation proves incorrect, there is a "Type I" differing site condition. The U.S. Court of Federal Claims has set out the requirements for a successful Type I differing site condition claim under a federal contract:

1. The contract documents must have affirmatively indicated or represented the subsurface or latent physical conditions which form the basis of plaintiff's claim;

2. the contractor must have acted as a reasonably prudent contractor in interpreting the contract documents;

3. the contract must have reasonably relied on the indications of subsurface or latent physical conditions in the contract;

4. the subsurface or latent physical conditions actually encountered within the contract area must have differed materially from the conditions indicated in the same contract area;

5. the actual subsurface conditions or latent physical conditions encountered must have been reasonably unforeseeable; and

6. the contractor's claimed excess costs must be shown to be solely attributable to the materially different subsurface or latent physical conditions within the contract site.[26]

This test seems reasonable and fair; when the owner's contract documents misrepresent conditions in the field, the owner should compensate the contractor for the cost of dealing with actual, different conditions.[27] Yet, until the early 1900s, the common law provided no sure relief to the contractor. Where the contract was silent regarding the risk of unforeseen subsurface conditions, that risk was allocated to the contractor:

> Where one agrees to do, for a fixed sum, a thing possible to be performed, he will not be excused or become entitled to additional compensation, because unforeseen difficulties are encountered.[28]

Application of this principle led to harsh results, justified by the proposition that the contractor could have addressed this risk by inserting appropriate contract

---

[26] Youngdale & Sons Constr. Co. v. United States, 27 Fed. Cl. 516 (1993).

[27] Of course, the owner is not liable if the contractor did not rely upon the incorrect information. *See* Comtrol, Inc. v. United States, 294 F.3d 1357 (Fed. Cir. 2002).

[28] *Spearin*, 248 U.S. 132, 136 (1918).

terms.[29] Contractors probably recognized the futility of negotiating protective clauses with the government, and instead included large contingencies in their bids to account for the risk.

Eventually, the U.S. Supreme Court recognized this potential for "an extravagant price based on conjecture of conditions,"[30] and held that incorrect subsurface information in the contract documents would support a claim of *misrepresentation*.[31] In short order, the federal government inserted a "Changed Conditions" clause in its construction contracts allowing recovery for "Type I" differing site conditions.

Roughly ten years later, the federal changed conditions clause was expanded to include "Type II" differing site conditions:

> Unknown physical conditions at the site, of an unusual nature, which differ materially from those ordinarily encountered and generally recognized as inhering in work of the character provided for in the contract.[32]

Today, most standard form contracts contain a differing site conditions clause providing compensation for "Type I" and "Type II" conditions.[33] In providing explicit relief for Type I differing site conditions, these clauses confirm the common law: even in the absence of such a clause, there would be a cause of action for misrepresentation or breach of warranty. The Type II differing site condition, however, is purely contractual — absent an explicit contractual allowance, conditions different from those usually encountered are the contractor's risk. Common-law arguments such as mutual mistake are possible, but the absence of a Type II differing site conditions clause in the contract puts the contractor at a decided disadvantage.[34]

Much of the difficulty in establishing a Type I differing site condition comes from proving what was "indicated" in the contract documents. Often, the contractor uses the information provided in the contract documents to draw reasonable conclusions regarding subsurface conditions at the worksite.

> [I]t is not necessary that the 'indications' in the contract be explicit or specific; all that is required is that there be enough of an indication on the face of the

---

[29] "If the parties have made no provision for a dispensation, the rule of law gives none. It does not allow a contract fairly made to be annulled, and it does not permit to be interpolated what the parties themselves have not stipulated." Dermott v. Jones, 69 U.S. 1, 8 (1864).

[30] Christie v. United States, 237 U.S. 234, 241 (1915).

[31] *Christie*, 237 U.S. 234, 241; Hollerbach v. United States, 233 U.S. 165 (1914); United States v. Atlantic Dredging Co., 253 U.S. 1 (1920).

[32] 48 C.F.R. § 52.236-2 (2004) (federal differing site condition clause).

[33] *See, e.g.,* AIA Doc. A201, General Conditions, ¶ 4.3.4 (1997); EJCDC Doc. No. 1910-2, General Conditions, ¶ 4.2 (1990).

[34] Hall Contracting Corp. v. Entergy Servs., Inc., 309 F.3d 468 (8th Cir. 2002); *see also* Green Constr. Co. v. Kansas Power & Light Co., 1 F.3d 1005, 1009 (10th Cir. 1993) ("[A]bsent fraud, the party who agrees to complete construction for a fixed cost must absorb any losses resulting from unforeseen conditions.").

contract documents for a bidder reasonably not to expect subsurface or latent physical conditions at the site differing materially from those indicated in this contract.[35]

Two cases from the U.S. Court of Federal Claims demonstrate some of the difficulties presented by inferences drawn from the contract documents. In *Weeks Dredging & Contracting, Inc. v. United States,*[36] the plaintiff was low bidder on a $9 million dredging project on the Tennessee-Tombigbee Waterway in the southeastern United States. The project covered some 30 miles of river, and required removal of over seven million cubic yards of material. Weeks premised its bid on a physical review of the site, and on the log of 156 borings taken by the government along the alignment of the project. The borings showed layers of different material, including gravel of various size and "eutaw," a clay-like material. In order to estimate the quantity of these materials, Weeks identified the depth of each layer shown at one boring, and then extrapolated a line to the depth shown for that same material at the next boring (a relatively standard practice).

In performing the work, however, Weeks encountered more large gravel and eutaw than it had estimated, and the dredging was far more difficult and costly. Weeks ultimately submitted a $3.6 million Type I differing site conditions claim, asserting that the conditions actually encountered were different from those shown by the contract borings.

In evaluating Weeks's claim, the court concluded that the pre-bid borings were a direct representation by the government, but only of the "character and nature" of the materials involved.[37] The court rejected Weeks's claim that the borings could be used to create a geometrical calculation of the anticipated quantities of gravel or eutaw. The presence of numerous sand and gravel mining operations along the river, along with the well-known tendency of river flow to deposit sediment irregularly, should have alerted Weeks to the potential for wide variations in the location and depth of the various materials. The court held that a reasonable bidder would have taken these circumstances into account in estimating the project, and thus the quantities of gravel and eutaw actually encountered were *foreseeable.*[38] Weeks's differing site conditions claim was denied.

In *H.B. Mac, Inc. v. United States,*[39] the plaintiff signed a $6 million contract to construct a maintenance facility for the Army in Hawaii. The contract called for construction of structures in two contiguous areas, but provided borings only in one of the two. The contractor prepared its bid on the assumption that subsurface conditions were generally uniform across the site.

[35] Foster Constr. C.A. & Williams Bros. Co. v. United States, 435 F.2d 873 (Ct. Cl. 1970); *cf.* Mojave Enters. v. United States, 3 Cl. Ct. 353, 357 (1983) (differing site conditions claim precluded because government made no representations as to subsurface conditions).
[36] 13 Cl. Ct. 193 (1987), *aff'd,* 861 F.2d 728 (Fed. Cir. 1988).
[37] 13 Cl. Ct. 193, 220-21.
[38] 13 Cl. Ct. 193, 235-40.
[39] 153 F.3d 1338 (Fed. Cir. 1998).

Instead, silty material and groundwater combined to require an expensive sheet-pile excavation support system in the area without borings. The contractor submitted a Type I differing site conditions claim for its additional costs. The Army contested the claim, citing *Weeks* for the proposition that the borings provided by the government were not incorrect.

Although the trial court held that H.B. Mac *was* entitled to extrapolate information from the borings and assume they represented conditions at the other side of the worksite,[40] the Court of Federal Claims reversed, ruling that the contractor's reliance *was not* reasonable given that the borings were taken at a distance from the project site, and the location of the project on an alluvial plain near the ocean and several streams.

In both *Weeks* and *H.B. Mac,* the success of a Type I differing site conditions claim hinged upon the way the contractor interpreted the government's borings. It is difficult to find a consistent test among the reported decisions on Type I differing site conditions claims. From case to case, emphasis may shift from economic hardship to strict construction of contract; emphasis can be placed on precisely what the contract documents *said*, or what was implied, and inconsistent contract provisions can add to the confusion.

Contracts often include a disclaimer that any borings or subsurface information is provided for information only. A close competition can arise when a Type I differing site conditions claim based upon incorrect subsurface information meets up with a contractual disclaimer. Concepts of fairness and equity are often urged, but a court inclined toward "strict construction" may limit its focus to questions of technical accuracy in the contract documents. On federal contracts, disclaimers are often rejected where there are express representations of site conditions. The court may resolve the ambiguity created by the two clauses against the government drafter, or base its conclusion on considerations of fairness.[41] Nonetheless, the effect of such disclaimers should not be discounted, particularly where the claim is based on interpretation of the contract documents and not an explicit error.

State courts are less consistently supportive of differing site conditions claims where the contract includes a disclaimer clause. In *Brown Brothers, Inc. v. Metropolitan Government of Nashville & Davidson County,*[42] the successful bidder on a roadbuilding contract relied on the owner's "Estimated Earthwork Quantities" showing an estimated volume for rock excavation that proved far too low. However, the contract also provided that bidders "shall rely exclusively upon their own estimates, investigation and other data which are necessary for full and complete information upon which the proposal may be based."[43]

Faced with what appeared to be a straightforward Type I differing site conditions claim based on estimates provided in the contract, the Tennessee court

---

[40] 36 Fed. Cl. 793 (1996).

[41] United States v. Seckinger, 397 U.S. 203, 210 (1970); Celeron Gathering Corp., 34 Fed. Cl. 745, 752 (1976); Department of Transp. v. P. DiMarco & Co., 711 A.2d 1088 (Pa. Commw. Ct. 1998); *cf.* Millgard Corp. v. McKee/Mays, 49 F.3d 1070 (5th Cir. 1995).

[42] 877 S.W.2d 745 (Tenn. Ct. App. 1994).

[43] 877 S.W.2d 745, 746.

concluded that "[p]arties to a contract are free to allocate risks and burdens between themselves as they see fit."[44] Emphasizing that "nothing in the record . . . indicates that the inaccuracy of the defendant's estimates constitutes negligence or misrepresentation," the court concluded that ". . .without some proof of negligence on the part of Metro, the burden of risk may not be removed from the shoulders of the contractor."[45]

In *Sanders Co. Plumbing & Heating, Inc. v. City of Independence*,[46] the Missouri Court of Appeals held that a boilerplate disclaimer could negate "*implied* or *suggestive* representations," but "does not negate . . . positive representations of material fact."[47] This distinction seems useful, but applying the test undoubtedly will yield varied results. The *Sanders* decision includes concurring and dissenting opinions, which neatly summarize two very different philosophies that can be brought to bear in these cases. The concurring opinion notes that enforcing the disclaimer would deliver a "windfall to the public entity and a crushing burden to the contractor. . . ."[48] The dissent argued the contract's subsurface information was not actually incorrect, but rather the contractor's interpretation of that information was incorrect, and thus no relief was justified.[49]

The theory of differing site conditions appears to be limited to conditions that existed at the time the contract was signed. Manmade conditions that arise after the contract is executed may not qualify as differing site conditions under the clause. In *Olympus Corp. v. United States*,[50] the court reasoned that differing site conditions clauses are a concession by the government, intended to alleviate circumstances that skew a contractor's bid. Since post-award events could have no bearing on the bids, the court considered a differing site conditions clause inapplicable.[51]

Virtually all differing site conditions clauses require prompt notice to the owner, permitting the owner an opportunity to inspect the conditions before they are disturbed. Failure to provide timely notice can be deadly. On federal projects, a court may be willing to overlook late notice if there was no prejudice to the owner.[52] State law is often less forgiving.[53]

---

[44] 877 S.W.2d 745, 749.

[45] 877 S.W.2d 745, 748.

[46] 694 S.W.2d 841 (Mo. Ct. App. 1985).

[47] 694 S.W.2d 841, 846 (citing United States v. Spearin, among other cases).

[48] 694 S.W.2d 841, 848.

[49] 694 S.W.2d 841, 850 ("There is not one iota of evidence that the 'auger boring' logs did not truly and correctly disclose subsurface soil conditions and ground water as of April-June, 1974 [two years prior to the contract]. . . . Moreover, the uncontradicted evidence was that ground water levels sporadically change.").

[50] 98 F.3d 1314 (Fed. Cir. 1996).

[51] 98 F.3d 1314, 1317, citing 4A John Cosgrove McBride, Government Contracts § 29.10[1] (1996) (The court's logic shows an interesting similarity to the common law of mutual mistake of fact.).

[52] *See, e.g.,* Dawco Constr., Inc. v. United States, 18 Cl. Ct. 682, 693 (1989), *rev'd on other grounds*, 930 F.2d 872 (Fed. Cir. 1991); Frederick Snare Corp. v. Maine-N.H. Interstate Bridge Auth., 41 F. Supp. 638 (D.N.H. 1941).

[53] *See, e.g.,* Hall Contracting Corp. v. Entergy Servs., Inc, 309 F.3d 468 (8th Cir. 2002); Glynn v. City of Gloucester, 21 Mass. App. Ct. 390, 487 N.E.2d 230, *rev. denied*, 396 Mass. 1107, 489 N.E.2d 1263 (1986).

[2]   Other Types of Defects

It would be difficult to categorize the wide range of possible defects that give rise to claims. Some of the more common examples are plans and specifications that are incomplete and plans and specifications that contain conflicting information. In each instance, the owner has warranted the accuracy of the plans and specifications, and the contractor who discovers the defect during construction should be entitled to recover its extra costs for remedying the defect.

In *Airprep Technology, Inc. v. United States*,[54] the plaintiff was hired to design and fabricate a bag-house for dust collection at an experimental plant being built for the Department of Energy. The specifications provided values for various operating pressures and temperatures. The dispute centered on a designation of "Inlet Gas Pressure Operating Range." Airprep interpreted this to mean the air pressure at the point where air entered the bag-house — since the bag-house was porous by design, air pressure would drop within the structure.

The government adopted a different interpretation of the meaning of "Inlet Gas Pressure Operating Range." By the government's view, this was the internal operating pressure within the bag-house. Airprep ultimately refused to complete the work and the government terminated the contract for default. Airprep then filed a claim to reverse the default termination and for damages.

The court found Airprep's interpretation of the specifications reasonable, and further stated:

> In sum, [the government] did not establish either that its interpretation of [the contract] was correct, or that a reasonable contractor, faced with [the specified] inlet gas pressure . . . would have any reason to think the operating pressure inside the baghouse would also be in that range. There is therefore no proof that the baghouse that Airprep was willing to deliver could not meet the actual contract requirements, *as opposed to the new ones imposed by [the government]*.[55]

Thus, the court concluded the specification was not ambiguous, and the government's interpretation amounted to an entirely new undertaking. This direction was held to constitute a cardinal change, which excused Airprep's refusal to proceed and justified reversal of the default termination.

A specification that calls for nonexistent products has been held defective. In *Appeal of M.A. Mortensen Co.*,[56] the plaintiff contracted with the government for construction of a medical facility in Alaska. The specification included firestopping at beam penetrations in fire-rated walls. Under "Acceptable Manufacturers and Products," the specification stated that any firestopping system listed by Underwriters Laboratories was acceptable. Mortensen ultimately determined that UL did not list *any* firestopping system. Mortensen had to devise and construct its own system, and recovered the additional cost involved.

---

[54] 30 Fed. Cl. 488 (1994).
[55] 30 Fed. Cl. 488, 507 (emphasis added).
[56] ASBCA No. 53,394 (Oct. 4, 2004).

In *Caldwell & Santmyer, Inc. v. Glickman*,[57] the specifications for a laboratory building project listed certain equipment as "vendor furnished/vendor installed." Shortly after the bid, the low bidder was asked to review its pricing because its price was some 41 percent lower than the next bidder. The low bidder indicated it had not priced this equipment, on the assumption others were furnishing and installing it. He was allowed to withdraw his bid. The contract was awarded to the second-low bidder, Caldwell & Santmyer.

The government soon discovered, however, that Caldwell & Santmyer had made the same assumption. The government asked Caldwell & Santmyer to submit a corrected bid and directed that no work proceed on the contract. Caldwell & Santmyer said they had made no mistake, and declined to submit a corrected bid. The government, facing an inevitable claim for additional compensation based upon the ambiguous specification, chose instead to terminate the contract for convenience. Caldwell & Santmyer appealed, but the termination was upheld as appropriate, since the ambiguous specification precluded an "even playing field" for all bidders.

One interesting case of an alleged defective specification arose in *Hercules Inc. v. United States*.[58] There, chemical manufacturers brought suit to recover their litigation and settlement costs in resolving the "agent orange" class-action suit by Vietnam War veterans. The Hercules plaintiffs argued that because they produced the defoliant in compliance with the government's specifications, the government should be liable for their costs and expenses in defending and settling the tort claims brought by the veterans. The Supreme Court ruled against Hercules, holding that although the *Spearin* doctrine applied to the *performance* of the contract in question, the implied warranty did not require the government to pay the costs of defending and settling third-party claims against the contractor.[59]

[E] Negligence or Intent Not Required

When an owner breaches the implied warranty by providing defective plans and specifications, the contractor does not need to show negligence, fraud, or any other wrongdoing on the part of the owner in order to recover its extra costs. The contractor need only show that:

1. The plans and specifications were defective;

2. The contractor reasonably relied on the plans and specifications; and

3. Its extra costs were caused by the defective plans and specifications.[60]

---

[57] 55 F.3d 1578 (Fed. Cir. 1995).

[58] 516 U.S. 417, 116 S. Ct. 981 (1996).

[59] 516 U.S. 417, 425.

[60] Christie v. United States, 237 U.S. 234 (1915); W.H. Knapp Co. v. State, 18 N.W.2d 421 (Mich. 1945).

Similarly, the six-part test for a Type I differing site conditions claim[61] does not require intent or negligence. Nonetheless, considerations of fault can enter into the court's consideration, particularly in state court.[62]

[F]   When the Owner Is Not Liable

Although as a general rule the owner is liable for extra costs a contractor incurs as a result of defective plans and specifications, there are some exceptions in which the contractor will be held responsible for either (1) the cost of making the project function as intended, or (2) the cost to correct the defects in the plans and specifications.

[1]   Contractor's Failure to Follow Plans and Specifications

If the contractor fails to follow the requirements of the plans and specifications, no claim for implied warranty will lie.[63] Included in this rule is the implicit requirement that the contractor be unaware of the defect during performance. Knowledge of the defect would invoke the contractor's notice obligations.

In *Mega Construction Co. v. United States,*[64] a contractor was terminated for default after a 22,000-square-foot floor slab began to show signs of substantial cracking. The contractor sought to overturn the termination by proving that the cracking was due to the government's defective specifications. After termination, in order to reduce cracking, the government modified the slab specification to reduce the spacing of both the reinforcing steel and the control joints in the slab.

The U.S. Claims Court refused to set aside the termination. The court held that the contractor could not rely on the owner's implied warranty because the contractor had deviated from the plans and specifications by installing the reinforcing steel under rather than in the slab. Even though the specifications were defective, the contractor was not entitled to any relief because it failed to comply with the specifications.

[2]   Patent Discrepancies

Most contracts require that the contractor review the plans and specifications and call to the owner's attention any discrepancies. If the contractor sees a patent discrepancy in the plans, it is obligated to notify the owner of that discrepancy.[65]

---

[61] See § 7.02[D][1].

[62] *See* Brown Bros. v. Metropolitan Gov't of Nashville & Davidson County, 877 S.W.2d 745 (Tenn. Ct. App. 1994).

[63] Al Johnson Constr. Co. v. United States, 854 F.2d 467 (Fed. Cir. 1988); Mega Constr. Co. v. United States, 29 Fed. Cl. 396 (1993).

[64] 29 Fed. Cl. 396.

[65] *See, e.g.,* AIA Doc. A201, General Conditions, ¶ 3.2 (1997), "Review of Contract Documents and Field Conditions by Contractor"; FAR 52.236-4, "Physical Data" (1999); *see also* Clearwater Forest Indus., Inc. v. United States, 650 F.2d 233 (Ct. Cl. 1981).

When a contract term is subject to more than one reasonable interpretation, that term is ambiguous.[66] Ordinarily, the contract is interpreted against the drafter under the general rule of *contra preferentum*. But this rule does not apply when the ambiguity is *patent*: where the ambiguity is *"so 'patent and glaring' that it is unreasonable for a contractor not to discover and inquire about [it]."*[67] Even if the contractor did not discover a patent ambiguity before bidding, no recovery will be allowed for costs arising out of that patent ambiguity.[68] These rules apply equally to patent defects in the contract documents.[69] The contractor who knowingly enters into a contract aware of the fact of defective specifications has no chance of recovery.[70]

Importantly, if the contractor has knowledge of a patent mistake prior to submitting a bid, but fails to notify the owner of the mistake, the contractor's claim for extra work based upon that mistake will be denied. The obligation of the contractor to call the mistake to the owner's attention is not dependent solely on whether the contractor actually knew of the mistake. Instead, the obligation is based upon whether the contractor, as a reasonably prudent contractor, should have known of the mistake. If the contractor should have known, then knowledge of the mistake is presumed, and the contractor cannot recover for any extra costs arising out of the mistake.[71]

[3]   Failure to Conduct Site Inspection

Most contracts contain clauses requiring the contractor to perform a reasonable site inspection.[72] Defects in the plans and specifications do not excuse a contractor from its duty to conduct a reasonable site inspection, and a contractor who fails to conduct a reasonable site inspection will not be entitled to recover extra costs even if the plans and specifications are defective.[73]

As with patent discrepancies, the contractor cannot take advantage of defective plans and specifications if a reasonable site inspection would have revealed those defects. The contractor is held to a reasonable standard and is imputed to have that knowledge that a reasonably prudent contractor would have acquired from a reasonable site inspection.[74]

---

[66] Jowett, Inc. v. United States, 234 F.3d 1365, 1368 (Fed. Cir. 2000).

[67] Beacon Constr. Co. v. United States, 161 Ct. Cl. 1, 314 F.2d 501, 504 (1963); *see also* Triax Pac. v. West, 130 F.3d 1469 (Fed. Cir. 1997); HPI/GSA-3C, LLC v. Perry, 364 F.3d 1327 (Fed. Cir. 2004).

[68] NVT Techs., Inc. v. United States, 370 F.3d 1153 (Fed. Cir. 2004); *cf.* H&M Moving, Inc. v. United States, 499 F.2d 660 (Ct. Cl. 1974).

[69] Space Corp. v. United States, 470 F.2d 536 (Cl. Ct. 1972); Highway Prods., Inc. v. United States, 530 F.2d 911 (Ct. Cl. 1976).

[70] Johnson Controls, Inc. v. United States, 671 F.2d 1312 (Ct. Cl. 1982); Robins Maint., Inc. v. United States, 265 F.3d 1254 (Fed. Cir. 2001). *Cf.* E.L. Hamm & Assocs., Inc. v. England, 379 F.3d 1334 (Fed. Cir. 2004).

[71] Unicorn Mgmt. Corp. v. United States, 375 F.2d 804 (Ct. Cl. 1967).

[72] See § 7.05[A].

[73] McCormick Constr. Co. v. United States, 18 Cl. Ct. 259 (1989), *aff'd*, 907 F.2d 159 (Fed. Cir. 1990); Clark v. United States, 5 Cl. Ct. 447 (1984), *aff'd*, 770 F.2d 180 (Fed. Cir. 1985).

[74] Umpqua River Navigation Co. v. Crescent City Harbor Dist., 618 F.2d 588 (9th Cir. 1990).

In *Mojave Enterprises v. United States*,[75] a contractor's failure to conduct a reasonable site inspection from which it could have more reasonably ascertained the quantity of rock to be removed resulted in denial of its claim. The court's decision was strongly influenced by the fact that nothing in the bid documents could or did induce the contractor to form an incorrect opinion about the amount of subsurface rock it would encounter. Nothing was represented in a more favorable condition than what was actually encountered. There was no bid document that contained any specific representation or estimate as to the quantity or quality of the excavation required. Because a reasonable site inspection would have uncovered the true nature of the site conditions, the fact that the plans and specifications were defective did not give rise to a claim by the contractor.

Sherman Smoot Co. of Ohio v. Ohio Department of Administrative Services[76] involved construction of a prison. The contractor encountered subsurface soil conditions, which made footing construction more expensive. The Court of Claims denied a claim for differing site conditions, at least in part because the contractor failed to make a pre-bid site inspection. On this point, the Ohio Appeals Court noted that the area where problems were encountered during construction was 15 to 35 feet below the surface, and reversed the lower court's decision.[77]

§ 7.03   MISREPRESENTATION

[A]   Misrepresentation as Breach of Implied Warranty

[1]   Misrepresentation in Plans or Specifications

When an owner makes a representation in either plans or specifications, the owner has an obligation to make the representation accurate. If the owner's representations are not accurate, the owner may have breached the implied warranty that the plans and specifications are accurate and may be liable for misrepresentation.[78] The cases discussed in this section provide examples of instances where courts have held owners liable for misrepresentation where the plans or specifications they supplied proved to be inaccurate.[79]

In *Acchione & Canuso, Inc. v. Commonwealth Department of Transportation*,[80] the Pennsylvania Department of Transportation solicited bids for a contract to perform 13,131 linear feet of trenching. The project involved three different types of trenching; the contractor estimated the cost per linear foot for each type of trenching would be $13, $23, and $52 respectively. Based on the estimated quantities, the contractor's combined bid price was $24 per linear foot.

---

[75] 3 Cl. Ct. 353 (1983).

[76] 136 Ohio App. 3d 166, 736 N.E.2d 69 (2000).

[77] 136 Ohio App. 3d 166, 177-78, 736 N.E.2d 69, 77.

[78] See § 7.02 [A].

[79] **Sections 7.03[B]** and **7.04** go into more detail about claims of misrepresentation based upon affirmative misrepresentation or the owner's failure to disclose material information.

[80] 501 Pa. 337, 461 A.2d 765 (1983).

After the contract was awarded, the state more than doubled the size of the project by adding almost 18,000 linear feet of trenching. The additional trenching was needed due to omissions in the original plans and specifications. The amount of the least expensive trenching increased by almost 50 percent, but the amount of the most expensive trenching needed increased by 336 percent. Despite the changed circumstances, the state denied the contractor's claim for extra compensation.

The Supreme Court of Pennsylvania held that the increased expenses incurred by the contractor to perform the additional trenching was a direct result of the contractor's reliance on misrepresentations in the plans and specifications, thereby entitling the contractor to compensation for the extra work.

In *Gogo v. Los Angeles County Flood Control District*,[81] the contract called for excavation work and construction of a dam. The owner's specifications noted that another company, pursuant to a separate contract with the owner, was performing quarrying operations that would reduce the amount of excavation the contractor would have to perform. According to the specifications, the other company would excavate down to a certain level, and then the contractor would excavate from that level downward.

The contractor performed a site inspection with the district's resident engineer, who showed the contractor the limits of the necessary excavation. Based on the specifications and subsequent representations of the engineer, the contractor estimated that the excavation would consist of 10,000 cubic yards of rock and 52,000 cubic yards of loose material. The contractor submitted a composite bid price of 60 cents per cubic yard for the excavation.

After the contractor bid the job, the other company, with the authorization of the owner, stopped its quarrying operations five feet higher than had been planned. The contractor protested that this created 40,587 additional cubic yards of material, mostly solid rock, which would need to be excavated. The district threatened to sue for breach of contract unless the contractor proceeded with the job. The contractor proceeded under protest and then sued to recover its added costs.

The court held that the district, which knew that the other contractor would stop excavating five feet higher than it represented to the contractor, misled the contractor in the plans and specifications and by the advice given by the resident engineer. The court held that when a public agency induces a contractor to believe that certain conditions actually exist and the contractor relies on that information, the contractor is entitled to recover the value of the extra work necessitated by the conditions being other than as represented.

In *Morris, Inc. v. South Dakota Department of Transportation*,[82] Morris contracted to provide aggregate for a paving project. The state's plans included data on a state option pit, including pit bore data representing the quantity and quality

---

[81] 45 Cal. App. 2d 334, 114 P.2d 65 (1941).
[82] 1999 S.D. 95, 598 N.W.2d 520 (1999).

of material available. Morris used the data supplied by the DOT in preparing its quote.

Once production began at the pit, Morris was unable to produce the required aggregate due to clay seams running throughout the material, which were not indicated on the pit data supplied by the DOT. It was later learned that the data provided by the state was more than ten years old, and the material indicated in the borings had been removed from the pit in the interim. Eventually, the DOT agreed with Morris that the required material was not in the pit and entered into a construction change order to haul rock from another source to blend with the pit material in an attempt to meet project specifications.

The DOT compensated Morris for the additional haul under the construction change order, but refused to compensate Morris for the delays and extra costs incurred in trying to obtain the necessary material from the pit.

The South Dakota Supreme Court held that Morris had relied upon the information furnished by the state to prepare its bid, and that contractors are entitled to expect the data provided to be accurate. The court ruled that the state was not entitled to judgment as a matter of law because the state's use of stale data in the bid package created a question as to whether the state acted in good faith. The court further held that a general exculpatory clause in the bid documents had no effect because the positive specifications made by the state were obviously intended to be used by the bidding contractors in formulating their bids.

[2] Misrepresentation Stemming from Differing Site Conditions

Misrepresentation as a breach of the implied warranty frequently arises in the context of differing site conditions. Construction contracts often include exculpatory clauses where the owner disclaims responsibility for the accuracy of the data it provides regarding the site conditions (a "differing site conditions clause"). When a contract contains a differing site conditions clause, courts sometimes focus on the specific terms of that clause. However, where a contract does not contain a differing site conditions clause (and sometimes even when such a clause is included in the contract) courts apply the concept of implied warranty to determine owner and contractor liability.

The general definition of a misrepresentation of a site condition that gives rise to a breach of the implied warranty of plans and specifications is:

1. The physical condition of the site was materially different from the condition represented in the plans and specifications;

2. The contractor was reasonably justified in relying on the representations by the owner; and

3. The extra costs claimed by the contractor were actually caused by the unexpected site conditions.

The contractor must show that a representation of a material condition was in the contract and that the representation did not accurately reflect the true condition. If the contractor can establish these facts, then the owner is liable for the damages the contractor incurred as a result of relying on the representation.[83]

[3] Sovereign Immunity

As a general rule, government entities are shielded by sovereign immunity from suits stemming from their exercise of discretionary functions. For example, in *Kiska Construction Corp., U.S.A. v. Washington Metro. Area Transit Authority*,[84] the Washington Metropolitan Area Transit Authority (WMATA) contracted with Kiska to construct two subway tunnels in Washington, D.C. The specifications described a potential water level in a tunnel that was substantially different from that actually encountered and, importantly, different from the owner's soil consultant's predictions of what would be encountered. The contractor did not learn of the soil consultant's opinion until after problems were encountered. Kiska brought suit, alleging fraudulent misrepresentation and/or negligent misrepresentation.

The appellate court affirmed the dismissal of Kiska's misrepresentation claims on sovereign immunity grounds. The court ruled that the decision of what to include in the IFB was a discretionary function, and therefore Kiska's claims based on misrepresentation were barred by the doctrine of sovereign immunity.

In other cases, however, courts have held that sovereign immunity does not shield government from claims for misrepresentation or fraud in actions based on misrepresentations in plans or specifications in a construction contract. In these cases, the courts have not held the government entity liable for misrepresentations as such, but instead ruled that the misrepresentation constitutes a breach of the implied warranty of the accuracy of the plans and specifications.[85]

[B] Elements of Affirmative Misrepresentation in Contract

An affirmative false statement of fact in a contract may expose the owner to liability based upon misrepresentation and breach of the implied warranty.[86] To support a claim of affirmative misrepresentation in contract, a contractor must prove five elements: (1) that the owner made an affirmative misrepresentation (2) of material facts, (3) which induced the contractor to enter into the contract, and that (4) based upon the contractor's reasonable reliance upon the

---

[83] Hollerbach v. United States, 233 U.S. 165 (1914).

[84] 321 F.3d 1151 (D.C. Cir.), *cert. denied*, 540 U.S. 939 (2003).

[85] *See, e.g.,* E.H. Morrill Co. v. State, 65 Cal. 2d 787, 793-94, 56 Cal. Rptr. 479 (1967); Arthur L. Sachs, Inc. v. City of Oceanside, 151 Cal. App. 3d 315, 320-21, 198 Cal. Rptr. 483 (1984).

[86] Liability for misrepresentation may also arise as a result of the owner's failure to disclose material information. See § 7.04.

misrepresentation, (5) the contractor suffered harm as a result of the misrepresentation.[87]

[1]   Affirmative Factual Misrepresentation

According to the Restatement of Contracts, a misrepresentation is "an assertion that is not in accord with the facts."[88] Such an assertion may be made either verbally or in writing.[89] The question of whether something is an affirmative or "positive" assertion of fact depends heavily on the particular facts.[90] The cases that follow help illustrate how courts have conducted this type of inquiry.

[a]   Affirmative Misrepresentation Found

In *Midwest Dredging Co. v. McAninch Corp.*,[91] a subcontractor on a highway construction project brought an action against the Iowa State Department of Transportation (DOT) for breach of the implied warranty. One portion of the contract, entitled Special Provision 244 (SP-244), required that the embankment material to be used as support under the pavement of the highway be taken from a site named "borrow C." SP-244 required that the material from borrow C be hydraulically dredged at the borrow site and pumped to the construction site. Before opening the contract to bids, the DOT took 21 test borings to determine the subsurface conditions in borrow C. Based upon these test results, DOT determined that hydraulic dredging and transportation of the embankment material was feasible, and estimated the total contract cost based upon this assumption.

Soon after beginning the dredging project, however, Midwest (the subcontractor hired to do the dredging work) began to encounter problems with rocks too large to fit through their transfer pipes. After a few months, Midwest presented the DOT with a report that borrow C was not hydraulically dredgable. Midwest proposed various alternative procedures, but all were rejected by the DOT. Soon after, Midwest declared insolvency, and sued both McAninch (the general contractor) and the DOT, alleging that its losses on this job contributed significantly to its financial problems. The trial court held in favor of Midwest.

---

[87] *See* Restatement (Second) of Contracts §§ 159 to 172 (1981). Courts may vary on the wording of the elements, but these five represent the basic principles required of affirmative misrepresentation claims. *See, e.g.*, Unnerstall Contracting Co. v. City of Salem, 962 S.W.2d 1 (1998) (describing misrepresentation in six elements: (1) positive representation (2) of a material fact, (3) which is false or incorrect, (4) lack of knowledge by a contractor that the positive representation of the material fact is false or incorrect, (5) reliance, and (6) damages).

[88] Restatement (Second) of Contracts § 159 (1981).

[89] *See, e.g.*, Douglas Northwest, Inc. v. Bill O'Brien & Sons Constr., Inc., 64 Wash. App. 661, 828 P.2d 565 (1992).

[90] Sanders Co. Plumbing & Heating Inc. v. City of Independence, 694 S.W.2d 841, 847 (Mo. Ct. App. 1985) ("what is and what is not a 'positive representation' will always be a question to be answered by the trier of fact case-by-case").

[91] 424 N.W.2d 216 (Iowa 1988).

The appellate court agreed, holding that the DOT had breached its implied warranty. The DOT had not merely provided the test boring results to Midwest, but drew up plans based upon its tests, and required that a specific dredging and piping technique be employed. By so doing, the DOT made a false affirmative representation that material in borrow C could be hydraulically dredged and piped in accordance with its plans and SP-244.

[b] Affirmative Misrepresentation Not Found

In *Burgess Mining & Construction Corp. v. City of Bessemer*,[92] the contractor sued the owner to recover for additional work for the construction of an airport. The contract provided that "the contractor *may* secure topsoil and sub-base material from within the project limits. . . . [t]he contractor *may* obtain this material from within the construction limits of the project." (Emphasis supplied.) The contractor claimed that this provision of the contract was a representation by the city that the contractor would be able to use material from the construction site. The Alabama Supreme Court held that by using the permissive word "may," the contract did not impose liability on the city for the contractor's additional costs if it could not find suitable material on the construction site.

In *Wiechmann Engineers v. California State Department of Public Works*,[93] a contractor sued for misrepresentation and breach of the implied warranty after it discovered subsurface boulders along the length of the project site. The court denied the contractor's claim because the state had not made representations of any kind about subsurface conditions. Additionally, the contractor knew that the state had performed certain subsurface tests, yet did not request any information about what the tests had revealed. Lastly, the contractor's general manager conceded that while visiting the site twice prior to submitting the bid he had noticed boulders along the length of the project, but nevertheless had not asked for information about the subsurface conditions. The court explained "a careless contractor cannot convert his own lack of diligence into a case of fraudulent concealment" and held that the state had not misrepresented factual matters or concealed material information.

[2] Materiality

A false statement of fact in a contract must be material for it to be actionable. Often, the materiality of an assertion will depend heavily on the statement's effect on the economic determinations that led the contractor to enter into the contract. The following case involves a material assertion of fact that led to owner liability.

In *State Road Department v. Houdaille Indus. Inc.*,[94] a contractor brought suit against the Florida State Road Department to recover for additional work done

---

[92] 294 Ala. 74, 312 So. 2d 24 (1975).
[93] 31 Cal. App. 3d 741, 107 Cal. Rptr. 529 (1973).
[94] 237 So. 2d 270 (Fla. Dist. Ct. App. 1970).

during construction of the Everglades Parkway. For five months, the Road Department had four survey crews complete survey work and subsoil investigations in preparation of plans and specifications. Houdaille successfully bid on two projects involving clearing, grubbing, and subsoil excavation work. The plans drafted by the Road Department specified that 408 yards of muck were to be moved, and 622,968 cubic yards of embankment material were to be taken from a borrow canal. However, these estimates were far different from the actual amounts involved. The contractor claimed that it was entitled to recover damages based upon the grossly inaccurate plans and procedures.

The appellate court affirmed a judgment in favor of the contractor, noting that because "the subcontractor encountered muck in quantities astronomically in excess of those represented in the plans," the contractor's entire method of construction operation had to be changed. The court ruled that the failure of the Road Department to procure and submit accurate soil bearings to prospective contractors constituted a *material* false representation in the invitation to bid.

[3]   Inducement to Enter Contract

The material misrepresentation must have induced the contractor to enter into the contract. Whether the contractor is "induced" to enter the contract is a matter of subjective intent, as is whether the party was *in fact* induced to act.[95] Thus, there is likely some interplay between the materiality of the misrepresentation (the second element) and the inducement, because the more material a misrepresentation is, the more likely the contractor was induced to enter into the contract because of that misrepresentation.

The following case is an example of a contractor claiming that he was induced into signing a contract by the fraudulent misrepresentations of the owner. In *Frontier-Kemper Constructors, Inc. v. American Rock Salt Co.*,[96] American Rock Salt Co. (ARSCo), the owner of a salt mine, contracted with Frontier-Kemper Constructors, Inc. to build an extension of the mine. After the owner withheld $3 million in liquidated damages for delayed completion of the project, the contractor brought suit seeking more than $27 million in punitive damages (plus punitive damages) claiming three types of fraudulent inducement. Specifically, the contractor alleged that during contract negotiations the owner: (a) misrepresented the amount of financing it had available to it, (b) misrepresented the manner in which the mine would be constructed, and (c) withheld information concerning problems at the site that would adversely affect construction.

The court rejected the contractor's claims, holding that the defendant's statements regarding the amount of financing it had available to it—even if true—were not actionable, because during the contract negotiations, the owner did not owe a fiduciary duty to the contractor. The court also held that if the owner

---

[95] Restatement (Second) of Contracts § 167 (1981).
[96] 224 F. Supp. 2d 520 (W.D.N.Y. 2002).

changed the requirements of how the mine would be constructed, the contractor's remedy was limited to the change order provision of the construction contract. Lastly, the court found that the contractor's claim that the owner fraudulently withheld information about adverse site conditions was without merit.

[4]   Justifiable Reliance

Inducement to enter a contract alone is not adequate to support a misrepresentation claim if the contractor's reliance on the assertion was not reasonable or justifiable under the circumstances. For example, if the changed condition was foreseeable, then there will be no owner liability for misrepresentation. The following case illustrates this principle.

In *Basin Paving Co. v. Mike M. Johnson, Inc.*,[97] a town requested bids for a waste water and water system project. In anticipation of the project, the town had boring tests performed along the project site and drawings made based on the boring tests. The contractor encountered more rock than it had anticipated based on the town's test results, and filed suit against the town, seeking additional compensation. The contractor asserted that the amount of rock present was a changed condition because it differed from the amount shown in the drawings based on the boring tests. The court, however, decided that the presence of rock in any amount was not a changed condition entitling the contractor to additional compensation. The court found that the town made no representations as to what the contractor would find under the surface, and the contract not only referenced the possible presence of rock, but placed the burden of predicting its presence on the contractor. Prospective bidders also had been advised to examine the pipeline routes carefully to determine the likelihood of encountering rock formations. The court ruled that the contractor could not recover additional compensation for a changed condition if the complained-of condition was foreseeable.

[5]   Harm Caused by the Misrepresentation

A contractor must also prove that it was harmed as a result of the misrepresentation. As the cases throughout this section indicate, the harm alleged is often that the contractor was forced to expend additional resources or time as a result of the misrepresentation.

§ 7.04   FAILURE TO DISCLOSE SUPERIOR KNOWLEDGE

Owners are obligated to disclose superior knowledge of information material to the work. This duty grows out of the implied obligation of good faith and fair

---

[97] 107 Wash. App. 61, 27 P.3d 609 (Wash. Ct. App. 2001), *rev. denied*, 145 Wash. 1018, 41 P.3d 483 (2002).

dealing,[98] and the implied warranty that the owner's plans and specifications are accurate.[99] Owners have an incentive to disclose such information in order to assure accurate bids, but may be reluctant to disclose too much detailed information for fear of triggering claims based upon differing site conditions.[100] Owners generally hedge this risk by providing information, but also attempt to disclaim the contractor's ability to rely upon its accuracy, and require bidders to investigate all material site conditions prior to bidding.[101] Such disclaimers, if interpreted too broadly, could effectively negate contractual differing site conditions provisions, and compel contractors to submit much higher bids than conditions would ordinarily warrant.[102] By the same token, an owner does not become an insurer merely by providing information, and the owner should not be responsible for the contractor's failure to evaluate all material information relating to the work.[103] Resolving these issues involves a fact-intensive inquiry, which often turns upon whether the owner had exclusive control of undisclosed material information, and whether the contractor took reasonable steps to obtain all information important to its bid.

[A] The Owner's Obligation

If an owner possesses superior or special knowledge that is vital to the performance of a contract and that information is unknown or not reasonably available to the contractor, the owner must disclose it. If the owner fails to disclose its superior knowledge, and the contractor is misled as a result, the owner has breached its contract with the contractor.[104] For example, in *Bradley Construction, Inc. v. United States*,[105] the Court of Claims held that the government's implied duty to disclose superior knowledge arises when (1) a contractor undertakes to perform without vital knowledge of a fact that affects the cost or duration of the work; (2) the government is aware that the contractor has no knowledge of and no reason to obtain

---

[98] *See* John Cibinic, Jr. & Ralph C. Nash, Jr., Administration of Government Contracts 184 (2d ed. 1985).

[99] Wiechmann Eng'rs v. California State Dep't of Pub. Works, 31 Cal. App. 3d 741, 107 Cal. Rptr. 529 (1973); J.A. Thompson & Son, Inc. v. State, 51 Haw. 529, 465 P.2d 148 (1970).

[100] *See Owner Disclosure of Superior Site Condition Knowledge,* Constr. Claims Monthly (Sept. 2004).

[101] See §7.05.

[102] *See* P.T. & L. Constr. Co. v. New Jersey Dep't of Transp., 108 N.J. 539, 531 A.2d 1330, 1340 (1987) ("[s]hould we err by giving too much force to the contract documents that would limit recoveries such as those awarded here, bid prices will have to be inflated to cover the risk"); Stenerson v. City of Kalispell, 193 Mont. 8, 629 P.2d 773 (1981).

[103] *See* Cook v. Oklahoma Bd. of Pub. Affairs, 736 P.2d 140 (Okla. 1987).

[104] J.F. Shea Co. v. United States, 4 Cl. Ct. 46 (1983). At least two states, however, do not appear to recognize the superior knowledge doctrine. American Demolition, Inc. v. Hapeville Hotel, LP, 202 Ga. App. 107, 413 S.E.2d 749 (1991) (contractor assumed all site condition risks); Hendry Corp. v. Metropolitan Dade County, 648 So. 2d 140 (Fla. Dist. Ct. App. 1994), *rev. denied,* 659 So. 2d 1087 (Fla. 1995) (owner not liable for undisclosed superior knowledge absent affirmative misrepresentation); *see Owner Disclosure of Superior Site Condition Knowledge,* Constr. Claims Monthly (Sept. 2004).

[105] 30 Fed. Cl. 507, 510 (1994).

such information; (3) any contract specification supplied misleads the contractor or does not put the contractor on notice to inquire; and (4) the government fails to provide the relevant information. Similarly, in *Welch v. State*,[106] the court held that a cause of action for nondisclosure may arise in three instances: when (1) the owner makes representations but does not disclose facts that materially qualify the information disclosed; (2) the facts are known or accessible only to the owner, and the owner knows that they are not known or reasonably accessible to the contractor; or (3) the owner actively conceals information from the contractor.[107] The court held that the contractor did not have to prove an affirmative misrepresentation or intent to conceal to recover for extra work. The mere nondisclosure of information, combined with a statement of facts likely to mislead, is sufficient to state a cause of action for breach of the implied warranty of plans and specifications.

[B]   When Owner's Knowledge Is Not "Superior"

The owner will be liable, however, only when its knowledge is "superior", i.e., when it exclusively controls either the information or the means of acquiring it. The owner generally acquires superior knowledge when it conducts pre-bid studies or analyses,[108] or through its prior control of the project site.[109]

As will be discussed in more detail in **Section 7.05,** bidders will be charged with knowledge of all conditions that would have been revealed upon a reasonable site inspection, regardless of whether the owner specifically discloses the existence of those conditions. In addition, contractors are charged with knowledge of all information equally as accessible to them as to the owner. For example, if a review of municipal records would have revealed material information about the site, the contractor will be charged with knowledge of the contents of those records, even if the owner is actually aware of the information and the contractor is not.[110]

---

[106] 139 Cal. App. 3d 546, 188 Cal. Rptr. 726 (1983).

[107] 139 Cal. App. 3d 546, 555-56; *see* Warner Constr. Corp. v. State, 2 Cal. 3d 285, 293-94, 85 Cal. Rptr. 444 (1970).

[108] P.T. & L. Constr. Co. v. New Jersey Dep't of Transp., 108 N.J. 539, 531 A.2d 1330, 1340 (1987) (N.J. Department of Transportation failed to disclose prior study, not reasonably discoverable by contractor, that revealed that "working conditions at the site would impose unusual difficulties for a contractor.").

[109] Horton Indus. Co. v. Village of Moweaqua, 142 Ill. App. 3d 730, 492 N.E.2d 220 (1986) (municipality failed to disclose thousands of feet of existing drainage tile despite knowledge that, for years, individuals had been improperly tapping into municipal storm sewer); City of Indianapolis v. Twin Lakes Enters., Inc., 568 N.E.2d 1073 (Ind. App. 1991) (city failed to disclose that large obstructions had been dumped into reservoir at the location that became site of dredging under the contract).

[110] Hydromar Corp. of Delaware & E. Seaboard Pile Driving, Inc., JV v. United States, 25 Cl. Ct. 555, *aff'd*, 980 F.2d 744 (Fed. Cir. 1992) (government not liable on superior knowledge claim when dredging contractor failed to examine boring logs explicitly mentioned in contract documents); McCormick Constr. Co. v. United States, 18 Cl. Ct. 259 (1989), *aff'd*, 907 F.2d 159 (Fed. Cir. 1990) (well-drilling contractor was not misled when he had opportunity to obtain information regarding test drilling in project area, but failed to do so).

In *Hardwick Bros. Co. v. United States*,[111] the Court of Claims held that the contractor could not recover on a theory of superior knowledge because the allegedly vital information in the government's possession — old Missouri River channel locations in the levee area, river slope data, complete topographic maps, the Corps's Construction Reference Plane data used for designing river navigation projects, the Corps's General Design Memorandum for the levee construction, indication of swampy areas, drainage data, and rainfall data, as well as other technical data — was either known or should have been known by an experienced and reasonably prudent contractor, or could have been discovered if the contractor had exercised due diligence.

In *J.F. Shea Co. v. United States*,[112] the contractor entered into a contract with the Department of Interior to build an aqueduct. The contractor claimed that it encountered subsurface conditions that materially differed from the "indications" in the contract, causing it to install more steel rib supports in the aqueduct than originally anticipated.

The contractor alleged that the Department of Interior failed to disclose or make available to bidders several prior geological reports. A single subsequent report was made available, but it did not mention the earlier reports. The contractor argued that the report that was made available was misleading because it led the bidders to believe that there were no other reports available, so that the contractor was prevented from acquiring the true facts. The court noted that when the government has superior knowledge it is under a duty to disclose that information, but it went on to say:

> The government is under no duty to disclose information, such as an opinion or conclusion of its geologists, where the knowledge of both the government and the bidder is based on data equally available to both parties and where more conclusive data is available but neither party chooses to obtain it.[113]

These authorities underscore the principle that the owner will not be held liable for the contractor's failure to investigate reasonably information material to its bid, but that the owner will be liable if it withholds material information exclusively within its possession.

§ 7.05   EXCULPATORY CLAUSES

[A]   Site Investigation

A site investigation clause is not, strictly speaking, construed as an exculpatory provision. A site investigation clause generally will not protect the owner

---

[111] 36 Fed. Cl. 347 (1996).

[112] 4 Cl. Ct. 46 (1983).

[113] 4 Cl. Ct. 46, 53; *see* Max Jordan Bauunternehmung v. United States, 10 Cl. Ct. 672, 679 (1986), *aff'd*, 820 F.2d 1208 (Fed. Cir. 1987) (government did not withhold superior knowledge that portions of work could only be performed by specialized subcontractors, when that fact was disclosed in the bid solicitation, and the identities of the subcontractors was in the public domain).

from potential liability for any and all differing site conditions that arise during the project,[114] particularly where the contract also contains changed conditions provisions.[115] Instead, a site investigation clause shifts risks arising from conditions that could have been discovered upon reasonable investigation by the contractor.[116]

What constitutes a "reasonable investigation" depends upon a number of factors, including the circumstances under which the contract was bid, whether the contractor was afforded reasonable access to the site,[117] whether the owner disclosed all material information in its exclusive possession or control,[118] and whether the contractor was afforded sufficient time to make an adequate investigation.[119] For example, in *Frederick Snare Corp. v. Maine-New Hampshire Interstate Bridge Authority*,[120] the parties entered into a contract for building foundations for a bridge over the Piscataqua River connecting Portsmouth, New Hampshire to Kittery, Maine. The advertisement for bids was dated December 2, 1938, with responses due by December 16, 1938. Snare did not receive the bidding plan and contract documents until December 12, 1938. The contract provided as follows:

> Each bidder must inform himself of the conditions relating to the construction and labor under which the work is to be performed . . . . [A]t the time of the opening of the bids each bidder will be presumed to have inspected the site and to have read and to be thoroughly familiar with the Plans and Contract Documents (including all addenda). The failure or omission of any bidder to receive or examine any form, instrument or document shall in no wise relieve any bidder from any obligation in respect of his bid.

The bid documents inaccurately depicted the depth of bedrock beneath the river bed. As a consequence, Snare had to excavate and blast more material than it anticipated, and sought its extra costs from the defendant. The defendant argued that the site investigation clause barred Snare's recovery. The Court rejected this argument and awarded Snare a portion of its extra costs. The Court found that, based upon the short bid period, the government knew that the bidders could not obtain accurate information regarding the condition of the riverbed, and that,

---

[114] United States v. Spearin, 248 U.S. 132 (1918); *see* Welch v. State, 139 Cal. App. 3d 546, 551, 188 Cal. Rptr. 726 (1983).

[115] Frederick Snare Corp. v. Maine-New Hampshire Interstate Bridge Auth., 41 F. Supp. 638 (D.N.H. 1941).

[116] P.T. & L. Constr. Co. v. New Jersey Dep't of Transp., 108 N.J. 539, 531 A.2d 1330, 1335 (1987).

[117] *Owner Disclosure of Superior Site Condition Knowledge*, Constr. Claims Monthly (Sept. 2004).

[118] See § 7.04.

[119] *See* Cook v. Oklahoma Bd. of Pub. Affairs, 736 P.2d 140 (Okla. 1987); *see also* Christie v. United States, 237 U.S. 234 (1915); Alpert v. Commonwealth, 357 Mass. 306, 258 N.E.2d 755, 764 (1970) (21-day bid period not sufficient for contractor to make adequate test borings); Peter Salvucci & Sons, Inc. v. State, 110 N.H. 136, 268 A.2d 899 (1970).

[120] 41 F. Supp. 638 (D.N.H. 1941).

under the circumstances, the site investigation clause did not trump the differing site conditions clause.

A reasonable investigation does not require that the contractor be a trained geologist or other specialized expert, nor does it require that the contractor hire such experts or conduct technical investigation.[121] If, however, a reasonable investigation would have revealed the allegedly differing condition, then the contractor's claim may be barred.

[B] Disclaimer of Reliance on Information Provided by the Owner

Closely related to site investigation clauses are clauses that disclaim the accuracy or completeness of information provided by the owner. One such provision reads as follows:

> Contractor acknowledges that Owner makes no representation or warranties with respect to the accuracy of studies, reports or other information furnished by the Owner, or the information or opinions therein contained or expressed. Contractor further represents that this is not relying on Owner for any information, data, inferences, conclusions, or other information with respect to site conditions, including the surface and sub-surface conditions of the Site and surrounding areas.

The underlying policy of this provision is that information provided under its terms is not part of the contract. Accordingly, if it proves to be inaccurate, the owner cannot be held liable. Some courts have held such disclaimers effective,[122] while others have ruled it ineffective.[123] The courts appear to reach different conclusions based upon their assessment of whether the contractor reasonably relied upon the information furnished by the owner. Whether the contractor's reliance was reasonable depends upon the facts and circumstances of each case. For example, a court may be more inclined to disregard or nullify such a provision when the owner intentionally withholds material information, discloses inaccurate information, or when it is standard practice for the contractor to rely upon information provided by the owner.[124] On the other hand, a court may be more inclined to enforce

---

[121] Flores Drilling & Pump Co., AGBCA No. 82-204-3 (1982); Cook v. Oklahoma Bd. of Pub. Affairs, 736 P.2d 140, 148-49 (Okla. 1987).

[122] Wiechmann Eng'rs v. State Dep't of Pub. Works, 31 Cal. App. 3d 741, 107 Cal. Rptr. 529 (1973) (disclaimer effective where contractor failed to examine test borings to determine subsurface conditions); see Cook v. Oklahoma Bd. of Pub. Affairs, 736 P.2d 140 (Okla. 1987) (disclaimer effective where contractor failed to conduct reasonable investigation, which would have revealed wet soil conditions at project site).

[123] Stenerson v. City of Kalispell, 193 Mont. 8, 629 P.2d 773 (1981) (reasonable inspections would not have revealed any information not contained in the municipality's erroneous plans, and to determine that the plans were inaccurate would have required a resurvey of the entire site); see Jack B. Parson Constr. Co. v. State, 725 P.2d 614 (Utah 1986) (general site inspection clause does not impose duty on bidders to conduct additional testing where reasonable physical inspection appears to confirm the accuracy of the state's specific representations).

[124] See Stenerson v. City of Kalispell, 193 Mont. 8, 629 P.2d 773 (1981).

this disclaimer when it made available all the information it had, and additional information was readily available to the contractor.[125] In such circumstances, the contractor may have a difficult time proving that it relied upon the inaccurate information provided by the owner.

[C] Contractual Disclaimer of *Spearin* Warranty

The implied warranty of plans and specifications survives general contract clauses that disclaims responsibility for the accuracy of information provided by the owner, or that require contractors to examine the site and check the plans.[126] There is a split of authority, however, regarding whether the *Spearin* warranty survives more specific contractual disclaimers.

In *Rhone Poulenc Rorer Pharmaceuticals, Inc. v. Newman Glass Works,*[127] the owner specified a type of opaque glass and listed three manufacturers from whom it could be purchased. Newman acquired the specified glass from one of the listed manufacturers and installed it. Newman's contract provided that its work would be free from faults and defects and required Newman to remove and replace any portions of the work found by the owner to be defective. The opacifier coating delaminated from the glass, but Newman refused the owner's request that the glass be removed and replaced.

The Third Circuit Court of Appeals held that Newman's contractual obligations to remove and replace defective work far exceeded the site inspection or plan review obligations that had been held ineffective to negate the implied warranty. Accordingly, the circuit court held that Newman's contractual obligations trumped the implied warranty.[128]

A contrary result was reached in *Trustees of Indiana University v. Aetna Casualty & Surety Co.*[129] The owner and its architect specified that a certain kind of brick be used in constructing buildings. The contractor warranted that the work would be of good quality, and free from faults and defects, in conformance with the contract documents. The brick proved to be excessively porous, and to have an unusually high water absorption rate, which caused it to deteriorate rapidly. The evidence showed that the defective bricks had been underfired during the manufacturing process. The owner argued that the bricks were suitable as specified, and

---

[125] Wiechmann Eng'rs v. State Dep't of Pub. Works, 31 Cal. App. 3d 741, 107 Cal. Rptr. 529 (1973); J.A. Thompson & Son, Inc. v. State, 51 Haw. 529, 465 P.2d 148 (Haw. 1970); *Owner Disclosure of Superior Site Condition Knowledge,* Constr. Claims Monthly (Sept. 2004).

[126] Spearin v. United States, 248 U.S. 132, 136 (1918); Sherman R. Smoot Co. of Ohio v. Ohio Dep't of Admin. Serv., 136 Ohio App. 3d 166, 176, 736 N.E.2d 69, 76 (1990).

[127] 112 F.3d 695 (1997), *reh'g denied,* 112 F.3d 703 (1997).

[128] The dissent in *Rhone Poulenc* argued that the express warranty extended only to the contractor's own work, and that the contractor should not be held liable if the contractor followed the specifications provided but the results proved unsatisfactory. *See* W.H. Lyman Constr. Co. v. Village of Gurnee, 403 N.E.2d 1325 (Ill. App. Ct. 1980) (suggesting that contractual provisions transferring *Spearin* risk to contractor might be unconscionable).

[129] 920 F.2d 429 (7th Cir. 1990), *abrogated on other grounds by* Watson v. Amedco Steel, Inc., 29 F.3d 274 (7th Cir. 1994).

were merely defectively manufactured. On this basis, the owner argued that the *Spearin* warranty extended only to the adequacy of the specification, not as a guarantee that the particular bricks would be free of manufacturing defects. The Seventh Circuit Court of Appeals held that the trial court did not err in finding that the contractor's express warranty was trumped by the implied warranty of suitability.

While the Seventh Circuit did not fully analyze the disclaimer issue, its holding has been echoed in other cases. For example, in *Charles R. Perry Construction, Inc. v. C. Barry Gibson & Associates, Inc.*,[130] the Florida Court of Appeals held that the contractor only warranted that it would use new exterior siding materials acquired from a specified vendor, and that those materials would be installed in accordance with the manufacturer's instructions. The court implicitly held that the express warranty that all work would be of good quality and free from defects was limited to those portions of the work under the contractor's control, and was insufficient to trump the implied warranty of plans and specifications.

§7.06   CONCLUSION

Examining the language of the contract documents is a critical first step in resolving any construction dispute. The contract language is intended to reveal what the parties intended and how they allocated known and unknown risks. Sometimes, however, the contract documents are incomplete, erroneous, ambiguous, contradictory, or confusing. In addition, there is a substantial, and often conflicting, body of case law interpreting and applying specific contract provisions, as well as implied warranties that arise from the contract by operation of law. These basic legal principles, as applied to specific contracts, may help the parties, mediators, arbitrators, and court bridge the gaps between contract language and expectations that breed disputes.

---

[130] 523 So. 2d 1221 (Fla. App. 1988); *see also* Central Ohio Joint Vocational Sch. Dist. Bd. of Educ. v. Peterson Constr. Co., 129 Ohio App. 3d 58, 716 N.E.2d 1210 (1998) (change order modified express disclaimers and rendered them ineffective to negate implied warranty).

CHAPTER 8

CHANGES RESULTING FROM AMBIGUOUS SPECIFICATIONS

Randall L. Erickson

§ 8.01   INTRODUCTION

The most carefully drafted construction contract often contains numerous ambiguities, particularly in the specifications, which are usually long, detailed, and extremely complex. Ironically, parties' attempts to avoid such ambiguities often create ambiguity. Many factors contribute to such a situation. For example, in trying to delineate carefully each detail of the work to be performed, the parties, who are rushed, often inadvertently use inconsistent terms. Also, efforts to meld terminology from different documents are often the cause of ambiguities.

Invariably, in the initial euphoria of a project, parties cannot imagine that a dispute could arise. In an effort to preserve this perceived cordiality, they often remain silent on issues that, if promptly addressed, would have avoided misunderstandings and disputes later. Further, they usually believe that, if a dispute does arise, they will be able to resolve it without difficulty.

Ambiguities can result from three sources: inconsistent language, unclear language, or an absence of language. In the latter two situations, the ambiguity is likely to be difficult to recognize because each party assumes its interpretation is the only possible one. Although the first situation may seem to be one that only careless drafters would encounter, such a conclusion would be wrong. The detail of the specifications and drawings in the typical construction contract lends itself to minuscule, yet important and often costly, ambiguities. This situation is compounded because lawyers, who typically draft and review contracts, usually lack the technical expertise required to discover and eradicate technical inconsistencies. Indeed, lawyers rarely get involved in reviewing such specifications.

All of these problems are compounded further by the nature of the construction process itself. The time allocated to do everything is incredibly compressed. By the time an owner decides to contract for the building of a project, it is often urgently needed. Construction must begin as soon as possible and be completed without delay. The bidding process is rushed. Contractors and subcontractors often have inadequate time to carefully review specifications and prepare their bids. Moreover, the bidding process provides little or no incentive to discover and resolve ambiguities. It is in the bidders' best interests to simply assume that any possibly ambiguous term refers to the less expensive alternative so that a low bid can be submitted. The assumption is that problems can be resolved later. Therefore, most ambiguities are first discovered and brought to light during the performance stage of the contract, when the parties who have adopted their respective interpretations and priced the contract accordingly have no room for flexibility. The owner does not wish to pay more for something it feels has already been contracted for (and typically cannot afford to do so in any case), and the contractor typically has left no margin for error in its bid.

If the contractor discovers the ambiguity, it will issue a Request for Information to the owner or to the architect, which may demand work the contractor had not anticipated or not included in the preparation of its bid. More typically, however, the contractor will simply commence building in accordance with its interpretation of the contract. The owner will thereafter discover the discrepancy and demand that the work be performed in accordance with the owner's interpretation. In either case, the contractor will issue a change order request to the owner asking the owner to agree to modify the contract and pay the contractor for the additional work. Usually, the owner will deny this request.

At this point, the parties cannot afford the luxury of a long, drawn-out court battle. Substantial delay would cause monumental financial harm to both parties. As a result, the contractor will complete the project in accordance with the owner's demands, and thereafter file a Request for Equitable Adjustment. At that point, the litigation begins.

§ 8.02 DEFINING AMBIGUITIES

The first step for a court in most litigation arising from a Request for Equitable Adjustment is to determine whether the contract is, in fact, ambiguous. Whether a contract is ambiguous is a question of law.[1] Generally, courts will conclude that an ambiguity exists if a contract is reasonably susceptible to more than one interpretation.[2] However, courts apply this test in a variety of ways. For example, in *Community Heating & Plumbing Co. v. Kelso,* the contractor interpreted the contract as requiring conduit sleeves on new manholes only, but the government claimed that the contract required conduit sleeves on some existing manholes as well. The contractor claimed that the contract was ambiguous, but the federal circuit court applied the test for ambiguity rather strictly and rejected the contractor's claim, saying: "That the parties disagree with a specification, or that a contractor's interpretation thereof is conceivable, does not necessarily render that specification ambiguous."[3] The court went on to hold that the appellant's interpretation was not reasonable, and the contract was therefore not ambiguous. It commented that "substantial evidence" supported the government's interpretation, relying in part on the manner in which other bidders interpreted the contract.

Similarly, in *Olander Contracting Co. v. Gail Wachter Investments,*[4] the City of Bismarck, Olander Contracting Co., and Gail Wachter Investments entered into a water and sewer construction contract connecting a ten-inch sewer line from

---

[1] Community Heating & Plumbing Co. v. Kelso, 987 F.2d 1575, 1579 (Fed. Cir. 1993) (citing Newsom v. United States, 676 F.2d 647, 649, 230 Ct. Cl. 301 (1982)).

[2] *See, e.g., id.* ("A contract is ambiguous if it is susceptible of two different and reasonable interpretations, each of which is found to be consistent with the contract language."); Edward R. Marden Corp. v. United States, 803 F.2d 701, 705 (Fed. Cir. 1986) ("It is a generally accepted rule, which requires no citation of authority, that if a contract is reasonably susceptible of more than one interpretation, it is ambiguous."); *but see* Froeschle Sons, Inc. v. United States, 891 F.2d 270 (Fed. Cir. 1989) (criticized *Marden* stating that no reliance on the ambiguous contract term or technical exhibit to the contract was demonstrated); Appeal of Centex Constr. Co., ASBCA No. 33,279, 88-2 BCA (CCH) ¶ 20,541 (1988) (Contract was ambiguous because "[o]n its face, it was susceptible to two different interpretations."), *rev'd without opinion by* Centex Constr. Co. v. United States, 864 F.2d 149 (Fed. Cir. 1988).

[3] 987 F.2d 1575, 1579 (Fed. Cir. 1993), corrected on rehearing Community Heating & Plumbing Co. v. Kelso, 1993 U.S. App. LEXIS 31453 (Fed. Cir. 1993).

[4] 2002 N.D. 65, 643 N.W.2d 29 (S. Ct. 2002), *rev'd and remanded on other grounds,* 2003 N.D. 100; 663 N.W.2d 204 (S. Ct. 2003).

Wachter's housing development to Bismarck's existing 36-inch concrete sewer main and installing a manhole at the connection, to be paid for by Wachter. The contract provided that the engineer may order work done on a force account basis or the city of Bismarck may require the contractor to do work on a force account basis. Olander installed the manhole, but it collapsed within a few days. Olander installed a second manhole, with a larger base supported by pilings, but it failed a few days after it was installed. Olander then placed a rock bedding under the sewer main, replaced 78 feet of the existing concrete pipe, and installed a manhole a third time on a larger base. Olander sued Wachter and Bismarck for damages of $456,536.25 for extra work required to complete its contract. The contract required Olander to "perform unforeseen work, for which there was no price included in the contract, whenever it is deemed necessary or desirable in order to complete fully the work" and provided that "extra work will be paid for." The contract did not define unforeseen work or extra work, and did not specify which party was required to pay for such work. The parties presented plausible arguments for contrary positions. The contract was, therefore, ambiguous. The trial court properly received extrinsic evidence of the parties' ambiguously expressed intentions and properly submitted to the jury the factual questions of whether or not Olander performed extra work for which it was entitled to be paid and, if so, which party or parties were required to pay for it.

When there is only one meaning, however, there is no ambiguity. In *Jowett, Inc. v. United States*,[5] the U.S. Army Corps of Engineers awarded a contract to Jowett, Inc. to construct a three-story air-conditioned office building. Jowett submitted a claim for additional expenses incurred in insulating cold-air supply ducts as instructed by the contracting officer. The contracting officer denied the claim, and Jowett sued for an equitable adjustment. Jowett submitted affidavits from executives at four construction firms disagreeing with the government's interpretation of the paragraph that concerned insulating ducts. The affidavits attested that it was not "standard practice in the greater Baltimore/Washington area" to insulate supply ducts in ceilings. The Court of Federal Claims declined to accord any weight to these affidavits. The contract obligated Jowett to insulate all "supply ducts; return air ducts [and] . . . plenums." However, Paragraph 3.3 excused Jowett from insulating "return ducts in ceiling spaces . . . [and] ceilings which form plenums." There was no term in the contract that had an accepted industry meaning different from its ordinary meaning, nor was there a term with an accepted industry meaning that was omitted from the contract. Jowett had not established that there was an ambiguity in the contract language by reference to trade practice and custom. Affidavits describing a supposedly common industry practice of not insulating air supply ducts in ceilings are simply irrelevant when the language of the contract was unambiguous on its face. It was well established that the government can vary from the norm in the trade when contracting for goods and services. Finally, the affidavits stated that the industry executives would not read this contract as requiring the insulation of the cold-air supply ducts in the ceilings. Jowett

---

[5] 234 F.3d 1365 (Fed. Cir. 2000).

urged that the affidavits showed that the contract unambiguously exempted the ducts at issue from the duct insulation requirement. However, affidavits that those familiar with trade practices in the construction industry would interpret the specifications differently are irrelevant, unless they identify a specific term that had a well-understood meaning in the industry and that was used in, or omitted from, the contract. Jowett's generalized affidavits thus provided no basis for upholding its interpretation of the contract, one that would vary the plain language of the contract. The contract unambiguously required Jowett to insulate the cold-air supply ducts inside the ceiling spaces of the office building.

In *HRE, Inc. v. United States*,[6] a contractor sought to interpret a contract provision that it claimed was ambiguous by resorting to an AIA document that had been used by the contract drafter. This case involved a contract to install and insulate pipe in a federal office building. During performance, the government ordered the contractor to insulate condenser pipe that the contractor had installed but left uninsulated. The contractor performed the work but sought an equitable adjustment claiming that the work was not required under the contract. In particular, the contractor claimed that a provision of the contract did not require those areas to be insulated. However, the Board rejected that argument, concluding that the contract unambiguously required the insulation of those areas in another provision of the contract through the language "unless otherwise specified, insulate low temperature piping." In answer, the contractor argued that the drafting history of an AIA document called "Masterspec," a set of work standards widely used in the construction industry and that had been used in drafting the contract at issue, showed that the drafter of the subject contract had left out a reference to condenser piping. As such, the contractor argued that the failure to include the reference to the condenser pipe in the portion of the contract that was taken from the "Masterspec" meant that the contract's general insulation requirement did not cover the condenser piping, The court refused to allow the extrinsic evidence from the "Masterspec" because there was no ambiguity in the contract. The court held that "outside evidence may not be brought in to create an ambiguity where the language is clear."[7]

Further, in *Appeal of W.G. Yates & Sons Construction Co.*,[8] a contractor sought to recover costs incurred to secure another supplier when the government rejected the contractor's first choice of a supplier. In this case, the contractor had been awarded a contract for the construction of a maintenance hangar under which the contractor was responsible for the design, fabrication, and installation of motorized hangar doors. The contract required that the supplier meet certain specifications including having installed at least ten similar door systems, which were equal to or exceeded specified dimensions, and which had been operational for at least five years. The contractor based its bid on a supplier that had installed several door systems, only three of which were comparable to the dimensions required by

---

[6] 142 F.3d 1274 (Fed. Cir. 1998).

[7] 142 F.3d 1274, 1276.

[8] ASBCA No. 47,213, 98-2 BCA (CCH) ¶ 29,742 (Apr. 29, 1998).

the bid documents. After the contract had been awarded, the government rejected the contractor's supplier because it did not satisfy the bid requirement that the supplier must have installed ten "similar" systems. The contractor argued that the term "similar" was latently ambiguous and should be construed against the government. According to the ASBCA, the term "similar" meant "nearly corresponding; resembling in many respects, somewhat like, and having a general likeness or sameness in all essential particulars." The board concluded that the supplier's interpretation of "similar" was not reasonable because such a reading did not take into account the size of the doors that constituted the supplier's previous projects. The board held that ambiguity does not necessarily inhere where parties disagree over the meaning of a term. The contractor also contended that the "similar" term included both hangar doors and sliding blast doors. The court rejected that, because such an interpretation would not give full effect to each provision of the contract.

At times, however, courts are very lenient in finding that ambiguity exists. For example, in *Edward R. Marden Corp. v. United States*,[9] the federal circuit noted that the appellant's reading of the contract differed from the government's. It then concluded: "These differing views, without more, are sufficient to convince us that there was indeed a[n] . . . ambiguity in the contract."[10] In an even looser analysis, the court in *United States v. Turner Construction Co.*[11] *assumed* that the contract in question was ambiguous, saying, "It is unlikely that this dispute would be before this court if the contract were truly clear." In *Interstate General Government Contractors, Inc. v. Stone*,[12] the court concluded that the contract, which used conflicting terms, was ambiguous because "[t]aken as a whole, the contract fail[ed] to express clearly the intentions of the parties." There was little discussion of whether the conflicting terms reasonably could have been reconciled.

In *Appeal of the State of New Hampshire*,[13] H.E. Sargent, Inc. was the successful bidder on a contract for the State Department of Transportation. The invitation for bids contained a bid item for Common Excavation (Item 203.1), in addition to bid items for the placement of excavated soils in the road embankment (Item 203.6 Embankment-in-Place) and in four designated off-site locations (Item 203.61 Embankment-in-Place, Surplus Excavation Placement). There was a difference of 238,610 cubic yards of soil between that which was to be removed under Item 203.1 and that which was to be placed under Items 203.6 and 203.61. A special attention provision indicated excavation unit prices were intended to reflect the effort to excavate the material only, and were not to include the placement of material. The "surplus" material disposal sites were not intended to provide a location for placement of all surplus material. The contractor was responsible for disposal of any additional surplus excavation. Sargent disposed of 123,719 cubic yards of soil at locations other than at Embankment-in-Place and

[9] 803 F.2d 701 (Fed. Cir. 1986).
[10] 803 F.2d 701, 705.
[11] 819 F.2d 283, 285 (Fed. Cir. 1987).
[12] 980 F.2d 1433, 1434 (Fed. Cir. 1992).
[13] 147 N.H. 426, 790 A.2d 131 (S. Ct. 2002).

the four off-site storage areas designated at the time of the bid. Sargent sought $247,438 for disposal of the material. A DOT hearings officer denied the claim on the basis that Sargent's interpretation of the contract, which permitted payment, was unreasonable. Sargent appealed to a board, which found that Sargent was entitled to be paid because the contract language was ambiguous and should be construed against the state. The state appealed.

Sargent argued that the plain language of the special attention provision required that it include only the cost to excavate soils in Item 203.1 and to provide separate unit prices for the disposal of all excavated material under either 203.6 or 203.61, whether used as fill in the road embankment, deposited off-site in the four designated areas, or taken off-site and disposed of in waste areas subsequently approved by the state. Consequently, it argued that it underbid Item 203.1 because it did not include any costs associated with disposal. The provision made clear that no costs for the placement of material within the project limits or designated waste sites were to be included in Item 203.1, but instead were to be identified separately in bid Items 203.6 and 203.61. In addition, the special provision relating to excavation of embankment items required materials within Item 203.61 to be placed in locations designated in only four specific surplus disposal sites that were to be paid under Item 203.61. Finally, the earthwork summary provided estimated quantities of soil to be excavated or placed under Items 203.1, 203.6, and 203.61. If Sargent were correct in its interpretation, then the estimated number of cubic yards of soil estimated under Item 203.1 should have equaled the number of units under Item 203.6 plus Item 203.61. The estimated amount, however, differed by 238,610 cubic yards of soil between that which was to be removed under Item 203.1 and that which was to be placed under Items 203.6 and 203.61. This difference should have alerted Sargent to its misinterpretation. The contract was not ambiguous when read as a whole. The board's interpretation was unreasonable and its finding reversed.[14]

§ 8.03 METHODS EMPLOYED TO AVOID AMBIGUITY

Parties employ various devices at the contract formation stage in attempts to avoid ambiguities. After litigation has begun, courts read contracts in a manner that resolves as many ambiguities as possible without undermining the clear intentions of the parties.

Parties to construction contracts encounter more opportunity for ambiguity than most contracting parties because construction contracts are lengthy, complex, and usually incorporate detailed specifications by reference. In order to avoid ambiguity that can result from conflicting documents, parties often incorporate a precedence-of-documents clause that predetermines the order of importance of the

---

[14] *See also* United Excavating & Wrecking, Inc. v. Drake Constr. Co., 2002 Ohio 3773 (2002) (contract was not ambiguous that permitted the subcontractor to temporarily store the cinders and later dispose of them at the borrow pit and did not entitle the subcontractor to an additional $7 per cubic yard).

different documents incorporated in the contract. Generally, the precedence-of-documents clause operates to resolve conflicts between specifications and drawings. For example, in *Appeal of Hull-Hazard, Inc.*,[15] the specifications were held to govern where the drawings showed two mirrors in each bathroom while the specifications called for one mirror per bathroom. Similarly, in *Appeal of Colville Contractors*,[16] the specifications required that the contractor install monitoring equipment according to the manufacturer's instructions. However, the drawings indicated installation in a fashion contrary to the manufacturer's instructions. Since the manufacturer's instructions were part of the specifications, the instructions were held to govern. In addition to drawings, a precedence-of-documents clause can operate to subordinate other documents to the specifications. For example, in *Tarlton Construction Co. v. General Services Administration*,[17] the specifications were held to govern rather than a conflicting contract provision that incorporated the National Electrical Code by reference.

When a precedence-of-documents clause is used, parties are more easily able to resolve ambiguities that result from conflicting documents (as opposed to conflicting language within a document, which is not generally impacted by a precedence-of-documents clause). Such an easy resolution provides the parties with a clear-cut method of resolving disputes, avoiding litigation, and therefore limiting legal fees.

However, the precedence-of-documents clause has its drawbacks. First, such a clause is not always effective. Courts usually refuse to apply the clause if the inconsistency between the documents is not a clear conflict. For example, in *Jamsar, Inc. v. United States*,[18] the court upheld the board's decision that refused to apply a precedence-of-documents clause. In *Jamsar*, the work in controversy was shown on the drawings, but no mention of it was made in the specifications. The board held that mere silence in either the drawings or the specifications did not constitute a conflict between them. Because most inconsistencies between documents are not cases of completely incompatible requirements, such a holding substantially decreases the effectiveness of precedence-of-documents clauses.

Another problem with precedence-of-documents clauses is that they are somewhat arbitrary and often do not reflect the true intentions of the parties. For example, an owner may insert a precedence-of-documents clause into a contract, providing that in case of discrepancy between the specifications and the drawings, the specifications control. Many owners will choose the specifications over the drawings in a precedence-of-documents clause because they have more faith in the specifications, which are usually more detailed. However, experience has shown that architects and engineers are more prone to make minor adjustments or clarifications on the drawings, as opposed to the specifications. Indeed, in most instances, neither owners nor contractors (nor their lawyers) can accurately predict

---

[15] ASBCA No. 34,645, 90-3 BCA (CCH) ¶ 23,173 (June 29, 1990).
[16] ASBCA No. 45,157, 96-1 BCA (CCH) ¶ 28,098 (Dec. 18, 1995).
[17] GSBCA No. 10,528, 94-1 BCA (CCH) ¶ 26,279 (July 27, 1983).
[18] 442 F.2d 930, 194 Ct. Cl. 819 (1971).

which of the two should control in any given situation. It is possible that either could reflect the true intentions of the parties (or their designer). Therefore, although precedence-of-documents clauses do lower litigation-related costs by providing a clear standard to follow in case of conflicting documents, they do so at a substantial cost in accuracy and may be inconsistent with real life in the case of specifications and drawings.

Moreover, precedence-of-documents clauses are initially somewhat limited. They take effect only if one document is clearly in conflict with another document but both documents are consistent within themselves. Such situations are rare. More often than not, the confusion emanates from vague or inconsistent language within the document itself.

Parties also use the bidding process to attempt to discover and clarify language that could create ambiguity. Conferences are held among the owners, designers, architects, engineers, contractors, and subcontractors in order to discuss the specifications and raise questions about them. However, as previously discussed, the primary incentives of the bidding process undermine and sometimes even prevent the discovery and clarification of ambiguities.

However, parties to a contract are usually unable to avoid all ambiguity. Two examples of recent unpublished cases illustrate. In the first, a contractor stopped work on a project after the owner filed bankruptcy and ceased payments. Several years later, the property was purchased by a new owner, who then hired the same contractor to complete the work. The contract provided that the contractor "will cause all warranties of work and equipment installed, either existing or to be installed, to be fully operational and that all warranties will apply" and that "all work and building conditions are to be completed in a first class workmanship-like manner." Upon completion of the project, the owner claimed that the contractor had violated those provisions of the contract by failing to replace certain appliances and equipment, saying that because the warranties had run on the equipment, it violated the first provision, and because the equipment wasn't new, it violated the second. The contractor claimed that the contract had not been violated because the overall intent of the contract was *completion* of the project. Moreover, the contractor claimed that the equipment was "first-class" although it was not completely new. These different readings of the contract demonstrate how common ambiguity can be. Almost any provision of a contract can create ambiguity because most language can reasonably be interpreted in many ways.

In the second example, the owner contracted for improvements with a contractor under a contract to which only the two of them were party. Sometime later, the tenant decided to become a party to the contract as well, and the contract was modified accordingly to become tripartite. However, as is often the case when a contract is modified, the specifications were never changed to reflect the modification. They continued to reflect a bipartite alignment. In the end, the oversight created a minefield of ambiguity because it was impossible to determine to whom obligations were owed and who had authority under the specifications.

After litigation has begun, courts use their own methods to avoid a finding of ambiguity. Judges and juries have great freedom to interpret contract language, subject to the plain-meaning rule. According to some commentators, the *plain-meaning rule,* which prohibits judges and juries from looking beyond the contract itself when the language is clear,[19] springs from fear and distrust of judges and juries.[20] The Missouri Court of Appeals applied the plain-meaning rule to deny a contractor's extra work claim in *Chester Bross Construction Co. v. Missouri Highway & Transportation Commission.*[21] The Missouri Highway and Transportation Commission contracted with Chester Bross Construction Co. for highway improvements. The contract required Bross to construct a temporary barricade or gravel slope on exposed pavement edges to prevent vehicles' tires from dropping off of the pavement's exposed edge. Special Provision § 619.4.1 said, "Measurement of edge treatment will be made to the nearest linear foot for the units actually constructed." Standard Specification § 619.5.1 said, "Payment shall include all materials and labor necessary to eliminate the need for [edge treatment] or [to] construct, maintain, replace, relocate, remove and dispose of edge treatment." In its solicitation, the commission indicated that the linear footage of pavement edge treatment needed was 25,951, about one-half of the length of repaving on one side of the road. Bross constructed a wedge slope pavement edge along the length of the project except for side roads and driveway entrances. Bross later removed and disposed of those wedge slopes so that it could grade out a shoulder for the new pavement. Bross then constructed another wedge slope because of the larger drop-off from the pavement to shoulder base. Bross constructed a total of 194,210 linear feet of pavement edge treatment. After Bross completed the pavement edge treatment, the commission increased the contract's quantity of pavement edge treatment to 100,273 linear feet by a change order. Bross later filed a $375,748 claim against the commission for the remaining 93,937 linear feet of pavement edge treatment that it constructed. The commission denied the claim because the additional 93,937 linear feet of edge treatment was reconstruction or actually replacement of edge treatment previously constructed, paid for, removed, and then replaced as a result of the construction methods that Bross chose to employ. Bross sued the commission for breach of contract. The circuit court ruled that Standard Specification § 619.5.1 precluded payment for the additional 93,937 linear feet, because the commission's initial payment for pavement edge treatment included replacement or relocation of the edge treatment. Bross appealed.

Bross believed that "actually constructed" in § 619.4.1 meant that it should be paid for every linear foot of edge treatment that it actually laid down, even when it removed the first edge treatment so it could grade the shoulder and then re-laid an edge treatment. Bross contended that, because the first edge treatment that it constructed had a steeper slope than the second, the second construction was not a

---

[19] Community Heating & Plumbing Co. v. Kelso, 987 F.2d 1575, 1578 (Fed. Cir. 1993) ("[W]here a contract is not ambiguous, the wording of the contract controls its meaning and resort cannot be had to extraneous circumstances or subjective interpretations." (Citation omitted.)), *corrected on reh'g,* 1993 U.S. App. LEXIS 31453 (Fed. Cir. 1993).

[20] *See* J. Sweet, Legal Aspects of Architecture, Engineering and the Construction Process 511 (3d ed. 1985) [hereinafter Legal Aspects].

[21] 84 S.W.3d 149 (Mo. App. 2002).

"replacement." It also contended that the second construction was not a "relocation" because "it was not simply the initial edge treatment moved to a new location—it used a different material and a different quantity of material." The slopes' steepness and the type or quantity of material used did not make any difference. The payment provision specifically said that payment was for "all materials and labor" necessary to replace or to relocate the edge treatment. Regardless of the slopes' steepness or whether Bross constructed them with different or more material, it still was an edge treatment that Bross replaced or relocated because of its construction practices. When Bross constructed the additional 93,937 linear feet, it was replacing the edge treatment by "placing it again" or by "putting it in place of" the previous edge treatment. It also was relocating the edge treatment by "laying it out in a new location." The ordinary meaning of "relocate" was to locate or allocate again: establish or lay out in a new place. The commission's payment for 100,273 linear feet of edge treatment, therefore, included payment for Bross' replacing or relocating the edge treatment. The circuit court properly granted summary judgment for the commission.

However, appellate courts have indicated that language only occasionally is clear enough to invoke the plain-meaning rule.[22] As a result, courts typically consider many factors, including course of performance, custom in the industry, and circumstances surrounding the formation of the contract to avoid a finding of ambiguity. Statements and acts by the parties before the dispute arose can be particularly determinative. Courts, however, will not examine undisclosed intentions of the parties; they may only consider the objective meaning of actual communications.

Courts also use canons of interpretation to understand a contract. A *canon of interpretation* is basically a rule of thumb that applies common sense in order to construe contract terms. One such rule, *expressio unius est exclusio alterius*, provides that, in cases when a contract includes a list of items, only the items on the list are relevant and any item that is not included in the list, but logically could have been, is not relevant. Often, however, such lists are preceded by the term "including but not limited to." Use of this introductory phrase precludes operation of the *expressio unius* doctrine and makes the list useful only as an example. Another canon of interpretation, *ejusdem generis,* requires that the meaning of a general term in a contract be interpreted in accordance with specific examples or drawings that refer to it.

Courts use other seemingly commonsense methods for resolving disputes. For example, if a general provision of a contract is in conflict with a specific provision, courts often assume that the objective intention of the parties is reflected in the specific provision and will resolve the ambiguity in favor of the specific provision. Also, courts attempt, whenever possible, to read contracts in such a way as to give effect to the whole contract, that is, they will assume that no provision of the contract is superfluous or redundant. For example, in *Turner Construction Co. v.*

---

[22] Legal Aspects at 511.

United States,[23] Turner Construction sought $321,424 in damages, as a pass-through claim for its electrical subcontractor for what it contended was an ordered change imposed by the VA Contracting Officer in the operating rooms (ORs) in the medical center addition. The VA maintained that the contract required two-hour fire-rated protection for the emergency electrical system and that, pursuant to the contract specifications and the National Electrical Code (NEC), the feeders and panelboards in the ORs were part of the emergency system. The VA subsequently directed Turner and Richardson to effectuate the required fire protection via mineral-insulated (MI) cable. Turner disputed that the contract called for two-hour fire-rated protection for the OR feeders and panelboards, arguing that the contract drawings evinced a clear intent otherwise. Turner argued that, by negative inference, the drawings demonstrated that two-hour fire-rated protection was not intended for the OR panelboards and feeders. Drawing 1-E37, "Electrical Emergency Power Riser Diagram," had a note that the penthouse emergency feeders were required to change from simple conduit and wire to MI cable prior to penetrating the third floor (containing the ORs). Turner reasoned that because the penthouse-feeder requirement of MI cable was explicit, the lack of such a specific requirement for the OR feeders (in Drawings 1-E37 and 1-E42) was properly construed by both it and its electrical contractor as signifying mere conduit-and-wire feeders, without the two-hour fire-rated protection.

The drawings themselves established that the: (1) conduit wiring referred to wiring size, not fire protection requirements; (2) panelboards in question and their feeder wiring were part of the critical emergency electrical system branch circuitry; and (3) NEC provisions governed the installation of all electrical circuits. Turner ignored the fact that: the penthouse-wiring transition through the OR third floor was evidently a "special condition" (as addressed in Drawing 1-E1); conduit-and-wire designations were ones indicating wiring size (as addressed in Drawings 1-E1 and 1-E37), not fire-protection requirements; pursuant to Specification 16111, two-hour fire-rated protection could be accomplished either by MI cable or within a two-hour rated and approved "enclosure," and therefore, the drawings' references to conduit and wire did not preclude two-hour fire protection, so long as the conduit-and-wire option was within an approved enclosure. The court found no conflict between specific and general terms in the contract, nor any ambiguity on whether the contract calls for two-hour fire-rated protection for the OR panelboards and feeders. The complaint was dismissed. However, on appeal in *Turner Construction Co. v. United States*,[24] the court reversed their finding and remanded with instruction for determination of costs incurred by the contractor to add fire-rated to ordinary feeders, which were not specified in the contract and therefore deemed as a material change to the contract. The specifications were determined to be clear and unambiguous.

However, both of these methods, although sound in theory, can be somewhat arbitrary in practice. Often, the parties' intent is reflected in a general, rather than

---

[23] 54 Fed. Cl. 388 (2002).
[24] 367 F.3d 1319 (2004).

a specific, provision of a contract. In many cases, specific provisions are added as afterthoughts and have not been carefully considered. Likewise, many parts of contracts often are superfluous and redundant, but are left in the contract by careless drafters or in hopes that they will better protect a party's rights. In any event, when courts have used all of the above methods to try to resolve the dispute, yet the objective intention of the parties remains unclear such that the contract is reasonably susceptible to more than one interpretation, an ambiguity exists.

Similarly, courts will imply an obligation of good faith and fair dealing on the parties when interpreting a contract to avoid harsh results. Breach of the implied duty of good faith and fair dealing will support a jury award of breach of contract damages for differing site conditions. For example, in *Environmental Protection, Inspection & Consulting, Inc. v. City of Kansas City*,[25] the City of Kansas City, Missouri awarded EPIC the construction contract on the replacement spillway for the new zoo project. EPIC was required to build a cofferdam to dam up the water to allow excavations for the spillway. Although the walls of the cofferdam held the water back, water seeped from beneath the cofferdam. The seepage required pumping. Through its own investigation, EPIC determined that the water flowed from a layer of porous shot rock under the cofferdam. The city's representatives directed EPIC to remove the rock. EPIC found out about a rock haul road submerged in the lake near the cofferdam. Although the city and its engineers knew of the submerged road's existence, the bidding materials and the contract for the spillway project contained no reference to it. The materials composing the road consisted of packed rock that was porous and allowed water seepage. In its last payment application, EPIC sought payment of $11,080. The city denied the application but recognized that the zoo spillway project was 98 percent complete. On the negligence action, the jury awarded EPIC $40,000 after reduction for 20-percent fault. For breach of contract, the jury set damages at $561,200. Challenging the breach-of-contract judgment, the city asserted its entitlement to a JNOV. When the contractor encountered changed conditions, the contract required a written claim to allow the city to inspect. For the contractor to be entitled to additional compensation, the director had to find that the changed conditions required work not contemplated by the contract. The contractor specified that the director's decision should determine whether the claim was justified, and the Director's decision should be final and binding on the parties. The city argued that EPIC could not prove entitlement under any contractual provision to extra compensation for work caused by changed conditions because the director had sole, absolute discretion to approve or disapprove additional payment. However, the appellate court noted that the city overlooked the good-faith requirement implied in contracts. EPIC presented evidence of the existence of the submerged rock haul road, the city's knowledge of it, and the failure to disclose it in the contract documents and during project consultations. The city urged EPIC to continue its work to complete the spillway, which it did. EPIC provided the city with written change order requests, the majority of which were not approved. The contract's implied

---

[25] 37 S.W.3d 360 (Mo. App. W.D. 2000).

covenant of good faith and fair dealing obligated KCMo to pay for work caused by changed conditions and work not contemplated by the contract. The trial court did not err in overruling the city's motion for JNOV.

§ 8.04   GENERAL RULE: CONTRA PROFERENTEM

When an irreconcilable ambiguity exists, the general rule, often referred to as *contra proferentem,* construes contract ambiguities against the drafter or supplier of the ambiguous language.[26] Courts apply *contra proferentem* whenever there are two differing, reasonable interpretations, regardless of which interpretation is more reasonable. In fact, courts will not engage in any inquiry whatsoever of which interpretation is the more reasonable. The policy and origin for this rule are well stated by Justin Sweet:

> One basis for this guide is to penalize the party who created the ambiguity. Another, and perhaps more important, rationale is the necessity of protecting the reasonable expectations of the party who had no choice in preparing the contract or choosing the language. This rationale has its genesis in the interpretation of insurance contracts. Frequently insureds were given protection despite what appeared to be language precluding insurance coverage. This preference recognizes that insurance policies are difficult to read and understand and the insured's expectations as to protection are derived principally from advertising, sales literature, and salespeople's representations. Giving preference to the insured's expectations may also rest upon judicial conclusions that insurance companies frequently exclude risks that should be covered.[27]

Contra proferentem is applied mainly when one party has clearly been the one to choose the contract term. Generally, in accordance with the policy that underlies it, the rule of *contra proferentem* is not applied to contracts that are heavily negotiated. In cases of extensive negotiation, both parties are deemed to have chosen the contract terminology.

In many cases, parties to construction contracts have chosen to use standard contract forms prepared by the American Institute of Architects (AIA) or the National Society of Professional Engineers (NSPE). When such standard forms are used, courts differ regarding when to apply *contra proferentem* and which factors to consider in making such a decision.

In Legal Aspects,[28] Justin Sweet provides a framework of factors that courts consider in making the determination of whether to apply *contra proferentem* in such cases. Professor Sweet comments that, most importantly, courts look to the

---

[26] *See, e.g.,* United States v. Turner Constr., 819 F.2d 283, 286 (Fed. Cir. 1987) ("Contra proferentem . . . requires that a contract be construed against the party who drafted the document. . . . [It] correctly requires the drafter to use care and completeness in creation of a contract."); Interstate Gen. Gov't Contractors, Inc. v. Stone, 980 F.2d 1433, 1434 (Fed. Cir. 1992) ("The law is well settled that ambiguities in a contract are to be resolved against the drafter of the contract.").

[27] Legal Aspects at 513.

[28] Legal Aspects at 514-15.

surrounding facts and circumstances that led the parties to use the standard agreement. Particularly, if one party chose the agreement while the other was completely unfamiliar with it, courts tend to apply *contra proferentem* against the party who chose the agreement. Second, the courts consider the degree to which the standard form has been changed as an indication of the degree of negotiation between the parties. If any substantial amount of negotiation occurred, courts are reluctant to apply *contra proferentem*. Third, courts consider the intentions and motivations of the drafting organization. For example, the AIA drafts contracts for architects, and the agreements tend, therefore, to favor the architects' interests. Such a factor would sway a court in favor of applying *contra proferentem* against the architect. Finally, courts try to determine the true intention of the parties with regard to the particular clause, if some intention exists. Often, the parties had no intention regarding the clause and may even have been unaware of it. Because these factors are subjective, the cases on point are in disarray, and any case that turns on this issue will be highly unpredictable.

§ 8.05 EXCEPTION FOR GOVERNMENT CONSTRUCTION CONTRACTS: PATENT AMBIGUITY DOCTRINE

The doctrine of patent ambiguity applies to government contracts and is an exception to the general rule of *contra proferentem*. It requires that a contractor investigate any patent ambiguities in a contract before submitting a bid. In other words, it places upon contractors a duty to inquire and provides that a breach of the duty will prevent the contractor from recovering additional compensation for performing work under an ambiguous clause. If a contract is patently ambiguous, the contractor must inquire, regardless of the reasonableness of its interpretation.[29]

The policy for the doctrine of patent ambiguity has been explored by many courts but was most clearly expressed by the court in *Newsom v. United States*:[30]

> The doctrine of patent ambiguity . . . prevents contractors from taking advantage of the Government; it protects other bidders by ensuring that all bidders bid on the same specifications; and it materially aids the administration of Government contracts by requiring that ambiguities be raised before the contract is bid on, thus avoiding costly litigation after the fact.[31]

---

[29] Community Heating & Plumbing Co. v. Kelso, 987 F.2d 1575, 1578 (Fed. Cir. 1993) (citations omitted), *corrected on rehearing*, 1993 U.S. App. LEXIS 31453 (Fed. Cir. 1993). *See also* Conner Bros. Constr. Co. v. Brown, 113 F.3d 1256 (Fed. Cir. 1997) (patent ambiguity existed where specification clearly prohibits placement of conduit in concrete that is less than three inches thick, while electrical drawings show conduit in floor slabs that, according to structural drawings, are only two-and-a-half inches thick).

[30] 676 F.2d 647 (Ct. Cl. 1982).

[31] 675 F.2d 647, 649 (citation omitted).

The court later noted:

> [W]e emphasize the negligible time and the ease of effort required to make inquiry of the contracting officer compared with the costs of erroneous interpretation, including protracted litigation. While the court by no means wishes to condone sloppy drafting by the Government, it must recognize the value and importance of a duty of inquiry in achieving fair and expeditious administration of Government contracts.[32]

In *S.O.G. of Arkansas v. United States*,[33] the Court of Claims expressed similar notions, saying:

> The rule that a contractor, before bidding, should attempt to have the Government resolve a patent ambiguity in the contract's terms is a major device of preventative hygiene; it is designed to avoid . . . post-award disputes . . . by encouraging contractors to seek clarification before anyone is legally bound . . . . In addition to its role in obviating unnecessary disputes, the patent ambiguity principle advances the goal of informed bidding and works toward putting all the bidders on an equal plane of understanding so that the bids are more likely to be truly comparable. Conversely, the principle also tends to deter a bidder, who knows (or should know) of a serious problem in interpretation, from consciously taking the award with a lower bid (based on the less costly reading) with the expectation that he will cry "change" or "extra" if the procuring officials take the other view after the contract is made.[34]

Many courts express similar reluctance to "penalize a contractor because of a contract that was poorly drafted by the government."[35] But they conclude that public policy, particularly the policy of reducing costs in government contracts, requires them to do so.

Courts have construed rather strictly the contractor's duty to inquire regarding patent ambiguities. For example, in *Community Heating & Plumbing Co. v. Kelso*,[36] the court held that the duty to inquire is not satisfied when the reply from the government is nonresponsive: "[i]t is not enough under the duty to inquire that a contractor merely make an initial inquiry."[37] In that case, the appellant read the contract as requiring certain work only on new, as opposed to existing, manholes and related its interpretation very clearly to the government in a letter. The government never responded specifically to that portion of the letter. Because the government never affirmed the appellant's interpretation, the court held that the appellant's duty to inquire had not been satisfied.

---

[32] 675 F.2d 647, 651.

[33] 546 F.2d 367 (Ct. Cl. 1976).

[34] 546 F.2d 367, 370-71.

[35] *See, e.g.*, Interstate Gen. Gov't Contractors v. Stone, 980 F.2d 1433, 1436 (Fed. Cir. 1992).

[36] 987 F.2d 1575 (Fed. Cir. 1993). Community Heating & Plumbing Co. v. Kelso was affirmed in part pertaining to specifications being unambiguous, and reversed and remanded for matters unrelated to specifications.

[37] 987 F.2d 1575, 1580.

[A] Latent vs. Patent

Newsom v. United States[38] declared that the determination of whether an ambiguity is patent or latent "cannot be made upon the basis of a single general rule. . . . Rather, it is a case-by-case judgment based upon an objective standard."[39] The court added that it "is not a simple yes-no proposition, but involves placing the contractual language at a point along a spectrum."[40]

The test for determining whether an ambiguity is patent or latent was most recently discussed in *Stroh Corp. v. General Services Administration*,[41] in which the board said:

> The test for "(w)hat constitutes the type of omission sufficient to put (a contractor) under obligation to make inquiries cannot be defined generally, but on an ad hoc basis of looking to what a reasonable man would find to be patent and glaring." The legal standard under which a prospective contractor is charged with a duty to alert the Government to a patent ambiguity is an objective one:
>
>> Contractors are businessmen, and in the business of bidding on Government contracts they are usually pressed for time and are consciously seeking to underbid a number of competitors. Consequently, they estimate only on those costs which they feel the contract terms will permit the Government to insist upon in the way of performance. They are obligated to bring to the Government's attention major discrepancies or errors which they detect in the specifications or drawings, or else fail to do so at their own peril. But they are not expected to exercise clairvoyance in spotting hidden ambiguities in the bid documents, and they are protected if they innocently construe in their own favor an ambiguity equally susceptible to another construction . . . .
>> "[T]he most critical factor in deciding cases regarding the duty to inquire is the degree of scrutiny reasonably required of a bidder in order to perceive the discrepancy. . . ." [A] contractor has "only a finite time in which to prepare (its) bids and cannot be expected to note every potential problem of interpretation no matter how minor."
>
>> The cases in which the courts and boards have charged a contractor with knowledge of a patent ambiguity usually involve rather clearcut discrepancies, obvious omissions, or drastically conflicting provisions on the face of the contract documents. . . .
>
>> In determining whether an ambiguity created a duty to inquire, the courts and boards have also, when appropriate, considered a variety of other factors, such as the conduct of other bidders, the amount of recovery sought compared to the total contract price, the amount of time available to review the contract documents and prepare a bid, and whether the contractor stood to gain anything of significance as a result of its interpretation.[42]

---

[38] 676 F.2d 647 (Ct. Cl. 1982).
[39] 676 F.2d 647, 649-50.
[40] 676 F.2d 647, 649-50.
[41] GSBCA No. 11,029 (Feb. 24, 1993).
[42] *Id.* (citations omitted).

In *Stroh,* the contractor had contracted with the government to replace an air-conditioning system. A clause in the contract required that the contractor not interfere with the government's use and occupancy of the building. The government later claimed that that clause prevented the contractor from removing the existing air-conditioning system during the summer months. The contractor disagreed, but complied with the government's demand to refrain from starting work until October 15 and claimed damages for delay. The board, commenting that the government's interpretation of the clause in question was "rather subtle," agreed with the contractor that the ambiguity was not patent.[43]

In another case, *Appeal of Centex Construction Co.,*[44] the board determined that the ambiguity was patent because it "would have become readily apparent" upon a visit to the site.[45] In *Centex,* the contract required that buggy walks remain operational at the end of the day. The contractor interpreted that clause as requiring all buggy walks that had been torn down to be rebuilt. However, the appellee claimed that the clause required the contractor to provide temporary lighting for the buggy walks at night.

[B]   Reasonable Reliance

If a government contract contains a latent ambiguity, then the contractor may recover for work performed under it, provided that the contractor can prove it reasonably relied on its interpretation of the ambiguity in preparing its bid. *Fruin-Colnon Corp. v. United States*[46] held that, in order to recover, the contractor must rely on its interpretation *at the time of the bid;* reliance in performance is insufficient.[47] Likewise, in order for a subcontractor's reliance to be imputed to the general contractor, the general contractor must show that the subcontractor relied in preparation of its bid.[48] The court commented that allowing a contractor to recover for reliance during performance would "raise some troubling questions" and could provide the contractor with a windfall.[49]

In *Froeschle Sons, Inc. v. United States,*[50] the court held that if a contractor is itself unaware of an ambiguity or inconsistency, it may adequately establish reliance by proving that a subcontractor relied on the interpretation and there was

---

[43] *Id.*

[44] ASBCA No. 33,279, 88-2 BCA (CCH) ¶ 20,541 (1988), *rev'd without opinion by* Centex Constr. Co. v. United States, 864 F.2d 149 (Fed. Cir. 1988).

[45] *Id. See also* Seville Constr., Inc. v. United States, 35 Fed. Cl. 242 (1996), *aff'd,* 108 F.3d 1395 (Fed. Cir. 1997) (patent ambiguity in drawings concerning fire damper placement accompanied by failure of contractor to seek clarification renders contractor claim for equitable adjustment invalid).

[46] 912 F.2d 1426 (Fed. Cir. 1990).

[47] 912 F.2d 1426, 1429.

[48] 912 F.2d 1426, 1430.

[49] 912 F.2d 1426, 1432.

[50] 891 F.2d 270 (Fed. Cir. 1989). Froeschle Sons, Inc. was remanded with appeal instructions for determination of ambiguous specifications being latent or a patent discrepancy. Matter was affirmed in part wherein discrepancy was determined to be patent, and reversed as to latent discrepancy in plans.

no wide discrepancy in the bids of other subcontractors.[51] The general contractor need not prove that it specifically included that subcontractor's price in its bid.[52] Many cases have refused to allow a contractor to recover even for a very costly ambiguity without a showing of reliance at the time of the bid.[53]

§ 8.06   NOTICE OF OTHER PARTY'S INTERPRETATION

Several cases have held that, regardless of the degree of ambiguity or even of the degree of reliance, notice of the other party's interpretation and failure to object will preclude recovery. For example, in *Service Engineering Co.*,[54] the board said:

> The law is well-established that if, at the time of contracting, one of the contracting parties knows of the other party's interpretation of contract language and fails to question that interpretation, that interpretation will be held to have been adopted as the proper expression of the intent of the parties.[55]

In another case, *East West Research, Inc.*,[56] the board refused to allow recovery because the "appellant was aware of the interpretation of the [Government] representative. . . ." When appellant accepted the award without protest, it adopted the interpretation of the Government.

§ 8.07   CONCLUSION

The focus of this chapter has been on legal outcomes. However, the importance of ambiguities in the real world is that, regardless of how a court may rule, ambiguities create a losing situation for all parties involved. Ambiguities waste an incredible amount of time, money, and energy. They are, even more than most litigable issues, extremely costly. This is so for several reasons. First, they are hidden. At the contract formation stage, parties must expend a huge amount of time drafting and reviewing documents in such a way so as to exclude any possible hint of inconsistency. Second, when they involve specifications, they are extremely technical. Therefore, lawyers are not qualified (generally) to find them. Third, they are highly fact-specific; thus, courts cannot easily dispose of them. (For example, summary judgment is generally not appropriate when ambiguity is involved.) Finally, because resolving them is so time-consuming, ambiguities detract from the resolution of other issues that may be more important.

---

[51] 891 F.2d 270, 272.

[52] 891 F.2d 270, 272.

[53] *See, e.g.*, Edward R. Marden Corp. v. United States, 803 F.2d 701, 705 (Fed. Cir. 1986); Robinson v. Bowen, 867 F.2d 600, 604 (10th Cir. 1989); *but see* Froeschle Sons, Inc. v. United States, 891 F.2d 270 (Fed. Cir. 1989) (criticized *Marden* stating that no reliance on the ambiguous contract term or technical exhibit to the contract was demonstrated).

[54] ASBCA No. 40,272, 92-3 BCA (CCH) ¶ 25,106 (1992).

[55] ASBCA No. 40,272, 92-3 BCA (CCH) ¶ 25,106.

[56] ASBCA No. 30,096, 89-1 BCA (CCH) ¶ 21,422 (1988).

CHAPTER 9

CHANGES THAT RESULT FROM DELAYS AND INTERFERENCES

John S. Mrowiec
Edward B. Keidan

§ 9.01 CONSEQUENCES OF DELAY

The consequences of delay on a construction project can be significant, to both the contractor and the owner.[1] For an owner facing delays on a project, some possible damages include loss of use of the project (which may include both rent for currently occupied premises and lost rental income for the facility being constructed), extended construction administration costs, and the cost of funds (through extended construction loan interest and increased interest rates).

For a contractor or subcontractor, the consequences of delay might include some or all of the following: increased time-related costs such as material or labor escalation, idle equipment costs, additional supervision, site general conditions costs (such as trailer rental, utilities, insurance, and bond), overtime, general and administrative and other home office overhead costs, and interest on delayed revenue. Acceleration and inefficiency costs must also be considered.

§ 9.02 ROUTINE AND INTENTIONAL CHANGES

In most construction contracts, owners retain the right to delay or suspend the work for short periods of time without responsibility for additional compensation to the contractor. In such cases, construction contracts routinely provide that the parties will enter into a change order documenting the minor delay or extension and extending the contract time if the delay is on the critical path.

Parties may also enter into change orders when the contractor's performance is intentionally delayed for value-engineering or cost-saving reasons, and the completion date is extended accordingly by the change order. There are many situations in which the parties, by mutual consent, intentionally delay the contractor's performance in contracts and agree on the consequences, such as an extension of the contract time or additional compensation.

When events occur that delay the contractor's performance, it must be determined whether the events entitle the contractor to a change order changing either the contract price or the contract time, or both, or whether the contractor must bear the consequences of the delay. Generally, if acts of the owner cause the delay, then the delay is usually both excusable and compensable, and the contractor is entitled to a change order both extending the contract time and compensating the contractor for its additional costs due to the delay. If the delay is caused by factors beyond the control of both the contractor and the owner, then the delay is normally excusable but not compensable, and accordingly, the contractor is entitled to an extension of the contract time but not entitled to additional compensation. And if the delay is due to the acts or omissions of the contractor, then the delay is usually neither excusable nor compensable, and accordingly, the contractor is usually not entitled to either an extension of the contract time or any additional compensation.

---

[1] Special acknowledgement and appreciation is given to James J. Myers and Charles B. Molineux, former authors of previous related chapters.

§ 9.03   DELAY, DISRUPTION, AND ACCELERATION

A *delay* is an event that causes increased time of performance and consequently causes the completion date of the contract to be accomplished later than planned. *Disruption,* on the other hand, is a reduction in efficiency caused by an unanticipated event. A disruption can be caused by inadequate site conditions or other similar hindrances that do not necessarily result in an increased time of performance. A contractor encountering disruption may finish the project within the contractually specified completion date, but incur costs from inefficient work sequencing or other costly methods that must be employed to ensure performance of the contract. *Acceleration* is a compression of time to perform work. Acceleration occurs when there is an increase in the rate of performance above that anticipated at the time of contract. While disruption is distinct from acceleration, disruption is frequently caused by acceleration, such that contractors often will make claims for disruption and acceleration (and even delay as well).

A delay can be categorized as either excusable or inexcusable. These two categories are generally defined in the contract. A contract allocates risks, and the contractor will inevitably assume a certain number of these risks. If the delay is created by a risk that the contractor agreed to accept (for example, a mechanical breakdown of equipment) or a delay caused by the contractor (for example, the failure to properly coordinate its subcontractors and suppliers), then the delay will be deemed inexcusable, and if necessary, the contractor might be required to absorb the cost of acceleration or pay liquidated damages. The contractor may also be responsible for costs incurred by subcontractors through a domino effect resulting from the delay.

On the other hand, an excusable delay is caused by the occurrence of a risk that the contractor refused to accept under the contract, or a delay outside of the contractor's control and without the fault of the contractor. An excusable delay justifies an extension of contract performance time, excusing the necessity of meeting the contract's deadline. This entitlement to a time extension is generally predicated on the delay having an effect on the critical path of the schedule. Common examples of excusable delays include late contract award, denial of site access or late notice to proceed, late owner-furnished equipment or work, owner changes, design errors or omissions, unanticipated unusual weather, acts of God, acts of governments, war, and labor strikes.

An excusable delay might, but not necessarily, entitle the contractor to additional compensation. Accordingly, excusable delays are further divided into either compensable or noncompensable delays. Excusable compensable delays generally result from owner-created delays. Such a delay entitles the contractor to both time and money for increased costs resulting from the delay. By contrast, excusable noncompensable delays typically include delays for which no party is at fault. Severe weather provides a classic example of an event frequently categorized as excusable but noncompensable.

Other important issues are the criticality of the delay (critical project delays extend the project completion date), and concurrency (when there are two or more sources of delay during the same time period). And a common barrier to

228

compensable damages for delays is a no-damages-for-delay clause that limits a contractor's remedy to time extensions.[2]

Owners sometimes fail to recognize that the same types of inefficiencies result when a delay occurs and a time extension fails to follow. This type of situation can constitute a constructive change and is frequently called *constructive acceleration*. The classic example of a constructive acceleration occurs when an owner unjustifiably refuses to grant a time extension to offset a delay and, instead, demands that the expanded work be performed within the original contract duration. In order to recover for constructive acceleration, there must be an excusable delay, timely notice provided of that delay, a proper request for a time extension, a refusal or postponement of the decision on that request, an action by direct order or coercion to complete within the unextended performance period, and the contractor must actually accelerate and incur additional costs.

Types of costs incurred by contractors in acceleration typically include premium time and additional supervision, and may also include more home office involvement and/or lost productivity (for example, acceleration may lead to moving the work into less favorable weather conditions).

§ 9.04   CAUSES OF DELAY

The cause of a delay will dictate whether the delay is excusable or inexcusable, and whether it is compensable or noncompensable. The cause of delay can also dictate whether the delay is concurrent and, therefore, requires apportionment. Because the classification of a delay is dictated by its source, the causes of each delay must be defined before the liability and possible damages can be addressed. The conduct of different parties and even nature itself can be blamed as the source of delay.

[A]   Conduct of Another Party

Compensable delay is generally defined as delay outside of the control of the contractor, and within the control of the other contracting party (whether owner or general contractor).

[1]   Owner

When an owner signs a contract with a general contractor, a number of duties arise, including the express contractual duties and implied duties noted below at **§§ 9.05** and **9.06**. The first of these duties to take effect is typically the duty to furnish access to the jobsite to the contractor. Because an owner may have to acquire the land where the project will be built, this duty sometimes proves to be more difficult to fulfill than a layperson might expect. An owner must supply the site

---

[2] See § 9.05[A].

within a reasonable time, or within the time dictated by the contract, or be liable for the resulting delay.[3] Such a breach of contract can also occur if the owner bids the project in phases and the delay of an earlier phase results in an inability of the owner to deliver the site to the next contractor on time.[4] Such delays have been found to be constructive changes or suspensions.[5]

And where the contract does not specify a deadline for the issuance of a notice to proceed, the owner must issue the notice to proceed within a reasonable time.[6] A delayed issuance of the notice to proceed beyond a reasonable time may justify a time extension.[7]

Similarly, a delay in payment or failure to provide financing is the responsibility of the owner.[8] But any delay in payment must be material.[9]

And an owner has contract administration responsibilities that can delay the project. For example, a failure to provide survey information and timely approval of utility relocation may constitute an excusable and compensable delay.[10]

An owner is also required to coordinate its activities. Subparagraph 6.1.3 of AIA Document A201 (1997) specifically incorporates this implied duty into the terms of its standard agreement by providing that the owner shall coordinate the activities of the owner's forces. This duty of coordination exists even (or perhaps especially) where the owner has multiple prime contractors or a construction manager.[11] An owner can also be responsible for delays in delivering materials or supplies that it agreed to provide.[12] In addition, an owner can be responsible for late

---

[3] Howard Contracting, Inc. v. G.A. MacDonald Constr. Co., 71 Cal. App. 4th 3 (2d Dist. 1998); Blinderman Constr. Co. v. United States, 695 F.2d 552 (Fed. Cir. 1982); Walter Kidde Constructors, Inc. v. State, 434 A.2d 962 (Conn. Super. Ct. 1981); Joseph Corman Corp. v. United States, 246 F. Supp. 602 (D. Mass. 1969); Fritz-Rumer-Cooke Co. v. United States, 279 F.2d 200 (6th Cir. 1960).

[4] Worcester v. Granger Bros., 19 Mass. App. Ct. 379, 474 N.E.2d 1151 (1984).

[5] Merrit-Chapman & Scott Corp. v. United States, 439 F.2d 185 (Ct. Cl. 1971); McKee v. United States, 500 F.2d 525 (Ct. Cl. 1974); Baltimore Contractors, Inc. v. United States, 12 Cl. Ct. 328 (1987).

[6] Joseph Corman Corp. v. United States, 246 F. Supp. 602 (D. Mass. 1965).

[7] Indiana & Michigan Elec. Co. v. Terre Haute Indus., 507 N.E.2d 588 (Ind. Ct. App. 1987); U.S. Steel Corp. v. Missouri Pac. R.R. Co., 668 F.2d 435 (8th Cir. 1982); Gasparini Excavating Co. v. Pennsylvania Turnpike Comm'n, 187 A.2d 157 (Pa. 1963); Abbett Elec. Corp. v. United States, 162 F. Supp. 772 (1958); Ross Eng'g Co. v. United States, 92 Ct. Cl. 253 (1940); *see also* Goudreau Corp., DOTCAB No. 1895, 88-1 BCA (CCH) ¶ 20,479 (1988).

[8] Medema Homes, Inc. v. Lynn, 647 P.2d 664 (Colo. 1982).

[9] *See* Graham Constr. & Maint. Corp. v. Village of Gouverneur, 646 N.Y.S.2d 720 (1996) (three-week progress payment delay and owner's refusal to increase contract price for alleged differing site conditions did not justify contractor's termination of the contract).

[10] Horton Indus. Inc. v. Village of Moweaqua, 492 N.E.2d 220 (Ill. App. 1986).

[11] *See* Amp-Rite Elec. Co. v. Wheaton Sanitary Dist., 580 N.E.2d 622 (Ill. App. 1991), *app. denied*, 587 N.E.2d 1011 (1992); Julian Speer Co. v. Ohio State Univ., 680 N.E.2d 254 (Ohio 1997); North Harris Junior College Dist. v. Fleetwood Constr. Co., 604 S.W.2d 247 (Tex. Civ. App. 1980); L.L. Hall Constr. Co. v. United States, 379 F.2d 559 (1966); Hoffman v. United States, 340 F.2d 645 (1964).

[12] Peabody N.E., Inc. v. Town of Marshfield, 689 N.E.2d 774 (Mass. 1998); Arcon Constr. Co. v. South Dakota Cement Plant, 412 N.W.2d 876 (S.D. 1987); Mobil Chem. Co. v. Blount Bros. Corp., 809 F.2d 1175 (5th Cir. 1987); U.S. Fid. & Guar. Co. v. Orlando Utils. Comm'n, 564 F. Supp. 962 (M.D. Fla. 1983); Haney v. United States, 676 F.2d 584 (Ct. Cl. 1982); H. John Homan Co. v. United States, 418 F.2d 522 (Ct. Cl. 1969).

selections of finished goods and unnecessary changes.[13] And, analogous to the duty to coordinate is the obligation to obtain building permits and other licenses.[14]

Another duty implied in law is an owner's obligation to cooperate with the contractor.[15] The duty to cooperate may be breached, for example, when an owner imposes unreasonable testing requirements.[16] This implied duty to cooperate is frequently provided as an express term in a standard contract.

And the owner must manage the changes process. An owner may be liable for delays in issuing change orders,[17] disorderly issuance of change orders,[18] and delays in clarifying the scope of the changes.[19]

Similarly, an unreasonable delay in shop drawing review is generally compensable to the contractor.[20] The AIA Document A201 (1997), Paragraph 3.12.5, requires review of shop drawings with "reasonable promptness."

The most important of all duties imposed on the owner and always expressly provided in every contract is the obligation to pay. Not only could a contractor obtain damages for reasonable costs of shutdown, delay, and start-up caused by late payment, but a contractor can also justifiably suspend performance until paid.[21]

Finally, the owner's interference (action or inaction by the owner that delays the progress of the work) is discussed at § 9.08.

[2] Architect/Engineer

Because the architect/engineer (A/E) represents the owner in a typical design-bid-build construction project, many of the owner-created delays just discussed could be caused by the A/E acting as an agent for the owner. However, the contractor's claims are against the owner and not the A/E.[22] Because the owner

---

[13] Schlothauer v. Gusse, 753 F. Supp. 414 (D. Mass. 1991).

[14] *See* AIA Doc. A201, ¶ 3.7.1 (1997).

[15] Peter Kiewit Sons' Co. v. Summit Constr. Co., 422 F.2d 242 (8th Cir. 1969); Wood v. Lucy, Lady Duff-Gordon, 222 N.Y. 88, 118 N.E. 1082 (1917); *see also* A. Corbin, Corbin on Contracts 640, 654-55.

[16] Haney v. United States, 676 F.2d 584 (Ct. Cl. 1982); Jack Stone Co. v. United States, 344 F.2d 370 (Ct. Cl. 1965).

[17] Santa Fe, Inc., VABCA No. 1943, 84-2 BCA (CCH) ¶ 17,341 (1984); J.A. Ross & Co. v. United States, 115 F. Supp. 187 (Ct. Cl. 1953); Anthony P. Miller, Inc. v. United States, 77 F. Supp. 209 (Ct. Cl. 1948).

[18] Alrae Constr. Co., VABCA-No. 970, 73-1 BCA (CCH) ¶ 9872 (1973); Total Property Servs., ASBCA No. 45,883, 94-1 BCA (CCH) ¶ 26,369 (1993); DeMauro Constr. Corp., ASBCA No. 12,514, 73-1 BCA (CCH) ¶ 9830 (1972).

[19] Jess Howard Elec. Co., ASBCA No. 44,437, 96-2 BCA (CCH) ¶ 28,343 (1996).

[20] Sterling Millwrights, Inc. v. United States, 26 Cl. Ct. 49 (1992); Fehlhaber Corp. v. State, 410 N.Y.S.2d 920 (1978).

[21] *See* AIA Doc. A201, ¶ 9.7.1 (1997); *See* Franklin Pavkov Constr. Co. v. Ultra Roof, Inc., 51 F. Supp. 2d 204 (N.D.N.Y. 1999); White River Dev. Co. v. Meco Sys., Inc., 806 S.W.2d 735 (Mo. Ct. App. 1991).

[22] *See* Edward L. Bledsoe, 04-1 BCA ¶ 32,400 (Nov. 20, 2003) (where owner gave Bledsoe wrong site plan resulting in delay for redesign; Bledsoe entitled to delay damages against owner).

impliedly warrants the adequacy of the plans and specifications given to the contractor, these delays are compensable. In a typical design-bid-build construction project, both the A/E and the contractor have a contractual relationship with the owner but not with each other. Consequently, even when a delay results from defective plans or specifications, a contractor generally cannot seek liability from the A/E because there is a lack of privity.[23]

[3]   Contractor

Contractors are liable for inexcusable delays to both the owner and to subcontractors.[24] Furthermore, if the contract so provides, a contractor must pay liquidated damages. The owner may also be justified in withholding payment[25] or terminating the contract for breach. However, an owner can waive its right to a contractual remedy, and a waiver can be implied by the actions of the owner.[26] Also, as previously discussed, a party generally cannot easily obtain damages for concurrent delays.

Types of contractor-caused delays are numerous and various. A short list of possibilities might include delayed mobilization, delayed submission of bonds, management problems, inadequate resources, failure to coordinate subcontractor's schedules, supply delays, untimely shop drawing submittal, inadequate labor force, and defective workmanship.

[4]   Subcontractors

A contractor is generally responsible for the delays caused by its subcontractors. If the delay is inexcusable and the contractor cannot absorb the delay within the remaining time of the contract, then the contractor will be liable to the owner. The contractor may sue the subcontractor for any resulting damages, but the problem of concurrent delay frequently arises in such claims.

[5]   Suppliers

If a contractor cannot, after reasonable effort, obtain materials, then the consequential delay is generally considered excusable but not compensable. However, the shortage must be unforeseeable, and the supplier must be free of fault. Also, if the supplies are available elsewhere at a higher price, the contractor cannot claim an excusable delay. Added expense does not constitute unavailability.

---

[23] Bonan v. United Pac. Ins. Co., 462 F. Supp. 869 (D. Mass. 1978).

[24] Manuel F. Spence & Son, Inc. v. Commonwealth, 16 Mass. App. Ct. 290, 450 N.E.2d 1105 (1983).

[25] See AIA Doc. A201, ¶ 9.5.1 (1997).

[26] Fanning & Doorley Constr. Co. v. Geigy Chem. Corp., 305 F. Supp. 650 (D.R.I. 1969).

[B] Force Majeure

"Force Majeure" delays are generally defined as events not caused by any of the project participants and outside of their control. These types of delays are typically listed in the contract. In general, these types of delays are excusable but not compensable. In other words, time, not money, is generally the remedy for such delays. Typical provisions excuse delay "beyond the contractor's control," and also provide specific examples of such events.

These types of delays are generally characterized as excusable delays, and entitle the contractor to an extension of the contract time if the delay is on the critical path and consequently delays the end date of the contract. A typical excusable-delay clause is found in the AIA Document A201 (1997) contract:

> 8.3.1 If the Contractor is delayed at any time in the commencement or progress of the Work by an act or neglect of the Owner or Architect, or of an employee of either, or of a separate contractor employed by the Owner, or by changes ordered in the Work, or by labor disputes, fire, unusual delay in deliveries, unavoidable casualties or other causes beyond the Contractor's control, or by delay authorized by the Owner pending mediation or arbitration, or by other causes which the Architect determines may justify delay, then the Contract Time shall be extended by Change Order for such reasonable time as the Architect may determine.

As noted in the AIA provision, examples of force majeure delays include:

(i) "Adverse weather conditions not reasonably anticipatable" or "unusually severe weather."[27] Such weather conditions (a) must have been abnormal, (b) must not have been reasonably anticipated, and (c) must have had an adverse effect on the construction schedule.

Key issues with weather include: (1) How does one distinguish "normal" weather from "abnormal" or "unusually severe" weather?; and (2) How does one measure the impact of abnormal weather on the schedule? Special issues to consider with respect to weather delays are: (a) Do periods of especially good weather offset periods of bad weather?;[28] and (b) What if the days granted at the end of the project are in a less favorable weather season than when the delay occurred?[29]

---

[27] 48 C.F.R. § 52.249.10 (1990); FAR 52.249-10(b).

[28] *Compare* Roger Johnson Constr. Co. v. Bossier City, 330 So. 2d 338 (La. App. 1976) (contractor must demonstrate that it took advantage of good weather period), with Office of Chief of Engineers, Department of the Army, Modifications and Claim Guide, EP 415-1-2 at C-23 (July 1987) (time extension issued for unusual weather in one month even though previous months' weather was better than average).

[29] *See* Urban Planning & Heating Co. v. United States, 408 F.2d 382 (Ct. Cl. 1969) (granting extension with winter days may be inequitable for lost summer days); *see also* J.D. Hedin Constr. Co. v. United States, 347 F.2d 235 (Ct. Cl. 1965) (where government-caused delays force the contractor into more costly operations, compensable).

(ii) labor disputes (may not be excusable if caused by the contractor's unfair labor practices);[30]

(iii) acts of God (generally defined as tornados, hurricanes, earthquakes, fire, severe flood, and the like);

(iv) unusual delays in transportation;

(v) "unavoidable casualty"; or

(vi) "any cause beyond the Contractor's control."[31]

However, there are a few limited exceptions that make such delays inexcusable. If the contractor causes the event to occur, the delay will be inexcusable.[32] Similarly, foreseeability of the event at the time of bid may make the delay inexcusable.[33]

And there are some instances when such delays are both excusable and compensable. For example, while adverse weather is generally excusable but noncompensable, where weather delays push the work into a higher wage period or into winter conditions, the contractor may be entitled to compensation. Similarly, a nonweather delay that forces work into winter conditions may entitle the contractor to compensation.[34]

§ 9.05   EXPRESS CONTRACT PROVISIONS REGARDING DELAY AND SCHEDULING

The general principles listed above can, of course, be varied by the provisions of any particular contract. Some contract provisions related to delays and scheduling include the following:

a. Time is of the essence (and contract time is reasonable). For example, AIA Document A201, ¶ 8.2.1 (1997) states: "Time limits stated in the Contract Documents are of the essence of the Contract. By executing the Agreement the Contractor confirms that the Contract Time is a

---

[30] *See* Cuyamel Fruit Co. v. Johnson Iron Works, 262 F. 387 (5th Cir. 1920).

[31] *See* AIA Doc. A201, ¶ 8.3.1 (1997); *see also* EJCDC Standard General Conditions of the Construction Contract, ¶ 12.03A (1996) (any unanticipated event beyond the control of the contractor); International Institute for the Unification of Private Law (UNIDROIT), 1994 Principles of International Commercial Contracts, art. 7.1.7 (1994). Several courts have found that unavailability of specified materials may fit within this definition. *See* Acton Constr. Co. v. State, 383 N.W.2d 416 (Minn. Ct. App. 1986) (cement shortage was "unforeseen and severe"); J.D. Hedin Constr. Co. v. United States, 408 F.2d 434 (Ct. Cl. 1969).

[32] *See* 48 C.F.R. § 52.249-10 (1990) (fire excusable delay unless caused by contractor).

[33] *See* Codelfa Constr. Party Ltd. v. State Rail Auth., 149 C.L.R. 337 (1982) (contractor not entitled to time extension for inability to work a planned third shift where local law did not permit third shift).

[34] *See* Wilner v. United States, 26 Cl. Ct. 260 (1990).

reasonable period for performing the work." Without such a provision, the time limits may be found to be guidelines, and not contract requirements.[35]

b. "Date of the Agreement." AIA Document A201, ¶ 8.1.2 (1997) states: "The date of commencement of the Work is the date established in the Agreement." A similar AIA provision, at A101, ¶ 3.1 (1997) states: "The date of commencement of the Work shall be the date of this Agreement unless a different date is stated below or provision is made for the date to be fixed in a notice to proceed issued by the Owner." Other similar provisions include a date for the notice to proceed.

c. Substantial Completion. The AIA defines substantial completion, at AIA Document A201, ¶ 9.8.1 as "the stage in the progress of the Work when the Work or designated portion thereof is sufficiently complete in accordance with the Contract Documents so that the Owner can occupy or utilize the Work for [its] intended use."[36] In the absence of a contractual definition, a typical definition by a court includes the concept that the facility is "usable for its intended purpose."[37] The consequences of substantial completion are typically defined by the Contract, and may include payment of final progress payment (possibly subject to a retainage reduction for punchlist), commencement of warranty period, owner assumption of operation and maintenance, owner's right to occupancy, and cessation of owner's delay damages or liquidated damages.[38]

d. Schedule as contract document. Whether any schedule prepared by the owner or contractor is or is not a "contract document" depends on the language of the particular contract. Regardless, the owner's acceptance of the contractor's schedule likely means that the schedule will be used as the contractor's approved plan for performance of the work. Contracts may, but do not always, address requirements for schedule update frequency, scheduling techniques and schedule content (i.e., number of activities, activity codes, manpower and equipment requirements, etc.), and remedies for noncompliance with these items.[39]

---

[35] Burgess Constr. Co. v. M. Morrin & Sons Co., 526 F.2d 108 (10th Cir. 1976); DeSombre v. Bichel, 118 N.W.2d 868 (Wis. 1963).

[36] See AIA Doc. A201, ¶¶ 9.8.2-9.8.5 (1997) for procedures for substantial completion, punchlist, and final completion.

[37] Husar Indus., Inc. v. A.L. Huber & Sons, 674 S.W.2d 565 (Mo. Ct. App. 1984); Ducote v. Arnold, 416 So. 2d 180 (La. Ct. App. 1982); see also United States f/u/b Control Sys., Inc. v. Arundel Corp., 814 F.2d 193 (5th Cir. 1987) (substantial completion occurs "when facility is operationally functional").

[38] See Aetna Cas. & Sur. Co. v. Butte-Meade Sanitary Water, 500 F. Supp. 193 (D.S.D. 1980) (contract may provide that liquidated damages accrue until final completion, but absent such language, liquidated damages cease on substantial completion).

[39] See T. Driscoll & M. Lankenau, Scheduling Specifications—Getting Better or Will Time Tell?, 1 URS Claims Res. (Winter 2004).

In addition to the provisions listed above, many contracts contain "changes" clauses.[40] These clauses allow for equitable adjustment of cost or time of the contractor's performance. Contractors often use these clauses to justify delay costs.

In federal construction contracting, contractor claims for additional compensation for delays frequently are pursued and analyzed under the suspension of work clause found in government fixed-price construction contracts.[41] The federal differing-site-conditions clause[42] might apply in particular situations.[43] In the correct context, the federal contract changes clause[44] also has been utilized to support an award of delay damages to a federal construction contractor who encountered delay caused by owner-ordered changes.[45] Some federal claims courts have stated that the same fact pattern might entitle a contractor to delay damages under both the suspension-of-work clause and the changes clause.[46]

Similarly, in state court construction contracting decisions, many decisions are analyzed under the implied covenant not to hinder or delay.[47] Other decisions invoke the concept of "change."

Contract provisions such as no-damages-for-delay clauses or direct-costs-only for delay clauses vary the general principles that have been developed in the absence of contract clauses.[48]

[A]   No-Damages-for-Delay Clauses and Exceptions

Many owners attempt to include no-damages-for-delay clauses in the prime contract. Although the language used varies, all contain language attempting to preclude the contractor from recovering these types of damages. The effect of these clauses is somewhat offset by strict construction, and by judicially recognized exceptions to the harsh language of the clauses. Because of the harshness of these clauses, courts often will strictly construe these provisions against the drafter.[49]

---

[40] *See* AIA Doc. A201 (1997) at § 7 (including both Change Order and Construction Change Directive provisions).

[41] 48 C.F.R. § 52.242-14 (2004). *See, e.g.,* George Sollitt Constr. Co. v. United States, 64 Fed. Cl. 229, 2005 U.S. Claims LEXIS 52, *8-9 (Fed. Cl. 2005).

[42] 48 C.F.R. § 52.236-2 (2004).

[43] *See, e.g.,* Baldi Bros. Constructors v. United States, 50 Fed. Cl. 74, 78-79, 83, 85 (2001).

[44] 48 C.F.R. § 52.243-4 (2004).

[45] *See, e.g.,* Coley Properties Corp. v. United States, 593 F.2d 380, 385 (Ct. Cl. 1979).

[46] *See, e.g.,* Manuel Bros. v. United States, 55 Fed. Cl. 8, 50 (2002) (contractor denied recovery for failure of proof), *aff'd*, 95 Fed. App. 344 (2004).

[47] *See, e.g.,* Amp-Rite Elec. Co. v. Wheaton Sanitary Dist., 580 N.E.2d 622 (Ill. App. 2d Dist. 1991); Havens Steel Co. v. Randolph Eng'g Dist., 613 F. Supp. 514, 530 (W.D. Mo. 1985).

[48] See discussion in § 9.05[A].

[49] *See* J&B Steel Contractors, Inc. v. C. Iber & Sons, Inc., 642 N.E.2d 1215 (Ill. 1994) (such exculpatory clauses "are enforceable, though they are construed strictly against those who seek their benefit"); U.S. Indus., v. Blake Constr. Co., 671 F.2d 539 (D.C. Cir. 1982).

A no-damages-for-delay clause typically contains language similar to this:

> It is expressly understood and agreed that Contractor shall not be entitled to any damages or compensation from the Owner on account of delay or suspension of all or any part of the Work, Contractor acknowledging that delays are inherent in construction projects and Contractor having assessed that risk and having fully included that risk assessment within the Contract Sum.

Although the clause may be written in different forms, the essence of the clause is the statement that the contractor will not hold a party liable for increased costs incurred because of delay. Some include a further provision that the sole remedy for delay will be a time extension.

By contrast, the AIA does not contain a no-damages-for-delay provision. Instead, at A201 ¶ 8.3.1 (1997), the AIA document states:

> If the contractor is delayed at any time in progress of the Work by an act or neglect of the Owner or Architect, or of an employee of either, or of a separate contractor employed by the Owner, or by changes ordered in the Work, or by labor disputes, fire, unusual delay in deliveries, unavoidable casualties or other causes beyond the Contractor's control, or by delay authorized by the Owner pending arbitration, or by other causes which the Architect determines may justify delay, then the Contract Time shall be extended by Change Order for such reasonable time as the Architect may determine.

And Paragraph 8.3.3 goes on to state: "This paragraph 8.3.3 *does not preclude recovery of damages for delay by either party* under other provisions of the Contract Documents." (Emphasis added.)

The general rule is that no-damages-for-delay clauses are enforceable. However, these provisions are strictly construed against those that seek their benefit. Moreover, such clauses are subject to exceptions. Exceptions vary by state.[50] For example, in Illinois the Supreme Court has found that exceptions exist to the no-damages-for-delay provisions for (i) delay caused by "bad faith, concealment or misrepresentation," and (ii) delay "not within the contemplation of the parties."[51] Delay is "not within the contemplation of the parties" when it is unforeseeable or results from obstructions that do not naturally arise from the performance of the work itself or the subject of the contract. In addition, Illinois Appellate Courts have recognized two other exceptions: (iii) delay

---

[50] *See, e.g.*, Green Int'l, Inc. v. Solis, 951 S.W.2d 384 (Tex. 1997) (Texas recognizes four exceptions: (i) uncontemplated delay; (ii) delay caused by fraud or bad faith; (iii) unnecessarily long delay such that it is abandonment; and (iv) delay not specifically enumerated in clause); United States f/u/b/o Evergreen Pipeline Constr. Co. v. Merritt-Meridian Constr. Corp., 90 Civ. 5106, 1994 U.S. Dist. LEXIS 14882 (S.D.N.Y. 1995), *aff'd in part, vacated in part on other grounds*, 93 F.3d 153 (2d Cir. 1996) (New York recognizes four exceptions: (i) uncontemplated delay; (ii) bad faith; (iii) unreasonable delay amounting to abandonment; and (iv) delay resulting from a fundamental breach of contract).

[51] J&B Steel Contractors, Inc. v. C. Iber & Sons, Inc., 642 N.E.2d 1215 (Ill. 1994); John Burns Constr. Co. v. City of Chicago, 601 N.E.2d 1024 (Ill. App. 1st Dist. 1992).

of "unreasonable duration," and (iv) delay attributable to "inexcusable ignorance or incompetence of the engineer."[52] Similarly, the Wisconsin Supreme Court recognizes three exceptions: (i) "fraudulent conduct of the engineer," (ii) "orders made in bad faith and to hamper the contractor," and (iii) "orders unnecessary in themselves and detrimental to the contractor and which were the result of inexcusable ignorance or incompetence on the part of the engineer."[53] By contrast to Illinois, the Wisconsin Supreme Court has expressly refused to recognize an exception for "delays not reasonably to be expected at the time of contracting."[54]

Other courts have found exceptions for fraud,[55] unreasonable duration,[56] and unintended or uncontemplated delay.[57]

What about contract provisions that do not bar damages for delay, but instead attempt to limit severely the types of allowable damages for delay? A federal court interpreting Illinois law found that the exceptions to no-damages-for-delay provisions should similarly apply to clauses permitting limited recovery of delay damages.[58] However, the court noted that the application of these exceptions should be determined on a case-by-case basis, including an examination of the following factors: (i) the extent of damages recoverable (i.e., the more limited the damages, the greater the likelihood that the exceptions will apply); (ii) the harshness of the result; (iii) who determines the amount of recoverable damages; and (iv) whether the reason for the cause of the delay falls within the parameters of an exception.[59] Other courts are more inclined to enforce these clauses.[60]

In addition, an owner's failure to grant a time extension may constitute a breach of the contract, such that the owner is precluded from reliance on the no-damages-for-delay provision.[61] And in many states, one exception to the no-damages-for-delay provisions is for "active interference," for example, if the delay was caused by the owner's unreasonable actions or bad faith.[62] At the subcontractor level, where the prime contractor provided inaccurate drawings, failed to timely respond to requests for information, changed project managers three times, and

---

[52] *J&B Steel Contractors*, 642 N.E.2d 1215.

[53] First Sav. & Trust Co. v. Milwaukee County, 148 N.W. 22 (Wis. 1914).

[54] John E. Gregory & Sons, Inc. v. A. Guenther & Sons, Inc., 432 N.W.2d 584 (Wis. 1988).

[55] Clark-Fitzpatrick, Inc. v. Long Island R.R. Co., 198 A.D.2d 254 (N.Y. App. Div. 1993); Northeast Clackamass County Elec. Coop., Inc. v. Continental Cas. Co., 221 F.2d 329 (9th Cir. 1955).

[56] United States f/u/b/a Williams Elec. Co. v. Matrix Constructors, Inc., 480 S.E.2d 447 (S.C. 1997); McGuire & Hester v. City & County of San Francisco, 247 P.2d 934 (Cal. Ct. App. 1952).

[57] Clifford R. Gray, Inc. v. City Sch. Dist. of Albany, 277 A.D.2d 843 (N.Y. App. Div. 2000); White Oak Corp. v. Department of Transp., 585 A.2d 1199 (Conn. 1991); Corinno Civetta Constr. Corp. v. City of New York, 502 N.Y.S.2d 681 (1986).

[58] Mellon Stuart Constr., Inc. v. Metropolitan Water Reclamation Dist. of Greater Chicago, No. 93 C 6241, 1995 WL 239371 (N.D. Ill. Apr. 21, 1995).

[59] *Id.* at *8.

[60] *See* Reliance Ins. Co. v. United States, 20 Cl. Ct. 715 (1990).

[61] United States f/u/b Pertun Constr. Co. v. Harvestors Group, Inc., 918 F.2d 915 (11th Cir. 1990).

[62] *Newberry Square Dev. Corp.* v. Southern Landmark, Inc., 578 So. 2d 750 (Fla. Dist. Ct. App. 1991); Peter Kiewit Sons' Co. v. Iowa S. Utils. Co., 355 F. Supp. 376 (S.D. Iowa 1973).

failed to coordinate its subcontractors, a Pennsylvania Court concluded that a sub-contractor's claims were not barred by a no-damages-for-delay provision because of the active interference by the prime contractor.[63] See § **9.08** regarding Interferences.

[B]   The Effect of Change Orders

Not infrequently, the owner and contractor are able to agree that a cause for delay is excusable and thus agree on a change order extending the contract time for the period caused by the delay. Change orders are amendments to the contract. The change order adds or deletes work from the contract, increases or decreases the contract price, and sometimes adjusts the date of completion.

But change orders have another legal effect. They may operate as a "release" or as an "accord and satisfaction." Depending on the language of the change order, a release or accord and satisfaction will preclude the party receiving the increased compensation or time from recovering amounts beyond the amount stated in the change order, because the change order extinguishes the disputed items.

Change orders may act as a bar to additional or future claims for delay damages. Change orders typically contain release language waiving all claims that are the subject of the change order. If a contractor agrees to a change order containing general release language, the contractor may be found to have waived claims for delay damages, even if the delay damages were unknown at the time.[64]

Disputes often arise about whether a change order constitutes full settlement for a delay or interference claim. Sometimes the contractor fails to appreciate the true impact of the delay or disruption at the time of the signing of the change order. Other times, the contractor appreciates the impacts, but the owner disagrees and demands that the contractor sign the change order "now, as is." On some occasions, both parties agree that there will be impacts that they either cannot, or choose not to, quantify presently. They then address these impacts in the change order language.

A contractor forced to sign a change order "now, as is" without any reservation of rights language may claim that it was under duress, such that the change

---

[63] ILM Sys., Inc. v. Suffolk Constr. Co., 252 F. Supp. 2d 151 (E.D. Pa. 2002).

[64] Jackson Constr. Co. v. United States, 62 Fed. Cl. 84 (2004); ILM Sys., Inc. v. Suffolk Constr. Co., 252 F. Supp. 2d 151 (E.D. Pa. 2002) (change order barred later claim for labor overruns); Safeco Credit v. United States, 44 Fed. Cl. 406 (1999); Castle Constr. Co. v. Owens & Wood P'ship, 590 So. 2d 186 (Ala. 1991) (change order for direct costs of extra work waived pre-existing claim for delay that had provided that cost of change could not be determined until the project was complete); Joe Lemoine Constr., Inc. v. United States, 36 Fed. Cl. 4 (1996) (change order altering the sequence of work bars a later time extension request); Progressive Bros. Constr. Co. v. United States, 16 Cl. Ct. 549 (1989); Trembley v. Theiss, 152 A.D.2d 793 (N.Y. App. Div. 1989); Algernon Blair, Inc., ASBCA No. 25,825, 87-1 BCA (CCH) ¶ 19,602 (1987); Bromley Contracting Co., HUDBCA No. 85-969-C3, 87-3 BCA (CCH) ¶ 20,024 (1987).

order should not bar future claims. In *Pellerin Construction, Inc. v. Witco Corp.*,[65] the contractor signed a contract modification that barred future delay or disruption claims. The contractor argued that, at the time it signed the modification, it was running a $1 million operating deficit and had received only one payment in three months. But the court held that the contractor's problems were not determinative of duress. For duress to be found, the court stated, the construction manager must have improperly threatened the contractor. There was no evidence of such threats. In fact, in this case, while the modification was being negotiated, the construction manager paid $1.2 million in progress payments. Thus, the court found the modification to be binding and dismissed the contractor's claims. By contrast, in *C&H Commercial Contractors, Inc. v. United States*,[66] the court concluded that, despite the language of the contract modifications, the contractor's delay claims were not barred. Although the court stated that the language of the modifications "could hardly be more clear" in failing to contain any reservation of rights and in releasing all claims, C&H's president and vice-president testified that the Air Force's contracting officers had repeatedly assured them that they would be entitled to submit a subsequent claim for delay and impact costs, despite the express language in the modifications to the contrary. And one of the Air Force's contracting officers not only testified that she gave those assurances, but this was confirmed in an internal Air Force memo: "We all explained that the clause included in each modification saying that the amount agreed on for the modification was the full compensation was not intended to preclude the contractor's rights to file a future claim, but meant that the amount of the modification represented the equitable adjustment for the particular work identified in the modification. . . ." Under these circumstances, the court concluded that the government's "outrageous" conduct did not constitute an accord and satisfaction, because the modifications were obtained through the government's misrepresentations. Accordingly, the court held that the modifications were voidable to the extent they barred impact and delay claims.

An express, clear reservation of rights can successfully allow the contractor the ability to claim additional delay damages in the future.[67] However, at least one court has concluded that a reservation of rights in one change order may not be sufficient to reserve delay damages where subsequent change orders contained no reservation.[68]

---

[65] 169 F. Supp. 2d 568 (E.D. La. 2001). *See also* Strickland Tower Maint., Inc. v. AT&T Communications, Inc., 128 F.3d 1422 (10th Cir. 1997) (to prevail on claim for economic duress, requires proof of a "wrongful act," which is more than a disparity in bargaining position); Vulcan Painters, Inc. v. MCI Constructors, Inc., 41 F.3d 1457 (11th Cir. 1995) (evidence did not prove economic duress, and settlement and release were clear and unambiguous).

[66] 35 Fed. Cl. 246 (1996); *see also* Williams Trucking Co. v. JW Constr. Co., 442 S.E.2d 197 (S.C. Ct. App. 1994) (where subcontractor entered into release under duress, release was vitiated).

[67] Gainesville-Alachua County Reg'l Airport Auth. v. R. Hyden Constr., Inc., 766 So. 2d 1238 (1st Dist. 2000); Vicari, General Contractor, Inc. v. United States, 47 Fed. Cl. 353 (2000); Valco Constr. Co., ASBCA No. 39,550, 90-2 BCA (CCH) ¶ 22,854 (1990); Wright Assocs., ASBCA No. 3371, 87-3 BCA (CCH) ¶ 20,043 (1987).

[68] John Price Assocs. v. Davis, 588 P.2d 713 (Utah 1978).

And contractors attempting to reserve rights in a change order must do so clearly. Ambiguous language in a change order may not save later impact claims. For example, in *Centex Bateson Construction Co. v. West,*[69] Bateson, the VA, and subcontractors established a "Supplemental Agreement" change order methodology, in which each Supplemental Agreement included the following standard language:

> This Supplemental Agreement constitutes full and complete compensation due to the Contractor for all costs, direct and indirect, resulting from the modifications set forth herein with the exception of the reservations listed below:

> Reference J.W. Bateson Company, Inc. letter dated January 5, 1988 entitled 'Reservation of Rights on Change Orders' and the Senior Resident Engineer's letter dated March 24, 1988 concerning same.

Bateson's January 5, 1988, letter referenced in each Supplemental Agreement attempted a reservation of rights for later "impact costs" claims:

> It should be expressly understood that all Amendments/Modifications will be executed by J.W. Bateson Company, Inc. for full compensation for all money and time associated with the changed work, including all direct and indirect costs, but the contractor expressly reserves the right to seek additional time and compensation at a later date for impact or suspension of work.

> "Impact costs" shall be deemed to include, but not by way of limitation, extended home office overhead; extended job site overhead; idle labor; idle equipment; escalated labor, material and equipment costs; loss of productivity; inefficiencies, dilution of supervision; stacking of trades; extended warehouse and other storage costs, and other time related costs recognized by boards and courts.

The VA's response letter limited the broad nature of the reservation:

> The Veterans Administration does not necessarily agree with our definition/interpretation of "Impact Costs." The Veterans Administration's agreement to the language in your January 5, 1988 letter in no way waives the 10% limitation on overhead related directly to supplemental work.

Bateson's electrical subcontractor, Dynalectric Co., asserted a claim for labor inefficiencies and other impact costs. Bateson sponsored Dynalectric's claims against the VA. The VA denied the claims. After a lengthy hearing, the Veterans Affair Board of Contract Appeals agreed with the VA. The board determined that the Supplemental Agreements served as "accords and satisfactions" for the electrical subcontractor's claims. The board concluded that the Supplemental Agreement reservation language was unambiguous, and that the only fair meaning of the Supplemental Agreement was that only "unknowable costs" were reserved.

---

[69] 2000 U.S. App. LEXIS 16089 (Fed. Cir. 2000) (unpubl.).

Dynalectric's claims either were, or should have been, known at the time of the Supplemental Agreements, according to the Board, and therefore Dynalectric had already been compensated for those costs through the Supplemental Agreements. While the board agreed that the impact on unchanged work was unknowable at the time of the Supplemental Agreements, the Board ruled that Bateson had failed to prove that the VA was liable for those costs.

Bateson appealed to the United States Court of Appeals for the Federal Circuit. In affirming the board, the court specifically noted that the Supplemental Agreements were "often executed after work covered by the Agreement had been completed. Thus, most direct and indirect costs . . . could be included in the Supplemental Agreements." The court agreed with the board that the Supplemental Agreements barred all impact claims that were knowable at the time of the agreements. And with respect to the "unknowable" claims for impact on unchanged work, these were barred because Dynalectric failed to prove such impacts occurred.

Finally, where the parties agree on a change order in resolution of disputed claims, the language of the change order may condition the effectiveness of the contractor's release of other claims on the occurrence of some event, such as actual payment of the compromised amount, within a specified time period. In that situation, if the owner fails to pay within the specified time, the contractor is no longer obligated to accept the compromised amount. The failure of payment will mean the contractor will have its rights renewed to claim the full amount, and the owner will have its original defenses. But what happens when the parties agree to settle for a compromised amount, they sign a settlement "change order," but there is no deadline for payment of the amount, and the owner never pays? In *Dick v. Geiger*,[70] owner and contractor agreed to a change order amount of $3 million on disputed issues. Owner signed the change order and made an initial payment of $350,000 on those amounts, and then filed for bankruptcy. Contractor proceeded with a proof of claim in bankruptcy, and also filed suit against the owners of the company personally. The owners sought to dismiss the claims, arguing that the change order constituted a release, regardless of actual receipt of payment. In interpreting the language of the release, the court held that the change order, while expressly contemplating the possibility of owner's bankruptcy, nevertheless provided for a release, without conditioning that release on actual receipt of payment. Therefore, the court concluded that the claims against the owners of the company personally were barred, and contractor was left only with a claim for the undisputed amount in owner's bankruptcy.

[C]   Constructive Change Orders

Although many delay and interference claims by contractors involve formal written change orders, a written directive (or even an expressed oral directive) may

---

[70] 783 N.E.2d 368 (3d Dist. 2003).

not be required to obtain relief. Courts often recognize the legal fiction of constructive changes and constructive change orders. A constructive change occurs when actions of the owner or its agent imply that the terms of the contract have been altered.

The constructive change doctrine is well established in government contract litigation and fully accepted by the United States Claims Court. "When a contractor performs work beyond the work required under the contract but without a formal change order, and it is perceived that such work was informally ordered by the government or caused by the fault on the part of the government, a constructive change can be found to occur."[71] In *Calfon Construction, Inc. v. United States*,[72] the claims court articulated the standard for a constructive change:

> To recover under the contract's changes clause on the basis of a constructive change—for work beyond that required by the contract, but without a formal change order—the contractor must show that the requirements of the contract were enlarged and that the additional work was not volunteered, but was ordered by a government officer having the requisite authority.[73]

Courts typically will focus on whether or not a delaying event or interference was foreseeable to conclude whether or not the event fell outside the scope of the contract.[74]

While using the above standard, a district court recently found a constructive change had occurred when a contractor, who was selected to deactivate a ship owned by the United States, received the ship in a condition substantially worse than expected.[75] The court noted that the unforeseen condition of the ship enlarged the scope of the contract and that the contracting officer directed the contractor to complete the job. Because the contractor did not volunteer to do the extra work, the contractor was entitled to an equitable adjustment.

This doctrine serves a purpose beyond the obvious intention of providing restitution to contractors forced to perform delayed or additional work outside the contract. "One of the purposes of allowing constructive changes is to ensure that the contractor will proceed with the work pending resolution of disputes."[76] Thus, both the owner and the contractor benefit from the doctrine of constructive change.

In sum, any event that creates a delay will be designated a "change" by operation of law so long as the work was outside the contract, a person of authority nevertheless directed that the extra work be performed, and the contractor did not volunteer its services. Furthermore, a court will typically find that work was outside the scope of the contract if the court deemed the additional work to be unforeseeable.

---

[71] American Line Builders, Inc. v. United States, 26 Cl. Ct. 1155, 1180 (1992).

[72] 18 Cl. Ct. 426 (1989), *aff'd*, 923 F.2d 872 (Fed. Cir. 1990).

[73] *Id.* at 434 (citing Len Co. & Assocs. v. United States, 385 F.2d 438, 181 Ct. Cl. 29 (1967)).

[74] Green Constr. Co. v. Kansas Power & Light Co., 1 F.3d 1005 (10th Cir. 1993).

[75] Olympic Marine Servs., Inc. v. United States, 792 F. Supp. 461 (E.D. Va. 1992).

[76] American Line Builders, Inc. v. United States, 26 Cl. Ct. 1155, 1180 (1992) (citing J. Cibinic & R. Nash, Administration of Government Contracts 321 (2d ed. 1986)).

§ 9.06   IMPLIED CONTRACTUAL DUTIES RELATED TO DELAY

In addition to express contractual provisions, construction contracts contain implied contractual duties that may affect the rights and obligations of the parties when a delay occurs on the project. These implied duties include:

a. The duty not to hinder, obstruct or unreasonably delay performance of the contract. In the context of construction delays, courts often hold that the owner owes this implied duty not to hinder, obstruct, or delay the contractor's work.[77]

b. An implied covenant of good faith and fair dealing. In most states,[78] the courts acknowledge that every contract contains this implied covenant.[79] This implied covenant imposes a duty to cooperate and not to hinder the occurrence of a condition to the other party's performance. For example, a party who benefits from a condition, such as a deadline, must cooperate and not hinder the other's ability to meet the condition.

c. An implied warranty of plans and specifications. In federal government contracts, the owner warrants that the plans and specifications it supplies to a contractor are suitable for the intended purpose, that is, that the plans and specifications, if followed, will result in satisfactory performance.[80] This implied warranty is known as the *Spearin* doctrine, and has been adopted by many states on nonfederal public projects and on private contracts.[81] The implied warranty is not overcome by clauses in the contract requiring the contractor to examine the site, check the plans, or assume responsibility for the work until completion and owner's acceptance. When defective construction documents delay completion of the

---

[77] Luria Bros. & Co. v. United States, 369 F.2d 701, 708 (Ct. Cl. 1966); Bat Masonry Co. v. Pike-Paschen Joint Venture II, 842 F. Supp. 174 (D. Md. 1993); Peter Kiewit Sons' Co. v. Summit Constr. Co., 422 F.2d 242, 257 (8th Cir. 1969); Havens Steel Co. v. Randolph Eng'g Co., 613 F. Supp. 514, 530 (W.D. Mo. 1985); Amp-Rite Elec. Co. v. Wheaton Sanitary Dist., 580 N.E.2d 622 (Ill. App. 2d Dist. 1991).

[78] This is not true for every state. For example, in Indiana, the implied covenant of good faith and fair dealing is limited to contracts for sales of goods governed by the Uniform Commercial Code (which may apply to construction supply contracts) and to fiduciary relationships. *See* First Fed. Sav. Bank of Indiana v. Key Markets, Inc., 559 N.E.2d 600 (Ind. S. Ct. 1990); Morin Bldg. Prod. Co. v. Baystone Constr. Co., 717 F.2d 413 (7th Cir. 1983).

[79] *See* Mellon Stuart Constr., Inc. v. Metropolitan Water Reclamation Dist. of Chicago, No. 94 C 1915, 1995 U.S. Dist. LEXIS 3493 (N.D. Ill. Mar. 20, 1995) (where owner failed to grant adequate time extensions, placed inordinately long holds on essential project activities, inexcusably failed to provide an architect, and failed to approve of shop drawings and to respond to RFIs, the jury could conclude that, singly or in combination, owner had breached the duty of good faith and fair dealing); SCS of Wis., Inc. v. Milwaukee County, 244 Wis. 2d 286, 628 N.W.2d 439 (2001).

[80] United States v. Spearin, 248 U.S. 132 (1918).

[81] *See* W.H. Lyman Constr. Co. v. Village of Gurnee, 403 N.E.2d 1325 (Ill. App. 2d Dist. 1980); Fidelity & Deposit Co. of Maryland v. City of Sheboygan Falls, 713 F.2d 1261, 1271 (7th Cir. 1983) (interpreting Wisconsin law); Connersville Country Club v. F.N. Bunzendahl, Inc., 222 N.E.2d 417 (Ind. App. 1966); Centex Constr. Co. v. James, 374 F.2d 921 (8th Cir. 1967).

contract, the contractor is entitled to recover all costs proximately resulting from the owner's breach of implied warranty.[82] Such a warranty
applies despite the fact that the architect/engineer (A/E) produced the
documents. The delay created by design defects will include the delay
from the defect itself and any additional delay resulting from the time
needed by the A/E to design a correction.[83] However, a court will not
allow a delay claim grounded on defective design plans and specifications unless the contractor follows the documents or can prove that its
deviation, however so slight, did not contribute to the delay. For example, in *Al Johnson Construction Co. v. United States*,[84] a court granted a
time extension for delays created by problems with the access road, but
it refused to grant an extension for a delay caused by a "berm failure."
The plans specified a 22-foot-high berm to be built against coffercells
designed to retain the river during construction. A rainstorm raised the
level of the river before the contractor built the berm to full height. The
berm liquefied and sloughed into the contractor's excavation. The court
stated that because the contractor had not completed the berm, it bore the
"difficult burden" of proving that its nonconformance to the specifications had no logical relationship to the failure of the berm.

d. Failure to disclose superior knowledge. A party may breach the contract
by failing to disclose superior knowledge of facts or information important to the performance of that contract, which the other party could not
be expected to have known.[85]

§ 9.07 CONSEQUENCES OF CONSTRUCTIVE CHANGES DUE TO DELAY

A constructive change of the terms of a construction contract can impact the
performance of the contract in a number of ways. The most obvious consequence
of a constructive change is time overruns. The damages associated with overruns
result from the costs incurred during the delay period and include fixed overhead,
rescheduling costs, equipment rentals, storage costs, finance charges, and wage

---

[82] J.L. Simmons Co. v. United States, 412 F.2d 1360 (Ct. Cl. 1969); Chaney & James Constr. Co.
v. United States, 421 F.2d 728, 732 (Ct. Cl. 1970) (all delays due to defective or erroneous specifications are per se unreasonable and hence compensable); Laburnum Constr. Corp. v. United States, 325
F.2d 451, 163 Ct. Cl. 339 (1963).

[83] *Id.*

[84] 854 F.2d 467 (Fed. Cir. 1988).

[85] *See* Horton Indus., Inc. v. Village of Moweaqua, 492 N.E.2d 220, 227 (Ill. App. 5th Dist. 1986)
(even though contract required contractor to replace all existing underground utilities without additional compensation, whether shown on plans or not, owner's failure to disclose field tile system's
use as sewer and failure to provide survey entitled contractor to recover delay damages); Edward R.
Marden Corp. v. United States, 442 F.2d 364 (Ct. Cl. 1971); Helene Curtis Indus., Inc. v. United
States, 312 F.2d 774 (Ct. Cl. 1963).

increases. A time overrun can also be compounded if a contractor is forced to postpone further construction because the project could not be completed before the occurrence of adverse seasonal weather.[86] To prove these types of damages, a contractor frequently must provide scheduling documentation that utilizes the critical path method so as to demonstrate that the critical path, and not a secondary task with sufficient float, was affected by the change.

A time overrun can also frustrate a contractor's plan of early completion and a resulting bonus. Notwithstanding the possibility of earning a bonus, the primary motivation for completing a project early is to save all the costs listed in the preceding paragraph that are necessary to maintain an active construction force. A contractor may also be attempting to avoid adverse seasonal weather that may likely begin before the project deadline date. Courts recognize that these costs are no less real simply because they occurred prior to a completion date. Therefore, they will allow a contractor to recover such losses. As stated by the district court in *Sun Shipbuilding & Dry Dock Co. v. United States Lines, Inc.,*[87] "Costs due to delay are no less damaging merely because they occur fortuitously before a contract deadline rather than after."

Constructive changes can also result in a loss of efficiency. Because a constructive change by definition is an implied change, it is frequently accompanied by disputes between the contractor and owner. These disputes can create a substantial distraction to supervisors and the trades that can result in a measurable loss in productivity. In addition, a change in the sequence of work can create substantial loss in efficiency and result in damages.[88] A subcontractor may also have a valid claim against a general contractor if the subcontractor is forced to work out of sequence and wait until another trade creates an obstruction that hinders future work in the area.

A contractor may be required to respond to a constructive change by accelerating its work. Constructive acceleration occurs when a contractor is required to accelerate the schedule of a project because an owner demands that the original performance date be met despite the justification of a time extension due to a constructive change. Inefficiencies result from overtime, trade stacking, rescheduling, overcrowding of workmen, the increased cost of requiring materials promptly, finance charges resulting from cash flow burdens, and the failure ever to reach optimal productivity because the reduced time spent on each item prevents a work crew from taking full advantage of the benefits of the learning curve.

§ 9.08 INTERFERENCE

Interference can be any action or inaction by which the contractor's contemplated method of performance is affected. Broadly speaking, this might include change orders from the owner, refusal to allow a method, delays and disruptions,

---

[86] *See* Al Johnson Constr. Co. v. United States, 854 F.2d 467 (Fed. Cir. 1988).

[87] 439 F. Supp. 671 (E.D. Pa. 1977).

[88] Youngdale & Sons Constr. Co. v. United States, 27 Fed. Cl. 516 (1993).

changed site conditions, defective specifications or drawings, and unavailability of equipment or materials. Delay due to unreasonable owner interference is compensable.

[A]   Basic Rule: Contractor Selects Method

The basic rule is that the contractor is free to choose its method of performance of the required work provided that it is not inhibited by the contract. A few examples: (a) a painter may want to paint the second floor from a ladder, from a truck, from a scaffold, or some other method; or (b) a foundation contractor placing concrete below groundwater level may want to use interlocking steel sheeting, a wellpoint dewatering system, soldier beams and lagging combined with pumps, or slurry wall. The choice is the contractor's, and the risks and costs will vary.

The basic rule is slightly qualified in that the method of performance chosen by the contractor must be "workmanlike" and in conformance with industry standards.[89] Thus, the contractor is responsible for compliance not only with state and federal statutes that bear on the safety or labor components of its performance, but also with any requirements written into the contract. In addition to government regulations, contracts also incorporate by reference industry publication to govern the standards of performance. These may specify the types of equipment or time-honored methods that are acceptable for a given job. The experienced contractor recognizes these limitations to its choices of methodology before bidding on the contract.

Even when the contractor's method of performance is allowable within the terms of the contract, it may nonetheless be doomed to fail. An inexperienced contractor may not anticipate costs that a more experienced contractor could have foreseen, for example, availability of low-cost materials was prematurely relied upon,[90] the site may not have been properly inspected prior to bidding, sequencing may have been badly planned, or the method of construction or transportation of materials or labor may have included unnecessary, albeit permissive, risks.

In *D.L. Muns Engineering & Building Contractors*,[91] a subcontractor chose to repair a pier from a poorly anchored floating barge in rough winter weather. Amendments to the contract later allowed a nearby condemned pier to be used as

---

[89] *See* Santa Fe, Inc., VABCA Nos. 1898, 2167, 87-1 BCA (CCH) ¶ 19,527 (1986).

[90] But even experienced contractors must be careful to include any conditions to their bid expressly in the contract. *See* Mat-su/Blackard/Stephan & Sons v. Alaska, 647 P.2d 1101 (Alaska 1983). The contractor had outbid its competitors in a paving contract by relying on rights to a gravel pit near the paving project site. Neighbors appealed to the Zoning Board of Examiners, which then overruled the grandfather rights to the pit, and the contractor had to find another source. The contractor was not relieved of its duty to proceed at the bid price, and could not claim mutual mistake. "The fact that the state knew MBS [the contractor] intended to remove gravel from the Spendlove source does not, without more, show that use of the Spendlove source was an implied condition in the contract between the parties." 647 P.2d 1101, 1105. Of course, in the public contract situation, the conditioning of a bid will usually cause it to be deemed nonresponsive.

[91] ASBCA No. 30,104, 87-2 BCA (CCH) ¶ 19,709 (1987).

a work station once its piles were stabilized. Still, the subcontractor persisted in its risky method and did not even attempt to properly anchor the barge. Its claims for impossibility of timely performance were rejected by the federal board on the grounds that alternate methods of performance were available and that the contractor assumed the risk when it contemplated using the barge prior to bidding.[92] The subcontractor also made a bad decision about the method of driving sheet piles. It began at the outer edge of the pier. Not until the waves had knocked down the sheet pile did the subcontractor begin working from shoreside outward.[93] Having noted the general point that method is usually a matter of contractor choice, it is also important to note a few related points:

1. The method must be in accordance with good construction practice. This is a concept that obviously changes as the industry changes. What was once acceptable may not be acceptable today.

2. The method must be in accordance with contract requirements. These requirements might address design questions, even indirectly. For example, a complicated steel truss roof structure can possibly be assembled on the ground, but placing it in position might require special handling to avoid stresses for which, however temporary, the steel has not been designed.

3. A method might be directed by the contract or merely recommended. Varying from the directed method would require a contract change. Even if the contractor's work is usable, if it does not comply with a contract requirement it may be rejected or ordered redone.[94]

[B] Reasonable Interpretation of Contract

Most contracts impose parameters within which the contractor must choose its method of performance. Frequently, the subject of litigation is whether the chosen method of performance is within a reasonable interpretation of the contract. For example, in *Santa Fe, Inc.,*[95] a contractor had to install approximately 5,000 light fixtures and hoped to save time and labor by using a powder-actuated stud gun to shoot studs one-and-a-half inches into the underside of prestressed concrete joists and beams in a concrete ceiling. The resident engineer consulted with the manufacturer of the prestressed beams and joints, who indicated that "it would not be responsible for the prestressed members if studs were shot into the bottoms thereof."[96] The prohibition of the contractor's method was affirmed by the senior resident engineer. When the contractor then came up with an alternate method of

---

[92] *Id.* at 99,808.

[93] *Id.* When the prime contractor terminated the subcontractor and took over the work, it used a "leapfrog" method of working landward to seaward.

[94] *See* Allen & Whalen, Inc. v. United States, 172 Ct. Cl. 603 (1965).

[95] VABCA Nos. 1898, 2167, 87-1 BCA (CCH) ¶ 19,527 (1986).

[96] *Id.* at 98,696.

performance, its claim for a price increase and time extension was denied. On appeal, however, the board held that (1) it was acceptable industry practice to shoot prestressed joists with a powder-actuated stud gun; (2) the contract drawings and specifications did not prohibit this method; and (3) the "government could elect to hold appellant to a stricter standard, but it must, accordingly, compensate the contractor for its extra work."[97]

[C] Interference by Owner/Government

The owner always has an incentive to keep a tight rein on costs. The owner seeks to prevent inefficiency and to make sure that all requirements for the pre-scribed quality of workmanship and materials are being properly implemented—in short, to get the job done right the first time. This incentive may motivate the owner to interfere with the method of performance that the contractor has chosen.

The general rule, as expressed by a federal board of contract appeals, is that "improper *imposition* of a specific method of performing contract work, or improperly *restricting* a contractor's choice of methods, which increases a con-tractor's costs, constitutes a constructive change for which an equitable adjustment is required."[98] Complementarily, "[w]here a particular method of performance is *permitted* by the terms of the contract, and the Government *rejects* that method, any resultant extra costs are compensable as a constructive change to that con-tract."[99] The case of *Harold Bailey Painting Co.*[100] provides an example. A con-tractor chose spray painting as its method of performance, only to receive objections from the government, which then *directed* that rollers be used. The court held for the contractor, stating:

> In the absence of a contract provision prohibiting painting by spraying, appel-lant *could* accomplish its painting work by either rolling or spraying. To require appellant to paint by rolling is to change appellant's method of per-formance to a more expensive one. To the extent appellant incurred additional costs as a result of being required to do so, it is entitled to an equitable adjust-ment under the "Changes" clause.[101]

---

[97] *Id.* at 98,698. *See also id.* at 98,697: "The Government may impose a standard on the contrac-tor that is different or stricter than the industry standard, but it must do so with specificity in the con-tract itself." (quoting WRB Corp. v. United States, 183 Ct. Cl. 409 (1968); Tufano Contracting Corp. v. United States, 174 Ct. Cl. 398, 356 F.2d 535 (1966)); "The government may of course hold a con-tractor to a method of performance not specified in the contract, but if it does so the government has changed the contract and must compensate the contractor for any extra costs it incurs in performing the change." (quoting Erickson Air Crane, 83-1 BCA (CCH) ¶ 16,145 at 80,213 (1983); Otto Randolph, Inc., ASBCA No. 11,539, 66-2 BCA (CCH) ¶ 5928 (1966)).

[98] Long Servs. Corp., PSBCA No. 1606, 87-3 BCA (CCH) ¶ 20,109 (1987) (citing Bill Wright Painting & Decorating, Inc., ASBCA No. 33,343, 87-1 BCA (CCH) ¶ 19,666 (1987); Otto Randolph, Inc., ASBCA No. 11,539, 66-2 BCA (CCH) ¶ 5928 (1966)).

[99] Warren Oliver Co., VABCA Nos. 1657, 1807, 87-3 BCA (CCH) ¶ 19,977 at 101,227 (1987) (citing J.B. Williams Co. v. United States, 196 Ct. Cl. 491, 450 F.2d 1379 (1971)).

[100] ASBCA No. 27,064, 87-1 BCA (CCH) ¶ 19,601 (1987).

[101] *Id.* at 99,172 (citing CWC, Inc., ASBCA No. 28,847, 84-2 BCA (CCH) ¶ 17,282 (1984)).

Objecting to the equipment to be used on a job is but one form of interference with the contractor's method of performance. Interference with contractor's personnel, subcontractors, or trades may also be deemed interference. Of course, the ultimate interference by the owner would be to terminate the contract.[102]

Interference by *third* parties, such as environmentalists, may or may not lead to some owner liability depending, of course, upon superior knowledge, contract provisions, and degree of cooperation by the owner with the contractor. When that interference leads to a delay, for example, pushing summer foundation work into winter, the contractor's methods of doing work (protecting concrete pours, and so forth) will be affected.

One of the motives for interference by the owner is the prospect of figuring out a shorter critical path for performance. A directed change in the contractor's method of performance that results in greater efficiency can lead to a "deductive change order." The owner can subtract from the accepted bid amount any savings that the contractor realizes as a result of the ameliorative interference. Therefore, if worker-hours, materials expenses, or other costs are decreased by the interference, the owner can pay less than the contract price when it proves that the savings resulted from its change orders. This is also known as a "downward adjustment."

Unfortunately, however, the interference often has the opposite effect, namely, disruption, delays, and increased expense to the interfering party. The low-bid system can lead to a method of performance where the labor, equipment, and sequencing are tightly figured with little room for error. Under such circumstances, there is limited elasticity to rebound from a change order, and the contractor may be forced to abandon its chosen method of performance entirely. The likely result is additional expense not only to start anew, but also to compensate the contractor's efforts prior to the change order.

If the designer's determination of the cost is not reasonable, the contractor may successfully challenge it. For example, in *RaDec v. School District*,[103] a contractor was permitted to recover additional payment for earthwork, because an architect's determination that the cost of the revised sitework plan reduced the contract amount was patently erroneous and equivalent to bad faith, according to the Supreme Court of Nebraska.

The contract provided that the costs of changes were to be determined by the architect. The architect revised the earthwork plan so that no fill dirt would be needed at the site, rejected the contractor's proposed credits due to the change, and issued a unilateral change deducting $189,000 from the contract. The contractor sued, claiming $85,000 additional payment for the change. The trial court awarded $80,269.

---

[102] *See* Richerson Constr., Inc., GSBCA Nos. 11,161, 11,263 (11,045)-Rein, 11,430, 93-1 BCA (CCH) ¶ 25,293 (1992) (quoting Liles Constr. Co. v. United States, 197 Ct. Cl. 164, 173-74, 176, 455 F.2d 527, 531, 533 (1972): "There is no greater interference with the manner and method of performance, short of termination of the work, than the ordered replacement of the craftsmen originally chosen to do the work.").

[103] 248 Neb. 338, 535 N.W.2d 408 (1995).

The appellate court concluded that the architect's determination had no reasonable basis or was patently erroneous and constituted a gross mistake as would necessarily imply bad faith. As a result, the court concluded that the contract provision authorizing the architect to resolve the cost of the change was not binding on the contractor.

[D] Unintentional Interference

More often than not, the owner's interference is unintentional. The specifications or preliminary surveys may have been defective, or there might be greater restrictions than anticipated at the time of bidding, such as delays, interruptions, and site conditions not foreseen by either party. These circumstances often result in constructive change orders.

It may well happen that a change of method is forced upon the contractor rather than initiated by it when a change in design is directed. Of course, the owner may be unaware of the impact of the design change it wishes to make. For example, on a rockfill dam construction contract in West Virginia, the Corps of Engineers directed a contractor to use rock from a particular quarry area downstream of the dam axis not earlier listed in the contract documents. The designated area was at a much lower elevation than the original upstream quarries, and from that new location, a substantially uphill haul was required as contrasted with the downhill haul from the original quarries. It was obvious that the contractor's method of placement of rock was changed and made more costly when the bottom-dump wagons on the jobsite could not be used and powerful trucks had to be substituted for the uphill haul.[104]

And whether the owner directs the change or simply suggests the change may make a difference. The difference between a suggestion and a direction can be a subtle one. A suggestion usually follows a request for advice, while a direction can be a solicited or an unsolicited order. However, an order leading to changes in the method of performance is compensable, although a mere suggestion is not. The test is often whether or not the order was in writing.

In *Donald R. Stewart Associates,*[105] the contractor followed a government representative's suggestion (alleging it was an order) to use clay for backfill, only to be ordered later by the same representative to replace it with gravel. It was held that "a non-coercive suggestion, made because the contractor was having difficulty, does not constitute direction or entitle the contractor to compensation for a construction change."[106] The government representative asserted that "he resisted all requests for directions and confined himself to making suggestions."[107] Absent

---

[104] Western Contracting Co., ENGBCA. The claim was settled during appeal.
[105] AGBCA Nos. 84-226-1 et al., 92-1 BCA (CCH) ¶ 24,705 (1992).
[106] *Id.* at 123,311 (citing OFEGRO, HUDBCA Nos. 88-3410-C7, 89-4469-7, 91-3 BCA (CCH) ¶ 24,206 (1991)).
[107] *Id.*

a written direction, it would be difficult to prove that such a communication is anything other than a suggestion.

[1] Site Access/Conditions

Obstructing access to the worksite can have not only a delay impact, but also a disruptive effect on the contractor's sequencing and overall coordination of work to such an extent that performance must be totally reconfigured.

[2] Failure to Remove Obstructions

In *Caesar Construction, Inc.,*[108] the government breached its implied duty not to interfere with the contractor's performance. It failed to remove, after a timely request, melting snow piles it deposited near the excavation site, which led to additional pumping expenses to remove the water that flowed into the excavation site. It is important to note that water from other sources—rainfall and a broken drainage pipe—was also being pumped from the excavation site. Although the contractor made no effort to erect a barricade against drainage into the excavation as is customary in the industry, and in spite of the fact that no *delay* was shown to be caused by the additional pumping, the court awarded the contractor for its *added effort* as a result of the government's nonfeasance. Strangely, however, the court required no proof as to the approximate amount that was attributable to the melting snow. Rather, it limited the period of the damage to the original contract schedule not including the period of reworking a faulty foundation.[109]

A more routine case involving excess water on the construction site is *C.M. Lowther, Jr.*[110] In a contract to remove and replace asbestos insulation around piping runs in the crawl space of a building, removal was specified of the upper six inches of contaminated soil in the crawl space. Water overflowed from a nearby government machine room, increasing the weight and expense of removal, as well as disrupting the method of vacuuming with a particular piece of equipment that did not function well with sticky, tacky soil. Although it was determined that the vacuuming equipment selected would have clogged even under ordinary conditions, the contractor nevertheless recovered on the basis that the added weight of the saturated soil forced it to make many more disposal trips than anticipated (in order to comply with weight limits on state roads).

---

[108] ASBCA No. 41,059, 91-1 BCA (CCH) ¶ 23,639 (1990).

[109] *But see* James Lowe, Inc., ASBCA No. 42,026, 92-2 BCA (CCH) ¶ 24,835 (1992) (although the government breached its duty to cooperate in the repair of a broken sewer line by failing to reduce water pressure timely to enable repair, the contractor could not recover because it failed to segregate the amount of pumping to repair the damaged sewage line from the amount of pumping required for other water located on the construction site).

[110] ASBCA No. 38,407, 91-3 BCA (CCH) ¶ 24,296 (1991).

[3] Rehandling and Refusal to Allow Storage

An obvious way in which a contractor reduces cost and outbids competitors is by having access to construction materials closer to the jobsite, cutting the time of hauling to the site. By sequencing the work to minimize transportation of heavy equipment and materials to and from the jobsite, the contractor may achieve a less expensive performance.

In *Construction Management Engineers, Inc.,*[111] the government refused to allow storage of structural steel on a road leading to both the construction site and a medical facility, as it would have interfered with ambulance access. The subcontractor presented a constructive change claim for triple handling of the steel as a result of having to store the steel off-site. The board denied the claim, stating that there was no express agreement that the steel could be stored on the access road. It noted contract language that the "storage of materials on the government premises shall be confined to areas authorized or approved by the contracting officer."[112]

Similarly, in *Boro Developers, Inc.,*[113] the board denied a claim for additional handling of materials as a result of denial of storage near an airstrip. It determined that the contractor did not reasonably interpret a contract provision requiring the contractor to put a "foreign object damage curtain" between materials and the runway. The contractor could not prove that access was denied for reasons other than its unwillingness to construct the damage curtain.

---

[111] ASBCA No. 31,627, 91-2 BCA (CCH) ¶ 23,781 (1991).
[112] *Id.* at 119,110.
[113] ASBCA No. 40,146, 90-3 BCA (CCH) ¶ 23,192 (1990).

CHAPTER 10

CHANGES RESULTING FROM IMPOSSIBILITY OR IMPRACTICABILITY OF PERFORMANCE

Jon T. Anderson

§ 10.01   INTRODUCTION

Impossibility and *impracticability* are generally recognized grounds for the discharge of construction contract obligations. By definition, impossibility and impracticability relate to occurrences beyond the control of the contracting parties and, therefore, are not obviously subjects justifying "changes" to contractual obligations. However, in proper circumstances, events of impossibility or impracticability may allow modifications in contractors' and other parties' performance obligations, including restitution for incurred costs and provided benefits and adjustments to compensation and extensions of contract time. Commonly used construction industry risk allocation provisions are important in devising such relief. Treating a situation of impossibility or impracticability like a "change" focuses on the contracting parties' assumptions of risk and the character of their actions in light of the impossibility or impracticability experienced.

§ 10.02   IMPOSSIBILITY AND IMPRACTICABILITY DOCTRINE

"Impossibility," as applied to issues of contract performance, is normally traced to nineteenth-century common-law doctrinal innovation that provided for discharge in situations when a party's performance was precluded by "actual" or "objective" impossibility beyond the contracting party' control.[1] "Impracticability," frequently called "commercial impracticability" and sometimes "commercial impossibility," is a later development, based on judicial reluctance to enforce a contract against a nonperforming party when its performance is commercially unreasonable but not objectively impossible.[2] The *Restatement (Second) of Contracts* consolidated the two expressions of contractual excuse or discharge under the cover of "impracticability."[3] The Restatement approach (and

---

[1] Williston on Contracts § 1931 (3d ed. 1978) [hereinafter Williston] (citing Taylor v. Caldwell, 122 Eng. Rep. 309 (Q.B. 1863) (excuse of rental contract when theatre burned)). *See also* J.H. Schlegal, *Of Nuts, and Ships, and Sealing Wax, Suez and Frustrating Things—The Doctrine of Impossibility of Performance*, 23 Rutgers L. Rev. 419 (1969); R.A. Posner & A.M. Rosenfeld, *Impossibility and Related Doctrines in Contract Law: An Economic Analysis*, 6 J. Legal Stud. 83 (1977) [hereinafter Posner & Rosenfeld]; Annotation, *Modern status of the rules regarding impossibility of performance as a defense in action for breach of contract*, 84 A.L.R.2d 12 (1962); 3 National Institute of Construction Law, Inc., Construction and Design Law ch. 24 (1991).

[2] The doctrine is often traced to Mineral Park Land Co. v. Howard, 156 P. 458 (Cal. 1916), which treated a tenfold increase in a contractor's costs as the equivalent of impossibility. *Cf.* Natus Corp. v. United States, 371 F.2d 450, 456 (Ct. Cl. 1967) ("impossibility predicated upon 'commercial impracticability' "); Tombigbee Constructors v. United States, 420 F.2d 1037, 1049 (Ct. Cl. 1970) ("commercial impossibility").

[3] Restatement (Second) of Contracts § 261 cmt. 11 (1979) (Impracticability of Performance and Frustration of Purpose). Section 261 is the basic rule, providing:

> Where, after a contract is made, a party's performance is made impracticable without his fault by the occurrence of an event the non-occurrence of which was a basic assumption on which the contract was made, his duty to render that performance is discharged, unless the language or the circumstances indicate the contrary.

the similar principles earlier set forth in the Uniform Commercial Code) has been influential, although doctrinal debate continues[4] and the Restatement's liberalization of doctrine has not been wholly accepted by the courts.[5]

The traditional rule was that no obligation arose among the parties with respect to a contract impossible of performance upon execution. Impossibility "doctrine" extends this excuse of performance to include limited incidents of later-arising, "supervening" impossibility. Conventional impossibility doctrine further distinguished between "objective" (it cannot be done) and "subjective" (the party cannot do it) impossibility, with only the former establishing an excuse of performance.[6] Impossibility analysis was normally considered applicable only in limited circumstances: when performance was rendered impossible due to changes in law, when the subject matter of the contract or something necessary for contract performance was destroyed, or when a person necessary for contract performance

---

Comment d to § 261 notes:

> Although the rule stated in this Section is sometimes phrased in terms of "impossibility," it has long been recognized that it may operate to discharge a party's duty even though the event has not made performance absolutely impossible. This Section, therefore, uses "impracticable," the term employed by Uniform Commercial Code § 2-615(a), to describe the required extent of the impediment to performance.

The implementation of Restatement (Second) of Contracts § 261 in the Uniform Commercial Code is in article 2, § 2-615(a), which states in part that:

> Delay in delivery or non-delivery in whole or in part by a seller who complies with paragraphs (b) and (c) is not a breach of his duty under a contract for sale if performance as agreed has been made impracticable by the occurrence of a contingency the nonoccurrence of which was a basic assumption on which the contract was made or by compliance in good faith with any applicable foreign or domestic governmental regulation or order whether or not it later proves to be invalid.

[4] *Compare* Posner & Rosenfeld *with* R.A. Hillman, *An Analysis of the Cessation of Contractual Relations*, 68 Cornell L. Rev. 617 (1983); R.A. Hillman, *Court Adjustment of Long-Term Contracts: An Analysis Under Modern Contract Law*, 1987 Duke L.J. 1. *See also* M.J. Frug, *Rescuing Impossibility Doctrine: A Postmodern Feminist Analysis of Contract Law*, 140 U. Pa. L. Rev. 1029 (1992) [hereinafter Frug]. New instances for the potential application of impossibility and impracticability doctrine constantly arise. M. Baker, *"A Hard Rain's A-Gonna Fall"—Terrorism and Excused Contractual Performance in a Post September 11th World,* 17 Transnat'l Law. 1 (2004); P. O'Connor, *Allocating Risks of Terrorism and Pandemic Pestilence: Force Majeure for an Unfriendly World,* 23 Constr. Law. 5 (Fall 2003); and R.A. Guidry, *The Steel Price Explosion: What Is an Owner or a Contractor To Do?,* 24 Constr. Law. 5 (Summer 2004), identify points of current concern, although generally concluding that impracticability doctrine is of problematic utility.

[5] *See, e.g.,* Jennie-O Foods, Inc. v. United States, 580 F.2d 400, 409 (Ct. Cl. 1978): "The commercial impracticability standard can be easily abused; thus this court has not applied it with frequency or enthusiasm. It is not invoked merely because costs have become more expensive than originally contemplated."

[6] *See generally* Restatement of Contracts § 455 (1932) ("Impossibility . . . not due to the nature of the performance, but wholly due to the inability of the individual promisor . . . [does not] discharge a duty created by a contract."); Williston §§ 1931-37.

[7] *See, e.g.,* Restatement (Second) of Contracts § 261 cmt. a (1979) ("impossibility" is understood not to require "literal or actual impossibility").

died. Current expressions expand the scope and qualify the application of the doctrine.[7] The essentials are, of course, these:

1. That a party's performance in fact be precluded or very seriously impaired, not simply made more difficult;

2. That the impossibility not be due to the fault of the party excused, and

3. That the specific risk of impossibility not have been assumed by the party seeking discharge.[8]

Although the consistency of impossibility doctrine is certainly subject to question,[9] there is wide acceptance of its generally stated principles.

Traditional impracticability (or commercial impracticability) doctrine focuses on the commercial incidents of a specific party's contract performance, excusing such when (in typical formulations) the party's performance, though not impossible, involves "excessive and unreasonable difficulty or expense"[10] or when "the attendant costs of performance bespeak commercial senselessness."[11] The doctrine is obviously a substantial qualification of the objective focus of conventional impossibility doctrine. Commercial impracticability is often the standard used in federal contracts cases considering impracticable contract requirements. Although used widely, it is not universally accepted,[12] and the decisions considering the excuse often express hesitancy about its appropriateness.[13] Except in obviously extreme cases, an assertion of commercial impracticability often appears as an attempt by a contracting party to escape the consequences of what turned out to be a bad bargain,[14] and it is impossible to predict the extent of difficulty that will allow relief.[15]

---

[8] *See, e.g.*, Opera Co. v. Wolf Trap Found., 817 F.2d 1094, 1097-102 (4th Cir. 1987) (general review of impossibility doctrine); Chase Precast v. John J. Paoriessa Co., 566 N.E.2d 603, 605 (Mass. 1991) (consideration of relationship between impossibility and frustration).

[9] *See, e.g.*, Posner & Rosenfeld at 84 (noting "pervasive dissatisfaction with the prevailing doctrinal articulations" possibly reflecting "an inability to develop a coherent positive theory consistent with the typical outcomes in the recurring cases"). *See also* Frug at 1047 ("impossibility doctrine . . . lack[s] a coherent essence").

[10] Schmeltzer v. Gregory, 72 Cal. Rptr. 194, 198 (Ct. App. 1968) (citing Mineral Park Land Co. v. Howard, 156 P. 458 (Cal. 1916)). *See also* Transatlantic Fin. Corp. v. United States, 363 F.2d 312, 316 (D.C. Cir. 1966) (one of the "Suez Canal" cases).

[11] Natus Corp. v. United States, 371 F.2d 450, 457 (Ct. Cl. 1967).

[12] Huffines v. Swor Sand & Gravel Co., 750 S.W.2d 38, 40 (Tex. App.—Ft. Worth 1988) (the conclusion is qualified); Hanover Petroleum Corp. v. Tenneco, Inc., 521 So. 2d 1234, 1240 (La. Ct. App.) ("The common law doctrine of commercial impracticability has no application under Louisiana law"), *writ denied*, 526 So. 2d 800 (La. 1988).

[13] Jennie-O Foods, Inc. v. United States, 580 F.2d 400, 409 (Ct. Cl. 1978).

[14] *See, e.g.*, Southern Dredging Co., ENGBCA No. 5695, 92-2 BCA (CCH) ¶ 24,886 at 124,116 (1992) (rejecting contention that fuel cost increases following invasion of Kuwait made performance of dredging contract commercially impracticable; "neither abnormal price increases nor unusual trade conditions change this basic principle regarding a contractor's assumption of the risk of increased performance costs in a fixed price contract").

[15] *See, e.g.*, A.O. Sykes, *The Doctrine of Commercial Impracticability in a Second-Best World*, 19 J. Legal Stud. 43, 73-83 (1990) (reviewing the principal commercial impracticability cases—*Mineral Park, Florida Power & Light, Waldinger*—and finding inconsistent and nonpersuasive reasoning).

Restatement (Second) of Contracts also addresses the principle of "frustration of purpose," a complementary approach leading to the discharge of contract performance:

> Where, after a contract *is* made, a party's principal purpose is substantially frustrated without his fault by the occurrence of an event the non-occurrence of which was a basic assumption on which the contract was made, his remaining duties to render performance are discharged, unless the language or the circumstances indicate the contrary.[16]

This approach is applicable in situations when performance is neither impossible nor commercially impracticable but is nonetheless excusable because, due to circumstances beyond the contracting party's control, the value of the performance has become so worthless that it would be unjust or commercially senseless to require performance. Although of general application, the excuse of "frustration" is somewhat disfavored[17] and has not been widely employed in construction industry cases.[18]

The excuses of contractual performance defined by the terms "impossibility," "impracticability," and "frustration"—simply *impracticability* hereinafter—are qualified in application by numerous, detailed precepts only suggested by the previous summary descriptions. Any assertion of the doctrines should be based upon

---

[16] § 265 cmt. 11 (1979).

[17] *See, e.g.,* United States v. Southwestern Elec. Coop. Inc., 869 F.2d 310, 315 (7th Cir. 1989) (applying Illinois law; refusing to void a power sales contract due to unexpected construction cost increases: "Under Illinois law the defense is not to be applied liberally and the party seeking rescission must show that (1) the frustrating event was not reasonably foreseeable and (2) the value of counterperformance has been totally or nearly totally destroyed by the frustrating event."). *See also* Dudley v. St. Regis Corp., 635 F. Supp. 1468, 1472 (E.D. Mo. 1986). N.R. Weiskopf, *Frustration of Contractual Purpose—Doctrine or Myth?,* 70 St. John's L. Rev. 239, 242 (1996), questions whether frustration is a "true legal doctrine or shibboleth," noting "the inescapable conclusion is that the courts typically do not permit purchasers of goods and services to escape contractual liability because of supervening frustration of bargaining objective unless, of course, the parties are found to have so agreed." Conlon Group, Inc. v. City of St. Louis, 980 S.W.2d 37 (Mo. App. 1998) exemplifies the point. The case concerned a redevelopment plan involving a developer's renovation of existing structures into a mixed-use complex including a parking garage; the structures proved incapable of supporting a garage load without "gutting" and major reconstruction, and the developer requested authorization to demolish the existing structures and construct new buildings. *Id.* at 39. When the redevelopment authority denied the request, the developer sued for inverse condemnation contending it was relieved from obligations under the redevelopment plan due to "commercial frustration." The decision turned on the developer's purchase of the redevelopment property in an "as is" condition and without "any type of engineering . . . analysis. It then failed to . . . investigat[e] the structural soundness of the buildings" before entering into the redevelopment agreement. *Id.* at 41. The otherwise compelling economic facts of the case were obviously insufficient to overturn the contractual risk allocation reflected in the "as is" provision.

[18] T.G. Galligan, Jr., *Extra Work in Construction Cases: Restitution, Relationship, and Revision,* 63 Tulane L. Rev. 799, 843-45 (1989) [hereinafter Galligan] (because "frustration" is a disfavored doctrine and is not based on considerations precluding performance, where the contractor continues work, claims will be treated as "extra work" cases rather than as involving "frustration").

a thorough study of these specific rules. Specific details of interest include at least the following:

1.   Impracticability bears an obviously close relationship to the excuse of contract obligations obtained through a "mutual mistake of fact."[19]

2.   Impracticability doctrine is always qualified by the principle that a party seeking relief may have assumed the risk that performance would be impossible or commercially impracticable.[20]

3.   A promisor will generally be held obliged to attempt to avoid impracticability through alternative means of performance, even though more expensive.[21]

4.   The current Restatement continues the principle that temporary impracticability suspends but does not discharge performance, and that partial impracticability does not (normally) excuse the performance of other obligations.[22]

5.   Application of the doctrine to construction industry problems is substantially affected by the common use of risk allocation provisions, though there remains uncertainty about the effect of contractual agreement relating to impracticability.[23]

6.   Restitution is the normal mechanism to adjust the equities of the parties affected by contractual impracticability.[24]

7.   Impracticability is typically asserted as a defense to a claim for breach of contract, and, as such, the burden of proof lies on the party raising the claim.[25]

It deserves constant emphasis that, although relief of performance by reason of impracticability has been long accepted, the discharge of contract obligations is still the exception and not the rule, and application of the doctrine requires satisfaction of stringent criteria.

Current academic comment on impracticability focuses on the general inadequacy of doctrine to provide predictability or consistent explanations of the

---

[19] *See, e.g.,* R.A. Hillman, *An Analysis of the Cessation of Contractual Relations,* 68 Cornell L. Rev. 617, 618 (1983) (noting that the separate treatment of material breach, good-faith termination, material mistake, frustration, and impracticability can be "misleading to the extent that they suggest that fundamentally different considerations govern their adjudication").

[20] Williston § 1972A.

[21] *See, e.g.,* Blount Bros. Corp. v. United States, 872 F.2d 1003 (Fed. Cir. 1989) (aggregate supply specification): "The contractor has the burden to prove that it explored and exhausted alternatives before concluding the contract was legally impossible or commercially impracticable to perform."

[22] Restatement (Second) of Contracts § 269 (1979) (Temporary Impracticability or Frustration), § 260 (Partial Impracticability).

[23] See § **10.03[B]**.

[24] See § **10.03[A]**.

[25] Williston § 1978B.

decisions.[26] The decisions reflect a somewhat different concern, focusing on the role of risk "foreseeability." This may be of interest to construction industry practitioners in that the uncertain doctrinal role of foreseeability could affect the use of relatively standard contractual provisions intended to address recurring impracticability situations.[27] Under Restatement § 261, the nonoccurrence of impracticability is treated as a "basic assumption" underlying the parties' agreement (and, therefore, the occurrence of impracticability discharges performance), but the parties are also treated as contracting with reference to "foreseeable" risks. The "foreseeability issue" is whether the fact the parties' contract includes a provision addressing a risk must mean that the risk is "foreseeable." If the provision adequately addresses the risk, then any concern should be nominal. But if not, the mere fact of contract treatment may establish "foreseeability" and thus preclude application of the discharge rules, which are intended to reach an equitable result.

Justice Souter's plurality opinion in *United States v. Winstar Corp.*[28] upheld the enforceability, through a breach of contract action, of presumed government contracts controlling accounting for supervisory goodwill as affected by later regulatory change accomplished through the Financial Institutions Reform, Recovery & Enforcement Act of 1989 (FIRREA). The opinion includes a summary of the impossibility doctrine as applied to government contracts, focusing on the specific impossibility risk of government regulatory action. The decision as a whole—the plurality opinion, concurrences, and dissents—has occasioned much comment, principally focused on the "unmistakability doctrine"—that is, the principle that " 'sovereign power ... governs all contracts subject to the sovereign's jurisdiction, and will remain intact unless surrendered in unmistakable terms.' "[29] On more-or-less standard government contract issues—such as the compensation questions considered in this chapter—the decision is of mixed significance. On the one hand, the Federal Circuit has treated Justice Souter's recitation of accepted impossibility-impracticability doctrine, as set out in Restatement (Second) of Contracts

---

[26] *See* Posner & Rosenfeld at 84. *See also* M.J. White, *Contract Breach and Contract Discharge Due to Impossibility: A Unified Theory*, 17 J. Legal Stud. 353 (1988); C.P. Gillette, *Commercial Relationships and the Selection of Default Rules for Remote Risks*, 19 J. Legal Stud. 531 (1990).

[27] *Compare* Waldinger Corp. v. CRS Group Eng'rs, Inc., 775 F.2d 781 (7th Cir. 1985) ("failure to provide a contractual excuse against the occurrence of a foreseeable contingency may be deemed to be an assumption of an unconditional obligation to perform") *and* Eastern Air Lines, Inc. v. McDonnell Douglas Corp., 532 F.2d 957, 991 (5th Cir. 1976) ("Exculpatory provisions which are phrased merely in general terms have long been construed as excusing only unforeseen events which make performance impracticable.") *with* Foster Constr. C.A. v. United States, 435 F.2d 873, 887-89 (Ct. Cl. 1970) (allocation of risk resulting from changed conditions provision) *and* Big Chief Drilling Co. v. United States, 26 Cl. Ct. 1276, 1292 (1992) (same risk allocation for noninclusion of changed conditions clause).

[28] 518 U.S. 839, 116 S. Ct. 2432, 135 L. Ed. 2d 964 (1996).

[29] 518 U.S. at 872, quoting Bowen v. Public Agencies Opposed to Soc. Sec. Entrapment, 477 U.S. 41, 52, 106 S. Ct. 2390, 91 L. Ed. 2d 35 (1986). *See, e.g.,* J.I. Schwartz, *The Status of the Sovereign Acts and Unmistakability Doctrines in the Wake of Winstar: An Interim Report,* 51 Ala. L. Rev. 1177 (2000); M.P. Malloy, *When You Wish Upon Winstar: Contract Analysis and the Future of Regulatory Action,* 42 St. Louis U. L.J. 409 (1998).

§ 261, as of doctrinal significance.[30] On the other hand, contemporaneous federal contract decisions on affirmative adjustment claims by construction and supply contractors have not recognized clear doctrinal effect from *Winstar.*[31] However, this is not to suggest that *Winstar* may not ultimately have significance with respect to government contract claims of the type discussed in this chapter.[32]

The courts express inconsistent views of the general subject, from "the parties should be bound unless their contractual purpose was frustrated by a completely unforeseeable [event] and the test of foreseeability should be an objective one; not a subjective inquiry into the state of mind of the parties"[33] to "[p]laintiff's argument that an event of force majeure must be unforeseeable must be rejected,"[34] and dismissing "the obsolete rule that foreseeability, whether reasonably likely or not, bars the application of the doctrine."[35] However, despite dispute

---

[30] *See* Seaboard Lumber Co. v. United States, 308 F.3d 1283, 1294 (Fed. Cir. 2002) (declaratory relief actions by timber companies seeking relief from timber harvesting contracts that had become noneconomic):

> The Supreme Court has reformulated the common law doctrine of impossibility as follows: [W]here, after a contract is made, a party's performance is made impracticable without his fault by the occurrence of an event the non-occurrence of which was a basic assumption on which the contract was made, his duty to render that performance is discharged, unless the language or the circumstances indicate the contrary. United States v. Winstar Corp., 518 U.S. 839, 904, 116 S. Ct. 2432, 135 L. Ed. 2d 9674 (1996) (quoting Restatement (Second) of Contracts § 261). This defense requires Seaboard to show that (i) a supervening event made performance impracticable; (ii) the non-occurrence of the event was a basic assumption upon which the contract was based; (iii) the occurrence of the event was not Seaboard's fault; and (iv) Seaboard did not assume the risk of occurrence. *See Winstar Corp.*, 518 U.S. at 904-10, 116 S. Ct. 2432.

[31] *See, e.g.*, Raytheon Co. v. White, 305 F.3d 1354, 1367-68 (Fed. Cir. 2002) (claim for price adjustment partially based on commercial impracticability for purpose of developing a monetary claim for a termination settlement proposal on a military supply contract; review of commercial impracticability doctrine cites Restatement (Second) of Contracts § 261 but does not refer to *Winstar*); I.W. Matteson, Inc. v. United States, 61 Fed. Cl. 296, 320 (Fed. Cl. 2004) (damages action under Corps of Engineers fixed-price dredging contract for failure to obtain spoil areas; impracticability principles are derived from *Raytheon;* Jennie-O Foods, Inc. v. United States, 217 Ct. Cl. 314, 580 F.2d 400, 409 (1978); *Seaboard,* 308 F.3d 1283; but *Winstar* is referred to only as a secondary citation).

[32] *Cf.* J.I. Schwartz, *The Status of the Sovereign Acts and Unmistakability Doctrines in the Wake of Winstar: An Interim Report,* 51 Ala. L. Rev. 1177, 1199: "[T]he Court of Federal Claims and Federal Circuit are actively engaged in sorting out the status of the government's sovereignty defenses—seeking to elucidate the points left obscure by the Supreme Court's *Winstar* decision."

[33] United States v. Buffalo Coal Mining Co., 345 F.2d 517 (9th Cir. 1965) (unanticipated difficulty in mine rehabilitation). *See also* Savage v. Peter Kiewit Sons' Co., 532 P.2d 518, 522 (Or. 1967): "One purpose of a contract is to shift reasonably foreseeable business risks to the party promising the performance so that the promisee can devote his energies and capital to other matters."

[34] Sabine Corp. v. ONG W., Inc., 725 F. Supp. 1157, 1170 (W.D. Okla. 1989) (long-term gas purchase contract).

[35] Opera Co. v. Wolf Trap Found., 817 F.2d 1094, 1104 n.14 (4th Cir. 1987) (excuse of theatre performance contract due to power outages and weather). Although U.C.C. § 2-615 is often understood to be the practical equivalent of Restatement (Second) of Contracts § 261, the factor of "foreseeability" has been applied in cases under the U.C.C. so as to limit its applicability in situations of commercial impracticability. *See* R.A. Guidry, *The Steel Price Explosion: What Is an Owner or a*

concerning foreseeability, the overall advantages of addressing contractual risks relating to impracticability are such that developed construction contract practices should not be affected.

§ 10.03 CHANGES RESULTING FROM IMPRACTICABILITY

Although the *discharge* of a party's performance is by definition a change in a party's contract, the existence of an excuse for performance does not necessarily justify any other kind of adjustment of a party's contract obligations.[36] There are a number of circumstances, however, in which situations of impracticability have led to relief that included adjustments in contract obligations beyond the simple discharge, total or partial, of a party's performance. The frequent use of risk allocation provisions in construction industry contracts is an obvious ground for such action. The most developed line of analysis is reflected in federal government contract decisions in which government-issued specifications resulting in performance impracticability have sustained equitable adjustments under standard changes clauses, as well as governmental liability for breach of warranty. Some state court decisions follow the reasoning of the federal cases although, without the administrative structure construing standard provisions underlying federal changes doctrines, other legal theories are normally used to sustain relief. Further, restitution principles are commonly utilized to adjust contracting parties' obligations in situations when overall performance has been totally or partially discharged due to impracticability.

[A] Restitution

The use of partial performance and restitution principles for the provision of relief when contractual performance has been discharged because of impracticability

---

Contractor To Do?, 24 Constr. Law. 5, 7-8 (Summer 2004) (discussing Eastern Air Lines, Inc. v. Gulf Oil Corp., 415 F. Supp. 429, 441 (S.D. Fla. 1975) (fuel requirements contract: "even if Gulf had established great hardship under U.C.C. § 2-615 . . . Gulf would not prevail because the events associated with the so-called energy crises were reasonably foreseeable at the time the contract was executed. If a contingency is foreseeable, it and its consequences are taken outside the scope of U.C.C. § 2-615[.]")). This factor continues to be predominant in claimed commercial impracticability decision under the U.C.C. *See, e.g.*, Watson Labs., Inc. v. Rhone-Poulenc Rorer, Inc., 178 F. Supp. 2d 1099, 1112 n.10 (C.D. Cal. 2001) ("Under . . . 2-615, contract performance will only be excused due to impracticability when the purportedly excusing events were unforeseen at the time the contract was executed.").

[36] *See* 17A Am. Jur. 2d Contracts § 673 at 681 (1991) ("While a real impossibility may release a party from performance, it does not stand for performance so as to enable such party to sue and recover as if he had performed."). *But see* Cook v. Deltona Corp., 753 F.2d 1552, 1558 (11th Cir. 1985) (Florida law; inability to perform development contract due to dredge and fill problems): "But change is what impossibility is about. . . . Impossibility accommodates the tension between the changes a party bargains to avoid and the changes, unbargained for and radical, that made enforcement of the bargain unwise."

is allowed by traditional doctrine[37] and provided for by the current Restatement expression of impracticability.[38] Although now widely accepted, the application of restitution to cases of impracticability is arguably exceptional and is not invariably provided.[39] It should also be recognized that restitution may apply in favor of either the party relieved of performance or the other contracting party, depending on the balance of benefits under the contract and the parties' respective equities.[40]

When all parties' further performance has been discharged due to impracticability, restitution traditionally has been allowed as a means of avoiding the "unjust enrichment" that may have occurred through performance preceding discharge. For this purpose, the measure of restitution reflects the benefit provided by such performance, and the courts have recognized a number of specific techniques of valuation.[41] The limitation of restitution to the benefit provided constitutes a significant restriction upon the scope of relief. Especially in construction industry cases, it would normally exclude most preparatory costs and costs incurred in attempted performance of an impracticable contract not resulting in a usable construction product.[42] Sections 272(2) and 377 of the current *Restatement (Second) of Contracts* set forth an extension of restitution relief for impracticability to include compensation, in appropriate cases, of the discharged party's "reliance interest."[43] Although § 377 qualifies this recognition by linking reliance to benefit, § 272(2) is not expressly so limited. The authorities cited in support of the unlimited rule are the leading decisions that have allowed construction contractor relief

---

[37] *See* Williston §§ 1972-74 at 226:

> But where the party excused by impossibility has partly performed the contract on his side before the impossibility arises, or where the other party has partly or wholly performed without receiving compensation, justice requires the imposition of a quasi contractual obligation on the party receiving such performance to pay its fair value.

[38] Restatement (Second) of Contracts § 272(1) (1979) states that in any case governed by impracticability doctrine, "either party may have a claim for relief including restitution under the rules stated in §§ 240 and 377 [concerning equivalent exchanges of part performance and restitution]." Restatement (Second) of Contracts § 272(2) provides that if the rules of Restatement chapter 11 (Impracticability of Performance) and Restatement chapter 16 (Remedies) "will not avoid injustice, the court may grant relief . . . as justice requires including protection of the parties' reliance interests."

[39] A. Kull, *Mistake, Frustration, and the Windfall Principle of Contract Remedies*, 43 Hastings L.J. 1, 33-35 (1991) (the historical treatment of impracticability was to leave the parties as they were; the allowance of restitution derives largely from building contract cases where work was interrupted due to destruction of the premises).

[40] Restatement (Second) of Contracts § 377 cmt. a (1979).

[41] *See, e.g.*, D.B. Dobbs, Remedies ch. 4 (1973) (summarizing valuation approaches); H. Mather, *Restitution as a Remedy for Breach of Contract: The Case of the Partially Performing Seller*, 92 Yale L.J. 14, 16-21 (1982) (noting various valuation techniques).

[42] *But see* Galligan at 810 (arguing that in construction cases the courts not only "stretch the benefit concept, but they measure recovery in ways that suggest that unjust enrichment is not the only relevant criterion").

[43] J.M. Perillo, *Restitution in the Second Restatement of Contracts*, 81 Colum. L. Rev. 37, 40-41 (1981) (contending that §§ 158 and 272 of the Restatement expand the relief available in situations of impracticability by recognizing that a "right of action for reliance is permitted").

for pre-discharge expenditures in attempted performance of the impracticable obligations.[44] The Restatement view is therefore construable as allowing for contractor restitution relief not defined solely by the benefit provided, at least in situations when some breach of duty by the other contracting party may be found.[45]

There is skepticism that the Restatement's contemplated extension of restitution relief to include reliance has been much followed,[46] but the principal authorities are useful if not dispositive.

Even if the requirement of benefit remains a limitation upon restitution recoveries, the scope of restitution relief in construction cases has always been wider than strict doctrine might suggest.[47] This primarily occurs by means of a flexible interpretation of the benefit requirement that treats partial or attempted performance as a benefit to the recipient, as a divisible or separate contract, or as

---

[44] *See* Restatement (Second) of Contracts § 272 cmt. c (1979) (citing Northern Corp. v. Chugach Elec. Ass'n, 518 P.2d 76 (Alaska), *on reh'g*, 523 P.2d 1243 (Alaska 1974), *on appeal from trial after remand*, 562 P.2d 1053 (Alaska 1977); Hol-Gar Mfg. Corp. v. United States, 360 F.2d 634 (Ct. Cl. 1966)). See also **§ 10.03[C] and [D]**.

[45] That is, presumably the parties' actions in *Hol-Gar* and *Northern Corp.* met the criteria for treatment under § 272(2) (not qualified by benefit) rather than § 377.

[46] R.R. Anderson, *Monetary Recoveries for Reliance and in Restitution Under Article 2 of the U.C.C.*, 22 U.C.C. L.J. 248, 261 (1990) ("Little judicial authority exists for allowing the recovery of reliance damages in excuse cases.") (citing as allowing recovery only Northern Corp. v. Chugach Elec. Ass'n, 518 P.2d 76 (Alaska 1974); National Presto Indus. v. United States, 338 F.2d 99 (Ct. Cl. 1964), *cert. denied*, 380 U.S. 926 (1965); Albre Marble & Tile Co. v. John Bowen Co., 155 N.E.2d 437 (Mass. 1959), *on appeal after trial*, 179 N.E.2d 321 (Mass. 1962)). A. Kull, *Rationalizing Restitution,* 83 Cal. L. Rev. 1191, 1204-05 (1995) disputes the applicability of restitution to the recovery of reliance expenditures in conditions of contractual avoidance and characterizes restitution decisions not based upon benefit to the recipient as "remedies that are restitutionary in form as a means of escape from a disrupted contractual exchange." Restatement (Third) of Restitution and Unjust Enrichment § 34 (T.D. No. 3, 2004), comment d, confirms that, in cases of avoidance, "the [restitution] defendant's liability is measured by net enrichment, not by the claimant's loss" and that "the recipient's liability in restitution for the claimant's part performance may be reduced by the recipient's expenditures in reliance on the interrupted transaction." The comment concludes: "The effect . . . is to allocate to the restitution claimant the losses flowing from the disruption of the parties' bargain. . . . By deducting losses from the recovery in restitution . . . this makes the incidence of losses from supervening circumstances a function of the contractual sequence of performance," which is "ordinarily a subject of conscious bargaining" and may therefore "legitimately be regarded as a function of the parties' agreement." However, Cochran v. Ogletree, 536 S.E.2d 194 (Ga. App. 2000) interestingly illustrates the process. The case involved claims by a property owner for return of deposits relating to two purported construction contracts and by the builder "for their losses" under one of the contracts. At least one of the contracts was held void for vagueness. *Id.* at 538. The court concluded that "[t]he theory of unjust enrichment applies when there is no legal contract and when there has been a benefit conferred," and, therefore, the owner recovered its deposit, less an award of quantum meruit based on "an expectation by the plaintiff [builder] that services be rendered at an agreed price, and at the time they were rendered, plaintiff became obligated to pay . . . even though the written contract was void." *Cochran*, 536 S.E.2d 194, 199. The decision has no identification or quantification of benefit but only an identification of a reliance interest (under a void agreement). It is difficult to envision a clearer upholding of a reliance interest through a restitutionary recovery.

[47] *See* Galligan at 810.

specifically requested and thus converted into a benefit notwithstanding its objective character.[48]

Albre Marble & Tile Co. v. John Bowen Co.[49] illustrates the utility of such analysis. The Massachusetts court was unwilling to adopt a rule allowing restitution for reliance expenditures, but it recognized that the subcontractor's preparatory work had not provided any benefit. Restitution for the subcontractor's costs therefore was rationalized by treatment of the subcontract scope of work as the equivalent of a "special request" for subcontractor activity, a recognized ground for quasi-contractual recovery.[50]

National Presto Industries v. United States[51] faced somewhat similar considerations. The case involved a contractor's claim for losses incurred through unanticipated difficulties in manufacturing artillery shells using a new process. The opinion rejected recovery for breach[52] and based relief on "mutual mistake" sustaining a reformation of the contract so as to split the losses incurred: "Reformation, as the child of equity, can mold its relief to attain any fair result within the broadest perimeter of the charter the parties have established for themselves. Where that arrangement has allocated the risk to neither side, a judicial division is fair and equitable."[53] Although cited by the Restatement as supporting the recovery of reliance expenditures through restitution, the decision in fact illustrates a relaxed application of the requirement for benefit, because the court determined that the contractor's period of attempted, disappointing performance should be treated as providing benefit to the government.[54] Of course, as demonstrated by the California decision in *C. Norman Peterson Co. v. Container Corp.*,[55] the scope of restitution relief when performance continues, even though the contract itself may be treated as impracticable, may be very great and even exceed that provided by the abandoned contract.

Although the relief provided through restitution may appear limited, there are approaches allowing more extensive recoveries in appropriate cases. In any event, in the classic situation where impracticability discharges performance,

---

[48] *See, e.g.,* Williston at § 1977. *Compare* Albre Marble & Tile Co. v. John Bowen Co., 155 N.E.2d 437, 440-41 (Mass. 1959) (noting that the principle requiring benefit "is unworkable if the concept of benefit is applied literally" and sustaining restitution recovery "for those expenditures made pursuant to the specific request of the defendant").

[49] 155 N.E.2d 437 (Mass. 1959).

[50] *Id.* at 440.

[51] 338 F.2d 99 (Ct. Cl. 1964), *cert. denied,* 380 U.S. 926 (1965).

[52] *Id.* at 106.

[53] *Id.* at 112.

[54] *Id.* at 111 n.21; *compare* Safina Office Prods. v. General Servs. Admin., GSBCA No. 10,024, 93-1 BCA (CCH) ¶ 25,485 at 126,958-59 (1993) (rejecting a $500,000 claim on a $150,000 software contract, noting "the parties have unwittingly entered into a 'commercially impossible' contract, i.e., one that simply could not be performed within the economic ambit of the contract," but concluding "we find the crucial *National Presto* element of benefit to the Government missing, and we will not reform the contract on the basis of mutual mistake.").

[55] 218 Cal. Rptr. 592 (Ct. App. 1985) (restitution in excess of guaranteed price); see § 10.03[D].

restitution must be considered the primary vehicle for an equitable adjustment of the contracting parties' interests.

[B]   Contractual Provisions Treating Impracticability

Impracticability doctrine recognizes and, indeed, is based upon the potential that the parties will contractually allocate various risks, including that of performance impracticability.[56] Risk allocation provisions are common in construction industry contracts, including specific clauses addressing performance problems associated with impracticability. Any analysis of contract *changes* arising out of events of impossibility-impracticability will therefore necessarily focus, in the first instance, on the contractual adjustments for such situations expressly authorized by the parties' agreement. However, notwithstanding the express doctrinal recognition of the role of contractual risk allocation provisions in *Restatement (Second) of Contracts* § 261, the effect of such provisions upon the application of impracticability doctrine is not conclusively resolved.[57]

Common construction industry contract provisions dealing with impracticability include force majeure provisions; provisions concerning the risk of loss of construction; differing site, changed, or concealed conditions clauses; termination provisions; excusable delay; and, of course, more or less standard changes clauses.[58] This listing is obviously not exhaustive of contract stipulations affecting risk allocation or impracticability analysis. The relevant common factor of such provisions is that they either expressly or by implication establish a contractual allocation of the performance risk arising out of a specified type of event and frequently authorize an adjustment in the parties' contract, often through the vehicle of a change order.

There are numerous court decisions that interpret the most commonly used risk allocation provisions in construction contracts.[59] The cases naturally consider

---

[56] Restatement (Second) of Contracts § 261 (1979).

[57] See § **10.02** for discussion of § 261. *Compare* J. Sweet, Legal Aspects of Architecture, Engineering and the Construction Process § 27.03(B) (4th ed. 1989) ("the common law doctrine of impossibility is not likely to be employed if there is a force majeure provision, which grants relief under specified circumstances to the performing party") *with* Florida Power & Light Co. v. Westinghouse Elec. Corp., 826 F.2d 239, 262 (4th Cir. 1987) (relief from contract to remove and dispose of spent nuclear fuel: "[T]he doctrine of impossibility-impracticability does not depend on nor is it limited in its application by the specific language of the contract."). P.J.M. Declercq, *Modern Analysis of the Legal Effect of Force Majeure Clauses in Situations of Commercial Impracticability*, 15 J.L. & Com. 213 (1995) is an interesting and detailed examination of Professor Sweet's point.

[58] *See* R.F. Cushman & G.L. Blick, Construction Industry Forms (Aspen Publishers 1988 & Supp. 1993); W. Sabo, Legal Guide to AIA Documents (Aspen Publishers, 3d ed. 1992 & Supp.). Federal standard contract provisions are included in the Federal Acquisition Regulations (FAR), 48 C.F.R., pt. 52.

[59] *See* Annotation, *Construction and effect of "changed conditions" clause in public works or construction contract with state or its subdivision*, 56 A.L.R.4th 1042 (1987); Annotation, *Validity and construction of "no damage" clause with respect to delay in construction contract*, 74 A.L.R.3d 187 (1976).

a wide variety of circumstances and, therefore, do not permit easy summarization. It is elementary that such provisions may present issues of contract validity, interpretation, and effect.[60] Although "changes analysis" is simple in principle, the results are sometimes difficult to reconcile, the facts are often complicated, and the notice and other procedural requirements are difficult to follow.[61]

The special treatment under a changes clause of performance issues attributable to impracticable specifications is discussed in some detail in § 10.03[C]. The federal doctrine on this subject has not been extended to include impracticability within the scope of other commonly used risk allocation provisions, such as the differing-site-conditions or suspension-of-work clauses, although the predicates of the doctrine—government assumption of risk and a change order authorization—are present.[62] At least one decision considering the consequences of unreasonable delay under a suspension-of-work clause, however, has affected an important component of the federal defective specification cases—expansive use of a contract authorization to provide an equitable adjustment. In *Fruehauf Corp. v. United States*,[63] an unreasonable 15-month delay, expressly stated to be the fault of neither the government nor the contractor, was held to justify an equitable adjustment. The suspension-of-work clause excluded adjustment for causes other than an act of the contracting officer,[64] but notwithstanding this limitation, the court allowed the contractor's claim for compensation attributable to the long delay under the suspension clause modification provision. The court reasoned: "Neither party can reasonably be held to have foreseen this development. . . . [U]nder the

---

[60] *See* Eastern Air Lines, Inc. v. McDonnell Douglas Corp., 532 F.2d 957, 988-92 (5th Cir. 1976) (interpretation of force majeure clause: "if a promisor desires to broaden the protections available under the excuse doctrine he should provide for the excusing contingencies with particularity and not in general language"); Foster Constr. C.A. v. United States, 435 F.2d 873, 880-81, 886-89 (Ct. Cl. 1970) (history and application of the modern changed conditions clause: "The purpose is thus to take at least some of the gamble on subsurface conditions out of bidding.").

[61] Sabine Corp. v. ONG W., Inc., 725 F. Supp. 1157, 1169 (W.D. Okla. 1989) (insistence upon contractually required notice in order to invoke a force majeure provision). *But see* Galligan at 1157 (noting that the courts frequently utilize "implied waiver" and similar principles in order to allow recoveries where some performance in fact occurs). *Cf.* Brinderson Corp. v. Hampton Roads Sanitation Dist., 825 F.2d 41, 45 (4th Cir. 1987) (though no Virginia law on point, applying federal constructive notice decisions to excuse a contractor's failure to provide formal notice of a differing site condition).

[62] The standard government contract suspension-of-work (FAR 52.212-12) and differing-site-conditions (FAR 52.236-2) provisions both authorize contract modifications. The differing-site-conditions provision is uniformly construed as a governmental assumption of risk with respect to the defined conditions. *See, e.g.,* Foster Constr. C.A. v. United States, 435 F.2d 873 (Ct. Cl. 1970). Further, Merritt-Chapman & Scott Corp. v. United States, 528 F.2d 1392, 1397 (Ct. Cl. 1976), expressly noted the possibility of an adjustment under the suspension clause for nongovernment-caused delays, in the circumstance that "while at the same time, the contractor is prevented from working by other causes." It is, therefore, somewhat surprising that the impracticability cases do not appear to arise out of such circumstances.

[63] 587 F.2d 486 (Ct. Cl. 1978). The court's discussion suggests that it thought some fault, if only administrative passivity, lay with the contracting officer. *Id.* at 496-97.

[64] *Id.* at 495 (citing Merritt-Chapman & Scott Corp. v. United States, 528 F.2d 1392 (Ct. Cl. 1976)).

circumstances, the only equitable way to allocate such unforeseen risk . . . is by way of an equitable adjustment under the suspension of work clause."[65]

Unusual as the result in *Fruehauf* appears, the idea that a provision excluding or limiting relief for delays (in *Fruehauf*, conditioning an adjustment upon contracting officer action) may itself define a level of performance disruption that justifies compensation has been accepted in other limited circumstances. In *Corinno Civetta Construction Corp. v. City of New York*,[66] the court considered contractor delay claims against a broad public contract no-damages-for-delay clause, precluding compensation claims "or delay . . . occasioned by any act or omission to act of" the public entity.[67] The New York Court of Appeals noted four exceptions to such claim preclusion, and held:

> The [second] exception [for uncontemplated delays] *is* based on the concept of mutual assent. Having agreed to the exculpatory clause . . . the contractor intended to be bound by its terms. It can hardly be presumed, however, that the contractor bargained away his right to bring a claim for damages resulting from delays which the parties did not contemplate at the time.[68]

It is clear that the decision was grounded on an assumption of contractee fault for delay, but the Opinion also, throughout, distinguishes between the three exceptions expressly grounded on contractee fault and the second, nonspecific "uncontemplated delays" exception.[69] The court's language thus recognized that the considerations underlying impracticability could support an adjustment, notwithstanding the no-damages clause, for an unreasonable delay not caused by the contractee and beyond the parties' contemplation.[70] The considerations of foreseeability and risk assumption used to sustain relief in these cases are very similar to those defining application of impracticability doctrine. In a proper case, therefore, it is at least possible that the consequences of impracticability may be addressed through the provided or inferred adjustment provisions.

[C]   Defective Specification Decisions

The most developed body of decisions treating impracticability as a change are federal government contract cases. Performance difficulties attributable to

---

[65] *Id.* at 497. The amount and components of the equitable adjustment were not before the court; the opinion reversed to allow determination "of the amount of equitable adjustment to which plaintiff is entitled on a reasonable allocation of an unforeseen risk encountered by both parties."

[66] 502 N.Y.S.2d 681, 493 N.E.2d 905 (1986).

[67] *Id.* at 685 n.1.

[68] *Id.* at 686.

[69] *Id.* at 688.

[70] *But see* John E. Gregory & Son, Inc. v. A. Guenther & Sons Co., 432 N.W.2d 584 (Wis. 1988):

> the adoption of a "no damage for delay" clause shows that the parties realize that some delays cannot be contemplated at the time of the draft of the contract. . . . [T]he doctrine of mutual assent supports our conclusion that delays not contemplated . . . should not be an exception to the rule that [such clauses] should be enforced.

government specifications that reach the stringent levels required by impracticability doctrine are recognized both as excusing the government contractor's performance and as sustaining other modifications of the government contract.[71] In such cases, contractors have obtained relief both in the form of damages for breach of contract and as an equitable adjustment under a standard federal contract changes clause.[72] In a sense, the cases are simply extreme instances of changes driven by deficiencies in government plans, specifications, and other contract documents treated as a breach of the government's implied warranty under *United States v. Spearin*,[73] and their "true" standing as impracticability cases can therefore be questioned.[74] But the reliance on impracticability to sustain an affirmative adjustment under a changes clause is an unusual and significant extension of a doctrine devised to discharge contract performance, capable of being applied beyond the federal contracting arena.[75]

Federal impracticability doctrine is explained and applied in a significant number of cases.[76] The decisions arise, of course, out of performance problems

---

[71] *See* R.C. Nash, Government Contract Changes ch. 13C at 13-36 through 13-51 (1989) [hereinafter Nash]; S.L. Schooner, *Impossibility of Performance in Public Contracts: An Economic Analysis*, 16 Pub. Cont. L.J. 229 (1986); J.M. Vogel, *Impossibility of Performance—A Closer Look*, 9 Pub. Cont. L.J. 110 (1977) [hereinafter Vogel]; G.A. Cuneo & E.H. Crowell, *Impossibility of Performance: Assumption of Risk or Act of Submission*, 29 Law & Contemp. Probs. 531 (1964).

[72] *See, e.g.*, Hol-Gar Mfg. Corp. v. United States, 360 F.2d 634 (Ct. Cl. 1966) (equitable adjustment); Big Chief Drilling Co. v. United States, 26 Cl. Ct. 1276 (1992) (damages).

[73] 248 U.S. 132 (1918), *as interpreted in* Hol-Gar Mfg. Corp. v. United States, 360 F.2d 634, 638 (Ct. Cl. 1966): "When the Government contracts for supplies to be manufactured in accordance with Government specifications, there is an implied warranty that if the specifications are followed, a satisfactory product will result."

[74] *See* Vogel at 116 ("[c]onflicting or defective specifications should not be included in the area of impossibility for the simple reason that the true issue of impossibility never arises"); Nash at 13-3 ("the problem is not that the specifications contain detailed errors but that the work called for cannot be done at a reasonable cost or reasonable within the bounds of the work contracted for").

[75] The Alaska Supreme Court used the federal impracticability-constructive change in its first opinion in Northern Corp. v. Chugach Elec. Ass'n, 518 P.2d 76, 83-84, but later withdrew the constructive change component, 523 P.2d 1243, 1246 (1974).

[76] Hol-Gar Mfg. Corp. v. United States is often referred to as the origin of the doctrine. Foster Wheeler Corp. v. United States, 513 F.2d 588 (Ct. Cl. 1975), discussed in the text, is the more comprehensive decision. Other significant opinions include R.M. Hollingshead Corp. v. United States, 111 F. Supp. 285 (Ct. Cl. 1953) (considering a storage/shipment requirement for DDT, contended to be "impossible of performance," as to which the court agreed that the government's specification "implicitly represented that if the specifications were complied with, satisfactory performance would result"); Jennie-O Foods, Inc. v. United States, 580 F.2d 400 (Ct. Cl. 1978) (summarizing the doctrine with respect to commercial impracticability and confirming that the contractor needs to attempt alternative methods of performance); Piasecki Aircraft Corp. v. United States, 667 F.2d 50 (Ct. Cl. 1981) (contractor assumption of risk under performance specification); Tombigbee Constructors v. United States, 420 F.2d 1037 (Ct. Cl. 1970) (literal impossibility not required). As an illustration of the expansive use of impracticability analysis as an affirmative basis for claim, note the statement in Appeal of D.E.W. & D.E. Wurzbach, ASBCA No. 50,796, 98-1 BCA ¶ 29,385 at p. 9427, 1997 WL 734987:

> Appellant's recovery is not limited by the contract price when a contract is converted from a default termination to a convenience termination on the basis of impossibility.

caused a contractor by a government specification that cannot be performed or cannot be performed at a reasonable cost. They involve both affirmative contractor

---

The rationale for this exception is that the issuance of impossible specifications is a breach of the Government's implied warranty of the adequacy of its specifications.

Wurzbach primarily concerned application of the loss ratio used to determine recoverable costs in a termination for convenience settlement, and the fact that, on contracts in a loss position, such settlements typically cannot exceed the contract price nor include profit on the recoverable costs. However, the board noted there could well be difficult issues involved in "separat[ing] the losses caused by the Government's [deficient design] from those caused by [the contractor]."

Other recent interesting considerations of impracticability doctrine at the board of contract appeals level include Appeal of Reflectone, Inc., ASBCA No. 42,363, 98-2 BCA ¶ 29,869, 1998 WL 354206. The contract at issue there concerned the development and supply of "aerial refueling simulators" under a fixed-price incentive price contract approximating $34 million (98-2 BCA at p. 1842) on which the contractor alleged a cost overrun exceeding $16 million and claimed recovery on theories of impossibility of performance, superior knowledge, mutual mistake, breach of implied warranties, failure to cooperate, and out-of-scope work. The decision denied the impossibility claim on the grounds that the integration work involved was difficult, not impossible, and "[e]ven if the integration . . . did go beyond the state of the art . . . a contractor may bind itself to do so." *Id.* at p. 1868. As to commercial impracticability:

> Reflectone also contends that, under *Foster Wheeler*, the contract was commercially impracticable because the cost and time of performance was significantly greater than expected due to unanticipated development work. 513 F.2d at 598. Relying principally upon our decisions in *Numax Electronics, Inc.*, ASBCA No. 29,080, 90-1 BCA ¶ 22,280 and *Johnson Electronics, Inc.*, ASBCA No. 9366, 65-1 BCA ¶ 4628, Reflectone asserts that, where there is evidence of significant delay or unanticipated development, or both, impracticability has been found without addressing the issue of cost. The cost issue is apparently of concern to Reflectone because its cost increase (which allegedly was approximately 44 percent) would not, by itself, establish commercial impracticability. (Citations omitted.) In this regard, we view the level of the cost increases experienced by Reflectone together with the lack of any relaxation of specifications that were so difficult, costly and time consuming as to be commercially impracticable to be enough to distinguish this case from *Tombigbee Constructors v. United States*, 420 F.2d 1037, 1049 (Ct. Cl. 197), upon which Reflectone also relies. (98-2 BCA at p. 1868.)

Concerning the above, it is difficult to read the *Numax Electronics, Inc.* and *Johnson Electronics, Inc.* decisions as dispensing with "cost" as a component of impracticability analysis. *Numax* is an entitlement decision, reversing a Contracting Officer's denial of a claim for equitable adjustment ($903,225 on a fixed-price contract value of $2.1 million) on the grounds that mass production of the "slide assembly" was commercially impracticable though not impossible. *Johnson* concerned a default termination converted to a termination for convenience, and, therefore, its discussion of impracticability was in the context of an excuse of performance, not an affirmative adjustment; however, the case does clearly focus upon time for performance as indicative of the impracticable character of the obligation imposed upon the contractor. 1964 WL 427 at *9.

No significant doctrinal changes are indicated in recent federal contracts judicial decisions. However, Raytheon Co. v. White, 305 F.3d 1354, 1368 (Fed. Cir. 2002), includes a convenient summary of the magnitude of adjustment required for consideration of commercial impracticability in federal contracts: Even assuming the cost overrun was 57 percent rather than 24 percent, an overrun of that size does not by itself establish commercial impracticability. *See, e.g.*, Gulf & W. Indus. Inc., 87-2 BCA (CCH) ¶ 19,881 at 100,575 (1987) (finding a contract with a claimed 70-percent overrun not commercially impracticable). Nor, as the board recognized, were the delays and low yields associated with the guidance section production contracts so extraordinary as to demonstrate impracticability of performance. *See* Soletanche Radio Nicholson (JV), 94-1 BCA (CCH) ¶ 26,472 at 131,774

claims and defenses against government claims.[77] Doctrine concerning impracticability in the decisions is conventional, currently relying upon Restatement principles, except as affected by specific, developed grounds of decision.[78] Because the federal decisions are all nonjury, the opinions provide detailed factual explanations of the nature of performance difficulties encountered and of the procedures employed to develop the claim at issue. Apart from the contractor's satisfaction of impracticability criteria, the courts' analyses focus primarily on the issue of risk assumption, that is, did the contractor assume the risk of contractual impossibility-impracticability? Risk assumption evaluates not only the particular performance requirement (specification) at issue, but also the parties' roles in the development, adoption, and modification of the specification. The decisions seldom involve genuine "technical impossibility" and most frequently consider significantly increased costs of performance with reference to "commercial impracticability." The changes analysis applied in the leading cases is conventional "constructive change" reasoning, that is, in view of the situation confronting the contractor, the contracting officer should have issued a change order modifying the specification at issue to relieve the contractor of performance impracticability. Changes analysis includes consideration of contractor notice and actual or excused compliance with change order procedures.[79] As noted, it is questionable whether the federal decisions as thus summarized constitute "true" impracticability cases. The fundamental basis of decision relied upon is the government's responsibility for the specification at issue, typically grounded on the "implied warranty" of sufficiency long ago recognized in *Spearin*, or the government's failure to disclose superior information. But while the conceptual precision of the decisions can be debated, contract appeals boards and contract courts expressly treat the situations as involving impracticability.

The critical components of the federal impracticability-changes doctrine— assuming performance was in fact impracticable—are the analysis of the contract

---

(1993) (finding commercial impracticability when compliance with the specification would have taken more than 17 years at a cost of more than $400 million, rather than 720 days and $16.92 million); Numax Elecs., Inc., 90-1 BCA (CCH) ¶ 22,280 at 111,916 (1989) (finding commercial impracticability when the contractor obtained a yield of only 3090 acceptable units out of 8000, or 3.75 percent); Whittaker Corp., Power Sources Div., 79-1 BCA (CCH) ¶ 13,805 at 67,688-89 (1979) (granting relief where what the parties thought would be a seven-month production contract turned into an unsuccessful four-year development effort with a 148-percent cost overrun).

[77] Hol-Gar Mfg. Corp. v. United States, 360 F.2d 634 (Ct. Cl. 1966) (involved a request for equitable adjustment); Piasecki Aircraft Corp. v. United States, 667 F.2d 50 (Ct. Cl. 1981) (involved a contractor attempt to convert a default termination into one for the convenience of the government); Blount Bros. Corp. v. United States, 872 F.2d 1003 (Fed. Cir. 1989) (involved a proposed deductive change order).

[78] For example, the respective assumptions of risk derived from the type of specification at issue. *See* Wilson Constr., Inc., AGBCA No. 89-178-1, 92-2 BCA (CCH) ¶ 24,798 at 123,717 (1992): "The general rule [of Government liability for defective specifications] . . . applies only to design specifications [citation omitted]. . . . No warranty is implied by performance specifications." *See also* Consolidated Diesel Elec. Corp., ASBCA No. 10,486, 67-2 BCA (CCH) ¶ 6669 (1967).

[79] For application of constructive change principles in a contended situation of impracticability, *see* Wilson Constr., Inc., AGBCA No. 89-178-1, 92-2 BCA (CCH) ¶ 24,798 at 123,718 (1992).

documents to determine which party (if either) has assumed the risk of impracticability[80] and, if it is the government, the contractual analysis to determine the bases for contract adjustment.

The "assumption of risk" determination outlined in the decisions has at least two components. First, the cases involve a detailed and developed analysis of the specific contract provisions and documents at issue, typically, a specification. The analysis develops a characterization of the specification and identifies the party responsible for the specification.[81] Characterization by itself is often enough to sustain a conclusion of assumption of risk because the developed rule of thumb generally distinguishes between design and performance specifications.[82] However, the cases demonstrate varying results for similar specification types;[83] therefore, the courts recognize that a detailed factual inquiry into the origin, sponsorship, and purpose of the specification at issue may be appropriate.[84]

---

[80] *See, e.g.*, Foster Wheeler Corp. v. United States, 513 F.2d 588, 594 (Ct. Cl. 1975): "If a contractor proves 'impracticability,' *i.e.*, 'commercial impossibility,' of a contract, it is entitled to recover its costs of attempting to perform the contract, provided that the contractor did not assume the risk of impossibility."

[81] *Id.* at 600 ("The risk that contract specifications will prove impossible . . . may lie with the Government, the contractor, or both (in the case of mutual mistake of fact)."); *id.* at 598 ("Two factual questions [are] determinative: (1) which party had the greater expertise in the subject matter of the contract? and (2) which party took the initiative in drawing up specifications and promoting a particular method or design?"); *id.* at 601 (evidence evaluated in the case).

[82] Wilson Constr., Inc., AGBCA No. 89-178-1, 92-2 BCA (CCH) ¶ 24,798 at 123,717 (1992). Willamette Crushing Co. v. State, 932 P.2d 1350 (Ariz. App. 1997) is a state court decision examining the variable scope of risk assumption driven by the differing types of specification. The contract involved was for highway construction "to be completed within 360 working days and . . . to be staged according to a specified Traffic Control Pattern (TCP)." The contractor contended that the time could not be met using the state's TCP and obtained permission to use its own. The claim involved was for the cost overrun incurred through use of the contractor's own TCP, which necessarily involved a contention that the state's TCP was defective or precluded timely completion. The decision rejected application of a *Spearin* warranty to the state's TCP and also denied relief on a contention of "commercial 'impossibility or impracticability' " (932 P.2d at 1354). As to the latter, the contractor argued "that 'time impossibility' can support a claim for commercial impracticability," relying on federal contract precedents, which the Arizona court distinguished as "not *American Ship* [*Building v. United States*, 228 Ct. Cl. 220, 654 F.2d 75 (1981)]-type performance specification cases; they are *Spearin*-type cases in which the design specifications tightly circumscribed the contractor and misled it regarding some physical condition relevant to the job and the bid." *Id.* at 1355. The contractor's claim was therefore denied "[b]ecause the State's TCP contained no hidden physical defects and because Wildish did not have to use the State's TCP." *Id.* at 1356. However, the relatively small (10 percent) cost overrun, although absolutely quite large for a small contractor ($2+ million), was presumably also a factor in the court's conclusion that commercial impracticability had not been proven.

[83] *Foster Wheeler*, for example, involved a performance specification, which was held to be defective.

[84] Foster Wheeler Corp. v. United States, 513 F.2d 588, 601 (Ct. Cl. 1975) (demonstrates a review of evidence on this point). *See also* Hol-Gar Mfg. Corp. v. United States, 360 F.2d 634, 638 (Ct. Cl. 1966) ("Here the governing specifications were entirely drafted by the defendant."). *Cf.* J.A. Maurer, Inc. v. United States, 485 F.2d 588, 595 (Ct. Cl. 1973) ("if the contractor, from a stance of superior expertise, asks for and obtains leave to perform according to methods defined and stated by him, he impliedly warrants" the sufficiency of his method).

The second component of the assumption of risk analysis is abbreviated in the current cases. It is little more than recognition that, because the specification has caused a situation of contractual impracticability, the specification must be "defective," or not in compliance with the government's implied warranty of specification sufficiency.[85] The conclusion of specification deficiency, then, translates into a governmental assumption of the risk of impracticability because the government's implied warranty necessarily includes an implied warranty that performance of the specification is "possible."[86] The legal conclusion following from this assumption of risk is, of course, that the government has breached its implied warranty by providing an impracticable specification.

When the government has assumed the risk of impracticability, the contractual analysis that follows also includes two significant innovations, although both are now sufficiently accepted as to be considered unexceptional. The first is the frequent application of "constructive change" considerations. These various factors allow a contracts tribunal to treat the contractor's and government's actions (normally, the contractor's request for a modification of the impracticable specification and the contracting officer's refusal or belated concurrence) as accomplishing a constructive change within the scope of the contract changes clause.[87] The second is an expansion of the "equitable adjustment" authorized by the changes clause for such change to include the contractor's *pre*-change order (or, even, notification) costs of attempted performance of the impracticable specification. This latter point is not a necessary conclusion from the standard changes clause, which authorizes an adjustment only for the cost of performing changed work.

---

[85] *See, e.g., id.* at 594-97 (review of evidence showing performance was "commercially and absolutely impossible"); *id.* at 598 (conclusion: the contract "contained specifications which were impossible to meet, either commercially or within the state of the art"); *see also* Blount Bros. Corp. v. United States, 872 F.2d 1003 (Fed. Cir. 1989).

[86] Blount Bros. Corp. v. United States, 872 F.2d 1003, 1007.

[87] As demonstrated in Hol-Gar Mfg. Corp. v. United States, 360 F.2d 634 (Ct. Cl. 1966). The analytical step of treating impracticability as a constructive change and therefore as sustaining compensation through an equitable adjustment is difficult without reliance upon the extensive "changes" law developed around federal contracts. The Alaska Supreme Court backed away from this step in Northern Corp. v. Chugach Elec. Ass'n, 523 P.2d 1243, 1246 (Alaska 1974). Other state courts have demonstrated similar reluctance, though without necessarily precluding effective relief. *See* Sentinel Indus. Contracting Corp. v. Kimmins Indus. Serv. Corp., 743 So. 2d 954, 965 (Miss. 1999) (subcontractor suit for breach of contract based on failure to approve requested change orders on a project for dismantlement of an ammonia plant), in which the court commented:

> The trial court erred in instructing the jury on "constructive change orders," a concept not recognized under Mississippi law. However, the instruction is in line with our previous decisions allowing recovery for extra compensation without regard for written change orders where the owner imposes extra-contractual work while denying change order requests.

However, the concept has been readily accepted in other jurisdictions. Julian Speer Co. v. Ohio State Univ., 680 N.E.2d 254, 257 (Ct. Cl. of Ohio 1997) (breach of contract claim for uncompensated changes in construction of bioscience building): "The state's verbal instructions to build the project other than as included in the specifications create a 'constructive change order' that is a proper basis to allow recovery of additional costs (citation omitted)."

The rationale for the expansion is usually traced to the early impracticability-change decision in *Hol-Gar Manufacturing Corp. v. United States*,[88] citing the constructive change-defective specification decision in *J.W. Hurst & Son Awnings, Inc.*[89] *Hurst* involved a contractor's claim for costs incurred in the performance of defective but not impracticable specifications that the contracting officer had refused to modify. The board noted the considerations underlying treatment of the government's action as a constructive change and rationalized the appropriate equitable adjustment as follows:

> Faulty design and mistakes in specifications causing extra work have been held to provide a basis for price adjustment under the "Changes" clause, even though the change constituted a relaxation of the specification to achieve an attainable result. . . . Where, as here, the change *is* necessitated by defective specifications and drawings, the equitable adjustment to which a contractor is entitled must, if it is to be equitable i.e., fair and just, include the costs which it incurred in attempting to perform in accordance with the defective specifications and drawings. Under these circumstances the equitable adjustment may not be limited to costs incurred subsequent to the issuance of the change orders.[90]

Hol-Gar involved a negotiated contract for the design and supply of generator sets required to comply with an elaborate design and performance specification. The contractor's preproduction sample did not satisfy requirements. The contractor then submitted a number of engineering proposals and contended that "the only solution was to change the specifications to permit" a substitution.[91] The contracting officer agreed, and a "Supplemental Agreement" was executed, in which the contractor agreed to make no claim for additional costs resulting from the substitution, but "reserve[d] the right to submit a claim for costs incurred in attempting to meet the original specifications."[92] The court treated this claim as allowable in accordance with the reasoning set forth in *Hurst*, holding:

> [T]he change in specifications made useless some of the expenditures plaintiff had made . . . and it must be included in its cost of performance. Since the necessity for the change was not due to plaintiff's fault, but to faulty specifications, an equitable adjustment requires that plaintiff be paid the increase in its costs over what they would have been had no change been required.[93]

---

[88] 360 F.2d 634. The case involved a negotiated, fixed-price contract for the design and fabrication of generator sets pursuant to elaborate government specifications. *Id.* at 635. The contractor's preproduction samples did not meet the specification, the contractor contended that "the only solution was to change the specifications," and the parties entered into a "supplemental agreement" that amended the contract by relaxing the specification and allowing a substitution. *Id.* at 637. The contractor agreed no claim would be made for additional costs of the substitution but "reserve[d] the right to submit a claim for costs incurred in attempting to meet the original specifications." *Id.*

[89] ASBCA No. 4167, 59-1 BCA (CCH) ¶ 2095 (1959).

[90] *Id.* at 8964-65 (citations omitted).

[91] 360 F.2d 634, 637 (Ct. Cl. 1966).

[92] *Id.*

[93] *Id.* at 638.

It should be emphasized that the court in *Hol-Gar* did not conclude that the specification was impossible. Rather, after holding that an equitable adjustment including attempted performance costs was appropriate, the court went further and said:

> But whether or not costs incurred prior to the change come within the "Changes" article, plaintiff is nevertheless entitled to recover damages for breach of warranty. [citing Spearin and other authorities] If the warranty is breached, i.e., the specifications are defective, the plaintiff is entitled to damages equal to the amount expended in trying to comply with the defective specifications.[94]

It was with respect to this conclusion that the court set forth its factual conclusion that the specification at issue had caused impracticability.[95]

The conclusion pointed to by *Hol-Gar* and *Hurst* was made express in *Foster Wheeler*, a leading impracticability decision.[96] In *Foster Wheeler*, although the government did issue a change of specification, the contractor's claim for the costs of attempted performance under the assertedly impracticable specification was not based on the changes clause. The court recognized that the contractor was not asserting a claim that the revised specification (if considered a change) had increased its costs of performance within the meaning of the clause.[97] Notwithstanding the absence of a formal or even arguably constructive change order, however, the Claims Court explained the allowance of costs of attempted performance simply by citing *Hurst* and *Hol-Gar* and concluding that:

> We hold that the . . . contract was impossible to perform, that the government must bear the risk of impossibility, and that plaintiff has not waived its claim. Plaintiff is thus entitled to recover an equitable adjustment, pursuant to the "Changes" clause, of costs incurred in attempting to meet faulty specifications.[98]

Obviously, the development of changes analysis, culminating in the *Foster Wheeler* approval of compensation for the costs of attempted performance under a changes provision even without a change order, has significant implications for numerous impracticability situations. F.J. Baltz and D.S. Herzfeld, *Impracticable Specifications*,[99] is a useful review of the doctrine and cases.

---

[94] *Id.*

[95] *Id.*: "The plaintiff tried for almost three years to attain the desired performance by following the original specifications; but it was only after the original specifications were changed . . . that it was able to comply with the specifications."

[96] 513 F.2d 588 (Ct. Cl. 1975). The case involved performance of a fixed-price supply contract for the design and fabrication of shock-hardened boilers required to demonstrate compliance with a "shock hardness" performance specification. *Id.* at 590. The court's conclusion was that the contract included "specifications which were impossible to meet, either commercially or within the state of the art," although the contractor's noncompliant boilers were accepted by the government. *Id.* at 593, 598.

[97] *Id.* at 592-93.

[98] *Id.* at 602.

[99] 34 Procurement Law. 3 (No. 2, 1999).

The federal impracticability-changes cases occur, of course, within the unique and now well-developed contractual and administrative procedures applicable to federal contract disputes. This limits their easy application to nonfederal cases. However, two aspects of the decisions point to wider utility.

First, federal changes analysis as developed through *Foster Wheeler* means that an impracticability attributable to defective government-provided specifications along with a changes provision allows compensation for a contractor's attempted costs of performance as a contractual equitable adjustment. Contractor and government/owner activity sufficient to meet constructive change criteria could provide the change order normally thought necessary to sustain an equitable adjustment, as demonstrated by the initial ground for contractor relief recognized by the Alaska Supreme Court in *Northern Corp. v. Chugach Electrical Ass'n.*[100] But the *Foster Wheeler* decision also suggests that, even absent such implication of the change order process, compensation as an equitable adjustment can be appropriate, a point expressly remarked upon in the more recent claims court decision in *Big Chief Drilling Co. v. United States.*[101]

Second, the federal doctrine is ultimately grounded on the government's implied warranty of specification sufficiency. *Hol-Gar*, as noted, is good authority for the unexceptional proposition that the provision of relief for impracticability caused by specification deficiencies constituting a breach of the implied warranty can also be provided through damages and need not depend upon constructive change or other considerations uniquely applicable to changes analysis. There is wide acceptance of the principle that a party furnishing a specification impliedly warrants its sufficiency.[102] However, outside the federal arena, it may be difficult to apply the changes analysis required to sustain compensation for impracticability under a changes provision, as shown by the Alaska court's withdrawal of its initial constructive change decision.[103] As discussed in the next section, the alternative ground for relief from impracticability noted in *Hol-Gar* may therefore be the specific application of federal impracticability doctrine of more general use.

---

[100] 518 P.2d 76, 83-84 (Alaska 1974): "we hold that [owner's] insistence after it was, or should have been, aware that performance could not be accomplished by the ice haul method constituted, in effect, a compensable change order in the contract."

[101] 26 Cl. Ct. 1276 (1992). See § **10.03[D]**.

[102] *See* J. Sweet, Legal Aspects of Architecture, Engineering and the Construction Process §§ 27.05, 28.02, 29.03 (4th ed. 1989).

[103] Northern Corp. v. Chugach Elec. Ass'n, 523 P.2d 1243, 1246 (1974):

> Upon reconsideration, we prefer not to rest our opinion on the rationale of an implied change order, for the reason that it involves the establishment of not only a fictional date when a change order becomes effective, but in addition involves a fictional change order itself. . . . We hold that under the circumstances here involved, where Chugach had the technical expertise to inform itself as to ice conditions prior to insisting on performance, Chugach thereafter impliedly warranted that method in the same manner as if it had unilaterally established the specification at the time the contract was entered.

[D] Adjustments Through Breach and Other Contract Actions

Even without analysis supporting an equitable adjustment as a change, performance problems attributable to impracticability can lead to relief other than simply restitution for a wholly or partially discharged contract. The controlling considerations underlying such relief are the contracting parties' respective assumptions of risk and their conduct before and after the condition of impracticability is recognized. As in the federal impracticability cases, the owner/government's implied warranty of contract document/specification sufficiency is critical to a conclusion that the contractor did not assume the specific performance risk involved. Because such cases by definition do not involve an equitable adjustment under a contract provision, the legal theories sustaining relief are those common to numerous construction industry disputes: breach, misrepresentation, abandonment, and reformation of contract obligations.

The Alaska Supreme Court's *Northern Corp.* decision must be considered the paradigm.[104] As previously noted, the court initially determined that contractor recovery for the attempted costs of performance of an impracticable contract (method of performance) could be sustained as an equitable adjustment based on a constructive change: the owner should have issued a change order when the contractor provided proper notice of performance problems. This ground for relief was then expressly withdrawn, on the reasoning that it employed excessive fictions, and recovery was predicated simply as a damages action for breach of (the owner's) implied warranty of specification sufficiency because of the owner's insistence upon performance in accordance with an impracticable method. The court's approval of an action for damages should probably be construed as mooting its speculation concerning restitution recovery although the Alaska court's final decision reaffirmed "the mitigation factor relating to [contractor's nonrecovery for] performance after knowledge of impossibility."[105] The overall result of the Alaska court's opinions was the development of a damages remedy for impracticability with no remaining link to the requirement of benefit apart from the mitigation factor and not dependent upon a specialized constructive change analysis. In impracticability cases when the implied warranty of specification sufficiency may have application, the *Northern Corp.* decisions provide a useful, comprehensive analysis leading to an equitable result.

Indeed, the persuasiveness of the Alaska court's analysis is indicated by the Oklahoma law decision of *Miller v. City of Broken Arrow.*[106] A sewer pipe installation contractor's noncompletion of contract due to deficient specifications for trench bottom stabilization (which the owner's engineer refused to change) was excused, applying Oklahoma impossibility doctrine. Citing *Northern Corp.,* the court found the owner was also "obligated to bear the losses or damages incurred

---

[104] Unlike the other cases discussed, it does not involve a contractor's substantial performance of the impracticable contract (or specification) and, thus, is more clearly a decision allowing compensation relief with respect to impracticability.

[105] Chugach Elec. Ass'n v. Northern Corp., 562 P.2d 1053, 1057 (Alaska 1977).

[106] 660 F.2d 450 (10th Cir. 1981).

[by the contractor] as a result of [its attempted] compliance with the [deficient and impossible to perform] plans and specifications."[107] As in *Northern Corp.,* the essential ground of decision was the owner's provision of specifications impossible to perform, maintained despite the contractor's repeated efforts to obtain relief.[108]

The recent Claims Court decision in *Big Chief Drilling Co. v. United States* confirms the substitutability of a damages remedy in a case where changes analysis failed, at least as long as there is some basis for finding government-owner risk assumption based on the *Spearin* implied warranty. The case involved drilling and casing in accordance with defective specifications that substantially increased the contractor's cost of performance. The contractor had requested and been denied relief from the specifications.[109] As previously noted, the differing-site-conditions clause of the standard federal general conditions of the contract had been "specifically deleted," and the plaintiff did not rely upon any other risk allocation provision.[110] Although not a classic impracticability case in that the contractor accomplished substantial performance, the Claims Court relied upon the performance impracticability authorities to sustain an equitable adjustment for "monies expended in trying to comply with the defective specifications" in justifying compensation for costs of performance to the defective specification. Significantly, the court further noted that in such circumstances, the authorities "seem to pass over the need to find either a direct or constructive change in order to trigger entitlement to damages under the Changes clause."[111] However, rather than treating the contractor's claim as one for an equitable adjustment, "the court chooses to award plaintiff damages based on theories of breach of contract," on the reasoning that the government's issuance of defective specifications "constitute[d] a significant breach of the implied warranty" of specification sufficiency, reaching the level of a cardinal change.[112]

A relatively recent California decision suggests still another approach to the issue of contractual impracticability, at least when (as in *Big Chief*) *the* parties have continued their prosecution of the work. *C. Norman Peterson Co. v. Container Corp.*[113] involved a contractor's claim for cost overruns arising out of

---

[107] *Id.* at 458.

[108] *Id.* at 457.

[109] 26 Cl. Ct. 1276, 1304-05 (1992).

[110] *Id.* at 1292. See discussion in § **10.03[B]**.

[111] *Id.* at 1304. Note, with respect to this observation, the intriguing comment in Warner Constr. Corp. v. City of L.A., 85 Cal. Rptr. 444, 451, 466 P.2d 996 (1970), considering requested and not provided modifications to a retaining wall construction contract, that there are "no valid grounds for distinction between contracts which contemplate amendment and those which do not" since "all contracts can be amended by consent of the parties." Warner is an interesting pre-bid misrepresentation case (failure to disclose information relevant to interpretation of borings), but relief was provided under a claim for breach of contract in the owner's refusal to issue a change order under a differing-site-conditions provision.

[112] *Id.*; see § **10.02**.

[113] 218 Cal. Rptr. 592 (Ct. App. 1985). The *Peterson* construction contract abandonment approach has been approved by the California Supreme Court although its application to public

its performance of a fast-track, plant rehabilitation contract. The evidence was that "the project was poorly engineered, and there were an extensive number of changes which were beyond the contemplation of the parties when the contract

---

contracts has been foreclosed. In Amelco Elec. v. City of Thousand Oaks, 38 P.3d 1120 (Cal. 2002), the California Supreme Court held that abandonment could not be applied against a public entity ("the notion of competitive bidding would become meaningless"), but it approved the abandonment doctrine for private construction contracts " 'when an owner imposes upon the contractor an excessive number of changes such that it can fairly be said that the scope of the work under the original contract has been altered' " (Amelco, 38 P.3d at 1125, citing C. Norman Peterson, 172 Cal. App. 3d at 640) and provided that there is " 'a finding that both parties intended to disregard the contract.' " (Id., citing C. Norman Peterson, 172 Cal. App. 3d at 643). An unpublished decision, Taiho Dev. Enter. Co. v. Lee, 2004 WL 1179431 (Cal. App. 1 Dist. 2004) (Note: California Rule of Court 977(a) prohibits citation or reliance upon opinions not certified for publication or ordered published except as specified by Rule of Court 977(b)), demonstrates one application of the doctrine, treating it as raised by the pleading of a common count (Id. at *4) and sustained by "evidence of a substantial departure from the provisions of the original construction contract. . . . [T]he scope of the work was significantly changed. . . . [Owner] used other subcontractors to do the work reserved for [plaintiff]. . .the parties almost never referred to the contract . . . [and] orally modified the payment terms and extra work request procedure[.]" (Id. at *7.) Professor Sweet's characterization of the restriction upon the abandonment approach in the California Supreme Court's Amelco decision aptly gists the concern raised by the intermediate appellate court decision under review in the case. See J. Sweet, The Amelco Case: California Bars Abandonment Claims in Public Contracts, 32 Pub. Cont. L.J. 285, 307 (2003) ("What the court is telling us is that the abandonment concept is too powerful a claims weapon to be in the hands of the contractor.").

Recognition of the construction contract abandonment approach outside California is mixed. J.A. Jones Constr. Co. v. Lehrer McGovern Bovis, Inc., 89 P.3d 1009 (Nev. 2004) involved and largely sustained a structural concrete subcontractor's claims for breach, fraud, abandonment, and quantum meruit arising out of a host of design and construction issues relating to an exposition center expansion project. One ground of appeal was the trial court's requirement that the subcontractor "choose to either sue on the contract or for quantum meruit." J.A. Jones, 89 P.3d 1009, 1018-19. The Nevada Supreme Court held this to be error, noting, as to abandonment and citing both C. Norman Peterson and Nevada authority, that the facts for application of the theory had been established—"in effect directed . . . to perform work inconsistent with the . . . contract which specifically described the efficient manner and time frame in which Jones was to perform its work" and "Jones testified . . . it agreed to perform . . . on the belief that it would be paid . . . on terms other than those identified in the contract" (Id. at 1019)—and therefore quantum meruit recovery was in order. Id. In effect, the court treated abandonment as an unexceptional conclusion to draw about a significantly disrupted contract and quantum meruit as the expectable measure of relief for the contractor. See also the unpublished decision in Tulsa Steel Mfg. Co. v. South Coast Structural, Inc., 2002 WL 864394 (Cal. App. 2 Dist. 2002) (Note: California Rule of Court 977(a) prohibits citation or reliance upon opinions not certified for publication or ordered published except as specified by Rule of Court 977(b)), involving claims between a project structural steel supplier and its erection subcontractor, in which the Court observed that "[t]he contractor who completes the project in an abandoned contract is entitled to recover the reasonable value of its services on a quantum meruit basis" and holding that the pleading of a common count for quantum meruit was the effective equivalent of pleading an abandonment action. Id. at *8.

In contrast, in R.M. Taylor v. General Motors Corp., 187 F.3d 809, 813-14 (8th Cir. 1999), concerning contracts for conveyor system construction in automobile plants, the Circuit Court reversed a $21+ million quantum meruit recovery and rejected abandonment in the contended "abuse [of] the contract change-order provisions by ordering changes outside the scope of the original contracts," noting "[t]he abandonment doctrine has not been so expanded under Michigan

was first executed," and, further "[m]any of these changes were made without following the procedures provided for in the written contract."[114] The contractor
asserted claims both for breach and for quantum meruit on a theory of abandonment—in effect, a contention that performance under the contract had become
impracticable, though the work (as changed) had not. The court upheld recovery
on the theory of abandonment, noting the parties' continued prosecution of the
work but without comprehensive compliance with contract adjustment procedures.
It concluded that "once it is found that the terms of a construction contract have
been abandoned, the contractor who completes the project is entitled to recover the
reasonable value of its services on a quantum meruit basis" and that the "abandonment" in the particular case included the guaranteed maximum provisions of the
contract (which, therefore, did not limit the contractor's recovery). In reaching this
conclusion, the court expressly stated that the precipitating cause of the abandonment was the owner's prior breach of its implied warranty of specification sufficiency, as demonstrated by the unplanned nature and excessive number of
changes.[115]

Iannuccillo v. Material Sand & Stone Corp.[116] is a breach of contract case
involving a useful demonstration of the critical terms in *Restatement (Second) of
Contracts* § 261. The case concerned a landowner's damages claim against a contractor that had partially but not substantially performed an excavation contract
and a payment claim by the contractor. The work was impacted by numerous problems, but the critical point was the discovery of a ledge that the parties dispute
whether removal was part of the contract. "The property lay untouched [for seven
years] while the instant suit was pending" until owner hired another contractor to
complete the site development.[117] The contractor contended that "this unexpected

---

law" and "[e]ven if . . . excessive or untimely change orders could support . . . implied abandonment
under Michigan law, the evidence does not support such a finding in this case," comparing the case
to *C. Norman Peterson* in which " 'hundreds of changes' were ordered without following contractual
change-order procedures" (citing *C. Norman Peterson*, 218 Cal. Rptr. 592, 599). L.K. Comstock &
Co. v. Becon Constr. Co., 932 F. Supp. 906, 907, 935 (E.D. Ky. 1993), involving a subcontractor's
claim against a general contractor to the effect that "changes which occurred during performance of
[the] contract in work to be performed by [the] subcontractor constituted abandonment or cardinal
change entitling subcontractor to restitution," also distinguished *C. Norman Peterson* on the ground,
"[m]ost critically . . . Comstock not only finished the job . . . but repeatedly reaffirmed its adherence
to the contract established by the parties." In other words, there was no intention to abandon the contract. However, demonstrating that any good authority is subject to expansive use, in General Motors
Corp. v. Northrop Corp., 685 N.E.2d 127, 141 (Ind. App. 1997), a mixed federal and California law
decision growing out of an advanced technology defense contract, the *C. Norman Peterson* decision
was cited as authority for the recovery of additional expenses arising from "reasonable reliance upon
defective specifications provided by a private party."

[114] 218 Cal. Rptr. 592, 599.

[115] 218 Cal. Rptr. 592, 600 (citing Souza & McCue Constr. Co. v. Superior Court, 370 P.2d 338,
20 Cal. Rptr. 634 (1962)) (implied warranty of correctness of plans and specifications); Warner
Constr. Corp. v. City of L.A., 466 P.2d 996 (Cal. 1970) (owner liability for misrepresentation in failure to disclose knowledge of difficulties affecting contractor performance).

[116] 713 A.2d 1234 (R.I. 1998).

[117] 713 A.2d 1234, 1237.

discovery coupled with [owner's] intransigence in failing to renegotiate . . . forever extinguished its obligation under the contract."[118] The Rhode Island Supreme Court affirmed the trial court's finding of impracticability, noting *inter alia* that "the nonexistence of the ledge was a basic assumption of the parties," a point confirmed by the fact that the actual blasting cost to remove the ledge ("closer to $40,000") was four times the contracting parties' contractual estimate of a shared cost of $10,000.[119] "Accordingly, we hold that the discovery of the ledge so increased the burden upon the defendant . . . that further performance . . . was rendered impracticable."[120] However, although the defendant was relieved of its performance obligation, the court nonetheless held it liable for the return of payments proportional to the work within the scope of the original contract but performed by the replacement contractor.[121] And, separately, the contractor was held entitled to its contractually-agreed share of blasting costs on the ledge in fact expended, even though substantial performance was not provided since some benefit was provided sufficient "to forgo strict adherence to the general rule" for providing contractual relief.[122]

Although as a matter of logical consistency construction contract changes ought to flow from some contractual authorization, it is apparent that in an impracticability case, the great disruption of the parties' contract that has occurred leads the courts to search for grounds to provide relief. In all the three cases noted in this section, a changes provision was available, but relief from impracticability was provided on different reasoning in each case.

[E] Project Continuation Despite Impracticability

As the authorities discussed in the earlier sections have indicated, the most probable occurrence of a change resulting from impracticability is when the parties, notwithstanding the occurrence, determine to continue with their enterprise. Because the parties' contract as originally entered into is by definition impossible to perform in such circumstances, the parties' continued performance is also, by definition, a change. In most such situations, the mere continuation of the work will presumably reflect some satisfactory accommodation between the parties. But the authorities indicate that there are several relevant legal theories whereby the parties' conduct can be evaluated and proper adjustments made. These range from the contractually defined procedures approved in the federal contract cases to the principles of restitution and noncontractual recovery, and the allowance of damages for breach approved in other decisions.[123] It is apparent that some

---

[118] 713 A.2d 1234, 1238.

[119] 713 A.2d 1234, 1239.

[120] *Id.*

[121] 713 A.2d 1234, 1240.

[122] *Id.*

[123] To recap: breach of implied warranty in *Big Chief*, breach of contract in failure to issue change order in *Warner Construction*; noncontractual recovery (quantum meruit) for abandonment in *C. Norman Peterson*; equitable allocation of costs through reformation in *National Presto*.

continuation of the project is the primary consideration in developing a case that permits the courts to ensure that justice is done in such circumstances.

§ 10.04 CONCLUSION

Because impracticability is an excuse of performance, the mere occurrence of impracticability affecting contract performance need not lead to a conclusion that the contracting parties' contractual relationship has changed. But litigation indicates that changes analysis—and, as much, the predicate underlying federal changes analysis—is a useful technique for addressing impracticability. The result is not always expressed as a change order-equitable adjustment, but the result, in a proper case, is not greatly different.

CHAPTER 11
THE CARDINAL CHANGE

Kenneth C. Gibbs
James L. Ferro

§ 11.01   DEFINITION OF CARDINAL CHANGE

A cardinal change is a breach of contract by the owner that occurs when an owner effects an alteration in the work so drastic that the contractor is required to perform duties materially different from those for which it contracted.[1] A cardinal change is so profound that the contractor is not limited by the provisions of the contract in recovering costs and damages from the owner.[2] One court has stated that the purpose of the cardinal change doctrine is "[t]o provide a breach remedy for contractors who are directed by the government to perform work which is not within the general scope of the contract."[3] Although a changes clause in the contract allows the government to make changes within the scope of the contract, it does not authorize a cardinal change.

Definition of a *cardinal change* might be: (1) increased time to contract completion; (2) increased cost of raw material; (3) a requirement that different raw material be used; (4) different equipment or tooling requirements; (5) increased labor demands or the requirement of more skilled laborers; (6) a percentage increase in the size of the project; or (7) an increase in the number of items to be produced.[4]

In effect, a cardinal change can free the contractor from the terms of its bid and of the contract and allow it to recover the reasonable value of the labor and materials provided to the project plus reasonable markups for overhead and profit.[5] "[D]amages may include compensation for pecuniary loss, such as profits that could have been realized but for the breach, that are a consequence of the breach."[6]

Courts have described the nature of the changes necessary to a finding of a cardinal change as "substantial,"[7] "material,"[8] "radical,"[9] "profound,"[10] "drastic,"[11] and "fundamental."[12] Other courts have described the circumstances that give rise

---

[1] Allied Materials & Equip. Co. v. United States, 569 F.2d 562, 215 Ct. Cl. 406 (1978).

[2] 569 F.2d at 564.

[3] Edwin R. Marden Corp. v. United States, 442 F.2d 364, 369, 194 Ct. Cl. 799 (1971).

[4] Powell, *The Cardinal Change Doctrine and Its Application to Government Construction Contracts*, 24 Pub. Cont. L.J. 377 (No. 3, Spring 1995).

[5] *See* Allied Materials & Equip. Co. v. United States, 569 F.2d 562 (Ct. Cl. 1978); Wunderlich Contracting Co. v. United States, 351 F.2d 956, 173 Ct. Cl. 180 (1965).

[6] Big Chief Drilling Co. v. United States, 26 Cl. Ct. 1276, 1321 (1992) (quoting Town of N. Bonneville v. United States, 11 Cl. Ct. 694, 726, *aff'd in part, rev'd in part*, 833 F.2d 1024 (Fed. Cir. 1987) (mem.), *cert. denied*, 485 U.S. 1007, 108 S. Ct. 1470 (1988)).

[7] Allied Mills, Inc. v. St. John, 275 Ala. 69, 71, 152 So. 2d 133 (1963).

[8] County of Greenlee v. Webster, 25 Ariz. 183, 194, 215 P. 161 (1923).

[9] 25 Ariz. 183, 196, 215 P. 161, 165.

[10] Allied Materials & Equip. Co. v. United States, 569 F.2d 562, 564, 215 Ct. Cl. 406 (1978).

[11] Luria Bros. & Co. v. United States, 369 F.2d 701, 707, 177 Ct. Cl. 676 (1966). *See also* Saddler v. United States, 287 F.2d 411, 152 Ct. Cl. 557 (1961); Ruckman & Hansen, Inc. v. Delaware River & Bay Auth., 244 A.2d 277 (Del. 1968).

[12] Air-A-Plane Corp. v. United States, 408 F.2d 1030, 1033, 187 Ct. Cl. 269 (1969).

to a cardinal change as an "abandonment of contract,"[13] which can occur not necessarily from one change but from the cumulative impact of many changes. Taken individually, these changes would not amount to a cardinal change. One court stated the doctrine as follows:

> In the specific context of construction contracts, however, it has been held that when an owner imposes upon the contractor an excessive number of changes such that it can fairly be said that the scope of the work under the contract has been altered, an abandonment of contract properly may be found. In these cases, the contractor, with the full approval and expectation of the owner, may complete the project. Although the contract may be abandoned, the work is not. Under this line of reasoning, the trial court was well justified in determining that, by their course of conduct, the parties had abandoned the terms of the written contract . . . . [14]

However, analyzing a sheer number of changes as being "excessive" does not automatically mean that a cardinal change has occurred. A determination of a cardinal change can only be reached by considering the circumstances surrounding the changes, including an analysis of the magnitude as well as the quantity of the changes:

> The number of changes is not, in and of itself, the test by which it should be determined whether or not alterations are outside the scope of a contract. This court decided in Magoba Construction Co. v. United States, 1943, 99 Ct. Cl. 662, that the Government had not breached a construction contract in which it had made 62 separate changes. On the other hand, obviously, a single change which is beyond the scope of a contract may be serious enough to constitute an actionable breach of that contract.[15]

Factors weighed and considered by the courts in determining the applicability of the cardinal change doctrine include the following:

1. The adequacy or completeness of the design documents at the start of the project;

2. The totality of the changes, including the number, magnitude, nature and quality, costs, and complexity (in relation to the original contract);

3. The amount of time spent on redesign or completion of the design during the course of the project;

---

[13] Opdyke & Butler v. Silver, 111 Cal. App. 2d 912, 245 P.2d 306 (1952); Daugherty Co. v. Kimberly-Clark Corp., 14 Cal. App. 3d 151, 92 Cal. Rptr. 120 (1971); C. Norman Peterson Co. v. Container Corp. of Am., 172 Cal. App. 3d 628, 218 Cal. Rptr. 592 (1985); H.T.C. Corp. v. Olds, 486 P.2d 463 (Colo. Ct. App. 1971); Olbert v. Ede, 338 Wis. 2d 240, 156 N.W.2d 422 (1968).

[14] C. Norman Peterson Co. v. Container Corp. of Am., 172 Cal. App. 3d 628, 640, 218 Cal. Rptr. 592, 598 (1985) (citations omitted).

[15] Saddler v. United States, 287 F.2d 411, 413, 152 Ct. Cl. 557 (1961).

4. The extent to which the change order or other contract procedures were followed during the course of the project in the administration of the changes;

5. The extent of the owner-caused delays in the work and the effect of such delays on the duration of the contract;

6. Whether the conditions under which the contractor expected to perform its work were substantially altered or whether the owner caused the contractor to change its planned means and methods of prosecution of the work;

7. Whether the completed project is substantially the same as the project contemplated by the parties; and

8. The extent to which the additional costs can be quantified and tracked to specific changes, the condition of the contractor's records relating to the changes and costs, and whether the condition of the records was affected by the owner.[16]

As a general rule, the General Accounting Office (GAO) will not review protests involving contract modifications because modification protests are matters of contract administration not within the scope of the GAO's bid protest function. However, the GAO will review modifications that are beyond the scope of the original contract to determine whether the modification should have been bid on competitively in accordance with statutory requirements or justified as a sole-source procurement.[17]

Traditionally, the GAO has followed the same approach with respect to task or delivery orders. In establishing a statutory scheme for task and delivery order contracts, the Federal Acquisition Streamlining Act of 1994 (FASA) permits a protest in connection with the issuance of a task or delivery order only on the ground that the order increases the scope, period, or maximum value of the contract.[18] The task and delivery order protest provisions are codified at 10 U.S.C. § 2304c(d) and 41 U.S.C. § 253j(d).

In considering protests of beyond-the-scope modifications, the GAO looks at whether there is a material difference between the work required under the modification or order and the terms of the original contract. Evidence of a material difference may be found in such factors as the type of work, performance period, or costs. Because the reason for the inquiry is to ensure the integrity of the competitive process, the critical issue is whether the change is one that potential offerors reasonably could have anticipated at the time of the initial contract.[19]

---

[16] *See, e.g.,* C. Norman Peterson Co. v. Container Corp. of Am., 172 Cal. App. 3d 628, 218 Cal. Rptr. 592 (1985).

[17] W. Woods, *General Accounting Office Reining in Out-of-Scope Work*, 33 Procurement Law. 27 (No. 4, Summer 1998).

[18] *Id.* at 27, citing Pub. L. No. 103-355, §§ 1004 and 1054.

[19] Woods at 27.

The GAO examines the modifications from the viewpoint of whether it limited competition for the work. The standards that the GAO used to determine whether a modification should have been bid on competitively may also be used to determine whether the modification constitutes a cardinal change. A review of the following several decisions suggests that the GAO enforces contract limitations on the services to be provided while discounting broad descriptions of potential future modifications.

In *MCI Telecommunications Corp.*,[20] the modification of an AT&T-dedicated transmission services contract permitted AT&T to design and maintain customized networks for agencies. MCI Telecommunications Corporation protested the modification. The original specifications had advised of the possibility of changes to the contract to improve services, features, or other requirements because of the rapidly changing telecommunications environment. The GAO determined the modification to be outside of the contract despite the broad descriptions of the type of future changes to be expected. The GAO focused on the difference between providing transmission services, which generally end at a customer's service delivery point, and network outsourcing, which requires involvement with the customer's private network.[21]

In *Sprint Communications Co.*,[22] MCI held a contract for bandwidth management and switching services. The contract stated that the contractor would not be required to provide access to the network or transmission services. Sprint protested when MCI's contract was modified to add an additional service with a transmission component. The GAO found the type of work initially required with the contract as modified to be materially different and sustained the protest.

In *Comdisco, Inc.*,[23] the GAO sustained a protest involving three task orders issued under Information Technology Omnibus Procurement (ITOP) contracts awarded by the Department of Transportation. The solicitation had advised that task orders would be issued to obtain a wide variety of support resources related to information resource management. The value of any hardware or software acquired, however, was to be limited to 25 percent of the value of a task order. The three task orders required the contractor to provide replacement computer equipment for up to six weeks. The GAO found that the task orders effectively constituted leases of the equipment the contractor was to provide. Because the agency failed to show that the value of the equipment was within the 25-percent limitation specified in the solicitation, the GAO concluded that the task orders were outside the scope of the ITOP contract.

In *Ervin & Associates, Inc.*,[24] the underlying contract required a broad range of administrative, accounting, and analytical support services in connection with Federal Housing Administration assets, such as mortgage notes. Two days before the contract expired, HUD issued a task order for due diligence services to support

---

[20] B-276659, 97-2 CPD 90 (Sept. 29, 1997).
[21] Woods at 27.
[22] B-278407.2, 98-1 CPD 60 (Feb. 13, 1998).
[23] B-277340, 97-2 CPD 105 (Oct. 1, 1997).
[24] B-278850, 98-1 CPD ___ (Mar. 23, 1998).

a portfolio reengineering demonstration program that had not been authorized at the time the contract had been awarded and was not mentioned in the solicitation. The $15 million not-to-exceed value of the modification was one-half of the maximum value of the entire contract. The GAO sustained the protest, concluding that the task order was not of the type that potential offerors reasonably could have anticipated.[25]

In a second case with the same name, *Ervin & Associates, Inc.*,[26] the contract was for management studies and analytical services covering any of the functions for which HUD was responsible. Ervin & Associates had competed unsuccessfully for the contract and protested two task orders as outside the scope of the contract. The GAO compared the terms of the contract and the proposed task orders in a number of areas: the organizational components and programs for which services may be requested, the types of services, and the degree of flexibility described in the contract. The GAO denied the protest because the contract described the anticipated services in such broad, general, and flexible terms that potential offerors reasonably would have anticipated being asked to perform nearly any type of management support services.[27]

The GAO also expressed its concerns about overly broad statements of work in task order contracts in letters this year to the army and the air force. The letters advised the agencies that all-encompassing work statements that do not reasonably describe the scope of services that will be required do not provide potential offerors notice of the work that will be within the scope of the resulting contract.[28]

Even though it is well established by the United States Court of Federal Claims that a cardinal change is a breach of contract by the government, the doctrine is seldom used by contractors to justify an actual physical abandonment of, or walkoff from, the project,[29] notwithstanding the fact that there is case authority supporting actual physical abandonment under appropriate conditions.[30] The essence of the cardinal change doctrine has been to allow the contractor to recover additional damages, whether in terms of a total cost claim, a change in unit prices, or other extra-contractual adjustments. As a practical matter, few contractors can afford to risk the damages that would be assessed against them if such an actual physical abandonment were found to be improper.[31]

---

[25] Woods at 28.

[26] B-279083, 98-1 CPD ___ (Apr. 30, 1998).

[27] Woods at 28.

[28] Woods at 28, citing Letter to the Acting Secretary of the Army, B-277979, 98-1 CPD 51 (Jan. 26, 1998).

[29] *See* C. Vacketta & T. Wheeler, *A Government Contractor's Right to Abandon Performance*, 65 Geo. L.J. 27, 41 (1976).

[30] *See* Peter Kiewit Sons' Co. v. Summit Constr. Co., 422 F.2d 242 (8th Cir. 1969) (applying South Dakota law); Allied Materials & Equip. Co. v. United States, 569 F.2d 562, 215 Ct. Cl. 406 (1978).

[31] *See* C. Vacketta & T. Wheeler, *A Government Contractor's Right to Abandon Performance*, 65 Geo. L.J. 27, 30 (1976).

§ 11.02   ORIGINS IN STATE COURTS

A basic tenet of contract law is that a breach of contract entitles the aggrieved party to damages. Such damages are intended to give the damaged party the benefit of the bargain and to put the party in the position it would have been in but for the breach. These damages may include lost income or profits if portions of a contract are deleted, or extra costs if added work is required by the other party.[32]

For example, in *McMaster v. State of New York*,[33] a contractor agreed to supply and cut hard sandstone for use in the exterior facings of the walls of buildings to be constructed at the Buffalo State Asylum for the Insane. The Asylum buildings to be constructed included an administration building, five male wards designated "A" through "E," five female wards designated "A" through "E," and several outbuildings, including a laundry, an icehouse, and two barns. After the central building, the outbuildings, and the five male wards had been completed, state managers ordered the contractor to remove all stone from the grounds within ten days. The five female wards were never built. The McMaster court affirmed the Court of Claims finding that the contractor was entitled to lost profits in the sum of $ 75,000 due to the State's breach of contract in omitting from the construction the five female wards. The court found that the State "certainly had no right to omit entirely the construction of all or any of the buildings."[34] "The refusal of the state to build them [the five female wards] and to allow the contractors to furnish and cut the stone for them constituted a breach of the contracts which made it liable for damages."[35]

As early as 1923, a state court had dealt with circumstances that involved cardinal change-like conditions and had allowed recovery in quantum meruit. In *County of Greenlee v. Webster*,[36] the Arizona Supreme Court found that the county's "many alterations in the plans and specifications, resulting in the alteration of the quantity, location and extent of the work as originally estimated and described in the contract . . . were unreasonable and had the effect of changing the general character of the contract."[37] The court agreed with the plaintiff contractor that

> [T]he changes in the alignment of the road were material and substantial changes in the contract, which . . . greatly increased the rock excavation, . . . compelled the use of pack animals instead of wagons to move excavated material, increased the cost of blasting on account of passing through a settlement of houses, also because of several railroad crossings, and necessitated the removal of material three times in connection with construction of said crossings.[38]

---

[32] *See generally* 4 Corbin on Contracts, Breach of Contract §§ 943-58 at 806-50 (1951), 389-418 (Supp. 1992); 5 Corbin on Contracts, Damages as Remedy for Breach § 1094 at 508-14 (1951), 199-201 (Supp. 1992).

[33] 108 N.Y. 542, 15 N.E. 417 (1888).

[34] *Id.* at 551, 15 N.E. 417, 420.

[35] 108 N.Y. 542, 554.

[36] 25 Ariz. 183, 215 P. 161 (1923).

[37] *Id.* at 185, 215 P. 161, 162.

[38] *Id.* at 194, 215 P. 161, 164-65.

The *Webster* court went on to find that the proper basis for recovery for this extra work was the reasonable value of the labor rendered and material furnished. Another area of origin of this doctrine is the Washington state courts, which have developed a line of cases relating to recovery of damages in quantum meruit for "cardinal change-like" conditions.[39] This line of cases originated from early cases that sought to eliminate the ability of a public entity to change radically the work of contractors beyond that which was contemplated in their contracts with the public entity.[40] In *Kieburtz v. Seattle*,[41] the Washington State Supreme Court found:

> It is undoubtedly a general rule that where a municipality lets work of a public nature to a contractor to be performed according to specific plans and specifications at a stated price for the completed work, and afterwards radically or materially changes the plan of the work so as to increase the cost of performance or orders and directs the contractor to perform work or finish material not within the contemplation of the original contract, the municipality becomes liable to the contractor for the increased cost of the work, or for the extra cost of the labor and material.[42]

The *Kieburtz* court found that the contractor who built two reservoirs for the city was entitled to damages caused by the changes as well as its lost profits from the deleted portions of the original contract work.

§ 11.03 ORIGINS IN UNITED STATES COURT OF FEDERAL CLAIMS

Although the principles of the cardinal change doctrine had been used in state courts, it was the U.S. Court of Federal Claims[43] that popularized the term "cardinal change" as a shorthand method of referring to changes beyond the scope of the changes clause in government contracts. The cardinal change doctrine developed in the Court of Federal Claims to deal with those contractors' claims in which the government had breached its contracts by ordering changes that were outside the scope of the changes clause.[44] The changes clause in a government contract grants to the "contracting officer" the authority to make changes to the work within the general scope of the contract.[45]

---

[39] Many of these cases are summarized in Nelse Mortensen & Co. v. Group Health Coop., 17 Wash. App. 703, 713-19, 566 P.2d 560 (1977).

[40] *See* Atwood v. Smith, 64 Wash. 470, 177 P. 393 (1911).

[41] 84 Wash. 196, 146 P. 400 (1915).

[42] *Id.* at 203, 146 P. 400, 403.

[43] The Federal Courts Administration Act of 1992, Pub. L. No. 102-572, 106 Stat. 4506 (1992), changed the name of the United States Claims Court to the United States Court of Federal Claims. The United States Claims Court had been created by the Federal Courts Improvement Act of 1982, Pub. L. No. 97-164, 96 Stat. 25 (1982), and it inherited substantially all of the jurisdiction formerly exercised by the United States Court of Claims. For purposes of this chapter, the authors will use the current name, the United States Court of Federal Claims, or Court of Federal Claims.

[44] American Air Filler Co., Comp. Gen. Dec. B-188408, 78-1 CPD 1 136, *motion for reconsideration denied*, 78-1 CPD 1 443 (1978).

[45] American Line Builders v. United States, 26 Cl. Ct. 1155, 1177 (1992).

In a typical government contracts case, the government argued that virtually any changes required by the contracting officer were within the broad language of the changes clause. The contractor, on the other hand, argued that the changes clause had limits, that the changes ordered by the government were beyond the scope of the clause, and that such changes constituted a breach of the contract. In ruling on these disputes, the court needed a shorthand method to describe those changes that were beyond the purview of the changes clause and thus a breach of contract.[46]

The first significant Court of Federal Claims case that discussed the cardinal change doctrine was *General Contracting & Construction Co. v. United States*.[47] The contractor agreed to construct several buildings and additions to several others at the Veterans Hospital in Somerset Hills, New Jersey. After the contract was signed, but before the contractor began work, the contracting officer notified the contractor, in the Notice to Proceed, to omit Nurses Building No. 17 from the construction. A later change order deleted the building and reduced the contract price by $99,000.

The court found that the contracting officer's authority to make changes pursuant to the standard form changes clause "did not vest him with the authority to eliminate entirely from the contract Building 17." It held that this was a cardinal change to the contract itself and was a "plain breach of the contract" by the government.[48] The contractor was awarded its damages, its direct losses for payments to subcontractors in connection with the elimination of the building, and losses comprised of anticipated profits and overhead.

Although the *General Contracting* case was decided in 1937, it was not until the 1960s that the cardinal change doctrine became popularized, beginning with the often-cited case *Saddler v. United States*.[49] In *Saddler*, the contractor agreed to provide materials and labor for the construction of a levee embankment pursuant to a contract based upon unit prices for estimated quantities of embankment, backfill, and stone riprap. After construction had begun, a severe flood inundated the worksite and forced abandonment of the project for several months. The government then elected to redesign the original plans and specifications, including a change from 5,500 to 7,950 cubic yards of embankment. The contractor and government agreed on these new amounts with no increase in unit prices. After the contractor's work had once again resumed, the government requested additional work, increasing the quantity of the embankment to more than 13,000 cubic yards, and offered a change order based on the same unit price. The contractor proceeded under protest and claimed damages for its extra costs.

The court held that "[t]he nature of this particular contract was so changed by the added work, albeit the same kind of work specified in the original specifications, as to amount to a cardinal alteration falling outside of the scope of contract."[50] As

---

[46] *See, e.g.*, KECO Indus., Inc. v. United States, 364 F.2d 838, 176 Ct. Cl. 983 (1966), *cert. denied*, 386 U.S. 958 (1967).

[47] 84 Ct. Cl. 570 (1937).

[48] *Id.* at 579-80.

[49] 287 F.2d 411, 152 Ct. Cl. 557 (1961).

[50] 287 F.2d at 414-15.

a result, the court did not limit the contractor to the unit price, and the contractor was awarded damages for the labor, travel, and engineering expenses that were chargeable to the extra work.

Another widely cited case, *Wunderlich Contracting Co. v. United States*,[51] illustrates the limits of the cardinal change doctrine. In *Wunderlich*, a general contractor agreed to construct a VA hospital complex for the government in 1950 just before the outbreak of the Korean War. This 14-building hospital complex was the largest high-class construction venture ever undertaken in Salt Lake City, and because there was no prototype of this facility elsewhere, the architect had serious problems with the design of the project.

Construction was seriously delayed and hindered due to the inadequacy and ambiguities of the plans and drawings. Extensive alterations and corrections were ordered by the government, and the contractor prepared a series of 470 estimates for submission based on its costs for labor, materials, and equipment. Most of these estimates were approved because they reflected actual additional costs. They were memorialized by the issuance of 35 change orders. The contractor was also impacted by an increase in the price of materials, equipment, and wages because of the onset of the Korean War. The contractor was further impacted by the competition for skilled labor in the Salt Lake City area and with emergency military projects and other war-related construction.

The court acknowledged that the 35 change orders were extensive but found that they were not "so extensive" as to constitute a cardinal change. The court also found that "[m]anifestly, plaintiff's performance has been lengthier and costlier than anticipated at the time the bid was submitted, but in the long run they constructed essentially the same project as described in the contract."[52] During and after the mid-1960s, the attempted use of the cardinal change doctrine became widespread, leading to an increase in cases decided by the Court of Federal Claims. Many of these cases are discussed in the following sections.

§ 11.04 APPLICABILITY OF CARDINAL CHANGE DOCTRINE

As discussed in § 11.01, there are a number of key factors that the practitioner should consider in analyzing the propriety of the cardinal change doctrine in any given factual situation. **Section 11.04[A]** illustrates the circumstances in which the cardinal change doctrine is applicable. **Section 11.04[B]** illustrates those factual circumstances when the cardinal change doctrine has been found to be inappropriate.

[A] Circumstances That Support Use of the Cardinal Change Doctrine

The following are examples of cases in which the cardinal change doctrine was applied. The representative cases include those in which significant portions

---

[51] 351 F.2d 956, 173 Ct. Cl. 180 (1965).
[52] 351 F.2d 956, 966.

of the work were deleted. In one, 5 of 15 buildings were deleted; in another, one building that was 10 percent of the contract price was deleted. Included are cases in which changes caused dramatic cost increases: a 300-percent increase in back-fill costs and a 50-percent increase in overall costs in one case and a 40-percent increase in direct labor costs in another. Additional cases are included where the number and complexity of the changes were found to be cardinal changes. In one, the contractor was required to change his method of removing excavated material in a contract to construct and improve 33 miles of road; in another, over 16,000 hours of redesign time was spent on the project after the contractor began work. In still another case, the owner was required to construct 100 additional detours beyond the 28 called for in the highway construction contract.

A change in the conditions under which a contract is to be performed can result in a cardinal change. In *Westinghouse Electric Corp. v. Garrett Corp.*,[53] the court found that a prime contractor's failure to supply timely to the subcontractor source control drawings that were necessary for the subcontractor's work amounted to a constructive and a cardinal change in the way the subcontractor could perform his work.

For example, in *Peter Kiewit Sons' Co. v. Summit Construction Co.*,[54] a sub-contractor was required to modify its backfilling procedures and perform them in three phases. The piping had been layed in a manner that was much more difficult than the backfilling in a two-phase operation without any piping as agreed in the contract and specifications. The material change caused a 300-percent increase in backfill costs and a 50-percent increase in the cost of performing the overall sub-contract. The subcontractor was entitled to damages for this substantial breach of contract and change in scope.

In *General Contracting & Construction Co. v. United States*,[55] the United States Court of Federal Claims found that the government's elimination of an entire building from a hospital complex project and the resulting reduction by 10 percent in the contract price amounted to a cardinal change or alteration of the contract.

In *McMaster v. State of New York*,[56] the deletion of 5 of the 15 planned build-ings at a state hospital was a cardinal change in the design and scope of the proj-ect. The change entitled the contractor to damages.

In *Black Lake Pipe Line Co. v. Union Construction Co.*,[57] pipeline contrac-tors were entitled to damages in quantum meruit for extra work performed beyond the scope of their contracts because of requirements by the owner for approval and acceptance of the work. The court found that the owner's interpretations of the contract specifications were changes to the contract causing the contractors to per-form excessive and additional work.

---

[53] 437 F. Supp. 1301 (D. Md. 1977).
[54] 422 F.2d 242 (8th Cir. 1969).
[55] 84 Ct. Cl. 570 (1937).
[56] 108 N.Y. 542, 15 N.E. 417 (1888).
[57] 19 Tex. Sup. Ct. J. 318, 538 S.W.2d 80 (1976), *overruled on other grounds*, Sterner v. Marathon Oil Co., 32 Tex. Sup. Ct. J. 266, 767 S.W.2d 686 (1989).

In *Airprep Technology, Inc. v. United States,*[58] the Claims Court determined that defective specifications may be a cardinal change. The contractor's president testified that baghouse specifications typically contain all the information necessary to design and build the baghouse, including the positive or negative pressure under which the baghouse is to operate. In *Airprep,* the specifications were not clear as to whether the designated pressure applied to operating pressure inside the baghouse.

The contractor stated that if the indicated pressure was for internal operation, an entirely different baghouse would result. Further, if that was so, the old baghouse could not be retrofitted, required much thicker steel, and could not have been fabricated on site as the contractor had intended. The court concluded that the specifications were ambiguous and that the government interpretation would have resulted in an entirely different project. Thus, the court determined that there had been a cardinal change as a result of the ambiguity.

Krygoski Construction Co. v. United States[59] involved a contract for the removal and disposal of asbestos during a demolition and restoration project of an abandoned U.S. Air Force airstrip and missile site. The original bids for the demolition work and asbestos removal were based on estimates developed by the Corps of Engineers on the quantities of asbestos in the buildings. Krygoski Construction bid the lowest, at $414,696. When Krygoski Construction conducted a predemolition survey as required by the contract, however, it found more asbestos than estimated in the original projections, especially in the building's floor and roofing. After verifying Krygoski Construction's results, the Corps estimated that the new asbestos removal would cost at least $320,000 more than the original bid projection. The contracting officer determined that because Krygoski Construction had not commenced any work and the contract would cost the government nearly 25 percent to 33 percent more than originally intended, the price increase was a "cardinal change" in the contract's terms justifying a convenience termination under the Competition in Contracting Act (CCA).[60]

The government's contract with Krygoski Construction contained a variations-in-estimated-quantities (VEQ) clause covering a variety of asbestos abatement services. The VEQ clause allowed Krygoski Construction to remove more asbestos, if found, at the contract unit price and allowed for adjustments in the overall contract price to reflect payment for the additional removal. The insertion of the VEQ clause in the original contract meant that the government had anticipated variations in asbestos quantities, at least for the work to which the VEQ clause applied. The Court of Appeals for the Federal Circuit determined, however, that the asbestos found in the floor and roofing by Krygoski Construction was not subject to the VEQ clause protections. The court instead explained that the government was required to resolicit the contract to account for the increase in

---

[58] 30 Fed. Cl. 488 (1994).

[59] 94 F.3d 1537 (Fed. Cir.), *reh'g & reh'g en banc denied,* 1996 U.S. App. LEXIS 30308 (Fed. Cir. Nov. 7, 1996), *cert. denied,* 520 U.S. 1210, 117 S. Ct. 1691 (1997).

[60] M. Garson, *Krygoski and the Termination for Convenience: Have Circumstances Really Changed?,* 27 Pub. Cont. L.J. 117, 131-32 (No. 1, Fall 1997).

asbestos abatement quantities, which was an unexpected occurrence falling outside the scope of the contract and a "cardinal change" under the Competition in Contracting Act, especially at the $8.78 removal price per square foot offered by Krygoski Construction. The court further stated that the newly discovered asbestos, if considered within the scope of the contract at all, would be included under a fixed-price section of the contract, under which Krygoski Construction would have to remove the additional asbestos without recovering payment for the increased work. According to the court, under this second line of reasoning, the termination for convenience was extremely fair to Krygoski Construction.[61]

A contractor was entitled to recover the reasonable value of his additional work in *Allied Mills, Inc. v. St. John.*[62] This work was not within the scope of the original excavation agreement, and the work resulted in a substantial change in the excavation and sloping work performed.

In *County of Greenlee v. Webster,*[63] changes in the location and route of a roadway that resulted in greatly increased rock excavation required the contractor to change his method of removing the excavated material, increased the cost of blasting, and added additional work due to several railroad crossings. These changes were found to be radical and material changes to the general character of the contract to construct and improve some 33 miles of road.

An abandonment of contract was found and the contractor allowed to recover its total costs on a paper mill modernization project when hundreds of changes caused extra work and expense for the contractor.[64] The contractor's direct labor and material costs increased over 40 percent from the original contract amount. The plans were so incomplete and poorly engineered that the owner practically redesigned the entire project during the course of construction, spending over 16,000 hours of redesign time. In addition, these changes were presented to the contractor without following the change order procedures required by the contract.

A Colorado court found that extensive changes required by an owner that were "too numerous to list, . . . over 40 major changes" constituted an abandonment of contract even though only preliminary plans were available (and admittedly were incomplete and without specifications) when the contract was signed.[65]

In *Rudd v. Anderson,*[66] an abandonment of contract was found when homeowners requested a total of 29 changes to a remodeling contract on their homes, 15 of which were substantial. The labor and materials involved for the changes exceeded the cost of the original contract.

A combination of major changes and the cumulative effect of minor changes made "almost from day-to-day to the end of the project" were found to constitute

---

[61] Garson at 133-34.

[62] 275 Ala. 69, 152 So. 2d 133 (1963).

[63] 25 Ariz. 183, 215 P. 161 (1923).

[64] C. Norman Peterson Co. v. Container Corp. of Am., 172 Cal. App. 3d 628, 218 Cal. Rptr. 592 (1985).

[65] HTC Corp. v. Olds, 486 P.2d 463 (Colo. Ct. App. 1971).

[66] 153 Ind. App. 11, 285 N.E.2d 836 (1972).

a legal abandonment of the contract in *Schwartz v. Shelby Construction Co.*[67] The major changes in the construction plans for this large apartment complex included material structural changes, complete relocation of the bathrooms in 160 of the units, moving the locations of sinks, water heaters, and bathtubs, and the installation of additional drains.

Contract abandonment was also found in *Baerveldt & Honig Construction Co. v. Dye Candy Co.*[68] Numerous changes, some material and substantial, others trivial, so modified and changed a contract to reconstruct a fire-damaged building "that it amounted to an abandonment hereof," and the resulting building was materially different from the building provided for in the original contract.

The requirement by the state engineer that the contractor construct 100 detours in addition to the 28 called for in the contract for construction of 6.11 miles of state highway was found to be a "qualitative change in the nature of the work outside the contemplation of the contract."[69]

A Nebraska court found that the owner's "substitution of cohesive clay for cohesive granular fill material in the construction area was a substantial change in conditions which materially altered the nature and cost of the pile-driving and foundational work performed by the subcontractor," resulting in a cardinal change.[70]

In *Olbert v. Ede*,[71] a contract to build a single-family home was found to be abandoned when the owner made 69 changes during construction, many of which were very substantial, including structural and mechanical changes and changes in the materials used. The evidence also showed that during the course of construction, the owner frequently contracted directly with other contractors and suppliers who made installations at the site without regard to the contract. The plans and specifications were abandoned to such an extent that it was impossible to trace the original contract work performed.

An Arkansas court found a cardinal change had resulted from the owner's breach of the warranty of correctness of plans and specifications when the plans and specifications were deficient and incomplete, causing substantial changes and additions in the work.[72] The contractor had agreed to remodel the interior of housing units with approximately 5 percent of the work to be devoted to new construction. On beginning construction, the contractor was required to perform additional work, including work on the roof, floors, and plumbing systems, that was not within the scope of the contract. This caused delays and hindrances to the contractor's work, resulting in added costs.

In a California case, an abandonment of contract was found when a project had been "completely redesigned" after the contract was executed. An experienced

---

[67] 338 S.W.2d 781, 788-89 (Mo. 1960).

[68] 357 Mo. 1072, 1080-81, 212 S.W.2d 65 (1948).

[69] Tufano Contracting Corp. v. State, 269 N.Y.S.2d 564, 25 A.D.2d 329 (1966).

[70] Omaha Pub. Power Dist. v. Darin & Armstrong, Inc., 205 Neb. 484, 495, 288 N.W.2d 467 (1980).

[71] 338 Wis. 2d 240, 156 N.W.2d 422 (1968).

[72] Texarkana Hous. Auth. v. Johnson Constr. Co., 264 Ark. 523, 573 S.W.2d 316 (1978).

manager testified that the project was "the most poorly engineered and designed that he had ever seen; and that this poor engineering resulted in enormous change orders . . . ."[73] The court also found that abandonment of contract may be implied on the acts of the parties, "where the scope of the work undertaken greatly exceeds that called for under the contract."[74]

In *Luria Bros. & Co. v. United States*,[75] a contractor was awarded damages resulting from delay caused by defective original specifications. These specifications misrepresented the nature of the bearing value of the material underlying the foundations of the project, an airplane hangar. The court found that these misrepresentations were so extensive that the changes required to complete the structure were beyond the scope of the original contract, and that they were of such a magnitude that they constituted a contract breach.

In *Edward R. Marden Corp. v. United States*,[76] the Court of Federal Claims remanded the case to the commissioner for further proceedings on the issue of evidence of a cardinal change. Evidence was based on contractor allegations that reconstruction of the hangar building after the first hangar constructed collapsed was based upon defective plans and specifications. The court held:

> By any standard the events alleged would have been deemed to have materially altered the nature of the contractor's undertaking. If plaintiff's allegations are true, then it performed work which was not essentially the same work the parties bargained for when the contract was awarded. Our decision on this point is based on the sheer magnitude of reconstruction work caused by the alleged defective specifications.[77]

Conduct in addressing the change may be considered, along with the scope of the change, in determining whether a cardinal change has occurred. Even a few changes of smaller magnitude can be considered cardinal, if they are poorly designed and the changes are sloppily executed. However, if the owner addresses changes promptly, efficiently, and with sensitivity to the impact on the contractor, perhaps even numerous sizable changes would not rise to the level of cardinal changes.[78]

In *Sehulster/Pre-Con v. Traylor Bros./Obayashi Corp.*,[79] a California Court of Appeals interpreted the rule in *Amelco Electric v. City of Thousand Oaks*[80] (holding contractor could not claim abandonment against a public owner) as applying only to contractor claims made directly to public owners. The court held

---

[73] Daugherty Co. v. Kimberly-Clark Corp., 14 Cal. App. 3d 151, 155, 92 Cal. Rptr. 120 (1971).

[74] *Id.* at 156, 92 Cal. Rptr. at 123 (citing Opdyke & Butler v. Silver, 111 Cal. App. 2d 912, 916, 245 P.2d 306 (1952)).

[75] 369 F.2d 701, 177 Ct. Cl. 676 (1966).

[76] 442 F.2d 364, 194 Ct. Cl. 799 (1971).

[77] 442 F.2d 364, 370.

[78] Powell, *The Cardinal Change Doctrine and Its Application to Government Construction Contracts*, 24 Pub. Cont. L.J. 377 (No. 3, Spring 1995).

[79] 111 Cal. App. 4th 1328 (2003).

[80] 27 Cal. 4th 228, 38 P.3d 1120, 15 Cal. Rptr. 2d 900 (2002).

that *Amelco* does not preclude a subcontractor on a public project from recovering from the prime contractor under an abandonment theory.

Sehulster arose when Traylor Brothers contracted with the City of San Diego to build a tunnel and subcontracted with Sehulster for the manufacture and supply of tunnel ring segments. After Traylor Brothers made substantial changes to its purchase order, Sehulster submitted a claim for cost overruns it attributed to the changes. When Traylor Brothers rejected the claim, Sehulster sued for a breach of contract and abandonment, and Traylor Brothers cross-complained against the city for indemnity. The jury awarded Sehulster $2.8 million in damages and determined that Traylor Brothers was entitled to 30 percent indemnity from the city.

The court of appeals affirmed the abandonment award but reversed the indemnity determination. It found that "the public policy considerations underlying the Supreme Court's decision [in *Amelco*] do not apply in the context of two contracting private entities." Since the court also found that Traylor Brothers was not entitled to implied contractual indemnity under the particular facts of the case, it declined to consider whether *Amelco* would preclude a contractor from recovering from the public owner under an implied contractual indemnity theory where it has incurred liability under an abandonment theory.

In *J.A. Jones Construction Co. v. Lehrer McGovern Bovis, Inc.*[81] the Supreme Court of Nevada found that there was sufficient evidence of a cardinal change in a construction contract to submit a subcontractor's cardinal change claim to a jury where the subcontractor presented testimony demonstrating material impacts on its contractual scope of work, where the cost of the entire project totaled over $8.8 million after J.A Jones anticipated the costs to be $5.5 million, with experts testifying that $4 million of the total costs stemmed from changes. The court found that although there was no change in the final project, a cardinal change could still occur because the court looks to the entire undertaking of the contractor, rather than the final product, when applying the cardinal change doctrine.

As the preceding cases illustrate, there is a wide variety of factual circumstances that have been found to be sufficient for the application of the cardinal change doctrine. The doctrine can be applied when there is a dramatic change in a single factor or when there are changes to many of the factors.

[B]   Circumstances Insufficient to Support Use of the Cardinal Change Doctrine

The following cases include those in which the degree of change was not significant enough to result in the application of the cardinal change doctrine. In some of these cases, the court found that the changes were within the contemplation of the contract, while in others, the dollar value of the change was insufficient. Still others show that the court found that the changes did not materially alter the essence of the contract.

---

[81] 89 P.3d 1009 (2004).

Even dramatic changes in conditions do not necessarily result in a cardinal change. A New York court found that a disclaimer by the city for any responsibility for the accuracy or completeness of information concerning existing conditions in its contract for street improvements relieved the city of responsibility. At issue was the contractor's excavation of over 600 cubic yards of rock when the job drawings showed only 20 cubic yards of rock to be excavated and the specifications estimated about 100 cubic yards.[82]

Regardless of the number of changes, a contractor must make a reasonable effort to maintain sufficient records to demonstrate the additional cost of the multiple modifications. A contractor cannot rely on abandonment to recover all its cost overruns. In *Amelco Electric v. City of Thousand Oaks*,[83] the City of Thousand Oaks solicited bids for electrical work to be performed in the construction of the Civic Arts Plaza. The project was managed by Lehrer McGovern Bovis, Inc. (LMB). Amelco Electric was awarded the contract. Amelco asserted that LMB improperly shifted engineering documentation responsibilities to Amelco. Amelco also expressed concern that the electrical drawings being issued did not identify all revisions, or contain all prior revisions, and gave examples of how these omissions interfered with its performance. Amelco requested a change order and $203,759 in additional funds to update the drawings. LMB refused.

Amelco accepted this decision, did not hire any additional personnel to do the work, and signed a change order for zero dollars and zero additional time, because LMB verbally promised that "things are going to get better." Although Amelco maintained daily records of its work activities, it was unable to produce documentation of instances in which its performance of a work directive or change order was delayed or interfered with by LMB's actions, and for which it was not compensated. The person responsible for actually recording the information in the contractor's daily log testified he would not record changes. Amelco's vice president asserted that the sheer number of changes made it "impossible" to keep track of the impact any one change had on the project or on Amelco. Amelco conceded that it was inefficient in performing the work, but assigned responsibility for virtually all of that inefficiency to LMB. Amelco submitted a $1.7 million total cost claim for costs allegedly resulting from the noncaptured costs of the change orders. Amelco sued under an abandonment theory of liability, where existing case law held that a contractor could recover from a private owner for the reasonable value of its services where the owner had made so many changes to a contract that it could have abandoned the contract. The jury found that the city had both breached and abandoned the contract, and awarded Amelco $2,134,586. The court of appeals affirmed the decision, concluding that as a matter of law a public works contract could be abandoned. The California Supreme Court reversed.

In *Amelco,* the California Supreme Court reversed the opinion of the trial court and the appellate court, holding that a contractor cannot recover against a public owner under the theory of abandonment. The court relied upon California's

---

[82] Constanza Constr. Corp. v. City of Rochester, 537 N.Y.S.2d 394, 147 A.D.2d 929 (1989).
[83] 27 Cal. 4th 228, 38 P.3d 1120, 15 Cal. Rptr. 2d 900 (2002).

void contract rule that prohibits a contractor from being paid for work performed under a contract that is subsequently declared void because the pubic owner was not authorized to award the contract in the first place. In *Amelco*, the court extended the application of this rule from problems that arise during the bidding of a contract to problems that arise during performance. The court concluded that allowing abandonment claims in the public works context would render the concept of competitive bidding meaningless.

In addition, changed conditions will not afford relief to a contractor when the contractor should have discovered or anticipated those changed conditions.[84] For example, in *Hensel Phelps Construction Co. v. King County*,[85] the painting subcontractor on an 18-story jail project was forced to operate under an accelerated timetable because of delays in the start of the project. This resulted in a stacking of trades and an increased amount of touch-up work. The contractor was denied recovery because the contract provided for such occurrences and the magnitude of these changed conditions was within the contemplation of the contract.

In *KECO Industries, Inc. v. United States*,[86] the contractor agreed to produce 270 refrigeration units of which 170 were to be electrically powered and 100 were to be gas powered. The government then directed that the 100 gas units be changed to electric. The court found that this change was within the scope of the original contract and, therefore, not a cardinal change.

In *F.H. McGraw & Co. v. United States*,[87] the Court of Federal Claims found that even when changes to the plans and specifications were "extensive and complicated, [and] would materially effect and curtail the work of the mechanical trades and thus the finishing trades . . . such changes were not sufficient to constitute a Cardinal Change." The project involved construction of two ten-story wings to an existing hospital building, a separate three-story building, several connecting corridors, and alterations to the boilerhouse building for the Veterans Administration. Once the work was fully in progress, the VA issued stop orders halting work on a large portion of the project pending its decision on certain design changes. The changes contemplated involved switching and moving certain operating units of the hospital from floor to floor. This included the morgue and embalming rooms, general office space, handicraft workshops, patients' dining rooms, serving kitchens, dishwashing rooms, offices, wards, and operating suites. Other changes affected the mechanical installation necessary to service the changed locations of these various facilities.

The Court of Federal Claims found no cardinal change in *Magoba Construction Co. v. United States*,[88] in which the contractor was to remodel a building to house the post office and courthouse in Brooklyn, New York, for $2,050,000. The court found that the 62 changes made during the course of the

---

[84] V.C. Edwards Contracting Co. v. Port of Tacoma, 83 Wash. 2d 7, 13, 514 P.2d 1381 (1973).

[85] 57 Wash. App. 170, 787 P.2d 58 (1990).

[86] 364 F.2d 838, 176 Ct. Cl. 983 (1966), *cert. denied*, 386 U.S. 958 (1967).

[87] 130 F. Supp. 394, 131 Ct. Cl. 501 (1955).

[88] 99 Ct. Cl. 662 (1943).

project, causing a net increase of approximately $80,000 to the contract, did not constitute a breach and were reasonable in light of the size of the project.

Similarly, in *Aragona Construction Co. v. United States*,[89] the court found no cardinal change when work done was "essentially the same work as the parties bargained for when the contract was awarded."[90] "[T]he changes did not materially alter the nature of the bargain into which the plaintiff had entered or cause it to perform a different contract."[91] The hospital building, when completed, was in the same location, looked the same, and had the same number of rooms and floors and the same facilities as the one shown on the original plans and specifications. Apart from the substitution of materials, it differed not at all from the building that had been contemplated when the contract was awarded.[92]

An owner that pays for additional work does not breach the contract by abandoning it as long as the amount of additional work is reasonable. In *Bartz v. Hewitt*,[93] Hewitt constructed a home for Bartz. Although the contract required a down payment of $33,500, the buyer gave the contractor $50,000 based upon the understanding that there would be changes to the contract's specifications. The buyer also obtained a construction loan in the amount of $100,000 to be released in five scheduled payments. The contractor received three of the scheduled payments as it progressed through various stages of construction. When the bank released the fourth scheduled payment together with a portion of the fifth payment, the buyer refused to sign the check over to the contractor because the contractor had not completed all of the required work. Although the buyer relented and delivered all of the fourth scheduled payment the next day, the contractor filed a mechanic's lien against the property in the amount of $38,500 and ceased work on the home. The buyer filed suit, alleging breach of contract and the contractor counterclaimed for unpaid labor and materials. The trial court found that the contractor had breached the contract and awarded the buyer $47,604.95. The contractor appealed.

The contractor argued that the buyer frustrated its ability to construct the home. The contractor asserted that the buyer unreasonably demanded changes that were so numerous and extensive that they not only resulted in substantial delays, but also reflected the buyer's abandonment of the contract as written. The contractor further contended that the buyer refused to pay for the changes, and wrongfully withheld funds. The contract expressly provided for changes, and the buyer's expert, a contractor with over 30 years of experience, testified that neither the number nor the nature of the changes sought was unusual. The record contained a list of agreed-to change orders the contractor prepared describing the changes, noting that changes during construction were permitted and listing the delays, only a few days of which could have been attributed to the changes. The contractor's

---

[89] 165 Ct. Cl. 382 (1964).
[90] *Id.* at 390.
[91] *Id.*
[92] *Id.* at 391.
[93] 745 N.Y.S.2d 146, 296 A.D.2d 723 (2002).

claim that the buyer refused to pay for the changes was contradicted by the buyer's acknowledgment of its obligation to pay for the cost of changes as completed and by its payment of a sum in excess of the down payment to be applied toward anticipated changes. Affirmed.

[C] Lessons Learned from Application of the Cardinal Change Doctrine

Upon a review of the above cases and the courts' applications of the factors identified, it appears that there is no rule of thumb, bright-line test, or other clear and consistent system for determining whether a given set of factual circumstances falls within the cardinal change doctrine. In fact, the authors have reviewed several cases in which the facts appear to satisfy the factors and fall within the parameters of the cardinal change, but in which the courts have declined to so find. Determination of whether a cardinal change has occurred appears to be an intensely factual, rather than a legal, analysis, and there is no certainty of the outcome of a given factual situation.

Numerous, sizable changes, if addressed promptly, efficiently, and with sensitivity to the impact on the contractor, may not rise to the level of cardinal changes.[94]

It is also easy to overlook the importance of time in a cardinal change. Courts have denied a cardinal change because of the contractor's failure to prove that the changes were responsible for the project delay.[95] Increased time of completion is a factor to be evaluated when considering whether a cardinal change has occurred.

Use of the cardinal change concept will not only continue, but also increase. As contracts limit more and more the costs that contractors may recover for delays and changes, contractors become less and less willing to perform changes or wait out delays. Instead, it appears that contractors are challenging the owner's right to require the contractor to perform the changed or delayed work. Cardinal change is often the theory under which the owner's right to insist on changed performance is challenged.

§ 11.05 RECOVERABLE DAMAGES

Upon a finding of a cardinal change, the contractor is normally entitled to recover the reasonable value of the additional work. However, as is shown in the following situations, some courts have awarded additional damages, including damages for overhead, profit, anticipated profit, delays, and damages based on a contractor's total costs for the work of improvement.

---

[94] Powell, *The Cardinal Change Doctrine and Its Application to Government Construction Contracts*, 24 Pub. Cont. L.J. 377 (No. 3, Spring 1995).

[95] Bramble & Callahan, Construction Delay Claims §§ 13.12 *et seq.* (Aspen Publishers, 3d ed., 2000 & 2004 Supp.).

[A] Quantum Meruit

In *Allied Mills, Inc. v. St. John*,[96] additional and different sloping and excavation work from that which was part of the written agreement formed a subsequent oral contract that entitled the contractor to recover his extra costs in quantum meruit. This included additional costs for excavation at the unit price specified in the written contract and additional costs for use of additional equipment including a front-end loader, bulldozer, and dump trucks.

An abandonment of contract based upon extensive changes required by the owner, including over 40 major changes, entitled the contractor to recover his costs in quantum meruit in *HTC Corp. v. Olds*.[97] This included the reasonable value of his labor and materials, notwithstanding the fact that the original contract provided payment on a cost-plus basis with a guaranteed maximum cost provision.

In *Schwartz v. Shelby Construction Co.*,[98] the reasonable value of material, labor, and services was awarded to a contractor. The court found a legal abandonment of the contract caused by the conduct of the parties based upon a number of major changes to the construction and cumulative effect of numerous minor changes. Similarly, an award of quantum meruit for the reasonable value of work and labor performed by a contractor was affirmed when the conduct of the parties showed that the old contract was abandoned and the parties were operating under a new implied contract.[99]

A subcontractor performing site work, excavation, and backfilling work was entitled to damages in quantum meruit in *Peter Kiewit Sons' Co. v. Summit Construction Co.*[100] This included actual expenditures plus 15 percent for overhead and profit for completed work based upon the general contractor's requirement that the work be performed in a materially different fashion that resulted in a change in the scope of the work.

Quantum meruit recovery was allowed in *Black Lake Pipe Line Co. v. Union Construction Co.*[101] The pipeline contractors were required to perform extra work beyond the scope of their contracts due to the owner's interpretations of the contract specifications.

A reasonable value for the services rendered and materials furnished by the contractor was the measure of damages in *Olbert v. Ede*.[102] The contract to build a single-family home was found to be abandoned in light of the substantial changes during the course of construction. There were 69 changes, including substantial structural mechanical changes and material changes.

---

[96] 275 Ala. 69, 70, 152 So. 2d 133 (1963).

[97] 486 P.2d 463, 465, 467 (Colo. Ct. App. 1971).

[98] 338 S.W.2d 781, 792-93 (Mo. 1960).

[99] Baerveldt & Honig Constr. Co. v. Dye Candy Co., 357 Mo. 1072, 1081-82, 212 S.W.2d 65 (1948).

[100] 422 F.2d 242 (8th Cir. 1969).

[101] 19 Tex. Sup. Ct. J. 318, 538 S.W.2d 80 (1976), *overruled on other grounds*, Sterner v. Marathon Oil Co., 32 Tex. Sup. Ct. J. 266, 767 S.W.2d 686 (1989).

[102] 338 Wis. 2d 240, 156 N.W.2d 422 (1968).

A written contract does not prevent recovery in quantum meruit after the owner accepted a subsequent verbal modification. For example, in *Abington Constructors, Inc. v. Madison Paper Industries*,[103] Madison Paper Industries requested bids on a project to reconstruct a dam. Cofferdams were necessary because work below the water level of a river was required. The bidding instructions placed responsibility on the bidder to be familiar with the site terrain. When the contractor visited the site to conduct an inspection, the river flows were too high for it to survey the river and the contractor declined to revisit the site. In its bid, the contractor represented that it carefully studied the subsurface conditions at the site. The parties agreed to a purchase order that referenced the project manual as well as the contractor's bid form. Prior to awarding the contract, the owner had issued an addendum stating that it would pay replacement costs for cofferdams in the event of floods. The district court found that the contractor committed a breach, although not in bad faith, by failing to conduct its own investigation.

The contractor experienced additional costs due to water levels and river bottom configurations that were different from specifications in the project manual. The contractor stated in a letter that it was compiling the costs associated with the unexpected conditions and requested a change order. Later, a series of floods caused extensive delay on the project. The contract provided that when high water flows caused delay, the contractor would be granted an extension of time. The owner also indicated that it would cover some, if not all, of the additional costs caused by the faulty specifications and high water flows. The contractor relied on this statement in continuing to work on the project during subsequent high water flows even though it was entitled to a time extension, and it worked seven days a week in hopes of completing the project on schedule. The contractor also sent a written memo seeking a change order and reiterating that the costs associated with repairs due to the flooding would be covered pursuant to the addendum of the contract. At several subsequent construction meetings, the owner indicated either that it was reviewing the cost overruns or that they would be dealt with at the end of the job, never stating that it refused to pay. The owner's internal documents showed that it set aside $100,000 for anticipated extra costs.

The contractor claimed additional costs under a number of liability theories including quantum meruit, unjust enrichment, mutual mistake, impracticability, and breach of contract. The district court found that although the parties had a contract, the contractor was entitled to quantum meruit recovery for the additional work and granted the contractor the reasonable value of its services. The owner appealed, contending that quantum meruit recovery was not available under Maine law when the parties had negotiated a contract. The appellate court stated that the fact that an express contract had been made did not prevent the parties from making another one concerning the same subject matter. Further, the fact that a contract has been put into express words did not prevent modification by implication from the conduct of the parties and from surrounding circumstances. If good-faith efforts in the field to overcome adverse conditions and get on with the job could

---

[103] 215 F.3d 1311 (2000) (unpublished decision).

always be trumped by the original written contract, the arteries of commerce, particularly in construction, would harden. The contractor was entitled to recovery in quantum meruit. The evidence supported the district court's conclusion that the elements of quantum meruit existed. The judgment of the district court was affirmed.

[B] Total Costs

A total cost recovery was allowed to a contractor who performed modernization work at a paper mill in *C. Norman Peterson Co. v. Container Corp. of America*.[104] There were hundreds of changes, many of which were significant, that increased the contractor's direct labor and material costs (not including profit or overhead) to $8,194,000. This was $3,405,000 more than the original contract amount of $4,789,000. This total cost award was also based upon the fact that the owner had expended 16,414 hours of redesign time on the project after the contractor began work and that many of the changes were made without following procedures required by the contract. The court held that the contractor was entitled to recover the unpaid reasonable costs of its work. Further, it established that the contractor's total costs were the best indication of the reasonable value of that contractor's work because the contractor was unable to keep accurate cost records due in large part to the fault of the owner.

In *Amelco Electric v. City of Thousand Oaks*,[105] the California Supreme Court, although ruling that the "abandonment of contract" legal doctrine cannot be asserted against a public entity, reasoning that this theory of recovery was in direct contravention with the public policy underlying the competitive bidding statutes, nevertheless held that the "total cost method" of measuring damages can be applied against the public entity. However, the contractor must satisfy the four-part test annunciated in *Servidone Construction Corp. v. United States*.[106] This test requires that the contractor establish (1) the impractability of proving actual losses directly; (2) that the contractor's original bid was reasonable; (3) that the contractor's actual costs were reasonable; and (4) that the contractor was not responsible for the added costs.

In *Omaha Public Power District v. Darin & Armstrong, Inc.*,[107] a Nebraska court allowed a contractor recovery pursuant to the total cost method. It found this method "permissible when no other method was feasible and the supporting evidence was substantial." The court then held that:

> The acceptability of the total cost method hinges on proof that: (1) the nature of the particular losses make it impossible or highly impractical to determine them with a reasonable degree of accuracy; (2) the bid or estimate was realistic;

[104] 172 Cal. App. 3d 628, 641-42, 218 Cal. Rptr. 592 (1985).
[105] 27 Cal. 4th 228, 38 P.3d 1120, 15 Cal. Rptr. 2d 900 (2002).
[106] 931 F.2d 860 (1991).
[107] 205 Neb. 484, 495, 288 N.W.2d 467 (1982).

(3) the actual costs were reasonable; and (4) the contractor was not responsible for the added expenses.[108]

[C]   Time and Materials/Cost Plus

In *Opdyke & Butler v. Silver*,[109] in which an abandonment of contract was found, the maximum price provision of the written contract was disregarded. The contractor was entitled to damages on a straight cost-plus-10-percent basis, which had been orally agreed to by the parties.

In *Rudd v. Anderson*,[110] substantial changes were made to a home remodeling contract so as to cause an abandonment of that contract. The court determined that the measure of value for the total remodeling construction work was the reasonable value of the work, based upon expert testimony that "the charges made for the labor and materials were reasonable and . . . the workmanship was average or above average."

[D]   Overhead and Profit

In *Texarkana Housing Authority v. Johnson Construction Co.*,[111] a contractor had been delayed in the completion of the original contract by 68 days due to the cardinal changes caused by the owner. The court found that the contractor was entitled to extended job costs and a pro rata share of home office overhead costs of $233.21 per day for each of the 68 days.

In *McMaster v. State of New York*,[112] lost profits were awarded to a contractor. The state had deleted 5 of the 15 planned buildings at a hospital complex in Buffalo, New York.

A case indicating a trend to expand the types of damages recoverable under a cardinal change is *Allied Materials & Equipment Co. v. United States*.[113] A contractor brought an action to recover anticipatory profits and other damages on the ground that the Army breached its contract by selling to plaintiff's competitors certain equipment that pursuant to the contract the plaintiff was to use in performing its obligations to supply cylinder assemblies. The Court of Claims disagreed with the government's contention that the cardinal change doctrine applied only when a plaintiff seeks extra costs incurred because of a deviation from contract terms. The court found:

> Inherent in this statement, however, is the fallacious assumption that the cardinal change concept's applicability is dictated by the nature of damages sought

---

[108] *Id.* at 496-97, 288 N.W.2d 467, 474.
[109] 111 Cal. App. 2d 912, 245 P.2d 306 (1952).
[110] 153 Ind. App. 11, 19, 285 N.E.2d 836, 841 (1972).
[111] 108 N.Y. 542, 15 N.E. 417 (1888).
[112] 569 F.2d 562, 215 Ct. Cl. 406 (1978).
[113] 569 F.2d 562, 563-64 (citations omitted).

by a plaintiff. This is simply not so. Under established case law, a cardinal change is a breach. It occurs when the Government effects an alteration in the work so drastic that it effectively requires the contractor to perform duties materially different from those originally bargained for. . . .

We have certainly never intimated, however, that the contractor is limited to a suit for extra costs incurred in performing duties fundamentally outside the scope of the contract, and we have never held that the applicability of this doctrine is in any way dependent on the nature of damages sought by the contractor. Although the typical case, thus far, has featured a plaintiff who undertook to perform despite the alteration of contractual obligations, this does not preclude a suit by a contractor who, for one reason or another, has not completed the contract. Undoubtedly, the cautious contractor might often proceed under the revised contract because of doubt whether he could invoke the Cardinal Change Doctrine. But if he has been prevented from performing, as in any breach case, the award of anticipatory profits is an appropriate remedy.[114]

The case was remanded to the district court for determination of whether there was a breach not remediable by an equitable adjustment under the contract.

[E]   Delay Damages

In *Tufano Contracting Corp. v. State of New York*,[115] the state required that a contractor performing reconstruction on a state parkway construct 128 detours although the contract required no more than 28. The contractor was entitled to recover in quantum meruit costs for all detours above the number required by contract. In addition, the contractor was entitled to damages caused by the delay to the entire project resulting from the construction of the additional detours.

§ 11.06   THE FUTURE OF THE CARDINAL CHANGE DOCTRINE

[A]   California Approach

In *Amelco Electric v. City of Thousand Oaks*,[116] the California Supreme Court recently found that the abandonment of contract doctrine was "fundamentally different" from the doctrine of cardinal change. The court also held that a contractor may not recover for abandonment of contract on a public project, reasoning that allowing abandonment claims on public works would render the concept of competitive bidding meaningless. While the *Amelco* court did not address whether a cardinal change claim would be applicable as against a public project, it appears likely that it will also be prohibited, as its application would have the same effect upon the competitive bidding process.

---

[114] 269 N.Y.S.2d 564, 25 A.D.2d 329 (1966).
[115] *Id.*
[116] 27 Cal. 4th 228, 38 P.3d 1120, 115 Cal. Rptr. 2d 900 (2002).

Subcontractors, however, are allowed to recover from their prime contractors on both private and public jobs.[117]

Abandonment of contract and cardinal change claims are still allowed as against private projects.[118] Until *Amelco*, there was general agreement among members of the California Construction Bar that the doctrine of abandonment of contract had equal application to public and private works of construction. The question now is whether the states referenced below, in which the courts have not yet ruled on the application of abandonment of contract or cardinal change to public construction projects, will follow California, utilizing the sanctity of public bidding to deny application of the doctrines.

[B]   States Allowing Recovery on Public Projects

Puerto Rico and eight states have allowed recovery or have recognized a contractor's right to recover on an abandonment of contract or cardinal change theory on public projects. These states include Arizona, Arkansas, Illinois, Maine, New York, Oregon, Washington, and Wyoming.[119]

[C]   States Allowing Recovery on Private Projects

The District of Columbia and 18 states allow recovery for cardinal change or abandonment of contract claims on private jobs.[120] These states include: Alabama,

---

[117] Sehulster Tunnels/Pre-Con v. Traylor Bros./Obayashi Corp., 111 Cal. App. 4th 1328 (2003).

[118] *See* Dodge v. Harbor Boat Bldg. Co., 99 Cal. App. 2d 782, 222 P.2d 697 (1950); Opdyken Butler v. Silver, 111 Cal. App. 2d 9, 12, 245 P.2d 306 (1952); Daugherty Co. v. Kimberly-Clark Corp., 14 Cal. App. 3d 151, 92 Cal. Rptr. 120 (1971); C. Norman Peterson Co. v. Container Corp. of Am., 172 Cal. App. 3d 628, 218 Cal. Rptr. 592 (1985).

[119] Arizona: County of Greenlee v. Webster, 25 Ariz. 183 (1923); Arkansas: Housing Auth. of Texarkana v. E.W. Johnson Constr., 264 Ark. 523 (1978); Illinois: Cook County v. Harms, 108 Ill. 151 (1883); Maine: Claude Dubois Excavating v. Kittery, 634 A.2d 1299 (Me. 1993); New York: Westcott v. State, 36 N.Y.S.2d 23 (1942); Oregon: Hayden v. Astoria, 74 Or. 525 (1915); Washington: Kieburtz v. City of Seattle, 84 Wash. 196 (1915); Wyoming: Scherer Constr., LLC v. Hedquist Constr., Inc., 18 P.3d 645 (Wyo. 2001); Puerto Rico: Paul N. Howard Co. v. Puerto Rico Aqueduct & Sewer Auth., 744 F.2d 880 (1st Cir. 1984).

[120] Alabama: Hutchinson v. Cullum, 23 Ala. 622 (1853); Colorado: H.T.C. Corp. v. Olds, 486 P.2d 463 (Colo. App. 1971); Indiana: Rudd v. Anderson, 285 N.E.2d 836 (Ind. App. 1972); Kentucky: L.K. Comstock & Co. v. Becon Constr. Co., 932 F. Supp. 906 (E.D. Ky. 1993); Louisiana: Nat Harrison Assocs., Inc. v. Gulf States Utils. Co., 493 F.2d 1405 (5th Cir. 1974); Maryland: Westinghouse Elec. Corp. v. Garrett Corp., 437 F. Supp. 1301 (D. Md. 1977); Michigan: R. M. Taylor, Inc. v. General Motors Corp., 187 F.3d 809 (8th Cir. 1999); Minnesota: Fuller Co. v. Brown Minneapolis Tank & Fabricating Co., 678 F. Supp. 506 (E.D. Pa. 1987); Missouri: Baerveldt & Honig Constr. Co. v. Dye Candy Co., 212 S.W.2d 65 (Mo. 1948); Nevada: Paterson v. Condos, 55 Nev. 134 (1934); Ohio: Oberer Constr. Co. v. Park Plaza Inc., 179 N.E.2d 168 (Ohio. Ct. App. 1961); Oklahoma: Watt Plumbing, Air Conditioning & Elec., Inc. v. Tulsa Rig, Reel & Mfg. Co., 533 P.2d 980 (Okla. 1975); Pennsylvania: E.C. Ernst, Inc. v. Koppers Co., 476 F. Supp. 729 (W.D. Pa. 1979); Rhode Island: Clark-Fitzpatrick, Inc./Franki Found. Co. v. Gill, 652 A.2d 440 (R.I. 1994); South Dakota: Peter Kiewit Sons' Co. v. Summit Constr. Co., 422 F.2d 242 (8th Cir. 1969); Texas: National

Colorado, Indiana, Kentucky, Louisiana, Maryland, Michigan, Minnesota, Missouri, Nevada, Ohio, Oklahoma, Pennsylvania, Rhode Island, South Dakota, Texas, Utah, and Wisconsin. These states, like California before *Amelco,* do not yet have any reported decisions concerning the application of the cardinal change/abandonment-of-contract doctrine on a public project.

[D]   Mississippi Says No

A federal district court has found that Mississippi law does not allow contractors to recover abandonment-of-contract or cardinal change claims on public or private projects. The seminal case establishing this approach is *Litton Systems, Inc. v. Frigitemp Corp.*[121] Litton Systems had hired Frigitemp as a subcontractor for construction of helicopters for the federal government. Litton sued Frigitemp for backcharges and Frigitemp counterclaimed, alleging a cardinal change, *inter alia,* and sought recovery for extra work in quantum meruit. The district court granted Litton's motion for summary judgment on Frigitemp's cardinal change claim, refusing to follow U.S. Court of Federal Claims cases, and holding that such a claim was not recognized under Mississippi law.[122]

[E]   States Without Reported Decisions

Courts in the 22 remaining states have not yet ruled on the application of abandonment-of-contract or cardinal change claims in any published decision.[123]

It appears that these states would most likely follow the position that the U.S. Court of Federal Claims and a majority of the states (which have considered the issue) have adopted and allow cardinal change/abandonment-of-contract recoveries on public and private projects, unless the state has a very strong public policy favoring public/competitive bidding on public jobs, which could furnish the rationale to disallow this doctrine on public projects.

[F]   United States Court of Federal Claims

As is illustrated in **§ 11.03** and the sections that follow, the cardinal change doctrine is well established in the United States Court of Federal Claims. *Becho, Inc. v. United States*[124] provides a summary of the current status of the federal law on cardinal changes: In *Becho,* the court held that the government may not impose

---

Envtl. Serv. Co. v. Homeplace Homes, Inc., 961 S.W.2d 632 (Tex. App. 1998); Utah: Rhodes v. Clute, 53 P. 990 (Utah 1898); Wisconsin: Olbert v. Ede, 156 N.W.2d 422 (Wis. 1968); District of Columbia: Blake Constr. Co. v. C. J. Coakley Co., 431 A.2d 569 (D.C. Ct. App. 1981).

[121] 613 F. Supp. 1377 (S.D. Miss. 1985).

[122] *Id.* at 1382-84.

[123] *See* A. Silberman, *Abandonment and Cardinal Change on State and Local Construction Projects,* 39 Procurement Law. 17 (No. 3, Spring 2004).

[124] 47 Fed. Cl. 595 (2000).

obligations on a contractor far exceeding anything contemplated by their contract, and if the government orders a drastic modification in the performance required by the contract, the order is considered a "cardinal change," which constitutes a material breach of the contract.[125] "Each case must be analyzed on its own facts and in light of its own circumstances, giving just consideration to the magnitude and quality of the changes ordered and their cumulative effect on the project as a whole."[126] In determining whether a cardinal change has occurred in a government contract, factors to consider include: (1) whether there is a significant change in the magnitude of work to be performed; (2) whether the change is designed to procure a totally different item or drastically alter the quality, character, nature, or type of work contemplated by the original contract; and (3) whether the cost of the work ordered greatly exceeds the original cost.[127]

---

[125] *Id.* at 600.
[126] *Id.* at 601.
[127] *Id.*

CHAPTER 12

CHANGES RESULTING FROM TERMINATION

Michael T. Callahan

12.01   TERMINATION ACCORDING TO A CONTRACT PROVISION

Although termination is one form of rescission of the contracting parties' rights, obligations, and duties after one or more parties has partially performed,[1] this chapter focuses on the termination of one party according to a contract provision, a more narrow view of termination and one closer to that anticipated when ending the performance of a contractor or subcontractor.

Either party may terminate the contract if the other party violates an express condition allowing for termination as a remedy within the contract. Termination pursuant to a failure to comply with an express contractual provision defining acts justifying termination is known as "default" termination.[2] Many contracts also permit termination without a default in a clause often entitled "Termination for Convenience."

§ 12.02   TERMINATION FOR CONVENIENCE

[A]   Generally

The termination-for-convenience clause permits contracts to be modified by either partial or complete termination for convenience without any breach or default.[3] The court in *District of Columbia v. Organization for Environmental Growth*[4] explained that the termination-for-convenience provision is a powerful tool for a public or private owner that is not balanced by a comparable right or advantage to the contractor.

Termination for convenience is available only when permitted by the contract. Although originally found only in federal government contracts, the right to terminate a contract for convenience is increasingly found in private construction contracts.[5] The Associated General Contractors of America Document No. 200, Standard Form of Agreement and General Conditions Between Owner and Contractor, provides that the owner may terminate for its convenience at Paragraph 11.4. The 1997 revisions to the American Institute of Architects (AIA) Document A201, *General Conditions of the Contract for Construction*, added a termination-for-convenience clause for the first time to AIA documents. Article 14.4.1 states that "[t]he Owner may, at any time, terminate the Contract for the Owner's convenience and without cause." Article 14.4.3 permits the contractor to recover payment for completed work and other costs incurred because of the termination, along with reasonable overhead and profit for the work that was terminated.

---

[1] Construction Law § 4.11[1] (Steven G.M. Stein ed, 1998).

[2] Construction Law § 4.13 (Steven G.M. Stein ed, 1998).

[3] M. Heley & M. Bloomquist, *The Design Professional's Role in Termination of the Contractor*, 17 Constr. Law. 3 (No. 2, Apr. 1997) (citing Linan-Faye Constr. Co. v. Housing Auth., 847 F. Supp. 1191, 1198 (D.N.J. 1994), *rev'd on other grounds*, 49 F.3d 915 (3d Cir. 1995)).

[4] 700 A.2d 185 (D.C. 1997).

[5] Justin Sweet, Legal Aspects of Architecture, Engineering and the Construction Process 747 (5th ed. 1994) (citing EJCDC General Conditions No. 1910-8, ¶ 15.4).

Exercising the termination-for-convenience clause requires the contractor to stop work, place no further orders, cancel any orders that were placed, and perform other acts designed to terminate performance and protect the interests of the owner. The terminated contractor may recover costs of unavoidable losses and expenditures incurred to preserve and protect the owner's property.[6] Most termination-for-convenience provisions in private contracts also allow the contractor to recover the cost of work to date, any demobilization or incidental costs, and either a designated or reasonable profit based on the value of the work performed.[7] However, depending on the terms of the clause, the owner may not be responsible for a contractor's anticipated profit on the entire job, but only for the portion of the work that the contractor completed prior to the termination for convenience.[8]

Under government contracts, duties of the parties change upon convenience termination. The contractor need not continue performance and the government is not obligated to pay for work performed after the termination. After termination, the contractor is also under no duty to correct defects in work performed prior to termination, and the government cannot charge the contractor to correct its defective work. The government remains liable, however, for continuing costs and the costs attributable to any unterminated portion of the contract.[9] The contractor need not incur any additional costs for any of these excused duties.

[B] Deductive Change or Termination for Convenience?

[1] Significance of the Decision

There are no clear guidelines for determining whether a deductive change or a partial termination for convenience is more appropriate. A board decision, *Steve Holmes*,[10] described the problem this way:

> . . . [t]he Government may alter the scope of the work under a contract through the use of either the Changes clause or the Termination for Convenience clause. . . . Since the rights of the parties differ markedly depending on what vehicle is utilized, there has developed a series of decisions attempting to draw the appropriate parameters as to which clause should be utilized in a given situation. Boards have looked to two tests in determining this issue: (1) was there a reduction in the scope of work without the substitution of other work; and (2) was the reduction major rather than minor?

---

[6] *Id.* at 747. See **§ 12.02[D]**.

[7] M. Heley & M. Bloomquist, *The Design Professional's Role in Termination of the Contractor*, 17 Constr. Law. 3, 8 (No. 2, Apr. 1997) (citing Linan-Faye Constr. Co. v. Housing Auth., 847 F. Supp. 1191, 1198 (D.N.J. 1994), *rev'd on other grounds*, 49 F.3d 915 (3d Cir. 1995)).

[8] Kenneth Cushman & A. Krauss, *Landmines on the Way to Termination*, Construct! 7, 13 (Summer 1997).

[9] Joseph West, *Practical Advice Concerning the Federal Government's Termination for Convenience Clause*, 17 Constr. Law. 26, 27 (No. 4, Oct. 1997).

[10] AGBCA No. 4, 90-1 BCA (CCH) ¶ 22,628 (1990).

The decision is important because amounts recovered under the two clauses are different.

Administrative costs, attorneys' fees, and other expenses incurred in preparing cost estimates and negotiating a settlement are allowed when the government has terminated a contract for its own convenience. These costs may not be allowed when the deletion is made under a changes clause. Deductive change orders are handled by reducing the existing contract price by the cost, including overhead and profit, that would have been incurred to perform the deleted work.[11]

Federal Acquisition Regulations provide for an equitable adjustment of the prices of the remaining portion of the contract in case of termination.[12] In an equitable adjustment situation, contractors may receive reasonable profit on the work they have done, but cannot recover anticipatory profits or consequential damages. Equitable adjustments are intended to leave the contractor in proportionately the same position it would have occupied had the parties originally contracted for the lesser amount of work. As a result, equitable adjustments do not increase the profit margin or reverse a loss position.[13]

If the government deletes work under a changes clause, the original contract price is reduced by the cost of the deleted work and the profit reasonably attributable to the deleted work. Deleting the cost of the work and the profits from the work leaves the contractor in the same position it would have been in if the deleted work had never been part of the contract.[14]

If the contractor is in a position to make a substantial profit on the contract, it may be able to retain a greater portion of its anticipated profits in a deductive change situation. Under the changes clause, only reasonable profit attributable to the deleted work is lost. The contractor keeps its substantial profit on the remaining work. In the partial termination-for-convenience situation, the contractor receives a "reasonable" profit on the work actually performed.[15]

If the contractor is in a loss situation, the opposite is true. If there is a deductive change, the contract price is reduced by the cost of the deducted items and the corresponding anticipated profit, leaving the contractor to suffer the whole loss and possibly aggravating the situation. In the partial termination situation, the loss ratio applies, reducing the amount of the anticipated loss by the amount of reduction in the work called for by the contract. In the loss situation, the contractor bears only part of the loss.[16]

In general, if the contractor anticipates a large profit, then the deductive change is preferable because it allows the preservation of maximum profit. In a

[11] Joseph West, *Practical Advice Concerning the Federal Government's Termination for Convenience Clause*, 17 Constr. Law. 26, 31 (No. 4, Oct. 1997) (citing Bruce Constr. Corp. v. United States, 324 F.2d 516 (Ct. Cl. 1963)).

[12] FAR 52.249-2(1).

[13] Joseph West, *Practical Advice Concerning the Federal Government's Termination for Convenience Clause*, 17 Constr. Law. 26, 31 (No. 4, Oct. 1997).

[14] *Id.*

[15] *Id.*

[16] *Id.*

small profit or loss situation, the partial termination is preferable because the contractor will recover settlement and other special costs not recoverable under the changes clause, as well as reducing projected losses proportionately.[17]

[2] Courts Have Different Approaches

The court and boards have followed three different approaches in deciding whether the decision was proper.[18] A number of cases hold that the contracting officer has discretion as to which clause to use, except when major portions of the work are deleted.[19]

In contrast, in *Nager Electric Co. v. United States*,[20] the Court of Claims suggested that only a cardinal or fundamental change would require use of the termination-for-convenience clause in pricing a deletion of work. To the same effect was *Arboreal, Inc.*,[21] which, in addition to inquiring whether the deduction altered the original bargain between the parties, also asked whether "the deletion eliminates identifiable items or a certain quantity of work [termination] . . . or whether the deletion constitutes a reduction in the scope of work." The board also stated that the "contemporaneous treatment of changes by the parties is also a factor."

In *Arboreal*, only 3 percent of the work was deleted, and the parties treated the action as a reduction in the scope of work. Similarly, in *American Construction & Energy, Inc.*,[22] a 12-percent reduction in work, coupled with the parties' treatment of the reduction as a change, mandated the use of the changes clause. The latter reason was the sole rationale for pricing a deduction under the changes clause found in *Kinetic Engineering & Construction, Inc.*[23] In *Steve Holmes*, the government had reduced a tree-planting contract by 11 percent. The board noted that there were no reductions in scope, and that another case had held that a 20-percent scope reduction was a "major change." However, the cases have also articulated a distinction between deletion in identifiable items or quantity and deletion in scope. The distinction is vague, as virtually all deletions are deemed to be a reduction in work scope.

In *Skidmore, Owings & Merrill*,[24] the ASBCA formulated a third possible test. That test distinguished between partial termination and deductive change on whether the government's need for the item continued: If the government no longer needs the item, then a partial termination for convenience is preferred. If the need continues, then a deductive change should be used. This distinction is not often followed.[25]

---

[17] *Id.*

[18] *Id.*

[19] R. Nash & J. Cibinic, Government Contracts 1119 (3d ed. 1980).

[20] 16 Cont. Cas. Fed. (CCH) ¶ 80,367 (Ct. Cl. 1971).

[21] AGBCA No. ____, 88-2 BCA (CCH) ¶ 20,635 (1988).

[22] ASBCA No. 34,934, 88-1 BCA (CCH) ¶ 20,361 (1988).

[23] ASBCA No. AS-30,726, 89-1 BCA (CCH) ¶ 21,397 (1988).

[24] ASBCA No. 5115, 60-1 BCA (CCH) ¶ 2570 (1960).

[25] Joseph West, *Practical Advice Concerning the Federal Government's Termination for Convenience Clause*, 17 Constr. Law. 26, 31 (No. 4, Oct. 1997).

Krygoski Construction Co. v. United States[26] represents the most recent decision explaining restraints on the government's use of a partial termination for convenience. In *Krygoski*, a Court of Appeals for the Federal Circuit (CAFC) panel reaffirmed prior decisions that the contracting officer's decision to terminate for convenience breached the contract only if the decision was made in bad faith or abused contracting discretion. *Krygoski* expressed that when a contracting officer must choose, the ease of administration usually suggests that modification should be selected. This standard conflicted, however, with the decision in *Torncello v. United States*.[27] In *Torncello*, the court found that a termination-for-convenience clause may not be properly invoked unless the government can demonstrate that the circumstances of the bargain or the expectations of the parties have changed.[28] Rehearing en banc of the *Krygoski* decision was unfortunately denied, and the Supreme Court denied Krygoski Construction's petition for certiorari, leaving unanswered the question of which standard controls the government's ability to terminate for convenience.[29]

The two major pre-*Krygoski* termination-for-convenience decisions created an extremely narrow *Torncello* changed-circumstances rule. In *Salsbury Industries v. United States*,[30] the CAFC decided that *Torncello* stood for the proposition that when the government contracts with a party knowing that it will not honor the contract, it cannot avoid a breach claim by using the convenience termination clause. This interpretation of *Torncello* effectively injected an intent element into the *Torncello* rule. Five years later, in *Caldwell & Santmyer, Inc. v. Glickman*,[31] the CAFC not only cited the *Salsbury* changed-circumstances interpretation with approval, but also found no breach when the government contracts in good faith but, at the same time, has knowledge of facts supposedly putting it on notice that at some future date it may be appropriate to terminate the contract for convenience. The CFAC appeared to apply the *Torncello* breach standard only to instances in which the government had precontract knowledge of the circumstances requiring the termination and a precontract intent to terminate.[32]

The government's contract with Krygoski Construction contained a variations-in-estimated-quantities (VEQ) clause that allowed Krygoski Construction to remove more asbestos than anticipated at the contract's price per unit. The insertion of the VEQ clause in the original contract meant, according to the panel, that the government had anticipated variations in asbestos quantities. The CAFC determined, however, that the asbestos found in the floor and roofing by Krygoski

---

[26] 94 F.3d 1537 (Fed. Cir.), *reh'g & reh'g en banc denied*, 1996 U.S. App. LEXIS 30308 (Fed. Cir. Nov. 7, 1996), *cert. denied*, 520 U.S. 1210, 117 S. Ct. 1691 (1997).

[27] 681 F.2d 756 (Ct. Cl. 1982) (en banc).

[28] M. Garson, *Krygoski and the Termination for Convenience: Have Circumstances Really Changed?*, 27 Pub. Cont. L.J. 117, 119-20 (No. 1, Fall 1997).

[29] *Id.* at 120-21.

[30] 905 F.2d 1518 (Fed. Cir. 1990).

[31] 55 F.3d 1578 (Fed. Cir. 1995).

[32] M. Garson, *Krygoski and the Termination for Convenience: Have Circumstances Really Changed?*, 27 Pub. Cont. L.J. 117, 130-31 (No. 1, Fall 1997).

Construction was not subject to the VEQ clause protections. The court instead explained that the government was required to resolicit the contract to account for the increase in asbestos quantities, an unexpected occurrence falling outside the scope of the contract and a "cardinal change" under the Competition in Contracting Act, especially at the removal price per square foot offered by Krygoski Construction. The panel further stated that the newly discovered asbestos, if considered within the scope of the contract at all, would be included under a fixed-price section of the contract under which Krygoski Construction would have to remove the additional asbestos without recovering payment for the increased work. According to the court, the termination for convenience was extremely fair to Krygoski Construction.[33]

Viewed from Krygoski Construction's perspective, the government promised to pay Krygoski Construction for asbestos removal services that the government knew would arise from Krygoski's contractually required pre-demolition survey. Yet when Krygoski Construction found more asbestos than the government had anticipated, the government used Krygoski Construction's figures to rebid the asbestos work at a lower price. In other words, the contractual promise to Krygoski Construction turned out to be: "If your survey is close to our self-admitted rough estimates, we'll honor your contract and modify it under the VEQ clause items. If your survey is too far away from our estimates, we'll deny you VEQ coverage and find someone else at a lower price. But thanks for the survey."[34]

District of Columbia v. Organization for Environmental Growth, Inc.[35] stated that, where the changed circumstances test applied, changed circumstances could be manifested by the government's growing unhappiness with the contractor's performance. The court explained that dissatisfaction with performance may itself be regarded as a change in circumstances and that it would be irresponsible for the district to remain silent in the face of increasing evidence of misfeasance by a government contractor.[36]

Opponents of the *Krygoski* decision have warned that limitations of the bad faith or abuse of discretion standard could have undesirable economic impacts on the government procurement market.[37] Yet contracts terminated for convenience occur in only 0.4 percent of all contract actions. In other words, the likelihood of a termination for convenience occurring is one out of every 250 contract actions. This slim chance hardly seems like a probability that would deter market entry and significantly increase the prices the government pays for goods and services. In addition, the low termination-for-convenience probability most likely is attributable to the government's disinclination to terminate for convenience.[38]

---

[33] *Id.* at 133-34.

[34] *Id.* at 135.

[35] 700 A.2d 185 (D.C. 1997).

[36] W. Shirk, *Terminations for Convenience More Difficult to Overturn in District of Columbia*, 33 Procurement Law. 3, 4 (No. 2, Winter 1998).

[37] M. Garson, *Krygoski and the Termination for Convenience: Have Circumstances Really Changed?*, 27 Pub. Cont. L.J. 117, 137 (No. 1, Fall 1997).

[38] *Id.* at 139-40.

The American Bar Association Section of Public Contract Law subcommittee proposed to establish a new FAR termination-for-convenience standard. The draft proposal to amend FAR 49.101(b) would force the government to abide by private law standards of contractual "good faith" in its contractual obligations.[39] The proposal reads:

> The government when exercising its rights to terminate for convenience . . . must act consistently with those contractual good faith duties to which private parties are held. This means, in part, that the government, whether knowingly or not, (1) may not attempt to recapture an opportunity foreclosed at the time of contracting, and/or (2) may not act inconsistently with the justified expectations of the parties at the time of contracting.[40]

[C] Exercising the Election to Terminate for Convenience

[1] Administrative Procedure

[a] Standard Form Contract Termination Clause

Administrative procedures for local public and private parties that use standard form contracts are relatively simple. For example, the Associated General Contractors of America Document No. 200, Standard Form of Agreement and General Conditions Between Owner and Contractor, provides that the owner may terminate for its convenience at Paragraph 11.4.1 "upon written notice" to the contractor. The contractor is required to "immediately" stop work and follow the owner's instructions for shutdown and termination procedures, and "strive to minimize" any further costs.

[b] Federal Contract Termination Clause

Termination procedures for United States government contracts in FAR Part 49 include subparts 49.1, 49.2, and 49.5. Under the federal procedure, after the contracting officer issues a notice of termination, the contracting officer responsible for the termination (TCO) is responsible for negotiating any settlement with the contractor, including a no-cost settlement if appropriate.[41]

In the interest of expediting a termination settlement, the TCO may request specially qualified personnel to determine qualitative and quantitative allocability of termination inventory.[42] No distinction is made between cost-reimbursement

---

[39] Id. at 147-48.

[40] ABA Termination Subcommittee Proposed Amendment to FAR 49.101 (Draft of May 22, 1997).

[41] Joseph West, *Practical Advice Concerning the Federal Government's Termination for Convenience Clause*, 17 Constr. Law. 26, 28 (No. 4, Oct. 1997).

[42] Id. at 31 (citing FAR 49.105(b)(4)(ii)).

contracts, under which the government clearly has title to all property acquired and for which the contractor has a government property accountability requirement, and fixed-price contracts, under which the government has no title and the contractor has no such government property record-keeping responsibility.[43]

The government has no contractual or other basis for imposing an allocability review of residual contractor property as a result of the termination for convenience of a fixed-price contract. Any allocability requirement is based upon the assumptions either that the contractor had a government property accountability requirement from the inception of the contract with respect to contractor property, or that the contract was converted into a cost-reimbursement contract at termination, making all acquired property government property. Neither assumption is consistent with the "property" provisions of fixed-price contracts. Under a fixed-price contract, the rebuttable presumption is that all contractor property charged to the contract was properly consumed in the normal course of contract performance, except that which is physically stored when the contract is terminated for the convenience of the government.[44]

The only fixed-price contract property for which the contractor has an obligation to maintain property accountability records is: special tooling and special test equipment, but only if the special tooling or test equipment clause is in the contract;[45] facilities and special test equipment acquired by the contractor and the government;[46] special direct-purchase materials;[47] and government-furnished property.[48]

An allocability review also duplicates the Defense Contract Audit Agency's (DCAA) incurred cost audit, usually performed in response to the contractor's termination settlement proposal. The DCAA has the responsibility for determining incurred cost reasonableness, including the allocability to the contract of the costs of contractor property. To the extent that the DCAA requires assistance to determine if a specific quantity of any item was reasonably required for the performance of the contract, such assistance should come from the government's program office that has the technical competence to make such a determination, and not from the property administrator, who performs a function largely unrelated to the technical requirements of performance.[49]

In *Fairchild Industries, Inc. v. United States,*[50] which involved a fixed-price incentive contract, the appellate court reversed the Court of Federal Claims and stated that the Air Force bore none of the contractor's risk and was liable for payment only when the work, "line item by line item, succeeded and was accepted."

---

[43] William Murphy, *Fixed-Price Contract Terminations for Convenience: Allocability Reviews of Termination Inventory,* 34 Prof. Law. 22 (No. 1, Fall 1998) (citing FAR 45.5).

[44] *Id.* at 23.

[45] *Id.* at 22 (citing FAR 52.245-17 and 18).

[46] *Id.* at 22 (citing FAR 52.245-2(c)(3)).

[47] *Id.* at 22 (citing FAR 52.245-2(c)(4)).

[48] *Id.* at 22 (citing FAR 52.245-2(c)(1)).

[49] *Id.* at 23-24.

[50] 71 F.3d 868, 873 (Fed. Cir. 1995).

The court ruled that the provision for progress payments gave the government a priority security interest in the contractor's work product rather than title to the completed work, because progress payments are loans from the government, to be repaid from the contract price and not partial purchases, and that the government's security interest in the contractor's inventory secures funds loaned to the contractor through progress payments.[51]

Allocability reviews for fixed-price contracts effectively require the contractors to create typical government property accountability records after the fact. This post-project documentation is to show the quantities acquired, the unit prices, the quantities consumed, the record of consumption, the residual inventories on hand, and that the item was of the quality required by the contract. Allocability reviews are inconsistent both with the terms of fixed-price contracts and with the rebuttable presumption that the contractor was at risk during performance of the contract and acquisition of the property in question.[52]

[2] Bad Faith

An overriding condition for one party to terminate another party is the necessity that the owner or contractor that terminates act in good faith. When the contract specifies that the contractor or owner can terminate the agreement for default, the inquiry is whether the default was reasonably genuine and not prompted by bad faith.[53] If a termination for default was in bad faith, the party that terminates does not collect is additional performance costs and the party that had been terminated collects the reasonable value of it performance costs.

To show bad faith, the terminated contractor must establish that the party that terminates has an improper motive. Invocation of a termination for convenience by a state to save money is not a bad-faith termination. Consider *Capital Safety, Inc. v. State of New Jersey, Division of Buildings & Construction.*[54] The New Jersey Division of Buildings and Construction entered into a contract with Capital Safety, Inc. for removal of asbestos from a division building. The division was required to evacuate the building before the contractor could begin work. The division encountered difficulty relocating its employees and ordered the contractor to suspend all work. The contractor submitted a claim for the damages it incurred as a result of suspension, which the division paid. A supplemental agreement authorized the Division to terminate the contract for convenience without payment of additional damages if it determined that termination was in the public interest. The only limitation was that the division could not exercise this authority in bad faith.

---

[51] William Murphy, *Fixed-Price Contract Terminations for Convenience: Allocability Reviews of Termination Inventory*, 34 Prof. Law. 22, 24 (No. 1, Fall 1998) (citing Marine Midland Bank v. United States, 687 F.2d 395 (Ct. Cl. 1982), *cert. denied*, 406 U.S. 1037 (1983)).

[52] *Id.* at 25-26.

[53] Construction Law § 4.13[2] (Steven G.M. Stein ed., 1998) (citing Paul Hardeman, Inc. v. Arkansas Power & Light Co., 380 F. Supp. 298 (E.D. Ark. 1974)).

[54] 848 A.2d 863 (N.J. Super. Ct. App. Div. 2004).

The division vacated the suspension order and directed the contractor to proceed with asbestos removal but then notified the contractor it was still experiencing difficulty relocating its employees and equipment and therefore would be unable to make the building available. The contractor submitted a claim for additional delay damages. After unsuccessfully attempting to negotiate an agreement limiting the contractor's claim, the division exercised its right to terminate the contract. The contractor brought a breach of contract action. The contractor's complaint asserted that the division's inability to relocate the workers was not a valid basis to invoke the termination-for-convenience provision of the contract. The trial court dismissed the contractor's complaint. The contractor appealed.

The division's inability to provide the contractor access due to the division's inability to relocate its employees and equipment was one of the contingencies that the parties had in mind when they included the termination-for-convenience provision in the supplemental agreement. Before the division terminated the contract, the contractor had made a settlement offer under which the State would have been required to pay the contractor for costs of demobilization plus an unspecified additional amount of delay damages for remobilization. If the division had not invoked the termination-for-convenience provision, it would have been exposed to an open-ended and potentially very substantial claim for delay damages. The division could not be found to have acted in bad faith because its motive in terminating the contract was not to harm the contractor but instead to serve the financial interests of the State by avoiding exposure to a claim for additional delay damages. Summary judgment was affirmed.

Similarly, a contractor's termination of a subcontractor is not bad faith if it conforms to the notice provision in a termination clause that allows termination with or without cause. In *Roof Systems, Inc. v. Johns Manville Corp.*,[55] Gilbane Building Company contracted to build two schools for the Houston Independent School District. The contractor subcontracted the roofing and sheet metal work for both schools to Roof Systems, Inc. The subcontract contained a termination-for-convenience clause. The subcontract required the subcontractor to provide the district a warranty on the roof systems as a condition of final payment. The material supplier asserted that it would not issue its guaranty unless the roof systems were installed by a certified installer. The subcontractor was not a certified installer. However, the subcontractor claimed it arranged for a certified installer, Total Roofing Services, Inc., to install the roof systems. The material supplier denied that it approved the subcontractor's proposed sub-subcontractor arrangement. The material supplier eventually informed the contractor that the warranty would not issue under any circumstances. The contractor stated that the subcontractor was not in conformance of the contractual requirements and failed to make required progress and terminated the subcontractor after the required 48-hour notice. The contractor contracted with another company to install the roof systems. The subcontractor sued the contractor for breach of contract. The trial court granted a no-evidence motion for summary judgment filed by the contractor. The subcontractor appealed.

---

[55] 130 S.W.3d 430 (Tex. App. 2004).

The contractor was allowed to terminate the subcontractor's contract for convenience, with or without cause. Nevertheless, the subcontractor contended the contractor could not rely on the termination-for-convenience clause because the contractor specifically cited the subcontractor's failure to maintain the progress schedule in its termination notice. However, a general contractor was not bound by its first announced reason for terminating a subcontract absent bad faith by the general contractor or a change of position in reliance by the subcontractor. The subcontractor maintained that the contractor failed to negate any bad faith on its part or any reliance on the subcontractor's part. The contract allowed termination upon 48 hours' notice. Therefore, the contractor's compliance with contract terms negated any bad faith attributable to timing of the termination notice. There was no bad faith on the contractor's part. The trial court did not err in granting the contractor's motion for summary judgment.

Bad faith sufficient to show that a termination for convenience was a breach of contract applies to the conduct of the termination, not the conduct during the administration of the project. In *District of Columbia v. Organization for Environmental Growth, Inc.*,[56] the court reviewed a decision by the District of Columbia Contract Appeals Board holding that the contractor was entitled to common law damages, including lost profits, because the district acted in bad faith in terminating Organization for Environmental Growth's (OFEGRO) contract and was barred by *Torncello* from invoking the termination-for-convenience clause.[57] The court noted that the only effective restriction on the exercise of the termination-for-convenience mechanism was a demonstration by the contractor of the contracting officer's bad faith. The court held that though the record was replete with evidence of confusion, miscommunication, and incompetence, the testimony before the board and the documentary exhibits failed to show any specific intent on the part of district officials to injure OFEGRO. The court observed that a showing of bad faith in the *execution or performance of the contract* would have been insufficient to overturn a termination for convenience: "What must be demonstrated by a contractor is bad faith *in the termination of the contract.*"[58]

[D] Determining the Amount of the Convenience Termination

[1] Federal Convenience Termination Cost Principles

[a] According to the Termination Clause

The basic principle in the settlement of federal government fixed-price contracts is fair compensation.[59] The contractor is free to negotiate for any amount it

---

[56] 700 A.2d 185 (D.C. Aug. 28, 1997).

[57] W. Shirk, *Terminations for Convenience More Difficult to Overturn in District of Columbia*, 33 Procurement Law. 3 (No. 2, Winter 1998).

[58] *Id.* at 21 (emphasis added).

[59] Joseph West, *Practical Advice Concerning the Federal Government's Termination for Convenience Clause*, 17 Constr. Law. 26, 29 (No. 4, Oct. 1997) (citing FAR 49.201(a)).

feels is fair, limited only by reasonableness and contract price. However, the total payments to the contractor generally cannot exceed the contract price. Because fair compensation is the articulated goal, the use of business judgment is the standard in federal government contracts, instead of strict accounting principles.

Costs that may be recovered are identified by the contract, usually in the termination clause itself, and appropriate procurement regulations. The federal government has a variety of standard form termination-for-convenience clauses that define what costs may be recovered by the terminated contractor. One such clause for a federally funded corporation reads:

> 9. TERMINATION—. . . As compensation to Company for such termination or suspension, Amtrak shall pay Company its actual, necessary, reasonable, and verifiable expenses as a direct consequence of such termination or suspension. . . . In no event shall Amtrak be liable for lost or anticipated profit or unabsorbed indirect costs or overheads, nor shall Amtrak's liability for such termination or suspension expenses exceed the unpaid balance of the Order price. The right of reimbursement set forth herein shall be Company's exclusive remedy in the event of such termination or suspension.

Ideker, Inc.[60] held that the contracting officer's use of the method of computing damages prescribed by the termination-for-convenience clause was proper.

Allowable costs after a termination for convenience, plus a reasonable profit, are determined by the cost principles of FAR Part 31. Costs that have arisen from the contract and have not yet been reimbursed are compensable if they are reasonable, allocable, and were not specifically designated as unallowable when the costs were incurred.[61] The FAR deals specifically with termination costs and serves as a supplement and modification to other cost principles.[62]

In addition to un-reimbursed costs to perform the work, termination may require the contractor to incur some costs that would not have been incurred had the contract been completed. These expenses include inventory and disposal of contract items, negotiating subcontractor termination claims, settling contractor claims against the subcontractors, termination claim preparation, and indirect costs related to salary and wages incurred as settlement expenses.

[b] Pre-award Costs

In the event of termination for the convenience of the owner, recovery may include certain start-up and preparatory costs incurred prior to contract award. In *Barsh Co.*,[63] the Postal Service notified Barsh that it would be awarded a contract

[60] ENGBCA Nos. 4389, 4602, 87-3 BCA (CCH) ¶ 20,145 (1987).
[61] Joseph West, *Practical Advice Concerning the Federal Government's Termination for Convenience Clause*, 17 Constr. Law. 26, 29 (No. 4, Oct. 1997) (citing FAR 31.201).
[62] *Id.* at 29 (citing FAR 31.205-42).
[63] PSBCA No. 4481, 2000-2 BCA (CCH) ¶ 30,917 (2000).

for the construction of security improvements at a federal building. A pre-construction conference prior to the award caused Barsh to believe that the project was on a tight schedule. Barsh prepared subcontracts, purchase orders, bonds, and job cost files. Subsequently, the contract was awarded to Barsh, but three weeks later the contract was terminated for the convenience of the government. Barsh's termination settlement proposal included costs for these pre-award activities, but the Postal Service opposed recovery of any pre-award costs. In considering Barsh's appeal, the board noted that these costs were incurred after Barsh learned that it would receive the contract and reasonably believed there was urgency to the project. The board found that these costs were incurred in order to meet the tight contract schedule. However, Barsh's costs incurred prior to submitting its bid proposal were not recoverable. The bid proposal costs that were eliminated from its recovery included costs for estimating, negotiating subcontract prices, and its proposal preparation costs.

[c]   Costs of Completed Work

Generally, recovery is limited to the actual cost of the completed work. If the contract is terminated for the convenience of the owner because the work is impossible to perform, the contractor may be able to recover performance costs in excess of the contract price, even if the contractor was in a loss position at the time of termination. Although this may not be the case otherwise, the impossibility of performance results in a situation where the usual limitations on the amount and type of damages may not apply.[64]

[d]   Lost Labor Productivity

Lost productivity may be recovered as part of the cost of the work, but the proof of the lost productivity may be difficult to provide.[65] In *Defense Systems Corp.,*[66] the Navy terminated two contracts it had with Defense Systems for default. Defense Systems appealed the terminations and submitted claims for equitable adjustments to both contracts. The board changed the default termination to a termination for convenience on appeal. The contractor claimed it had incurred $1,388,371 in labor inefficiency caused by the government. The claimed amount was derived by subtracting from the total direct labor cost charged to the contract the direct labor cost included in the defective specification and other claims, and the alleged "planned direct labor" for the work performed up to the time the contractor stopped work. The "planned direct labor" cost was based on a budget prepared by the contractor's job management team.

---

[64] D.E.W., Inc. & D.E. Wurzbach, A Joint Venture, ASBCA No. 50,796, 2000-2 BCA (CCH) ¶ 31,104 (2000).

[65] See **Chapter 18**.

[66] ASBCA Nos. 44,131R, 44,835R, 50,562, 50,563, 50,997, 50,998, 2000 ASBCA LEXIS 45; 2000-1 BCA (CCH) ¶ 30,851 (Mar. 16, 2000).

However, the direct labor amount in the budget was the dollars left for labor after subtracting from the contract price the amounts required for materials, overhead, general and administrative expenses, and "whatever profit" management wanted to include. The board stated that the record did not include the bid estimate documents or any other credible evidence supporting the bid price and the labor costs included when the job was bid. The testimony and the report of the contractor's expert assumed the allocated bid price was realistic. The board found that the labor inefficiency claim failed for the lack of proof that the claimed costs were the result of defective specifications or government-responsible cause.

[e] Profit

A terminated contractor is allowed a fair and reasonable profit on costs for preparation and work done by the contractor for the terminated portion of the contract work. However, the FAR specifically prohibits the recovery of anticipatory profits and consequential damages. Any reasonable method may be used to arrive at a profit factor, but the FAR sets forth nine factors for consideration when negotiating profit.[67] The termination settlement may be for a lump-sum payment without segregating profit.[68]

The percentage of the profit the contractor is entitled to may be based upon the actual profit percentage the contractor would have earned on the entire contract had it not been terminated for convenience, rather than the profit percentage defined in the contract for changed work. For example, in *Charles G. Williams Construction, Inc.*,[69] the contract was terminated for convenience after the contractor completed Phase 1 of the improvements to a medical center. The contractor claimed a 10-percent profit mark-up on the costs of the work prior to termination, based upon the fact that the 10-percent profit factor was used for earlier change order work approved by the government. The board, however, ruled that the appropriate measure of profit was the profit margin the contractor would have earned if the contract were not terminated. A government audit reflected that if the Phase 2 work was not terminated by the government, the contractor would have earned only 3.61 percent profit. The board applied the 3.61-percent profit factor to the cost of the work completed in calculating the contractor's recovery for the termination for convenience.

If a contractor would have sustained a loss had the contract been completed, the termination settlement amount must be adjusted to reflect the loss. Not only will the contractor be denied profit on the completed work, but the contractor also will not be able to recover all of its incurred costs on a losing contract.[70] However,

---

[67] Joseph West, *Practical Advice Concerning the Federal Government's Termination for Convenience Clause*, 17 Constr. Law. 26, 30 (No. 4, Oct. 1997) (citing FAR 49.202).

[68] *Id.* at 29 (citing FAR 49.201(b)).

[69] ASBCA No. 49,775, 2000-2 BCA (CCH) ¶ 31,047 (2000).

[70] Joseph West, *Practical Advice Concerning the Federal Government's Termination for Convenience Clause*, 17 Constr. Law. 26, 30 (No. 4, Oct. 1997) (citing FAR 49.203).

a long-standing exception to the general rule limiting recovery in a termination for convenience, when the contract is to be performed at a loss, may permit some profit recovery. When the government has substantially contributed to the increased costs and it is not possible to separate that portion of the loss from the portion caused by the contractor, profit may be recovered.[71] This exception applies to conversions of default terminations into terminations for convenience. In *D.E.W. & D.E. Wurzbach*, the primary reason for the defective work that initiated the default termination was that the design specification provided by the government was impossible; this fact permitted profit to be recovered. In *Wurzbach*, the board placed one limitation on the contractor's ability to recover profits on a losing contract. The board stated that profit would not be allowed if the deficiencies in the work stemmed from the contractor's gross disregard of its contractual obligations. In that situation, the costs of performing such grossly deficient work will be considered unreasonable and unallowable.

[f] Claims Preparation and Settlement Expenses

Most of the termination cost disputes center on the cost of claims preparation or settlement proposal and presentation expenses. When reasonably incurred, legal, accounting, clerical, and other costs are allowable. Claim preparation costs are allowable regardless of whether they are incurred by in-house personnel or by outside consultants.[72]

Termination settlement expenses, subcontract settlements, and other direct-charged termination costs are direct costs to which general and administrative expenses (G&A) or any other indirect cost may be allocated. Other indirect costs may include payroll taxes, fringe benefits, occupancy costs, and immediate supervision costs.[73] No contractual or regulatory provision precludes the allocation of G&A to termination settlement expenses and the settlement of subcontractor claims. However, FAR 31.205-42(g) and (h) and the settlement proposal forms[74] show G&A cost as an element of total costs before settlement expenses and subcontractor settlements. That placement of G&A costs on the termination settlement proposal forms may often be misused to support an argument that G&A costs are not allocable to settlement expenses and subcontract settlements.[75] Two cases have recognized the propriety of recovering G&A on termination settlement expenses and that G&A is not precluded by either the termination clause or the Federal Procurement Regulations.[76]

---

[71] *Id.* (citing D.E.W. & D.E. Wurzbach, A Joint Venture, ASBCA No. 50,796, 98-2 BCA (CCH) ¶ 29,385 (1998)).

[72] *Id.* at 29.

[73] *Id.* (citing FAR 31.205-42(g)).

[74] *Id.* (citing Standard Forms 1435 through 1438; *see* FAR Pt. 53).

[75] William Murphy, *Applying G&A Costs to Termination Settlement Expenses and Subcontract Settlements*, 33 Prof. Law. 13 (No. 3, Spring 1998).

[76] *Id.* (citing Kollmorgen Corp., Electro-Optical Division, ASBCA No. 28,480, 86-2 (CCH) BCA ¶ 18,919 (board allowed application of full overhead and full G&A to contractor's settlement

Statutes mandate that Cost Accounting Standards (CAS) be the law with respect to the measurement, assignment, and allocation of costs to contracts with the government.[77] Whatever the FAR or their standard forms may say or imply with respect to cost allocation, CAS controls. Any conflicts must be resolved in favor of CAS.[78] CAS 410, 402, and 406 relate to termination settlement expenses and the allocation of G&A costs to such expenses. CAS 410, Allocation of Business Unit General and Administrative Expenses to Final Cost Objectives, requires the allocation of G&A costs to final cost objectives as contracts, including termination settlement expenses and subcontractor settlements. CAS 410 has no provision for the elimination of a final cost objective from the G&A allocation base. It requires using a G&A base that is representative of the total activity of the business unit. The Federal Acquisition Regulations fail to cite CAS 410.[79]

The FAR termination cost principles address the allowability of eight categories of costs. Two of these categories are "settlement expenses" and "subcontractor claims."[80] In Subparagraph (g)(1)(iii), costs of indirect labor that are direct charged as settlement expenses should normally be burdened only with payroll taxes, fringe benefits, occupancy, and immediate supervision costs. Literally applied, this would be in direct conflict with the CAS prohibition of "fragmenting" and must therefore fail because CAS controls with respect to allocation of costs. With one exception, FAR does not expressly address the application of G&A costs to termination costs.[81]

If contractor personnel who charge their time directly to termination settlement tasks are normally indirect personnel, the indirect pool should be reduced for their labor costs plus applicable payroll taxes, fringe benefits, occupancy costs, and supervision that are included in the termination claim.[82]

The government may attempt to impose on the contractor some termination costs that may not be necessary. For example, government contractors have no obligation to perform or support allocability reviews of contractor property under terminated fixed-price contracts. Under a fixed-price contract, the rebuttable presumption is that all contractor property charged to the contract was properly consumed in the normal course of contract performance, except that which is physically on hand when the contract is terminated for the convenience of the government. Government-required accountability reviews are inconsistent both with the terms of fixed-price contracts and with the fundamental concept that the

---

expenses); Thiokol Chem. Corp., ASBCA No. 17,554, 76-1 BCA (CCH) ¶ 11,731 (1976) (burdening contractor's settlement expenses and subcontract settlements with G&A was allowable under the termination cost principles of Armed Services Procurement Regulations; such burdening would not constitute double recovery)).

[77] Id. (citing Pub. L. No. 100-679, § 5(f)(3), 41 U.S.C. § 422(f)(3)).

[78] Id. (citing Boeing Co., ASBCA No. 28,342, 85-2 BCA (CCH) ¶ 18,435 (1985)).

[79] Id. at 14 (citing FAR 52.249-6, Termination Clause, and FAR 52.249-2, Fixed Price Contract Termination for Convenience Clause).

[80] Id. (citing FAR 31.205-42).

[81] Id. at 15 (citing FAR 31.205-42).

[82] Id.

contractor was 100 percent at risk during performance of the contract and acquisition of the property in question.[83]

[2] State and Local Convenience Termination Cost Principles

Determining reimbursable termination costs under a contract not governed by federal contracting rules is different. The termination-for-convenience clause in state, local, and private contracts often defines the costs that a contractor that is terminated for convenience may recover. For example, the Associated General Contractors of America Document No. 200, Standard Form of Agreement and General Conditions Between Owner and Contractor, provides at Paragraph 11.4.2 that the contractor is entitled to be paid for the work performed to date and "any proven loss, cost or expense" in connection with the work, "including all demobilization costs and a premium set forth below."

Mobilization and demobilization costs are recovered based on the terminated contractor's cost policy and industry practices. In *Quality Asphalt Paving, Inc. v. State*,[84] Quality Asphalt Paving, Inc. and the state contracted for a highway construction project. However, after performance began, the state terminated the contract under the termination-for-convenience clause because a buried utility cable conflicted with the project plans. The contractor submitted to the state a claim for termination costs. The contractor claimed $767,067 of the $1 million its successful bid specified for mobilization and demobilization costs. The state and the contractor disagreed about claims for mobilization costs, demobilization costs, and standby costs. Although the contractor's project bid included an amount for the "mobilization and demobilization" item, it was the standard practice of the industry, and of the contractor, to charge only mobilization costs to a project, and to charge demobilization costs as part of mobilization for the next project. The contractor appealed the state commissioner's hearing officer awarding the contractor $ 449,621 for the item. The contractor appealed the commissioner's decision to the superior court, which affirmed the commissioner's decision permitting recovery of mobilization costs. The contractor and the state appealed.

The contractor first argued that as a matter of contract interpretation, it was entitled to recover $767,067 of the $1 million its bid allocated for mobilization and demobilization costs because it was an "agreed price." The state responded that the hearing officer did not err by basing the cost award on expert testimony, supporting evidence provided by an audit report, and the hearing officer's own expertise. The contractor claimed that its normal policy regarding demobilization was inapplicable to the project because the termination left the contractor without a new job to which to charge the demobilization costs. Although the termination was unexpected, it was a foreseeable possibility when the contractor bid on the state's project. The court held that the industry standard and the contractor's own policy

---

[83] William Murphy, *Fixed-Price Contract Terminations for Convenience: Allocability Reviews of Termination Inventory*, 34 Prof. Law. 22 (No. 1, Fall 1998).

[84] 71 P.3d 865 (Alaska 2003).

regarding demobilization costs constituted substantial evidence supporting the hearing officer's decision to deny the contractor additional demobilization costs.

In *Jeffrey B. Peterson & Associates v. Dayton Metropolitan Housing Authority*,[85] the Ohio Court of Appeals determined that a contract, which listed the permitted costs that may be recovered in the event of a termination for convenience, did not permit recovery of any other costs. Dayton Metropolitan Housing Authority awarded a contract to Jeffrey B. Peterson & Associates to replace the roofs, fascia, gutters, and down spouts. According to the contract, work was to be completed within 90 days. The contractor began work, but a number of problems caused delay and the work was not finished on time. The authority terminated the contract for default. The contractor filed suit for breach and wrongful termination of the contract. A magistrate found that the authority had breached the contract. However, the magistrate limited the contractor's damages to costs listed when the contract was terminated for convenience. The trial court adopted the magistrate's decision. The contractor appealed.

The magistrate and trial court both felt that the contract limited damages. The termination-for-convenience clause said that the authority was liable for "reasonable and proper costs" resulting from the termination. The contract did not define the term "reasonable and proper costs," nor did it contain an express limitations clause that restricted damages. However, the termination clause said that the authority "shall be liable . . . upon the receipt . . . of a properly presented claim setting out in detail" five listed items. The five items included: (1) the cost of work performed to the date of termination; (2) the cost of settling subcontractor claims; (3) the cost of preserving work; (4) the cost of presenting the termination claim; and (5) reasonable profit on the work performed. Since the authority specifically mentioned only five categories, the appellate court stated that the intent was to exclude any items that were not mentioned. The appellate court limited the termination claims to the five categories of listed items.

A terminated contractor who fails to secure releases or waivers of liens being filed by subcontractors may not forfeit its right to recover under substantial performance. *TA Operating Corp. v. Solar Applications Engineering, Inc.*[86] involved TA Operating Corporation, an owner who had contracted with Solar Applications Engineering to construct a prototype multi-use truck stop for a fixed price. Confusion over the construction plans caused delays. Upon substantial completion, the owner sent the contractor a punch list of additional items that needed to be finished. After disputing some items, the contractor began work on the list items and filed a lien affidavit against the project as a precautionary measure because the time for payment of a portion of the retainage had passed, without any payment from the owner. The owner understood the lien affidavit to be a request for final payment. The owner sent notice to the contractor that it was in default for not completing the list items and for failing to secure legally effective releases or waivers of the liens that the subcontractors had begun filing against the project.

---

[85] 2000 Ohio App. LEXIS 3259 (2d Div. July 21, 2000).
[86] 2005 Tex. App. LEXIS 2350 (2005).

The contractor submitted a final application for payment in the amount of the unpaid retainage. The owner terminated the contractor for failure to complete the punch list items and refused to make final payment. The contractor sued the owner for breach of contract under the theory of substantial performance. The contractor counterclaimed. The trial judge entered judgment for the contractor. The owner appealed.

The owner did not dispute that the contractor substantially performed the agreement or that the owner was able to use the building for its intended purpose, yet the owner argued that the contractor forfeited its right to recover because it did not submit legally effective releases or waivers of liens with its application for final payment as required by the contract. The owner argued that recovery under the doctrine of substantial performance was not allowed when all conditions to final payment had not been met. The contractor argued that imposing a forfeiture would have negated the purpose of the doctrine of substantial performance, which was to protect the right to compensation from being forfeited by omissions or defects that did not deprive the owner of the essential benefit for which it contracted. Even if the contract provision at issue were a condition precedent to the owner's contractual obligation to pay the contractor for the work it performed, the contractor was entitled to compensation because equity would not have permitted the enforcement of a forfeiture in an inequitable, oppressive manner.

[3] Subcontractor Costs

In *McDonnell Douglas Corp. v. United States*,[87] the court held that subcontractor termination settlements involving a fixed-price incentive contract could be included in the termination cost recovery, unless the government proved collusion or lack of arm's-length bargaining. The *McDonnell Douglas* decision suggests that when the TCO disagrees with the contractor's judgments with respect to subcontract settlements in which the contractor is at risk, the government's burden to prove that the settlement is not reimbursable as a termination cost is very heavy.[88] In addition, the government will not pay the contractor any amount for loss of anticipatory profits or consequential damages from the termination of any subcontract.[89]

It is important for the contractor to understand that the termination-for-convenience clause is not a mandatory flow-down provision. Contractors generally must negotiate with their subcontractors for inclusion of the termination-for-convenience clause in subcontracts. Without a termination-for-convenience clause, the contractor may be liable under state law for breach of the subcontract if the

[87] 40 Fed. Cl. 529 (1998).
[88] William Murphy, *Fixed-Price Contract Terminations for Convenience: Allocability Reviews of Termination Inventory*, 34 Prof. Law. 22, 24 (No. 1, Fall 1998).
[89] Joseph West, *Practical Advice Concerning the Federal Government's Termination for Convenience Clause*, 17 Constr. Law. 26, 28 (No. 4, Oct. 1997) (citing FAR 49.108-3).

government terminates the contractor's contract for convenience. Although the contractor's liability to subcontractors may include lost profits and consequential damages, the contractor will be unable to recover those costs from the government. With a termination-for-convenience clause, a subcontractor may not recover lost profits or any other category of cost precluded in the clause. For example, in *T.I. Construction Co. v. Kiewit Eastern Co.*,[90] the termination clause in the subcontract permitted the subcontractor to be compensated for all completed work prior to the termination and for reasonable closeout costs. The clause also said that the subcontractor was not entitled to any compensation for loss of anticipated profits or unallocated overhead. The subcontractor claimed that the termination-for-convenience clause was invalid and unenforceable and that it was entitled to all its lost profits. The appeals court disagreed. The court enforced the termination-for-convenience clause and barred the subcontractor from collecting damages for lost profits not permitted under the clause.

§ 12.03 TERMINATION FOR DEFAULT

[A] Generally

[1] Standard Clauses

A construction industry standard form contract generally provides that either party can terminate for certain defaults by the other party. For example, the 2000 edition of the Associated General Contractors of America Document No. 200, Standard Form of Agreement and General Conditions Between Owner and Contractor, provides for the owner's termination of a contractor at Paragraph 11.3. Paragraph 11.5 provides for the contractor's right to terminate the contract. The American Institute of Architects standard form A201 also provides for termination by either the contractor or the owner. Similarly, the American Institute of Architects standard form A401 provides that a contractor may terminate a subcontractor if the subcontractor fails to perform properly or if the subcontractor fails to begin correction of its defective performance after receipt of written notice.

[2] Notice

All termination clauses define the circumstance that may permit either party to terminate for default. A contract's termination clause often provides a "cure" period in which the recalcitrant party may correct its performance and avoid a termination. The American Institute of Architects standard form contract A401 imposes a two-step process for termination. The first "notice" required by the AIA forms defines a seven-day period within which the subcontractor must begin the correction of its defective performance. This period is designed to provide the subcontractor time to cure past defects and provide assurances that there will be no

---

[90] 1992 U.S. Dist. LEXIS 19213 (E.D. Pa. 1992).

future defaults. A second seven-day period provides the parties with the time to plan new arrangements necessary by the termination. The Associated General Contractors of America (AGC) forms provide similar two-step notice requirements prior to termination. Under the AGC contract forms, a contractor must "commence and satisfactorily continue correction of the default" within seven days of receipt of a notice to cure. If the contractor fails to commence and satisfactorily continue to correct the defective work, the owner may provide a second notice that it intends to terminate the agreement, and after 14 additional days, the owner may terminate the contract by "written notice." Termination for default will only be enforced if the party that terminates strictly complies with its notice obligations prior to termination.[91]

However, if a contractor has failed to complete at the contractor's completion date, an owner may terminate a contractor without notice. In *Jeffrey M. Brown Associates, Inc. v. Rockville Center, Inc.*,[92] the exhibits the contractor attached to its complaint revealed to the appellate court that it was not entitled to an extension of time. Jeffrey M. Brown Associates, Inc., the contractor, entered into a fast-track contract with Rockville Center, Inc. to design and build a retail pavilion and theater on the owner's land. The contract provided that time was of the essence because the owners had to meet an occupancy schedule for their incoming tenants and required a final certificate of occupancy at a certain date. The contractor completed enough work on the theater portion of the project to receive a temporary occupancy permit from the city, while work on the retail portion of the project continued. Disputes arose concerning the quality of the contractor's work and delays in construction. To ensure completion of the project, the parties entered into a settlement agreement under which the contractor agreed to complete its work by a fixed date. A 15-day cure period allowed the contractor to cure any breaches after completion. The owner notified the contractor that it had not achieved substantial completion. This triggered the 15-day cure period. On the completion date, the city's chief inspector wrote a letter to the owners that a final certificate of occupancy would not be issued until a defect in an expansion joint was repaired. The owners deemed the contractor to be in default and terminated the contract. The contractor sued, alleging the owners breached the contract, as amended by the settlement agreement, by terminating the contractor and by refusing to pay the contractor. To achieve final completion, the contractor was contractually required to obtain a final certificate of occupancy that it did not obtain. The consequence of the contractor's failure to achieve completion was the contractor's default, and the risk that it could be terminated with no notice or opportunity to cure. The owners were free to terminate the contract and take back the escrowed funds when the contractor could not demonstrate it was entitled to a time extension and defaulted. The contractor failed to state a claim for breach of contract.

The notice period in a termination clause may be modified by the parties' actions during the contract performance period. *AXA Global Risks U.S. Insurance*

---

[91] Construction Law § 4.13[1] (Steven G.M. Stein ed., 1998).
[92] 7 Fed. Appx. 197 (4th Cir. 2001).

Co. v. Sweet Associates, Inc.[93] involved Sweet Associates, Inc. who hired as the general contractor for a library expansion project at the State University of New York at Albany. In connection therewith, Sweet entered into a subcontract with Atlantic Wall Systems to provide labor, materials and equipment. As required by the subcontract, Atlantic guaranteed its performance by procuring a performance bond from plaintiff. From the beginning, Sweet found Atlantic's work deficient. When Atlantic failed to remedy the problems, Sweet requested a meeting with Atlantic and its surety, ultimately meeting with Atlantic. When the quality of work did not improve, Sweet gave formal notice to Atlantic, by letter dated December 31, that it sought to terminate the subcontract if the default was not cured within the 15-day period provided therein. Sweet, Atlantic, and the surety thereafter scheduled a meeting for January 21, which resulted in a letter by Sweet to the surety, dated January 27, conditionally withdrawing its prior notice of default yet "reserving the right to declare [Atlantic] to be in default upon three (3) days written notice." No objection to the shortened time frame was made. Atlantic continued work on the project. Twice more Sweet sent default notices, this time to both Atlantic and the surety. Neither objected to the shortened cure period. In response to the third default notice, Atlantic advised Sweet that, due to its failure to pay in a timely manner, Atlantic's subcontractors were refusing to continue work, thus accounting for the problems that Sweet noted. Sweet nonetheless made a demand upon the surety, as Atlantic's surety, to complete the remaining work. The surety complied, again without objection to the shortened cure period. After finishing the work on the project, the surety commenced an action against Sweet and others for breach of contract. The contractor counterclaimed for damages caused by the surety's delay in completing the work. The surety moved for partial summary judgment on the issue of liability due to Sweet's failure to comply with the 15-day notice to cure provision of the subcontract. The supreme court granted the surety's motion and the contractor appealed. Despite protestations that the shortened period was a modification of the contract that was not properly implemented, the issue was a waiver of the 15-day provision and the surety's failure to object to the shortened notice provision that Sweet unilaterally drew into their agreement. There was an intention to waive the contractual notice provision once the original notice of default was conditionally withdrawn.

[3] Third-Party Certification

The receipt of a certificate from a third-party such as an architect that a contractor's default is sufficient to justify the termination may be necessary before an owner is permitted to terminate.[94]

---

[93] 302 A.D.2d 844 (N.Y. App. Div. 2003).
[94] Construction Law § 4.13[1][a] (Steven G.M. Stein ed., 1998).

[4]   Improper Default Termination Changed to Termination for Convenience

In a contract with a termination-for-convenience clause, a party may terminate a contract for default and then, if it is found that the termination is wrongful, change the termination to one for convenience. Although accepted without question in federal contract administration, the rule may equally apply to private contracts. In *Millgard Corp. v. EE Cruz/Nab/Frontier-Kemper, Joint Venture,*[95] the EE Cruz/Nab/Frontier-Kemper, Joint Venture terminated Millgard Corporation for default. Millgard sought as damages for wrongful termination anticipated profits and home office overhead on work not performed. The joint venture claimed that under Paragraph 9(a) of the subcontract, it had the unilateral right to terminate the subcontract. Under the clause, the subcontractor was not entitled to lost profits if the subcontract was terminated for convenience. The JV moved for summary judgment.

The joint venture offered as an affirmative defense to its termination of its subcontractor Millgard that "if the Subcontract was not properly terminated, then the termination of the subcontract was for convenience" under Paragraph 9(a). New York and Second Circuit law did not appear to have addressed this issue directly. The court held that the JV was not bound by its initial rationale for default termination, provided that it was not acting in bad faith, and Millgard did not change its position in reliance upon the initial reason given for termination.

Failure to follow the procurement rules is not sufficient breach of contract to justify a default termination. Consider *Women's Development Corp. v. City of Central Falls.*[96] The low-income housing finance program used public money to develop low-income and moderate-income housing. The state distributed the money to participating municipalities on a statewide basis through a competitive bidding process. The City of Central Falls applied for and obtained money to support a local program known as the centennial urban renewal enterprise. The Women's Development Corporation represented that it possessed significant expertise in administering this kind of housing-development project. The city entered into a contract with the Women's Development Corporation. The Women's Development Corporation was responsible for property acquisition, design, development, construction, financing, and overall administration of the project. A new mayor subsequently took office and according to the plaintiff, the city's attitude toward the project dramatically changed. The mayor refused to release the funds relating to the three approved requisitions. The city failed to pay the plaintiff for these services. The plaintiff filed a breach-of-contract claim against the city. The city terminated the development contract for cause. Even though the city had not previously complained about the developer's deficient performance, the termination letter cited the developer's failure to provide accurate documentation as justification for terminating the contract. The letter also stated

---

[95] 2003 U.S. Dist. LEXIS 21287 (S.D.N.Y. 2003).
[96] 764 A.2d 151 (R.I. 2001).

that the developer had failed to cooperate with an audit of the project, had submitted false and misleading invoices, and had made material misrepresentations to secure approval of various elements of the project. The trial court found that the evidence of the breaches was uncontradicted and each of the breaches in and of themselves was very material, and that even assuming that none of the breaches was material, then all of them taken together were extraordinarily material. The trial court awarded the city monetary relief. The Women's Development Corporation appealed.

The Women's Development Corporation argued that it had not materially breached the contracts by its failure to adhere to various contractual provisions when it performed under the contracts. The developer argued that the contract breaches were immaterial and that, given its substantial performance under the contract, the trial justice erred in granting the city judgment as a matter of law on its breach of contract claims. The plaintiff's mere failure to include anti-kickback and EEO language in its subcontracts, to obtain prior written approval from the city before subcontracting various services, and to use competitive-bidding procurement procedures was not shown to have deprived the city of any reasonably expected contractual benefits. The city also failed to establish that any of these omissions or failures on the plaintiff's part could not have been cured had the city brought these matters to the plaintiff's attention in a timely fashion. The city failed to prove that any of the plaintiff's omissions or failures resulted in any actual harm to the city or that they had served to frustrate the parties' expectations in any material way. Therefore, the appellate court held that the breaches of contract cited, whether considered individually or collectively, did not, as a matter of law, constitute evidence of the plaintiff's material breach of contract justifying termination, nor did they justify the city's nonpayment for the work performed by the Women's Development Corporation under the contracts.

[5] Terminated General Contract Also Terminates Subcontract

A subcontractor's contract is terminated when the general contractor's contract is terminated if the subcontractor's work is to assist the general contractor in the performance of the general contract. Consider *Carolina Casualty Insurance v. Ragan Mechanical Contractors Inc.*[97] Latco Construction Company, Inc. contracted with the DeKalb County Board of Education for the construction of a school. The contractor obtained performance and payment bonds, and these were issued jointly by two sureties. The contractor subcontracted with Ragan Mechanical Contractors, Inc. for the mechanical, HVAC, and plumbing work. The subcontract provided that if the board of education terminated "any part" of the general contract "which includes the Subcontractor's Work," then the subcontract was also terminated. The board issued a stop-work directive. The subcontractor stopped working but was not paid for all of the work it performed on the project, although the contractor was paid for the work. The board terminated the

---

[97] 584 S.E.2d 646 (Ga. Ct. App. 2003).

contractor's "right to proceed" on the project, stating that it considered the contractor to be in default. The board demanded that the co-sureties discharge their obligations under the performance bond. The co-sureties subsequently agreed to complete the contractor's general contract. The subcontractor sought payment from the contractor and co-sureties under the payment bond. The co-sureties refused to pay the subcontractor, taking the position that the subcontractor failed to perform its obligation to complete its work under the subcontract even though the general contract had been terminated. The trial court granted the subcontractor's motion for partial summary judgment, and denied the co-sureties' motion. The co-sureties appealed.

Although the parties agreed that the subcontract incorporated the general contract by reference, the subcontractor did not agree to be directly bound to the board under that contract. Rather, the subcontractor agreed to perform its work in compliance with the general contract and subject to the approval of the contractor and the board. The subcontractor's primary undertaking was to perform its work for the benefit of the contractor and for the purpose of enabling the contractor to meet its obligations under the general contract. In that connection, the subcontractor assumed toward the contractor all of the obligations and responsibilities that the contractor assumed toward the board. In addition, the subcontractor agreed to start work when notified by the contractor and to complete work at times as would enable the contractor to comply with the main contract. Thus, while the contractor was obligated to the board to perform work under the general contract, the subcontractor was obligated to the contractor under the subcontract to assist in performing that work. The appellate court found that when the board terminated the contractor's obligation to perform, the subcontractor's obligation to assist in that performance was also terminated.

In contrast, a party that terminates a contractor may elect to take control of the subcontractor and as a result become liable for the subcontractor's costs to perform after the contractor's termination. *Encore Construction Corp. v. S.C. Bodner Construction, Inc.*[98] examines when the owner's responsibility for subcontractor costs begins if the subcontractor performed according to the owner's requests, but before the notice period in the termination clause had ended and the contractor was terminated.

Encore Hotels and S.C. Bodner Construction entered into a contract for the construction of a hotel. The contract provided for a ten-day notice of termination. Bodner subcontracted with Imperial Marble Corporation for materials to be used and with Summit Construction for the installation of the materials Imperial would provide. On February 4, Encore sent a letter that terminated Bodner. Imperial shipped its first installment of materials to the construction site on February 4, and Encore's project superintendent instructed Summit's superintendent to unload the materials and begin installation. Summit learned on February 6 that Bodner had been terminated. Encore's project superintendent indicated to Summit that Encore had taken over the project. He asked Summit to remain at the site and continue to

---

[98] 765 N.E.2d 223 (Ind. Ct. App. 2002).

install the materials Imperial had provided. Summit continued installing the materials through February 16, and it returned to the site on February 20 to install more materials. Imperial shipped additional materials to the site on or about February 12, 14, 17, 18, and 20. Bodner never received from Encore any payment for the materials provided by Imperial or the work completed by Summit, and neither Bodner nor Encore had paid either subcontractor.

Encore asserted that the contract was not actually terminated until February 14, ten days after the letter was mailed to Bodner. Encore conceded that it became liable to the subcontractors after the contract terminated and it took over the construction site on and after February 14. The letter could be read as terminating the contract ten days after the date of the letter, as the letter specified it was being submitted pursuant to the contract. The notice letter could also be read to refer to Encore's election to terminate the contract, and not to the termination itself that would take effect ten days later. The day after the letter was mailed, but before Bodner received it, Bodner's president received a telephone call that "at this date from here on out [Bodner] was receiving no more money to work on the project." Encore took over the job site as of February 4, the date the letter was mailed. Encore obtained a forklift so that Summit could unload some materials on February 4. Summit prepared a "mock-up" of the marble installation and it was approved. Encore's letter of February 4 did not afford Bodner the ten days' notice called for in the agreement, as it stated the termination would occur "now," and Bodner was given no opportunity to cure any breach of the agreement or to notify the subcontractors of its termination.

Encore perpetrated an "actual wrong" when it asked Imperial and Summit to provide labor and materials for the project after the date when it terminated Bodner, and then refused to pay. Encore allowed the delivery of Imperial's materials during the period from February 4 through February 20, it made no effort to return the materials, and it allowed them to be installed after it had terminated Bodner. Encore asked Summit to remain at the site and to continue installing the materials, and it promised that Summit would be paid. Encore was unjustly enriched by its retention of the benefits that Imperial and Summit provided and for which Encore did not pay.

[6]   Waiver of Right to Terminate by Default

[a]   Defective Work

The right to terminate for default can be waived by a variety of actions. For example, an owner waives the right to rescind a building contract when the homeowners treat the contract as still in force. *Hiblovic v. Cinco-T.C., Inc.*[99] involved a contract between Cinco-T.C., Inc. and the Hiblovics for the sale of a residential lot and construction of a house. The sale was to close after completion of the house, and the contract stated that the house would be deemed completed at such time

---

[99] 2005 Mo. App. LEXIS 567 (2005).

that it was ready for occupancy. The contract required the homeowners to close even if certain items remained incomplete, so long as the items did not prevent comfortable occupancy of the house. During the course of construction, the homeowners noticed cracks in the foundation and reported to the contractor that the foundation had failed. The homeowners wanted to rescind the contract. The contractor offered a settlement of the claim of an additional warranty on the foundation and a retaining wall at no charge if the homeowners did not rescind the contract. The homeowners accepted the offer and negotiated language for the warranty. The contractor provided the negotiated warranty and constructed a retaining wall at no charge. The homeowners participated in finishing construction of the house by requesting revisions to the plans and selecting particular color patterns and floor coverings. Nevertheless, the homeowners later refused to close and informed the contractor of their intent to rescind the contract. The homeowners filed suit, and the contractor filed a counterclaim. The trial court entered judgment in favor of the homeowners. Both parties appealed.

The homeowners contended that the foundation wall failed, thus granting sufficient basis for the homeowners to revoke the contract. When the contractor offered the homeowners a settlement of the claim, the homeowners accepted the offer. The homeowners further participated in finishing construction of the house by requesting revisions to the plans and selecting particular color patterns and floor coverings. The homeowners waived their right to rescind the contract by participating in finishing the construction of the house, encouraging the contractor to continue with the construction of the house, executing five different change orders, and making color and floor selections for the house. There was a waiver of the right to rescind a building contract where the contract was treated, by the homeowners, as still in force. The homeowners' point on appeal was denied.

[b] Waiver of Timely Performance

A contract may also be terminated for default for failure to meet the contract completion date. The right to terminate for default for failure to meet contract completion dates may also be waived by permitting a contractor to continue to perform after the contract completion date. However, for construction contracts, "continued performance alone will not ordinarily support a claim of waiver." When the government preserves its rights, a contractor cannot convert that forbearance into conduct amounting to a waiver. In *Abcon Associates, Inc. v. United States*,[100] the court considered whether the government waived the delivery schedule under the contract and, therefore, wrongfully terminated the contractor. The Unites States Postal service awarded Abcon Associates, Inc. a contract for the extension of the loading dock and the installation of three freight elevators at a USPS Processing and Distribution Center. Under the terms of the contract, the contractor was to commence performance within ten days of receipt of the notice

---

[100] 44 Fed. Cl. 625 (1999).

to proceed and to complete performance within 510 days. Work under the contract was divided into two phases, each with its own completion deadline. Phase I was further divided into phases 1a and 1b. Phase 1a was to commence immediately and be completed by April 1. Phase 1b was to commence immediately and be completed by December 1. Phase 2 was to commence on April 1 of the following year and be completed by October 1. The contractor received the notice to proceed on May 1. The notice to proceed identified September 23 as the completion date for all work. The contractor commenced performance of Phase 1 in May. Shortly thereafter, the contractor discovered discrepancies between the project drawings and the actual conditions in the USPS facility.

The December Phase 1b completion deadline passed without completion of the project. By a December 17 letter, the contracting officer's representative informed the contractor that it was in default and that the government could terminate the contract if the contractor did not cure the default. During the same month, the government began withholding the liquidated damages stipulated in the contract. In a February letter, the contracting officer again notified the contractor that the government was considering terminating the contract. This letter indicated that the default was based on a failure to submit an acceptable project schedule. At a meeting later that month, the contracting officer indicated that some of the performance problems were not entirely the contractor's fault. The Phase 1a deadline of April 1 passed without completion. Phase 2 was not commenced as required by the contract. The contractor offered a new schedule that included completion of Phase I by August 23 and of Phase 2 within three months thereafter. In May and June, the contractor received design solutions for the outstanding problems. The contractor continued to perform while liquidated damages mounted.

By August, the contractor submitted requests for additional compensation and time to complete the contract. The contractor based its requests on what it perceived to be design defects, differing site conditions, or government-directed changes. The government authorized the release of a portion of the liquidated damages that it had retained. The authorization was made despite the fact that the contractor continued to represent that it could not prepare an accurate construction schedule and that Phase 1 was incomplete.

The contractor's proposed Phase 1 deadline of August 23 passed without completion. The October 1 contract deadline for Phase 2 passed without delivery. On October 3, the contractor received a payment equal to the full amount of liquidated damages collected to date by the government. The contractor submitted a formal request for an extension of the contract performance date on October 15. The contracting officer issued a written rejection of the request. The contractor's proposed Phase 2 completion date passed without delivery. During the entire duration of the contract, the contractor continued to work on the project, and the government continued to review the contractor's work and to make payment. On December 30, the contracting officer unilaterally modified the contract and withheld liquidated damages for the period from the original contract completion date through termination. By letter of December 31, the contracting officer terminated the contract for failure to make progress.

The court concluded that the government's December and February letters reserved its rights to terminate for default. The government's assessment of liquidated damages and refusal to grant a time extension supported this conclusion. Other conduct, such as the interim release of liquidated damages and continued contract payments, was seen as an effort to mitigate the effects of the subcontractor's failure to perform.

In *William M. Hendrickson, Inc. v. National Railroad Passenger Corp.,*[101] Amtrak issued the first of four purchase orders to Hendrickson to manufacture air conditioning units. All four Amtrak purchase orders issued to Hendrickson included NRPC 69, a three-page stand-alone document that contained 31 "conditions of purchase." The clauses of NRPC 69 relevant to Hendrickson's breach of contract claim provided:

> 8. DEFAULT—(A) Amtrak may . . . terminate the whole or any part of this Order in one of the following circumstances: if Company (1) fails to make delivery of the Supplies within the time specified herein as "delivery date" or any extension thereof. . . . At its sole option, Amtrak may require a cure of the failure involved rather than terminating the Order in whole or in part. If Company does not cure the failure within the period specified by Amtrak, then Amtrak shall have the right at that time to terminate the whole or any part of the Order. . . .

> 10. DELIVERY DATE—(A) Company agrees to deliver the Supplies no later than the date specified in the Order as "Delivery at Destination". . . . Because time is of the essence hereof, Company will commence and prosecute the work . . . with due diligence and dispatch and make deliveries as specified. (B) If Company encounters or anticipates difficulty in meeting the Order delivery schedule, Company shall immediately notify Amtrak in writing, giving pertinent details; provided however that this data shall be informational only in character and shall not be construed as a waiver by Amtrak of any delivery schedule or date or of any rights or remedies provided by the law or this Order. . . .

> 20. NON-WAIVER—No waiver by Amtrak of any breach on the part of Company or any of its obligations herein contained shall constitute a waiver of any subsequent breach of the same or any other of such obligations. . . .

Amtrak became concerned that Hendrickson was not delivering the units quickly enough to meet Amtrak's needs. Before it issued the fourth purchase order, Amtrak informed Hendrickson that its delivery needs were 16 units/month. The fourth purchase order issued by Amtrak contained the following delivery dates: 20 units April 1; 16 units May 3; 16 units June 1; 16 units July 1; 16 units August 1; and 16 units September 1. Hendrickson failed to deliver units according to the dates in the fourth purchase order. Amtrak requested a meeting with Hendrickson to discuss the delivery schedule for units to be supplied under the

---

[101] 47 U.C.C. Rep. Serv. 2d (Callaghan) 1284 (E.D. Pa. 2002).

fourth purchase order. Hendrickson proposed a new delivery schedule. Amtrak accepted this delivery schedule. Hendrickson made deliveries on the fourth purchase order, but the deliveries did not adhere to the new delivery schedule that the parties agreed.

The director of Amtrak's Procurement Department sent Hendrickson a Notice to Cure in response to Hendrickson's failure to adhere to the delivery schedule in the original purchase order and the subsequent schedule agreed to by both parties. The notice stated that unless such condition was cured within ten days of receipt of the notice, Amtrak would terminate subject contract for default under clause entitled "Default." Hendrickson responded to the Notice to Cure and identified two problems that negatively affected its ability to deliver units according to schedule:

(1) Amtrak had returned 22 of 33 units recently delivered by Hendrickson. O'Neill asked that Amtrak assign an Amtrak employee to communicate with Hendrickson the reasons for the returns.

(2) Sporadic Purchase Orders. Hendrickson stated that the sporadic nature of the purchase orders had caused Hendrickson to "tear down" its production line on two occasions, requiring it to spend time and resources to recreate the production line.

In attempting to offer an acceptable cure to Amtrak, Hendrickson met with Amtrak's Chief Mechanical Officer to discuss the needs of Amtrak's Mechanical Department with respect to Hendrickson's delivery of the units. The Chief Mechanical Officer informed Hendrickson that 8 car sets, or 16 units, per month would be sufficient to meet the needs of the Mechanical Department, but that Amtrak's Purchasing Department, not the Mechanical Department, made the determination regarding what constituted an acceptable cure. Hendrickson responded that, at that time, it was capable of supplying 8 units per month, but could gradually increase its production to 16 units per month. Hendrickson indicated that it would present this delivery schedule as a proposed cure to the Purchasing Department. On April 17, Amtrak sent a notice of termination of contract to Hendrickson. Hendrickson contended that Amtrak breached the final contract between the parties when it notified Hendrickson of its termination of the contract in April. The delivery dates in the purchase order and a subsequent schedule agreed to by the parties were essential terms of the contract. Amtrak did not cause Hendrickson's inability to perform according to schedule.

Hendrickson failed to perform according to the schedules agreed to by the parties and, therefore, was in default of the contract. The terms of the contract between Hendrickson and Amtrak clearly and explicitly authorized Amtrak to terminate the contract for default if Hendrickson failed to deliver according to the dates in the purchase order and "any extension thereof." Hendrickson did not deliver in accordance with the original schedule or the subsequent schedule. Amtrak's termination was proper. Moreover, it was reasonable for Amtrak to conclude that Hendrickson would not be able to deliver the remaining units under the contract by the final delivery date. Weeks before Amtrak sent Hendrickson the notice to cure, Hendrickson had delivered only 28 of the 60 units that the new schedule required it to deliver by that time. Thus, in order to complete delivery by the final delivery date of April 4, Hendrickson would have had to have delivered 72 units in just over a month.

The plain language of the contract between the parties made clear that the delivery dates were essential terms of the contract. Clause 10 of the contract stated that "time is of the essence." Clause 8, the default clause, identified failure to deliver according to the specified delivery dates as a cause for default termination. Moreover, the required delivery dates themselves were clearly laid out in both the original schedule and the schedule Hendrickson itself developed.

The dates were not arbitrary, as Hendrickson contended. Amtrak made clear to Hendrickson that the delivery dates for the fourth purchase order were established in order to coincide with Amtrak's refurbishment program. Despite this fact, Hendrickson argued that its failure to deliver according to these dates was excusable because the dates in the first three purchase orders were not feasible, Hendrickson did not adhere to them, and Amtrak did not require Hendrickson to adhere to them. Regardless of what occurred under the prior three contracts, Hendrickson could not rely on course of dealing when it was aware that the delivery dates were not arbitrary but were developed to allow Amtrak to coordinate the installation of Hendrickson units with its overhaul effort. Furthermore, under the U.C.C., express terms of an agreement trumped course of dealing. Finally, the explicit terms of the contract also made clear that Hendrickson's failure to deliver according to the delivery dates in the first three purchase orders did not excuse its failure to deliver timely on the fourth purchase order. Clause 20 of NRPC 69, Non-Waiver, also would apply to any argument that Amtrak waived its right to object to Hendrickson's late deliveries under the fourth purchase order when it permitted Hendrickson to propose the amended schedule. The delivery dates in the fourth contract not only were not arbitrary but were essential terms of the contract.

The termination of a contractor for being behind schedule can often work against the owner when it has not properly considered all the delays and claims of the contractor. The case of *District of Columbia et al. v. Kora & Williams Corp.*,[102] is an example of what can happen. Kora & Williams Corporation (K&W) ran afoul of the government on a major job at Union Station. Congress had given the District of Columbia the responsibility for completing the parking garage along with developing the railroad access facilities at the station. Restoration of the station itself was to proceed at the same time as the district's work. The restoration was the responsibility of the Union Station Redevelopment Corporation, another public body. The funds for the district to do this work were to be provided by the Federal Highway Administration (FHWA).

---

[102] 743 A.2d 682 (D.C. 1999).

The district contracted with K&W to perform the construction work. Before long, K&W and the district were arguing over change orders, time extensions, and claims that ran into the millions of dollars, money that the district did not have available. K&W was late. Its late performance jeopardized the success and completion of the restoration contract overseen by the Redevelopment Corporation, which began to press its claims for more than $6 million if the garage and the link being constructed by the district were late. In addition to the claims, the Redevelopment Corporation began campaigning to get the district to terminate K&W. If K&W was terminated for default, its surety would have to finish the work and carry or absorb its costs over the approved contract balance. This meant that the district could use the funds it received from the FHWA for K&W's unresolved change orders and claims to ease its own funding problems on the contract. The district's contracting officer relinquished its responsibility for the default decision to the then City Administrator, who made the termination decision for pre-textural reasons not related to the rights of K&W and the duties and responsibilities of the district as a party to the K&W contract. Entitlement to time extensions, a time adjustment for change orders, excusable delay, and responsibility for delay were never considered as part of the termination decision. K&W appealed its termination to the District of Columbia Contract Appeals Board and sought conversion of the termination into one of convenience rather than the default mode rendered by the district. The board found that the district used the TERMINATION-DELAYS clause of the contract as a pretext to: (1) obtain additional funds from FHWA based on K&W's outstanding claims and change orders; (2) obtain reprocurement funds from the surety; and (3) appease Union Station Redevelopment Corporation, which was threatening to assess damages against the district. The mass of evidence summarized in the board's findings left the court unable to reject the board's conclusion that the termination decision was "shaped by ulterior motives" rather than a reasonable exercise of the contracting officer's discretion. K&W and its surety were also awarded total costs of $12,410.991 plus interest at 4 percent per annum.

[c] *Interference*

As a general rule, the prevention or hindrance of another party's performance of a contract constituted a material breach of the contract and excused the nonperformance of the nonbreaching party and waived the right to terminate. In *William M. Hendrickson, Inc. v. National Railroad Passenger Corp.*,[103] Hendrickson claimed that its failure to deliver according to schedule was excused because Amtrak substantially interfered with Hendrickson's ability to perform by returning units as defective that were not defective, withholding funds, and not providing Hendrickson with a steady flow of orders for its units.

---

[103] 47 U.C.C. Rep. Serv. 2d (Callaghan) 1284 (E.D. Pa. 2002).

While evidence was introduced that Amtrak returned a substantial number of units to Hendrickson for various defects, Hendrickson failed to prove that Amtrak returned units for failures that did not exist, that Amtrak failed to identify the defects in machines returned, and that Amtrak intentionally sabotaged units causing them to fail. To prove its allegations, Hendrickson relied primarily on the testimony of Hendrickson's president. Without documentary proof, the district court concluded that testimony was not credible. In contrast, Amtrak officials credibly testified to the problems that Amtrak experienced with Hendrickson units. The manager of Amtrak's Mechanical Department testified to receiving calls and complaints from Amtrak maintenance personnel about Hendrickson units breaking down, and offered documentary evidence of a significant number of Hendrickson warranty failures. The warranty failures became so numerous that Amtrak officials called a meeting with Hendrickson's president in order to discuss the problems. The significant number of warranty failures also prompted Amtrak to conduct quality assurance inspections of Amtrak units upon their delivery to Amtrak. A former director of equipment maintenance for Amtrak testified to the quality assurance failures that Amtrak experienced with Hendrickson units. Amtrak introduced the quality control inspection reports, which established that Amtrak returned at least 14 units to Hendrickson for failing quality control inspection. Moreover, Hendrickson admitted to Amtrak that its performance was deficient. Immediately after receiving the notice to cure, Hendrickson sent a letter that stated that it "was not attempting to offer excuses for our poor performance." Hendrickson did not prove that Amtrak prevented it from delivering on time by returning nondefective units, or by failing to identify the defect in units it did return. In addition, there was no evidence that Amtrak intentionally sabotaged Hendrickson units causing them to break down.

Lastly, Hendrickson alleged that Amtrak's sporadic purchase orders prevented it from making timely deliveries on the fourth purchase order. This was no justification for nonperformance. Amtrak was under no duty to award Hendrickson a steady flow of orders. Even if this were a viable excuse, Hendrickson failed to prove that the sporadic orders interfered with its performance. According to Hendrickson, the sporadic nature of the purchase orders caused Hendrickson to tear down its production line, only to have to rebuild it once Amtrak issued a new order. Yet, the evidence presented at trial established just the opposite. The fourth purchase order was issued, more than twice the number of the third purchase order, to be delivered at 16 units per month for six months. Thus, there would have been no reason for Hendrickson to tear down its production line during the fourth contract and, indeed, there was no evidence that Hendrickson did so. Even at the time that Amtrak issued the fourth purchase order, Hendrickson had not yet completed delivery on the third purchase order. Thus, it is not clear why Hendrickson would have been forced to tear down its production line between the third and fourth purchase orders.

Hendrickson failed to prove that Amtrak was the cause of its failure to perform and that its default was excusable. Amtrak's termination for default was justified by Hendrickson's failure to deliver units according to the original schedule in the purchase order and the amended schedule and because Hendrickson's default was not excused. Because Amtrak had paid Hendrickson for all units delivered to Amtrak under the fourth purchase order, Amtrak was not liable to Hendrickson.

[B]   Failure to Make Progress

[1]   Assurance That Work Will Be Completed Timely

In addition to terminating a contractor for failure to complete on time, many termination clauses permit termination for failure to progress. Under federal contract law, a contractor's failure to make satisfactory progress gives the government the basis to request assurance that the contract work will be completed in a timely manner and that corrective measures will be taken to "cure" the default, even though the circumstances at the time may not justify termination for default. The contractor's failure or refusal to provide such assurances to the government may be grounds to terminate the contract for default.[104]

Failure to provide adequate assurances of timely performance constitutes a breach of the contract, justifying termination of the contract for default. For example, in *Danzig, Sec. of Navy v. AEC Corp.*,[105] the Navy awarded AEC Corporation a contract to complete the construction of a Naval and Marine Corps Reserve Training Center. The contract called for the completion of the project by October 14. The contractor was behind schedule as a result of financial difficulties. A cure notice was issued by the owner. The contractor provided a schedule with a new projected completion date. The owner agreed not to terminate the contract for default if the contractor continued to make progress according to the new schedule. The contractor submitted a revised schedule with another extended completion date. The contractor's surety later froze the project's bank account. The owner sent the contractor another cure notice. The owner was concerned that the decreasing number of man hours devoted to the job was delaying the job. Although the contractor responded to the second cure notice, the owner gave the contractor a letter directing them to show cause why the contract should not be terminated for default. The contractor did not respond to the owner's show-cause letter, and the owner terminated the contract for default. The contractor appealed the termination. The Armed Services Board of Contract Appeals held that the termination was not valid. The owner sought reconsideration.

The owner argued that the contractor failed to give adequate assurances that it could complete the contract on a timely basis, or even that it could continue to make progress toward completion, and justified the owner's decision to terminate

---

[104] Danzig v. AEC Corp., 224 F.3d 1333 (Fed. Cir. 2000). *See also* Morganti Nat'l, Inc. v. United States, 49 Fed. Cl. 110 (2001) (court affirmed default termination after contractor failed to demonstrate its ability to make progress to complete work at an extended completion date agreed by the government).

[105] 224 F.3d 1333 (Fed. Cir. 2000).

the contract for default. The appellate court found that the contractor's performance after the new completion date had been established gave the owner a reasonable basis for concern that the contract would not be completed at the extended completion date. The court further stated that the owner was therefore entitled to issue a cure notice demanding a correction of the slow pace of the work or a satisfactory explanation of how the contractor planned to complete the work on a timely basis. The contractor's responses to the cure notice did not adequately explain how its slow progress was the result of delay caused by the government. The court also found that the contractor's conduct also clearly failed to provide the requisite assurance that it would complete the project on a timely basis. The owner was entitled to regard the contractor's failure to provide such assurance as a breach of the contract, justifying termination of the contract for default. Reversed and remanded.

Long delays to activities identified by the schedule as critical, such as a subcontractor's substantial delay in submitting steel shop drawings and starting to fabricate steel, justifies a contractor's termination before the project is completed. For example, in *Intermetal Fabricators, Inc. v. Losco Group, Inc.*,[106] the Losco Group renovated two properties for the United States Postal Service. The contractor subcontracted with Amboy Steel, Inc. to perform the steel fabrication, installation, and miscellaneous metals. With the contractor's consent, Amboy assigned the subcontract to Intermetal. The subcontract provided that all steel work was to be completed within 200 days of execution. The subcontract also provided that the shop drawings were to be submitted by the subcontractor to the general contractor within two weeks of the signing of the subcontract. The contractor testified that the subcontractor repeatedly delayed the project and otherwise breached the subcontract. No shop drawings were submitted within the two-week period. The contractor also complained that the subcontractor delayed ordering the steel. The subcontractor submitted a requisition for $117,256.22. The contractor refused payment because the contractor had already been overpaid for the work completed, and the subcontractor was not performing the remaining work under the subcontract. The contractor later terminated the subcontract.

The contractor argued that it properly terminated the subcontract because the subcontractor repeatedly delayed the project, breached various provisions of the subcontract, and refused to fulfill its performance obligations under the subcontract. The subcontractor argued that its termination was improper because the contractor breached the subcontract by failing to pay the monies owed on the project. The court found that the subcontractor failed to deliver timely the initial shop drawings. One year after the execution of the initial subcontract, the subcontractor had not yet submitted a full set of approved shop drawings and had not begun fabrication or erection of the steel. Although the subcontractor argued that the architect's failure to answer questions caused the delayed submission of the drawings and the eventual commencement of steel fabrication and erection, the court noted

---

[106] 2000 U.S. Dist. LEXIS 11622 (S.D.N.Y. 2000).

that the subcontractor offered no explanation for delay before the questions were submitted to the architect. The court found that a dispute over payment for prior jobs between the subcontractor and its detailer had caused at least some of the delay, and that the subcontractor's failure to retain timely the detailer also contributed to the delay. The subcontractor also failed to order the steel for the project timely. Once steel fabrication and erection began, the subcontractor's inability to meet its own obligations to pay for labor and material caused additional project delays. The subcontractor substantially delayed and abandoned work on the project and justified the termination of the subcontract for failure to progress.

In *Harley Paws, Inc., d/b/a Three Dog Bakery v. Mohns, Inc.,*[107] correction of defective work would not permit completion on the contract date and justified termination for failure to progress. Mohns, Inc. and Harley Paws, Inc. contracted for the remodeling of a retail store. Mohns told Harley Paws that the construction should be completed in approximately five weeks. Based on that information, Harley Paws scheduled its grand opening for September 26. Construction commenced in early August and continued until September 11, when disputes developed primarily involving: (1) the modification, possible delay, and additional costs involving the construction of the store's cabinetry; and (2) the rescheduling of the faux finisher, who was scheduled to do the finishing painting on September 12, but could not because Mohns had failed to complete the preliminary painting. The additional costs for cabinets was resolved through an informal mediation meeting with Harley Paws' attorney on the afternoon of September 11. During the mediation, Harley Paws and Mohns agreed to a change order on the cabinets. Hours later, however, when Harley Paws discovered defects in the drywall and learned from Mohns' president that the store would not be completed by the grand opening date, Harley Paws fired Mohns and arranged for other contractors to complete the remodeling. Harley Paws subsequently sued Mohns for breach of contract. The court concluded that Mohns had breached the contract. In its findings of fact, the court explained that, given the need to be ready for the September 26 opening, the parties clearly understood that "time was of the essence." The court concluded "that the termination on the 11th of the contract and the hiring of replacement contractors was reasonable."

The facts supported the trial court's conclusion that Harley Paws breached the contract. The work had not progressed as scheduled, and by September 11, it had become evident that the work would not be completed within the contracted time. Mohns had substantially underestimated the cost of the cabinetry, and as of September 11, Mohns did not know who would construct the cabinets or when they would be installed. The contractors who replaced Mohns testified that Mohns' workmanship had been shoddy and, as a result, the scheduled subcontractor's work was delayed, further indicating that the job would not be completed on schedule. Evidence also established that the new contractors worked 12 to 13 hours a day to complete the project by September 23. The court implicitly found that Mohns' words and actions constituted an anticipatory breach. These findings

---

[107] 639 N.W.2d 223 (Wis. Ct. App. 2001).

were not clearly erroneous, and the facts found by the trial court constituted an anticipatory breach.

In *In re Stone & Webster, Inc.*,[108] Maine Yankee Atomic Power Company hired Stone & Webster Engineering Corporation (SWEC) to decommission Maine Yankee's Wiscasset nuclear power generating facility. Under the Decommissioning Agreement, SWEC was responsible to complete the project on time and on budget. Article 11, Termination for Cause, governed Maine Yankee's right to terminate the Agreement for cause. Article 11.1 provided that Maine Yankee had the right to terminate the Agreement in the event of the insolvency of the contractor. Section 11.2 provided that Maine Yankee may terminate for cause in the event that SWEC failed to perform substantially or breached the Agreement. Article 11.4 provided that "[i]f Contractor fails to substantially perform under the Contract Documents or if Contractor materially breaches any of the terms of the Contract Documents . . . Maine Yankee shall have the right, without any further liability to Contractor . . . [to terminate the agreement, obtain performance from another contractor, and/or sue the Contractor for breach]." SWEC was obligated to complete the work in accordance with the milestone schedule. That provision required SWEC to complete the physical work of the project by April 30, 2004.

Problems with SWEC's performance on the decommissioning project occurred early. SWEC was unable to pay its bills or its subcontractors; SWEC failed to develop an adequate project schedule; and SWEC failed to make adequate progress on the project. Early schedules that SWEC submitted did not include all of the licensing and permitting tasks, was not resource-loaded, and included false logic. SWEC implemented a series of workshops in hopes of getting an approved schedule. Despite SWEC's efforts, the final SWEC schedule still did not include all work activities, particularly in the area of licensing and permitting, and lacked sufficient details. Maine Yankee terminated the Agreement based upon SWEC's insolvency and because SWEC had not adequately performed under the contract. Both purported grounds for termination were provided under the contract. Specifically, Maine Yankee stated that SWEC had not provided an acceptable project schedule, had not made adequate progress in completing the work, had not obtained the necessary regulatory approvals, had not administered the work, had failed to provide adequate assurances of its ability to complete performance, and had failed to pay its subcontractors and suppliers as required by the Decommissioning Agreement. Soon thereafter, SWEC filed voluntary petitions for bankruptcy relief. Maine Yankee assumed the role of the contractor on its project, and proceeded with the decommissioning of the power plant. Maine Yankee filed proofs of claim in the bankruptcy cases against SWEC. SWEC objected to Maine Yankee's claims, arguing that Maine Yankee did not properly terminate the Decommissioning Agreement for either insolvency or failure to perform.

SWEC failed to meet its obligation to make adequate progress completing the work. First, the April 28 schedule update reflects that, as of just prior to termination, SWEC projected that the physical work would be completed by January 5, 2005.

---

[108] 279 B.R. 748 (Dist. Del. 2002).

Second, as of December 1999, the project was "significantly" behind schedule and over budget. Maine Yankee noted that according to SWEC's April 2000 monthly report, SWEC had earned only $20.8 million of the planned $25.7 million (approximately 80 percent) during the 2000 calendar year. The April 2000 monthly report also reflects that during the month of April, SWEC started only 48 percent of the tasks and completed only 53 percent that were intended to be started and completed that month. Moreover, based on its earned value, SWEC only earned 75 to 85 percent of its projected earned value in 1999 and 80 percent in 2000, which demonstrated that SWEC was behind schedule. Last, Maine Yankee noted that these inadequacies, when combined with SWEC's financial difficulties at the time and commensurate deterioration of employee morale, loss of job site personnel, and difficulties with subcontractors confirmed that SWEC breached its obligations to make adequate progress toward completing the work. It was clear that, as of the termination date, SWEC had problems progressing with the work at the Maine Yankee site and was substantially behind schedule. With the specter of SWEC's increasing financial difficulties, and the corresponding inability to pay subcontractors and to retain its own employees, Maine Yankee had no reason to think that SWEC's performance would improve to an acceptable level. Based on the fact that SWEC was behind schedule and was earning far less than the expected earned value at the time of termination, Maine Yankee was within its right to terminate SWEC on this ground.

[2] Excusable Delay Must Be Considered

If the owner contributed to the delay, in other words, the delay was "excusable," the termination is wrongful and the terminated contractor may collect damages for breach. However, a leading treatise explained that "a contractor is not entitled to relief upon the mere occurrence of an event that qualifies as an excusable delay. The contractor must show that the event caused delay to the overall completion of the contract."[109] A subsection of that treatise entitled "Delay of Overall Completion Required" discusses the case law establishing that a contractor "is not entitled to an excusable delay unless it can prove that the time lost delayed the completion of the job. It is not sufficient to establish that some work was prevented; the work prevented must be work that will delay the overall completion of the job."[110]

In *Roberts & Schaefer Co. v. Hardaway Co.*,[111] the design-build contract required subcontractor Hardaway to provide a critical path method (CPM) schedule

---

[109] Morrison Knudsen Corp. v. Fireman's Fund Ins. Co., 175 F.3d 1221 (10th Cir. 1999)(citing J. Cibinic & R. Nash, Administration of Government Contracts 577 (3d ed. 1995) (citing Essential Constr. Co., 1978 ASBCA LEXIS 228, ASBCA No. 18,491, 78-2 BCA (CCH) ¶ 13,314 at 65,122; AB-Tech Constr., Inc., 1982 VABCA LEXIS 12, VABCA No. 1531, 82-2 BCA (CCH) ¶ 15,897 at 78,823-11)).

[110] *Id.* (citing J. Cibinic & R. Nash, Administration of Government Contracts 577, 579 (3d ed. 1995).

[111] 152 F.3d 1283 (11th Cir. 1998).

to the design-build contractor, Roberts & Schaefer. After work on the project was delayed, Roberts & Schaefer expressed their dissatisfaction with Hardaway's progress and scheduling effort. When the scheduling effort and progress did not improve, Roberts & Schaefer terminated Hardaway. In its letter of termination, Roberts & Schaefer listed Hardaway's wrongful acts, including:

> . . . (3) Hardaway failed to cooperate in its contractual duty to develop and follow a work schedule,. . . (5) Hardaway failed to cooperate with R & S . . . to do the work and develop a schedule that would ensure timely completion. . . .

The district court found that Roberts & Schaefer had caused substantial delays to Hardaway, concluded that the termination was wrongful, and awarded Hardaway damages. In Roberts & Schaefer's appeal, it argued that Hardaway did not use a CPM, so it was impossible to ascertain the critical path for the construction work required by the contract, and thus impossible to determine the impact or proportion the cause of any particular delay. After a thorough review of the record, but without additional explanation in its opinion, the appellate court determined that the argument lacked merit and affirmed the damage award. Apparently, the court believed Roberts & Schaefer's substantial delays explained and forgave Hardaway's failure to progress.

In *Morrison Knudsen Corp. v. Fireman's Fund Insurance Co.*, Morrison Knudsen Corporation (MK), a federal contractor, terminated its subcontractor, Ground Improvement Techniques (GIT), for default and sued GIT for damages. GIT counterclaimed for wrongful termination. The United States Department of Energy hired MK to manage cleanup of radioactive mill tailings at sites around the country. MK subcontracted with GIT to clean up the Slick Rock, Colorado, site. GIT hired several lower-tier subcontractors. The subcontract's default-termination clause incorporated essentially verbatim the standard federal Default clause for fixed-price construction contracts.[112] The clause allowed MK to terminate GIT if the work had been delayed, not for excusable reasons, but by GIT's lack of diligence:

> A. If [GIT] refuses or fails to prosecute the work. . .with the diligence that will ensure its completion within the time specified in this Subcontract, including any extension. . .[MK] may . . .terminate [GIT's] right to proceed. . . .
> B. [GIT's] right to proceed shall not be terminated and [GIT] not charged with damages under this article, if:
> (1) The delay in completing the work arises from causes. . .beyond the control and without the fault or negligence of [GIT]. [A list of examples followed.]

The sole issue of liability at trial was whether the default-termination was wrongful. By terminating GIT, MK indicated a belief that GIT was so far behind schedule, without adequate excuse, as to show a lack of diligence that made the

---

[112] 175 F.3d 1221 (citing 48 C.F.R. § 52.249-1-(1997)).

project's timely completion uncertain. In challenging the termination, GIT claimed that it had been entitled to extensions of time for various "excusable delays" under the subcontract. GIT attributed these to MK's defective specifications, failure to timely secure permits, rigid interpretations of specifications and safety requirements, and propensity to reject proposed work plans. During the contractor's performance, GIT requested extra compensation and extensions of time because of delays to, changes in, and increased costs of the work that GIT attributed to MK. GIT's central theory was that its plan to complete the project before the contract completion date displeased MK, who could not then earn the maximum possible fees from DOE. MK, in GIT's view, thus sought to hinder and delay the work. MK, on the other hand, attributed the delays and increased costs to errors, omissions, and delinquencies by GIT and its subcontractors.

On appeal, MK argued that a contractor was not entitled to an excusable delay unless it proved that the delay was on the project's critical path and that it would delay completion of the entire project. GIT responded that MK had not identified any part of the contract or any cases using the terms "critical path" or "criticality." MK did not claim that the contract expressly referred to the critical path or required that excusable delays affected the project's overall completion. It argued instead that the latter requirement was a well-established rule of federal contracting law. The appellate court found MK's description of federal-contracting law correct.

MK neither argued that GIT's "excusable delays" did not in fact cause overall delay, nor asserted that it ever did so at trial. In other words, that it never argued one of GIT's claimed delays was not "excusable" because the delay had not affected overall completion. MK did argue that case law required GIT to show that each individual delay caused an overall delay. But it never asserted a link between that legal argument and the outcome in the dispute: it said nothing inconsistent with an assumption that each delay claimed by GIT did in fact contribute to overall delay. The appellate court concluded that the district court's description of the law, while not faultless, was not reversibly erroneous.

[C]   Determining the Amount of a Default Termination

[1]   Recovery for the Party That Terminates

[a]   Additional Performance Costs

In a default termination, the owner collects its additional costs to complete the terminated contractor's work from the contractor. The amount the owner is due is often subject to dispute.

In *In re Stone & Webster, Inc.*,[113] a federal bankruptcy court ruled that an owner that had terminated a contractor for failure to progress did not have to reduce its additional costs to perform to match the terminated contractor's

---

[113] 279 B.R. 748 (Dist. Del. 2002).

aggressive completion schedule. Maine Yankee Atomic Power Company hired Stone & Webster Engineering Corporation (SWEC) to decommission Maine Yankee's Wiscasset nuclear power generating facility. Maine Yankee terminated the agreement based upon SWEC's insolvency and because SWEC had not adequately performed under the contract. Both purported grounds for termination were provided under the contract.

SWEC contended that Maine Yankee could not recover damages associated with delays unless they proved that those delays were chargeable to SWEC and would not have been avoided by SWEC. SWEC argued that because Maine Yankee failed to prove that the delay was chargeable to SWEC, Maine Yankee's damages must be reduced by at least $2.17 million, which is the amount that SWEC's expert calculated as the cost for supervisory labor associated with the six-month delay. The court did not believe that any adjustment was required for delay costs. The court found that SWEC breached the agreement and that Maine Yankee mitigated its damages by weighing other contractors' bids against its own self-performance bid. Conceptually, Maine Yankee was therefore owed damages based on the cost of completion for the SWEC scope of work. The fact that Maine Yankee projected that it would not complete that scope of work until six months after the date of completion in the agreement did not mean that any "delay" costs adjustments were properly compensable to SWEC. So long as the damages that Maine Yankee was recovering were based on Maine Yankee's cost to complete the SWEC scope of work, it was proper for Maine Yankee to recover that entire amount.

Even if the court were to conclude that such delay costs were owed, it would still not have awarded any such costs in this instance. The expert's analysis presumed that SWEC would have completed the project on time. However, based on SWEC's own projections at the time of termination, it was projecting to finish the work three months later than Maine Yankee was projected to finish. Although Maine Yankee's subsequently produced "aggressive" schedule targeted an on-time completion date, in light of SWEC's inability to stay on schedule under the agreement, the court did not find that schedule to be credible evidence that indicated that SWEC would complete the work any earlier than Maine Yankee projected. But for termination, these delay costs were costs that SWEC—not Maine Yankee—would have had to bear. Therefore, the court disagreed that a delay claim adjustment was required or warranted. The court concluded that Maine Yankee was within its right to terminate the agreement for cause. Maine Yankee proved damages, recoverable from SWEC, in the amount of $20.8 million. The court, therefore, estimated Maine Yankee's allowable claim at that amount.

[b] Terminated Contractor's Set-offs

SWEC asserted that Maine Yankee's damages failed to credit SWEC's claims against Maine Yankee. The court found Maine Yankee liable to SWEC in the amount of $1,227,524.64 for work performed and invoiced before termination, but suspended an award of damages due to the potential mutuality of debts that might permit a set-off. Maine Yankee argued that it had already given SWEC credit for the full $1.2 million claimed, because under a damages formula of the agreement, the amount of SWEC's offset claim, not having been paid, was not subtracted from the "remaining Agreement funds." Maine Yankee explained that if it now had to pay the amount, Maine Yankee's damages would simply increase by the same amount, offsetting in full any need to pay that amount.

Maine Yankee needed to pay amounts then due and owing under the agreement. If Maine Yankee properly terminated the agreement, Maine Yankee was not liable to SWEC for any damages arising from that termination (i.e., a breach of contract action). The damages formula in the contract intrinsically accounted for the amount owed to SWEC. First, the unpaid agreement funds were calculated by determining the difference between the payments Maine Yankee had made to SWEC under the Decommissioning Agreement and the total contract price. Maine Yankee's total damages award was the difference between Maine Yankee's cost to complete the remaining scope of work and the unpaid agreement funds that it would have owed to SWEC under the agreement. If Maine Yankee had paid SWEC the $1.2 million it owed in May 2000, that would have decreased the "unpaid agreement funds" by that amount. Since the unpaid agreement funds were subtracted from the cost to complete in order to determine the damages, Maine Yankee's damages award would have risen by that same amount. As Maine Yankee did not pay the $1.2 million to SWEC, its present damages estimate was already reduced by that amount from the damages it would have requested had it paid the $1.2 million. Therefore, no set-off for the $1.2 million was necessary. SWEC should, however, be compensated for the interest on that amount. The court reduced Maine Yankee's net damages award by $450,000.

SWEC also argued that any payment of a claim to Maine Yankee would be premature, because Maine Yankee had not yet completed the work and provided SWEC with the receipt for that work. Second, Maine Yankee's actual costs were presently unknown, because it would take it approximately two-and-a-half more years to complete the decommissioning work. The agreement required that the damages arising from any breach of the Decommissioning Agreement be fully liquidated before payment. In other words, Maine Yankee's damages claim was contingent, because, under the Agreement, it could not recover for costs due to a breach before it incurred those costs. Because of the contractual provision that required the court to treat Maine Yankee's claim as a claim that is not to be paid until the decommissioning work was complete, the court applied its conclusions as to the appropriate measure of damages to fix the dollar amount of Maine Yankee's claim, but such damages might be subject to adjustment to the extent they differed from the actual costs. Maine Yankee proved damages, recoverable from SWEC, in the amount of $20.8 million.

[2]   Recovery for the Party That Is Improperly Terminated for Default

An improperly terminated contractor recovers its breach of contract damages. In addition, profit is permitted for an improperly terminated contractor even though the termination-for-convenience clause prohibits recovery of any profit. In *The Millgard Corp. v. EE Cruz/Nab/Frontier-Kemper, Joint Venture*,[114] the EE Cruz/Nab/Frontier-Kemper, Joint Venture argued that the termination-for-convenience clause operated as a bar to anticipated profits even in the event that a trier of fact determined that the Joint Venture breached the subcontract. The Joint Venture insisted that even though they did not terminate Millgard for convenience, the fact that they could have done so meant that Millgard never could have reasonably anticipated profits in the event of breach. Thus, the mere inclusion of a right to terminate for convenience in the contract negated any liability for lost profits regardless of whether this ground of termination was or was not properly invoked. The termination-for-convenience provision was not intended to have such broad and dire consequences for subcontractors. If this were correct, one would anticipate the literature and the cases in the construction industry to have reflected this, which was not the case. Accordingly, the motion for summary judgment was denied.

---

[114] 2003 U.S. Dist. LEXIS 21287 (S.D.N.Y. 2003).

CHAPTER 13

NOTICE REQUIREMENTS FOR CHANGES AND RELATED CLAIMS

Michael L. Orndahl

§ 13.01   INTRODUCTION

It's an all-too-common scenario. Sometime during or near the end of a construction project, the contractor, in an effort to minimize losses or maximize profit, reviews the cost report to see where more money was spent than planned, identifies areas where the owner (or perhaps a subcontractor) may have been the cause of higher costs, prepares a request for additional compensation, and sends it off to the (unsuspecting) party where the blame has been put.

The reaction is understandable. The owner may express surprise or outrage, point out the contract provision that requires the contractor to give timely written notice of the reason for a request for more money, ask (rhetorically) why the clause was not complied with, and summarily deny the request.

Sometimes the failure to comply strictly with a contract notice provision relating to changes in the work and other events can be overcome. But such failure is just one more hurdle in the claims process, one that can be avoided by proper contract administration and, to a lesser extent, careful contract drafting.

The purpose of the notice provision seems clear: to provide the other contracting party against whom a claim may be made an opportunity to investigate the facts giving rise to the claim while they are still fresh and to mitigate any resulting damages.[1] Both the fairness and necessity of the provision ensure its place in virtually every construction contract. In addition, various statutes governing recovery by providers of labor and material on federal or public construction contracts or the enforcement of money claims against public owners contain notice requirements.[2]

Despite the obvious need for contractual and statutory notice in a variety of construction contexts, the notice issue is still one of the most litigated in construction law. As one court, commenting on the proliferation of litigation over the notice provisions of the federal Miller Act,[3] has stated:

> It may be that Congress thought the procedural requirements it prescribed for laborers and materialmen to enforce the right to sue for their pay which is accorded them by the Miller Act were so plain, simple and easy to comply with that there would seldom be questions about them. But experience is to the contrary and the courts are continually called on to determine whether one deviation or another from the strict letter of the Act necessitates denial of the protection to laborers and materialmen, which the Act aims to provide.[4]

---

[1] New Pueblo Constructors, Inc. v. State, 144 Ariz. 95, 696 P.2d 185 (1985).

[2] See § **13.07**.

[3] 40 U.S.C.S. §§ 270a-270f (Law. Co-op. 1978 & Supp. 1993); see § **13.07[A]**.

[4] United States ex rel. Hopper Bros. Quarries v. Peerless Cas. Co., 255 F.2d 137, 143 (8th Cir. 1958), *cert. denied*, 358 U.S. 831 (1958), cited in Okee Indus., Inc. v. National Grange Mut. Ins. Co., 225 Conn. 367, 623 A.2d 483, 487-88 (1993). In addition, in CTI/DC, Inc. v. Selective Ins. Co. of Am., 392 F.3d 114 (4th Cir. 2004), the court discussed the purpose of notice requirements in the context of Maryland Public Bond statute. The court, in determining the adequacy of notice under Maryland's "Little Miller Act," stated:

> While the statute as a whole is designed to afford additional protection to subcontractors, the notice requirements aim to protect the general contractor. Interpreting the

This chapter explores the bases for notice requirements, what they contain, and the extent to which they are enforced. Typical notice provisions in some of the more commonly used forms are examined, as well as statutory uses. Finally, a few ideas on the negotiation and administration of these clauses are presented.

The chapter deals with notice requirements when the federal, public, or private owner is the object of the notice because the vast majority of cases and statutes arise in this context. However, the principles are the same when analyzing compliance with notice provisions in other contracts, such as subcontracts and purchase orders, or when an owner must provide notice to the contractor before withholding amounts for stated acts of default.[5]

§ 13.02 NOTICE REQUIREMENT CHARACTERISTICS

While notice provisions vary among contracts and statutes, they all have common characteristics of form, content, timeliness, and designated recipient.

[A] Form

Notices generally must be given in writing, and thus a most contentious issue in this area is whether the failure to give written notice can be circumvented. A writing minimizes disputes over whether the notice was given at all.[6] In addition, the details of the event or occurrence for which notice is required may be more extensive than could be accomplished sufficiently orally.[7] Consequently, courts will usually enforce an express written notice requirement when doubt about the giving of the notice or adequacy of its content exists.[8]

---

notice provisions of the Federal Miller Act, the First Circuit stated "[t]he notice provision serves an important purpose: it establishes a firm date after which the general contractor may pay its subcontractors without fear of further liability to the materialmen or suppliers of those subcontractors."

Id. at 119, citing United States ex rel. Water Works Supply Corp. v. George Hyman Constr. Co., 131 F. 3d 28, 32 (1st Cir. 1997).

[5] See.,e.g., State Highway Dep't v. Hall Paving Co., 127 Ga. App. 625, 194 S.E.2d 493 (1972) (it was held that the state sufficiently complied with the spirit of a contractual requirement that notice be given to the contractor when the contract duration for performance had expired because the state provided weekly reports from which the contractor should have derived the information to be contained in the notice).

[6] United States ex rel. Excavation Constr., Inc. v. Glenn-Stewart-Pinckney Builders & Developers, Inc., 388 F. Supp. 289 (D. Del. 1975) (written notice avoids misunderstanding between the parties).

[7] A related issue, not discussed in this chapter, deals with the standard contract requirement that modifications must be in writing. See S. Stein, Construction Law § 14.06 (1993).

[8] Maxton Builders, Inc. v. Lo Galbo, 68 N.Y.2d 373, 502 N.E.2d 184, 493 N.Y.S.2d 825 (1986); State Line Contractors, Inc. v. Commonwealth, 356 Mass. 306, 249 N.E.2d 619 (1969). Whether written notice requirements will be strictly construed will depend on the particular jurisdiction. Federal courts tend to have a liberal interpretation of notice requirements while some states apply a very strict interpretation. In Perini Corp. v. City of New York, 18 F. Supp. 2d 287 (S.D.N.Y. 1998), Perini Corp. contracted with the City of New York to upgrade the Coney Island Water Pollution

Whether notice by facsimile constitutes proper written notice depends on the context in which the notice is provided. In *Dean Management, Inc. v. TBS Construction*,[9] the plaintiff, Dean Management, terminated its subcontract with defendant, TBS, and filed a complaint seeking damages. The trial court ruled that the contract barred written notice by fax and therefore the defendant did not receive written notice as required by the contract.[10] On appeal, the court stated that Article 5 of the contract allowed the plaintiff to terminate the contract with defendant under certain circumstances by providing 24 hours' "written notice." Since the contract did not define "written notice," the court concluded that the unambiguous and plain meaning of the term "written notice" included fax transmittals.[11]

Notice by facsimile was not allowed in the context of a statutory mechanic's lien notice. In *Season-4, Inc. v. Hertz Corp.*,[12] the court held that Section 24 of the Illinois Mechanic's Lien Act requires the lien claimant to serve the party in question "by registered or certified mail, with return receipt requested, and delivery limited to addressee only."[13] Therefore, the court found that notice by facsimile is not authorized under the statute.

[B] Content

The amount of detail required in change and other notice provisions may vary, but at a minimum, a notice usually includes a description of the event or occurrence causing the change, the effect on the contractor's work, and the amount of the change. A notice that does not convey an intent to assert a claim may not be effective.[14]

Plant. Because 55 percent of the plant was funded by an E.P.A. grant, the contract incorporated several federal regulations, including 40 C.F.R. § 33.1030(3)(d) ("Changes Clause"). In determining whether federal law or New York law applied in interpreting the requirements under the Changes Clause, the court discussed the standards of each. "Federal law, as developed by the Board of Contract Appeals and the Court of Claims, construes the notice provisions of the Changes Clause liberally; thus, a contractee's actual or constructive notice of the conditions underlying the claim excuses formal compliance when federal law is applied . . . . New York, on the other hand, requires strict compliance with notice provisions in public contracts as a condition precedent to the pursuit of compensation claims." *Perini*, 18 F. Supp. 2d at 293 (citations omitted). In Engineered Maint. Serv., Inc. v. United States, 55 Fed. Cl. 637, 642 (2003), the court, in determining the adequacy of notice under a differing-site-conditions clause, found that the first inquiry was whether there was proper notice of the differing site condition. If not, the contractor's claim would still be allowed if it could demonstrate that the government had actual knowledge of the differing site condition and that the government would not suffer any prejudice if the claim was allowed to proceed.

[9] 339 Ill. App. 3d 263, 790 N.E.2d 934 (2d Cir. 2003).
[10] 339 Ill. App. 3d at 265.
[11] 339 Ill. App. 3d at 270.
[12] 338 Ill. App. 3d 565, 788 N.E.2d 179 (1st Dist. 2003).
[13] 338 Ill. App. 3d at 571 (citing 770 ILCS 60/24).
[14] Lezzer Cash & Carry v. Aetna Ins. Co., 371 Pa. Super. 137, 537 A.2d 857 (1988).

In *CTI/DC, Inc. v. Selective Ins. Co. of America*,[15] the trial court granted the defendant's motion to dismiss on the grounds that plaintiff's complaint failed to stated a claim under Maryland's "Little Miller Act." Specifically, the defendant claimed that the complaint failed to allege compliance with the notice requirements under the Act. The Little Miller Act specifically requires that a 90-day notice be provided to the general contractor and that the notice "(i) shall state with substantial accuracy the amount claimed and the person to whom the labor or material is supplied."[16]

On appeal, the CTI/DC argued that a letter that it sent on December 3, 2002, should be construed as substantially complying with the content requirements of the Little Miller Act. The letter stated as follows:

RE: Cheverly Health Center

Subject: Request for Bonds

CTI/DC Inc. supplied ready mixed concrete to the referenced project. We have an outstanding balance of ONE HUNDRED TWELVE THOUSAND TWO HUNDRED AND SIXTY ONE DOLLARS ($112,261.00) ON INVOICES.

We respectfully request copies of the payment and performance bonds provided by your office to the Prince George's County as owner of the building.

The permit issued for this construction project is no. 2484200. The building is located directly across the street from the Prince George's Hospital Center on Hospital Drive in Cheverly, Maryland.

Your cooperation and prompt attention to this matter is appreciated.

CTI/DC's December 3, 2002, letter failed to identify the entity to which it supplied concrete. Regardless, CTI/DC argued that the letter, in conjunction with a meeting that took place prior to the mailing of the letter, provided the general contractor with actual knowledge of the subcontractor to whom it supplied concrete. The court stated that not only did the letter fail to state the name of the subcontractor to whom CTI/DC supplied concrete, the letter failed to reference any meeting or conversation held about the debt. The court held that "because CTI/DC's notice failed to state the name of the subcontractor or reference any conversation held about the debt," CTI/DC failed to comply with an explicit prerequisite for bringing suit under the "Little Miller Act." The name of the subcontractor is the crucial aspect of the "Little Miller Act's" notice requirements. "Absent this information, the safeguards built in by the legislature to protect the general contractor are vitiated because the general contractor is left to use his or her imagination to attempt to determine which subcontractor not to pay."[17]

Sometimes a "two-part" notice requirement will permit the giving of information sufficient to alert the owner to the fact that the contractor has suffered

---

[15] 392 F.3d 114 (4th Cir. 2004).
[16] Md. State Fin. & Proc. Code § 17-108(b)(2)(i).
[17] 392 F.3d 114, 120.

damage from an event under the responsibility of the owner and allow the later furnishing of data supporting the request for additional compensation.[18]

[C] Timeliness

The time within which the required notice must be provided varies, from "prompt" or "reasonable" to a stated period of days, usually no more than 30. In the absence of a specified period, a reasonable time limit will be implied.[19] The enforceability of time periods has been the subject of numerous judicial interpretations, a natural consequence because of the harsh results flowing from strict enforcement of time requirements.[20]

[D] Recipient

The last criterion that effective notice must meet is that it is given to the proper recipient. Who is the proper recipient sometimes is not obvious and brings into discussion concepts such as actual and apparent authority.[21] Issues involving waiver and estoppel also require examination of the conduct of authorized representatives of the owner.[22]

§ 13.03 FEDERAL CONTRACT CLAUSES

The study of the occurrence and enforceability of notice provisions is enhanced by reference to particular contracts of general use. As with most construction law

---

[18] *See, e.g.,* the federal changes clause, § 11.4.

[19] Austin Co. v. Vaughn Bldg. Corp., 26 Tex. Sup. Ct. J. 64, 643 S.W.2d 113 (1983).

[20] In Ryco Constr., Inc. v. United States, 55 Fed. Cl. 184 (2002), the court was required to determine the effect of the contractor's failure to give timely notice. The court stated that delay in providing notice provides some degree of prejudice to the government, but this will not necessarily require denial of the contractor's claim. Instead, "the existence of prejudice resulting from the dilatory notice usually serves to increase the burden of persuasion facing the contractor rather than to bar its claim entirely." *Ryco,* 55 Fed. Cl. at 197, quoting T. Brown Constructors, Inc. v. Secretary of Transp., 132 F.3d 724, 733 (Fed. Cir. 1997). *See also* Maxton Builders, Inc. v. Lo Galbo, 68 N.Y.2d 373, 502 N.E.2d 184, 493 N.Y.S.2d 825 (1986) (three-day time period enforced, despite argument that reasonable time period should apply because contract did not contain "time is of the essence" provision); Montgomery County Bd. of Educ. ex rel. Carrier Corp. v. Glassman Constr. Co., 245 Md. 192, 225 A.2d 448 (1967) (holding that notice must be mailed, but not necessarily received by the contractor, within 90 days from when the claimant last performed labor or furnished material); Southwest Eng'g Co. v. Reorganized Sch. Dist. R-9, Lawrence County, Marionville, 434 S.W.2d 743 (Mo. Ct. App. 1968) (holding that notice of the cause of the delay could be given at the conclusion of the delay rather than at the commencement, and that "the written request was defective in detail, but it was timely and it served the elementary purpose of the contract provision." *Id.* at 747).

[21] *See* Sweet, Legal Aspects of Architecture, Engineering and the Construction Process § 21.05 at 389 (4th ed. 1989).

[22] *See, e.g.,* Welsh v. Gindele & Johnson, 376 N.Y.S.2d 661, 50 A.D.2d 971 (1975) (architect was authorized representative of school district).

issues, the federal government's contracting scheme is a fruitful source of information. Federal construction contracts for fixed-price work usually contain notice provisions not only in the changes clause but also in other remedy-granting clauses. These clauses and the manner in which they are interpreted by the boards of contract appeals and the courts are examined in §§ **13.04** through **13.08**. Although the notice provision in each clause is different, the issues that arise and their treatment by the various tribunals are similar.[23]

[A] Changes

The relevant provisions of the federal changes clause with respect to notice are as follows:

(a) The Contracting Officer may, at any time . . . by written order designated or indicated to be a change order, make changes in the work within the general scope of the contract . . . .

(b) Any other written or oral order . . . from the Contracting Officer that causes a change shall be treated as a change order under this clause; *provided,* that the Contractor gives the Contracting Officer written notice stating (1) the date, circumstances, and source of the order and (2) that the Contractor regards the order as a change order. . . .

(d) [E]xcept for an adjustment based on defective specifications, no adjustment for any change under paragraph (b) of this clause shall be made for any costs incurred more than 20 days before the Contractor gives written notice as required.

(e) The Contractor must assert its right to an adjustment under this clause within 30 days after (1) receipt of a written change order under paragraph (a) of this clause or (2) the furnishing of a written notice under paragraph (b) of this clause, by submitting to the Contracting Officer a written statement describing the general nature and amount of proposal, unless this period is extended by the Government. The statement of proposal for adjustment may be included in the notice under paragraph (b) above.

(f) No proposal by the Contractor for an equitable adjustment shall be allowed if asserted after final payment under this contract.[24]

An early case expressed the minimum description that notice under the changes clause should contain:

Perhaps a claim registered pursuant to a Changes clause of a government contract need not specify that clause particularly as a basis for relief, but it must

---

[23] For a discussion about the notice provisions of three of the federal relief-granting clauses and a view of their effectiveness, *see* M. Weintraub, *"Appraisal Notice" Requirements in Federal Construction Contracts: Their Continued Validity,* 12 Pub. Cont. L.J. 40 (1981).

[24] FAR 52.243-4 (1987). The Federal Acquisition Regulations are found at Title 48 of the Code of Federal Regulations.

bear some of the attributes of a claim itself, purporting to be in the nature of a claim as of legal right as opposed to a request for grace. The letters contained in the plaintiff's exhibits do not even specify the amount of relief sought. They express mere ambiguous requests for adjustments as distinguished from demands predicated upon an expressed contractual right.[25]

Balanced against the need to have legally sufficient notice is the notion that "notice provisions in contract-adjustment clauses [should] not be applied too technically and illiberally where the Government is quite aware of the operative facts."[26] An example of a decision in which the court wrestled with these competing policies is *H.H.O. Co. v. United States.*[27] The contractor had relied on daily diaries, affidavits, letters, and various other materials, as well as oral complaints to the contracting officer's site representatives, as evidence that the government had constructive notice of the claims. Noting that "[t]he fact, however, that the contracting officer is aware of problems or contentions in performance is not the same as providing notice of a monetary claim against the government,"[28] the court denied the government's motion to dismiss and remanded the case for further proceedings.

Prejudice to the government works as an impediment to attempts to evade notice requirements in changes clauses as it does for other contractual avenues of relief. In *Calfon Construction Inc. v. United States,*[29] the contractor argued that its failure to give notice until well after the compensable events occurred did not deprive its right to pursue claims against the government. However, the Court of Claims ruled that the contracting officer would have pursued a more economical course of action had notice been given timely.

Another early case held that the 30-day notice period was not applicable to constructive changes.[30] However, paragraph (b) of the current changes clause specifically provides for notice in such circumstances, and thus, earlier case law to the contrary would likely not apply. There is some authority to the effect that a

---

[25] Specialty Assembling & Packing Co. v. United States, 298 F.2d 794, 796, 156 Ct. Cl. 252, 254-55 (1962).

[26] Hoel-Steffen Constr. Co. v. United States, 456 F.2d 760, 768 (Ct. Cl. 1972); see § 11.6. Though involving interpretation of the notice provision in a suspension-of-work-clause case, the holding of *Hoel-Steffen* was cited with approval as applying to the changes clause in Casson Constr. Co., 83-1 BCA (CCH) ¶ 16,522 (1983).

[27] 12 Cl. Ct. 147 (1987). To the same effect, *see also* Gulf & W. Indus., Inc. v. United States, 6 Cl. Ct. 742 (1984). *See also* Ryco Constr., Inc. v. United States, 55 Fed. Cl. 184, 197 (2002). Late notice will not necessarily bar a claim for additional compensation under the changes clause. Instead, the existence of prejudice on the part of governments will increase the burden of persuasion that the contractor must meet.

[28] *Id.* at 163. The court also sent back the questions of whether by considering the claims on the merits the contracting officer waived the notice requirement and whether the government was prejudiced by the lack of notice.

[29] 18 Cl. Ct. 426 (1989). *See also* E.W. Jerdon, Inc., 88-2 BCA (CCH) ¶ 20,729 (1988).

[30] Colo-Macco, Inc., 69-2 BCA (CCH) ¶ 7919 (1969).

contractor need not respond to the contracting officer's written directive if the consequences of the directive are not evident until later.[31]

Even when the notice period is not strictly enforced, claims under the changes clause may not be asserted after final payment. The point at which final payment occurs for this purpose, however, is not always easy to determine, turning on the facts and circumstances of a given case.[32] Actual or constructive notice that claims are still extant, as in other cases, may operate as relief from the otherwise terminal effects of final payment.[33]

[B]   Differing Site Conditions

Perhaps no construction contract clause is more dependent upon an enforceable notice provision than one that requires prompt notification to the government upon discovery of subsurface or hidden conditions. Because such conditions are usually in the path of further progress, a contractor is usually anxious to proceed with the work. On the other hand, the owner needs to examine the conditions before they are removed or covered up by the ensuing work to be able either to make such changes in the work that might mitigate the effects of the conditions or to have sufficient information to evaluate the contractor's subsequent claim for an increase in the time or cost of performance of the work. Prejudice to the government resulting from lack of or inadequate notice is usually easier to prove under the differing-site-conditions clause.

The notice clause of the differing-site-conditions clause reads in relevant part as follows:

(a) The Contractor shall *promptly, and before conditions are disturbed,* give a *written notice* to the Contracting Officer of (1) subsurface or latent physical conditions at the site which differ materially from those indicated in this contract, or (2) unknown physical conditions at the site, of an unusual nature, which differ materially from those ordinarily encountered and generally recognized as inhering in work of the character provided for in the contract.

And, as if for emphasis:

(c) No request by the Contractor for an equitable adjustment to the contract under this clause shall be allowed, unless the Contractor has given the written notice required, *provided,* that the time prescribed in (a) above for giving written notice may be extended by the Contracting Officer.[34]

---

[31] H.L. Yoh Co. v. United States, 288 F.2d 493, 153 Ct. Cl. 104 (1961). With respect to notice of overruns required under the limitation-of-cost clause, FAR 52.232-20, *see* Peerless Ins. Co., 83-1 BCA (CCH) ¶ 20,730 (1983).

[32] Gulf & W. Indus., Inc. v. United States, 6 Cl. Ct. 742 (1984) (citing numerous cases).

[33] Marine Elec. RPD, Inc., 84-3 BCA (CCH) ¶ 17,540 (1984).

[34] FAR 52.236-2 (1984) (emphasis added).

Despite the government's insistence that relief may be granted only upon the giving of written notice, the boards and courts will not enforce the requirement when the government has actual notice of the conditions.[35] Whether actual notice has been received, however, may be problematical and, of course, dependent upon the circumstances—and the circumstances are myriad.[36]

For example, when certain conditions are foreseen and the differing site condition is an exacerbation of the expected conditions, the differing site condition is less likely to be apparent from mere observance of the conditions. The contractor's argument that the government had actual notice of the conditions will likely fail.[37] When a government inspector was shown a sample of excavated material saturated with oil, this did not constitute actual notice because the sample was for a purpose different from demonstrating the existence of a differing site condition. In another case,[38] the contractor successfully advanced its differing-site-conditions claim based on actual notice. The government knew from the contractor's quality control reports that material different from core borings had been encountered, but it failed to examine the material while it was still stockpiled prior to removal.[39]

Another issue is the point at which the obligation arises to give the required notice. A contractor cannot give notice until the differing conditions become sufficiently apparent. In one case, the contractor could not have realized from the subtle changes in elevations before commencing work that excavated quantities would increase.[40]

In *Farnsworth & Chambers Co. v. United States*,[41] the Court of Claims addressed the issue of whether the government had sufficient notice of a differing site condition so as to comply with the notice provision of the clause. Notice had been provided to the government within the time required, but it was not specific with respect to the location of the condition. Government representatives were aware of the condition—a severe leakage of water back into a cofferdam—and had attributed the condition to faulty workmanship. The notice, however, treated the significant inflow as an unforeseen condition. The court held that the government had adequate notice that "something in the physical conditions was claimed to be amiss."[42] It further concluded that the fact that the contractor later made its claim more precise did not diminish the effectiveness of the original notice.

---

[35] *See* Cass, 70-1 BCA (CCH) ¶ 8270 (1970); Appeal of Powell's Gen. Contracting Co., 80-2 BCA (CCH) ¶ 14,680 (1980).

[36] For numerous examples, *see* Gov't Cont. Rep. (CCH) ¶¶ 10,300.25-.35, 21,820, 21,830 (1993).

[37] *See* Barnet Brezner, 65-2 BCA (CCH) ¶ 4902 (1965); Northeast Constr. Co., 67-1 BCA (CCH) ¶ 6195 (1967).

[38] AAAA Enters., Inc., 86-1 BCA (CCH) ¶ 18,628 (1985).

[39] Titan Pac. Constr. Corp., 87-1 BCA (CCH) ¶ 19,626 (1987); *see also* Nicholson Constr. Co., 85-3 BCA (CCH) ¶ 18,325 (1981); Delphcon/J.A.M.E., Joint Venture, 88-3 BCA (CCH) ¶ 21,107 (1988) (the government failed to take part in a survey to establish an excess quantity of muck); Holloway Constr. Co. and Holloway Sand & Gravel Co., 89-2 BCA (CCH) ¶ 21,713 (1989).

[40] C.E. Wylie Constr. Co., 85-1 BCA (CCH) ¶ 17,933 (1985). *See also* Edward R. Marden Corp., 85-2 BCA (CCH) ¶ 18,083 (1985).

[41] 346 F.2d 577, 171 Ct. Cl. 30 (1965).

[42] 346 F.2d at 581, 171 Ct. Cl. at 37.

Some contractor excuses for failure to give notice altogether fail to convince the tribunal. In *Penner*,[43] the contractor unsuccessfully argued that giving notice would have delayed the project. The board responded that under the differing-site-conditions clause, the government must make a prompt inspection and if it failed to do so, the contractor could recover its resulting delay costs.[44]

The government's own documents may be proof of actual knowledge. Letters or other communications from the government to the contractor may show that the government not only was aware of the condition, but also gave it consideration.[45]

Finally, lack of prejudice coupled with some knowledge of the facts giving rise to the differing site condition will operate as a waiver of the requirement, as seen in *Perini Corp.*[46] The government was aware that less quantities of grout were being used, though it did not know at the time that the contractor would equate the lesser quantity with a differing site condition. However, the government took no different approach to the contractor's performance than if it knew of the differing site condition in the first instance.

The requirement of formal notice under the differing-site-conditions clause may not be required if the contractor can demonstrate lack of prejudice on the part of the government. A key consideration in determining actual prejudice is whether the government had the ability to inspect the alleged differing site condition in order to be able to respond to the claim. In *Engineered Maintenance Services, Inc. v. United States*,[47] the contractor entered into a firm fixed-price contract to replace the steam and condensate lines at a government facility in Alabama.[48] The contracting officer eventually terminated the contract for failing to make adequate progress on the job. After the termination, the contractor requested an extension of time based on the differing site conditions that it had encountered.[49] The time extension was denied and the contractor filed this action. The government moved for summary judgment on the basis that the contractor failed to provide notice as required under the differing-site-conditions clause, and accordingly, the contractor could not demonstrate excusable delay. Without an excusable delay, the contractor would be in default and termination would be appropriate.[50]

FAR 52.236-2(a) requires that written notice be given promptly, and before conditions are disturbed, when the contractor discovers a differing site condition. The contractor, however, conceded that it did not strictly comply with the notice provision, but argued instead that the government had actual knowledge of the condition and that it was not prejudiced by the lack of formal notice.[51]

---

[43] 80-2 BCA (CCH) ¶ 14,604 (1980).

[44] *Id.* at 72,006.

[45] Schouten Constr. Co., 79-1 BCA (CCH) ¶ 13,630 (1978); Ruckman & Hansen, Inc. v. District of Columbia, 24 Cont. Cas. Fed. (CCH) ¶ 82,271 (1978).

[46] 78-1 BCA (CCH) ¶ 13,191 (1978).

[47] 55 Fed. Cl. 637, 642 (2003).

[48] *Id.* at 639.

[49] *Id.* at 640.

[50] *Id.* at 641.

[51] *Id.* at 642.

In determining whether the government was prejudiced, the court found that the contracting officer was aware of complaints made by the contractor through quality control reports and inspector's daily reports. However, these reports only indicated conditions that the government fully expected the contractor to encounter. Accordingly, the contracting officer did not make any site visits.[52] In addition, when the contractor encountered piping that was not indicated on the government's drawings, it indicated that it would not require an extension of time as a result thereof. The court stated:

> If the Court were to overlook EMS's failure to comply with the formal notice requirements of FAR Section 52.236-2(a) and find that actual notice was sufficient, the Government would surely suffer prejudice. It would be forced to defend against conditions anticipated in the contract of which it was not properly notified. Such insufficient notice directly precluded the Government from investigating the site and potentially minimizing extra costs that the contractor ended up having to incur.[53]

Accordingly, the court held that the contractor's differing-site-conditions claim was barred by lack of notice.[54]

[C] Suspension of Work

Another construction clause in which notice is important covers the situation when the work is suspended or delayed because of an act or omission of the government and the contractor is entitled to compensation because of that delay. The current suspension-of-work clause provides as follows:

> (c) A claim under this clause shall not be allowed (1) for any costs incurred more than 20 days before the Contractor shall have notified the Contracting Officer in writing of the act or failure to act involved (but this requirement shall not apply as to a claim resulting from a suspension order), and (2) unless the claim, in an amount stated, is asserted in writing as soon as practicable after the termination of the suspension, delay, or interruption, but not later than the date of final payment under the contract.[55]

Because of these monetary consequences, reasonable notice will allow the government to consider whether to accelerate the contractor's performance as a more cost-effective alternative to paying the contractor's delay damages. It also allows the government to maintain accurate records and perform necessary corrective measures.[56]

---

[52] Id.
[53] Id. at 643.
[54] Id.
[55] FAR 52.212-12 (1984).
[56] Morales, 89-2 BCA (CCH) ¶ 21,766 (1989) (citing Lane-Verdugo, 73-2 BCA (CCH) ¶ 10,271 (1973)).

The 20-day notice requirement may create a hardship. In one case, a board of contract appeals ruled that an eight-month delay in giving notice was too long.[57] However, in another case, an appeals board ruled that the government's requirement that a fully documented claim be submitted within 20 days of the delay was an overly strict reading of the clause.[58]

Compliance with the notice requirement of an earlier version of the current suspension-of-work clause was the issue in *Hoel-Steffen Construction Co. v. United States*.[59] The clause provided in part:

> No claim under this clause shall be allowed (i) for any costs incurred more than twenty days before the Contractor shall have notified the Contracting Officer in writing of the act or failure to act involved . . . and (ii) unless the claim, in an amount stated, is asserted in writing as soon as practicable after the termination of such suspension, delay, or interruption but not later than the date of final settlement of the contract. Any dispute concerning a question of fact arising under this clause shall be subject to the Disputes clause.[60]

Although the notice provision had not been strictly complied with, the government's representative had received definite complaints and was aware of the problems; the contractor had made oral complaints and had written two letters about the matter; and a meeting with the government was held on the point. The government "knew full well . . . what was troubling plaintiff"[61] and that it had the responsibility to remedy the difficulty complained of by the contractor. It is notable that the contractor's letters asked for different relief and referred to a different clause of the contract. The court, in ruling for the contractor, concluded with an expression of its attitude toward notice provisions:

> To adopt the Board's severe and narrow application of the notice requirements, or the defendant's support of that ruling, would be out of tune with the language and purpose of the notice provisions, as well as with the court's wholesome concern that notice provisions: in contract adjustment clauses not be applied too technically and illiberally where the Government is quite aware of the operative facts.[62]

[D] Default—Force Majeure

Similar to suspension of work is delay caused by force majeure found in the default clause,[63] except that the contractor is entitled to only a time extension and

---

[57] Moulder Bros., 89-2 BCA (CCH) ¶ 21,639 (1989).

[58] Building Maint. Corp., 79-1 BCA (CCH) ¶ 13,560 (1979).

[59] 456 F.2d 760 (Ct. Cl. 1972).

[60] *Id.* at 763, n.2.

[61] *Id.* at 767.

[62] *Id.* at 767-68.

[63] FAR 52.249-10 (1984).

not compensation.[64] Contrary to the approach taken in most other industry standard forms, when force majeure delays are in a stand-alone clause, force majeure delays are treated as excuses for default termination of the contract caused by delay in completion of the contract. Just as in nonfederal contracts in which timely completion is important, the government must be notified of the potential delay to consider whether acceleration of the work is a desirable alternative. The relevant portion of the default clause for fixed-price construction contracts concerning notice reads as follows:

> (b) The Contractor's right to proceed shall not be terminated nor the Contractor charged with damages under this clause, if
> (1) The delay in completing the work arises from unforeseeable causes beyond the control and without the fault or negligence of the Contractor. [Examples follow.]
> (2) The Contractor, *within 10 days from the beginning of any delay* (unless extended by the Contracting Officer), notifies the Contracting Officer *in writing* of the causes of the delay.[65]

The current clause requires notice within 10 days of the commencement of the delay. An early board decision did not require the contractor to forfeit the entire period of delay for failure to give timely notice, but granted an extension from the time that the contracting officer had notice of the delay.[66] This approach is similar to treatment given to late notice under the suspension-of-work clause in § 13.03[C].

[E] Final Payment

A very important provision is the requirement to notify the government of unresolved claims or requests for additional compensation prior to the contractor's acceptance of final payment for the work. Failure to give this notice will bar the contractor from being able to pursue such claims or requests administratively and before the boards or courts. Found in the payment clause, the notice provision reads as follows:

> (h) The Government shall pay the amount due the Contractor under this contract after . . .

---

[64] As any experienced construction lawyer knows, a noncompensatory time extension can be turned into one that includes money damages when the government refuses to grant a time extension based on force majeure. Certain requirements must be met: (a) the government must be given notice of the contractor's right to a time extension; (b) the government must refuse the request; (c) the contractor must notify the government that its refusal to grant the extension will require the contractor to accelerate the work; and (d) the contractor must actually accelerate. *See, e.g.,* 2 S. Stein, Construction Law § 16.12(3) (1990); B. Bramble & M. Callahan, Construction Delay Claims §§ 6.1-6.18 (Aspen Publishers 1992).

[65] FAR 52. 249-10 (1984).

[66] Rambo & Regar, Inc., I Cont. Cas. Fed. (CCH) ¶ 117 (1943).

(3) Presentation of a release of all claims against the Government arising by virtue of this contract, other than claims, in stated amounts, that the Contractor has specifically excepted from the operation of the release.[67]

The most common issue that arises under this clause is whether the excepted claims listed by the contractor are specific enough and in stated amounts. The leading case is *Mingus Constructors, Inc. v. United States*,[68] which considered whether the following exception was sufficient to reserve the contractor's claims: "Pursuant to correspondence we do intend to file a claim(s)—the amount(s) of which is undetermined at this time." The court ruled that the release was inadequate, stating:

> Exceptions to releases are strictly construed against the contractor. As in *H.L.C. & Associates*, the exception noted by Mingus on its release, even as supplemented by reference to its prior letters, is nothing more than a "blunderbuss exception" which does nothing to inform the government as to the source, substance, or scope of the contractor's specific contentions. Vague, broad exceptions as used by the contractor in *H.L.C. & Associates* and by Mingus in the present case are insufficient as a matter of law to constitute "claims" sufficient to be excluded from the required release.[69]

The court concluded that none of the special and limited circumstances under which a claim can be considered despite the execution of a release were present, such as post-release consideration of a claim; economic duress, fraud, or mutual mistake; or unilateral mistake.[70]

§ 13.04 EXCUSES FOR NONCOMPLIANCE

As demonstrated by the scenario introducing this chapter, contractors often fail to comply strictly with the terms of a notice provision. Courts and administrative tribunals, both federal and state, have considered several arguments for permitting

---

[67] FAR 52. 232-5 (1989).

[68] 812 F.2d 1387, 33 Cont. Cas. Fed. (CCH) ¶ 75,126 (Fed. Cir. 1987).

[69] 812 F.2d at 1393, n.6 (citing H.L.C. & Assocs., 367 F.2d 586, 589, 176 Ct. Cl. 285, 291, 11 Cont. Cas. Fed. (CCH) ¶ 80,495 (1966)). The reservation attached to that release read:

> The Eligible Builder reserves the right to assert claims against the United States . . . in the amount of $500,000.00 for damages suffered by the Eligible Builder . . . due to, but not limited to, damages caused by the Department of the Navy by the daily, constant, continuous, arbitrary and unreasonable interference with and disruption of the work of the Eligible Builder under said contract, the arbitrary rejection of work and materials of the Eligible Builder although said work and materials complied with the standards of workmanship and quality of materials required under the plans and specifications and said Housing Contract, all of which caused undue and unnecessary increased costs to the Eligible Builder and other damages in the performance of the contract by the Eligible Builder.

[70] *Id.* at 1395, 33 Cont. Cas. Fed. (CCH) ¶ 75,126 at 80,223.

claims for relief despite such failure. Because of the extensive federal experience in this area, as just described, state courts will sometimes look to the federal claims court and boards of contract appeals for guidance.[71]

[A] Actual Notice

A common excusable deviation from written notice is when the contractor provides oral notice to the owner.[72] When such notice is followed by written confirmation, such as a letter or minutes of a meeting, the courts usually allow a claim to be considered on its merits. In the absence of written follow-up, however, actual notice is more difficult to prove.

The issue of whether actual notice was sufficient to comply with the written notice provisions of a differing-site-conditions clause was dealt with in *Brinderson Corp. v. Hampton Roads Sanitation District.*[73] The contractor conceded that it did not give formal written notice until nine months after the conditions were encountered. However, it had orally complained about the swamp-like conditions in which its equipment was unable to move. In addition, the owner's soil consultants had seen the conditions and had abundant opportunity to investigate. The court held that the owner's actual notice of the conditions was sufficient compliance with the notice requirements.

In another case, oral notice of a claim by telephone did not comply with the written notice provisions of a payment bond.[74] Yet, in *Stone v. City of Arcola,*[75] when the owner's agent told the contractor that further requests for time extensions would be useless, the court held that this was proof of the owner's actual notice of the delay, and thus the contractor did not waive its delay claim. And in *Okee Industries, Inc. v. National Grange Mutual Insurance Co.,*[76] actual notice to a contractor that a subcontractor made a claim against the contractor's bond sufficed despite a notice letter to the contractor that was otherwise statutorily deficient.

A common scenario happens when unusual or severe weather causes delay and damage to the project, an event that is usually obvious to the owner. When notice requirements are not strictly complied with, actual notice is relatively easy to prove.[77]

---

[71] New Pueblo Constructors, Inc. v. State, 144 Ariz. 95, 696 P.2d 185 (1985); Brinderson Corp. v. Hampton Roads Sanitation Dist., 825 F.2d 41 (4th Cir. 1987) (applying Virginia law).

[72] Diagle v. Donald M. Clement Contractor, Inc., 533 So. 2d 1064 (La. Ct. App. 1988) (filing of lien constituted written notice required under public works statute within 45 days of recordation of notice of acceptance by the owner of the work, citing La. Rev. Stat. Ann. § 38:2247 (West 1989)).

[73] 825 F.2d 41 (4th Cir. 1987) (applying Virginia law).

[74] Lezzer Cash & Carry v. Aetna Ins. Co., 371 Pa. Super. 137, 537 A.2d 857 (1988).

[75] 181 Ill. App. 3d 513, 130 Ill. Dec. 118, 536 N.E.2d 1329 (1989). Citing secondary authority, the court also approved, without discussion, the theory that "waiver of a claim for delay does not correspondingly dictate that the party waiving the delay be held liable for the delay." 536 N.E.2d at 1337.

[76] 225 Conn. 367, 623 A.2d 483 (1993).

[77] New Pueblo Constructors, Inc. v. State, 144 Ariz. 95, 696 P.2d 185 (1985).

Actual notice in the context of a change provision was addressed in *Mike M. Johnson, Inc. v. County of Spokane*.[78] In *Johnson*, the contractor, MMJ, entered into two separate sewer installation contracts with the County of Spokane. After beginning the projects, the county revised a portion of the work and proposed change order #3, which provided for design changes, and altered the schedule. In addition, change order #3 provided for an increase in the price in the amount of $69,319 and an eight-day schedule extension. MMJ, without objection, proceeded to work under the change order. MMJ encountered numerous other problems during the course of the work, which led to a series of letters by which the contractor complained of these issues. At one point the county responded to an MMJ letter by stating:

> To the extent that [MMJ] may consider that letter any sort of formal notification of a claim pursuant to the contract, a request for additional time, a request for a change order, or a request for any other remedy allowed by the contract, the letter is rejected because it is too general and nonspecific regarding any relief or remedy which may have been requested. In this regard, you are referred to the applicable contract specifications. All requests for additional time to complete the contract, additional compensation or change order must be submitted within the time permitted and in the form specified in the contract documents. Spokane County simply cannot accept a letter, such as the July 24, 1998 letter, as anything other than an attempt to cause Spokane County to acquiesce in what might be later claimed to be some sort of attempt to modify our contract. As we have repeatedly advised you, Spokane County must insist that you follow the terms and conditions of our contract in every respect on both of these projects.[79]

Subsequently, MMJ filed suit based on its claims for additional compensation. The trial court granted summary judgment in favor of the county on the basis that MMJ failed to follow the contractual protest and/or claims procedures of the contract.[80] The appellate court reversed, finding that a genuine issue of material fact existed as to whether the county had actual notice of MMJ's claim excusing compliance with the claims procedures.

On appeal to the Washington Supreme Court, the Court refused to apply an actual notice exception to compliance with contractual provisions and further stated that there had been no waiver of these provisions by the county. The court explained:

> A waiver of a contract provision must be made by the party benefiting from the provision. Here, the county stood to benefit from the mandatory protest and claim procedures; thus, only the county could waive MMJ's compliance with the procedures. MMJ simply could not waive enforcement of the provisions for the county, and MMJ's notifying the county that it had concerns does not in

---

[78] 150 Wash. 2d 375, 78 P.3d 161 (2003).
[79] 150 Wash. 2d at 381-382.
[80] 150 Wash. 2d at 376.

any way evidence the county's intent to waive the contract's requirements. Moreover, to hold that a contractor's notice of protest to the owner serves to excuse the contractor from complying with mandatory claim procedures would render contractual claim requirements meaningless. There would be no reason for compliance, as the contractor could merely assert general grievances in order to secure a later claim. We hold that "actual notice' is not an exception to contract compliance.[81]

Actual notice in place of statutorily required notices under state mechanic's lien laws is generally disfavored. Although some states provide for a liberal construction of these notice requirements, in many states they are strictly construed. In *Mel Stevenson & Associates, Inc. v. Giles*,[82] Spec Building Materials, Inc. (Spec) supplied materials to the general contractor on a construction project owned by Giles. The general contractor refused to pay for a portion of the materials and Spec filed a materialman's lien. The trial court held that the lien was invalid for lack of notice as required by 42 O.S. 1981, § 142.1. On appeal, Spec argued that notice under the statute was not required because Giles had actual notice that it was supplying materials to the project. Rejecting this argument, the appellate court stated:

> Section 142.1 goes beyond knowledge that a supplier or subcontractor has contact with a project. Section 142.1 is a prerequisite to enforcement of a lien and gives the property owners the "benefit of a specific pre-enforcement notice of potential materialmen's liens as part of their rights."[83]

Accordingly, the court held that actual notice was insufficient to satisfy the notice requirements of 42 O.S. 1981, § 142.1.

In *Season-4, Inc. v. Hertz Corp.*,[84] the court addressed the notice requirement under Section 24 of the Illinois Mechanics' Lien Act. The court stated that actual notice cannot substitute for the written notice required by Section 24:

> We note, however, that "[t]he statute makes no exceptions for cases where the owner may have actual notice of the subcontractor's claim from some source other than those included in [s]ection 24." Suddarth v. Rosen, 81 Ill. App. 136, 140 (1967) (failure to serve statutory notice required dismissal of lien claimant's complaint regardless of whether the owners had notice of the claim from an alternative source).[85]

[B]   Waiver and Estoppel

A variation of actual notice is when oral notice is coupled with the owner's recognition that relief has been requested and the owner's subsequent consideration

[81] 150 Wash. 2d at 391.
[82] 103 P.3d 631 (Okla. Civ. App. 2004).
[83] *Giles* (citing C&C Tile & Carpet Co. v. Aday, 697 P.2d 175, 178 (Okla. Ct. App. 1985)).
[84] 338 Ill. App. 3d 565, 788 N.E.2d 179 (1st Dist. 2003).
[85] 338 Ill. App. 3d at 572.

of the contractor's request on the merits.[86] A variation of waiver is when the owner or its agent lulls the claimant into foregoing the required notice until after the period for filing has passed,[87] or when the owner tells the contractor that filing further claims is useless.[88]

In *Emma Corp. v. Inglewood Unified School District*,[89] Emma Corp. submitted the low bid to the District for a school construction project that included a 10-percent bid bond. After the submission, Emma discovered that it failed to include plumbing costs in its bid, causing the bid to be $800,000 too low. The applicable California statute allows a bidder to withdraw a bid under certain circumstances. Section 5103 states:

The bidder shall establish to the satisfaction of the court that:

(a) A mistake was made.

(b) He or she gave the public entity written notice within five days after the opening of the bids of the mistake, specifying in the notice in detail how the mistake occurred.

(c) The mistake made the bid materially different than he or she intended it to be.

(d) The mistake was made in filling out the bid and not due to error in judgment or to carelessness in inspecting the site of the work, or in reading the plans or specifications.[90]

Emma submitted a timely letter to the district requesting that its bid be withdrawn. The district realized that the letter did not comply with the content requirements of the statute but did not notify Emma of this fact.[91] In fact, several district authorities knew that the technical requirements of the statute were complex and that a contractor may not comply with those requirements to rescind its bid properly.

Following the receipt of Emma's letter, and without notice to Emma, the district met in an executive session were the district determined that it would not allow Emma to withdraw its bid because the letter had not complied with the technical requirements of the statute.[92] In addition, the district's representative informed Emma upon receipt of the letter that the district's legal counsel would contact them if any further information was required.[93]

---

[86] *See generally* 2 S. Stein, Construction Law § 6.09[3][b] (1993). Estoppel can be used by an owner as a defense against a contractor's assertion that, for example, the period within which a notice of claim must be given has not commenced. *See* Arnell Constr. Corp. v. Village of N. Tarrytown, 473 N.Y.S.2d 489, 100 A.D.2d 562 (1984) (contractor waived owner's notice of acceptance of the work by making a request for final payment).

[87] Welsh v. Gindele & Johnson, 376 N.Y.S.2d 661, 50 A.D.2d 971 (1975).

[88] Stone v. City of Arcola, 181 Ill. App. 3d 513, 130 Ill. Dec. 118, 536 N.E.2d 1329 (1989).

[89] 114 Cal. App. 4th 1018, 8 Cal. Rptr. 3d 213 (2d Dist. 2004).

[90] 114 Cal. App. 4th at 1026; Cal. Pub. Cont. § 5103.

[91] 114 Cal. App. 4th at 1020.

[92] 114 Cal. App. 4th at 1023.

[93] 114 Cal. App. 4th at 1024.

As a final insult, explicit instructions were given to several of the district's employees and representatives that "no agent or employee of the District would assist [Emma] in rescinding its mistaken bid; the district's agents and employees would decline to react to any withdrawal notification by [Emma], written or oral; the District's agents or employees would not answer or react to any question by [Emma] about the bid withdrawal process and, instead, would refer all inquiries to the outside legal counsel for the District."[94] When Emma discovered the district's position that Emma's initial letter did not comply with the statute, it instructed its attorney to send another letter requesting that its bid be withdrawn, which included all of the technical detail required by the statute.[95] This, however, occurred subsequent to the five-day notice period. The contract was then awarded to Emma and Emma refused to perform.

At trial, the court found that the district was estopped from enforcing the original bid. The appellate court affirmed. The appellate court discussed the rules governing estoppel against public entities:

> Equitable estoppel may be asserted against the government in some circumstances . . . . The requisite elements for equitable estoppel against a private party are: (1) the party to be estopped was apprised of the facts, (2) the party to be estopped intended by conduct to induce reliance by the other party, or acted so as to cause the other party reasonably to believe reliance was intended, (3) the party asserting estoppel was ignorant of the facts, and (4) the party asserting estoppel suffered injury in reliance on the conduct. . . . [T]he doctrine of equitable estoppel may be applied against the government where justice and right require it. . . . Correlative to this general rule, however, is the well-established proposition that an estoppel will not be applied against the government if to do so would effectively nullify a strong rule of policy, adopted for the benefit of the public. . . . The tension between these twin principles makes up the doctrinal context in which concrete cases are decided. . . . The government may be bound by an equitable estoppel in the same manner as a private party when the elements requisite to such an estoppel against a private party are present and, in the considered view of a court of equity, the injustice which would result from a failure to uphold an estoppel is of sufficient dimension to justify any effect upon public interest or policy which would result from the raising of an estoppel. . . .[96]

Under these circumstances, the *Emma* court held that where, as here, the public entity deliberately misled a bidder to prevent the bidder from timely complying with the bid withdrawal statutes, the public entity would be estopped from enforcing the bid.

Waiver of the right to claim for equitable adjustment may also arise out of failure to comply with the specifics of a notice requirement. However, the party

---

[94] 114 Cal. App. 4th at 1022.

[95] 114 Cal. App. 4th at 1023-1024.

[96] 114 Cal. App. 4th at 1030 (citing Medina v. Board of Retirement, 5 Cal. Rptr. 3d 634, 112 Cal. App. 4th 864, 868-69 (2d Dist. 2003)).

seeking to waive the right must strictly comply with the contract provision. In *Atlantic Coast Mechanical. v. R.W. Allen Beers Construction*,[97] R.W. Allen Beers hired Atlantic Coast Mech. (ACM) to perform certain mechanical work on a construction project in Augusta, Georgia. In April of 1998, ACM submitted a request for equitable adjustment. On April 29, 1998, Beers responded by letter stating that the request was "precluded by the terms of the trade contract agreement [subcontract] and various change orders and asked ACM to withdraw the request."[98]

The trial court granted summary judgment against ACM based in part on Beers assertion that ACM had not complied with Article 14(b) of the subcontract. Article 14(b) stated in relevant part:

> . . . [A]ny dispute concerning a question of fact arising under this Agreement which is not resolved shall be decided by [Beers], and [Beers] shall reduce its decision to writing and furnish a copy thereof to [ACM]. The decision of [Beers] shall be final and conclusive, unless within forty-eight (48) hours from the date of receipt of such decision, [ACM] issues written notice to [Beers] contesting same. If [ACM] does not contest [Beers's] final decision within the time period noted above, [ACM] shall be deemed to have waived any right to contest that decision. [ACM] shall carry on the Work and comply with its performance and scheduling obligations under this Agreement despite the existence of any dispute or legal proceedings, unless otherwise agreed in writing by the parties hereto.[99]

Beers argued that ACM's failure to respond to the April 29 letter within 48 hours as required by contract precluded it from asserting its request for equitable adjustment under Article 14(b) of the subcontract. The appellate court disagreed. It found that disputes addressed by Article 14(b) were those regarding "a question of fact arising under the Agreement." In the April 29 letter, however, Beers did not consider the merits of the claim. Instead, the letter only addressed whether ACM was legally entitled to assert its claim. "Thus, the dispute between the parties was not regarding a question of fact arising under the agreement."[100] Accordingly, the court found that ACM did not waive its claim by failing to respond to the Beers letter.

[C] Absence of Prejudice to the Owner

When actual notice is absent, a contractor is left to argue that the owner was not prejudiced by the lack of notice. However, this is when the courts and boards usually draw the line. An early case that considered a rather desperate attempt by the contractor to overcome lack of notice was *Eggers & Higgins v. United*

---

[97] 264 Ga. App. 680, 592 S.E.2d 115 (2003).
[98] 264 Ga. App. at 681.
[99] 264 Ga. App. at 682.
[100] 264 Ga. App. at 682.

States.[101] The court held that a delay of five-and-a-half years in providing notice of a claim was prejudicial in that the government was deprived of considering alternative actions.

A more recent case from the U.S. Court of Appeals for the Federal Circuit is *Mingus Constructors, Inc. v. United States,*[102] previously discussed, which reviewed a claims court decision holding that a contractor's exception to a final release was insufficient to preserve claims against the government. The lower court had based its ruling on the prejudice that resulted from the government's inability to analyze and present its case.[103] The appellate court rejected this rationale, stating:

> Furthermore, to the extent that the Claims Court relied on prejudice to the government as an independent ground for its decision, we disagree. The delay in the assertion of a claim by a contractor inevitably causes some degree of prejudice to the government; however, the existence of prejudice resulting from the dilatory notice usually serves to increase the burden of persuasion facing the contractor asserting its claims for equitable adjustment rather than to bar its claim entirely. Under proper circumstances prejudice to a party could be so overwhelming so as to permit entry of judgment in favor of the prejudiced party as a matter of law [citing *Eggers & Higgins*]. However, we do not believe that the case before us presents such a situation.[104]

Thus, the court held that prejudice generally is not a factor to be considered in determining whether a contractor has given the required notice.

State law is generally in accord. For example, in *Paterson-Leitch Co. v. Massachusetts Municipal Wholesale Electric Co.,*[105] a subcontractor ignored a dual notice provision of the subcontract that required notice of claim, first, to the owner's agent (the construction manager) and, second, to the owner within 14 days of the agent's adverse decision. On appeal, the court considered various of the subcontractor's contentions in an attempt to circumvent the failure to give notice, including that the owner was not prejudiced. Citing both Massachusetts law and prevailing authority elsewhere, the court upheld the notice requirement, ruling that lack of prejudice alone was not a determinant as to whether the requirement was followed.

Whether a party is prejudiced may be a consideration in assessing the reasonableness of the period during which the notice was given, if not expressly provided by contract or statute. In one case, an owner gave the contractor notice of a warranty defect 376 days after contract completion. Because of the lack of prejudice

---

[101] 403 F.2d 225 (Ct. Cl. 1968).

[102] 1812 F.2d 1387, 33 Cont. Cas. Fed. (CCH) ¶ 75,126 (Fed. Cir. 1987).

[103] Mingus Constructors v. United States, 10 Cl. Ct. 173, 178 (1986), 33 Cont. Cas. Fed. (CCH) ¶ 74,407 at 79,391.

[104] Mingus Constructors v. United States, 812 F.2d 1387, 1392, 33 Cont. Cas. Fed. (CCH) ¶ 75,126 at 80,220 (Fed. Cir. 1987) (citations omitted).

[105] 840 F.2d 985, 10 Fed. R. Serv. 3d (Callaghan) 902 (Bankr. D. Mass. 1988).

to the contractor, who had made several unsuccessful attempts during this period to repair the defect, the owner was deemed to have complied with "reasonable" notice.[106]

[D] No Single Identifiable Trigger

Sometimes the starting point of an event that triggers the commencement of a notice period is not easily determinable. For example, a series of storms, none of which individually would entitle a contractor to a time extension, may in the aggregate constitute an excusable weather delay. Such an event would not eliminate the need for notice, but it would likely excuse the giving of notice until after the storms had passed and weather data could be analyzed.

Another example is *J.A. LaPorte, Inc.*[107] The board held that failure to comply with a 20-day notice provision in the changes and suspension-of-work clauses of a federal contract did not bar a claim when no single government action was an identifiable event from which the contractor's delay in presenting the claim could be measured.

[E] Substantial Compliance

Some courts have used the concept of substantial compliance to permit less-than-complete fulfillment of formal notice requirements, though this notion is no more than a composite of the excuses already discussed. An early Supreme Court decision held that actual receipt of notice and unchallenged sufficiency of its content constituted substantial compliance with notice by certified mail.[108] Another case spoke of substantial compliance when an imperfectly worded letter, coupled with the contractor's actual notice of the claim and lack of prejudice, were sufficient to overcome strict compliance.[109]

§ 13.05 STANDARD FORMS

In addition to their presence in government contracts, notice provisions appear in widely disseminated industry forms. Some of those forms follow and are described with reference to their respective notice provisions.

[A] American Institute of Architects

Like the federal prime contract form, the equivalent form published by the American Institute of Architects contains several remedy-granting provisions,

---

[106] Austin Co. v. Vaughn Bldg. Corp., 26 Tex. Sup. Ct. J. 64, 643 S.W.2d 113 (1983).

[107] 75-2 BCA (CCH) ¶ 11,486 (1975).

[108] Fleisher Eng'g & Constr. Co. v. United States ex rel. Hallenbeck, 311 U.S. 15 (1940).

[109] Okee Indus., Inc. v. National Grange Mut. Ins. Co., 225 Conn. 367, 623 A.2d 483 (1993).

relief under which is conditioned upon notice to the owner or its agent.[110] Interestingly, the procedures under which a contractor may seek additional time and money are contained in several clauses in a single section entitled "Claims and Disputes."

For example, Subparagraph 8.3.1 sets forth the basis on which the contractor is entitled to an extension of time for force majeure and other causes. Subparagraph 4.3.8.1, however, states the manner in which a contractor may submit a claim for a time extension, requiring the inclusion of a cost estimate and the effect of the delay on prosecution of the work. Written notice must be provided in accordance with the claim time-limit clause, Subparagraph 4.3.3.

Similarly, the right of the owner to make changes is covered by Article 7 of the contract; suspension of the work for the convenience of the owner is found under Subparagraph 14.3. However, claims for additional cost based on, among other reasons, the failure of the owner to recognize a constructive change or for suspension of the work, must proceed in accordance with Subparagraph 4.3.7.

All of the above claims are subject to the same time limits. Subparagraph 4.3.3 provides for 21-day written notice after either party recognizes a condition giving rise to a claim or after the event giving rise to the claim, whichever is later.

The counterpart to the federal differing-site-conditions clause, "Claims for Concealed or Unknown Conditions," is found at Subparagraph 4.3.6. Contrary to the federal provision, which requires notification of differing site conditions to be given "promptly," the AIA clause specifies a 21-day notice period after conditions are first observed.

The AIA payment provisions allow the contractor to accept final payment without releasing claims for which written notice had previously been given and are identified as still unsettled when final payment is requested.[111]

[B]   Engineering Joint Contract Documents Committee

The engineers' form has a more traditional format, that is, the remedy-granting clauses and the procedures for asserting a claim under those clauses are generally stand-alone.[112] In addition, some of the clauses track with their federal counterparts with respect to notice.

For example, the clause governing changes in the contract price, found at Paragraph 13.2, contains a two-part notice provision like the federal changes clause. The engineers' clause provides for a 30-day written notice stating the general nature of the claim, followed by supporting data and the amount of the claim within 60 days of the occurrence or event giving rise to the claim. The time extension provision (¶ 12.1) follows a similar two-part notice scheme.

The suspension of work clause at Paragraph 15.1 refers to the clauses dealing with changes in contract price and time for the contractor's redress. Paragraph

---

[110] AIA Doc. A201, General Conditions of the Contract for Construction (1987).

[111] *Id.* at ¶ 9.10.1.

[112] EJCDC No. 1910-8 (1990).

4.2.3, "Notice of Differing Subsurface or Physical Conditions," requires prompt notice like the federal differing-site-conditions clause. Finally, the contractor will not waive claims "previously made in writing and still unsettled" by accepting final payment (¶ 14.15.2).

[C]   Associated General Contractors of California

Perhaps the most well-known form developed by general contractors is that published by the largest chapter of the Associated General Contractors.[113] With the exception of the differing-site-conditions clause, which requires prompt notice, all of the principal clauses providing relief to the contractor require "reasonable" notice. The drafters of the form apparently decided that establishing a specified certain number of days for any notice period was ill advised, given the wide variety of circumstances giving rise to claims for relief under those clauses.

§ 13.06   STATUTORY NOTICES

Not all notice provisions are contractual. Many are contained in laws that provide for the assertion of claims by prime contractors against public agencies. Others are in laws governing the payment of money to those who provide labor and material on federal, public, and private works of improvement. In some cases, these provisions are interpreted more strictly than when parties have included them in their contract, largely because legislative intent is sometimes given more force than the intent of the parties to a contract.

[A]   Miller Act

Most construction lawyers and their clients are familiar with the federal Miller Act,[114] a remedial statute that was enacted following the Depression and that has spawned much litigation. Generally, the Act provides for the payment of first-and second-tier subcontractors and first-tier suppliers to the general contractor. As a condition to enforcement of its statutory rights, a claimant must provide to the general contractor written notice of the amount of nonpayment no later than 90 days after having last furnished the labor or material the claimant was obligated to provide.[115]

The 90-day period is clear; however, a number of issues have arisen concerning the commencement of that period and its termination. In the words of the

---

[113] Form AGCC-1 (1988).

[114] 40 U.S.C.S. §§ 270a-270f (Law. Co-op. 1978 & Supp. 1993).

[115] *Id.* at § 270b(a). *See* Annotation, *Timeliness of notice to public works contractor on federal project, of indebtedness for labor or materials furnished,* 69 A.L.R. Fed. 600 (Supp. 1992); Annotation, *Sufficiency of notice to public works contractor on United States project under Miller Act (40 USCS § 270b(a)),* 98 A.L.R. Fed. 778 (Supp. 1992).

statute, the commencement of the notice period is "the date on which [the claimant] did or performed the last of the labor or furnished or supplied the last of the material" for which the claim is made.[116] A common question is whether the material last furnished was part of the original contract or was for the correction of post-performance warranty problems.

In *United States ex rel. Raymond A. Dergen, Inc. v. DeMatteo Construction Co.,*[117] the court held that special duct clips delivered two months after what had been thought as final delivery of the contract quantity were part of the original contract and not replacement parts. The factors leading to this conclusion were that the original shipment was incomplete, the same supplier completed the order, and the clips were supplied at no additional cost.[118] The court took the occasion to examine the underlying policy considerations of the Miller Act. It recognized the hardship a contractor faces over the uncertainty of when to pay what may turn out to be a defaulting subcontractor (who fails to pay the lower-tier Miller Act claimant with whom it has a contract). However, it concluded that the plain wording of the statute and its remedial purpose required the notice period to commence when the last of the material was furnished, even if sometime later than when the parties believe that final shipment occurred.[119]

A different sort of problem occurs when notice is given *before* the last of the labor or materials is provided. Recognizing that the Miller Act is to be given liberal construction to further the congressional intent that labor and material provided to federal projects be paid, and noting the consensus in other circuits that actual notice will suffice when technical compliance with the law is not found,[120] the court in *United States ex rel. Moody v. American Insurance Co.*[121] held that notice given prior to the end of contract performance is effective.[122]

The sufficiency of the required notice is frequently disputed. Often, a claimant first begins writing to the general contractor for assistance in securing payment from a recalcitrant subcontractor, then later makes it clear that the claimant is looking to the prime contractor for payment. Cited often is *United States ex rel. San Joaquin Blocklite v. Lloyd E. Tull, Inc.*[123] The court allowed a

---

[116] *Id.*

[117] 467 F. Supp. 22 (D. Conn. 1979).

[118] *Id.* at 25.

[119] *Id.* at 26.

[120] Unlike notice provisions in clauses providing relief under a contract, no cases have been found in which oral notice alone sufficed as actual notice. For example, in United States ex rel. Greenwald Indus. Prod. Co. v. Barlows Commercial Prod. Co., 567 F. Supp. 464 (D.D.C. 1983), the court held as sufficient a notice addressed to the wrong contractor but sent to an office staffed by personnel identical to both the addressee and the contractor to whom the material had been provided.

[121] 835 F.2d 745 (10th Cir. 1987).

[122] *See also* United States ex rel. Honeywell, Inc. v. A&L Mech. Contractors, Inc., 677 F.2d 383 (4th Cir. 1982) (the same effect despite a strong dissent that emphasized the administrative problems created for general contractors in having to deal with what may be erroneous or moot notices resulting from additional work, subsequent contract modifications, or negotiations between the parties).

[123] 770 F.2d 862 (9th Cir. 1985).

premature notice[124] to the contractor and a subsequent incomplete but timely notice to be read together to comply with the content requirements of a Miller Act notice.

Telephonic notice has been held to be insufficient notice from the prime contractor. The court relies on the purpose of written notice "to prevent misunderstanding between the parties and to afford certain minimal evidence of communication."[125]

When material is provided pursuant to multiple contracts, not an uncommon practice with suppliers, a question is whether a notice is needed for each contract or whether one notice after performing the last contract will suffice. In *United States ex rel. A&M Petroleum v. Santa Fe Engineers,*[126] the claimant made 15 deliveries of oil products, each in accordance with separate purchase orders. Citing extensive authority, the court concluded that notice after the last shipment sufficed for all deliveries.

[B] State Statutes

Many states have notice requirements for prime contractors who wish to preserve rights to claim or to maintain an action against a public entity arising from a claim.[127] In addition, virtually every state has laws that provide protection for those who contribute to the building of both public and private works. As with the Miller Act, all require notice to be given to the general contractor—and sometimes others as well-before a right to payment under the statute arises.

[1] Claims Against Public Entities

Written notice provisions in statutes governing claims by prime contractors against public agencies are generally liberally enforced, given the remedial purposes of such laws.[128] The preceding analysis is much the same: the excuses allowed for noncompliance with statutory notice provisions are similar to those for

---

[124] Contrary to United States ex rel. Moody v. American Ins. Co., 835 F.2d 745 (10th Cir. 1987), the Ninth Circuit does not accept as timely a notice given prior to the furnishing of the last of the labor and material.

[125] United States ex rel. Excavation Constr., Inc. v. Glenn-Stewart-Pinckney Builders & Developers, Inc., 388 F. Supp. 289 (D. Del. 1975) (citing Coffee v. United States, 157 F.2d 968 (5th Cir. 1946) and Apache Powder Co. v. Ashton Co., 264 F.2d 417 (9th Cir. 1959)). *See also* United States ex rel. P.W. Parker, Inc. v. George W. Pennington & Son, Inc., 504 F. Supp. 1066 (D. Md. 1980).

[126] 822 F.2d 547 (5th Cir. 1987).

[127] *See, e.g.,* N.Y. C.P.L.R. 9802 (McKinney 1981) (written verified claim must be filed against village within one year after cause of action accrued), N.Y. Educ. Law § 3813 (McKinney 1981) (notice of claim against school district must be given within three months after the accrual of the claim).

[128] Minsky v. City of L.A., 11 Cal. 3d 113, 520 P.2d 726, 113 Cal. Rptr. 102 (1974).

contractual notices. For example, a county failed to object to a contractor's failure to comply strictly with notice provisions governing claims by prime contractors. Notice was given to the department of public works, deemed to be representative for the board of commissioners to whom notice was required to be given. The court held that the contractor made substantial compliance with the statutory notice law.[129]

Some notice provisions are predicated on the accrual of a cause of action based on a contract or statutory claim. For example, a New York court held that a cause of action accrues when the claimant should have viewed the claim as having been rejected.[130] This could occur when a public entity tells a claimant, in writing or by its actions, that payment may not be honored.[131]

[2] Mechanic's Liens

Mechanic's liens provide security for payment against the property being improved and apply only to private contracts. Because of the greater part that financing institutions play in private development, they are often statutory recipients of notice along with the owner and the general contractor. Unlike public projects, the general contractor may obtain lien rights against the owner's property.

Generally, the legislatures and courts have mandated a policy of liberal construction of mechanic's lien requirements to effectuate fairly and reasonably the law's remedial intent.[132] While the statutory requirements must be complied with, substantial compliance may satisfy the requirements to accommodate the remedial intent of the law.[133]

[3] Bond Claims

Some statutory payment schemes apply to claims by subcontractors and suppliers against the payment bond provided by a general contractor to secure payment of labor and materials. In some states, the law applies to bond claims on

---

[129] E.E. Tripp Excavating Contractor, Inc. v. County of Jackson, 60 Mich. App. 221, 230 N.W.2d 556 (1975). *See also* Stromberg, Inc. v. Los Angeles County Flood Control Dist., 270 Cal. App. 2d 759, 76 Cal. Rptr. 183 (1969) (the court stressed: "The doctrine of substantial compliance cannot be predicated on a complete failure to comply with the mandates of the claims statute" (emphasis added), 270 Cal. App. 2d at 763).

[130] Memphis Constr. v. Village of Moravia, 398 N.Y.S.2d 386, 59 A.D.2d 646 (1977).

[131] Chem Constr. Corp. v. Board of Educ., 430 N.Y.S.2d 771, 105 Misc. 2d 980 (Sup. Ct. 1980).

[132] H&S Torrington Assocs. v. Lutz Eng'g Co., 185 Conn. 549, 441 A.2d 171 (1981); Truestone, Inc. v. Simi W. Indus. Park 11, 163 Cal. App. 3d 715, 209 Cal. Rptr. 757 (1984).

[133] 441 A.2d at 174. While many states provide for a liberal construction of the notice requirements for a mechanic's lien claim, other states provide that the notice requirement be strictly construed. *See* Season-4, Inc. v. Hertz Corp., 788 N.E.2d 179, 338 Ill. App. 3d 565 (1st Dist. 2003). In Wesco Dist. v. Westport Group, 03-03-00438-CV (Tex. App. 3d Dist. 2004), the court held that a notice required under the Texas Mechanic's Lien Act was timely mailed but returned postage due did not constitute substantial compliance.

private construction projects[134] as well as to those for public works.[135] In these cases, notice may have to be given to the surety on the bond as well as the contractor. Further, because the surety stands in the shoes of its principal, the surety has the defense of lack of notice that the debtor-contractor has. The provisions of the bond itself, even in the absence of a governing statute, usually require the claimant to give notice to the surety.[136]

Payment bonds provided pursuant to statute are usually given the same liberal interpretation as mechanic's liens.[137] Even so, written notice provisions can be strictly construed. One court stated that "this legislative policy of liberal construction does not control in those cases where the legislature has mandated certain requirements for perfecting a surety bond claim in clear unequivocal terms."[138] It ruled that neither actual notice nor lack of prejudice to the contractor and the surety waived the written notice requirement of the bond statute. Another court, however, held that service of the required notice by ordinary rather than certified mail, together with proof of receipt by the general contractor, was compliance with the payment bond statute.[139]

In addition, the particular language of the bond must be examined in conjunction with the surety notice requirement where a surety seeks to raise deficient notice as a defense to a claim on the bond. In *William J. Templeman v. United States Fidelity*,[140] the subcontractor, Premier, brought suit on the labor and material payment bond supplied under the Illinois Public Construction Bond Act. The trial court granted summary judgment to the surety on the basis that it failed to comply with the notice provision stated in Section 2 of the Act. Section 2 of the Act states in relevant part:

> Every person furnishing material or performing labor, either as an individual or as a subcontractor for any contractor, with the State, or a political subdivision thereof where bond or letter of credit shall be executed as provided in this Act, shall have the right to sue on such bond . . . Provided, however, that any person having a claim for labor, and material as aforesaid shall have no such right of action unless he shall have filed a verified notice of said claim with the officer, board, bureau or department awarding the contract, within 180 days

---

[134] *See, e.g.,* Cal. Civ. Code § 3097 (Deering 1986 & Supp. 1993).

[135] *Id.* at § 3091.

[136] When interpreting private or public bonds, a court may look to how provisions in similar statutory bonds are interpreted. For example, in Lezzer Cash & Carry, Inc. v. Aetna Ins. Co., 371 Pa. Super. 137, 537 A.2d 857 (1988), the court looked to Miller Act interpretations because of the similarity in the provisions of the bond at issue with those of the Act. *See also* Montgomery County Bd. of Educ. ex rel. Carrier Corp. v. Glassman Constr. Co., 245 Md. 192, 225 A.2d 448 (1967); Pi-Con, Inc. v. A.J. Anderson Constr. Co., 435 Mich. 375, 458 N.W.2d 639 (1990); Okee Indus., Inc. v. National Grange Mut. Ins. Co., 225 Conn. 367, 623 A.2d 483 (1993).

[137] Montgomery County Bd. of Educ. ex rel. Carrier Corp. v. Glassman Constr. Co., 245 Md. 192, 225 A.2d 448 (1967).

[138] Texas Constr. Assocs., Inc. v. Balli, 558 S.W.2d 513 (Tex. Civ. App. 1977).

[139] Pi-Con, Inc. v. A.J. Anderson Constr. Co., 435 Mich. 375, 458 N.W.2d 639 (1990).

[140] 317 Ill. App. 3d 764 (2000).

after the date of the last item of . . . materials . . . and shall have furnished a copy of such verified notice . . . with the agency awarding the contract.

The claim shall be verified and shall contain (1) the name and address of the claimant . . . ; (2) the name of the contractor for the government; (3) the name of the person, firm or corporation by whom the claimant was employed or to whom he or it furnished materials; (4) the amount of the claim; (5) a brief description of the public improvement sufficient for identification.

No defect in the notice provided for shall deprive the claimant of his right of action under this article unless it shall affirmatively appear that such defect has prejudiced the rights of an interested party asserting the same.[141]

On appeal, the surety argued that the subcontractor's notice did not comply with Section 2 since it did not state the amount due under the subcontract and it was not verified. The appellate court cited Paragraph 3 of the actual labor and material payment bond provided on the project. That paragraph provides, in relevant part:

No suit or action shall be commenced hereunder by any claimant:

a) Unless claimant, other than one having a direct contract with the Principal, shall have given written notice to any two of the following: the Principal, the Owner, or the Surety above named, within ninety (90) days . . . .[142]

In discussing the purpose of notice provisions in bond statutes, the court stated:

The notice provision of statutes governing bonds of contractors constructing public buildings and suits by materialmen in connection therewith protects the contractor and the contractor's surety from having to account to unknown suppliers and subcontractors by putting the burden on claimants to advise the contractor and surety of their participation on the project and to advise if they are not promptly paid and by giving the principal contractor the earliest possible notification that a materialman has not been paid and that the materialman may make either a future demand for payment or a future claim against the bond. Thus, the notice provision contained in the Bond Act is unquestionably of benefit to a surety.[143]

However, since the subcontractor had a direct contract with the general contractor, the principal on the bond, the plain language of the bond itself specifically exempted the subcontractor from giving written notice to the principal, owner, or surety of their intent to make a claim.

The court reversed the trial court's order granting summary judgment, stating:

In effect, USF&G asks to be permitted to issue a bond that provides no notice is required prior to suit, but when a claimant relies on that language, to avoid

---

[141] *Id.* at 768-69 (citing 30 ILCS 550/2).

[142] *Id.* at 770.

[143] *Id.* at 770, citations omitted.

payment by invoking the Bond Act, which contains a notice requirement. This we refuse. Instead, we construe the language contained in the bond issued and drafted by USF&G against USF&G and conclude as a matter of law that notice by Premier was waived.[144]

[4]   Public Works Payment Statutes

In some states, a provider of labor or material on a public work of improvement is entitled to maintain a claim for nonpayment against money, such as retention, owed by the public agency to the general contractor.[145] Upon timely notice from the claimant against the fund, the agency must withhold the amount claimed, in some cases together with an additional amount to cover the costs of prosecuting an action to recover the money.[146]

§ 13.07   CONTRACT FORMATION AND ADMINISTRATION

Because of the importance of giving appropriate notice as a condition to the enforcement of payment and other contractual and statutory rights on construction projects, consideration should be given to the drafting of notice provisions in private contracts, followed by rigorous contract administration during performance.

[A]   Formation

Although notice provisions in public contracts and remedial statutes are essentially immutable, the negotiability of most private contracts provides an opportunity to make sure that notice requirements are reasonable and capable of fulfillment. For example, time periods should be stated as specific durations instead of the vague "reasonable" or "prompt." True, the latter provides more flexibility, as fixed time periods do not take into account the wide variety of circumstances under which notice must be provided. However, notice provisions that are specific as to time are less likely subject to dispute and, when the content of the notice is brief, are easy to meet.

The scope of a written notice requirement should not be burdensome. A brief description of the event or occurrence giving rise to the request for relief and the contractor's belief that the owner is responsible for any resulting time or cost

---

[144] *Id.* at 771 (citing Barker v. Leonard, 635 N.E. 2d 846, 263 Ill. App. 3d 661 at 663 (1994)).

[145] *See, e.g.,* Cal. Civ. Code §§ 3179-3214 (Deering 1986 & Supp. 1993).

[146] *Id.* at § 3086. A claimant not in privity with the prime contractor must give a preliminary notice to the prime contractor and the public agency, personally or by registered or certified mail, within 20 days of first providing labor or material to the jobsite. The stop notice is perfected by serving it on the public agency in the manner described above any time after the furnishing of the labor and material, but no later than 30 days after the public agency records a notice of acceptance or completion or, if no filing is made by the public agency, 90 days after actual completion.

impact should be adequate to provide the owner with sufficient information with which to conduct an investigation and decide on a course of action. If more detailed information is desirable, that should be given in a follow-up notice after a period (which should be liberally extended) during which the contractor has time to collect, evaluate, organize, and present the information. This second "notice" should not be a condition precedent to granting relief; less painful alternatives, such as deducting the owner's increased expenses of investigation as a result of tardy notice, should be employed.

Notice should be designed to reach the owner, but the role of the owner's site representative should not be ignored. An owner who is paying the bills may be removed from the day-to-day activities of the project and may not want to trust to the adequacy of communications with site representatives. Nonetheless, allowing notice to be given to the site representative will increase the chance that the contractor will give notice when required, facilitate communications between the contractor and the site representative, and will lessen arguments over notice compliance.

[B]   Administration

Education about the importance of complying with written notice requirements should be made available to those who have to deal with contract administration and payment requests. Many seminars are available, and some purveyors will present in-house programs.

Project manuals tailored to specific projects can include all of the applicable notice provisions. Standard form notice letters tied specifically to these provisions can greatly aid field administrators. Blanks are left for the essential information that the contract or law requires to be provided.

CHAPTER **14**

PRELITIGATION ADVICE FOR CHANGE ORDER CLAIMS

Neal J. Sweeney
Jason B. Adkisson
Sarah-Nell H. Walsh

§ 14.01 THE CONSTANT POTENTIAL FOR LITIGATION

It is an unfortunate fact of life in construction that each situation suggesting the need for a change order to alter the contract time or price also entails the risk that the parties will disagree and litigation may result. That is not to say that litigation is inevitable. On the contrary, only a fraction of potential change order issues results in litigation; most are resolved on the site or at the project management level. Relatively few change order claims consume a disproportionate amount of time and resources in litigation. Fortunately, the considerations and approaches that must be followed in preparing to litigate change order claims can also contribute to their resolution through less costly informal processes, thereby disposing of the need for litigation.

This chapter will suggest an approach to change orders that provides the ability to succeed in litigation, but only after exhausting all practical efforts to avoid the need to litigate.

§ 14.02 EARLY RECOGNITION AND EVALUATION OF CHANGE ORDER ISSUES

The first step in requesting a change order or prosecuting a change order claim is to recognize the potential contractual basis for an adjustment in time or price. Early recognition is required to ensure that notice requirements are met and that costs and documentation needed to support the change order claim are maintained. Familiarity with contract clauses, technical requirements, and some fundamental contract and construction law concepts are needed to recognize the need for a change order and to avoid unknowingly providing or accepting a nonconforming quantity, quality, or method of performance. All project management personnel should be familiar with the contract terms, including the plans and specifications, the general conditions, and any special provisions so they can evaluate the performance actually demanded, compared to the performance specified in the contract. In-house educational programs, enhancing this ability and equipping job personnel to identify and handle possible change order claim situations, should also be considered. Education and awareness programs must also extend beyond office staff and should certainly include the project superintendent and, to a lesser extent, the foreman. Even if the lower-level field supervisors are not able to address fully every contractual issue that arises, they must be trained to recognize those situations and circumstances that require further scrutiny and review at a higher level.

Recognizing and evaluating potential change order claims requires developing a sense of context and scale in order to decide which issues actually merit a change order request. A change order should not be asserted for every minor or hypertechnical alteration of the project scope. Although a paper trail may be necessary to track the source and authorization of minor alterations in the plans and specifications and to document the actual as-built conditions, not every change entails an adjustment in price or time of performance. On the other hand, the cumulative effect of a myriad of minor changes incorporated during construction, particularly if they come late in the project, can be substantial and result in delays and extra cost. The ripple effect of the numerous changes, manifested as dollars and cents or as time lost to inefficiency, may justify a major change order. An effective program that identifies change orders includes targeting those incidents that are sufficiently meritorious and substantial to justify the cost of preparing and prosecuting them. Requesting change orders with little merit or significance will merely waste resources and squander credibility. Practicality and pragmatism should govern; pursuing change order claims on principle rarely makes business sense.

Most designers and owners do not understand the inconvenience and disruption that change orders can cause a contractor. Many projects begin with the announcement of anticipated changes, with the pre-change notice often continuing throughout the project. When notified of a particular change, contractors will place an informal "hold" on the area until the change order has been priced and the decision has been made as to whether to change the work. Costs for extended performance time or delays are usually not included for those early-announced changes. Eventually, the contractor must insist on a decision on the change, without fully knowing if the change will cause a delay, and the designer issues a last-minute proceed order. As these informal holds and last-minute proceed orders increase, the schedule may slip and overhead and field costs increase.

Although many standard-form Requests for Proposals have a place for the designer to check if contract work should be stopped pending preparation of the change order cost estimate, written instructions to stop are rarely volunteered. Therefore, the contractor should always inquire and, unless specifically instructed to stop, proceed with installation per the unchanged plans and specifications. However, if the contractor is certain the change will be authorized and provides ample written notice that it is stopping work in order to avoid unnecessary costs, it may be appropriate to stop without an express instruction to do so. In addition, the change order pricing proposal should indicate the absolute latest approval date to prevent any rework or delay.

Once it is determined that an issue merits a change order claim, comprehensive preparation and organization should be promptly undertaken. The dollar value associated with the changed work or associated time impact will generally dictate the level of effort and expense invested in this step. The facts, evidence, and documents relating to the change should be assembled, organized, and reviewed before they are lost or forgotten. If the work or impact of the change is ongoing, additional emphasis should be placed on the documentation and collection of information, which may establish the basis for the change order or its dollar value. A detailed discussion of project documentation is contained in **§ 14.03**. This preparation should be undertaken with an eye toward resolving the change order in the formal setting of an arbitration or litigation, while still seeking early resolution through informal and less onerous means. If early resolution is not achieved, complete preparation at an early stage provides important insight for developing a strategy and a factual foundation that can be relied upon as prosecution of the change order continues.

§ 14.03 DOCUMENTATION AND EVIDENCE TO SUPPORT CHANGE ORDER CLAIMS

Contract terms requiring formal notice of claims or changes within a specified time should always be followed. Formal notice letters, despite their importance, are only a fraction of the documentation required to prepare and prosecute a change order claim effectively. Documentation cannot be considered only when a change order issue arises; at that point, it may be too late. Establishing and maintaining a system of project documentation from the outset of the project is essential to proper management and presentation of change order claims. In fact, the failure to implement and utilize an adequate document control and change management system can be fatal to the successful pursuit of a future claim.

The first step in preparing a change order claim should be to investigate the claimant's own records and sources of information about the project and the change. Project records are generally voluminous. Although the review of the records must be sufficient in scope to cover the documents relevant to the claim and anticipated defenses, it must also be sufficiently focused and specific enough to avoid inundating the claim preparation process with unnecessary and irrelevant documents. Certain categories of documents almost always merit some consideration, such as the contract and related change orders, pay applications, daily logs or reports, bonds and insurance policies, correspondence files, internal memoranda, and e-mail.

Each company and each project should establish and enforce standard procedures relating to the creation, maintenance, and orientation of certain specific types of documentation.

[A] Correspondence

As a matter of routine, the project management should be drilled on the importance of complying with technical notice requirements in the contract. Discussion with other parties should likewise be confirmed in writing to the involved parties, with copies in the file. Such confirmation will help resolve any misunderstanding that might exist and also preserve the substance of the discussion if a dispute arises later. All of these steps are increasingly being done electronically, by e-mail.

The speed, ease, and informality of e-mail as a means of communication and documentation has many advantages, but it is important to be cautious in the use of e-mail, especially if it is used to replace formal correspondence. The perceived informality of e-mail should not be an excuse to fail to document and explain a position or situation clearly and comprehensively. Inappropriate and ill-advised off-the-cuff remarks that you would not put in a formal letter are just as bad when communicated by e-mail. Always keep in mind that e-mail is subject to the same discovery requests and requirements as paper documents; keep relevant e-mail correspondence in some sort of accessible format, to decrease the cost of complying with electronic discovery requests in potential future litigation.

[B]   Meeting Notes

Regular job coordination meetings between the various parties to the project, on a cumulative basis, cover more issues and contribute more to the exchange of information necessary to complete the work than all the correspondence on the project. Because such meetings are of great importance, one person should be designated to maintain the minutes or notes for each meeting. That person should record the subjects covered, the nature of the discussion, the future actions to be taken and by whom. The name, title, and affiliation of each participant should be listed. The notes should be concise but informative. The items discussed should be indexed or designated in such a manner that they can be located for future reference. The notes should then be distributed regularly to all participants and those affected.

The widespread use of computers has made it simple to maintain and update regular meeting notes, even though certain items will likely remain open to discussion through several meetings. At the opening of each regular meeting, the notes from the previous meeting can be reviewed to confirm their accuracy and the mutual understanding of the participants. By identifying those items that remain outstanding, the previous week's minutes can also serve as an agenda for the current meeting. Additionally, all project meeting minutes must be carefully identified and tracked in order that they can be put to the fullest possible use in identifying project problems or referenced for historical data at a later date.

[C]   Jobsite Logs or Daily Reports

Jobsite logs or daily reports are generally maintained by the project superintendent and often provide the best record of what happens in the field. They help keep management and office personnel informed of progress and problems. In the event of a claim, they are often among the most helpful documents in recreating the progress on the job and as-built schedules.

The daily log or report must be a part of the superintendent's daily routine. If updating it is too burdensome, it either will be ignored or will detract from the superintendent's primary function of getting the job built. Key information should be elicited briefly and concisely, requiring as little narrative as possible. The information covered should include:

- Manpower, preferably broken down by subcontractors or trades;

- Equipment used and idle;

- Major work activities;

- Any delays or problems;

- Areas of work not available;

- Safety and accidents;

- Oral instructions and informal meetings;

- Brief weather summary; and

- Jobsite visitors.

Use of a standard form can both ease the burden on the superintendent and better maintain the information in an organized, easily retrieved manner. The process can be expedited further by simply allowing the superintendent to dictate entries and having the report compiled by office staff.

All key project personnel, such as foremen, project engineers, and project managers, should also be encouraged to maintain personal daily logs, and procedures should be established to facilitate this effort. The information recorded should be similar to the job log or daily report, but not as extensive or detailed.

These types of routine, contemporaneous descriptions of work progress, site conditions, labor and equipment use, and the contractor's ability (or inability) to perform its work can provide valuable information necessary to reconstruct accurately the events of the project when preparing a claim. When maintaining these reports or logs, project personnel must be consistent in recording events and activities on the job, particularly those that relate to claims or potential claims. Failure to record an event, once the responsibility of a daily report or log is undertaken, carries with it the implication that the event did not occur or was insignificant, and also threatens the credibility of the entire log.

[D]   Standard Forms

Information flows constantly between project participants through a variety of media. Drawings are revised; shop drawings are submitted, reviewed, and returned; field orders and change orders are issued; questions are asked; and clarifications are provided. Cumulatively and individually, these bits and pieces of information are essential for building the job and also for reconstructing the progress of events on paper in the event of a claim. The standard procedures must include the means for providing, eliciting, recording, and tracking this mass of data so that it can be used during the course of the job and efficiently retrieved in an after-the-fact claim setting.

Routine transmittal forms should be customized to address specific, routine types of communications in order to expedite the process, but also to ensure that required information is provided. For example, separate specialized forms can be prepared for transmittal of shop drawings and submittals, requests for clarifications, drawing revisions, and, of course, field orders and change orders. When possible, the forms should provide space for responses, including certain standard responses that simply can be checked off or filled in. At a minimum, the forms should identify the individual sender, the date issued, and specific and self-descriptive references to the affected or enclosed drawings, submittal, or specification. If a response is requested by a certain date, that date should be identified on the form.

[E]   Photographs and Videotapes

Photographs and videotapes are a helpful, easy, and inexpensive means to monitor, depict, and preserve conditions of the work as those conditions change and the work progresses. They are particularly helpful in claims situations. One approach, incorporated in many contracts, is to accumulate a periodic pictorial diary of the job through a series of weekly or monthly photographs of significant milestones in the construction. This encourages personnel to take photographs of site conditions on a routine basis, perhaps concentrating on problem areas and those areas associated with crucial construction procedures and scheduling. Photographs are also the best evidence of defective work or problem conditions that may be cured or covered up and cannot be viewed later.

A professional photographer may be needed or required by contract, but generally jobsite personnel, with some instruction, are capable of handling the photography chores. Digital cameras capable of producing quality photographs should always be used, as they allow the photographer to check the content and clarity of the photos while still at the site and before conditions are altered.

Photos should always be identified with a notation as to time, date, location, conditions depicted, personnel present, and the photographer. If possible, these should be noted when the photograph is taken. If not, a log should be kept as the photos are taken and checked when the photos are printed, and the appropriate entries made on the back of the prints. Without this information correlated to specific photographs, the utility of the entire effort can be substantially undermined. File copies, negatives, or CD-ROMs (for use with digital cameras) should also be retained in an organized, retrievable manner.

Digital videocassette recorders are increasingly inexpensive and easy to operate. In some situations, video can be considerably more informative than still photographs, such as when attempting to depict an activity or the overall status of the project. (Static conditions, however, are best photographed.) A contemporaneous narrative voice-over accompanying the video will give the after-the-fact viewer a much better idea of what is being depicted and why. A monthly videotape is an excellent way of preserving and presenting evidence. Again, properly trained jobsite personnel can operate the video equipment and later testify in conjunction with the showing of the tape.

[F]   First-Hand Observation

Although documentation is certainly critical to any change order claim, it is not everything. At trial, witness testimony, perceptions, and recollections will gain the most attention. Those individual resources should not be overlooked when preparing change order claims. The more remote claim preparation is from the individuals actively involved in the field, the more likely there will be unpleasant surprises and inconsistencies as the claim is subjected to greater scrutiny in discovery or at trial. Consequently, the field personnel involved should be interviewed to confirm that management's second-hand understanding about the facts and circumstances of the change order claim is accurate and complete. As far as possible, project personnel should staff and assist in the claim preparation effort. At a minimum, field personnel should have the opportunity to review the claim at various stages of preparation, and certainly before it is submitted, to confirm its accuracy.

§ 14.04 EFFECTIVE COMMUNICATION REGARDING CHANGES

[A] Importance of Meetings

Regardless of the effort invested in planning and design, no project can be built precisely according to the plans and specifications. Inevitably, there will be hidden conflicts, problems with the site, changes in need or use, or better ways to do things, all of which may require changes. Communication between the project owner, design professional, contractor, and subcontractors is crucial to the effective recognition, implementation, and resolution of changes and change orders. All must recognize the need for a cooperative team approach, rather than adversarial conflict. The owner, designer, and general contractor must establish some method to both discover what is occurring at the jobsite, in terms of changes, and to relay suggestions, recommendations, and requirements as to how these potential change issues can be addressed and resolved. Satisfactory communication can be achieved only if the parties have personnel who will develop pleasant and confident working relationships with one another. Jobsite staff should have good rapport with the on-site personnel of the owner or designer so that they will report difficulties and seek recommendations for avoiding or resolving them. Efforts to develop this rapport should begin at the preconstruction conference and continue throughout the contract period.

Regular job meetings help to establish and maintain the required lines of communication on a construction site. Weekly, bi-weekly, or monthly meetings should be regularly scheduled and held. The choice of participants and the frequency will depend on the meetings' purpose and the status or level of activity on the job. Field coordination meetings should involve the project superintendent, subcontractor superintendents, and key foremen. Such brief but regular meetings aid the process of coordinating and scheduling the work at a grassroots level. These meetings also identify problem areas and information needed for progress before a situation becomes critical.

Regular meetings between the design professional's staff and the contractor are helpful for keeping up on the status of submittals, shop drawings, and areas requiring clarifications. Meetings between the contractor, architect, and owner should also take place, but probably on a less frequent basis. These meetings can be used to apprise the owner of important developments and to work out contractual issues. Further, the parties can discuss problems that are not being addressed on a more operational level and therefore require the owner's intervention. The contractor should be wary of allowing the owner to get too far removed from the construction effort.

[B] Partnering

Partnering is a process intended to instill and maintain joint recognition and pursuit of the common interest in successful project completion among all project participants. Through partnering, management for the owner, general contractor, and designer, as well as subcontractors and subconsultants, focus on teambuilding and problem solving. The basic approach of partnering may be more familiar to those involved in construction, primarily on a negotiated price basis. In the context of lump-sum price and competitive bidding in which much construction, particularly public works, takes place, partnering represents a significant departure from business as usual.

The partnering process must begin before construction begins because it requires the reeducation of project personnel, particularly those steeped in an "us versus them" approach to construction. The U.S. Army Corps of Engineers (Corps), through the use of partnering on its projects and the promotion of partnering by its officials, has done the most to increase awareness about partnering and educate the industry. In its *Partnering* pamphlet, the Corps describes partnering as "an agreement in principle to share the risks involved in completing the project, and to establish and promote a nurturing partnership environment."[1] This requires "each party . . . to understand the goals, objectives, and needs of the other—their 'win' situation—and seek ways that these objectives can overlap."[2] Partnering is in many respects the mutual reaffirmation of the same principles of communication, common sense, and enlightened self-interest necessary to avoid and quickly resolve disputes. With partnering, these principles are applied even earlier in the process.

The initial partnering meetings must develop: (1) a method of shared communication that maximizes the technical and administrative resources available to the partnering group; (2) a realistic timetable for information exchange as the project develops, and the construction milestones deemed critical for the project; (3) quality, efficiency, and safety parameters; (4) a budgeting and incentive system; (5) an ongoing, objective performance evaluation system; and (6) a creative dispute prevention/resolution process that fosters the trust built during the initial matrix development meetings.[3]

§ 14.05 ELECTRONIC DATA AND DISCOVERY: SPECIAL CONSIDERATIONS

Computers have revolutionized the day-to-day manner in which nearly all business is conducted, and the construction industry is no exception. Computers are present at every level of a construction project, from the design phase through

---

[1] *See* U.S. Army Corps of Engineers, *Partnering* 1 (1991).

[2] *Id.*

[3] Kunz, *Counsel's Role in Negotiating a Successful Construction Partnering Agreement*, 15 Constr. Law. 19 (No. 4, Nov. 1995).

final project closeout. All parties to a project need to understand how computer-generated materials (correspondence, e-mail, memoranda, drawings, submittals, etc.) are integral to the claims process. In addition, one must consider the potential adverse consequences associated with computer-generated materials, particularly due to the broad scope of discovery.

[A]   Duty to Preserve Electronic Documents

Under the Federal Rules of Civil Procedure, a party is under a duty to preserve what it knows or reasonably should know is relevant in the action, is reasonably calculated to lead to discovery of admissible evidence, is reasonably likely to be requested during discovery, or is the subject of a pending discovery request. This duty arises when one has notice that evidence is relevant to future litigation or when a party should have known that evidence may be relevant to future litigation.[4] While "extraordinary measures" need not be undertaken to preserve all potential evidence, unique, relevant evidence that might be useful to an adversary must not be destroyed.[5]

The Federal Rules of Civil Procedure do not distinguish between the duty to produce electronic data and the duty to produce traditional paper-based documents. Information that is stored, used, or transmitted in electronic form is subject to discovery pursuant to the same basic rules as paper documents. To interpret the Federal Rules of Civil Procedure in a manner that would preclude production of electronic material would defeat the goal of securing the just, efficient, and inexpensive determination of every action.

The general trend is that the duty to preserve evidence attaches at the time that litigation was reasonably anticipated. While the courts have not drawn a bright line in terms of defining when litigation should be "reasonably anticipated" by the parties, it is clear that the duty to preserve attaches when a complaint is filed with the court. However, the duty to preserve may arise before the complaint is filed if the defendant should have known that certain evidence was relevant to future litigation.[6]

[B]   What Evidence Must Be Preserved?

A party must preserve evidence that is properly discoverable under the Federal Rules of Civil Procedure, including electronic data such as e-mail, word processing documents, spreadsheets, etc. Information sought during discovery need not be admissible at the trial, if the information sought appears reasonably calculated to lead to the discovery of admissible evidence.[7] Therefore, the duty to preserve electronic evidence extends to a very broad universe of material.

---

[4] *See* Zubulake v. UBS Warburg LLC, 220 F.R.D. 212, 216 (S.D.N.Y. 2003).
[5] *Id.*
[6] *Id.* at 217.
[7] Fed. R. Civ. P. 26(b)(1).

Although a party does not need to undertake extraordinary measures to pre-serve all potential evidence, it must preserve evidence that it has notice is likely to be the subject of a discovery request, even before such a request is received. However, this does not mean that a party is under an obligation to preserve all e-mail potentially relevant to any future litigation. Nonetheless, any entity or person who anticipates being a party or is a party to a lawsuit must not destroy unique, rel-evant evidence that might be useful to an adversary.[8]

Once a party reasonably anticipates litigation, it should suspend its routine document retention/destruction policy and institute a "litigation hold" to ensure the preservation of relevant documents. Otherwise, documents could be destroyed, thereby subjecting the party to a spoliation claim. As a general rule, the duty to preserve does not apply to inaccessible backup tapes, such as those maintained solely for the purpose of disaster recovery, but it does pertain to accessible backup tapes, such as those used for information retrieval.[9]

[C] Financial Burden Associated with Electronic Discovery

Restoring and producing responsive communications from backup tapes may be expensive. The Federal Rules of Civil Procedure limit the frequency or use of certain discovery methods if the judge determines that "the burden or expense of the proposed discovery outweighs its likely benefit."[10]

This balancing test is frequently invoked in cases in which massive amounts of electronic documents have been deleted, some of which may prove to be rele-vant. Although such documents may have been deleted from an individual's com-puter or hard drive, these documents are often retrievable from backup tapes maintained for recovery in case of disaster. The backup tape recovery process requires three steps: cataloguing, restoring, and processing.

The leading authority, *Zubulake*, held that "whether production of such doc-uments is unduly burdensome or expensive turns primarily on whether it is kept in an accessible or inaccessible format."[11] The court broke electronic data down into five categories based on accessibility:

1. Active online data, such as magnetic disks and hard drives;

2. Near-line data, such as robotic storage devices and optical disks;

3. Offline storage/Archives, such as removable optical disks or magnetic tape data;

4. Backup tapes containing compressed data; and

5. Erased, fragmented, or damaged data.[12]

---

[8] *See Zubulake*, 220 F.R.D. at 217.

[9] Zubulake v. UBS Warburg LLC, 217 F.R.D. 309, 317 (S.D.N.Y. 2003).

[10] Fed. R. Civ. P. 26(b)(2)(iii).

[11] *See Zubulake*, 217 F.R.D. at 318.

[12] *See id.*

The first three categories are identified as accessible data, stored in a readily usable format, and the usual rules of discovery apply.

The recovery process is no doubt technologically sophisticated and costly. This again raises the question of which party is responsible for the cost of recovering deleted electronic documents. While the presumption under the Federal Rules of Civil Procedure is that the responding party bears the costs of production, a responding party can shift the cost of production to the requesting party if it shows undue burden or expense. In the first *Zubulake* decision, the court ruled that the following factors are to be considered in determining which party should incur costs of retrieving deleted electronic files:

1. The extent to which the request is specifically tailored to discover relevant information;

2. The availability of the information from other sources;

3. The total cost of production, compared to the amount in controversy;

4. The total cost of production compared to the resources available to each party;

5. The relative ability of each party to control the costs and its incentive to do so;

6. The importance of the issues at stake in the litigation; and

7. The relative benefits to the parties of obtaining the information.

The court held that the factors should be weighted in descending order and went on to group them into three categories in order of importance. The first two factors comprise the first and most important group, the marginal utility test. Since an e-mail contains the precise language used by the author, it is a particularly powerful form of proof at trial if offered as an admission by a party opponent.[13]

Factors three through five are the cost factors. The cost of production is usually very significant. The court normally compares the cost of restoration with the value of a potential verdict to make sure that the cost of restoration is not "significantly disproportionate" to the projected value of the case.

The least important group comprises factors six and seven. The sixth factor, the importance of the issues at stake in the litigation regarding the public interest in the suit's outcome, will rarely come into play. The seventh factor, the benefits to both parties, is least important because generally the requesting party will benefit from the production and the responding party will not. In cases where both parties would benefit, that factor may weigh against cost-shifting.

This list of factors is only a guide; the precise allocation of costs is a matter of judgment and fairness, not a mathematical formula with seven inputs. This analysis provides the court wide discretion in its final analysis of the appropriateness of cost-shifting and the amount actually shifted. Specifically, the court maintained that

---

[13] *See* Zubulake v. UBS Warburg LLC, 216 F.R.D. 280, 287 (S.D.N.Y. 2003).

"a list of factors is not merely a matter of counting and adding; it is only a guide" and that "the precise allocation [if the cost should be shifted] is a matter of judgment and fairness rather than a mathematical consequence of the seven factors."[14]

Where the court deems cost-shifting to be appropriate, normally the costs of restoration and searching shifts to the requesting party and the responding party still bears the cost of reviewing and producing electronic data once it has been converted to an accessible format. In summary, the court has wide discretion in its assessment of the seven factors as well as the ultimate decision to impose a partial or complete shift in cost.

§ 14.06   JOB COST RECORDS

Job costs should be properly maintained and monitored to help recognize potential change order issues as well as to price change orders accurately. The contractor must monitor its actual price expenditure against its individual budget or cost code items to evaluate its financial performance on the project.

The monitoring of costs and the process for doing so must be established before construction starts and begin before job costs are incurred. The original bid or estimate provides the starting point for developing the budget against which the actual costs will be compared. That original estimate, however, must be reviewed and adjusted to the results of subcontract buyout and corrections for errors in estimating that are revealed only after bid opening.

Although a certain level of detail and breakdown of categories of costs is necessary for actual and meaningful tracking, too much detail is impractical to maintain and enforce in the course of the project. The reliability of the tracking of most job costs will ultimately depend on the willingness and ability of field personnel to code labor hours and equipment and material use accurately to the appropriate cost category. The cost code system must therefore be user-friendly and the individuals responsible for coding costs properly trained to do so.

Once the system for monitoring costs is established, it must be rigorously maintained throughout the entire project or it is a wasted effort. If job cost records are properly maintained, variances and overruns will be evident, alerting the contractor to problem areas, hopefully in time to mitigate overruns. Substantial overruns may also highlight potential claim issues, which should be brought to the attention of the owner and design professional. Accurate and reliable job cost records permit company management to evaluate the financial status of the project on a regular basis, without having to rely exclusively on the second-hand reports of project personnel, who might prefer not to share bad news.

§ 14.07   PROJECT SCHEDULING

Proper attention to scheduling is necessary on every project, although the extent of scheduling required may vary greatly. As with project costs records, a

---

[14] *Id.* at 289.

properly maintained and updated schedule can help identify potential change order issues as well as prove the time and disruptive impact of changes to the work.

The effective implementation of a schedule ensures that all parties to the project—owner, contractor, subcontractors, and design professional—agree that the schedule will govern the project. Ideally, this understanding should be spelled out in the prime contract and subsequent subcontracts. General contractors should not rely on a subcontract's generic flow-down provision, but should spell out the subcontractors' obligations with respect to the schedule in the flow-down clause or in a separate clause.

Agreeing to abide by the schedule is not enough. To make the schedule an effective tool, all parties must actively participate in its creation, by providing realistic durations for work activities and by sharing concerns or insight regarding schedule logic relating to those activities. The party ultimately responsible for bringing the project in on time must reserve the right and power to determine the final form of the critical path method (CPM) schedule. Although the input of all parties is necessary, a general contractor will generally not be able to accommodate all of the conflicting demands of the trades and still produce a workable schedule. Nonetheless, no schedule can be etched in stone. To be an effective tool, it must be adjusted to reflect the changing circumstances of the project. Therefore, all parties have a continuing obligation to maintain it.

The need for accurate and timely information to update the CPM must be emphasized at the outset of the project, at weekly job meetings, and through monthly update procedures. To facilitate the update process, the party with scheduling responsibility should establish procedures and possibly standard forms for the other project participants to use. This may include the submission of "fragnets" with any change order proposals that are claimed to have a time impact. The extent and sophistication of these efforts will vary with the size and complexity of the project and the nature of the schedule, but the underlying need to update and maintain an accurate schedule is a constant.

§ 14.08 PRACTICAL TIPS FOR PROMPT RESOLUTION OF CHANGE ORDER CLAIMS

Although claims and disputes are part of the construction process, they need not and should not dominate it. When they arise, efforts should be redoubled to resolve them as quickly as possible. The complexity, time, and cost of arbitration and litigation naturally favor negotiation and settlement. Alternative dispute resolution (ADR) procedures, such as arbitration, certainly are options for expeditiously resolving disputes. However, management should not rely on these sophisticated and involved techniques to the exclusion of more traditional, routine, and grassroots approaches that resolve disputes at the earliest possible time.

An approach favoring prompt resolution should be part of a claims policy, and project personnel and management should be educated and trained accordingly. Although contract provisions regarding notice of claims and other technical requirements should be complied with, other lines of communication on the project should not be overlooked as a means of bringing a change order claim to quick resolution and avoiding the need to have the disputes process run its full course. It is far easier and less expensive to resolve problems in the field, where they arose, than in the courtroom. Even if early settlement is not achieved, the negotiations force the claimant to examine the merits of its claim, revealing the strengths and weaknesses of the claim at an early stage.

Comprehensive and careful preparation greatly enhances the likelihood of early resolution and settlement. A party attempting to settle a claim should know its own case intimately, anticipating as many of the opposing party's points as possible despite the absence of discovery. A well-prepared claim document is helpful both as a starting point and as a reference during settlement discussions. Those with first-hand, detailed knowledge of the underlying facts are also essential to any negotiating effort. There is simply no substitute for the person who experienced the project's problems on a daily basis.

[A]   Evaluate Cost Impact of Change

The issue of liability generally receives the most attention and focus in construction disputes. Does a differing site condition exist? Who caused the delay and is it compensable? However, the issue of damages, costs that flow from the events giving rise to liability, is just as important. Too often, the issue of calculating and proving damages is given a back seat, with little precision or scrutiny applied until the eve of trial. That approach can result in an entirely misguided claim effort, missed opportunities for settlement, and loss at trial or in arbitration. An early analysis of damages can help determine whether a claim really exists and the best means of preparing and positioning the claim for the affirmative recovery sought.

[B]   Prepare and Submit a Comprehensive Claim Document

Effective change order claim preparation and presentation involves promoting understanding, while making the claim appear substantial and well supported. A good technique is to use a *claim document*, a written synopsis of the claim that can be presented to the opposition at the early stages of the dispute. Like every other aspect of claim preparation, the claim document serves two alternate purposes. Its immediate and primary goal is to bring about a prompt and satisfactory resolution of the claim. Failing that, the claim document will provide a blueprint for further prosecution of the claim.

The claim document allows the claimant to explain its grievance in a comprehensive fashion. Preparing the document requires the claimant to refine and synthesize the claim from beginning to end. The claim document should be viewed as a story, with a clear and definite theme that can be readily communicated, understood, and remembered. The theme should be the strongest argument supporting the claimant's theory of recovery. There will certainly be a number of facts gathered in support of the claim, but trying to present and argue each of these facts will simply overwhelm and confuse the reader, and the claim document's persuasive value will be lost.

The primary communicative component of the claim document is the factual narrative. Although this narrative will certainly focus on the claimant's point of view, it should not be overly argumentative or combative. To the extent possible, the facts presented should be permitted to speak for themselves. The writing style should be clear and precise, but should not read like technical specifications. The narrative should be comprehensive and logically organized so it can be used as a resource throughout negotiations and further prosecution of the claim. If the matter is so complex that the narrative is exceedingly long, an executive summary should be prepared.

The factual narrative is often followed by a written discussion of the applicable legal principles that support and illustrate the theories on which the claim is based. Assistance from an attorney experienced in construction claims is generally required to fashion the legal arguments and otherwise to ensure that the factual narrative is presented in a manner consistent with the applicable legal principles. The need for or extent of a legal discussion is generally geared to the expertise or experience of the ultimate decision maker for the opposition. For example, in federal construction contracts, certain theories of entitlement are so firmly established and recognized on all levels that no (or only a limited) legal discussion is required. In other situations, the legal discussion may be a crucial element in causing the other side to recognize its liability and exposure. A one-time owner may have no concept of a differing site condition or why the contractor should be compensated for it. Even though local government entities contract regularly, claims against them might require a lengthy legal decision because the elected officials ruling on them might not immediately recognize the need to settle a claim.

The pricing of the change order and support for such calculations is every bit as important as establishing liability for the claim. The claim document must reflect the damages and include a specific dollar figure, fairly detailed cost analysis, and breakdown. Supporting information and sources should be identified, and appended if not too voluminous.

Finally, the claim document should be used to showcase and highlight the most persuasive documentary and demonstrative evidence. The most revealing documents should be quoted or even reproduced in their entirety in the body of the narrative. Those documents that do not merit incorporation into the text, but that are referenced in support of the claim, can be included in an indexed appendix that is cross-referenced with and organized like the factual narrative. In this manner, the narrative can be reviewed without having to sift through every bit of paper, although that backup is readily available should further review be desired.

In addition to documents, charts, graphs, drawings, and photographs, other demonstrative and visual evidence should be incorporated into the claim document as far as practical. Similarly, consideration should be given to including relevant reports by experts as attachments to the claim document as exhibits, with appropriate references to and quotes from the reports in the narrative.

In certain situations, the nature of the claim or the character or capacity of the opposition may counsel against submitting an extensive claim document. The opposition may not have the financial resources or genuine interest in resolving the claim by negotiation, which is a primary goal of the claim document. Instead, the opposition may seek a one-way flow of information, desiring to receive a detailed presentation of the claim, but unwilling to explain or document any response, defense, or counterclaim until trial. The claimant must evaluate whether pursuing the "race for disclosure" by providing a claim document will ultimately eliminate the roadblocks to negotiation and settlement, or simply better equip the opposition to defend the claim, without a commensurate benefit to the claimant. Generally, but not always, a sound, well-documented, and well-prepared claim should be able to withstand and be improved through feedback from the opposition's scrutiny. Moreover, even if the judgment is made that an extensive claim document should not be submitted, that conclusion does not necessarily mean that a claim document should not be prepared for internal use to organize the claim and prepare for whatever proceeding may follow. Of course, if formal claim submission is mandated by the contract, such a requirement should be followed, although the extent of the submission may vary.

[C]   Get Expert Legal and Technical Advice Early

Construction claims often require the assistance of experts to help solve problems and to assemble and analyze the facts. Prompt and cost-effective claim preparation may involve calling upon attorneys experienced with construction claims and other technical experts at an early stage. Of course, the use of outside assistance will depend on the size and complexity of the claim, but in most claims, such early involvement will facilitate prompt resolution or better preparation for trial and will be worth the investment. Skimping on experienced and qualified legal and technical support for a claim can prove very costly in the long run. Unfortunately, a legitimate claim that is initially supported by a flawed legal theory or technical analysis may be doomed.

The construction attorney who would ultimately present the claim to judge, jury, or arbitrators should be consulted to ensure that the claim and supporting documentation and evidence is being assembled and preserved in a manner consistent with favorable resolution of the claim in such a formal proceeding. However, this does not mean a construction attorney needs to take over the claim effort, and an attorney's involvement does not presuppose a resort to litigation or arbitration. On the contrary, it is simply another element of comprehensive preparation with the goal of contributing to the early resolution of claims.

By involving technical and accounting experts early, the claimant will likewise enhance its claim preparation efforts and leverage in negotiations or at trial. If a technical expert can participate during actual construction, when a claim is merely a probability, that option should be considered. At such an early stage, the expert may be able to suggest ways of mitigating damages or reducing the impact of an injurious condition. The expert may also be able to recommend methods of preserving evidence and of creating demonstrative evidence for use during negotiation, arbitration, or trial. Further, testimony based on first-hand observation of the construction will generally be more credible and persuasive than testimony based solely on second-hand input. If a claim merits prosecution, it also merits the best and most qualified technical expert in that subject who is available.

[D]   Use Demonstrative Evidence

Demonstrative evidence has the special advantage of presenting abstract, complicated, and extensive facts with pictures, clarifying oral testimony or documentary narrative in concrete terms. In addition, demonstrative evidence can spark interest and avoids the tedium of a relentless one-dimensional recitation of facts. The simple clarity demonstrative evidence provides is particularly effective in large, highly technical, complex construction claims. However, the utility of demonstrative evidence should not be overlooked in smaller, more straightforward disputes.

Demonstrative evidence ranges from photographs and videos to charts summarizing facts or making comparisons, such as a chart comparing as-planned manpower to as-built manpower in order to depict an overrun graphically. Charts and graphs are often used in connection with scheduling presentations, again usually comparing the as-planned schedule to the as-built schedule, with a focus on those problems creating delays. By displaying this information in an attractive visual format, in addition to written and oral presentations, the claim can be advanced in a more compelling and persuasive manner. The goal of the demonstrative presentation is lost if it is unclear, confusing, and not supported by facts.

Discussions regarding the importance and usefulness of demonstrative evidence and its persuasiveness generally can be found in trial advocacy materials. But there is no need to hold such a powerful and effective tool in reserve until trial. Demonstrative evidence should be developed and used to simplify the change order claim and persuade the other side as soon as possible.

[E]   Alternative Dispute Resolution as a Means of Avoiding Litigation

Alternative dispute resolution (ADR) is a new name for an old game. The "alternative" sought in ADR is to litigation. Negotiation has always been an alternative to litigation and it remains the primary vehicle for solving disputes. Many ADR techniques are merely forms of structured negotiation. In most other industries, arbitration is considered ADR, but in construction, it seems arbitration has acquired many of the negative aspects of litigation. Consequently, arbitration is not included in this discussion of ADR.[15]

First and foremost, ADR procedures aim at yielding settlements to avoid the costs and delays of litigation. ADR procedures may offer the additional affirmative benefit of avoiding the acrimony of purely adversarial proceedings. The hostility

---

[15] *See, e.g.*, T. Stipanowich, *Beyond Arbitration: Innovation and Evolution in the United States Construction Industry*, 31 Wake Forest L. Rev. 65 (1996).

litigation generates not only may undermine settlement efforts, but can damage important ongoing business relationships. Some ADR procedures can also offer greater opportunities to have very technical issues resolved on a purely technical basis by someone with knowledge and experience in a specialized field.

ADR procedures are generally flexible and allow participants to apply their own creativity in designing a procedure most suitable to their particular situation and dispute. Although several specific procedures have been developed within the last decade or so, in many respects ADR is little more than structured negotiation. The process is voluntary, so the parties are free to make their own rules. They can determine how much of the resolution process they want to control and how much they want to yield to a third party. Thus, the range can go from informal negotiation between management representatives all the way to a formal, adversary arbitration resulting in a binding award by an arbitrator.

The voluntary and consensual aspects of ADR procedures, and the extent to which they put the participant in control, are perhaps the most important ingredients of ADR's success. ADR procedures such as mini-trials and mediation require the active involvement of the parties themselves as key decision-makers and not merely as witnesses. The principals are required to confront the dispute and deal with the problems directly.

The participants' freedom to create and label their own procedures makes it difficult to apply hard-and-fast definitions to specific types of ADR. Some general working definitions of the more common procedures follow.

[1] Dispute Review Boards

Dispute review boards (DRBs) provide a structure and procedure for large projects to facilitate prompt resolution of disputes. The DRB is typically composed of three technical experts who have the opportunity to observe the construction first-hand. There are three principal benefits associated with DRBs: early attention to problems arising during contract performance; prevention and resolution of disputes before they grow into larger problems; and minimal costs compared to litigation.[16]

Although most documented use of DRBs is on large civil work projects, they can be employed on virtually any type of project. As a practical matter, a formal DRB procedure may be restricted to larger jobs, but the principles associated with DRBs and the use of technical experts to resolve disputes early and on the site should not be overlooked on any project, regardless of size.[17]

---

[16] *See* Frank Carr, Robert A. Rubin & Robert J. Smith, "Dispute Review Boards," 1992 Construction Law Update 112 (O. Currie & N. Sweeney eds., Aspen Publishers, Inc. 1992 (first published by John Wiley & Sons)).

[17] *See, e.g.*, Dispute Resolution Board Foundation Practices and Procedures Manual; Libbey, *Note & Comment: Working Together While "Waltzing in a Mine Field": Successful Government Construction Contract Dispute Resolution With Partnering and Dispute Review Boards*, 15 Ohio St. J. on Disp. Resol. 825 (2000).

[2] Mediation

Mediation basically involves introducing a neutral third party into the negotiations to assist the parties in arriving at their own solution to the dispute. The process is generally very informal and may involve little more than the mediator shuttling back and forth between the parties. The mediator may also hear evidence and arguments and otherwise be educated on the merits of the dispute and thereby be better able to advise the parties. However, a mediator renders no decision. Mediators may have technical expertise in the particular field of the dispute, but specialized skill and training in mediation and negotiation is generally deemed more important than technical background.[18]

[3] Mini-Trial

Mini-trials require each side to present a summary of its case to the party representatives with settlement authority but who were not involved in the transactions giving rise to the dispute. The presentation may be a soliloquy by an attorney or management representative, involve witnesses and experts, or combine those approaches with documentary and graphic evidence. After the presentations, which generally last less than two days, the party representatives engage in negotiations in an attempt to settle. Frequently, a neutral third party also sits in on the presentations. Depending on the format agreed upon in advance, the third party may act as a mediator to aid the negotiations or may render a nonbinding opinion on the dispute if initial efforts to settle fail.[19]

[4] Summary Jury Trial

A summary jury trial is similar in format to a mini-trial, but it generally more closely resembles a formal trial. Greater reliance is placed on attorneys and the observance of rules of evidence. The presentations are made before a mock jury of six and presided over by a judge. The jury renders an advisory verdict that then is supposed to serve as the basis of negotiations, usually with the aid of the presiding judge.[20]

[5] Settlement Judge

A settlement judge is a judge of the same court in which the litigation is pending but is not presiding over the case and will have no involvement in its

---

[18] *See* Michael B. Shane & Charles A. Cooper, "Mediation Disclosed: The View of the Mediator," 1995 Construction Law Update 183 (O. Currie & N. Sweeney eds., Aspen Publishers, Inc. 1995 (first published by John Wiley & Sons)).

[19] *See, e.g.,* Reba Page & Frederick J. Lees, *Roles of Participants in the Mini-Trial*, 18 Pub. Cont. L.J. 54 (1988).

[20] *See, e.g.,* T. Cook, *The Summary Jury Trial: A Summary of Issues in Dispute Resolution*, 1993 J. Disp. Resol. 359 (1993).

outcome. The settlement judge works with the parties like a mediator, but often takes a more aggressive approach than a mediator and can provide valuable insight and practical evaluations of the likely outcome of the case.[21]

[6]   ADR: A Fixture with Momentum

ADR is now a fixture in the construction industry and continues to gain in popularity. Agencies of the federal government have been very active in encouraging ADR. The U.S. Army Corps of Engineers, Office of Chief Counsel, has been very active in encouraging and implementing the use of ADR techniques in the Corps's extensive construction programs and in publicizing their lessons learned.[22] The Corps stresses training and indoctrination in ADR procedure and the use of those procedures at the earliest possible time. The opportunity to employ ADR does not end when litigation begins. On the contrary, many states and the federal government encourage ADR in an effort to ease crowded court dockets. The primary forums for litigating construction claims against the federal government, the Armed Services Court of Appeals and the U.S. Court of Federal Claims, have detailed ADR rules allowing and encouraging the parties to choose from a broad range of procedures to facilitate settlement.[23]

There is certainly much to be gained from the attention ADR has garnered as a special, particular type of conflict resolution. Still, ADR concepts should not be viewed as too specialized or complicated to be applied in the ordinary course of business. Although the concepts behind ADR—primarily the advantage of prompt resolution of disputes—should be practiced on a daily basis, complicated ADR procedures should not displace or become a substitute for informal and less structured negotiations that have for years sufficed to resolve most disputes. ADR procedures should remain an alternative, to be applied when more traditional approaches to settlement fail, and not be imposed as a substitute for litigation, arbitration, or whatever administrative process would lead to the final and formal adjudication of a claim. Not all parties or claims are amenable to settlement, and the rights of parties to their day in court must be preserved.

§ 14.09   ISSUES AFFECTING SUBCONTRACTORS

Much of the work on any given project is actually performed by subcontractors, not the general contractor who is in direct contractual privity with the owner.

---

[21] *See, e.g.*, R. Page & W. Jockish, *The Corps of Engineers Board of Contract Appeals Use of Alternative Dispute Resolution*, 24 Pub. Cont. L.J. 453 (1995).

[22] *See, e.g.*, Edelman & Carr, *The Mini-trial: An Alternative Dispute Resolution Procedure*, 42 Arb. J. 7 (Mar. 1987).

[23] *See* Carol N. Park-Conroy, "ADR in Federal Construction Contract Disputes: A Neutral Perspective," 2003 Construction Law Update 1 (N. Sweeney ed., Aspen Publishers, Inc. 2003). *See also* ASBCA "Notice Regarding Alternative Methods of Dispute Resolution," available at <http://www.adr.af.mil/iadrwg/asbcanot.html> (2005).

Consequently, most change order claims involve not only the owner and general contractor, but also one or more subcontractors. The inclusion of additional parties adds another link in the chain of contractual privity, increasing the complexity of presenting and resolving change order claims.

The burden and risk of this increased complexity generally falls on the general contractor. As a result, the general contractor must step gingerly, often walking a narrow line between the competing and generally inconsistent interests of the owner and subcontractor. If the general contractor unequivocally commits to the subcontractor's position that a change order is required, it may have difficulty avoiding liability to the subcontractor if the owner rejects the change order claim. Conversely, if the general contractor initially takes an adamant position against a subcontractor's change order request, persuading the owner to agree to the change order will be difficult even if the general contractor subsequently changes its position.

Generally, neither the owner nor the subcontractor is confronted with this risk of having to fight an issue on two fronts, and they may be able to use that risk as leverage in their respective dealings with the general contractor. Nonetheless, long before any change order issues arise, all the parties have an interest in establishing, or at least understanding, a consistent contractual and procedural framework for dealing with change orders on all levels.

[A]   Key Subcontract Clauses Relating to Change Orders

Through subcontracting, the general contractor seeks to spread the risks of project performance. The subcontract preparation phase requires extreme caution and diligence to ensure that the subcontract does not create greater risks by leaving dangerous gaps as the work is parceled out. The general contractor must therefore seek consistency between the obligations it assumes toward the owner in the prime contract and the obligations the subcontractor adopts in the subcontract. The general contractor must recognize the need to "flow down" to subcontractors the legal obligations owed to the owner, as well as the technical scope of work. In certain respects, the owner shares this goal of integrated allocation of risks and responsibility with the general contractor because it contributes to the smooth completion of the project, including the ability to implement changes in the work as need may dictate.

The subcontractor likewise wants access, albeit indirectly through the general contractor, to the change order process and payment from the owner. The entire subcontract and subcontract administration technique affects how this arrangement is ultimately implemented. The remainder of this section discusses some of the most crucial subcontract clauses.

[1]   Flow-Down Clause

A general flow-down clause in the subcontract is the critical starting point for bringing the subcontractor into the change order process. A flow-down clause contractually ties the subcontractor to the general contractor in the same manner or scope as the contractor is bound to the owner. The absence of such a clause can leave the general contractor exposed to additional liability because it renders the general contractor unable to demand of the subcontractor the performance that the owner can demand of the general contractor. In return for the protection created in the flow-down clause, the general contractor generally gives the subcontractor the same rights to claims, protest, and notice as the general contractor may have against the owner. In other words, the rights and duties flow both ways—upward to the general contractor, as well as downward to the subcontractor. This mutual obligation tends to keep the general contractor and subcontractor on even ground despite the lack of contractual privity between the owner and the subcontractor.

While a general flow-down clause is imperative, some of the issues, rights, and obligations relating to the change order process are so crucial that they should be addressed in separate subcontract language. These additional sections should be drafted with an eye toward consistency with the prime contract.

For example, in *L&B Construction Co. v. Ragan Enterprises, Inc.*,[24] the Georgia Supreme Court recognized and confirmed that flow-down clauses effectively impose on a subcontractor the incorporated duties as set forth in the general contract. The parties in L&B Construction did not dispute that the general contractor's contract agreement with the project owner contained an effective no-damages-for-delay clause. The issue was whether a flow-down clause could be construed to incorporate the no-damages-for-delay clause in the subcontract. Noting that Georgia law has long recognized the legitimacy of flow-down clauses as a technique to impose on a subcontractor some or all of the contractor's obligations to the owner, the Georgia Supreme Court stated that when a flow-down clause is used in a subcontract, no additional language is needed to impose such duties on the subcontractor. The court held that because the general contractor protected the owner from an action for delay damages, it necessarily followed that the subcontract afforded the general contractor the same protection from the subcontractor.

Another common pitfall occurs where the general contractor neglects to flow applicable Federal Acquisition Regulation clauses and other requirements down to the supplier when placing its order for materials or services for government contract work. Given the broad definitions of "subcontractor" used by the government in certain contexts, FAR clauses generally applicable to subcontractors and suppliers may also apply to a subcontractor or supplier notwithstanding the fact that these requirements are not expressly included in the subcontract or supply contract.[25] As a result, the supplier or subcontractor may not even be aware that its materials or performance will be used in the performance of a government contract. When a statute or executive order applies to subcontracts by their terms, the

---

[24] 267 Ga. 809, 482 S.E.2d 279 (Ga. 1997).

[25] *See, e.g.,* F. Baltz & J. Morrissey, *Do You Know if You Are a Government Contractor?: FAR Clauses Incorporated into Subcontracts Without Reference*, 34 Procurement Law. 36 (No. 4, Summer 1999).

requirements of the particular statute or executive order may be considered to be included in the subcontract as a matter of law, even though the general contractor has not specifically "flowed down" a FAR clause to its subcontractor. By contrast, when a FAR clause reflects a procurement objective rather than a statutory or executive order requirement, a court is less likely to declare that such a clause is included in a subcontract as a matter of law.

[2] Subcontract Scope of Work

Every subcontract must clearly and definitively define the scope of work to be performed by the subcontractor, but realistically, the subcontractor's work can never be completely defined. To compensate for this reality, the subcontract should also refer to all contract documents between the owner and the general contractor. When drafting a subcontract, general contractors should not rely exclusively on a general incorporation by reference with respect to description of bid items in the general contract, because the description may be too broad and can lead to later disputes between the general contractor and the subcontractor. The subcontract should contain a very explicit description of the subcontractor's duties. However, this description should be inclusive rather than exclusive, because one must be careful not to exclude items that could have otherwise been included by implication (that is, customary within the industry). Therefore, any listing of work items should include the proviso "including, but not limited to . . . ."

[3] Changes Clause and the Duty to Proceed

In addition to the general flow-down clause, it is advisable to address specifically the general contractor's right to implement changes in the subcontractor's work, whether the changes are initiated by the owner or the general contractor. It is crucial that such a provision specify that in the case of a dispute, the work will proceed while the dispute is being resolved.

The duty to proceed is essential. Without it, the right to require changes would be rendered hollow. The subcontractor could simply contend that there is some change or condition justifying extra time and money that must be agreed upon in advance. Without the duty to proceed, the subcontractor could attempt to stop the work or refuse to man the job each time a disagreement arises.

[4] Disputes Procedures

As noted above, subcontracts should also specifically address the dispute procedures to be followed when the general contractor and subcontractor cannot agree on change order claims. Generally, the general contractor should tie the subcontractor to the same remedies and disputes procedures as those in the prime contract with the owner, whether in court, arbitration, or an administrative disputes process. This approach typically benefits the general contractor because the rights of the subcontractor and owner can be resolved in the same forum, avoiding the potential for inconsistent results when the general contractor must resolve its dispute with the subcontractor elsewhere.

The construction industry favors arbitration as a forum for dispute resolution; many prime contracts and subcontracts require that the parties arbitrate disputes. Therefore, the general contractor should reserve the right in its subcontracts to consolidate any subcontract arbitration proceeding with other ongoing arbitrations between it and other subcontractors or the owner. Without such a right to consolidate, the general contractor is exposed to the risk of inconsistent results. However, the perceived advantage of arbitrating subcontract disputes may be lost if the general contractor is limited to litigating with the owner. A solution might be for the subcontract to provide for arbitration with subcontractors, at the general contractor's option. The contractor would then have the flexibility to choose the most advantageous forum for each dispute as it arises. Be aware, though, that the enforceability of such one-sided arbitration agreements is open to question.[26]

Generally, the courts will follow the dispute resolution procedure outlined in the contract, whether it is explicitly stated or incorporated by reference. For example, in *Lord & Son Construction, Inc. v. Roberts Electrical Contractors*,[27] a subcontractor sued the general contractor to recover additional expenses and damages attributable to delays in the project. In response, the general contractor sought to compel arbitration, arguing that the subcontract incorporated the terms of the general contract, which required that controversies be settled by arbitration. The court held that the incorporation by reference was enforceable, and the subcontractor was forced to comply with the provision requiring that all disputes be resolved by arbitration.

Not all flow-down or incorporation-by-reference clauses will automatically be deemed sufficient to incorporate an arbitration provision. For example, in *St. Augustine Pools, Inc. v. James M. Barker, Inc.*,[28] the court held that language in a subcontract that made the subcontract "subject to the general contract" was not sufficient to incorporate an arbitration provision.[29]

The construction industry also embraces less formal procedures designed to avoid or resolve disagreements quickly before they become full-blown disputes, such as partnering and mediation. For example, the 1997 edition of the *General*

---

[26] *See* W.L. Jordan & Co. v. Blythe Indus., Inc., 702 F. Supp. 282 (N.D. Ga. 1988) (enforcing the prime contractor's right under the Federal Arbitration Act unilaterally to opt in or out of arbitration). *See also* Willis Flooring, Inc. v. Howard S. Lease Constr. Co. & Assocs., 656 P.2d 1184 (Alaska 1983) (upholding unilateral arbitration provision). *But see* Stevens/Leinweber/Sullens, Inc. v. Holm Dev. & Mgmt., 795 P.2d 1308 (Ariz. Ct. App. 1990) (such clause is unenforceable under Arizona law as "so grossly inequitable that it runs counter to the philosophy of encouraging arbitration"); Iwen v. U.S. West Direct, 293 Mont. 512, 977 P.2d 989 (1999) (unilateral arbitration clause struck down); R.W. Roberts Constr. Co. v. St. Johns River Water Mgmt. Dist. for Use & Benefit of McDonald Elec., 423 So. 2d 630 (Fla. Dist. Ct. App. 5th Dist. 1982) (same).

[27] 624 So. 2d 376 (Fla. Dist. Ct. App. 1993).

[28] 687 So. 2d 957 (Fla. Dist. Ct. App. 5th Dist. 1997).

[29] *See also* Burgess Constr. Co. v. M. Morrin & Son Co., 526 F.2d 108 (10th Cir. 1975).

Conditions of the Contract for Construction, AIA Document A201, added language in Subparagraph 4.5.1 that requires mediation as a condition precedent to arbitration in disputes other than those involving aesthetic effect. Even if the prime contract does not include mediation or partnering provisions, the general contractor is not necessarily precluded from implementing them in his subcontracts, provided that it does not conflict with the general contractor's ability to flow down and enforce the formal disputes procedure from the prime contract.

Most flow-down clauses on federal government contracts require subcontractors to pursue claims involving the government before the appropriate board of contract appeals. However, subcontractors have successfully argued that they should be allowed to arbitrate rather than proceed before the board of contract appeals, where the basis of the subcontractor's claim did not involve the conduct or ultimate liability of the owner.

In *NavCom Defense Electronics, Inc. v. Ball Corp.*,[30] a subcontractor requested arbitration of its claim for the cost of redesigning antennas that failed the general contractor's inspection criteria, claiming that the criteria imposed by the general contractor were more rigorous than the government's specifications required. The general contractor submitted the subcontractor's claim to the contracting officer, who denied the claim. The general contractor then attempted to stay the subcontractor's arbitration demand and force the subcontractor to pursue its claim before the board of contract appeals. The court concluded that the subcontractor's claim did not challenge the government's conduct or suggest that the government was responsible for the subcontractor's claim. Therefore, the claim was not subject to the Contract Disputes Act, and the Act did not require the subcontractor to proceed before the board of contract appeals.

Similarly, in *Finegold, Alexander & Associates, Inc. v. Setty & Associates, Ltd.*,[31] the court ruled that a subcontractor was entitled to arbitrate its claim against a general contractor on a public contract. The court found that the subcontractor's claim did not "involve" the government.

The case of *BAE Automated Systems, Inc. v. Morse Diesel International, Inc.*[32] provides a contrasting view from the private sector. In that matter, the project owner and general contractor entered into a contract that established that disputes would be sent to a three-member dispute resolution board, with the owner, contractor, and architect each designating one member. The general contractor entered into a subcontract that incorporated the dispute resolution process as set forth in the prime contract. After the subcontractor substantially completed his contractual obligations, he submitted a claim for increased costs and the contractor advised him that the claim should be submitted to the board. The subcontractor disagreed, arguing that the dispute resolution process applied only to claims that were attributable to the owner's conduct, and not to claims that the subcontractor had against the general contractor. The court disagreed, concluding that

---

[30] 92 F.3d 877 (9th Cir. 1996).
[31] 81 F.3d 206 (D.C. Cir. 1996).
[32] 2001 U.S. Dist. LEXIS 6682 (S.D.N.Y. 2001).

the subcontract unambiguously incorporated the dispute resolution procedure set forth in the prime contract and clearly required the subcontractor to pursue and exhaust that remedy before commencing any other action. While this result may seem to be in sharp contrast with the two proceeding cases, it follows the policy that courts will encourage parties to participate in ADR before resorting to litigation.

The *BAE Automated Systems, Inc.* case illustrates that the better practice in drafting contracts that will include flow-down clauses is to include a specific dispute resolution provision in the subcontract. From the general contractor's perspective, the subcontract should include an option that allows it to elect either arbitration or litigation, allowing the most effective management of the flow-through of liability if the owner files a claim. Regardless of which dispute procedure is actually specified in the subcontract, the subcontractor needs to pursue that remedy diligently, exhaust all avenues of protest outlined in the subcontract, and prepare to be bound by the determination of its claims or rights under the specified dispute procedure.

[B] Pay-When-Paid Clause

[1] Obligations

Almost inevitably, disputes arise between general contractors and subcontractors centering around the contractor's obligation to make progress payments or pay retainage to the subcontractor before the contractor has received the corresponding payment from the owner. Many general contractors include a "pay-when-paid" or "pay-if-paid" clause in their subcontracts, which expressly makes the general contractor's payment obligation to the subcontractor contingent on the general contractor's receipt of payment from the owner.

All general contractors would prefer that the courts read a "pay-when-paid" clause as a condition precedent. However, courts generally do not favor conditions precedent in a contract and will not give them effect unless the condition is established by clear and unequivocal language.

Courts in a few states hold that pay-when-paid clauses create a condition precedent, so that the general contractor's obligation to pay the subcontractor for work performed is contingent on the general contractor receiving payment from the owner.[33] Nonetheless, a general contractor should be cautious in relying on general pay-when-paid language as an absolute defense to subcontractor claims, because the court may find that the condition has been fulfilled, even though the contractor has not been paid for that particular purchase order. For example, in *Urban Masonry Corp. v. N&N Contractors, Inc.*,[34] the court held that the general

---

[33] *See* Galloway Corp. v. S.B. Ballard Constr. Co., 250 Va. 493, 464 S.E.2d 249 (1995); Berkel & Co. Contractors v. Christman Co., 533 N.W.2d 838 (Mich. Ct. App. 1995).

[34] 676 A.2d 26 (D.C. 1996).

contractor's payment obligation was triggered by its entering into a "walk away" settlement with the owner.

Courts in most states have refused to accept lack of payment from the owner as an absolute defense to a subcontractor's demand for payment. In these states, the pay-when-paid clause is interpreted to permit the general contractor to delay payment to the subcontractor temporarily under the standard that payment within a reasonable period of time is acceptable.[35] For example, in *Main Electric, Ltd. v. Printz Services Corp.*,[36] the Supreme Court of Colorado determined that a payment clause did not expressly reflect the parties' intent to shift the risk of the owner's nonpayment from the general contractor to the subcontractor so as to qualify as a condition precedent and eliminate the general contractor's obligation to pay the subcontractor eventually.

Some states have gone even further, holding that pay-when-paid clauses are unenforceable. Both California and New York courts have held that pay-if-paid clauses are unenforceable as contrary to public policy.[37] Other states, such as Illinois, North Carolina, and Wisconsin, have declared pay-if-paid clauses void and unenforceable by statute. Maryland and Missouri have statutes that may affect the enforcement of these clauses in the lien situation. Texas has enacted a Trust Fund Statute that imposes personal liability on general contractors who wrongfully retain or divert funds received from the owner and owed to subcontractors.[38] As the law varies from state to state and this issue is frequently addressed in case law and statutes, it is important always to consult the current state law controlling a particular subcontract.

Because courts generally prefer not to enforce pay-when-paid clauses, a general contractor may want to consider adding language to the subcontractor form indicating that the pay-when-paid clause is a specific part of the bargain. The general contractor may also consider reciting separate consideration for the pay-when-paid clause. If the general contractor wants the benefit of the pay-when-paid clause to apply also to any payment bond surety, it should tie the language of the pay-when-paid clause to the surety's obligation under the payment bond. In that case, the payment bond surety may not have the obligation to pay a subcontractor until after the surety collects—an important consideration for general contractors because they often have the obligation to reimburse the payment bond surety. As most bonds are preprinted forms, special steps are required to include a pay-when-paid clause.

A general contractor must also carefully draft and adhere to its payment provision when there is a concern about a subcontractor's imminent default. Lack of proper payment can provide the basis for a subcontractor's default to be

---

[35] *See generally* B.C. Hart, Peter C. Hallis & Vincent J. Fahnlander, "Claims for Payment," Construction Subcontracting: A Legal Guide for Industry Professionals (O. Currie, N. Sweeney & R. Hafer eds., John Wiley & Sons 1990); *see also* 1 Construction Law § 3.8 (2004); *id.* § 4.3.

[36] 980 P.2d 522 (Colo. 1999).

[37] *See* William R. Clarke Corp. v. Safeco Ins. Co., 938 P.2d 372 (Cal. 1997); West-Fair Elec. v. Aetna Cas. & Sur. Co., 661 N.E.2d 967 (N.Y. 1995).

[38] Tex. Prop. Code §§ 162.001 *et seq.* (1995).

overturned and labeled a material breach of contract by the general contractor. A general contractor cannot demand that the subcontractor perform without being paid. When proper payment is denied, the general contractor may be precluded from recovering its losses and may be liable to the subcontractor for its wrongful action. The general contractor must protect itself by adhering to all the technical notice provisions and procedures for withholding funds, just as the subcontractor must adhere to all the technical prerequisites to receiving payment.[39]

Of course, a subcontractor may have different negotiating goals. If the pay-when-paid clause cannot be negotiated out of the contract, a subcontractor may try to make the language as general and generic as possible. The subcontractor will try to avoid the impression that the cost of the pay-when-paid clause has been included in the general contractor's price. If the general contractor has tied the payment bond to the pay-when-paid clause, the subcontractor may want to increase its price to account for the increased risk.

[2] Change Order Requests Under Pay-When-Paid Clauses

Even with all the appropriate subcontract clauses in place, general contractors must recognize that there are limits on cost burdens that can be placed on a subcontractor in proceeding with disputed change work. Those limits are not clearly defined; they are dependent on the circumstances and are ultimately a matter of reasonableness and fairness. Disputed extra work valued at $40,000 may be of little consequence to the general contractor on a $5 million project, and clearly be subject to the duty to proceed. If that same $40,000 in disputed extra work is then imposed by the general contractor on a painting subcontractor whose original subcontract was a mere $30,000, it is an entirely different situation, and the general contractor's ability to pass through and enforce the duty to proceed without immediate payment to the subcontractor is much less clear.

If the work that is the subject of a claim is only additional effort needed to accomplish satisfactory performance of the original contract objective, no basis exists to argue that the existing contract terms should not control the performance and acceptance of that work. However, if the work is extra work not originally covered or contemplated by the contract, the possibility arises of a whole new set of contractual terms and obligations. For example, in *Valley Steel Construction Inc. v. Addison Fabricators, Inc.*,[40] a contractor withheld payment to a subcontractor for an executed change order under a pay-when-paid clause because the owner had not paid the contractor. The court held that the change order was a subsequent agreement separate from the original contract, constituting an unconditional promise to pay the subcontractor, and thus was not subject to the pay-when-paid clause.

If it is the intent of the parties that payment for extra work authorized by change order be conditioned upon payment by the owner to the contractor for the

---

[39] Dickerson Florida, Inc. v. McPeek, 65 So. 2d 186 (Fla. Dist. Ct. App. 1995).
[40] 658 So. 2d 352 (Ala. 1994).

extra work, such intention must be set forth clearly and unambiguously in either the contract (for example, in the changes clause) or in the change order itself. The same principles of drafting that govern contingent payment clauses apply to change order payment provisions.

[C]   Order of Precedence Language

A general contractor will not typically rely on the flow-down of the terms of the prime contract to dictate all aspects of its relations with the subcontractor. A general contractor wants to include additional subcontract terms necessary to effectuate proper subcontract administration and to take advantage of any leverage the general contractor maintains over the subcontractor. In addition, most general contractors typically employ a subcontract form that fits into their established internal procedures and with which their personnel are familiar. These circumstances frequently add up to a subcontract that covers at least some and perhaps many of the same issues addressed in the prime contract, which have flowed down into the subcontract. The potential for conflicts and confusion must be recognized and addressed.

Typically, conflicts between the terms of the subcontract and the prime contract are resolved by including language in the general flow-down clause so that if such conflicts arise, the terms of the subcontract govern. Broad language may be a good starting point, but it should not be relied upon exclusively. Instead, prior to executing subcontracts, the general contractor should carefully compare the general and supplementary conditions of the prime contract with the subcontract form, and determine whether it is more advantageous to rely on the subcontract term or the conflicting prime contract term in that particular situation. Without such scrutiny, the subcontractor may not be integrated into the change order process.

[D]   Administration of Subcontractors

The balancing act required of the general contractor in crafting its subcontracts must be maintained throughout the project in its dealings with the owner and subcontractors on owner-initiated changes. The general contractor must function as a conduit between the owner and subcontractors, passing down the owner's directives for extra work and forwarding to the owner any subcontractor notices and change order claims. Unless the general contractor is prepared to side with either the owner or the subcontractor in the case of disputed work, it should avoid being judgmental or editorializing as it passes directives and demands back and forth. Routine transmittals and cover letters should be employed that maintain the necessary flow of paperwork, fulfill prime contract notice requirements, and clearly define the issue or item of work, but that do not bind the general contractor to either the owner's or the subcontractor's position.

Maintaining this type of neutrality is often difficult. Ideally, when the outcome of the disagreement is in doubt, the general contractor should remain neutral throughout the dispute resolution process, viewing it as a matter of owner versus subcontractor. Understandably, however, the owner, the subcontractor, or both will not quietly allow the general contractor to remain on the sidelines as a disinterested party. The owner and/or the subcontractor frequently become frustrated and angry at the fence-sitting general contractor, insisting on the contractor's contractual obligation to support their respective positions and attempting to push the contractor into some action. The general contractor must constantly consider all the circumstances and apply sound business judgment to determine which way to proceed on a particular change order claim. In some instances, that judgment may be appropriately affected by considerations beyond the merits of the particular change in dispute, such as long-term relations with an owner or subcontractor, or the ability to trade off a change order claim against concessions on an unrelated issue.

Eventually, the contractor may have to abandon its neutrality and commit to one position. If the general contractor does not commit to the subcontractor's claim, the general contractor risks losing the financial resources of the owner. For example, in *FDIC v. Peabody, N.E., Inc.*,[41] the Connecticut Supreme Court limited the ability of a general contractor to pass through to the state a subcontractor claim when the general contractor had not admitted liability to the subcontractor. The court in Peabody stated that, unlike private-sector claims, suits against the state may not be based upon the contingent liability of a party who may become liable at some point in the future. Contingent liabilities do not constitute a disputed claim under a contract with the state, necessary for a suit against the state under the state's waiver of sovereign immunity. Otherwise, subcontractors effectively would be able to prosecute their claims against the state indirectly through general contractors, thus increasing the complexity and volume of litigation against the state.

Regardless of the position the general contractor may take on the merits of a subcontractor change order claim, the procedures and paperwork employed on the subcontractor level should be meticulously maintained and should mirror those employed between the owner and general contractor in form, scope, and status. The general contractor should be readily able to track individual owner-initiated changes down to specific subcontractor change orders or line items on change orders. The general contractor must implement this discipline and enforce it on its subcontractors, and avoid and discourage the tendency to be less formal and precise on the subcontractor level.

In fact, subcontractors should be required to present change order pricing in the same form in which the general contractor is required to present pricing to the owner, with discrete pricing for each change. This approach makes the subcontractor pricing easier to understand and review. It also allows the general contractor to attach and incorporate the subcontractor's proposal in its own proposal to the owner. Each subcontractor change order or directive should use the same language as the owner-initiated change or directive and expressly cross-reference and incorporate that original document by reference, with a copy provided to the

---

[41] 680 A.2d 1321 (Conn. 1996).

subcontractor. Accurately describing the scope of a change and keeping it consistent on each level of privity is essential. Likewise, any limitations, waivers, or reservations incorporated into the owner's change or directive should be expressly passed through and included in the written communication with the subcontractor. Finally, it is best to make the finalization and execution of an owner change order the administrative predicate to issuing the reciprocal subcontractor change order. These measures provide consistency and maintain the administration of subcontractor change orders as a fully integrated component of the owner change order process.

§ 14.10   LIQUIDATING AGREEMENTS

[A]   General Principles

A "liquidating agreement" is a type of settlement agreement wherein the contracting parties settle the dispute between them (i.e., "liquidate") and agree to pass through some or all of the claims to a third party. In the construction setting, liquidation agreements are generally executed between the general contractor and one or more of its subcontractors in order to pass claims through to the project owner.[42]

Under traditional contract principles, subcontractors are not permitted to maintain an action against a project owner due to lack of contractual privity. The pass-through process is the standard method through which such claims are handled. Specifically, subcontractor pass-through claims evolved because federal law and the law of many states provide that subcontractors performing under public contracts do not possess standing to sue a government entity without first establishing privity of contract.

The federal law regarding these types of claims is known as the *Severin* doctrine, named for the case of the same name.[43] According to this doctrine, a subcontractor can pursue a claim against the owner in the general contractor's name only if the subcontractor is actually damaged. The fact that a subcontractor incurs additional costs is not sufficient to support a claim against the owner. In these circumstances, the general contractor and subcontractor often execute a liquidation agreement to avoid the *Severin* doctrine, thereby permitting prosecution of the subcontractor's claim against the owner.

---

[42] *See* Michael K. Love & Carl T. Hahn, "Pass-Through Claims, Flow Down Clauses and Subcontractor Choice of Law Issues," 1994 Construction Law Update (O. Currie & N. Sweeney eds., Aspen Publishers, Inc. 1994 (first published by John Wiley & Sons)).

[43] *See* Severin v. United States, 99 Ct. Cl. 435 (1943), *cert. denied*, 322 U.S. 733 (1944) (subcontractor pass-through claim denied on the grounds that exculpatory provision relieved general contractor of liability to subcontractor; the subcontractor therefore possessed no claim to pass on to the government). *See also* United States v. Blair, 321 U.S. 730 (1944) (articulating public policy rationale for allowing pass-through claims).

Liquidating agreements limit the general contractor's liability for owner-caused subcontractor claims. A standard liquidation agreement possesses three basic elements:

1. The imposition of liability upon the general contractor for the subcontractor's increased costs, thereby providing the general contractor with a basis for legal action against the owner;

2. A liquidation of liability in the amount of the general contractor's recovery against the owner; and

3. A provision that provides for the "pass-through" of that recovery to the subcontractor.[44]

In addition to saving costs incurred by the contractor when presenting the subcontractor's claim, a liquidation agreement also overcomes the subcontractor's inability to present its claim to the owner due to lack of contractual privity. Thus, the contractor confesses liability to the subcontractor for owner-caused changes or delays, the subcontractor, as a practical matter, releases the contractor from all other liability, the subcontractor presents its claim to the owner, and the subcontractor accepts whatever additional costs are recovered from the owner.

[B] Pass-Through Claims: Federal and State Recognition

In breach of contract actions against the federal government, general contractors have long been permitted to present subcontractors' claims on a pass-through basis against the government, even though the no-privity rule traditionally barred subcontractors from recovering directly against the government.[45] As long as the general contractor remains liable to the subcontractor for the subcontractor's damages, the general contractor will be permitted to bring an action against the government for the subcontractor's damages.[46]

A number of states also permit pass-through claims in cases involving state government entities.[47] In contrast, at least five states have not allowed a

---

[44] *See* Bovis Lend Lease LMB Inc. v. GCT Venture, Inc., 728 N.Y.S.2d 25, 27, 285 A.D.2d 68 (2001). *See also* Interstate Contracting Corp. v. City of Dallas, Tex., 320 F.3d 539 (5th Cir. 2003) (extensive discussion of liquidation agreements).

[45] *See, e.g.,* Interstate Contracting Corp. v. City of Dallas, Tex., 320 F.3d 539 (5th Cir. 2003); J.L. Simmons Co. v. United States, 158 Ct. Cl. 393, 304 F.2d 886, 888 (1962) (a prime contractor suffers actual damages if it has reimbursed its subcontractor for the subcontractor's damages, or if the prime contractor remains liable for such reimbursement in the future).

[46] *See* E.R. Mitchell Constr. Co. v. Danzig, 175 F.3d 1369 (Fed. Cir. 1999); W.G. Yates & Sons Constr. Co. v. Secretary of Army, 192 F.3d 987 (Fed. Cir. 1999).

[47] *See* Interstate Contracting Corp. v. City of Dallas, Tex., 320 F.3d 539 (5th Cir. 2003). *See also* Frank Coluccio Constr. Co. v. City of Springfield, 779 S.W.2d 550, 551-52 (Mo. 1989) (en banc); St. Paul Dredging Co. v. State, 107 N.W.2d 717, 724 (Minn. 1961); Roof-Techs Int'l, Inc. v. Kansas, 57 P.3d 538, 550-53 (Kan. Ct. App. 2002); Metric Constructors, Inc. v. Hawker Siddeley Power Eng'g, Inc., 468 S.E.2d 435, 438-39 (N.C. Ct. App. 1996); Board of County Comm'rs v. Cam Constr. Co.,

pass-through claim under certain circumstances.[48] Only Connecticut expressly rejects pass-through claims.[49]

[C]   Establishment of Pass-Through Claim and Related Considerations

As noted above, so long as the contractor is liable to the subcontractor for claims, the contractor is generally permitted to present the subcontractor's claims to the owner.[50] Stated differently, if the prime contractor is liable to the subcontractor for damages sustained by the subcontractor, the prime contractor itself is injured by the acts of the government and therefore has standing to sue the government in a pass-through suit on behalf of its subcontractor.[51] If the government seeks dismissal of the prime contractor's pass-through claim, it bears the burden of proof and must show that the prime contractor is not responsible for the costs incurred by the subcontractor.

The specific contours and requirements for pass-through claims vary from jurisdiction to jurisdiction. For example, some states permit pass-through claims only when there is a liquidating agreement in place that meets certain requirements.[52] Other states permit pass-through claims only when the prime contractor pleads the suit for the subcontractor and has an obligation to render the recovery to the subcontractor.

To collect on a subcontractor's claim from the owner, the contractor must show that some additional costs resulted from the owner's acts or omissions. This requirement is satisfied by the contractor establishing either that it has reimbursed the subcontractor for the subcontractor's additional performance costs or that the contractor remains liable for those costs. Liquidation agreements are therefore

---

480 A.2d 795 (Md. App. 1984); Kensington Corp. v. Michigan, 253 N.W.2d 781, 783 (Mich. Ct. App. 1977); Buckley & Co. v. New Jersey, 356 A.2d 56, 73-74 (N.J. Super. Ct. Law Div. 1975); D.A. Parrish & Sons v. County Sanitation Dist. No. 4, 344 P.2d 883, 888 (Cal. Dist. Ct. App. 1959); Schiavone Constr. Co. v. Triborough Bridge & Tunnel Auth., 619 N.Y.S.2d 117, 209 A.D.2d 598 (1994).

[48] *See, e.g.*, Board of Governors for Higher Educ. v. Infinity Constr. Servs., Inc., 795 A.2d 1127, 1129 (R.I. 2002); Farrell Constr. Co. v. Jefferson Parish, 693 F. Supp. 490, 498 (E.D. La. 1988); Department of Transp. v. Claussen Paving Co., 273 S.E.2d 161, 164 (Ga. 1980); Barry, Bette & Led Duke, Inc. v. New York, 669 N.Y.S.2d 741, 743, 240 A.D.2d 54 (1998); APAC-Carolina, Inc. v. Greensboro-High Point Airport Auth., 431 S.E.2d 508, 511-12 (N.C. Ct. App. 1993).

[49] *See* FDIC v. Peabody, N.E., Inc., 239 Conn. 93, 680 A.2d (1996) (applying sovereign immunity to reject pass-through claims unless the contractor admits liability and impleads the state on claims filed by the subcontractor against the contractor); Wexler Constr. Co. v. Housing Auth. of Norwich, 149 Conn. 602, 183 A.2d 262 (1962) (rejecting pass-through claims on the ground that a subcontractor could recover from the owner directly under a theory of implied contract).

[50] *See, e.g.*, W.G. Yates & Sons Constr. Co. v. Secretary of Army, 192 F.3d 987 (Fed. Cir. 1999) (federal circuit court held that the general contractor had standing to bring an action on behalf of its subcontractor).

[51] *See, e.g.*, E.R. Mitchell Constr. Co. v. Danzig, 175 F.3d 1369, 1370 (Fed. Cir. 1999).

[52] *See, e.g.*, Barry, Bette & Led Duke, Inc. v. New York, 669 N.Y.S.2d 741, 743, 240 A.D.2d 54 (1998).

typically drafted to make the contractor liable to the subcontractor, but only to the extent that the contractor recovers any part of the subcontractor's claim from the owner. For example, the AGC/ASA/ASC Standard Form Construction Subcontract, in Article 16.4.3, limits the contractor's liability to the subcontractor for any damages and claims caused by an owner's suspension, delay, or interruption for convenience, and provides that liability shall be fully extinguished by the contractor paying the subcontractor any additional time or money obtained from the owner on the subcontractor's behalf.[53]

Establishing specific liability is a key step in the successful presentation of a pass-through claim. For example, in *Mars Associates Inc. v. New York City Educational Construction Fund*,[54] the appellate court determined that because no specific liability existed between the contractor and the subcontractor, no owner liability existed for subcontractor claims submitted by the contractor. The liquidation agreement in question provided that the subcontractor would accept whatever sum, if any, the contractor received from the owner.[55]

Various limitation-of-liability clauses may also present problems for a contractor when attempting to pass through a claim. Specifically, the owner may argue that these terms prevent any contractor liability to the subcontractor, eliminating the possibility of a liquidating agreement pursuant to the *Severin* doctrine. However, these arguments do not always prevail. For example, in *Bovis Lend Lease LMB Inc. v. GCT Venture, Inc.*,[56] a New York appellate court held that a no-damages-for-delay clause in a subcontract did not preclude a contractor from entering into a liquidation agreement. The trial court had previously held that the express terms of the subcontracts precluded damages against the contractor for delays caused by the developer, and thus precluded the contractor from entering into the liquidation agreement without the consent of the developer. According to the appellate court, the clause was consistent with the general rule that, absent a contractual commitment to the contrary, a prime contractor was not responsible for delays that its subcontractors experienced unless the delays were caused by some agency or circumstances under the prime contractor's direct control. In this case,

---

[53] *See* AGC/ASA/ASC Standard Form Construction Subcontract, AGC Doc. No. 640/ASA Doc. No. 4100/ASC Form No. 52 (1994), art. 16.4.3. *See also* Schiavone Constr. Co. v. Triborough Bridge & Tunnel Auth., 619 N.Y.S.2d 117, 209 A.D.2d 598 (1994) (prime contractor permitted to sponsor claim on behalf of subcontractor under liquidating agreement with language similar to AGC/ASA/ASC form, which provided that the prime contractor had no liability to the subcontractor beyond any recovery from the owner).

[54] 513 N.Y.S.2d 125, 126 A.D.2d 178 (1987).

[55] *See also* Moore Constr. Co. v. Clarksville Dep't of Elec., 707 S.W.2d 1 (Tenn. Ct. App. 1985) (testimony that prime contractor would not be required to pay subcontractor any additional costs for delay unless the owner agreed to pay the prime determined an insufficient basis upon which to award damages); Triangle Sheet Metal Works, Inc. v. James H. Merritt & Co., N.Y.L.J. at 26 (N.Y. Ct. App. 1991) (subcontractor's claim against prime for delay caused by city, engineer, and other prime contractors dismissed because claim failed to offer evidence that prime was responsible for any of the delay).

[56] 728 N.Y.S.2d 25, 285 A.D.2d 68 (1st Dep't 2001).

the contractor assumed additional liability in an agreement subsequent to the original general contract and subcontracts through execution of the liquidation agreement.

This holding raises the question of whether liquidating agreements actually *improve* the rights of the subcontractor from those that it enjoys under a standard subcontract. However, the case also suggests that where the owner pre-approves subcontracts, the owner may possess a right to rely on limitations on subcontractors' rights to recover against the contractor as a defense against potential liquidating agreement claims. A prudent owner should therefore include preapproval provisions in its general contract agreement to require pre-approval of all subcontract forms.[57]

Full prime contract liability is not always required to establish a pass-through claim. In certain instances, conditional liability will suffice. For example, the court in *J.L. Simmons Co. v. United States*[58] determined that a specific type of conditional liability clause in a subcontract (through which the prime contractor remains conditionally liable to the subcontractor only when the former receives payment from the government) did not preclude suit by the prime contractor on behalf of its subcontractor.[59]

The existence of waivers also has a direct bearing on the application of the *Severin* doctrine. Multiple waivers suggest the subcontractor may have waived only certain claims rather than all claims, preserving the contractor's liability for the remaining subcontractor claims under the *Severin* doctrine.

One court held that the execution of multiple "Full and Final" releases created an ambiguity that warranted the consideration of extrinsic evidence to discern the parties' true intent.[60] Each release identified a specific amount of money as consideration, and none of the amounts identified correlated with the disputed amount. Although the releases each stated that they were "full and final," there would have been no need for the subcontractor to execute several such releases if they were in fact "full and final." The court concluded that issues of fact precluded a grant of summary judgment on whether the case was barred by the *Severin* doctrine.

Contractors must also consider the necessity of certifying a subcontractor's claim before proceeding under the terms of a liquidation agreement. Specifically, a contractor may be obligated to certify the accuracy of the subcontractor's claims under statutes that require certification of the contractor's claim, such as the federal Contract Disputes Act.[61]

---

[57] *See* S. Stein, 22 Const. Law Digest 23 (Dec. 2001).

[58] 158 Ct. Cl. 393, 304 F.2d 886 (1962).

[59] *See also* Kentucky Bridge & Dam, Inc. v. United States, 42 Fed. Cl. 501, 527 (1998) (where conditional liability on the part of a prime contractor to subcontractor, based on future payment by government to prime contractor, was considered sufficient liability to avoid application of *Severin* doctrine).

[60] *See* Perry-McCall Constr., Inc. v. United States, 2000 U.S. Claims LEXIS 84 (Ct. Fed. Cl. 2000).

[61] *See, e.g.*, Century Constr. Co. v. United States, 22 Cl. Ct. 63 (1990) (when prime contractor submits claim on behalf of subcontractor, prime must certify belief in accuracy of subcontractor's claim, not merely certify belief that subcontractor believes its claim is accurate).

If the contractor is required to certify a claim to the owner, as required in many government contracts, the parties need to include a provision covering certification of the subcontractor's claim and the steps to take if the contractor does not believe that the subcontractor's claim is certifiable. At a minimum, the contractor will need to possess a good-faith belief that the subcontractor's claim is valid and is not fraudulent before passing it through to the owner.

[D] State Legislative Action

In recent years, state legislatures have implemented statutory provisions related to pass-through claims on public projects. North Carolina Gen. Stat. § 143-134.2 is a sound example. That statute allows a contractor, on behalf of a subcontractor, to file an action against the owner based on a subcontractor claim arising out of or relating to labor, materials, or services from a subcontract with the contractor. The North Carolina statute provides: (1) that the owner cannot defend the contractor claim on behalf of a subcontractor claim because the subcontractor has not yet been paid for its claim, and (2) that the owner is not required to pay the contractor until the subcontractor submits proof to the court that the contractor has actually paid the claim to the subcontractor.[62]

[E] Liquidation Agreements and Joint Defense Doctrine

Prior to negotiating a liquidation agreement, the parties should consider the joint defense doctrine and agree on the extent to which it will apply. The joint defense doctrine is an extension of the attorney-client privilege when more than one party is involved and they share common interests. In ordinary circumstances, the disclosure to another party of otherwise privileged material will eliminate the attorney-client privilege. Similarly, if counsel for one party discloses strategies and estimates of success, the attorney work-product privilege will no longer apply. The joint defense doctrine allows parties that are jointly defending an action to preserve the attorney-client and attorney work-product privileges for communications and preparations in the joint defense. The joint defense doctrine, however, is not limited to communications regarding defensive matters. The scope of the privilege varies among the courts, with the Ninth Circuit in *Hunydee v. United States*[63] taking the most expansive approach.

A joint defense agreement should always be in writing. A written agreement identifying the common interest and the intent not to waive the privilege can assist in establishing the privilege. The common interest agreement should include statements that:

---

[62] *See* N.C. Gen. Stat. § 143-134.
[63] 355 F.2d 183 (9th Cir. 1965).

1. The parties have agreed to pursue a common claim;

2. The communications between the parties and counsel are for the purpose of pursuing a common purpose;

3. All communications are intended to be privileged;

4. No party will disclose any privileged information without the express written consent of the other party; and

5. The party receiving the information shall not have the right or the power to waive the privilege for the other party.

Finally, the common interest or joint defense agreement should also be separately written and signed so that it can be introduced as proof of the common enterprise or common defense without having to share the liquidation agreement.

CHAPTER 15

PREPARING AND DEFENDING A CLAIM FOR DAMAGES: A PRACTICAL GUIDE

David G. Surratt
Andrea A. Hight

§ 15.01   INTRODUCTION

Once a change order has been authorized, the next question to ask is, what is a proper measure of compensation for the change?

At first glance, the amount to be charged for a change order would seem to be a simple, straightforward mathematical calculation. To the contrary, the amount to be charged for a change order is often complicated, because there may be numerous ways to calculate the same change. Consider the following example: assume that an owner has recognized that a change has occurred; the only issue left to resolve is approving the method of calculation. In this example, during the course of construction, the architect decided to add a requirement that the heating and cooling ducts be wrapped with insulation. At the time the change was ordered, half of the ductwork had already been installed. The contractor had craftspersons working on the ducts every day and decided to do the added insulation work using the same forces currently on the job. What are the controlling contract provisions and what cost methods do they stipulate? How does the contractor segregate the cost to perform this change? Can the contractor recover the cost to estimate, order, and deliver the insulation to the jobsite? Is the cost recoverable and, if so, how is it measured? Is the contractor entitled to recover the fringe benefits of the workers who performed the work? What happens if the prevailing wage rises? Will the contractor be permitted to charge for supervision and overtime; if so, how are these costs measured? Furthermore, how does the owner verify that the contractor is charging the correct amount?

Although there is no uniform "cookbook" available to determine the proper recovery for such a change, a methodology should be employed to reach a reasonable result. First, the relevant contract provisions should be examined. One of the most frequently used standard forms of domestic construction contracts are those prepared by the American Institute of Architects (AIA).[1]

The AIA Document A201, *General Conditions of the Contract for Construction,* gives direction in Article 7 for handling changes in the work. Subparagraph 7.3.3, dealing specifically with construction change directives, provides the methods on which an adjustment in the contract sum shall be based. Should the contractor either not respond promptly to the methods and adjustment, or disagree with them, the architect decides price adjustments under the formulas expressed in Subparagraph 7.3.6, mainly cost plus a reasonable allowance for overhead and profit. Recoverable costs are then enumerated.

The AIA documents also provide that the preferable method of pricing a change order is by "forward pricing." Forward pricing is an agreement to a lump sum or unit prices made in advance of performing the work. In the event the parties cannot reach a forward-pricing agreement, then the work is performed and priced on the basis of actual cost plus a markup for overhead and profit, generally known as time and materials or T&M. The AIA change clause contemplates that the change will include the additional direct cost of labor, equipment, and material.

---

[1] *See* AIA Doc. A201, General Conditions of the Contract for Construction (1992).

However, changes often cause impact costs that are difficult to quantify as direct costs. Impact costs may be agreed upon and forward-priced as are other direct costs.

Generally, forward pricing of changed work results in prices that are too low. Owners frequently think that contractors make money on changes because their estimates are too high. In reality, contractors often lose money on changes because their estimates are in fact too low.

Seattle, Washington, officials implemented a forward-pricing method to compensate contractors for change order impacts. The system was implemented on a wastewater treatment project following settlement of impact claims that arose from delays and changes resulting from discovery of an archaeological find on the project site.[2] The owner and contractor agreed on impact factors for pricing future claims that might arise on the project. For example, change orders issued five weeks prior to the start of a scheduled construction activity were assigned a higher impact cost than change orders issued ten weeks prior to the start of an activity. If a change order was issued twelve weeks prior to a scheduled activity, the impact cost was zero. Impact cost factors included the timing of changes, the number of trades involved, the impact on schedules, and the cumulative nature of the disruption. Values assigned to impact factors were based on research done by the Construction Industry Institute (Austin, Texas). Of the 450 change orders, 148 were issued using this system for change order pricing on the project, totaling $860,000.

The implementation of a system that assigns a multiplier to costs in the event that future circumstances occur requires the development of a detailed CPM schedule to measure the impact of the change, and mandates accurate updating of the schedule on a regular basis. The details for this type of change order pricing can be determined in preconstruction meetings or partnering sessions. Most contractors will still reserve their rights to claim for costs not covered by the impact "estimate." Many systems still require the owner to audit the contractors' actual impact cost following project completion. Nevertheless, any system that helps the owner and contractor agree to equitable resolution of disputes is a benefit to both parties.

§ 15.02 METHODS OF PRICING A CHANGE ORDER

[A] Unit Pricing

Some contracts, particularly those for heavy and highway construction work, are priced on a schedule of unit prices (bid by the contractor) and estimated quantities (as computed by the architect or engineer).[3]

---

[2] *Change Orders Organized*, 235 Eng'g News—Record 11 (Sept. 1995).

[3] This section is in part adapted from W. Postner & R. Rubin, New York Construction Law Manual § 6.27 (1992). Reprinted from *New York Construction Law Manual* by permission of Shepard's/McGraw-Hill, Inc., copyright by Shepard's/McGraw-Hill, Inc. Further reproduction of any kind is strictly prohibited.

The reason for this pricing structure is that the exact quantities are indeterminable due to field conditions; thus, they cannot be calculated in advance. These contracts often state that the price of extra work will be based on "applicable" unit prices. Additionally, lump-sum contracts for building construction often include an agreed-upon schedule of unit prices intended to cover changes.

[1]   Scope of Work

One overlooked factor in evaluating the cost of a change order is the scope of work involved. The crew may have been routinely installing 1,500 feet of conduit per day on production-type work. Now, they are asked to plan and install 150 feet. The time measured on a per-foot basis may be two to four times greater. Because the extended initial planning and setup period is distributed over a much smaller scope of work, the result is likely to be reflected in more work hours per foot. When the learning curve effect is present, a small scope of work is always done on the learning end of the curve; the labor component may be several times greater than ordinarily required.[4]

[2]   Conditions at Time of Change

Change orders should be priced based on conditions that apply to the change. It is unfair to require contractors to price potential changed work on a unit-price basis as part of their original bids, or to price it using the unit cost of original unchanged work. Conditions at the time of a change are seldom the same as those prevailing at the time the original work was accomplished. Additionally, the loss of productivity associated with changes and interruptions almost invariably makes any changed work more costly on a unit basis.[5] With each change, the contractor estimates the work hours required, but due to the inability of any project personnel to anticipate fully the consequential effects of these changes, the actual work hours may be much greater than originally anticipated. As the number of changes increases, the differential between estimated work hours and actual work hours widens at an increasing rate.[6]

It is of little surprise that work bid at one rate may take two to four times more work hours when done as change-order work. This scenario leads to an important assumption: loss of productivity on changed work is the result of changes in the scope and complexity of the work and changes to the environment in which the work is done. The latter is probably most severe.[7]

---

[4] H. Thomas & C. Napolitan, *The Effects of Changes on Labor Productivity: Why and How Much*, Constr. Indus. Inst., Source Doc. 99 at 28 (Aug. 1994).

[5] W. Hester, J. Kuprenas & T. Chang, *Construction Changes and Change Orders: Their Magnitude and Impact*, Constr. Indus. Inst., Source Doc. 66 at 37 (Oct. 1991).

[6] Hester, Kuprenas & Chang at B2-5, B2-6.

[7] Thomas & Napolitan at 29.

[3]   Current Practice

Current practice is reasonably well developed to estimate the added labor hours for the work to be done. Contractor databases based on historical information can generally isolate the differences in pipe sizes, design detail, or changes in specification or quality requirements. Perhaps the most uncertainty arises when the scope of work is affected, as would be the case when a change is added and the quantity of new work is not very large. Here, the startup and mobilization effort cannot be spread over a large scope of work. Past research has shown that unit productivity can vary by as much as 3:1 because of scope reductions.[8] This fact is often obscured, largely because contractors are accustomed to reviewing cumulative productivity numbers or weekly summaries instead of unit data. Furthermore, changes in the work to be done or work content can cause labor productivity to vary by more than 2:1.[9]

[4]   Common Problems

The problems encountered in applying contract unit prices to change order work are illustrated by the following example:

Assume a situation in which rock must be chopped and removed from a subbasement to make room for plumbing pipes. An owner and contractor have agreed that a certain price will be paid for each cubic yard of rock removed. Thus, mere calculation of quantity multiplied by the unit price will yield the cost of the change. However, how is the quantity of the rock actually measured? Is the two-foot by two-foot intended trench dimension used, or is the expanded volume of chopped rock as it sits in a dumpster used? What about any overcut? Many contracts do not adequately address how work to be paid for on a unit-price basis is to be measured for payment.

Additionally, the contractor has gambled that the estimated unit cost adequately covers the work. Rock removal may be required at different locations, each having different characteristics, such as fill material, disintegrated rock, and solid rock. For each condition, the contractor may have estimated a unit price, estimated the quantity, added up the total costs, and taken a weighted average of unit cost and quantity to calculate a composite unit price for "unclassified" excavation. If, during the project, these quantities are altered disproportionately to one another so that a greater percentage of the removal consists of the more costly removal of solid rock, can the contractor readjust the unit price for "unclassified" excavation? Furthermore, what if the contractor provided a unit price for rock removal in the base contract, but a change order required rock removal for additional narrow, rock trenches? Is the "unclassified" excavation unit price *applicable* to this work? Assume further that the contractor underbid the cost to perform the base contract

---

[8] S. Sanders & H. Thomas, *Factors Affecting Masonry-Labor Productivity*, 117 J. Constr. Eng'g & Mgmt. 626-44 (No. 4, 1991).

[9] Thomas & Napolitan at 25.

rock removal. Should the contractor also take a loss on the change order? Again, most contracts are usually silent on such issues. However, when the parties have the foresight and ability to agree before the change to a method of measurement and calculation, the owner must simply verify that the units involved are properly tallied.

[5]   When Unit Pricing Does Not Apply

Generally, in a unit-price contract, the contractor is not entitled to more compensation than the contractual unit price for extra work unless the contractor can show bad faith or concealment of relevant information by the owner.[10] When, however, the increase in quantities of materials is not simply a numerical increase in materials required under the contract, unit prices do not apply.[11] As the New York Court of Appeals put it:

> It is perfectly true that steel *is* steel. But it *is* also true that when it is to be used in a manner totally different from that originally proposed on the basis of which bids were made and necessarily costing far more per ton, it may not reasonably, fairly, and in good faith be classified as similar.[12]

Similarly, when the increase or decrease in quantity is so large that it should be more accurately characterized as qualitative rather than quantitative, contractual unit prices may not apply.

A lump sum contract may also not be adjusted by unit costs if a schedule of unit prices has not been included. In *Randall & Blake, Inc. v. Metro Wastewater Reclamation District*,[13] Metro Wastewater Reclamation District, a political subdivision of the State of Colorado, and Randall & Blake, Inc. (RBI) entered into an agreement. Camp, Dresser & McKee (CDM) was the engineer. RBI's contract price was $2,742,222. Included in that amount was RBI's lump-sum bid of $1,409,528 for the construction of a new recreation structure (RS3). A portion of the work on the entire project required the placement of boulders, rip-rap, and filter gravel at specific locations, including the RS3 site. The complying type II bedding material discovered at the project site was used as bedding for the rip-rap in the river and on the banks throughout the project, including RS3. CDM suggested that a quantity change in type II bedding material, resulting from the use of on-site bedding material, justified a unit price reduction and, consequently, a contract price change. The parties failed to reach an agreement on any contract price change. Metro issued two change orders to the contract. The first purported to delete the type II bedding material as part of the foundation. The second changed the contract price based on the cost savings afforded by not having to purchase and

---

[10] Depot Constr. Corp. v. State, 224 N.E.2d 866 (N.Y. 1967) (lump-sum contract with unit prices for excavation less than or greater than specification estimate).

[11] Yonkers Contracting Co. v. New York State Thruway Auth., 25 N.E.2d 811 (N.Y. App. Div. 1966), *aff'd*, 245 N.E.2d 800 (N.Y. 1969).

[12] E.H. Smith Contracting Co. v. City of N.Y., 148 N.E. 655, 659 (N.Y. App. Div. 1925).

[13] 77 P.3d 804 (Colo. Ct. App. 2003).

supply the bedding material. CDM's calculation was based in part on unit cost savings of the bedding material. The contract price was reduced by $101,384 in Metro's favor. RBI filed suit against Metro, seeking the balance of the contract price of $101,384, plus interest. The trial court determined that the type II bedding material was bid on a unit-price basis and that the contract price should be adjusted to reflect that the estimate of type II bedding material differed materially from that which RBI had to supply. This appeal followed.

The contract plainly included both unit-price and lump-sum provisions, which were applied to different facets of the project. However, the contract plainly stated that the RS3 work was to be performed on a lump-sum basis. The bid form specified that RS3 should be bid on a "lump sum" basis, RBI bid a lump-sum price of $1,409,528 for RS3 work, and the specifications stated that the "measurement and payment for [RS3] shall be on a lump sum basis." This lump-sum price included full compensation for all costs associated with the RS3 construction. The unambiguous contract language and the parties' stated understanding clearly supported the determination that this was a lump-sum contract. The trial court's contract construction and interpretation was therefore incorrect. The judgment was reversed, and the case was remanded.

Generally, if a contractor's sole basis for requesting a higher unit price is that the amount of work is greater or less than that anticipated, the contractor may not recover. The contractor has assumed the risk of a variance in quantity. Some contracts expressly provide that the estimated quantities in the contract cannot be relied upon.[14] Similarly, an owner may be held to a unit price if it contends that it is entitled to a lesser unit price due to an increase in quantity.[15] If the change is *qualitative*, however, the contractor may be entitled to compensation for the extra work on a quantum meruit basis.[16] The distinction is based upon the court's opinion that "it would be inequitable to confine the bidder to a unit bid made to meet entirely different conditions."[17]

[6] Quantitative vs. Qualitative Changes

As the court pointed out in *Tufano Contracting Corp. v. State*,[18] in one sense, a change in quantity in a unit-price contract is "simply a quantitative increase over the number of [units] envisioned at the time of contracting." Where, however, "the additional involvement was not originally contemplated by the parties[,]" a qualitative

---

[14] Zurn Eng'rs v. California Dep't of Water Res., 138 Cal. Rptr. 478 (Cal. Ct. App. 1977).

[15] DeFoe Constr. Corp. v. Beame, 347 N.Y.S.2d 626 (1973); *see also* Perini Corp. v. United States, 381 F.2d 403 (Ct. Cl. 1967) (owner not entitled to reduction in unit price when contractor pumped a greater quantity of water than estimated); Kingsley v. City of Brooklyn, 78 N.Y. 200 (N.Y. 1879) (owner not entitled to reduction in contract price when contractor drove piles to a shallower depth than required at direction of owner).

[16] Depot Constr. Corp. v. State, 25 A.D.2d 707, 708 (N.Y. App. Div. 1965), *aff'd*, 224 N.E.2d 866 (N.Y. 1967).

[17] Foundation Co. v. State, 135 N.E. 236, 239 (N.Y. 1922).

[18] 25 A.D.2d 329 (N.Y. App. Div. 1966), *aff'd*, 257 N.E.2d 901 (N.Y. 1970).

change may result.[19] In *Tufano,* the contract called for the construction of 28 temporary road detours; 123 to 128 detours were actually constructed. The court held that an increase of this magnitude was not within the parties' contemplation and was qualitative, entitling the contractor to recover on a T&M basis, not on the contractual unit price. The T&M recovery applied only to the extra work, not to the 28 detours contemplated in the contract; those were compensated at the contractual unit price.

To determine whether a change is quantitative or qualitative, a close analysis of the contract and specific factual situation involved is necessary. A simple review of applicable cases can be misleading and confusing. For instance, it has been held that a near doubling of the amount of earth needed to complete a levee embankment was a qualitative change, entitling the contractor to increased costs plus 10 percent overhead,[20] whereas in another case, a 1,300-percent increase in the amount of grout provided was not, meaning that the contractor was paid its unit price for the additional grout.[21]

There are some determining factors that generally apply when analyzing whether a quantitative or qualitative change has occurred. First, if the contract specifically discusses different unit prices for different quantities of work or materials, the contractor will probably be held to the prescribed unit price. In *Depot Construction Corp. v. State,*[22] the contractor agreed to excavate a given quantity of work for a lump sum. Any excess or shortage was to be paid on a per-cubic-yard basis. Excavation over 600 cubic yards was to be paid at $22 per cubic yard. The total excavation was 2,982 cubic yards, almost five times the contract estimate. The court held that the contract placed the risk of the quantity on the contractor and limited the contractor's recovery to the unit price. Similarly, when a contract provided that a change in quantity would not result in a change of unit price, the contractor was not entitled to lost profits or a higher unit price when the amount of sheathing was reduced.[23]

Second, if the change in quantity was because of an honest error by the owner, it is more probable that the change will be considered quantitative.[24] Third, to be qualitative, the increase or decrease must be very large, although a large

---

[19] *Id.*

[20] Sadler v. United States, 287 F.2d 411 (Ct. Cl. 1961).

[21] DeFoe Constr. Corp. v. Beame, 347 N.Y.S.2d 626 (N.Y. Sup. 1973).

[22] 19 N.Y.2d 109, 224 N.E.2d 866 (N.Y. 1967).

[23] Camarco Contractors, Inc. v. State, 33 A.D.2d 717 (N.Y. App. Div. 1969), *modified on other grounds,* 271 N.E.2d 917 (N.Y. 1971); *see also* Leary v. City of N.Y., 118 N.E. 849 (N.Y. 1918) (actual rock excavation was 2,200 or 2,400 cubic yards; estimate was 1,800); Farub Found. Corp. v. City of N.Y., 49 N.Y.S.2d 922 (N.Y. Sup. 1944) (city used 13 percent of materials it estimated would be needed, resulting in greatly increased unit price; contractor held to contract unit price).

[24] *See* Yonkers Contracting Co. v. New York State Thruway Auth., 25 A.D.2d 811 (N.Y. App. Div. 1966), *aff'd,* 245 N.E.2d 800 (N.Y. 1969) (actual excavation 11 percent more than estimate); E.G. De Lia & Sons Constr. Corp. v. State, 1 A.D.2d 732 (N.Y. App. Div. 1955) (state estimated 4,850 feet of piling would be used; over 2,000 feet left at end of job); Farub Found. Corp. v. City of N.Y., 49. N.Y.S.2d 922 (N.Y. Sup. 1944) (city used 13 percent of materials it estimated it would need).

change may merely be quantitative.[25] For instance, an 11-percent change is quantitative,[26] while a 400-percent increase may be qualitative.[27] Finally, a change of method is usually a qualitative change. For example, if the depth of excavation is increased, and that increase requires the contractor to blast rather than mechanically dig, a qualitative change may result. In unit-price contracts, price adjustments are often triggered by variations in quantities that exceed the thresholds contemplated by the contract.

[7] Unbalanced Unit Price

A new unit price is determined after agreement for the amount of the adjustment. The presence of unbalanced unit prices often adds an obstacle to the process. An unbalanced unit price is one in which each bid item or breakdown of scheduled values in a lump-sum contract fails to carry its proportionate share of the overhead and profit in addition to the necessary costs for the item. The results are understated prices for some items and enhanced or overstated prices for others. Contractors seeking to obtain an advantage because of a possible inaccurate quantity estimate may quote prices below cost for items perceived to be under run and overstate prices for items on which a large overrun is anticipated.[28]

The dispute that arises from variation in quantities to be paid by an unbalanced unit price is whether a contractor is entitled to maintain its original profit structure, thereby continuing the advantage of the unbalanced bid. Two opposing theories relate to the basis for the equitable adjustment. Under one theory, an owner (or contractor) would expect to be entitled to relief from the overstated prices. Under the other, the owner must continue to pay the overstated (or understated) prices.[29] As a result of the second theory, if the unit prices are overstated, the owner will pay for the consequence of a bad quantity estimate and the failure to identify an unbalanced bid. If the unit prices are understated, the owner continues to pay only the understated unit prices, despite quantity overruns.

In *Burnett Construction Co. v. United States*,[30] the contractor submitted a severely understated price for water required for dust control on a road construction project. The contract unit price was $5.00 per thousand gallons. The actual performance costs were approximately $38.00 per thousand gallons. The contract

---

[25] *See* Seebold v. Halmar Constr. Corp., 146 A.D.2d 886 (N.Y. Sup. 1989) (unit price applied when subcontractor raked almost 90,000 yards of topsoil on contract that estimated 4,620 yards).

[26] Yonkers Contracting Co. v. New York State Thruway Auth., 25 A.D.2d 811 (N.Y. App. Div. 1966), *aff'd*, 245 N.E.2d 800 (N.Y. 1969).

[27] L.G. De Felice & Son v. State, 313 N.Y.S.2d 21 (Ct. Cl. 1970).

[28] F. Manzo, *The Impact of an Unbalanced Bid on the Change Order Process*, 3 Constr. Forum News 7 (No. 1, Oct. 1997).

[29] Manzo at 7, citing Manis Drilling, IBCA No. 2658, 93-3 BCA (CCH) ¶ 115,187 (1993) (although a contractor may legitimately unbalance its bid as a bidding technique, it does so at its own peril and must accept consequence that deletion of separately priced items may affect its profit or cost structure).

[30] 26 Cl. Ct. 296 (1992).

anticipated renegotiating unit overrun quantities when the quantities exceeded 115 percent of the estimated units. The contractor absorbed the cost of the unbalanced unit price for the first 115 percent of the work but was compensated for its costs for the overrun units over 115 percent.[31]

It is relatively easy to detect an unbalanced bid in the evaluation of a unit-price contract. In fixed-price, lump-sum contracts, the process is more difficult. The unbalancing of a bid is the shifting of part of the cost of work for one element of the work to another element of the work. A unit price that is materially unbalanced has shifted not only a disproportionate amount of overhead and profit, but also some portion of the actual cost of elements of work. In this situation, the unit price for some work can be understated and significantly less than the actual cost of that work, with an overstatement of prices for other aspects of the work. The degree to which this is accomplished determines whether a bid is simply mathematically unbalanced or materially unbalanced. In public-sector contracts, an unbalanced bid is objectionable because it constitutes an advance payment, may not ultimately prove to be the best offer, and is detrimental to the concepts underlying competitive bidding. In general, these characteristics are sufficient to warrant rejection of the bid, or, if procedures allow, a negotiation aimed at balancing the bid without changing the total bid.[32]

[8] Illustrative Cases

Below are some illustrative cases over unit pricing.

In *Claude Dubois Excavating, Inc. v. Town of Kittery*,[33] the contractor sued the town for breach of a sewer construction contract. The plaintiff was awarded the contract for the project based on its bid, even though the contract was not for a fixed price. This was a unit-price contract with prices for each discrete aspect of the project. The amount of the bid was the contractor's unit prices multiplied by the town's estimated number of units. The contract included the excavation of ledge materials at the rate of $140 per cubic yard. As the construction proceeded, the parties determined that more of the ledge would have to be removed than additionally anticipated. This raised the cost of the project well beyond the plaintiff's bid, and the town's engineers determined that the entire project would now cost nearly 20 percent more than the bid. The increase was well above the amount of the special bond. The contractor refused to lower its unit price and the town then deleted certain streets from the project so that it could remain within the amount of the revenue bond. The plaintiff then filed suit, seeking costs and lost profits from the alteration of the scope of the project. The court affirmed the summary judgment for the town, holding that the contract specifically provided that the town could decrease the quantity of work if the additional unanticipated ledge work would result in the project cost exceeding taxpayer approval.

---

[31] Manzo at 7-8.
[32] Manzo at 6.
[33] 634 A.2d 1299 (Me. 1993).

In *APAC-Carolina v. Greensboro-High Point Airport Authority*,[34] the plaintiff was the general contractor for an airport runway extension and taxiway project. The general contractor and a subcontractor sued the authority and its engineer for nonpayment of claims for undercut excavation that were not contemplated by the contract and were not mentioned by the defendants. The plaintiff's bid included a contract price for unclassified excavation at a per-cubic-yard rate. The bid did not include a price for undercut, replacement, or compaction work. The contract stated that all undercutting would be included in the broader category of unclassified excavation. Shortly after the subcontractor started grading work, the engineers directed the plaintiffs to undercut the subgrade to substantial depths. The plaintiffs protested that this was more complicated and time-consuming than the work estimated at the per-cubic-yard charge. In response to the subcontractor's request for additional compensation, the engineer threatened to shut down the job and impose liquidated damages. Thereupon, the plaintiffs performed the work under protest. The plaintiffs alleged that performance of the extra work caused delays resulting in the suspension of their work and they sought additional sums to cover the delay. Upon completion of the work, the authority made a payment to the contractor, but withheld a sum for liquidated damages and did not make payment on the extra work claims.

The court held that the general contractor could not assert the extra work claims on behalf of the subcontractor, because the additional subcutting did not meet the contract definition of extra work and the contract specifically treated the problem under the unclassified excavation category. The court held that the no-damages-for-delay provision in the contract was enforceable, and therefore, the plaintiffs could not recover delay damages.

In *Williams Trucking Co. v. JW Construction Co.*,[35] the contractor was hired to perform excavation, backfill, and grading work in connection with a mini-warehouse facility. The contractor started the work but stopped when a bulldozer sank into the ground. The parties then discovered that the property contained organic soil unsuitable for the project. Prior soil tests had revealed this condition, but the developer had failed to note the test results prior to contracting with the plaintiff.

The parties determined that the organic material should be removed and replaced with suitable soil. Such work was not contemplated by the original contract, so a change order was executed. Payment was to be made based on the amount of material replaced. The owner's representative, however, refused to use "truck counts" to determine the amount of such material. When the plaintiff started this replacement work, the owner did not provide an on-site soil representative as required by the change order. The plaintiff counted the load tickets from the trucks each night to verify the number of loads. Disputes subsequently arose over the work. The owner sent surveyors, after the work was completed, to drill test holes at random sites to calculate the volume removed and replaced. The plaintiff testified that the depth excavated to reach good soil varied greatly over the

---

[34] 431 S.E.2d 508 (N.C. App. 1993).
[35] 442 S.E.2d 197 (S.C. Ct. App. 1994).

entire site and that it had removed and replaced more materials than the surveyors calculated. The plaintiff's expert testified that truck counts were more reliable than random samples. When the contractor was recalled to the site to complete other work, it found that much of its grading had been ruined by other contractors, and $1,000 was allowed for regrading. The plaintiff continued to complain about the inadequacy of payment for the prior work; meanwhile, weather hampered the regrading work. The owner then terminated the contractor and hired a substitute to finish the plaintiff's work. The court affirmed the judgment for the plaintiff contractor, holding that there was sufficient evidence to show that the owner had failed to provide an on-site engineer as required and that this amounted to a breach of contract, preventing use of the change order method for determining the amount of removal and replacement work performed by the plaintiff. The court also found that the owner did not terminate the plaintiff for good cause.

In *Brown Brothers v. Metropolitan Government*,[36] the contractor alleged that the metropolitan government's warranty of its estimates of the amount of rock to be removed had been breached and that it was responsible for delays caused by relocation of utilities to permit the work to progress on this road extension project. The contract called for 139,845 cubic yards of rock excavation and 185,184 cubic yards of unclassified excavation (generally dirt). The contractor claimed that it actually removed more than 250,000 cubic yards of rock and only 67,000 of dirt. The contractor had calculated its bid based on $3.70 per cubic yard of rock and $1.10 per cubic yard of unclassified material. The difference in the extra rock excavation resulted in a cost overrun of $281,000. The contractor alleged that the government breached the implied warranty of accuracy by underestimating the amount of rock to be removed. The government argued that the information was provided merely for the convenience of the contractor and that the contract disclaimed any warranty of the accuracy of the estimates. The court affirmed the summary judgment for the government, holding that there was no warranty of the accuracy of the subsurface rock estimates. No delay damages could be recovered by the contractor for delays resulting from the utility relocation, as the risk of delay was specifically placed on the contractor by the contract and there was no showing that the government actively interfered with the contractor's operations.

[B] Variation in Quantities

In complex projects, unit pricing becomes more difficult, and the contractor usually assumes more risk.[37] Wrong estimates may result in windfall profits or substantial losses for one party or the other. Also, in instances in which the actual quantity is less than originally projected, the contractor may not be able to recover its fixed costs.

---

[36] 877 S.W.2d 745 (Tenn. Ct. App. 1993).

[37] This section is in part adapted from R. Rubin et al., Construction Claims: Prevention and Resolution 21-23 (2d ed. 1992). Used with permission from Chapman & Hall.

For example, assume a contract originally called for approximately 700 square feet of slab cutting and removal to create open space between two floors, but the architect redesigned the layout, reducing the slab cutting to 60 square feet. The actual price might greatly exceed the estimate, because the cost to deliver and set up air compressors constitutes a substantial fixed cost, which is no longer spread over a large amount of slab cutting.

Thus, a modern contractual approach may include a variation-in-quantities clause that sets a limit on how much the estimated quantity can vary before making some adjustment in price. For example, the contract for the San Francisco Bay Area Rapid Transit (BART) project provided that if the quantity of any unit-price item that amounted to 5 percent of the total contract bid price varied by greater than 25 percent, a change order would be issued.

Another form of a variation-in-quantities clause is generally known as a "split" quantities clause. This provision may be used in situations in which principal unit prices are susceptible to large variations. For example, the U.S. Bureau of Reclamation has stipulated that bidders would include in the first 65 percent of the total estimated quantity of a particular item "that part of the contractor's cost for construction facilities mobilization and demobilization, plant, fixed overhead, etc." The remaining 35 percent would include only the variable costs associated with completing the remaining 35 percent of this work, and hence this unit price could be used for any additional work. Under this system, the unit price would only be re-negotiated if the final quantity completed is less than 65 percent of the stipulated quantity. In such a case, an equitable adjustment would be made in accordance with the contract. Thus, a split-quantities clause, in comparison to a variation-in-quantities clause, should less often necessitate a need to calculate an adjustment during the project because the only reason to adjust a unit price would be because the actual quantity completed was less than 65 percent.

The AIA standard forms address variation in quantities.[38] The standard AIA variation-in-quantities clause is based on "material differences" and "substantial inequities," relatively imprecise terms. Note that the clause may be invoked by either the owner or the contractor.

Variation-in-quantities clauses can effectively spread construction risks, for both owners and contractors, more equitably. As an illustration, New York City's Third Water Tunnel involved tremendous overruns for unit-priced support steel for which the city had specified a lower-than-cost fixed unit price. Without any such clause, work stopped, a lawsuit was brought, and the project was delayed for years, during which time taxpayers incurred substantial maintenance costs to keep the partially driven tunnel from regressing. A variation-in-quantities clause, administered in good faith, ought to have averted this problem.

---

[38] *See* AIA Doc. A201, ¶ 7.1.4 (1992).

[C] Time and Materials

The "time and materials" (T&M) method of calculation is most often employed when the item of work is difficult to categorize into a particular unit-price item or when the scope or amount of the work cannot be fully determined in advance. This approach is typical when an emergency change is required.

For example, assume a project involved an acknowledged design defect in the waterproofing below an exterior marble terrace. Expensive marble slabs had to be removed, cleaned, and reset. Although historical cost figures were readily available to price the cost to set marble, the removal and cleaning were dependent on the strength of the particular grade of marble. Whatever stone could not be saved by careful removal and cleaning would have to be replaced. The most convenient resolution, especially in light of a constricted job schedule, would have been to perform this work on a T&M basis.

The owner, not the contractor, bears the risk if the work is performed on a T&M basis. This is because, by definition, the contractor on a T&M change will be reimbursed for its expenditures plus an agreed-upon fee or profit. Hence, the owner should seek to minimize this risk by keeping close watch on the time and materials as they are incurred. Detailed and verified record keeping is essential to this approach.

Time and materials may be less expensive than lump-sum under certain situations. Many owners have unnecessarily cost themselves a great deal of money in change orders by requiring their architect/engineer or construction manager to obtain firm quotations for all change orders in advance of approval of the proposed additional work. When the need for a change order develops and it is clear to all concerned, including the contractor, that the work in question must be undertaken and the owner requires a firm quotation in advance, unnecessary additional cost usually results. In this event, it is not unusual for the change order to cost from 200 percent to 500 percent of what it should cost. Although, it is true that labor and material accounting is difficult at best, and it is often true that the owner does not get work done under change orders for prices as reasonable as those under the main contract proposal. When it is clear to all concerned that there is no way to avoid the change order work, the T&M method will usually be best except when the lengths and quantity can almost never be set in advance, such as for foundation piling.[39]

§ 15.03 TYPES OF RECOVERABLE COSTS

[A] Labor

The contractor's payroll records establish who is paid what amount. These records may also delineate the particular project(s) or the particular activity(ies)

---

[39] G. Heery, Time, Cost, and Architecture 125 (1975).

on a given project toward which each individual's time has been allocated. Escalating labor costs may be relatively easy to prove if the escalation was subject to a union contract. Also, a change that accelerates a progress schedule often results in labor premiums in the form of overtime and shift work that should be reimbursable. Similarly, owner-caused delays and interruptions can create loss of productivity or loss of efficiency that, in turn, necessitates the expenditure of additional labor hours.

The contractor is generally reimbursed for the total cost it incurs to employ an individual for the number of hours charged to the change order. Labor costs for less-than-full-time employees at the site are apportioned. Payroll costs include, but are not limited to, salaries, wages, and fringe benefits. These benefits consist of social security contributions, unemployment compensation, excise and payroll taxes, workers' compensation, health and retirement benefits, bonuses, sick leave, and vacation and holiday pay applicable to the work.

AIA Document A201, Article 7, expresses a basic intent to reimburse the contractor's "reasonable expenditures." However, Subparagraph 7.3.6 does not itemize the numerous fringe benefits and ancillary labor-related costs. Thus, recovery of more discretionary payroll costs, such as bonuses, may be problematic under the AIA provisions.

Typically, with regard to physical labor, a union contract may be referred to in order to establish prevailing wages and benefits paid. However, what happens when a contractor is required to place a nonunion project manager on the project for a couple of weeks? Is the contractor allowed to recover a reasonable hourly rate for a project manager, or is the contractor entitled only to exactly what it pays for the particular individual?

[B] Materials

Material costs are often relatively easy to calculate and allocate. Typically, materials are purchased from a supplier, and the supplier submits a bill to the contractor. The contractor, in turn, passes this cost on to the owner. Thus, for example, a contractor on a T&M change can requisition for drywall materials by merely accumulating the respective bills from its supplier.

Complications may occur, however, when the materials have been taken out of the contractor's inventory. Suppose the contractor constructs a plumbing supply system out of copper pipe taken from its own warehouse. Suppose further that the price of copper has escalated dramatically since the time it was purchased. Should the contractor be reimbursed for what it paid for the copper pipe, or should recovery be based upon the fair market value of the pipe at the time of the work? What if the price of copper decreased and the contractor had actually paid more for the material? Also, should the contractor be reimbursed for the cost incurred to deliver the pipe to the jobsite?

The AIA General Conditions does not address the escalation in the price of copper. However, AIA Document A201, Subparagraph 7.3.6.2, does allow recovery for the cost of transporting the material(s). Also, monies received by the contractor as a result of the liquidation of surplus materials and equipment are to be paid to the owner. The contract form does not address the issue of how to price materials taken from the contractor's inventory.

Something else not addressed may be payment for materials that are subsequently changed. Once an owner pays for stored material, the owner may not recover the payment for changes in performance that do not permit the material to be used on the project.

[C] Equipment

Equipment cost is relatively easy to calculate if the equipment is rented at arm's length from an independent source and used solely for the particular change order work. On the other hand, cost recovery of equipment that is allocated to numerous operations on a project must be carefully documented for accurate apportionment.

The AIA treats the reimbursement of equipment cost the same as the cost of materials. For example, invoices paid by the contractor for the rental or purchase of jackhammers and compressors needed for the chopping of concrete decking would be reimbursable. Just as in materials, complications in the proper amount of recovery could occur, for example, when jackhammers and compressors are owned by the contractor. A reasonable rate for their use would have to be determined.

There are several means of arriving at a fair value for a contractor's self-owned equipment used on a project. Some contracts specify the use of industry manuals such as the Associated General Contractors of America (AGC) *Contractors' Equipment Manual* or the Rental Rate Blue Book to compute self-owned equipment costs. The AGC manual can provide a computed ownership expense by taking into account factors such as age, initial cost, useful life, operating hours, and maintenance and repair costs for each piece of equipment.

[D] Insurance and Bonding

Construction contracts normally require the contractor to carry comprehensive general liability insurance. If the contractor owns vehicles, it will also carry automobile liability insurance. The cost for automobile liability insurance is usually not a function of the amount of work the contractor performs. However, the general liability policy premiums are typically based, at least in part, on the amount of work performed and gross job payrolls.

Contractors sometimes lump insurance cost into the percentage charged for overhead. Contractors may, however, separately itemize a formulated percentage for insurance. This percentage is usually calculated by dividing the total premium by an expected sales/volume of work.

Performance and payment bonds may be purchased by the contractor at the request of the owner. Bond premiums are generally charged on the basis of the final contract price, as adjusted by change orders.

AIA Document A201, Subparagraph 7.3.6.4, allows recovery of the costs of all bonds, insurance, permit fees, and taxes related to changes in the work.

[E] Overhead

Main office or home office, overhead comprises all the costs incurred in the operation of an office. These costs include rental, utility, secretarial, estimating, marketing, bookkeeping, engineering, stationery, payroll, insurance, tax, and similar costs. Main office overhead is usually separated from job costs. Job costs are those costs that are directly related to the completion of the particular project. However, larger projects will often have some main office functions, such as secretarial and payroll work performed on the jobsite. Owner-caused delay could entitle the contractor to recovery of its overhead.[40]

[1] *Eichleay* Formula

Generally, owner-caused delay must have affected the critical path of the project in order for the contractor to receive compensation. The *Eichleay* formula[41] is one method used to allocate main office overhead to a particular project. The United States Court of Appeals for the Federal Circuit declared the *Eichleay* formula the only acceptable approach for calculating unabsorbed overhead for United States government projects, in *Wickham Contracting Co. v. Fischer.*[42] To succeed on an *Eichleay* claim, a contractor must document that the owner or client remained the sole cause of the delay.

This formula proportionally allocates the total cost of overhead over ongoing projects. In a simple example, if a particular project billed $1,000,000 during a particular time period, and the total amount billed for all contracts was $10,000,000 for the same period, 10 percent of the contractor's home office overhead would be allocated to that particular project.

When the suspension or delay period remains uncertain, and the contractor must stand ready to resume performance on short notice, the contractor is prohibited from cutting home office overhead costs or from obtaining additional work. Other reasons, such as exhaustion of bonding capacity, may also prevent the contractor from taking additional contracts. Examples of home office overhead affected by delay include the cost of weekly payrolls, Davis-Bacon reports, checks, W-2s, 941s, and other required tax forms.[43]

---

[40] Walter Kidde Constructors, Inc. v. State, 434 A.2d 962 (Conn. Super. Ct. 1981); Higgins v. Fillmore, 639 P.2d 192 (Utah 1981).

[41] Eichleay Corp., ASBCA No. 5183, 60-2 BCA (CCH) ¶ 2688, 2 Gov't Cont. Rep. (CCH) ¶ 485 (1960), *aff'd on reconsideration*, 61-1 BCA (CCH) ¶ 2894, 3 Gov't Cont. Rep. (CCH) ¶ 138(a) (1961).

[42] 12 F.3d 1574 (Fed. Cir. 1994).

[43] M. Kauffman & C. Holman, *The Eichleay Formula: A Resilient Means for Recovering Unabsorbed Overhead*, 24 Pub. Cont. L.J. 319 (No. 2, Winter 1995).

Extended overhead refers to the increase in overhead costs attributable to an extension in the time of contract performance. The extended performance time obliges a contractor to allocate more overhead to the contract than it contemplated when bidding the project. The terms unabsorbed overhead and extended overhead are frequently used interchangeably, though they remain conceptually different. The *Eichleay* formula is also applicable to extended overhead.

In *Jackson Construction Co. v. United States*,[44] a contractor was hired by the Army New York District Corps of Engineers to construct a building. The contractor, Jackson, brought suit to recover additional damages after he was paid $4,183,189. Jackson asserted a 120-day delay at the beginning of the contract that resulted from the relocation of a waterline that was located within the footprint of the new building. The Federal Court of Claims, after hearing the evidence, determined that Jackson was not entitled to any additional compensation, in part, because the contractor failed to meet its burden of proof on its claim for *Eichleay* damages and early completion.

The court articulated the elements of an *Eichleay* claim as a six-part framework. The contractor has the burden of proof and must establish its claim by a preponderance of the evidence. The six-part framework for evaluating a contractor's claim is as follows: (1) Was there a government-caused delay that was not concurrent with another delay caused by some other source?; (2) Did the contractor demonstrate that it incurred additional damages?; (3) Did the government issue a suspension or other order putting the contractor on standby?; (4) If not, can the contractor prove that there was a delay of indefinite duration where it could not bill a substantial amount of work and at the end of which it was required to be able to return to the contract immediately?; (5) Can the government satisfy the burden of production showing it was not impractical for the contractor to take other work?; (6) If the government meets the burden of production, can the contractor satisfy its burden of persuasion that it was impractical for it to obtain sufficient replacement work?[45] If the contractor meets these requirements, then the contractor may recover the unabsorbed used office overhead.

Furthermore, the court went on to state that if a contractor is trying to recover unabsorbed office overhead when the contract was completed on time, then the contractor must demonstrate that it incurred additional overhead by satisfying the *Interstate* three-part test for establishing an early completion delay.[46] In this case, the contract was completed inside the original contract time. Therefore, Jackson had to satisfy the *Interstate* test as well. Under the *Interstate* test, a contractor can recover the unabsorbed home office overhead on an early completion delay if it proves that it: (1) intended to finish early; (2) was capable of finishing early; and (3) would have actually finished early but for the government's actions.[47] In order to recover under the *Interstate* test, the contractor need not notify the government

---

[44] ___ Fed. Cl. _____, 2004 WL 2095579 (2004).

[45] *Jackson Constr. Co.*, citing P.J. Dick v. Principi, 324 F.3d 1364, 1373 (Fed. Cir. 2003).

[46] *Id.*, citing *P.J. Dick*, 324 F.3d at 1373.

[47] *Id.*, citing Interstate Gen. Gov't Contractors, Inc. v. West, 12 F.3d 1053, 1058 (Fed. Cir. 1993).

of its intent to finish the project early. However, the record must contain evidence of the contractor's intent, such as a bid estimate.

The Federal Court of Claims, in reviewing Jackson's claims in light of the aforementioned tests, determined that it did not meet either the *Eichleay* six-part framework or the *Interstate* three-part test. Jackson failed to prove the number of delays of the delay on the project's critical path, incorrectly calculated the daily contract overhead, and failed to meet all three elements of the *Interstate* test. Therefore, Jackson was not able to recover his claims for additional compensation against the government.

Article 7 of AIA Document A201 stipulates a reasonable allowance for overhead and profit for changes. What is reasonable? Commonly, instead of calculating an exact figure representing that portion of overhead allocable to the particular change (a very time-consuming prospect given the fact that overhead is allocable over numerous projects), a fixed percentage is added to the cost of the change. The 1997 edition of the *General Conditions of the Contract for Construction*, AIA Document A201, added language in Subparagraph 4.3.10.2 that included a mutual waiver of consequential damages, including home office overhead, "[d]amages incurred by the Contractor for principal office expenses including the compensation of personnel stationed there."

Federal government contracts also typically provide for the recovery of overhead and profit on changes. Thus, an allowance is typically included as part of an equitable adjustment.[48] In contrast to the AIA contract, the overhead rate for federal contract changes is that actually incurred, if such a rate is available at the time the equitable adjustment is computed.[49] When such a rate is not available, "standard" overhead rates may be applied.[50]

In some instances, federal contracts have permitted the reclassification of certain overhead costs to direct costs. Such reclassification is generally permitted when traditionally considered indirect costs can be directly attributable to the change. For example, a board of contract appeals has permitted a contractor to recover the cost of a foreman as a direct cost with an overhead percentage added to the cost.[51]

[2] Illustrative Cases

In *Daly Construction Inc. v. Garrett*,[52] the contractor appealed a decision of the Armed Services Board of Contract Appeals that denied its claims for delays

---

[48] Algernon Blair, Inc., ASBCA No. 10,738, 65-2 BCA (CCH) ¶ 5127 (1965); Sun Elec. Corp., ASBCA No. 13,031, 70-2 BCA (CCH) ¶ 8371 (1970).

[49] Keco Indus., Inc., ASBCA No. 15,131, 72-1 BCA (CCH) ¶ 9262, 14 Gov't Cont. Rep. (CCH) ¶ 228 (1972).

[50] *See, e.g.*, Industrial Research Assocs., Inc., DCAB No. WB-5, 71-1 BCA (CCH) ¶ 8680, 13 Gov't Cont. Rep. (CCH) ¶ 405 (1971).

[51] Triangle Elec. Mfg. Co., ASBCA No. 15,995, 74-2 BCA (CCH) ¶ 10,783 (1974).

[52] 5 F.3d 520 (Fed. Cir. 1993).

(518 days) attributable to the government's defective specifications. The delay resulted after the plaintiff discovered that the specifications for the transformer were defective, and represented the time needed to correct the defect and obtain the proper transformer to meet the corrected specifications. Representatives of the parties negotiated the cost of the delay. The Navy officer representing the government had authority to bind the government. The representatives agreed to $34,000 in home office overhead and $2,013 for direct costs. A formal modification was not issued, though, despite promises by the Navy. The contractor withdrew its initial appeal based on the representations of the officer and the Navy's counsel. Ultimately, the Navy formally denied the claim, and the board held that there was no binding agreement to pay the negotiated amounts. The contractor argued that the government's representatives had apparent authority to settle the matter and that the plaintiff had relied on their statements. The court affirmed the denial of the claims, holding that the plaintiff had failed to show that it was entitled to recover full extended overhead costs and had failed to reconstruct its costs related to the contract or show how the amount of its claim was reasonable.

In *Kirkham Constructors, Inc. v. United States*,[53] the contractor brought suit seeking an equitable adjustment for overhead increases sustained due to government delay. The contractor was to remodel a dining facility on an Air Force base. Several modifications were issued that increased the cost and delayed completion. The change orders executed for the adjustments compensated for the direct costs, but overhead and delay costs were not resolved. This was acknowledged in the contract amendment. The contractor requested an equitable adjustment of $133,000 for the impact on the unchanged work caused by the numerous change orders. The plaintiff sent another request for an equitable adjustment for unabsorbed home office overhead and field office cost caused by the defective specifications and failure of the government to provide timely direction.

The contracting officer advised the contractor that its request for an equitable adjustment was insufficient. The contractor treated this as a denial of its claim and requested a final decision. The contractor attached a certification of claim. The contractor appealed in an attempt to obtain a final decision, but the contracting officer's final decision was subsequently withdrawn without explanation. The Board of Contract Appeals ordered another final decision that was never rendered. Thereupon, the plaintiff filed this suit alleging that the withdrawal of the first final decision was equivalent to a denial of its claim. The court denied the government's motion to dismiss, holding that the contractor's claim was sufficiently specific, was properly certified, and was submitted during a dispute. This satisfied the requirements of the Contract Disputes Act and entitled the contractor to a determination of the claim on its merits.

In *Clark-Fitzpatrick, Inc./Franki Foundation. Co. v. Gill*,[54] the subcontractor sued the general contractor, whereupon the general filed a third-party action against the Department of Transportation, which counterclaimed against the general. The

---

[53] 30 Fed. Cl. 90 (1993).
[54] 652 A.2d 440 (R.I. 1994).

general contractor was awarded the contract to replace the bridge. Upon commencement of the work, problems arose leading to various disputes, the most important one being the unexpected behavior of the soils at the bottom of the bay. The department changed the pile-design concept, but disagreed with the general contractor on the additional cost. The department ordered the contractor to continue working under a force account, and the contractor filed suit seeking injunctive relief, termination of the contract, and damages. The parties entered into a termination agreement, whereupon the subcontractor filed this action seeking damages relating to the termination.

The court held that the contractor's failure to give formal notice to the department of extra remedial work was not a waiver of such claims. It was entitled to recover delay damages caused by the department's holding preconstruction meetings and delaying the award of the contract. The subcontractor was entitled to recover its additional overhead costs attributable to the department's breach, but was not entitled to recover for lost profits.

[F] Profit

Profit is usually included as part of the equitable adjustment and is almost always measured as a fixed percentage that is added to the cost of the change. Courts have typically allowed a "reasonable and customary allowance" for profit on contract changes.[55] When a credit change occurs (a net reduction to the cost of the project), some courts have held that profit should not be reduced.[56] However, some jurisdictions do reduce the contractor's profit if the change involves a reduction in the cost of the project.[57] AIA Document A201, Subparagraph 7.3.6, provides no reduction in profit in the event of a net reduction in the contract sum. EJCDC Document 1910-8, Subparagraph 11.6.2.5, provides to the contrary.

The calculation of the amount of profit is based upon the contract and the circumstances. AIA Document A201, Subparagraph 7.3.6, permits a reasonable allowance for profit. Most often, the rate of profit on change orders is established in the contract documents. However, when substantial changes take place, the parties may establish a rate, at the time of the change, that is reflective of the complexity of the work,[58] the risk assumed by the contractor,[59] or the amount of capital employed to complete the change.[60] In addition, when the parties cannot agree to a

---

[55] United States v. Callahan Walker Constr. Co., 317 U.S. 56 (1942); Jarosz v. Caesar Realty, Inc., 220 N.W.2d 191 (Mich. App. 1974).

[56] *See* Varo, Inc., ASBCA No. 16,146, 73-2 BCA (CCH) ¶ 10,206 (1973); Algernon Blair, Inc., ASBCA No. 10,738, 65-2 BCA (CCH) ¶ 5127 (1965).

[57] E.V. Lance Corp., ASBCA No. 9741, 65-2 BCA (CCH) ¶ 5076, 8 Gov't Cont. Rep. (CCH) ¶ 204 (1965).

[58] American Pipe & Steel Corp., ASBCA No. 7899, 1964 BCA (CCH) ¶ 4058 (1964).

[59] Cimarron Constr. Co., ENGBCA No. 2862, 69-2 BCA (CCH) ¶ 8003 (1969).

[60] Keco Indus., Inc., ASBCA No. 15,184, 72-2 BCA (CCH) ¶ 9576, 15 Gov't Cont. Rep. (CCH) ¶ 9 (1972).

price for a change, the courts will typically determine a reasonable price,[61] including overhead and profit.[62]

The 1997 edition of the *General Conditions of the Contract for Construction,* AIA Document A201, added language in Subparagraph 4.3.10.2 that included a mutual waiver of consequential damages, including profits lost on other projects as a result of delays on a current project, "[d]amages incurred by the Contractor . . . for loss of profit other than anticipated profits arising directly from the Work."

In *City of Beaumont v. Excavators & Constructors, Inc.,*[63] the excavation contractor was hired to perform street widening and other improvements for the city. The work, which was to be substantially completed within 220 working days, was finally completed within 240 working days. The telephone company did not know that the contract had been awarded until it received notice of a preconstruction meeting. The contractor completed the project within the allotted time period, was assessed no penalties for untimely performance, and made a 16.7-percent profit on the project. The contractor brought suit, however, claiming that it had been delayed in the performance of its work by the telephone company's delay in relocating its telephone poles and that it had sustained increased costs due to the delay attributable to re-sequencing the work. The contractor argued that it had to relocate and reassign its equipment and crews and incurred additional rental equipment charges and labor costs. The court reversed the judgment for the contractor, holding that no evidence or legal theory was advanced that would impose a duty on the telephone company to avoid delaying the contractor's performance. The city could not be held liable for any delay-related costs because of the no-damages-for-delay provision contained in its contract with the plaintiff.

§ 15.04 IMPACT COSTS

[A] Direct vs. Indirect Costs

[1] Direct and Indirect Costs Defined

The essential element of a changes clause is the determination of the proper level of compensation, positive or negative, as a result of a given change. This is generally referred to as the "equitable adjustment," generally seen as a corrective measure "utilized to keep a contractor whole" when the contract has been modified.[64] While direct costs are those directly incurred in order to complete a change, indirect costs or "impact costs" may be incurred in performing other items of the unchanged contract that have been affected by the change.

---

[61] Purvis v. United States, 344 F.2d 867 (9th Cir. 1965); Black Lake Pipe Line Co. v. Union Constr. Co., 538 S.W.2d 80 (Tex. 1976).

[62] Hensel Phelps Constr. Co. v. United States, 413 F.2d 701 (10th Cir. 1969).

[63] 870 S.W.2d 123 (Tex. App. 1993).

[64] Bruce Constr. Corp. v. United States, 324 F.2d 516 (Ct. Cl. 1963).

As a simple illustration, suppose that during the construction of a large art gallery, the owner decided that in addition to various forms of track lighting provided for in the contract drawings, she would like to have a large crystal chandelier hung in the center of each room. At this stage in the construction, the ceiling iron and drywall had already been installed. Had this change been ordered earlier, the direct cost of the change would have been the cost of the fixture, the materials necessary for its structural support, and the labor required to perform the installation. To perform this change at the time ordered, the contractor had to rip open part of the completed ceiling in order to install the structural support. The contractor incurred additional labor to remove and reinstall drywall. Furthermore, the removed drywall, as well as the scraps created from the newly installed drywall, had to be carted away. Should the contractor be compensated for the added labor and the cost of carting? What if the change has had an impact on the critical path of the project? Should the contractor be compensated for the additional time now necessary to remain on the project? Suppose, further, that the delay in completing this project has adversely affected the completion of other projects.

Generally, costs may be classified as direct and indirect. Direct costs are those most immediately connected with the work in question, while indirect costs are one step removed from direct costs, such as premiums, additional storage costs, and so forth. Indirect costs may also be referred to as impact costs. Indirect costs that are even further removed may be seen as unforeseeably remote and therefore unrecoverable.

[2]   Illustrative Cases

In *United States v. Becon Services Corp.*,[65] the subcontractor sought to recover for extra work performed on the project. The subcontractor received progress payments and made this additional claim for $1.2 million due to delay and inefficiencies caused by the general contractor. The subcontractor signed partial releases when the partial payments were made, but it sought to avoid the terms of those releases, claiming that they were the product of economic duress. The contract required that claims for additional work be itemized and presented within 10 days, but the subcontractor presented its first claim 14 months after substantial completion of the project. Thus, it could not recover under its claim. The court further rejected the subcontractor's economic duress argument because the only purported threat made by the general contractor involved a separate claim for $10,000.

In *Youngdale & Sons Construction Co. v. United States*,[66] the contractor sought to recover sums in addition to the contract price due to differing site conditions. The plaintiff, which was building officers' quarters on an Air Force base, encountered excess groundwater and subterranean rock formations. The plaintiff

---

[65] 837 F. Supp. 461 (D.D.C. 1993).
[66] 27 Fed. Cl. 516 (1993).

presented a claim for $1.6 million attributable to these conditions, using the total cost method to establish derivative damages.

The plaintiff bid $2.7 million on the project, which had an estimated cost of $3 million, and was awarded the contract. The plaintiff had not visited the site prior to bidding. In an inspection on the date of the notice to proceed, the plaintiff dug several potholes throughout the site. Within minutes, those holes were filled with 8 to 18 inches of groundwater. The soil removed from the holes was saturated. When the plaintiff brought this to the attention of the government, it was told that all jobs on the base experienced the same problem. The plaintiff alerted the government that it considered this to be materially different soil conditions from those indicated in the contract documents and considered this to be a compensable difference. Although the government acknowledged that the conditions were different from the contract drawings and specifications, it stated that such a condition was normal for the time of year and should have been anticipated by the plaintiff. It denied any monetary or time adjustments.

The plaintiff started the work, but was significantly delayed when equipment became mired in the muddy soil. The government reiterated its position that the contract documents were correct and that the plaintiff should proceed as planned. The government issued a cure notice for inadequate progress and threatened termination for "failure to begin substantial performance of the contract." Ultimately, the earthwork was performed with significant delays and additional costs. The plaintiff repeatedly submitted claims for differing conditions to the contracting officer. The plaintiff also challenged the contract boring logs with respect to differences in subterranean rock formations. The government claimed that the logs accurately depicted the actual site conditions and denied all the plaintiff's claims. The government threatened to assess liquidated damages for the delay and lack of performance and issued an unsatisfactory Contractor Performance Evaluation. However, it ultimately accepted the project as substantially complete and the plaintiff left the jobsite. The plaintiff continued to submit claims for increased costs attributable to differing site conditions for the actual costs incurred and the impact costs. The government paid the contract price less $46,750 in liquidated damages for the 187-day delay.

The court held that the plaintiff had failed to meet its burden of proving all the elements of a differing-site-conditions claim arising out of the rock problems. With respect to the groundwater issue, the court held that the contractor was not entitled to recover damages under the total cost approach, but could recover its direct costs. Therefore, the plaintiff was awarded those costs plus interest from the date the claims were received by the contracting officer.

In *State Department of Natural Resources v. Transamerica Premier Insurance Co.*,[67] a surety sought to recover from the state for damages suffered by the contractor after the state allegedly submitted defective plans and specifications that resulted in extra costs. These extra costs reached a point where the contractor's business collapsed. The contractor also sought to recover his personal losses.

---

[67] 856 P.2d 766 (Alaska 1993).

During the course of construction, problems arose from errors and discrepancies in the plans and specifications, and the department issued appropriate extra work and change orders. The department removed its on-site inspector to save money. After four months on the project, the contractor informed the department that he intended to file a claim for extra costs associated with defects in the plans. The contractor rejected the department's calculations for the cost of remaining extra work and change orders. The original contract was for $211,000 and the plaintiff submitted a claim for $156,000 in extra costs. The department awarded only $15,000 in extra costs. The plaintiff then brought his claim for consequential damages, arguing that debts incurred in prosecution of the project had destroyed his business. After unsuccessful attempts to obtain compensation through the administrative process, the plaintiff assigned his claims to the surety and this suit was filed.

The court affirmed the summary judgment for the state on the tort claims, dismissed the contractor's claims for personal injuries, and remanded the surety's consequential damage claims for further administrative proceedings. The Alaska Supreme Court held that the surety's consequential damage claims were potentially recoverable in a breach-of-contract claim, but found that there was no valid bad-faith claim against the state.

In *Mid-Western Electric v. DeWild Grant Reckert*,[68] the plaintiff electrical subcontractor sued the engineering firm that had prepared specifications for the installation of fire detection and fire suppression systems, under malpractice theories. The defendant was hired by the Air National Guard to prepare drawings and specifications for the project. The plans required input from several engineering specialties. The defendants sent the plans to another engineering company for part of the review. During the entire process, the Air National Guard reviewed and made changes in the plans and specifications. The plaintiff obtained the plans and specifications and bid on the contract. It used a general bid without a list of specific equipment and offered to supply all required equipment. The plaintiff's bid was significantly lower than the other bids. Because of the price discrepancy, the plaintiff repeatedly contacted its suppliers to assure that the equipment to be furnished was up to specifications. The plaintiff did not check the equipment list in the supplier's bid against the specifications, and when the list was submitted to the defendants, they determined that the equipment was insufficient in various respects.

The detectors did not meet specifications. The plaintiff made the installation, but the system failed to meet test specifications. The plaintiff contacted the manufacturer and repositioned the detectors, but the equipment still did not meet the specifications. The Guard then changed the specifications and agreed to pay the plaintiff an additional amount to meet the new standards, but refused to give the plaintiff full credit for the nonconforming detectors. The plaintiff then brought this suit against the engineers and the supplier of the detectors for the economic loss it had sustained. The supplier was dismissed from the suit and the jury returned a

---

[68] 500 N.W.2d 250 (S.D. 1993).

verdict for the plaintiff against the engineers in the amount of $45,000. The court reversed the judgment on the jury verdict, holding that the jury should have been instructed on the plaintiff's contributory negligence. It recognized, though, that purely economic damages could be recovered from the defendant engineers under malpractice theory.

[B] Recovery of Impact Costs

[1] *Rice* Doctrine

Typically, impact costs are claimed with regard to changes that result in critical path delay. Federal contracts at one time restricted the recovery of such costs.[69] In *United States v. Rice,* the construction of a veteran's facility was delayed when unsuitable soil conditions were encountered. As a result of the delay, the construction took place during the winter at decreased labor productivity and increased field overhead expense. The court held that an equitable adjustment was permissible for work changed by the plan and specification revisions, but no monetary adjustment would be made for any increase in the cost of the work not changed. Thus, no recovery was permitted for the increased labor and overhead expended to complete the project.

The restrictive *Rice* doctrine eventually was changed by revised standard federal government contract language as follows:

> If any such change causes an increase or decrease in the cost of, or the time required for performance of this contract, or otherwise affects any other provisions of this contract *whether changed or not changed by any such order,* an equitable adjustment shall be made in the contract price or delivery schedule, or both.[70]

Today, federal government contract changes entitle the contractor to an equitable adjustment to the work changed, as well as an equitable adjustment for increased costs resulting from the change, necessary to complete the unchanged work. The equitable adjustment encompasses the effect of a change order upon any part of the work, including delay expense, as long as the effect was "the necessary, reasonable and foreseeable result of the change."[71]

[2] Recoverable Costs

Examples of impact costs that may be recovered include unabsorbed overhead (overhead incurred if the project is shut down or idled),[72] salaries and benefits of

---

[69] United States v. Rice, 317 U.S. 61 (1942).

[70] FAR 52.243-1(b) (emphasis added).

[71] 32 Fed. Reg. 16,269 (Nov. 29, 1967).

[72] Eichleay Corp., ASBCA No. 5183, 60-2 BCA (CCH) ¶ 2688, 2 Gov't Cont. Rep. (CCH) ¶ 485 (1960), *aff'd on reconsideration,* 61-1 BCA (CCH) ¶ 2894, 3 Gov't Cont. Rep. (CCH) ¶ 138(a) (1961).

idle labor,[73] idle equipment owned or rented by the contractor,[74] additional bond premiums,[75] additional storage costs,[76] and so forth.

As an illustration, the Court of Claims decided a case involving the construction of a postal facility,[77] during which the Postal Service ordered numerous change orders that delayed completion of the project. The contractor asserted a claim for costs incurred by the delay. The court held that the contractor was entitled to recover increased costs of performance and impact costs as a result of the delay. These costs included payroll, premium time, taxes, and overhead.

[3] Recovery for Other Projects

However, recovery for costs incurred on other projects affected by the change is not permitted. For instance, one contractor was low bidder on several projects but could not accept the awards, because it had lost its bonding capacity. The contractor claimed that the loss of bonding capacity was directly attributable to maladministration of the contract in dispute by the governmental agency. The board of contract appeals dismissed this portion of its claim.[78] In general, courts have been reluctant to permit recovery of costs on one contract due to changes or delays from another contract.[79]

[4] No-Damages-for-Delay Clauses

Some state and local government contracts and private contracts incorporate no-damages-for-delay clauses in their contracts in order to shield against contractor claims for impact costs due to delays. No-damages-for-delay clauses have been upheld in many jurisdictions.[80] There are, however, numerous exceptions to the enforcement of such a clause.

---

[73] Weaver Constr. Co., ASBCA No. 12,577, 69-1 BCA (CCH) ¶ 7455, 11 Gov't Cont. Rep. (CCH) ¶ 379 (1969).

[74] W.G. Cornell Co. v. Ceramic Coating Co., 626 F.2d 990 (D.C. Cir. 1980); Mullinax Eng'g Co. v. Platte Valley Constr. Co., 412 F.2d 553 (10th Cir. 1969).

[75] Proserv, Inc., ASBCA No. 20,768, 78-1 BCA (CCH) ¶ 13,066 (1978).

[76] George Hyman Constr. Co., ENGBCA No. 4541, 85-1 BCA (CCH) ¶ 17,847, 27 Gov't Cont. Rep. (CCH) ¶ 320 (1985).

[77] Coley Properties Corp. v. United States, 593 F.2d 380 (Ct. Cl. 1979).

[78] Land Movers, Inc., ENGBCA No. 5656, 91-1 BCA (CCH) ¶ 23,317 (1991).

[79] General Dynamics Corp. v. United States, 585 F.2d 457 (Ct. Cl. 1978). In MLK, Inc. v. University of Kan., 940 P.2d 1158 (Kan. Ct. App. 1997), the contractor was not allowed to recover: 1. Lost profits (test was anticipation that MLK would lose profits on other projects when the contract was entered into, not when the MLK contract was terminated); 2. Loss of bonding capacity (previous MLK projects had claims against its bonds and other previous projects had been terminated); 3. Other consequential damages (MLK had the opportunity to avoid default on its SBA loan and failed to do so).

[80] *See also Recovering Consequential Damages from the Government: An Impossible Dream?*, 5 Nash & Cibinic: Rep. 20 (Apr. 1991).

A contractor wishing to recover impact costs from changes should first examine its contract. For example, the state of Washington denied the recovery of impact costs under a changed conditions clause because the sole contractual remedy for delay costs was an extension of time.[81] If a no-damages-for-delay or other claim-barring clause is not present, impact costs may be recovered.[82]

However, if a no-damages-for-delay clause is present, the contractor, in order to recover impact costs, will probably have to demonstrate that its claim falls within one of the applicable exceptions. For example, one of these exceptions is the contractor's claim that the delay was not intended or contemplated by the parties to be within the purview of the clause.[83] If the contractor cannot demonstrate that the clause meets one of the exceptions or that the clause does not apply to the change, recovery may be denied.

Assessing impact costs can be difficult. The more complex the project or change, the more difficult the assessment. For this reason, time extension and impact costs should be addressed in any change order. The contractor may reserve its right to later claim these costs or release all impact costs relating to the particular change.[84]

[C] Measuring Disruptions

[1] Identify the Locations and Resources

If a contractor knows the locations and resources required to perform each of its activities, the contractor may define the scope of possible disruptions and more accurately estimate the man-hour cost of a change order. With this information, the contractor should be able to minimize the disruptive effects of a change order by taking advantage of available float to postpone either the changed work or the unchanged work, or some of both.[85]

---

[81] *See* M. Brunner, Annotation, *Validity and Construction of "No Damage" Clause with Respect to Delay in Building or Construction Contract*, 74 A.L.R.3d 187 (1976). Donald B. Murphy Contractors, Inc. v. State, 626 P.2d 1270 (Wash. 1985).

[82] Shintech Inc. v. Group Constructors, Inc., 688 S.W.2d 144 (Tex. App. 1985).

[83] City of Houston v. R.F. Ball Constr. Co., 570 S.W.2d 75 (Tex. App. 1978); Western Eng'rs, Inc. v. State Road Comm'n, 437 P.2d 216 (Utah 1968); Ace Stone, Inc. v. Wayne Township, 221 A.2d 515 (N.J. 1966). *But see* Buckley & Co. v. City of N.Y., 121 A.D.2d 933 (N.Y. App. Div. 1986) (The contract provided procedures, which Buckley failed to follow, in order to modify the contract based upon "unanticipated subsurface" conditions. In addition, because the contract contained a no-damages-for-delay clause, the court denied the recovery of damages stemming from an eight-year delayed completion. The court stated that "while the conditions themselves may not have been anticipated, the possibility, however unlikely, of their arising was contemplated and addressed by the parties in their agreement." The court, in effect, issued an unreasonably strict and self-contradicting holding by ruling that unanticipated conditions were contemplated.).

[84] *See* NRM Corp. v. Hercules, Inc., 758 F.2d 676 (D.C. Cir. 1985).

[85] M. Finke, *A Better Way to Estimate and Mitigate Disruption*, 124 J. Constr. Eng'g & Mgmt. 490 (No. 6, Nov./Dec. 1998).

[2]   Effect on Profit

An ability to predict and quantify disruption can also allow a contractor to increase its profits. Missing opportunities to increase or maximize profits are even more regrettable when we consider that a contractor pricing a change order is usually in a much stronger bargaining position than when it submitted its bid for the original scope of work. To the extent a contractor fails to properly define the scope of possible disruption, or properly quantify such disruption, the risk increases that it will underestimate the man-hour costs of changes and such failures can preclude a contractor from later recovering any additional costs.[86] To minimize the disruptive working conditions will facilitate timely negotiated settlements for the value of the changed work, including the unavoidable disruption.[87]

[3]   Changes in Working Conditions

A change order can cause six different changes in working conditions:[88]

1. Resource diversions or skill dilution, requiring that the changed or disrupted and unchanged or disrupted work use the same resources and be performed at the same time.

2. Work area congestion, requiring that the changed and unchanged work be performed in the same area at the same time.

3. Stacking of trades, requiring that the changed and unchanged work be performed in the same area, be performed at the same time, and represent different types of work.

4. Dilution of supervision, requiring that the changed and unchanged work be performed at the same time and have the same supervisors.

5. Interruptions of otherwise continuous work, requiring that unchanged work be temporarily stopped while the changed work is performed.

6. Delay, requiring that the changed and unchanged work be performed at a different time and transforming the unchanged, but now delayed, work to become changed work.

[4]   Disruption Distribution Analysis

To measure disruption more accurately, an owner-contractor-agreed estimating methodology is needed that identifies the scope of possible disruption and generates estimates of disruption at the schedule activity level. The disruption

---

[86] *Id.* at 491.
[87] *Id.* at 492.
[88] *Id.* at 493-94.

distribution analysis is one way to estimate the disruption costs of the changed work. In a disruption distribution analysis, each activity in a contractor's scope of work is separately considered for increased performance costs as a result of the change. If it is determined that one activity can have no disruptive effect on another activity (because, for example, the potentially disrupted activity has already been completed), no disruption will be distributed to it.[89]

In disruption distribution, the total disruption distributed may be more or less than the man-hours of added or deleted work, or may equal zero. The disruption distributed through any causal relationship will be independent of the disruption sensitivity of other causal relationships for subsequent activities. Causal relationship sensitivities will change with time as the relevant working conditions change. When compared to current analytical methods, this new procedure will more accurately model disruption by first recognizing that the change-order-caused disruption man-hours added to unchanged activities can themselves disrupt other activities, both changed and unchanged; and second, allowing disruption to "flow" along each causal relationship.[90]

The disruption sensitivity of the causal relationship linking two activities will be a function of the linked activities' locations, times of performance, types of work, crew sizes and compositions, and supervisors. There are two sensitivity factors: qualitative and quantitative. Qualitative sensitivity factors indicate whether a pair of activities shares the same location, time of performance, resource type, or supervisor.[91] The information necessary to generate the qualitative factors includes each activity's resource or trade, supervisor, type of work, and location. The information necessary to create the quantitative factors includes each activity's crew size and composition. Disruption distribution for qualitative factors will require development of a comprehensive "location breakdown structure," similar to a work breakdown structure, in which each activity in the contractor's schedule will be identified by location. Like the work breakdown structure, the location breakdown structure should be a hierarchical, multi-level "tree" that can be summarized or rolled-up to different levels of detail. Performance dates for each activity will be available from the current critical path method schedule.[92]

Owner or designer reluctance to acknowledge that disruption costs result from changes deprives contractors of chances to minimize the disruptive impacts of changes. With cooperation from the designer and the owner, however, the contractor may mitigate the disruption effect of changed work.

The first step in mitigating disruption should be moving activities within their early start and late finish dates. As a result, in evaluating a change order, there will often be a trade-off between time extensions and disruption. As more time is given, activity early start and late finish dates will increase, making it easier to avoid disruptive working conditions by rescheduling the work. Even where

---

[89] *Id.* at 494.
[90] *Id.*
[91] *Id.*
[92] *Id.* at 495.

a project's critical path is unaffected, it may therefore sometimes be in an owner's interest to consider granting a time extension in return for an avoidance of disruption costs.[93]

Assuming that activity locations are going to be relatively fixed, disruption can be further mitigated most easily by adjusting activities' resources and supervisors. For example, resource and supervisor overlaps could be avoided by using roving dedicated change order crews. A dedicated change order crew performing its work during a second shift would be even more effective at avoiding disruption.[94]

The disruption distribution method in itself is not a complete, ready-to-use method for estimating and mitigating disruption. Disruption distribution requires detailed information and computations. It may be that the best use of disruption distribution will be to show how burdensome an accurate disruption analysis would be and why a simplified factor-based method as currently used should be accepted as reasonable to exchange for loss of accuracy.[95]

[D] Cumulative Impact of Multiple Changes

[1] Cumulative Impact Defined

When multiple changes on a project act in sequence or concurrently, there is a compounding effect; this is the most damaging consequence for a project and the most difficult to understand and manage. The net effect of the individual changes is much greater than a sum of the individual parts. Not only may increases in cost and time be required, but the project logic may also have to be redone.[96] The cumulative impact effect occurs when the project conditions have deteriorated to the point where work on an activity is adversely affected by another activity or by the mere nature of the site environment. No research has been conducted on this "ripple effect," although it has been acknowledged quite often by construction professionals. Defining when the ripple effect applies is often limited to a post-project analysis. One suggestion is that it occurs when the number of work hours devoted to changed work or rework exceeds 10 percent of the work hours devoted to the scope of work.[97] Cumulative disruption or impact is the disruption that occurs between two or more change orders and basic work. Cumulative impact does not include local disruption that can be ascribed to a specific change. It is the synergistic effect of the changes on the unchanged work and on other changes.[98]

---

[93] *Id.* at 496.

[94] *Id.*

[95] *Id.* at 496-97.

[96] Hester, Kuprenas & Chang, *Construction Changes and Change Orders: Their Magnitude and Impact*, Constr. Indus. Inst., Source Doc. 66 at 35 (Oct. 1991).

[97] Thomas & Napolitan, *The Effects of Changes on Labor Productivity: Why and How Much*, Constr. Indus. Inst., Source Doc. 99 at 25 (Aug. 1994), citing C. Leonard, *The Effect of Change Orders on Productivity*, 6 Revay Report 1-3 (No. 2, 1987).

[98] M. Finke, *Claims for Construction Productivity Losses*, 26 Pub. Cont. L.J. 311, 316-17 (No. 3, Spring 1997).

[2]   Difficulty in Measuring Cumulative Impact

The compounding effect of multiple project change is poorly understood, difficult to measure, and seldom reflected in the estimated cost of individual project changes. It becomes apparent when work cannot be completed on time and labor productivity does not measure up to the anticipated level of efficiency Project managers sometimes refer to the compounding effect of multiple project changes as the "ripple" effect.[99]

Many boards and courts have acknowledged that the disruptive impacts of changes and delays cannot be fully and accurately anticipated.[100] Few contractors maintain adequate jobsite records to allow evaluation of impact costs for individual change orders. Further, some contractors do not realize that they have incurred impact costs until final profit and loss statements indicate a sizable loss.[101] A pilot test confirmed that productivity information was not generally available in owner or contractor project files, especially for completed projects.[102]

In another study, it also concluded that construction firms either do not collect or do not preserve in easily retrievable manner the needed level of detail to analyze productivity, confirming earlier research. Although designers and contractors did not keep productivity data, they did maintain cost, labor-hour, schedule, and change information, all of which was available at the 25, 50, 75, 80, 85, 90, 95, and end-of-project milestones.[103]

The first objective of the research study was to identify and quantify the hidden cost of change. It was quickly discovered that it was impossible to estimate accurately all hidden costs associated with implementing change before the actual implementation. Even after project change is implemented, it is difficult to capture and account for the ripple effect.[104]

There may be many reasons why multiple change orders cannot be accurately priced until the project is over. Later change orders, including change orders that were priced prior to but authorized after a particular change order, might be made more expensive because of conditions created or changed by the first change

---

[99] C. Ibbs & W. Allen, *Quantitative Impacts of Product Change*, Constr. Indus. Inst., Source Doc. 108 at 4 (May 1995).

[100] Finke, *A Better Way to Estimate and Mitigate Disruption*, 124 J. Constr. Eng'g & Mgmt. 490 (No. 6, Nov./Dec. 1998), citing Roberts Constr. Co., GSBCA No. 5754, 81-1 BCA (CCH) ¶ 15,104 (1981) at 74,732; ACS Constr. Co., ASBCA No. 36,535, 89-1 BCA (CCH) ¶ 21,406 (1989) at 107,894; and Pittman Constr. Co., GSBCA No. 4897, 4923, 81-1 BCA (CCH) ¶ 14,847 (1981) at 73,298. *See also* Associated Mech. Contractors, Inc. v. Martin K. Eby Constr. Co., 964 F. Supp. 1576 (M.D. Ga. 1997) (court recognized that because subcontractor might be unable fully to account for delay costs until end of project, and that if pay application waived all cost claims not included in pay application, subcontractor would be required either to forego interim payments or forfeit rights to claim delay costs for which notice had been given).

[101] Ibbs & Allen at 10.

[102] Ibbs & Allen at 4.

[103] C. Ibbs, *Quantitative Impacts of Project Change: Size Issues*, 123 J. Constr. Eng'g & Mgmt. 308, 309 (No. 3, Sept. 1997).

[104] Ibbs & Allen at 32.

order. There is a complex interaction between multiple changes and a baseline scope of work. The first change requires that a contractor price two elements: the direct impact of the change on the base work and the indirect impact on the base work. The second change requires that a contractor price six elements: the direct and indirect impact on the base contract, the direct and indirect impact on the first change, and the direct and indirect impact on the second change. The third change creates 18 pricing elements a contractor must consider, with the number of pricing elements increasing according to the formula, $2 \times 3^{N-1}$, where N equals the sequential change number. In fact, for just the first three changes on a project, a contractor must account for 26 pricing elements, each of which represents a possible impact of a change.[105]

The owner may, for example, request a price for a proposed change but then delay authorizing it. In such a case, the baseline against which the contractor priced the change may no longer exist when the change is authorized. Moreover, other changes may be authorized in the time between the contractor's pricing and the owner's authorization. An ideal situation rarely occurs where change orders are individually implemented sequentially and promptly after they have been priced against a comprehensive and accurate baseline. If the first three changes on a project are priced individually but authorized at the same time, the contractor's pricing efforts will account for only those six elements representing the direct and indirect impacts of the changes on the baseline scope of work. The contractor will fail to account for the 20 elements representing the effects of the changes on each other and the effects of each individual change on those portions of the baseline affected by other changes.

As the time between pricing and authorization of changes increases, and as multiple changes are priced independently but authorized as a group, the chances increase of the conditions existing when the changes are authorized not being the conditions anticipated or existing when they were priced. Furthermore, the chances that some costs may be overlooked increase dramatically.[106]

[3] Causal Mechanisms

Causal mechanisms that link the disruptive changes to the changed working conditions may support estimated impact costs. Causal mechanisms could include shared resources or work areas. These shared resources or work areas should be objectively verifiable based on facts in the contractor's plan and project records, and therefore should not necessarily require expert opinion. It may be appropriate to trace causal mechanisms from well-defined groups of change orders rather than individual change orders.[107]

---

[105] Finke, *Claims for Construction Productivity Losses*, 26 Pub. Cont. L.J. 311, 331 (No. 3, Spring 1997).

[106] *Id.* at 332.

[107] *Id.* at 335.

Even a small number of changes, two or three, has a significant negative impact on labor productivity. Research discovered that the fine motor skills used by electricians are more adversely impacted by change than gross motor skills of heavy equipment operators.[108]

[4] Engineering and Construction Relationships

When comparing engineering and construction relationships, engineering change exhibited a stronger negative impact than construction change. For example, an engineering change that is not identified until construction begins will require additional engineering labor hours and coordination of material and other project resources, at a cost higher than the rework costs associated with identifying and resolving project change earlier in the project cycle. The late identification of project change will tend to disrupt work flow, reduce productivity, and increase project costs, thus negatively affecting overall project performance.[109]

The research indicated that construction change greater than 5 percent results in negative construction productivity or productivity less than planned. The more construction change, the more negative impact on construction productivity. When construction change approaches 34 percent, construction productivity is approximately 90 percent of normal.[110]

The largest number of projects in the study exhibited less than 4-percent growth. Thirty-seven percent of the projects were reduced in scope during the project construction phase. Twenty-nine percent exhibited growth in cost beyond 5 percent. The outlying or extreme range of project change areas accounted for project growth greater than 10 percent and scope reductions greater than 5 percent. These two areas accounted for 50 percent of the project change ratios. Seventeen percent of the projects showed growth between 11 and 50 percent.[111]

[5] Reduction in Project Scope

Project change caused by reduction in project scope is common when a primary goal is to bring a project in under or on budget. Project change has similar hidden costs, whether the change is an addition or reduction in scope. The ramifications and consequential costs can be excessive on staff, contractors, and suppliers. The hidden or unforeseeable costs of change increase with more project change; 20 percent of change on a project is a considerable amount.[112]

---

[108] Ibbs & Allen at 10.
[109] Ibbs & Allen at 51.
[110] Ibbs & Allen at 51-52.
[111] Ibbs & Allen at 63.
[112] Ibbs & Allen at 61-62.

[6]   Large Process-Oriented Private Project

Change in another study by Ibbs was measured from the original estimate, although it was acknowledged that using the original estimate as a basis for statistical analysis may lead to a built-in bias in the data analysis. Ibbs compared the estimate to the final contract cost regardless of whether the additional costs were approved as authorized change orders or claims were paid. In many cases, the contractor absorbed the impact of the change. Additional costs of performance were caused by both design-related and owner-directed changes. Ibbs's study concentrated on large, process-oriented private projects that differ from studies in many other sectors of the industry and the author's previous studies.[113]

Ibbs's study measured change by the increase in total installed cost (TIC) at selected design and construction milestone points. TIC included all engineering, procurement, and construction costs. Net and absolute difference were used to measure project change. If the initial and final facility cost values were identical, no recorded change was registered despite the fact that multiple changes might have canceled each other out.[114]

Most projects had less than 4-percent cost growth during the design phase. Similarly, change during construction was generally moderate. Combining the design and construction phases together showed a moderate 5-percent cost change.[115]

Compared to the change rates reported by J. Diekmann & M. Nelson,[116] Ibbs's change ratios were relatively low. Ibbs suggested the change rates may be lower than the other studies because private sector managers have more flexibility to negotiate with contractors, utilize different contract strategy techniques according to the project circumstances, and were more willing to modify scope when costs exceed budget. Thirty percent or more of the projects in the Ibbs study came in under the first cost estimate developed after a project moved into its design phase. On the other hand, approximately 20 percent of these projects did show substantial cost growth of 11 percent or more. The average was 26 percent, so even projects in the private sector resulted in major overruns.[117]

In each case, productivity declined noticeably as more change was incurred. Design phase productivity was 0.84 when there was 40 percent change on the project, and design productivity was 0.93 when there were no changes. By regression equation, every additional 10-percent change on a project hurts productivity by 2.48 percent.[118]

---

[113] Ibbs, *Quantitative Impacts of Project Change: Size Issues*, 123 J. Constr. Eng'g & Mgmt. 308 (No. 3, Sept. 1997).

[114] *Id.* at 309.

[115] *Id.*

[116] *Construction Claims: Frequency and Severity*, J. Constr. Eng'g & Mgmt., ASCE 111 (1985), and Hester, Kuprenas & Chang, *Construction Changes and Change Orders: Their Magnitude and Impact*, Constr. Indus. Inst., Source Doc. 66 (1991).

[117] Ibbs at 309-10.

[118] *Id.* at 310.

Design productivity averaged less than the planned value in all situations. Ibbs suggested one explanation for this was that turnkey contractors may be willing to expend extra design efforts to improve construction phase productivity.[119]

Construction productivity was equal to planned at a 6-percent change level for the typical project. Change occurring late in the construction job has a progressively more disruptive impact on productivity.[120]

Ibbs concluded that managers of private sector projects have some latitude to modify project scope as costs increase. Public sector owners, on the other hand, have less latitude, and consequently, their projects are probably more susceptible to change. Ibbs also concluded that the amount of change is proportional to the labor cost of that change. Large amounts of change are implemented less efficiently. Among many implications, this indicated that planning to avoid changes is perhaps more of a prudent investment than is generally thought.[121]

[7] Excessive Number of Change Orders

In some circumstances, an excessive number of change orders may cause the contractor to experience cost overruns in its overall project performance that exceed the direct cost of the individual changes or the local disruptive impacts of those changes. The contractor may attempt to recover any excess costs via a claim for the "cumulative impact" of the numerous changes.[122]

Courts and boards have recognized that a contractor's entitlement under the changes clause is not limited to the direct costs of multiple changes, but may also include the cumulative impact of multiple changes on distant, unchanged work. The theory of cumulative impact claims is that the contractor, when pricing changes individually and negotiating compensation for the direct changes, may not take into consideration the synergistic effect of all changes and may fail to foresee the so-called cumulative impact costs; it thereby obtains less than full compensation for the change order.[123] In *Appeal of Charles G. Williams Construction, Inc.*,[124] a project owner issued a series of 26 change orders to correct defective drawings and specifications. In addition to direct costs, each change order included a 15-percent overhead for indirect costs. The board ruled that this markup did not adequately compensate the contractor for the cumulative disruption of the performance and administration of the contract. The contractor was awarded additional compensation for cumulative impact costs. *Appeal of Atlas Construction Co.*[125] expressly recognized the cumulative impact costs and

---

[119] *Id.*

[120] *Id.*

[121] *Id.* at 310-11.

[122] Baltz & Morrissey, *Contractor's Claims for Cumulative Impact: Valid but Difficult to Recover*, 32 Procurement Law. 15 (No. 1, Fall 1996).

[123] Baltz & Morrissey at 15.

[124] ASBCA No. 33,766 (1989).

[125] GSBCA No. 8593 (1990).

awarded the contractor lost labor efficiency, additional costs for updating CPM schedules, and increased field office costs.[126]

In another case, Ebasco claimed that Exxon had breached the lump-sum, fixed-price, $106 million construction contract by ordering an estimated 98,000 change orders at Exxon's Santa Ynez oil and gas treatment facility in Santa Barbara, California, to build onshore process facilities as part of the plant expansion. The contract required the work to be completed in 22 months.[127] Because of initial delays caused by contractor interference and other causes, Exxon extended the schedule by 110 days and increased the contract amount by $4.3 million. Ebasco agreed to the new schedule and price based on Exxon's assurances that design was done and there would be no further problems with changes, drawings, and delays.

After extending the performance period and increasing the contract costs, however, there were as many as 200 changes a day for an estimated total of 98,000. Exxon ultimately issued at least 1,600 new drawings; 11,700 revisions to existing drawings; 3,600 cable schedule revisions; 1,700 modifications to the electrical bill of materials; 1,200 field change notices; and 1,000 changes to the mechanical line list. Ebasco claimed that many of the changes were issued without sufficient notice to permit it to reschedule its planned operation to accommodate the changes in an orderly or efficient fashion. The contractor claimed $62 million in a lawsuit filed by its former parent, Enserch Corp. The jury awarded $33.3 million to the contractor.[128]

[8] Disruption Theories

Two types of disruption theories exist: local and cumulative. *Local disruption* refers to the direct impact that changed work has on other unchanged work going on around it.[129] A contractor presenting a claim for cumulative disruption should decide initially whether it intends to recover synergistic cumulative disruption damages or local disruption damages that were unforeseeable at the time the individual changes were negotiated, due to the number and overlapping nature of the changes. In either case, the disruption limitations from prepriced or foreseeable work, foreseeable working conditions, mitigation of costs and damages, and responsibility for noncompensable disruption must be addressed.[130]

---

[126] *The Cumulative Impact of Multiple Changes*, 18 Constr. Claims Monthly 1 (No. 5, May 1996).

[127] *Jury Award Goes to Contractor*, 240 Eng'g News—Record 16 (No. 20, May 18, 1998).

[128] *Id.*

[129] M. Finke, *Claims for Construction Productivity Losses*, citing Triple "A" South, ASBCA No. 46,866, 94-3 BCA (CCH) ¶ 27,194 (1994) (cumulative impact has two aspects, either merely as an increment to direct or local disruption costs or as so conceptually distinct from local disruption as to constitute a separately compensable constructive change).

[130] *Id.* at 324.

[a] Proving Entitlement to a Cumulative Impact Claim

Multiple change orders do not automatically result in compensable cumulative impact costs, however.[131] In *Appeal of Freeman-Darling, Inc.*,[132] numerous change orders were found not sufficiently significant to have a substantial cumulative impact on the contractor's performance or administration of the contract. In *Southwest Marine, Inc.*,[133] the board denied the contractor's cumulative impact claim, concluding that the contractor had: (1) failed to show that after 202 change orders, the work differed significantly from the work anticipated under the original contract; and (2) failed to present evidence sufficient to convince the board that the change orders had actually caused Southwest Marine to experience labor inefficiency and other disruptive effects.[134]

To prove entitlement to a cumulative impact claim, the contractor must first prove: (1) the existence of a cumulative impact caused by the excessive and frequent changes; (2) that the cumulative impact of the excessive changes affected the work; (3) that the cumulative impact of the excessive changes increased the cost of performance; and (4) that the impact was not foreseeable when the change orders were priced. Other courts have also required the contractor to show that the contracting officer exceeded the permissible limits of discretion under the changes clause when the changes were issued, and materially altered the nature of the contractor's original bargain.[135] For these other courts, the theory of cumulative disruption further holds that the issuance of a large number of changes is itself a constructive change wholly separate and distinct from the individual changes themselves.[136]

[b] Proving Entitlement to a Local Disruption Claim

If a contractor elects to pursue local-yet-unforeseeable disruption associated with negotiated changes, the contractor should first show that the changes, although not necessarily constituting a cardinal change, were so numerous or overlapping or both that the contractor obtained less than a full recovery for the individual changes, because it was unable to foresee and account for all of the local disruption resulting from the individual changes. Second, it should prove that at the times the contractor negotiated the changes, it had no reason to know that it was not fully pricing the changes. The contractor must also show that the release or settlement language attached to the individual changes does not bar its claim. The contractor must then establish change-specific causation and produce a reasonable quantification of its damages.[137]

---

[131] *Cumulative Impact of Multiple Changes* at 1.
[132] GSBCA No. 7112 (1989).
[133] 94-3 BCA (CCH) ¶ 27,102 (1994).
[134] Baltz & Morrissey at 19.
[135] Baltz & Morrissey at 15.
[136] Finke, *Claims for Construction Productivity Losses* at 317.
[137] *Id.* at 324.

[c]   Synergistic Cumulative Disruption

If a contractor pursues synergistic cumulative disruption damages, the contractor should first be required to establish that a cardinal change occurred. Again, the contractor should also show that release or settlement language attached to the individual changes does not bar its claim. The contractor will then have to establish causation. The causal analysis required for a claim of synergistic cumulative damages, however, need not be change-specific to the extent required for local disruption claims. Finally, the contractor should produce a reasonable quantification of damages quantitatively distinct from its other claims.[138]

It is assumed that cumulative disruption is caused by an unreasonable or unforeseeable number of changes. Conversely, a reasonable or foreseeable number of changes does not cause cumulative disruption. One can establish, therefore, what constituted an unreasonable number of changes or change order man-hours on a particular project and identify when the project began to experience cumulative disruption. It is clear that labor productivity prior to the onset of cumulative disruption was unaffected because such work was performed under working conditions that existed prior to the onset of the cumulative disruption.[139]

Though much has been said about the cumulative impact of change orders, there have been no quantitative studies showing the magnitude of these effects. Projects in which the cumulative impact occurs are typically involved in litigation, so data are usually not available. However, studies at Pennsylvania State University indicated that their impacts can be as great as 7:1 or more. This figure seems quite large, but one must remember that these are very unsatisfactory projects. For projects not involved in claims, ratios as high as 4:1 have been documented. These conclusions are not presented as a tool for estimating losses of efficiency, but as an indicator that these orders of magnitude of efficiency losses can occur.[140]

Proving the cumulative, synergistic impact of changes can be difficult, because courts and boards have consistently held that the number of changes does not establish impact. Courts and boards have also expressed dissatisfaction with attempts to prove cumulative impact by comparing the original cost of the work to the cost as changed—a total cost comparison. Rather, a contractor is usually required to present contemporaneous documentation detailing the type and extent of the cumulative disruption. The contractor must present detailed proof of its alleged inefficient performance in the form of comparisons of the productivity achieved on the disrupted work versus normal productivity achieved on undisrupted work on the same or a similar project.[141] Many boards look for the testimony of experts to support the contractor's cumulative impact claim.[142]

---

[138] Id.

[139] Id. at 330.

[140] Thomas & Napolitan at 26.

[141] Bechtel Nat'l, Inc., NASA BCA No. 1186-7, 90-1 BCA (CCH) ¶ 22,549 (1990).

[142] Baltz & Morrissey at 15.

[9]   Identifying Working Conditions

When faced with a potential cumulative impact, a contractor should first identify all working conditions on the particular job that are likely to be adversely affected by a succession of changes. A contractor then must explain in its claim how performing those conditions caused a cost overrun.[143] Analysis of cumulative impact should focus on how a group of changes affects working conditions. Impact on working conditions may include:[144]

- effects on other work in the same area where changes are made;

- effects on other work to be performed by the same work force or equipment required for changes;

- schedule sequences that must be disrupted to accommodate changes;

- sequential activities that must be performed concurrently due to delays or acceleration arising from changes;

- changes that shift work into more adverse construction season;

- impacts of changes on availability of work force, crew size, and learning curve; and

- changed work delaying completion of follow-on unchanged work.

Working conditions may also include other various characteristics of the project, such as a remote location with a long-lead procurement, a finite number of available workers, special considerations about the types of materials or equipment that can be used, a project site with limited access, or other similar characteristics. Any of these factors could adversely affect a contractor's ability to address a large number of changes or other events and still maintain productivity.[145]

[10]   Contractor Checklist

Contractors contemplating the possibility of a cumulative impact claim should:[146]

- Whenever practicable, prepare and submit cumulative impact claims before completion of a project;

- Use available tools in scheduling and cost accounting programs to track impacts or numerous changes, even if those tools were not originally planned for use on the project; and

---

[143] G. Keating & T. Burke, *Cumulative Impact Claims: Can They Still Succeed?*, 20 Constr. Law. 30, 32 (No. 2, Apr. 2000).
[144] Keating & Burke at 31-32.
[145] Keating & Burke at 32.
[146] Keating & Burke at 35-36.

• When permitted by contract or the law of the jurisdiction, assert cardinal change (breach of contract) and constructive change (relief under the contract) as alternative theories in support of cumulative impact claims.

Cumulative impact of change orders can also relieve a contractor from the effect of certain contract provisions.[147] In *Acme Plastering Co. v. Boston Housing Authority*,[148] the turmoil and disarray caused by multiple change orders excused a contractor's deviation from the specifications. In *Castagna & Sons, Inc. v. Board of Education*,[149] issues relating to the cumulative impact of multiple change orders on a school building project (such as bad faith and willful, malicious, or grossly negligent conduct) could make a no-damages-for-delay clause unenforceable.[150]

§ 15.05   DEFENSE STRATEGY

The following questions can be used to shape a defense strategy to a change order claim.

UNIT PRICE CHANGES
1. Is the unit price chosen by the contractor "applicable" to the changed work?

2. How has the contractor measured the work for payment (for example, pay lines, overcut, in-place, or excavated quantities)?

3. Does the contract contain a variation-in-quantities clause? If so, is it applicable to the subject change order? Is claim made for the base contract quantity or just for the overrun quantity?

4. Is the contractor claiming a markup for overhead and profit to unit-priced items that already include a markup for overhead and profit?

TIME AND MATERIAL CHANGES

Labor
1. Has the contractor included personnel who should properly be included in overhead?

2. Were the wage rates that were claimed actually paid? (Beware of "composite" rates.)

3. Are all fringe benefits, tax markups, and insurance markups accurate? (Beware of an overall lump-sum percentage.)

---

[147] *Cumulative Impact of Multiple Changes* at 1.
[148] 490 N.E.2d 445 (Mass. App. Ct. 1986).
[149] 173 A.D.2d 405 (N.Y. App. Div. 1991).
[150] *See also* C. Norman Peterson Co. v. Container Corp., 218 Cal. Rptr. 592 (Cal. Ct. App. 1985) (so many changes permitted contractor to abandon contract and recover costs in quantum meruit).

Material
1. Are list prices being charged or are discounted prices that the contractor has actually paid being charged?

2. Is a credit given for surplus materials not used?

Equipment
1. Was the equipment rental based on an arms-length transaction or is the rental from a related company?

2. What is the basis for the pricing of self-owned equipment? Blue book, a percentage of blue book, AGC, some other method? Was the equipment already on the job for other purposes? Should the owner be charged only for operating expense, not ownership expense?

3. Is the equipment being charged for idle time? If so, could it have been used elsewhere? Does the idle time rate include operating cost?

4. Are charges being made for major overhauls and refurbishing of equipment?

5. Is a credit given for purchased equipment not fully consumed?

Overhead and Profit
1. Is the contractor double-dipping (in other words, charging for specific items that are usually included in overhead, such as supervisory labor, small tools, insurance, and the like)?

Other Changes
1. Is time extension addressed?

2. Are impact costs addressed? Is there a specific release of impact claims or a reservation of impact claims?

3. Has an adequate credit been given for omitted work or nonchanged work made easier by the change?

4. Has the proper "base line" been used to assess both the changed and the unchanged work?

The defense strategy may also consider whether the contractor may enforce the contract under which the claimed changes were performed. For example, in *Wright Brothers Builders, Inc. v. Dowling*,[151] the parties entered into an agreement to renovate approximately 2,817 square feet of the defendants' house and construct an addition of approximately 3,500 square feet. The plaintiff was to be paid on a cost-plus basis (10 percent for overhead and 7 percent for profit), and the preliminary budget was set at $528,360. The owner initiated a number of changes and upgrades, which raised the total contract budget to $875,579.

---

[151] 720 A.2d 235 (Conn. 1998).

Problems commenced when the work was nearing completion. After receiving billing no. 7, dated August 30, 1993, which showed the revised budget of $875,579, the owner expressed concerns about the cost of the job and failed to pay billing no. 7 in a timely fashion. Later, the owner and contractor signed a one-page document that provided that the contractor was to be paid $75,000 for additional work. Thereafter, the project was completed. The contractor claimed that $141,275 was due, whereas the owner claimed that only $67,474 was owed. The contractor claimed that the scope of work had been enlarged by the owner after the signing of the amendment. The defendants argued that the contract failed to satisfy two requirements of the HSSA, which were incorporated by reference into the state's home improvement act, and that these defects in compliance precluded the plaintiff from enforcing the contract. These sections require home improvement contractors to furnish two copies of the notice of cancellation to the homeowners with whom they contract to undertake home improvement services, by attaching two copies of the notice to the back of the homeowner's copy of the contract, and that each of the copies specifies the date of the transaction and the date by which the contract may be canceled.

The court found that the deviations from the precise specifications of the statute were of a minor and highly technical nature, and did not result in a lack of notice to the defendants that they had a right to cancel the contract within three days of signing it. The contractor had furnished one copy of the contract, to which was attached one copy of the notice of cancellation. Additionally, the contractor's failure to enter the required dates on the notice of cancellation did not rise to the level of noncompliance with the Home Improvement Act. The court concluded that the contract satisfied the requirements of the statute.

CHAPTER 16

SURETY ISSUES PERTAINING
TO CHANGES
Hugh E. Reynolds, Jr.

§ 16.01 INTRODUCTION

Payment or performance surety bonds may be required by statute. They may be required in a request for bids. The use of such bonds may also be required by the language of the contract or subcontract. The bonds are executed both by the bonded contractor (referred to as the *principal*) and by a surety that undertakes to guarantee completion of the performance of the work to which the contractor has obligated itself. Depending on the form of bond, the surety may obligate itself to provide money only up to a stipulated amount toward the cost of completing performance. In other bonds, the form may include either the right to complete performance (at the surety's option) or the obligation to complete the performance subject to the penal sum of the bond. In the case of payment bonds, the surety agrees to pay certain laborers and materialmen delineated in the bond if those bills are not paid by the contractor.

When there are changes in the work or in the conditions for performance of the work, the legal relationships may be altered between the surety and either the contractor (principal) or owner (obligee) or both. In some instances, these changes in the relationship can be quite drastic. They can even cost the obligee the protection of the bond.

In order to understand the reasons for these potential results, it is important to have a basic knowledge of general principles of suretyship law. Those general principles of suretyship law and the specific contractual provisions, either in the construction (bonded) contract or in the surety bond, control the resolution of problems that may arise as a result of changes in the work or the conditions for performance of the work. Generally, routine changes, whether processed by change orders or involving extra work for which equitable adjustments or extra compensation are required, do not materially influence the relationship between the surety on the one hand and either the contractor or the owner on the other. However, material changes may, under certain circumstances, change the legal obligations of the surety. It is possible to minimize the effect of any such change by the language of the contract or of the bond.

§ 16.02 GENERAL PRINCIPLES OF SURETYSHIP LAW

General principles of suretyship law apply to many surety relationships. Some are reasonably similar to the relationship between an owner, a contractor, and a surety on a construction project. Many are quite different. Furthermore, there may be a difference in the application of suretyship principles depending on whether a surety is a compensated or uncompensated surety. In the overwhelming bulk of cases, the surety issuing a bond on a construction project is a compensated surety.

In early suretyship law, most sureties were uncompensated. They issued instruments of suretyship as an accommodation to family members, business associates, or people from whom the surety wanted favors in return. The maxim of the law was: "The surety is a favorite of the law." This meant, among other things, that even minor changes in the underlying contract or relationship, which the surety agreed to perform upon a default by the principal, would release the surety unless the surety expressly consented to those changes. As professional and compensated sureties entered the business, the equities changed. The compensated surety is not the favorite of the law. Nonetheless, many "suretyship defenses" remain simply because of the nature of this three-party relationship. These remaining defenses apply whether the surety is compensated or uncompensated.

§16.03   SURETYSHIP RELATIONSHIP DEFINED

The American Law Institute has issued the *Restatement of the Law of Suretyship.* Part of the definition of *suretyship* contained in § 1 reads as follows:

§ 1. Scope; Transactions Giving Rise to Suretyship Status

(1) This Restatement applies (except as provided in § 3) and a secondary obligor has suretyship status whenever:

(a) pursuant to contract (the "secondary obligation"), an obligee has recourse against a person (the "secondary obligor") or that person's property with respect to the obligation (the "underlying obligation") of another person (the "principal obligor") to that obligee; and

(b) to the extent that the underlying obligation or the secondary obligation is performed the obligee is not entitled to performance of the other obligation; and

(c) as between the principal obligor and the secondary obligor, it is the principal obligor who ought to perform the underlying obligation or bear the cost of performance.

(2) An obligee has recourse against a secondary obligor or its property with respect to an underlying obligation whenever:

(a) the principal obligor owes performance of the underlying obligation; and

(b) pursuant to the secondary obligation, either:

(i) the secondary obligor has a duty to effect, in whole or in part, the performance that is the subject of the underlying obligation; or

(ii) the obligee has recourse against the secondary obligor or its property in the event of the failure of the principal obligor to perform the underlying obligation; or

(iii) the obligee may subsequently require the secondary obligor to either purchase the underlying obligation from the obligee or incur the duties described in subparagraph (i) or (ii).

(3) If the criteria of subsection (2) are fulfilled, the secondary obligor has suretyship status:

(a) regardless of the form of the transaction fulfilling the criteria;

(b) regardless of any term used by the parties to describe the secondary obligor or the secondary obligation;

(c) whether the secondary obligation is conditional or unconditional;

(d) whether or not the secondary obligation is known to the principal obligor;

(e) whether or not the obligee has notice that the secondary obligor has suretyship status; and

(f) whether or not satisfaction of the principal obligor's duty pursuant to the underlying obligation is limited to a particular fund or property.

In the construction arena, it is obvious that the *principal obligor* stands for the bonded contractor or bonded subcontractor. The *underlying obligation* is the construction contract or subcontract upon which the bond is issued. The *obligee* is the owner (or in the case of a subcontractor's bond, the general contractor). The *surety* is the company issuing the payment or performance bond or both.

A key part of this definition, one that affects the results when changes occur, is that the performance of the duty arises from the "underlying obligation." It is this obligation for which the surety owes performance, in whole or in part, of the duty of the contractor to the owner. Thus, if there is a change in the underlying obligation, does the surety's promise to perform remain in effect if the surety has not consented to the change? This is the question!

Other commonly used commercial suretyship instruments are governed by the same general principles. These include the guarantee of a loan by a third party, a surety bond issued to bond a public official, and the issuance of a bond on the performance of a supply contract. Often, the owners of a construction company execute indemnity agreements to protect the surety. Through these agreements, the surety writing construction bonds obtains promises of indemnity from individuals operating the bonded construction company in the event the surety suffers losses on its bonds. Such an agreement is, in part, an instrument of suretyship.

§16.04 DEFENSES OF THE SECONDARY OBLIGOR (BONDING COMPANY) AGAINST THE OBLIGEE (OWNER)

The *Restatement of the Law of Suretyship* provides excellent basic definitions of suretyship defenses. The basic definition appears in § 19 and reads as follows:

§ 19. Suretyship Status—Defenses of Secondary Obligor Against Obligee
    Suretyship status gives the secondary obligor a defense to its duties pursuant to the secondary obligation to the extent that:
        (a) the underlying obligation has been discharged by performance in accordance with its terms or other satisfaction by the principal obligor; or
        (b) there is a defense of the principal obligor to the underlying obligation that is available to the secondary obligor pursuant to § 34; or
        (c) the secondary obligor has available a "suretyship defense" (§§ 37-45); or
        (d) tender of performance by the principal obligor or secondary obligor discharges the secondary obligor pursuant to § 46.

For example, a contractor takes the position that it has fully performed the project. The owner takes the position that additional work needs to be performed that the contractor has refused to do. If it is determined that the contractor has in fact discharged the underlying obligation, then the surety is discharged. The surety has no obligation to the owner independent of the obligation of the contractor. Thus, the surety has no obligation to perform the disputed additional work.

The contractor has completed what is called for by the plans and specifications of the underlying agreement. The dispute is over additional work to which the contractor has agreed. Assume that the contractor either has failed to do the work or there is a dispute over whether it has been done properly. The surety may be discharged from any liability for performance of the disputed obligation depending on how one defines the "underlying obligation." Is the "other work" part of the bonded contract? Thus, the key to resolving this type of problem is to determine what is included within the "underlying obligation."

The contractor may submit change order documents to the owner, including pricing and time extensions pursuant to contract provisions. The owner refuses to process those documents, but insists that the work be performed. Assuming that the contract does not permit the owner to require continued performance under such circumstances (many contracts do permit this), it is arguable that the contractor has a defense so as to avoid performance of such work. Although this work may well be in implementation of the "underlying obligation," the principal may have a defense that negates the obligation to perform based on the owner's failure to implement the change order process properly. In this case, it may be that the underlying obligation has not been fully performed. However, the contractor may be excused from the performance of the additional work because of the breach by the owner. If the contractor is excused, so is the surety.

A clearer case arises if the owner has failed to pay the contractor. The contractor refuses to complete the principal obligation, terminating its continued performance for material breach by the owner. Assume, for purposes of the argument, that the contractor was correct. The material breach for nonpayment is a defense to continued performance of the underlying obligation by the contractor. This defense is also available to the surety according to § 16(b) of the definition.

Section 19 refers to later sections of the *Restatement of the Law of Suretyship*, specifically §§ 34 and 37 to 42.

§ 41. Modification of Underlying Obligation

If the principal obligor and the obligee agree to a modification, other than an extension of time or a complete or partial release, of the principal obligor's duties pursuant to the underlying obligation:

(a) any duty of the principal obligor to the secondary obligor of performance or reimbursement is correspondingly modified;

(b) the secondary obligor is discharged from any unperformed duties pursuant to the secondary obligation:

(i) if the modification creates a substituted contract or imposes risks on the secondary obligor fundamentally different from those imposed pursuant to the transaction prior to modification;

(ii) in other cases, to the extent that the modification would otherwise cause the secondary obligor a loss;

(c) to the extent that the secondary obligor is not discharged by
operation of paragraph (b) from its duties:
        (i) the secondary obligation is correspondingly modified; but
        (ii) if the modification of the underlying obligation changes
the amount of money payable thereunder, or the timing of such
payment, the secondary obligor may perform the secondary obligation as though there had been no modification;
        (d) the secondary obligor has a claim against the obligee to the
extent provided in § 37(4).

Although the application of these principals may be difficult in complex situations, the basic rule is fairly clear. If a modification in the underlying obligation
is so fundamental as to be the substantial equivalent of a substituted contract, the
surety is discharged. If a material modification increases the surety's loss, then it
may reduce the surety's obligation to that extent. This principle applies when the
modification was not so substantial as to constitute a fundamental change. It is
important to recall that these principles may be modified by contract. For example,
in most construction contracts, there are provisions modifying the application of
§ 37 precisely as written.

One additional section of the *Restatement* does not arise often, but may be
important in specialized cases related to the obligee's (owner's) nondisclosure of
events. It reads as follows:

**§ 47. Obligee's Non-disclosure of Events Giving Secondary Obligor Power
to Terminate Secondary Obligation**
        If, pursuant to the terms of the contract creating the secondary obliga-
tion, the secondary obligor has the power, upon the occurrence of a specified
event, to terminate the secondary obligation with respect to subsequent
defaults of the principal obligor on the underlying obligation or subsequently
incurred duties of the principal obligor, and:
        (a) such event occurs;
        (b) the obligee knows such event has occurred; and
        (c) the obligee has reason to know that the occurrence of such
        event is unknown to the secondary obligor; the secondary obligor is dis-
        charged from the secondary obligation with respect to defaults of the
        principal obligor that occur, or duties of the principal obligor incurred,
        thereafter and before the secondary obligor obtains knowledge of the
        occurrence of the event.

An example of this arises when the surety enters into a contract based upon standard AIA language that an architect will be supervising payments and provide at
least general examination of shop drawings and the like to monitor compliance with
the plans and specifications. At the time the contract is bonded, both the owner and
contractor know that the owner is not going to use an architect, but this is not disclosed to the surety. Rather, the surety receives a copy of the contract that calls for
participation by an architect. If in fact the nonparticipation of an architect becomes
material, either because of serious flaws in the shop drawings, obvious and serious
flaws in the work, or serious overpayments because there is no regularly established

system for compliance with the payment procedures, this may either discharge the surety or provide a pro tanto modification of the surety's obligations (in the case of overpayment).

§ 16.05 CHANGES PURSUANT TO THE TERMS OF THE CONSTRUCTION CONTRACT

Most construction contracts provide for changes in the work, which may be characterized in a number of ways. For example, the plans may call for 1,500 feet of pipe, but the ultimate construction requires 1,700 feet of pipe. The contractor is to be paid for the extra 200 feet of pipe, which can be done by way of a "change" in the work. Some deviations may involve "extra work" that does not involve a change in the plans and specifications. The plans and specifications may postulate that a certain concrete pad can be used in a certain place, for instance. It turns out that, because of other aspects of the design, it cannot be used in that place without extra work in terms of the total hours of labor required to install. Sometimes these problems occur as a result of "changed or unanticipated conditions"; sometimes they are simply inherent in the work. They often require additional work by the contractor, who may be entitled to extra compensation for that work, but not always.

Not surprisingly, most construction contracts routinely provide for all of these circumstances. For example, in the standard AIA Document A201 relating to general conditions of a construction contract, Article 7 deals with changes in the work:

> 7.1.1 Changes in the Work may be accomplished after execution of the Contract, and without invalidating the Contract, by Change Order, Construction Change Directive or order for a minor change in the Work, subject to the limitations stated in this Article and elsewhere in the Contract Documents.

Relative to our discussion of whether changes in the work may affect the obligation of the surety, this clause clearly designates the accomplishment of changes after the execution of the contract as something contemplated in the contract that will not "invalidate" the contract. Because the surety has bonded the performance of the contract, and the contract itself contemplates such changes, the case law is clear that changes pursuant to that clause and the other similar contract clauses do not alter the surety's obligation.

Article 7 or equivalent provisions in other contract forms contemplate changes that would be anticipated in the normal and routine construction project. Such changes, however, cannot be considered as limited to "minor change[s] in the work." After all, § 7.4.1 provides a simpler mechanism for handling "minor change[s] in the work." This clearly indicates that the procedures outlined in Article 7, §§ 2 and 3, may be "major" changes. But how major?

We can conclude that by executing a performance bond in which the surety agrees to the performance of the underlying construction contract, the surety has agreed to changes in the work contemplated by and implemented through contract provisions such as Article 7 in AIA Document A201.

Thus, even if there is no express language in the bond referring to such changes, they would be considered as incorporated into the bond, just as the entire construction contract, including documents incorporated by reference in the construction contract, is incorporated into the obligation imposed by the bond. However, as a word of warning, in the unlikely event that the bond expressly prohibits changes or expressly requires notification and approval by the surety before changes are implemented, the result could be different.

§ 16.06 CHANGES IN WORK PERFORMED: EFFECT ON SURETY

Routine changes implemented during the course of the construction contract and contemplated by such contract provisions as Article 7 of the AIA Document A201 are discussed in § 16.05. Those changes can include major changes. However, changes in the manner, method, or type of work to be performed also need to be considered because they are not necessarily covered by the specific change order provisions of a construction contract.

Generally, there are three issues in such cases. First, can the contractor be compelled to perform the changed work? Second, if the contractor does perform the changed work, is the contractor entitled to extra compensation? Third, is such a change so drastic that the contractor is performing a truly different contract than the one originally agreed to and, more importantly, *contemplated* by the parties when the bond was executed?

If the contractor can be compelled to perform the change, such compulsion must generally arise out of either what is implicit in the proper performance of the construction contract executed by the parties or because the contractor has made a serious error that increases or changes the required performance of the work in order to fulfill the contract. Since the bond, in effect, incorporates the contract obligations, in the former case, unless it is, in effect, a cardinal change, the bonding company would be held with the contractor.

There are two distinct tests for cardinal changes. First, a cardinal change is said to occur when the obligee makes an alteration of the work so drastic that it effectively requires the contractor to perform duties materially different from those originally bargained for.[1] This expression of the cardinal change doctrine is sometimes referred to as the "scope of the contract" test.[2] Second, in the context of projects awarded through a competitive bidding process, a cardinal change can occur when the contract is modified in such a way as to materially change the field of competition.[3] This expression of the doctrine, sometimes referred to as the

---

[1] P. Bruner, P. O'Connor & J. Hartnett, *The Surety's Response to the Obligee's Declaration of Default and Termination: "To Perform or Not to Perform That Is the Question,"* 17 Constr. Law. 11 (No. 1, Jan. 1997) (citing General Dynamics Corp. v. United States, 585 F.2d 457, 462 (Ct. Cl. 1978)). See also **Chapter 11**.

[2] *Id.* (citing Aragona Constr. Co. v. United States, 165 Ct. Cl. 382, 391 (1964)).

[3] *Id.* (citing Cray Research, Inc. v. Department of Navy, 556 F. Supp. 201, 203 (D.D.C. 1982)).

"scope of the competition" test, requires an analysis of the substance of the change rather than its magnitude.[4]

The surety should check for cardinal changes by applying the scope-of-the-contract test or the scope-of-the-competition test in the following situations:

1. When the contract increases substantially (for example, by more than 100 percent of the dollar value of the work to be performed);

2. When the method of performing the contract changes, so that the risks of performance are significantly altered;

3. In the competitive bidding context, when the method of performance changes in a way that a potential bidder could not reasonably have anticipated; and

4. When the method of payment to or financing of the contractor changes in such a way as to expose the surety to greater risk of loss.[5]

The same result generally would occur if the changes arise from the contractor's negligent performance, but this is subject to certain caveats. When extra work results from the manner or method of prosecuting the work, it may often occur because of errors not only by the contractor but also by the owner. As between the contractor and the owner, the contractor may have obliged itself to assume the extra costs associated with such errors even though the negligence of both parties contributed to the error. It is not entirely clear that the bonding company has assumed that particular obligation even though that obligation may be part of the conditions of the construction contract.

It is arguable that, by its surety agreement, the bonding company does not assume an obligation to indemnify the owner that is often incorporated in construction contracts. Rather, the bonding company's obligation is the completion of the work, not the performance of the agreement of indemnity. It is not clear from the cases what might happen in such a fairly unique instance.

Whether or not the contractor should be paid for such extra performance is relevant to the bonding company's obligation only under certain circumstances. For example, the bonding company would be entitled to the benefit of money moving from the owner to the contractor for extra work. This would be part of the contract balance available to complete the work if there is a default and should be available to pay bills incurred by the contractor in the performance of the work if the surety thereafter has to pay. Thus, if a contractor were forced to perform work without compensation because the owner used its economic advantage and payment was justly due for such work, the surety may argue that such a change in the nature of the work and the costs associated with it are a credit against its obligations under the bond because it should not have been disadvantaged by the "deal" between the contractor and the owner. These cases would be very fact-sensitive. The law on this point also is far from clear.

---

[4] *Id.* (citing Webcraft Packaging, Comp. Gen. Dec. B-194086, 79-2 CPD 120 (Aug. 14, 1979)).

[5] Bruner, O'Connor & Hartnett at 12 (citations omitted).

§ 16.07   EXTRA COSTS: EFFECT ON SURETY

The fact that performance of the work by the contractor costs more money than anticipated does not and cannot, in and of itself, operate to release or otherwise modify the surety's obligation. The surety agrees to perform if the contractor does not. If the contractor has misbid the job or misapprehended the scope of the work, that does not relieve the contractor of the responsibility to complete in accordance with the plans and specifications. Therefore, it would follow that the surety is not relieved either.

However, certain events that impose extra cost on the contractor may be indicative of causes that can affect the obligation of the surety.

Extra costs may provide evidence that the contractor has been misled under circumstances for which the owner would be responsible. If this is the case, and there is a material misrepresentation that would allow the contractor to terminate the contract for fraudulent misrepresentation, the surety would be released to the extent that the contractor is released. It is also arguable that if such a circumstance arises and the contractor collusively continues to perform with both the owner (obligee) and contractor, knowing the ultimate burden will be assumed by the surety, the surety may be entitled to assert the owner's misrepresentation or material breach even though the contractor has not. This is a very unique area with no case law one way or the other on the issue. In effect, any such case would be resolved by the basic principle of suretyship law: if the contractor is not responsible, the surety is not responsible.

Excessive extra costs may create a fact situation from which the contractor asserts either that it is entitled to extra compensation or that there has been a cardinal change. Thus, the costs themselves are not a grounds for either terminating the contract or receiving extra compensation. They are, however, evidence of other facts and circumstances that may justify either termination or extra compensation. To the extent the contractor is entitled to terminate or to extra compensation, the surety has the same entitlement.

Such extra costs may evidence that the contractor is performing out-of-scope work. Theoretically, at least, the surety has no responsibility for out-of-scope work. But is the surety entitled to some credit because contract funds have been expended for out-of-scope work without additional compensation to the contractor? This depletes the availability of such funds to pay for work for which the surety has obligated itself. This is a difficult question and very fact-sensitive. However, it may be raised if the facts show that the surety has been unfairly damaged in its position by the performance of the out-of-scope work and if the damage is material. Normally, in such cases, the surety's relief is a reduction in its exposure rather than relief from all liability.

Excessive extra costs, along with concrete evidence of either dramatically changed conditions that could not have been anticipated by the contractor or of considerable changes in the scope of the work, almost always create an issue in cardinal change cases. Cardinal change or fundamental change affecting a surety is discussed in **§ 16.08. Chapter 11** contains a thorough discussion of the effect of cardinal or fundamental changes as they relate to the contract relationship between the owner and the contractor.

Sometimes extra costs arise because of the conditions of performance rather than the actual completion of work pursuant to plans and specifications. These may be extra costs because of access problems, extra costs because of bad weather, extra costs because of inefficiencies in the work, or the like. In general, the principles discussed in this section are no different when the extra costs result from putting up the bricks and mortar or from working conditions. The key questions are:

- Who is responsible for those extra costs?

- Is the difference a material difference?

- Is the contractor entitled to compensation?

- What relief is available to the contractor and to the surety if the owner is responsible, there are substantial extra costs involved, and the owner refuses to provide additional compensation?

§ 16.08   MATERIAL CHANGES: EFFECT ON SURETY

Those material changes in the underlying contract that may increase the surety's risk may have the effect of reducing the surety's obligation to the extent its risk has been increased and it has been damaged. In general, this relates to material changes in the contract that should not reasonably have been anticipated by the surety. If it can still be said that even with such material changes, the contract being performed is essentially the same contract the surety bonded, then usually the surety is not relieved of liability but rather its exposure is reduced by the amount of the damage or increase in the risk. However, a *fundamental* or *cardinal change* is a change so significant that it can fairly be said the contract being performed is different from that which the surety bonded.

Employers Insurance of Wausau v. Construction Management Engineers, Inc.[6] provides an excellent example of what may happen and the legal consequences. In this case, Employers issued a subcontract performance bond in which the primary obligor was L.B. Samford, Inc., and the obligee was the primary contractor, Construction Management Engineers (CME). CME, in turn, had a general contract with the Department of the Navy for approximately $6.4 million to build a recruit depot at Parris Island, South Carolina. The Employers of Wausau bond issued on Samford was based upon a subcontract for $2.3 million, which required Samford to perform all of the work for the project, excluding general management of the project and 12 specific areas of construction. This contract was dated March 6, 1983. On March 7, 1983, Samford and CME entered into a contract that required Samford to perform all work (no exclusions) for 97 percent of the final contract amount ($6.4 million, as amended throughout the project). Samford was to authorize direct payment out of that amount by CME to other subcontractors and suppliers for their share of the work.

---

[6] 377 S.E.2d 119 (S.C. Ct. App. 1989).

What happened, in effect, is that Samford assumed the responsibility for general management of the project and absorbed the 12 excluded subcontracts into its contract. The March 7 contract specifically stated that it superseded any prior agreements or proposal. Wausau, not surprisingly, was not aware of the March 7 contract until Samford defaulted and Wausau was called upon to perform.

Wausau received a summary judgment of nonliability because the March 7 contract superseded the March 6 contract, and because the risk Wausau had assumed was changed from $2.3 million to $6.2 million. Summary judgment is granted only if there is no issue of fact. CME asserted that there were issues of fact, arguing that the March 7 contract was merely a "wraparound" contract that did not substantially change Samford's obligation. In other words, Samford was simply a conduit for the extra $4.1 million to the other 12 subcontractors.

The appellate court adopted the contractual argument of the trial court that the language of the contracts clearly showed that the bonded subcontract had been superseded. Hence, the contract bonded by the surety was no longer in existence and there was no "underlying obligation" for which the surety was responsible.

However, pertinent to this discussion, it also adopted the trial court's finding that the change of risk in the March 7 contract discharged Wausau as a matter of law. The Court of Appeals of South Carolina stated:

> The trial court also held the change in risk under the March 7 contract discharged Wausau as a matter of law. CME argues the trial court misconstrued the March 7 contract as a $6.2 million contract when actually it was for substantially less because CME paid other subcontractors directly and these funds were not directed through Samford. However, the contract on its face obligated Samford to perform all work of every nature for the complete project. Samford was ultimately responsible under the language of the contract. There is a substantial modification of the March 6 contract which only required Samford to perform certain specified work.[7]

Two other interesting issues discussed in this opinion sometimes apply to the surety under these circumstances. CME argued that Wausau could not deny liability because it should have investigated the circumstances, which would have revealed the March 7 contract. As the court said, "There is no evidence in the record Wausau had reason to be aware of the March 7 contract until after default by Samford. We fail to perceive any circumstances in the record which would impose a duty to investigate on Wausau."[8]

Disputes over alleged material changes in contracts often include factual arguments that the surety is estopped from denying the material change and claiming relief from liability because it was unaware of the change. It is clear that the surety has no duty of investigation. However, if the surety is aware of the material alteration and does not complain, that may very well produce a different result.

---

[7] *Id.* at 122.
[8] *Id.*

Another interesting aspect of the case is that Wausau did not claim that it was discharged from liability under its payment bonds. Thus, this case is silent concerning whether the cancellation of the obligation to the obligee cancels the payment bond when there are third-party beneficiaries. Although the case does not decide this, it may very well be that a court would hold that those subcontractors and suppliers whose account receivable was created in performing the work called for by the original (March 6) contract may be entitled to coverage. However, it seems unlikely that Employers would be obliged to cover unpaid bills incurred for those portions of the work that had been specifically excluded from the March 6 agreement, such as the 12 specific categories being handled by other and different subcontractors.

An example of a case holding that there was no "radical" or "fundamental" change is *American Druggists Insurance v. Thompson Lumber Co.*[9] In this case, the American Druggists Insurance Company bonded Zagger Construction Company, the general contractor. The claimants were unpaid subcontractors. Among other issues, the surety argued that because a basement had been added to the city hall, it was a fundamental change. The court disagreed, holding that it was not a fundamental change but "was fairly within scope of the contract and was not a radical change." It also pointed out that the Minnesota statute under which the bond was issued specifically stated, "[N]o assignment, modification, or change of the contract, or change in the work covered thereby, nor any extension of time for completion of the contract, shall release the surety on the bond."[10]

This case involved a payment bond that issued on a public contract, a situation in which courts tend to favor the claimant. It is conceivable that in a dispute between the owner and the contractor on private work, the addition of a basement to a structure not originally called for in the plans and specifications might be considered a cardinal change so as to relieve the surety of liability to the owner. These cases are always fact-sensitive.

It is important to recognize that there may be cases in which as between the contractor and the owner, the contractor is still bound by the new, fundamentally different contract. For example, in the *Employers of Wausau* case, it is clear that the bonded subcontractor, Samford, was bound by the $6.4 million contract because it had agreed to the cardinal change. The key to the case was that the surety had *not* agreed to the cardinal change. The cases discussed in **Chapter 11** involve a situation in which the contractor claims to be relieved of its original contract because the owner is seeking to enforce performance of an obligation that is cardinally changed from the original contract. Obviously, if the contractor prevails in such a case, the surety prevails as well. Thus, when a contractor agrees to a cardinal change but the surety has not, the contractor is bound but the surety is relieved. When there is a cardinal change to which neither the contractor nor the surety have agreed, neither is bound. When there is a cardinal change to which both the contractor and the surety have agreed, both are bound.

---

[9] 349 N.W.2d 569 (Minn. Ct. App. 1984).

[10] Minn. Stat. § 574.28.

It should be noted that when a cardinal or fundamental change is involved, the standard waiver by the surety of its right to be discharged because of alterations or changes does not apply. This is because a conclusion has been reached that this is not merely a change in the contract but, in fact, performance of a fundamentally different contract than the one the surety bonded. This then brings us back to a basic principle of surety law. The surety's obligation is the secondary obligation for performance of the contract it intended to underwrite, not of some other or different contract.

§ 16.09   CHANGES IN FAILURE TO FOLLOW PAYMENT PROVISIONS: EFFECT ON SURETY

It is a well-established principle of surety law that material changes in the payment provisions of a contract that adversely affect the surety operate to relieve the surety of all or a portion of its liability. Generally, this arises when the owner overpays the contractor or prematurely pays retainage.

Such deviations in the payment provisions generally operate to allow the surety to treat the improvident or premature payments as though they had not been made. Although there are some instances in which the deviation and payment procedures may be so material as to relieve the surety of all liability, in general, the surety's relief is pro tanto to the extent the surety has been damaged. Some of these cases involve contract changes. More often, what really happens is that the contractor and the owner do not follow the payment provisions of the contract. This, in effect, is a change through practice. However, the principle is the same whether there is some change in the contract provisions unknown to the surety or whether the contract provisions are not followed. Minor deviations in the payment provisions generally do not affect the surety's liability.

Thus, if a contractor under the payment schedule has earned $1 million on a $2 million contract, and there is a retainage of 10 percent, the contractor should normally be entitled to $900,000. If the owner has paid the contractor $1.3 million, the surety is entitled to credit for the $400,000 overpayment. In general, the owner cannot take credit for the $400,000 and claim that the unpaid balance of the contract price is the $1.1 million that should have remained unpaid if the owner had properly followed the contract provisions.

An early leading case illustrating this principle is *Home Indemnity v. United Railroad Co.*[11] The owner materially departed from the payment provisions of the contract without the consent of the surety and paid contract funds before they were due. In a finding for the surety, the Third Circuit stated that the surety "has the right to expect and demand that no payments will be made contrary to the terms of the contract."

A more recent case is *Reliance Insurance Co. v. Colbert,*[12] where there had been an alteration in the payment schedule by a contract addendum. The district

---

[11] 272 F. 607 (3d Cir. 1921).
[12] 365 F.2d 530, 535 (D.C. Cir. 1966).

court found that the alteration was not material and refused to release the surety from liability under the bond. The question was not pro tanto satisfaction but release because the claimant was not the owner (obligee) but the materialman (third-party beneficiary). As the *Colbert* opinion points out, prejudice must be shown in overpayment cases or in changes to the payment terms of the contract. If the prejudice proves impossible to measure, the surety must receive a discharge. If the prejudice is subject to measurement, the surety receives a partial discharge. In *Reliance* the surety's argument was that if it had known of the contract addendum, it would not have issued the bond. The case was then sent back on remand for determination as to whether there was prejudice and if it was subject to measurement.

Airtrol Engineering Co. v. United States Fidelity & Guaranty Co.[13] involved a bonded roofing subcontractor who defaulted in a contract with the air conditioning subcontractor on the project. The district court allowed the claim against the bonding company. This was reversed on appeal, citing to the general principle that a bonding company is entitled to expect that payments will be made by the owner to the principal in accordance with a contract. Payment should not have been made until materials were "jobsite installed." In this case, the relief was pro tanto relief for a premature payment in violation of the contract terms. Another case producing the same result is *Central Towers Apartments, Inc. v. Martin.*[14] These cases are reasonable examples of a number of cases on this issue.

A somewhat similar result may bind an unpaid supplier on a payment bond claim when the supplier agrees to release of funds that would otherwise protect the surety. In *Inland-Ryerson Construction Products Co. v. Brazier Construction Co.,*[15] the surety was entitled to the benefit of the retainage. An unpaid subcontractor agreed that it would take $19,000 immediate payment and would be paid from the retainage fund *after* the retainage was released and paid by the owner. The owner released the retainage to the contractor, who failed to pay the subcontractor. The subcontractor then sued the surety on the payment bond. As the court stated, "[T]he rule is based on the right of the surety to be subrogated to all means of payment; and if that is impaired by an agreement between the contractor and the subcontractor, he is released to the extent that his security is lost."[16]

On the other hand, a surety may agree to prepayment in advance. If the surety does, it cannot claim prepayment as a defense, either absolute or pro tanto, on the bond. In *United States ex rel. H&S Industries, Inc. v. F.D. Rich Co.,*[17] the contract bonded by the surety contained the following provision:

> [T]he surety (USF&G) and the principal (Cass) hereby jointly and severally agree with the obligee (Rich) that the obligation of said SURETY and its bond

---

[13] 345 So. 2d 1271 (La. Ct. App. 1977).

[14] 453 S.W.2d 789 (Tenn. Ct. App. 1969). *See also* Continental Ins. Co. v. City of Va. Beach, 908 F. Supp. 341 (E.D. Va. 1995) (owner's failure to inspect or test pipe before paying contractor entitled surety to recover cost of correcting defaulted contractor's defective work incurred while completing defaulted contractor's work under terms of performance bond with city).

[15] 500 P. 2d 1015 (Wash. Ct. App. 1972).

[16] *Id.* at 1019.

[17] 525 F.2d 760 (7th Cir. 1975).

shall be in no way impaired or affected . . . by any payment [under the subcon-
tract] before the time required therein . . . and such SURETY does hereby
waive notice of any and all such . . . payments . . . . [18]

The subcontract also contained the statement "first party [Rich] at its sole
option, may make prepayments without affecting the terms hereof nor the liability
on any bond given by the second party [Cass]." Under these circumstances, prepayments by Rich could not be used by the surety either as a pro tanto discharge or
as a release under the bond.

An interesting situation arises when the architect approves a payment that
operates as a prepayment because the architect's certificate is in error. The surety
may seek to assert that the architect, by contract, is acting as the "agent" of the
owner and the architect's error is the owner's error. In some cases (although none
that have gone to an appellate court), this assertion has been successful. It may be
argued that the surety may have a cause of action against the architect rather than
against the owner for such approval of premature payments. This creates a difficult
situation because the usual subrogation argument may not prevail and there is no
privity of contract. The owner is not damaged by the prepayments unless there is
insufficient money after the bond to protect the owner (if in fact the owner is not
responsible for the architect's error).

Continental Casualty Co. v. Public Building Authority[19] is a case that provides very little reasoning but holds that when there was no requirement of consent
by the surety, an architect's certificate of payment foreclosed an argument that
there was a prepayment. The owner, the surety, and the architect all had knowledge
that the contractor owed substantial amounts to several suppliers. The surety had
requested that no further payments be made without its consent. The court pointed
out that the surety's consent was not contractually required, and since the contract
merely called for a certificate from the architect, the owner was protected in making the payment.

It is the author's view that if ten courts passed on this same issue today, more
would find that the owner should not have released the payment than the opposite.
However, the issue here is not so much a matter of a change in the contract, but the
nature of the surety's equitable right to the fund created by the retainage.

The result in such a case today may turn on whether the owner has the authority to withhold payments upon completion of the contract because the owner knows
of unpaid labor and material bills. Lack of such a provision in the contract may
have been the key to the decision in the *Continental Casualty* case. But one is
unable to tell this from the opinion.

A case in which this issue clearly was involved is *J.R. Meade & Co. v.
Barrett & Co.*[20] In this case, the court held that since the owner had no authority to
withhold funds upon completion of the contract, even if there were unpaid bills,
the release of the funds by the owner did not relieve the surety of liability.

---

[18] *Id.* at 771.
[19] 238 F.2d 10 (5th Cir. 1967).
[20] 453 S.W.2d 632 (Mo. Ct. App. 1970).

These cases are very fact-sensitive and many of them are older ones. This is because the incidence of premature payments and disputes regarding premature payments is much less likely now than formerly. This is for two reasons. The first is that most contracts are performed under either the standard AIA form or similar ones. These forms provide for considerable administrative controls over the release of payment. They also give the owner significant authority to withhold payments because of unpaid bills, and so on. Furthermore, the issuance of bonds in which the surety agrees to premature payment, as occurred in the *F.D. Rich* case, rarely, if ever, occurs now.

Most cases today do not involve overpayment or prepayment during the course of the contract. Instead, they involve whether the owner has improvidently released the retainage or whether the owner can be forced to withhold making further payments when the contractor is in default. These cases turn on somewhat different principles than those germane to this chapter. For the most part, they do not involve issues relating to a change in the contract language or change in the payment practices. They tend to revolve around the competing equities to the balance of the contract price as between the owner, the contractor, the contractor's suppliers and materialmen and subcontractors, and the contractor's creditors.

§16.10 CHANGES IN TIME OF COMPLETION: EFFECT ON SURETY

As a general principle of law, if contract changes in the time of completion are material and increase the surety's risk, they could alter the surety's obligation either pro tanto or, in an extreme case, relieve it of liability.

For example, sureties issue what is a line of credit to a contractor. Thus, a contractor may have authority to have $100 million in bonded work at any one time. That is the cumulative total of the penal sums of the performance bonds issued by the surety on work in progress for which the surety still has some responsibility. The surety may examine each undertaking during underwriting, but the examination may be merely to ascertain if there have been changes in conditions or to catch obvious problems. Under such circumstances, time may be very important to the surety if it issues a bond that exceeds the line of credit.

The fact that time is material to the surety does not necessarily relieve the surety of liability, either in whole or pro tanto, if the owner materially changes the contract and extends the time for completion. There are two reasons for this. The owner may not understand that by extending the time of completion it is adding to the surety's risk, as could happen when the owner is providing for significant extra work or prepaying the contractor. However, if the owner recognizes that extensions of time without the approval of the surety might increase the surety's risk because of some particular fact situation, then the general principles that apply in the areas of changes in the work or changes in the payment provisions would apply to extensions of time. That is, if the owner knew that material extensions of time were increasing the risk to the surety, for example, that there were time-related securities available to protect the surety that would be depleted by a change in the time for completion, then the owner's potential responsibility for such a change may increase dramatically. Although one normally considers an extension of time as a possible change in the contract, it is clear that a contractual agreement to shorten the time, if it occurs, is far more likely to provide for relief to the surety. After all, the presumption is that extensions of time usually benefit the contractor. If they benefit the contractor, the assumption is that they also benefit the surety. As a practical matter, a contractor's requests for extension of time will almost always be considered appropriate, unless the owner has knowledge that it would greatly impair the rights of the surety and that the contractor is not entitled to an extension of time. If the contractor is entitled to an extension of time, the surety's bond agreement probably covers what is normal and routine in construction contracts, including extensions of time when warranted.

The safest way to evaluate any such situation is to apply the general rules to the aspects of changes or changed circumstances discussed in this chapter. An owner cannot make a change, materially increasing the surety's risk, without running a commensurate risk of losing all or some portion of the protection of the bond. The safest way to avoid this is to initiate the change only after notifying the surety.

§ 16.11   CHANGE ORDERS AND THE PAYMENT BOND SURETY

Change orders have other significance to payment bond sureties. For change orders that have been executed or recognized by the owner, the payment bond surety may be required to reimburse any subcontractor or supplier-claimant that has not been paid. The payment bond surety may not, however, be responsible to pay for extra work that has not been recognized under the contract. For example, in *Dawson Corp. v. National Union Fire Insurance Co.*,[21] a subcontractor claimed it was entitled to recover the cost of its additional work against the payment bond surety of a bankrupt general contractor. The labor and material bond provided by the surety in *Dawson* listed the general contractor as the principal and the owner as the obligee. The payment bond incorporated the provisions of the prime contract. The extra work the subcontractor claimed was based on work in addition to that expressly required under both the prime contract and the subcontract, but lacked any authorization by the owner to change the scope of work. The court determined that payment for additional work was not the responsibility of the owner/obligee without an approved change order from the owner. Because a change order was never issued nor modification executed, the court found that the surety had no obligation to pay the subcontractor under the payment bond.

In *Dawson*, the general contractor apparently did not cause or contribute to the subcontractor's additional costs. When the general contractor does contribute in some way to the subcontractor's additional performance costs, as in *disputed* change orders, subcontractors may be entitled to recover the costs of their additional work under the payment bond. For example, in *W.F. Magann Corp. v. Diamond Manufacturing Co.*,[22] the federal court determined that a subcontractor

---

[21] 285 N.J. Super. 137, 666 A.2d 604 (1995).
[22] 580 F. Supp. 1299 (D.S.C. 1984).

was entitled, under the Miller Act, to recover in quantum meruit from the prime contractor or the prime contractor's Miller Act payment bond surety the reasonable value of its services, materials, and equipment used on the project, together with interest from the time notice of the subcontractor's claim was given to the owner until the claim was paid. In *W.F. Magann*, the subcontractor claimed that the general contractor had breached the subcontract by refusing to recognize the subcontractor's claims for differing site conditions and defective specifications, refusing to grant reasonable time extensions, and threatening the subcontractor to make it drop its claims against the prime contractor and owner.

In recent years, a number of federal courts have allowed increased performance costs caused by delays to be recovered under a Miller Act payment bond despite the earlier decisions, provided the claimant on the payment bond did not cause or anticipate the delays.[23] For example, in *United States f/u/b Evergreen Pipeline Construction Co. v. Merritt Meridian Construction Corp.*,[24] a subcontractor sued a general contractor and its surety to recover its additional costs caused by delays. Although the contractor backcharged the subcontractor for costs attributable to project delays, the trial evidence indicated that the contractor had at the time of the backcharge received both time extensions and extra compensation for those delays from the owner but had failed to pass the adjustments to the subcontractor. The contractor had also advised the subcontractor that the owner was not paying the contractor for the delays. The subcontractor sued the contractor and its Miller Act surety. The subcontractor received a jury verdict on its breach of contract claim, including delay costs.

The subcontract included both a notice and no-damages-for-delay clause that barred compensation for any delays attributable to the contractor. The court found that the subcontractor's delay claim resulted in part from the contractor's failure to have the project site surveyed, along with the contractor's deceptive conduct. The Second Circuit remanded the case to determine whether the subcontractor complied with the subcontract's notice requirement.

The Second Circuit's decision demonstrated the court's willingness to allow recovery of delay costs notwithstanding the no-damages-for-delay clause. The court focused on exceptions to the enforceability of a no-damages-for-delay clause and indicated that the contractor's payment bond surety would be liable for delay costs if the subcontractor was later found to have given proper notice of its claim.[25]

Several policy considerations support an expanded interpretation of the Miller Act to include additional performance costs caused by delays. First, the Act is remedial in nature and should be liberally construed to protect those persons

---

[23] D. Douglas, B. McCarthy & E. Nelson, *Delay Claims Against the Surety*, 17 Constr. Law. 4, 6 (No. 3, July 1997) (citing Mai Steel Serv., Inc. v. Blake Constr. Co., 981 F.2d 414, 420 (9th Cir. 1992); United States ex rel. Lochridge-Priest, Inc. v. Con-Real Support Group, 950 F.2d 284, 288(89 (5th Cir. 1992); United States ex rel. T.M.S. Mech. Contractors, Inc. v. Millers Mut. Fire Ins. Co., 942 F.2d 946, 952 (5th Cir. 1991)).

[24] 95 F.3d 153 (2d Cir. 1996).

[25] A. Nahmias, *Delay Damages and the Miller Act Payment Bond Surety*, 19 Constr. Law. 36, 37 (No. 1, Jan. 1999).

providing labor and material on federal projects. Second, denying recovery of some costs of the work is not complete relief and frustrates the purpose of the Act. Third, denying recovery of actual costs could increase risks to perform federal projects and may reduce the number of subcontractors willing to take an increased risk. Finally, courts have allowed recovery of other costs not strictly "labor" or "materials," such as workers' compensation premiums.[26]

Delay damages typically include labor and material costs normally recoverable under a Miller Act payment bond. For example, increased labor and labor-related costs are likely to result from delay that is followed by acceleration. Delays can also increase material costs due to price escalation or lost discounts. Supervision, jobsite office, and other overhead costs include labor and materials as part of contract costs. Increased or extended overhead costs are typically recoverable on a Miller Act bond and should still be recoverable when increased by delays. Lost profits are not recoverable. Characterizing increased costs using labor and material categories typically recoverable on a surety bond should increase the likelihood of recovery. Delay damages that are difficult to demonstrate or are not clearly part of the labor and material costs for a specific project, such as unabsorbed home overhead and lost profits, will likely be denied.[27]

State courts also do not agree about whether a claimant may recover under payment bonds for state public works projects. *General Federal Construction, Inc. v. D.R. Thomas, Inc.*[28] pointed out that much of the controversy concerning recovery of delay damages is semantic. Where the claimant can define its costs in terms of "additional labor and materials" rather than "damages" for breach of contract, there is a greater chance of recovery. A better approach for the court would be to decide whether recovery of delay costs is consistent with the statutory purpose. In *Salvino Steel & Iron Works, Inc. v. Fletcher & Sons, Inc.*,[29] the Pennsylvania Superior Court determined that delay claims were not recoverable against a public works bond. The court found that the language of the bond matched the statutory language, and neither the statute nor the language of the bond expressly provided for recovery of costs incurred as a result of delays. As a result, the subcontractor could not recover on delay claims against the bond.[30]

The terms of the construction contract or subcontract may influence whether delay damages are recoverable under the payment bond. If the principal would not be liable for delay damages under the construction contract, then the surety also would not be liable because the liability of the surety usually matches the liability of the principal.[31]

---

[26] Douglas, McCarthy & Nelson at 6-7 (citing Watsabaugh & Co. v. Seaboard Surety Co., 26 F. Supp. 681, 869 (D. Mont. 1938), *aff'd*, 106 F.2d 355 (9th Cir. 1939)).

[27] Douglas, McCarthy & Nelson at 7.

[28] 52 Md. App. 700, 451 A.2d 1250, 1257-58 (1982).

[29] 398 Pa. Super. 86, 580 A.2d 853, 856 (1990).

[30] Douglas, McCarthy & Nelson at 8.

[31] Douglas, McCarthy & Nelson at 9 (citing United Aluma Glass v. Bratton Corp., 8 F.3d 756, 759 (11th Cir. 1993); Turner Constr. Co. v. First Indem. of Am. Ins. Co., 829 F. Supp. 752, 759 (E.D. Pa. 1993), *aff'd*, 22 F.3d 303 (3d Cir. 1994); F.W. Sims, Inc. v. Federal Ins. Co., 788 F. Supp. 149,

For example, in *United States f/u/b Seminole Sheet Metal Co. v. SCI, Inc.*,[32] the subcontract waived claims for delays caused either by the contractor or the owner. The court recognized that Florida courts enforce no-damages-for-delay clauses and that a contractor can normally rely on such a clause. The court ruled that the subcontractor's remedy against the contractor was limited to a time extension and upheld the district court's refusal to award delay costs to the subcontractor.

Most federal circuits have adopted or seem likely to adopt the rule holding Miller Act sureties liable for delay costs. Faced with an extended scope of liability, and considering that no-damages-for-delay clauses are respected in many states, sureties may consider such clauses as a new source of defense to delay-related claims, as long as they understand that states recognize several exceptions to enforcement and the principal's performance may have matched one of the exceptions.[33]

Courts that recognize exceptions to no-damages-for-delay clauses allow claimants to get around no-damages-for-delay or pay-when-paid clauses by holding that the actions of the general contractor or the owner voided those provisions or that the provisions were against public policy. Payment bond sureties attempting to avoid liability for delay damages should include specific language in the bond and not rely on no-damages-for-delay, pay-when-paid, and other similar clauses in either the subcontract or general contract.[34]

The payment bond surety's no-damages-for-delay defense will be strongest if the no-damages-for-delay clause is broadly written and specifically precludes the recovery of compensation or other damages of any kind or nature resulting from the delays. It may also be helpful if the no-damages-for-delay clause specifically excludes recovery of additional performance costs attributable to delay.[35]

In contrast, in *United States Fidelity & Guaranty Co. v. Borden Metal Products*,[36] the court held that a payment bond surety could not use the absence of a change order as a defense to a supplier claim if the claimant had no knowledge that the material or labor furnished was not part of the prime contract.

Claims against the payment bond brought after the time specified in the bond are generally honored.[37]

---

150 (E.D.N.Y. 1992); Republic Ins. Co. v. Prince George's County, 92 Md. App. 528, 608 A.2d 1301, 1305 (1992)).

[32] 828 F.2d 671 (11th Cir. 1997).

[33] Nahmias at 41.

[34] Douglas, McCarthy & Nelson at 9.

[35] Nahmias at 41.

[36] 539 S.W.2d 170 (Tex. Civ. App. 1976, *writ ref'd n.r.e.*).

[37] Lynbrook Glass & Architectural Metals Corp. v. Elite Assocs., 638 N.Y.S.2d 622 (App. Div., 2d Dep't 1996) (subcontractor that gave notice of its claim under a payment bond, after time limits required by the terms of the bond, could not recover even though surety had failed to raise the notice-of-claim defense in its answer to the suit, because subcontractor was strictly bound by the terms of the bond); Fisher Skylights, Inc. v. CFC Constr. Ltd. P'ship, 79 F.3d 9 (2d Cir. 1996) (one-year limitation period within which subcontractor was required to sue on a payment bond was not extended by surety's failure to give notice of denial of a claim on the bond within 90 days; subcontractor had filed a notice of claim with the surety, but had allowed the one-year statute to expire while waiting for surety to issue a denial of the claim).

ACCOUNTING FOR CHANGE ORDERS: HOW AND WHEN TO RECOGNIZE REVENUE FROM CHANGE ORDERS

Peter V. Badala
Mark O. Simundson

This chapter has been edited by Michael T. Callahan for the second edition. The authors gratefully acknowledge the assistance of Doug Rapp, CPA of The Barrington Consulting Group, Inc., in preparation of this chapter.

§ 17.01   INTRODUCTION

The general contractor on a highway construction project encounters toxic substances during excavation. The project owner instructs the contractor to suspend operations and issues a change order to compensate the contractor for the contractor's time-related costs during the suspension (for example, costs for supervision, idle equipment, and so forth) on a force-account basis. The force-account provisions of the contract call for payments based on predetermined labor and equipment rates.

Six months later, the project is still suspended. The contractor has submitted six monthly billings based on the agreed-upon force-account rates. The owner paid the first three billings in full; however, the owner has now taken the position that the contractor is not entitled to any additional compensation. The contractor's controller, who has been recording monthly income in connection with the change order, must now answer the following questions:

- Should any of the revenue that was recorded during the last six months be reversed?

- What about the billings related to the change order in future months in view of the fact that the suspension has not yet been lifted? Should any additional revenue be recorded, given the owner's position that the contractor is not entitled to any additional compensation?

Fortunately, the accounting literature provides guidance for the would-be controller. However, before beginning a discussion of contract change order accounting, it would be useful to first review some generally accepted accounting principles related to revenue recognition in general and the specialized accounting practices related to construction projects.

§ 17.02   REVENUE RECOGNITION: GENERAL CONCEPTS

Generally accepted accounting principles allow the recognition of revenue when the following events have occurred:

- Goods or services have been delivered to the buyer; and

- Assets such as cash or receivables have been received by the seller and their collectibility is reasonably assured.[1]

In addition to these general concepts, there are also specific guidelines related to construction contracts.

---

[1] AICPA Committee on Accounting Procedure, Accounting Research Bulletin No. 43: Restatement and Revision of Accounting Research Bulletins, ch. 1A, ¶ 1 (1953).

§ 17.03 ACCOUNTING FOR CONSTRUCTION CONTRACTS

In 1981, the Accounting Standards Division of the American Institute of Certified Public Accountants (AICPA) issued *Statement of Position 81-1: Accounting for Performance of Construction-Type and Certain Production-Type Contracts.*[2] *SOP 81-1* supplemented the limited guidance found in *Accounting Research Bulletin No. 45: Long-Term Construction-Type Contracts* and remains the most definitive pronouncement on the application of generally accepted accounting principles to construction contracts. Also in 1981, the AICPA Construction Contractor Guide Committee prepared the audit and accounting guide *Construction Contractors,* which also provided authoritative guidance to the construction industry and borrowed heavily from *SOP 81-1.*[3] The basic accounting issue addressed in the Statement of Position is the recognition of revenue and expenses—namely, the point in time at which contract revenue should be recognized as earned and construction costs should be recognized as expenses.[4]

The Statement of Position allows two different methods of accounting for long-term construction contracts: the percentage-of-completion method and the completed-contract method. Both methods are characterized by certain inherent advantages and disadvantages. *SOP 81-1* states that "the determination of which of the two methods is preferable should be based on a careful evaluation of the circumstances because the two methods should not be acceptable alternatives for the same circumstances."[5]

[A] Percentage-of-Completion Method

Under the percentage-of-completion method of accounting, income is recognized on a periodic basis even though it may take the contractor a number of years to fully complete the contract. The amount of income recognized in each period is a function of the contract price, the extent of construction progress on the project, the total estimated costs at the end of the project, and the income (gross profit) recognized in prior periods. If, at any time, a loss is anticipated in connection with a contract, then the entire loss would generally be recorded immediately.

SOP 81-1 recommends the use of the percentage-of-completion method of accounting when the following circumstances are present:

- Reasonably dependable estimates of construction progress, contract costs, and contract revenues are possible;

- "Contracts executed by the parties normally include provisions that clearly specify the enforceable rights regarding goods or services to be provided and

---

[2] Accounting Standards Division, AICPA, Statement of Position 81-1: Accounting for Performance of Construction-Type and Certain Production-Type Contracts (1981) [hereinafter SOP 81-1].

[3] The guide was updated in 1993.

[4] SOP 81-1 ¶ 2.

[5] SOP 81-1 ¶ 21.

received by the parties, the consideration to be exchanged, and the manner and terms of settlement";[6]

- "The buyer can be expected to satisfy his obligations under the contract";[7] and

- "The contractor can be expected to perform his contractual obligations."[8]

Obviously, these circumstances are present in connection with most commercial construction contracts. A key element of the percentage-of-completion method is the measurement of construction progress. Typically, contractors use estimates of the amount of work physically completed (that is, in place) as the basis of their measurement of progress. The Statement of Position references a number of practices commonly used in the industry (for example, cost-to-cost, efforts-expended, units of delivery, value-added) and suggests that any of them, as well as others, may be appropriate under certain circumstances. However, *SOP 81-1* does state that "the method or methods selected should be applied consistently to all contracts having similar characteristics."[9]

When a contract is completed, the contractor using the percentage-of-completion method must look back to the years in which the contract was open and compare the reported income with the income that would have been reported if the final costs and profit were known. If the contractor would have reported more income, interest is owed on the difference. When a disputed change order or claim is resolved in the contractor's favor, the look-back rules generally mean the contractor will owe the IRS interest. Any additional interest that may be owed because of the collection of additional income for a particular contract should be considered in the claim negotiations not only to understand if additional interest may be due, but also because the additional interest may be included in the final agreed amount. Look-back rules also may result in payments from the IRS. Contractors often optimistically underestimate their contract. As a result, when the contract is completed, the IRS owes them interest under the look-back provisions.

[B] Completed-Contract Method

Under the completed-contract method of accounting, the recognition of income is postponed until the project has been completed or substantially completed. (A project would be considered substantially complete if "remaining costs are not significant in amount."[10]) Costs and billings are accumulated, but no revenue, costs, or profit is reported on the income statement until the project is complete. *SOP*

---

[6] SOP 81-1 ¶ 23.

[7] *Id.*

[8] *Id.*

[9] SOP 81-1 ¶ 45.

[10] AICPA Committee on Accounting Procedure, Accounting Research Bulletin No. 45: Long Term Construction-Type Contracts ¶ 9 (1955).

81-1 recommends the use of the completed-contract method of accounting if the following circumstances are present:

• Reasonably dependable estimates are not possible;[11] or

• Inherent hazards make reasonably dependable estimates doubtful.[12]

The Statement of Position also states that the completed-contract method may be used if the financial condition and results of operations reported on that basis would not vary materially from those that would result from the percentage-of-completion method (for example, in circumstances in which a contractor has primarily short-term contracts).[13]

The one exception to the rule of nonrecognition until completion occurs if a loss is anticipated. If the contractor believes that construction costs will exceed the contract price at the end of the project, then the full amount of the loss must be recognized at once, regardless of whether or not the project has been completed.

The differences in results between the two methods can best be illustrated by example.

[C] Comparison of the Two Methods

TBCG Construction is the general contractor on a project to construct a wastewater treatment plant. The project is expected to take approximately three years to complete. The contract price is $30 million and TBCG Construction has estimated that it will incur construction costs of $27 million to complete the project.

At the end of year 1, TBCG has incurred costs of $9 million and has billed the owner for $10 million. The project is one-third complete, and the estimate of total costs to complete the project has not changed. In addition, no change orders have been required (you can tell that this is a fictional example); therefore, the contract price is still $30 million.[14]

Under the percentage-of-completion method, TBCG would recognize gross profit of $1 million at the end of Year 1 (based on the fact that the project is one-third complete and the total expected gross profit is $3 million). Under the completed-contract method, no income at all would be recognized. The difference between the costs incurred ($9 million) and the billings to the owner ($10 million) would be reported by TBCG as a liability on its balance sheet.

Assuming that the results in Year 2 were identical to the results in Year 1, TBCG would recognize an additional $1 million of income under the percentage-of-completion method at the end of the year. However, under the completed-contract

---

[11] SOP 81-1 ¶ 32.

[12] *Id.*

[13] SOP 81-1 ¶ 31.

[14] In this simple example, the amount of earned revenue under the percentage-of-completion method is assumed to be equal to the contractor's billings to the owner. In the real world, the two would typically be different.

method, no income would be recognized, and TBCG's net current liability in connection with the project would be $2 million (billings of $20 million less costs of $18 million).

In Year 3, TBCG completes the project. However, due to unanticipated cost overruns in some of the remaining activities, the final cost to complete the project was $27.5 million. Under the percentage-of-completion method, TBCG would recognize income equal to the final gross profit on the contract less the amount recognized in prior periods. However, because TBCG had already recognized gross profit of $2 million in prior years, $500,000 would be recognized at the end of Year 3. In fact, if final costs on the project had been $28.5 million, then TBCG would have recorded a $500,000 loss in Year 3 (final gross profit of $1.5 million less gross profit recognized in prior periods of $2 million).

Under the completed-contract method, TBCG would recognize income of $2.5 million upon completion of the project in Year 3. The reported results under the two different methods can be compared as follows:

TBCG Income Statement Comparison

		Percentage-of-Completion	*Completed-Contract*
Year 1	Contract revenue	$10,000,000	$ 0
	Contract costs	9,000,000	0
	Gross profit	$ 1,000,000	$ 0
Year 2	Contract revenue	$10,000,000	$ 0
	Contract costs	9,000,000	0
	Gross profit	$ 1,000,000	$ 0
Year 3	Contract revenue	$10,000,000	$30,000,000
	Contract costs	9,500,000	27,500,000
	Gross profit	$ 500,000	$ 2,500,000

As you can see, the total amount of income recognized over the life of the contract is identical under both methods. However, the timing of income recognition differs dramatically. Indeed, one of the criticisms of the completed-contract method is that it does not adequately reflect current performance when contracts extend into more than one accounting period and may result in irregular patterns of income recognition. If the operating results described above were material to TBCG's financial statements, and the circumstances of the contract did not preclude the preparation of reasonably dependable estimates, then *SOP 81-1* would require that TBCG use the percentage-of-completion method in accounting for this contract.

Among large public companies, the percentage-of-completion method of accounting is by far the most commonly used, favored by approximately 90 percent of the companies surveyed in *Accounting Trends & Techniques* from 1981 through 1991.[15] The completed-contract method is probably more popular among

---

[15] Accounting Trends & Techniques 295 (1983), at 314 (1987), at 347 (1991), at 328 (1992).

small and specialty contractors whose contracts generally do not extend beyond a single accounting period.

§ 17.04 ACCOUNTING FOR CHANGE ORDERS

Contract change orders result from a wide variety of circumstances. Increased scope, design deficiencies, differing site conditions, changes in requirements, work suspensions, and contractor requests are all potential causes of contract change orders. In addition, change order pricing can take a number of different forms, including lump sum, force account (that is, time and material), unit price, or deductive. Given the many different facts and circumstances that give rise to change orders, no one accounting treatment is appropriate for all situations. *SOP 81-1* states that the accounting for change orders should be based on the specific circumstances that are present. The accounting treatment cannot be determined until the terms, conditions, and underlying facts that gave rise to the change order are understood.

[A] Priced Change Orders

If the scope and the price of a change order have been approved by both the contractor and the owner, then contract revenue and costs should be adjusted in accordance with the terms of the change order. If the percentage-of-completion method is being used, then revenue, costs, and resulting income should be recognized as the change order work is completed. Under the completed-contract method, the recognition of revenue and costs would be deferred until the contract is complete.[16]

[B] Unpriced Change Orders

Often, the contractor begins performing change order work before the change order price has been established. The Statement of Position prescribes the following accounting treatment for unpriced change orders.

Under the completed-contract method, the costs associated with unpriced change orders should be deferred (that is, accumulated) as contract costs if it is probable that total contract revenue will equal or exceed total contract costs (including the cost of the change order).[17] Again, no revenue or profit would be recognized until project completion. If, on the other hand, total contract costs will *not* be recovered through contract revenue, then a loss should be recognized even though the project is not complete. Under this scenario, a change order could potentially increase or decrease the anticipated loss.

---

[16] SOP 81-1 ¶ 61.
[17] SOP 81-1 ¶ 62.

Under the percentage-of-completion method, the accounting treatment depends upon the contractor's expectations regarding the ultimate price of the change order.

- If it is *not* probable that the costs will be recovered through an adjustment in the contract price, then the costs should be expensed as they are incurred (with no revenue recognized).[18]

- If it is probable that the costs will be recovered through an increase in the contract price, then two different treatments are allowed. The contractor may defer the recognition of the costs until the parties have agreed on a contract price. Or the contractor may recognize the costs of the change during the period in which they are incurred and also recognize revenue to the extent of the costs incurred. Although both treatments would have an identical effect on the income statement's "bottom line" (that is, zero gross profit), reported contract revenue and costs in a given period may differ under the two approaches.[19]

- If it is probable that the contract price will be adjusted by an amount that exceeds the costs of the change order, *and the amount of the excess or profit can be reliably estimated,* then revenue, costs, and profit may be recognized as the change order work is performed based on its percentage of completion. However, revenue in excess of costs related to unpriced change orders should only be recognized when its "realization is assured beyond a reasonable doubt."[20]

As a practical matter, it may be extremely difficult for a contractor to estimate reliably the profit on an unpriced change order, particularly when the owner may be developing independent pricing proposals. Reliable estimates might be possible in a situation in which the past history on the project had demonstrated that the contractor's change order pricing proposals were always accepted by the owner without modification.

The flowcharts that follow (**Figures 17-1** and **17-2**) summarize the current guidelines for revenue and cost recognition in connection with both priced and unpriced change orders.

[C]   Meaning of the Term *Probable*

Probable is defined in the accounting literature to describe an event or events that are "likely to occur."[21] *SOP 81-1* references a number of circumstances that may indicate that cost recovery of unpriced change orders is probable, including

---

[18] *Id.*

[19] *Id.*

[20] *Id.*

[21] Financial Accounting Standards Board (FASB), Statement of Financial Accounting Standards No. 5: Accounting for Contingencies ¶ 3 (1975).

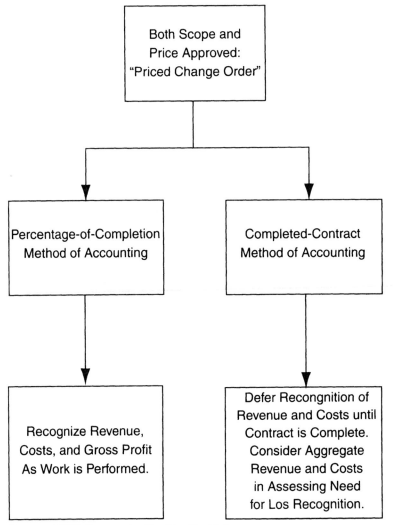

Source: AICPA Statement of Position No. 81-1.

FIGURE 17-1.   REVENUE AND COST RECOGNITION WITH RESPECT TO PRICED CHANGE ORDER.

the owner's written approval of the scope of the change, adequate segregation and documentation of change order costs, and a contractor's favorable experience in negotiating change orders in the past. Other factors that may also be relevant include the scope of work descriptions included in the original contract and prior change orders, as well as any specific contractual provisions related to changes in the work and the recovery of certain types of costs (including applicable markups).

Clearly, the guidelines related to when change order revenue may be recognized are subject to a certain amount of interpretation. One contractor's opinion of when cost recovery is "probable" may differ from another's. Consequently, many contractors have established more specific guidelines related to change orders. For

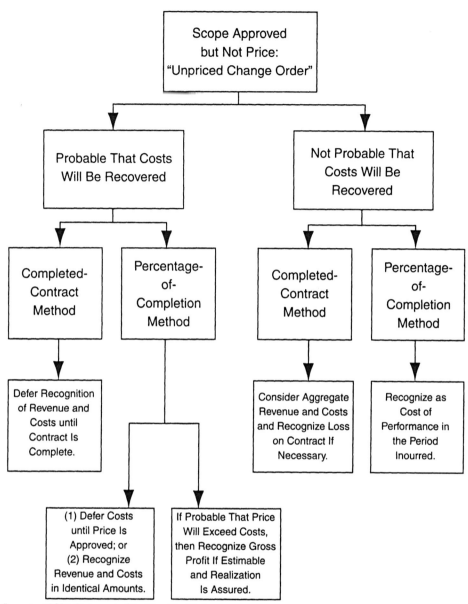

Source: AICPA Statement of Position No. 81-1,

FIGURE 17-2. REVENUE AND COST RECOGNITION WITH RESPECT TO UNPRICED CHANGE ORDER.

example, some contractors require a written document evidencing approval of the change by the owner before allowing unpaid work to be included in the recognition of revenue. Other contractors allow the inclusion of verbally approved changes in the determination of revenue but only after approval by key management. These specific guidelines are helpful in that they provide both project and accounting personnel with additional guidance for addressing the accounting problems that change orders introduce and also provide for a uniformity of treatment within an organization. Specific policies may also be helpful in preventing accounting abuses that might occur. For example, several years ago, a number of former officers of one company were charged by the Securities and Exchange Commission with filing false and misleading financial statements. One of the alleged practices of the company had been to recognize revenue and profit from change orders, even though the company had not billed its customers for many of the changes and rarely collected for them.

§ 17.05 DEFINITION OF COSTS

The accounting standards discussed above make numerous references to "costs" and "cost recovery"; therefore, it is important to understand how the accounting literature defines costs. *SOP 81-1* directs contractors to include the following in the determination of contract costs:

- "Direct costs such as material, labor and subcontracting costs";[22] and

- Indirect costs allocable to contracts such as "indirect labor, contract supervision, tools and equipment, supplies, quality control and inspection, insurance, repairs and maintenance, depreciation and amortization, and, in some circumstances, support costs, such as central preparation and processing of payrolls."[23]

With respect to indirect costs, the Statement of Position also states that the method of allocation must be "systematic and rational."[24] Selling, general, and administrative costs should ordinarily be treated as period expenses and not contract costs, except in certain situations.[25] (For example, under the completed-contract method, it may be more appropriate to treat general and administrative expenses as a contract cost to provide for a better matching of revenue and costs.)

§ 17.06 ACCOUNTING FOR CLAIMS

If change orders are in dispute or are unapproved with regard to both scope and price, then they should be evaluated as claims.[26] *SOP 81-1* provides for the recognition of additional contract revenue from claims only when it is probable that the claim will result in additional revenue and the amount of the additional revenue can be reliably estimated. These two conditions are met only when all the following circumstances are present:

---

[22] SOP 81-1 ¶ 72.
[23] *Id.*
[24] *Id.*
[25] *Id.*
[26] SOP 81-1 ¶ 63.

- There is a legal basis for the claim; or a legal opinion has been obtained stating that there is a reasonable basis for the claim.

- The additional costs were caused by factors that were unforeseen at the contract date and are not attributable to contractor deficiencies.

- The claimed costs are determinable and reasonable in relation to the work performed.

- The evidence supporting the claim is objective and verifiable.

If all of the above conditions are satisfied, then additional contract revenue may be recognized but only to the extent of the costs incurred.[27] In other words, no profit may be recognized from claims until an amount has been received or awarded.

The Statement of Position also condones a policy of recognizing revenue from claims only when the amounts have been received or awarded. If this particular practice is followed, then appropriate disclosures should be made in the footnotes to the financial statements.[28] **Figure 17-3** summarizes the accounting guidelines in connection with claims.

When the above conditions are not satisfied, the claims may not be recognized. For example, in *In re Raytheon Securities Litigation*,[29] the New York State Common Retirement Fund brought an action against Raytheon Company, alleging that defendants issued materially false and misleading statements concerning Raytheon Engineers & Constructors's (RE&C) financial performance in violation of Generally Accepted Accounting Procedures (GAAP). RE&C management estimated and tracked its contract losses on a regular, monthly basis in internal documents that detailed significant negative estimated profits on a number of contracts. The estimates were premised on the assumption that additional funding would be approved despite the fact that RE&C had been historically unsuccessful in securing such funding. For example, RE&C's 40 largest projects showed they required $251 million of additional funding in order to reach a negative estimated profit to completion of $171 million. Topping the list, the Saudi American General Electric PP9 power plant contract was listed with a negative estimated profit of $34,349,000 to completion, which was predicated on the assumption of securing $103,287,000 in additional funding from the client. Plaintiff alleged there was no reasonable basis for this assumption, noting that historically RE&C has been successful in collecting only 20 to 30 percent of the additional funding it had requested from its clients.

According to plaintiff, defendants violated GAAP in an effort to mask the extent of the losses that were occurring on RE&C contracts. Raytheon accounted for RE&C's long-term, fixed-price contracts under a percentage-of-completion method. Under GAAP, Raytheon was required to recognize the entire amount of

---

[27] SOP 81-1 ¶ 65.
[28] SOP 81-1 ¶ 66.
[29] 157 F. Supp. 2d 131, 2001 U.S. Dist. LEXIS 13348 (D. Mass. 2001).

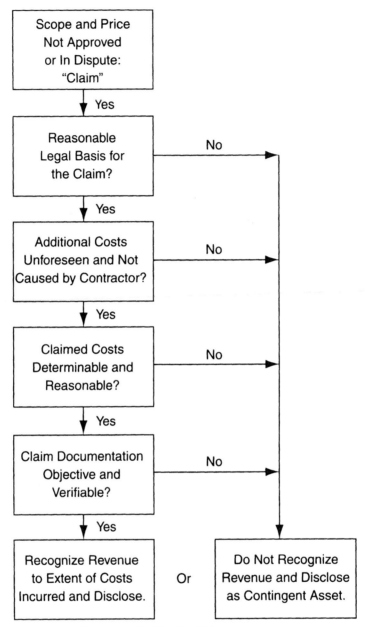

Source: AICPA Statement of Position No. 81-1.

FIGURE 17-3. ACCOUNTING FOR CLAIMS.

any losses estimated through the entire duration of the contracts as soon as those losses became probable and could be reasonably estimated. Financial Standards Accounting Board (FASB), *Statement of Financial Accounting Standards No. 5*, "Accounting for Contingencies" (SFAS No. 5), Paragraph 8, requires that an estimated loss shall be accrued by a charge to income if, based on the available information, the loss is probable and the amount of the loss can be reasonably estimated. In addition, under GAAP, Raytheon could not legitimately account for additional funding unless receipt of funds in excess of the contract price was probable and could be reasonably estimated. *SOP 81-1*, Paragraph 65, states that "[r]ecognition of amounts of additional contract revenue relating to claims is appropriate only if it is probable that the claim will result in additional contract revenue and if the amount can be reliably estimated." Based on these accounting principles, plaintiff estimated that Raytheon should have recognized a true loss totaling roughly $422 million on approximately 40 major contracts in process.

Plaintiff also alleged that Raytheon avoided recognizing $93 million in losses on ten inactive, completed RE&C contracts. The $93 million was booked as revenues in excess of actual client payments to cover cost overruns previously incurred. Raytheon categorized these contracts as subject to litigation or alternative dispute resolution. According to the plaintiff, the $93 million should have been written down as a loss in accordance with GAAP and Raytheon's own internal policies because there was no reasonable expectation of a recovery in that amount. For example, Raytheon failed to write off the Saudi Aramco Seawater Project although it was a closed project, it was in arbitration, and the historic relationship with the customer, as well as the contract terms, made recovery improbable.

Raytheon moved for dismissal. According to the court, the application of the accounting principles depended upon both a reasonable assessment of the probability of gain or loss and a reasonable valuation of the amount of the gain or loss. An application of GAAP that strayed beyond the boundaries of reasonableness would provide evidence of intent. Plaintiff's complaint detailed numerous instances of accounting legerdemain that all served to overstate the ledger of RE&C. The magnitude of the accounting overstatement resulting from the combination of the alleged GAAP violations was significant—more than $200 million in excess of a write-down of $310 million. Defendant Raytheon claimed that the documentation attached to the internal reports showed that Raytheon realistically "expected" to recover almost all of the $251 million and had made claims for reimbursement. This assertion was belied, however, by the listing of these contracts as "write-offs." By contrast, another report listed several contracts as "possible" write-offs. The use of the term "possible" to describe the contracts and its omission in the first list created a strong inference of contemporaneous knowledge of a serious GAAP problem. The plaintiff adequately alleged a claim with regard to the accounting irregularities at RE&C.

§ 17.07   BACK CHARGES

Back charges occur when work that is performed by one party should have been performed by someone else. For example, a general contractor may be forced to clean up after a subcontractor. Or an owner may be required to hire a substitute contractor to clear "punch-list" items because the original contractor neglected to do so. The costs that were incurred are then billed to the nonperforming party. Consequently, a contractor may be on both the receiving and the giving end of back charges.

Back charges that are billed to the contractor should be recorded as accounts payable and additional contract costs if it is probable that the amounts will be paid. Back charges that the contractor bills to others should be recorded as receivables and used to offset contract costs if it is probable that the amount will be collected. If the back charge is in dispute, then like disputed change orders, the back charge should be evaluated as a claim.[30]

§ 17.08   GOVERNMENT CONTRACTS

SOP 81-1 also applies to the financial reporting practices of federal government contractors. In addition, there are other pronouncements that provide guidance to entities performing government contracts, including Chapter 11 of *Accounting Research Bulletin No. 43*.[31] Federal government contractors are also subject to the standards promulgated by the Cost Accounting Standards Board (CASB). CASB standards address the procedures by which contractors may allocate costs to government contracts. CASB standards do not address financial reporting.

Constructive change orders are one of the significant nuances of government contracts. The accounting literature defines a constructive change to be a government act (or failure to act) that "has the effect of requiring the contractor to perform additional work or incur added costs and is not included in a formal change order."[32] Constructive change orders can present some significant challenges to contractors because government regulations require contractors to submit detailed cost and pricing documentation during change order negotiations. Frequently, the presence of a constructive change is not recognized until the costs associated with the change have already been incurred.

§ 17.09   CHANGE ORDER MANAGEMENT: SOME PRACTICAL CONSIDERATIONS

In the late 1980s, the Federal Construction Council's Building Research Board conducted a study of the causes and costs of contract change orders on both federal and nonfederal construction projects. Although the amounts by which contract prices increased due to change orders differed between organizations and project types, the increases frequently approached or exceeded 10 percent during the years under study.[33] These studies merely reinforced what people in the construction industry have always known—that change orders are an undeniable fact of life! In the 1990s, the Construction Industry Institute commissioned a series of

---

[30] SOP 81-1 ¶ 77.

[31] Accounting Research Bulletin No. 43: Restatement and Revision of Accounting Research Bulletins, ch. 11 (1953).

[32] AICPA Government Contractors Guide Special Committee, AICPA Audit and Accounting Guide: Audits of Federal Government Contractors 160 (1993).

[33] *The Federal Change Order Study*, Constr. Claims Monthly, Jan. 1988, at 1.

research projects that confirmed the Building Research Council's earlier studies.[34] Because they cannot be avoided, effective management is the only way to mitigate any disruptive impacts that change orders may have on a project.

The proper management of change orders depends on timely and effective communication between the project site and the home office. When a potential change is recognized at the project site, the home office should be notified so that the accounting and reporting requirements can be discussed and determined. At an early stage, the potential change should be reviewed by qualified project personnel who can make an educated assessment of the reasonableness of the claimed change in light of the scope of work and other contract provisions. In this manner, unsupportable potential changes can be "weeded out" before necessitating additional record keeping by project personnel and the home office accounting staff. The Construction Industry Institute describes several good change order management systems.[35]

[A] Cost Accounting

Ideally, a separate cost code or activity should be assigned to each potential change. If the contractor's cost report uses four-digit cost codes, then the 9000-series (9001, 9002, 9003, and so forth) can be reserved for potential changes. Although the administrative requirements increase with such a practice, the benefits can easily outweigh the costs. For example, if the scope of a potential change is approved, but the owner and contractor are unable to agree on price, then the price may be ultimately paid on a time and materials basis. If a separate cost account has been used to track the cost of the change, then the documentation needed for billing purposes is readily available. In addition, many potential changes never result in approved change orders and instead end up as claims. Actual contemporaneous job cost records provide compelling documentation in connection with the proving and pricing of claims.

For example, in *Com-Corp Industries, Inc. v. H&H Machine Tool Co.,*[36] the court considered whether time reports tailored to one specific project to collect additional performance costs indicated that the records were inherently untrustworthy. At trial, Com-Corp's accountant testified under both direct and cross-examination that employees working on the bezel project were instructed to log separately their hours spent completing the dies and submit them to Com-Corp with their time sheets. The accountant further testified that the records were then checked against the time sheets. On cross-examination, the accountant testified that the records were kept to track the additional costs on the bezel project. Finally,

---

[34] For example, *see* C. Ibbs & W. Allen, *Quantitative Impacts of Project Change*, Constr. Indus. Inst., Source Doc. 108 (May 1995).

[35] W. Hester, J. Kuprenas & T. Chang, *Construction Changes and Change Orders: Their Magnitude and Impact*, Constr. Indus. Inst., Source Doc. 66 (Oct. 1991); and Haggard, ed., *Project Change Management*, Special Publication 43-1 (Nov. 1994).

[36] 1996 Ohio App. LEXIS 4795 (1996).

the accountant testified that although the special time cards were specifically prepared for tracking the labor costs of the bezel project, Com-Corp tracked other
project costs in various ways. The jury awarded Com-Corp $1,082,619 in dam-
ages. H&H appealed. H&H argued on appeal that the use of special internal labor
reporting forms by Com-Corp to compile additional labor costs incurred while
performing tasks it claimed resulted from H&H's failures should not be considered business records.

The appellate court concluded that because the time reports were tailored to
one specific project did not indicate that the records were inherently untrustworthy
and that the trial court had not abused its discretion in admitting the special time
reports in affirming the award.

Of course, it may not be practical to set up separate cost accounts for each
potential change. For example, if the amount of the potential change is not
expected to be significant, then it may not be cost-effective to attempt to track the
costs of each change individually. On the other hand, many potential changes that
are initially perceived to be insignificant wind up being major sources of contention (and increased costs) on construction projects. This fact needs to be considered by the contractor in connection with accounting and reporting decisions.

[B]   Change Estimate File

All potential changes should be documented by a standardized "change estimate" form. The change estimates should be numbered sequentially and maintained in separate files. If the cost reporting system tracks the costs of potential
changes, then the change estimate number should correspond to the cost
account. For example, costs attributable to change estimate #3 would be
assigned to cost code #9003. The change estimate file should also include all the
following documentation:

1. Relevant correspondence;

2. Cost and time estimates;

3. Pricing proposals;

4. Schedule impacts;

5. Extra work reports or any other documentation required by the project
   owner;

6. Documentation of all approvals, whether written or verbal;

7. Current status; and

8. Final resolution.

Finally, a log of all the change estimates should be maintained. The log should
include a description of each change estimate, the date that the change was initiated, a reference to the approved contract change order number (if the change estimate resulted in a change order), the price of the approved change order, any

amounts in dispute, and the final resolution of the change estimate or the amounts in dispute.

[C]   Contract Change Order File

In addition to the change estimate files and log discussed in § 17.09[B], a control file of approved contract change orders should be maintained. A summary of contract change orders and revised contract amounts should be prepared and reconciled monthly to the progress billing information to ensure that change order work is being recorded and billed on a timely basis.

[D]   Benefits from Proper Change Order Management

Contractors reap a number of benefits from the effective management of change orders. First, the timely administration and billing of change order work gets money in the door faster. Second, accurate and complete cost reporting for changes can be valuable during the negotiation of change order prices. Finally, in the event that negotiations break down and a dispute arises, contemporaneous cost data will be available to assist in the pricing of the claim (which, all other things being equal, is much more persuasive than estimates developed "after the fact").

§ 17.10   ANSWER TO THE CONTROLLER'S DILEMMA

After reading this chapter, the controller should have found the answers to the questions raised in § 17.01. Assuming that the contractor in our example uses the percentage-of-completion method of accounting, the controller was correct in recording contract income in connection with the initial three months (you will recall that these amounts have been billed and collected). However, with respect to all other uncollected sums, the disputed change should be accounted for as a claim. If all the circumstances described in § 17.06 are present, then the contractor may recognize revenue but only to the extent of the costs incurred. If any of the circumstances described in § 17.06 are not present, or if the contractor chooses a more conservative accounting treatment, then no revenue would be recorded until payment is actually received by the contractor. The nature of the contingent asset would be disclosed in the financial statement notes.

CHAPTER 18

PROVING AND PRICING DAMAGES

Val S. McWhorter
Mark A. Smith

The original chapter by Val S. McWhorter and Mark A. Smith was supplemented by Michael T. Callahan.

§18.01 OBJECTIVES OF CHANGE ORDER CLAIM PRICING

This chapter provides practical advice on proving and pricing damages flowing from change order claims. Without demonstrating damage and quantifying it, the successful battle to prove the existence of a change will provide a hollow victory. Unless a contractor wants to dedicate personnel and finances to "ringing the bells of justice," its earliest focus should be on the ability accurately and persuasively to collect and present cost data supporting the injury or loss it believes it has suffered.

This chapter starts from the assumption that the elements of proof to establish the presence of a change have been satisfied and that the contractor must now look to the calculation of damages to establish the extent of recovery of the increased costs incurred. Under this circumstance, there are certain general goals and guidelines to be considered. Pricing construction damages that flow from changes should not be viewed as a "cookie cutter" operation (that is, in construction vernacular, there is no template). Rather, in determining how to identify and quantify damages, it is essential to understand what is being built and how each project is unique. Each construction project is different, with its own set of circumstances, design, personnel, equipment, and work environment. Although there are guidelines and certain general areas that should always be investigated, a successful damage presentation is the one that makes sense to the owner, or to a tribunal, taking into consideration the actual field circumstances.

The specific goal of pricing a claim based on changes to the work should be to identify and recover increased costs arising from the changes and to make a reasonable profit on the changed or added work. The measure of the increased costs can be viewed as "damages" or as an *equitable adjustment*—an administrative, contractual means for pricing what, in the absence of a changes clause, might otherwise be deemed a breach of contract. The "pricing of an equitable adjustment has the same underlying principle as the determination of contract damages: the objective to make the contractor whole when the government modifies a contract."[1]

In a contractual context, "the term 'damages' is used to mean compensation in money as a substitute for and the equivalent of the promised performance."[2] Further, in "determining the amount of this compensation as the 'damages' to be awarded, the aim in view is to put the injured party in as good a position as he would have had if performance had been rendered as promised."[3] This theory and approach have been widely accepted and followed by state and federal courts. For example, in *Brandon & Tibbs v. George Kevorkian Accounting Corp.,*[4] the court succinctly stated:

> The basic object of damages is compensation, and in the law of contracts the theory is that the party injured by a breach should receive as nearly as possible

---

[1] Lorentz Bruun Co., GSBCA Nos. 8504, 8505, 88-2 BCA (CCH) ¶ 20,719 at 104,699 (1988). *See also* Northwest Marine, Inc., ASBCA No. 43097, 92-2 BCA (CCH) ¶ 24,861 at 124,012 (1992).

[2] 5 A. Corbin, Corbin on Contracts, Pt. VI, topic B, ch. 55, § 990 at 3 (1963).

[3] *Id.* § 992 at 5.

[4] 277 Cal. Rptr. 40, 47 (Ct. App. 1990).

the equivalent of the benefits of performance (Civ. Code, § 3300; 1 Witkin, *Summary of California Law* (9th ed. 1987); Contracts, § 813, p.732; 5 Corbin, Contracts (1964) Damages, § 992, p.5.). The aim is to put the injured party in as good a position as he would have been had performance been rendered as promised.

This aim can never be exactly attained yet that is the problem the trial court is required to resolve.[5] Similarly, New Jersey permitted a contractor to collect its additional performance costs that unbalanced its bid in violation of the state procurement code in order to put the contractor in the position it occupied before the change in *M.J. Paquet, Inc. v. New Jersey Department of Transportation.*[6]

Federal precedent that has developed around standard changes clauses has defined an equitable adjustment with comparable boundaries. Although the term "equitable adjustment" has its primary origin in litigation surrounding the federal contract changes clause, it is worthy of note that the Federal Acquisition Regulation (FAR) contains no definition. This lack of official definition is, in the opinion of the authors, a proper approach because each construction contract and each change will have several unique facts in determining what is "equitable." The changes clause (FAR 52.243-4) defines the boundaries of such an adjustment when changes cause an "increase or decrease in the contractor's cost of, or the time required for, the performance of any part of the work under the contract, whether or not changed by any such order." In such circumstances, the focus in defining the adjustment is clearly on a contractor's cost:

> Since the purpose of an equitable adjustment is to keep the contractor whole when the contract has been modified by a change, the measure of the adjustment must relate to his altered position. . . . Accordingly, the proper measure of an equitable adjustment . . . is the difference between the reasonable cost of the work required by the contract and the actual reasonable cost to [the contractor] of performing the changed work, plus a reasonable amount for overhead and profit.[7]

As noted by the General Services Administration Board of Contract Appeals (GSBCA) in *Dawson Construction Co.,* the purpose of an equitable adjustment is to keep a contractor whole when a contract is modified. The measure of such an adjustment is not the value of what is received by the government or saved by the

---

[5] *See also* Barr v. MacGlothlin, 176 Va. 474, 484, 11 S.E.2d 617 (1940); Wanderer v. Plainfield Carton Corp., 40 Ill. App. 3d 552, 556, 351 N.E.2d 630 (1976); New York Water Serv. Corp. v. City of New York, 4 A.D.2d 209, 163 N.Y.S.2d 538, 539 (1957); Sofia Shipping Co. v. Amoco Transp. Co., 628 F. Supp. 116, 119 (S.D.N.Y. 1986); Intermountain Rural Elec. Ass'n v. Colorado Cent. Power Co., 322 F.2d 516, 522 (10th Cir. 1963); Chicago Painters & Decorators, Etc. v. Karr Bros., 755 F.2d 1285, 1290 (7th Cir. 1985).

[6] 794 A.2d 141, 171 N.J. 378 (S. Ct. 2002).

[7] Southern Paving Corp., AGBCA No. 74-103, 77-2 BCA (CCH) ¶ 12,813 at 62,364 (1977). *See generally* United States v. Rice, 317 U.S. 61 (1942), for early discussions of equitable adjustments.

contractor, but rather the altered financial position in which the contractor is placed by reason of the modification.[8]

Taking these general guidelines into consideration, a successful damage presentation should fit within these boundaries and be focused on cost, particularly because the contractor, if plaintiff or claimant, must bear the burden of proving its damages.

Damage calculations have become increasingly more creative with the use of sophisticated schedule analyses for determining delay and disruption damages and persuasive graphic presentations. Meanwhile, owners, including the federal government, have made efforts to limit recoverability of costs with special clauses and regulations while still seeking contract proposals or bids absent contingencies for changes. For example, despite the wording of the federal changes clauses that an equitable adjustment will be made for changes, the pricing-of-adjustments clause made available for use by federal agencies requires that all adjustments be prepared in conformance with cost principles set forth in the regulations. The clause can be limiting in its application from common law damages or what might otherwise be deemed "equitable." Similarly, FAR 31.602 requires use of the cost principles in pricing fixed-price modifications "whenever (a) cost analysis is performed, or (b) a fixed-price contract clause requires the determination or negotiation of costs." FAR 31.102 goes on to note:

> However, application of cost principles to fixed-price contracts and subcontracts shall not be construed as a requirement to negotiate agreements on individual elements of cost in arriving at agreement on the total price. The final price accepted by the parties reflects agreement only on the total price. Further, notwithstanding the mandatory use of cost principles, the objective will continue to be to negotiate prices that are fair and reasonable, cost and other factors considered.

Therefore, as a starter in pricing damages, one should be familiar with the general philosophies governing damages or equitable adjustment recovery, as well as specific limiting clauses in the contract or regulations.

§ 18.02   WHERE TO START

Most contractors on construction projects have budgets or other cost-control devices to measure their financial position on a job. Job cost records are therefore a good place to start in determining where the damages have occurred and where the fact finding effort should focus. If there are large cost overruns in identifiable bid items, the attention to costs should be centered on work items that are affected, including associated equipment and labor costs. If the contract is a lump-sum one with costs gathered by broad categories, such as equipment, materials (cement or

---

[8] GSBCA No. 5364, 82-1 BCA (CCH) ¶ 15,701 at 77,661, *reconsideration denied*, 82-2 BCA (CCH) ¶ 15,914 (1982).

aggregates, for example), or labor, overruns in those areas can help define the scope of the change and chart a course to measure damages.

In combination with the cost overruns identified through financial review, the pricing of changes should be governed by an understanding of the construction operations. This is best done with knowledgeable project personnel. These persons cannot only identify the direct effects of the change on performance, but they are most helpful in isolating impacts or ripples that flow from the change. If there is a constructive change, or if the contractor finds itself in the position of trying to identify the change that caused cost overruns, there is no substitute for interviews with project personnel, especially field superintendents or project managers and engineers. Those with a firsthand knowledge of how events affected their planned performance, their labor efficiency, or their equipment needs can help identify owner actions that result in changes or areas to investigate for damages.

Keep in mind, also, that these same individuals can provide factual support as either witnesses at a trial or in meetings with the owner. This interview process provides a good opportunity to evaluate their knowledge and credibility. To the extent that the cost overruns match with where field personnel believe changes occurred, a story will be pieced together that describes the events and the resultant damages.

Equally important is to confer with the contractor's record-keeping or accounting personnel to understand how costs in the field are accumulated and allocated to various cost accounts. Understanding the contractor's bid is also significant in evaluating whether recoverable damages have occurred, for it may be that the recorded "cost overruns" are measured against an inadequate bid. By reviewing and understanding the contractor's cost records and the actual conditions and events that were encountered during performance, the causal link between the change and the damages that flow from it can be established. This causal link is fundamental to successful damage recovery.

It is well established that for a contractor to recover an equitable adjustment following a change order, the contractor must show a cause and effect relationship between the change order and the costs sought to be recovered.[9] "Recovery of damages for a breach of contract is not allowed unless acceptable evidence demonstrates that the damages claimed resulted from and were caused by the breach."[10]

Mere proof of a breach and the existence of costs exceeding the contract price are insufficient for a successful recovery of damages. It is also insufficient to make "[broad] generalities and inferences to the effect that defendant must have

---

[9] *See* Wunderlich Contracting Co. v. United States, 173 Ct. Cl. 180, 351 F.2d 956 (1965).

[10] Boyajian v. United States, 423 F.2d 1231, 1235 (Ct. Cl. 1970); United States ex rel. Gray-Bar Elec. Co. v. J.H. Copeland & Son Constr., Inc., 568 F.2d 1159 (5th Cir.), *cert. denied*, 436 U.S. 957, 98 S. Ct. 3072 (5th Cir. 1978); Avedon Corp. v. United States, 15 Cl. Ct. 648 (1988) (although the contractor demonstrated the government caused unreasonable delay in a portion of its work, recovery was denied because the contractor failed to link the delay to any resulting increase in its costs and failed to distinguish delay or expenses attributed to the government's delay from that caused by other reasons).

caused some delay and damages because the contract took 318 days longer to complete than anticipated."[11] Moreover, when a plaintiff is unable to establish proximate cause between the breach and the damages and segregate the damages caused by the defendant from damages attributable to other factors, the award of damages will be difficult to sustain.[12]

To meet its burden then, a contractor must establish a relationship between the event (the change) and the damages (the cost increases). Often, particularly in construction contract claim situations, the causal link is directly tied to schedule-related issues, such as disruption of planned activities, resequencing of the work, delays in completion, and acceleration of the performance. If upon talking to project personnel it appears the damages may flow from a schedule-related cause, it will be necessary to compare and understand the differences between the contractor's planned performance (as-planned) and its actual performance (as-built).

There are far too many schedule issues to have them properly addressed in this chapter, but in pricing and proving construction changes, a familiarity with these concepts is critical. In the initial analysis, it is important to identify the existence of delays to or disruptions or suspensions of the work, the evidence of contractor efforts to overcome those factors, and the effect both those events may have had on overall increased costs.

§ 18.03   METHODS OF PRICING THE CHANGE

There are certain classic, well-established ways in which the pricing for an equitable adjustment can proceed: through a showing of actual, historical costs built up from a base of zero, or through the total cost or modified total cost method. A showing of actual costs, generally through the contractor's bookkeeping and other records, is generally the most persuasive way for a contractor to price an equitable adjustment, although by no means the only way. If the contractor has kept its books in such a manner that the costs related to the change order are segregated from its overall contract costs, there will be less resistance from the owner (or its auditor) to accept those costs as a true measure of the change. The more documentation a contractor produces, the more likely a court or board will decide that those documents reflect the costs for which the contractor is due an equitable adjustment.

A contractor's actual costs are considered to be reasonable costs in an analysis of change order pricing. As noted by the U.S. Court of Claims in the landmark decision of *Bruce Construction Corp. v. United States:* "As we have said above, there is a presumption that actual costs paid are reasonable. That presumption must be overcome by whichever party alleges its unreasonableness."[13]

---

[11] Wunderlich Contracting Co. v. United States, 173 Ct. Cl. 180, 351 F.2d 956, 969 (1965).

[12] S. J. Groves & Sons Co. v. Warner Co., 576 F.2d 524, 527 (3d Cir. 1978); Bath Iron Works v. United States, 34 Fed. Cl. 218 (1995) (contractor could not recover additional performance costs because it failed to establish relationship between event and damages; contractor merely presented proof that changes under a contract not the subject of its claim had caused additional work, rather than the contract under which it had brought its claim).

[13] 324 F.2d 516, 520 (Ct. Cl. 1963).

Efforts have been made by the federal government to overcome or modify the impact of the *Bruce* decision through legislation and implementing FAR provisions.[14] Specifically, the FAR provision provides that:

(a) A cost is reasonable if, in its nature and amount, it does not exceed that which would be incurred by a prudent person in the conduct of competitive business. . . . No presumption of reasonableness shall be attached to the incurrence of costs by a contractor. If an initial review of the facts results in a challenge of a specific cost by the contracting officer or the contracting officer's representative, the burden of proof shall be upon the contractor to establish that such cost is reasonable.

Nonetheless, many boards and courts continue to cite *Bruce* and follow the presumption of reasonableness it espouses and its preference for the use of actual costs as a basis for measuring damages or equitable adjustments. Accordingly, referral to a contractor's actual costs incurred is still the most favored approach by owners in evaluating change order requests.

Referral to and use of actual costs can take several forms. Pricing a change can follow what is commonly called a bottoms-up approach, or an attempt to start at zero and identify and accumulate all direct and indirect costs directly attributable to the change. This approach can pose many difficulties because of miscoding of costs or attempting to establish a firm causal link to each and every increased dollar spent. Oftentimes, the contractor's records simply do not provide adequate, accurate data to support such a pricing approach.

Actual costs can also be used to prepare a total cost or modified total cost analysis of damages. These methods were developed and accepted in circumstances when a bottoms-up approach was not possible or did not yield an appropriate or equitable adjustment.

The *total cost approach*, that is, the difference between bid and project cost as the amount of an equitable adjustment, is generally viewed with disfavor by boards and courts. It is appropriate, however, under certain specific circumstances and under fairly specific guidelines. The reasons it has been viewed with disfavor were set forth by the U.S. Court of Claims, as follows:

This theory has never been favored by the court and has been tolerated only when no other mode was available and when the reliability of the supporting evidence was fully substantiated. . . . The acceptability of the method hinges on proof that (1) the nature of the particular losses make it impossible or highly impracticable to determine them with a reasonable degree of accuracy; (2) the plaintiff's bid or estimate was realistic; (3) its actual costs were reasonable; and (4) it was not responsible for the added expenses.[15]

When used as a means of arriving at the amount of damages where causation has been established through credible evidence, the total cost method is acceptable when the nature of the losses incurred or the adequacy of the cost records prevent

---

[14] *See* FAR 31.201-3.
[15] WRB Corp. v. United States, 183 Ct. Cl. 409, 426 (1968).

more particularized allocation of costs to events. The total cost approach, or a modified one, may in fact be the most accurate measure for a change in the specifications or method of performance that is so significant as to affect most of the work.

A *modified total cost approach* is one that takes into account the concerns expressed by the court in *WRB Corporation*. Specifically, such an approach should acknowledge errors or misjudgments in the bid that would prevent it from being an accurate measure of what the work should have cost but for the change. Alternatively, a contractor could use as a baseline a modified bid or budget approach. Likewise, it may be necessary to abandon use of the bid altogether and develop a reasonable cost estimate of what the work reasonably should have cost, absent the change. By doing so, one of the hindrances of a total cost method is eliminated. As stated by the Armed Services Board of Contract Appeals: "In this appeal we are unaware of any better method by which the appellant could establish additional costs attributable to inefficiency than by establishing what the work reasonably should have cost and what the work did in fact cost."[16] Independent preparation of an estimate of the cost of the work from the bid documents, such as by an engineering or consulting firm, may provide persuasive evidence of the should-have-cost amount.[17]

Another hurdle to overcome in employing a total cost approach is the presumption in that methodology that the owner is responsible for all increased costs. Accordingly, this approach can be further modified to analyze, identify, and quantify all increased costs that the contractor recognizes are not the owner's responsibility, thereby enhancing the contractor's credibility and reducing the overall project costs by that amount in pricing the change.

If a court rejects the claimant's pricing method, it may allow recovery under a "jury verdict method." For a court to employ the jury verdict method in making an award, the contractor must first demonstrate clear proof of injury. Second, the court must also be satisfied that there is no more reliable method available for computing damages before it may adopt the jury verdict method. Last, to employ the jury verdict method, the evidence adduced at trial must also be sufficient to allow the court to make a fair and reasonable approximation of the plaintiff's damages.[18]

§ 18.04   LEVEL OF PROOF NEEDED

Once the most appropriate method (or sometimes the only available method) has been determined for pricing the change, it is helpful to know what level of proof will be expected at each stage of the change submission process. Although auditors and often owners attempt to persuade contractors that the change must be priced with absolute certainty and with an infallible causal link to each dollar, such is not the case. The courts and boards have made clear the fact that although

---

[16] Sovereign Constr. Co., ASBCA No. 17,792, 75-1 BCA (CCH) ¶ 11,251 at 53,606 (1975).

[17] Paul Smith Constr. Co., ENGBCA Nos. 2720, 2716, 70-2 BCA (CCH) ¶ 8524 at 39,650 (1970).

[18] *Bath Iron Works*, 34 Fed. Cl. 218 (1995).

the burden to prove the amount of money to which [the contractor] is entitled rests on [the contractor, the courts and boards] have also recognized that when entitlement has been proven but [a contractor] cannot prove or define its costs with exact data, he need not be sent away empty handed if a reasonable approximation of the extra costs can be made.[19]

The proof of damages need not be exact. The U.S. Court of Claims has held that the determination of the amount of damages "is not an exact science," and that it is not essential that the amount of damages "be ascertainable with absolute exactness or mathematical precision."[20]

When confronted with an inability to prove damages with certainty, the contractor need not abandon hope for recovery of damages caused by changes. The U.S. Court of Claims, citing long-standing precedent, described a "jury verdict" approach that would be appropriate under such circumstances:

> However, this inability to determine the precise amount of the damages attributable to the Government's breach of contract does not preclude the court from entering a judgment for the plaintiff. The ascertainment of damages is not an exact science. *Western Contracting Corp. v. United States,* 144 Ct. Cl. 318, 320 (1958). Hence it is not essential that the amount of damages be ascertainable with absolute exactness or mathematical precision. *Eastman Kodak Co. v. Southern Photo Co.,* 273 U.S. 359, 379, 47 S. Ct. 400, 71 L.Ed. 684 (1927); *Brand Investment Co. v. United States,* 58 F. Supp. 749, 102 Ct. Cl. 40, 44 (1944), *cert. denied,* 324 U.S. 850, 65 S. Ct. 684, 89 L. Ed. 1410. It is enough if the evidence adduced is sufficient to enable a court or jury to make a fair and reasonable approximation. *Hedrick v. Perry,* 102 F.2d 802, 807 (10th Cir. 1939).
>
> In estimating damages, the Court of Claims occupies the position of a jury under like circumstances; and all that the litigants have any right to expect is the exercise of the court's best judgment upon the basis of the evidence provided by the parties. *United States v. Smith,* 94 U.S. 214, 219, 24 L. Ed. 115 (1876).[21]

§ 18.05 COSTS TO INCLUDE

In contracting with the federal government, the issue of allowability under the FAR must be considered in the pricing of modifications to fixed-price contracts for construction.[22] Any cost for which a contractor feels it should be reimbursed by the government must be first *allowable* under FAR 31.201-2. To be allowable, the FAR requires that the cost must be:

---

[19] Louis M. McMaster, Inc., AGBCA No. 80-159-4, 86-3 BCA (CCH) ¶ 19,067 at 96,300 (1986).

[20] *See* Electronic & Missile Facilities, Inc. v. United States, 416 F.2d 1345, 1358 (Ct. Cl. 1969) (quoting in part from Specialty Assembling & Packing Co. v. United States, 355 F.2d 554, 572 (Ct. Cl. 1966)).

[21] Special Assembling & Packing Co. v. United States, 355 F.2d 554, 572-73 (Ct. Cl. 1966).

[22] *See* FAR 31.105.

1.   Reasonable;

2.   Allocable; and

3.   In conformance with generally accepted accounting principles and prac-
     tice, the terms of the contract, and the regulations in FAR 31.2.

"This section [FAR 31.201-2] makes plain that to be allowable, a cost must meet
all the criteria set forth therein."[23] Among those criteria to be considered are specific "unallowable" costs prescribed by FAR 31.205. The unallowable costs
should be excluded from any change order pricing. These FAR terms are made
applicable to construction contracts at FAR 31.105.

In general, a cost is considered *reasonable* if it "does not exceed that which
would be incurred by a prudent person in the conduct of competitive business."[24]
"A cost is allocable if it is assignable to one or more cost objectives on the basis of
relative benefits received or other equitable relationship."[25]

Regarding accounting practices, if the cost-accounting standards are applicable to a contract, then the contractor's allocation of its costs must be consistent
with the cost-accounting standards. If the cost-accounting standards are not applicable, the contractor's accounting standards must follow both FAR standards and
"generally accepted accounting principles."

After it has been determined that a cost is allowable, the FAR breaks costs
into separate categories for accounting and allocation purposes.

[A]   Direct Costs

Contractor-incurred costs are considered to be either direct or indirect in
nature. "The general rule is to first segregate out all charges [(costs)] that can be
identified with the specific objective in mind, leaving as indirect charges only
those where identification cannot be made."[26] This definition, as developed by
Boards of Contract Appeals, reflects both accepted accounting principles and the
definition found in the FAR.[27] Direct costs are defined in the FAR as:

> any cost that can be identified specifically with a particular final cost objec-
> tive. . . . Costs identified specifically with the contract are direct costs of the
> contract and are to be charged directly to the contract. All costs specifically
> identified with other final cost objectives of the contractor are direct costs of
> those cost objectives and are not to be charged to the contract directly or indi-
> rectly.[28]

---

[23] Boeing Co. v. United States, 202 Ct. Cl. 315, 329, 480 F.2d 854 (1973).

[24] FAR 31.201-3(a). *See* prior discussion regarding reasonableness and *Bruce.*

[25] FAR 31.201-4(a).

[26] Foster Constr. Co., DOTCAB 71-16, 73-1 BCA (CCH) ¶ 9869 at 46,150 (1972); *see also* Peter
Kiewit Sons' Co., ENGBCA No. 4742, 85-1 BCA (CCH) ¶ 17,911 at 64,429 (1985).

[27] ENGBCA No. 4742, 85-1 BCA (CCH) at 89,708.

[28] FAR 31.202(a).

Thus, a direct cost must be a dedicated cost; not only must it be identified and incurred specifically for a certain project, it must also benefit only that project. Consequently, the reimbursement for a direct cost is entirely allocable to its associated contract.

The most common direct costs in construction contracts are those attributable to direct labor, permanent materials, and equipment (either owned or leased). Depending on the nature of the project, other direct costs may include forms for concrete structures, consumable materials, special engineering, subcontracts, and small tools. It is generally best to include costs as direct costs, as opposed to an element of indirect or overhead costs, because as direct costs they are subject to 100 percent recovery, not just a part recovered by a percentage markup. Accordingly, it is recommended that an effort be made to determine the full extent to which costs can be property included as direct costs of a change.

Even if they can be identified directly with a project, not all expenses may qualify as costs under FAR. For example, in *Union Boiler Works, Inc. v. Caldera*,[29] the rental value of a contractor's fully depreciated equipment was not reimbursable under a cost-reimbursable contract. Under a cost-reimbursable contract, a contractor is entitled to recover rental costs paid for equipment it rents. When a contractor uses its own fully depreciated property, however, the rental value of that property ordinarily is not an allowable cost. The government may agree, however, to pay the contractor a reasonable amount for the use of the contractor's fully depreciated property.

[B] Indirect Costs

"Indirect costs . . . are residuals" of the contractor's incurred expenses after all of the direct costs have been identified.[30] The FAR defines *indirect costs* as:

> any cost not directly identified with a single, final costs objective, but identified with two or more final cost objectives, or an intermediate cost objective. . . . After direct costs have been determined and charged directly to the contract or other work, indirect costs are those remaining to be allocated to the several costs objectives.[31]

An indirect cost is a contractor-incurred cost that is expended for the benefit of two or more projects; the expense as a whole is not dedicated to any one contract. To be a reimbursable indirect cost, the cost must either benefit the contract to which part of the cost is allocated, or it must be necessary for the overall operation of the contractor's business.[32] In either case, the indirect cost is explicitly or implicitly of some benefit to the performance of the contract.[33] In describing indirect costs, the

---

[29] 156 F.3d 1374 (Fed. Cir. 1998).
[30] Foster Constr. Co., DOTCAB No. 71-16, 73-1 BCA (CCH) ¶ 9869 at 46,150 (1972).
[31] FAR 31.203(b).
[32] FAR 31.204-4.
[33] FAR 31.204-4(b).

FAR includes as common groups of indirect costs "manufacturing overhead, selling expenses, and general and administrative (G&A) expenses."[34]

Because an indirect cost as a whole is by definition expended on more than one contract, it consequently must be apportioned among them. It should first be noted that "indirect expensing . . . is not a science."[35] The FAR mandates the classification of costs into logical cost grouping (for example, general and administrative expenses) and then distributes "the grouping on the basis of the benefits accruing to the several cost objectives."[36] The distribution base must be an item universal to all of the contracts among which the cost grouping is being spread. This cost grouping provides a method of comparison by which all of the contracts incurring indirect costs may be judged on an equal, proportionate basis. "Some common bases include recorded accounting data such as direct labor hours and direct labor, and non-accounting data such as floor space, units produced and meter readings."[37]

Unallowable and allowable costs, if part of the base by which the indirect costs are being distributed, must bear their pro rata portion of the indirect costs.[38] When an indirect expense has been directly associated to an unallowable cost, the indirect expense is unallowable as well.[39]

[C] Profit

In addition to the recovery of direct and indirect costs, a contractor is entitled to recover profit on changed or added work.[40] The amount of profit on changed work should not be governed by the existence or extent of profit on the unchanged, base contract work.[41] On nonfederal contracts, the entitlement to profit and its amount varies by the state.

Profit on disputed changes may not be limited to the profit rates defined in the contract. For example, in *Amelco Electric v. City of Thousand Oaks*,[42] a California Appellate Court concluded that a contractor's breach of contract claim may include higher profit and overhead than permitted under the contract if it represents a reasonable value of its services.

---

[34] FAR 31.203(b).
[35] Aluminum Specialty Co., ASBCA No. 6228, 1963 BCA (CCH) ¶ 3859 at 19,201 (1963).
[36] FAR 31.203(b).
[37] G.J. Ginsberg & K.B. Weckstein, *A Pricing Roadmap*, Pricing of Claims A-16 (1987).
[38] FAR 31.203(c).
[39] FAR 31.206(a).
[40] New York Shipbuilding Co., ASBCA No. 16,164, 76-2 BCA (CCH) ¶ 11,979 at 57,438 (1976).
[41] Keco Indus., Inc., ASBCA Nos. 15,184, 15,547, 72-2 BCA (CCH) ¶ 9576 at 44,733 (1972); Stewart & Stevenson Servs., Inc., ASBCA No. 43,631, 97-2 BCA (CCH) ¶ 29,252 (1997) (profit added to modification on contract in which best and final offer was one-third less than original cost proposal because changes clause does not exclude recovery of profit and gives no instruction for circumstances when profit may or may not be allowed. While government is entitled to hold contractor to risk assumed at time of entering into contract, even if that risk means financial loss to contractor, it does not follow that contractor should be held to same risk for additional work not contemplated at time contract was entered. Additional work is subject to equitable adjustment including profit).
[42] 2000 Cal. App. LEXIS 570 (2d Dist. 6th Div., 2000).

[D]   Bond

In the event that there is a change order, the contractor may be required to purchase additional performance bond protection. "The increase in protection shall generally equal 100 percent of the increase in contract price. The Government may secure additional protection by directing the contractor to increase the penal amount of the existing bond or to obtain an additional bond."[43]

Thus, when an equitable adjustment is priced, the contractor should be reimbursed for its bond costs. The bond costs are generally segregated from all other costs and set out separately when the costs are totaled for an equitable adjustment claim.

Such bonding costs, required by the contractor in the general conduct of its business, are allowable under the FAR to the extent that such bonding is in accordance with sound business practice and the rates and premiums are reasonable under the circumstances.[44] Thus, bonding costs must meet a "reasonability" test much like other costs that the contractor seeks to affirm as allowable under a contract.

[E]   Home Office Overhead

A contractor's home office may provide valuable support to its field operation. For example, payroll may be handled from a central location, engineering and personnel services may be provided, financing is arranged, and management advice is given. These costs are generally for the benefit of more than one project and must, therefore, be borne in some relationship by all the projects.[45] Because these costs are mostly fixed costs and do not vary with the value or costs of ongoing projects, the home office overhead allocable to a specific project may vary over time depending on the value or number of ongoing contracts. Accordingly, if the adjustment for changes covers work performed over several years, different home office overhead rates may apply for markup of direct costs.

Typically, home office overhead costs become a factor if the change delays the work, as these fixed costs continue as the changed work delays the project beyond the scheduled or anticipated completion date.[46] The classic approach to calculating home office overhead has been use of an *Eichleay*-type formula.[47] This formula has come under growing criticism by the federal government, but it is still a useful and generally accepted means of calculating these costs.[48]

---

[43] FAR 28.102-2(a)(2).

[44] FAR 31.205-4.

[45] Eichleay Corp., ASBCA No. 5183, 60-2 BCA (CCH) ¶ 2688 (1960).

[46] J.D. Hedin Constr. Co. v. United States, 347 F.2d 235, 254 (Ct. Cl. 1965); Capital Elec. Co., GSBCA Nos. 5316, 5317, 83-2 BCA (CCH) ¶ 16,548 at 82,315, *rev'd on other grounds*, 729 F.2d 743 (Fed. Cir. 1984) (A court "will permit an allocation of home office overhead where [it is determined] that direct costs were in fact incurred as a result of conceded unreasonable delays.").

[47] *See* Eichleay Corp., ASBCA No. 5182, 60-2 BCA (CCH) ¶ 2688 (1960).

[48] *See generally* R. Nash, *The Eichleay Formula: Another Viewpoint*, 6 Nash & Cibinic Rep. No. 1, 17 (Jan. 1992).

The "*Eichleay* Method" of accounting for unabsorbed overhead (general and administrative costs) derives its name from a case involving the Eichleay Corporation, in which the plaintiff was awarded damages for overhead costs calculated under a relatively simple formula.[49] The approach employed in *Eichleay* compares total company results to results in a disputed contract during the life of the disputed contract. It involves three basic calculations, as set forth in **Table 18-1**.

The strength of *Eichleay* is that it is straightforward and, to some, logical. It is criticized, however, for certain perceived weaknesses: overhead is allocated on the basis of contract billings, yet billings do not generate overhead costs. (Allocation on the basis of costs, particularly in delays when costs continue beyond billings, would appear a reasonable alternate allocation method.) *Eichleay* also tends to understate the daily overhead rate because it includes the days of delay resulting from the disputed contract in the total contract days when calculating the average. This problem, and the allocation method, can be remedied with minor modifications to the approach. **Table 18-2**, for example, illustrates the impact of deleting days of delay in calculating the number of days included in the contract performance period.

In the "total direct cost" method, overhead is allocated to the disputed contract based on costs incurred rather than billings. **Table 18-3** illustrates a typical presentation format. This latter approach, which is also straightforward, can be modified slightly to approximate the same format of *Eichleay*. The direct cost approach can be subject to criticism, however. First, it does not consider differences in the cost components of the various contracts. It assigns the same rates to all, regardless of whether some might be primarily labor oriented and others might consist mostly of material or subcontractor costs. It is not, therefore, a good method for contractors who experience significant changes in the mix of contract costs from contract to contract.

The direct cost approach also may not reflect the true magnitude of overhead that should be allocated when long delays resulting in shutdowns are experienced on a project. If costs are not incurred on the project, overhead will not be allocated. When extended shutdowns occur, other methods of allocating overhead must be developed to account for idle capacity.

The United States Court of Appeals for the Federal Circuit declared the *Eichleay* formula the only acceptable approach for calculating unabsorbed overhead for United States government projects, in *Wickham Contracting Co. v. Fischer*.[50] An assertion that the *Eichleay* formula is applicable to all situations ignores inequities that may exist in the use of that method in a particular context and the fundamental differences between construction projects and manufacturing operations. The burden fluctuation method pronounced in *Allegheny Sportswear*[51] and *Lite/Manufacturing*[52] remains a logical and rational method for calculating damage in a manufacturing context, as use of the *Eichleay* formula may be in a

---

[49] *See* Eichleay Corp., ASBCA No. 5182, 60-2 BCA (CCH) ¶ 2688 (1960).

[50] 12 F.3d 1574 (Fed. Cir. 1994).

[51] ASBCA No. 4163, 58-1 BCA (CCH) ¶ 1684 (1958).

[52] ASBCA No. 4755, 58-2 BCA (CCH) ¶ 2009 (1958).

TABLE 18-1
***Eichleay* Overhead Calculation**

	Disputed Contract	*Other Contracts*	*Total*
Billings	$2,000,000	$57,500,000	$59,500,000
Cost	2,500,000	50,000,000	52,500,000
Gross Profit (loss)	($500,000)	$ 7,500,000	$ 7,000,000
General and Administrative Costs			$ 2,100,000
Contract Days	360		
Days of Delays	60		

Overhead Calculation

Overhead to Disputed Contract	($2,000,000 / $59,500,000) × $2,100,000 = $70,588
Daily Overhead rate at 360 contract days	$70,588 / 360 days = $ 196
Overhead to Disputed Contract at 60 days of delay	$196 x 60 days = $11,760

TABLE 18-2
Modified *Eichleay* Overhead Calculation

	Disputed Contract	*Other Contracts*	*Total*
Billings	$2,000,000	$48,000,000	$50,000,000
Cost	2,500,000	42,000,000	44,500,000
Gross Profit (loss)	($500,000)	$ 6,000,000	$ 5,500,000
General and Administrative Costs			$ 1,750,000
Contract Days	360		
Days of Delays	60		

Overhead Calculation

Overhead to Disputed Contract	($2,000,000 / $50,000,000) × $1,750,000 = $70,000
Daily Overhead rate at 300 contract days	$70,000 / 300 days = $ 233
Overhead to Disputed Contract at 60 days of delay	$233 x 60 days = $13,980

TABLE 18-3
Direct Cost Overhead Calculation

	Disputed Contract	*Other Contracts*	*Total*
Cost	$2,500,000	$48,000,000	$50,500,000
General and Administrative Costs			$ 1,750,000

Overhead Calculation

Overhead to Disputed Contract	($2,500,000 / $50,500,000) × $1,750,000 = $86,633

construction context. *Wickham Contracting*, in which the Federal Circuit concluded that the *Eichleay* formula should be used exclusively, concerned a construction dispute and referred to home office expenses as distinguished from "direct field costs." Such considerations do not exist in a manufacturing context.[53]

Courts and boards have held that the formula may not be used to recover unabsorbed home office overhead costs when (1) no element of uncertainty concerning scheduling exists; (2) the contract was completed ahead of schedule despite the delay; and (3) the project was substantially completed and demobilized before any delay.[54] In *Safeco Credit v. United States*,[55] the claims court determined that Safeco had not shown that it could not have taken on any other jobs during the contract period, and as a result, that it was not entitled to use the *Eichleay* formula.

[F] Project Overhead

Project overhead, also referred to as jobsite overhead, should be included as part of a calculation of equitable adjustments or damages as well. These charges can take two forms—a percentage markup on direct costs, or a daily rate to reflect delay costs.

There are certain overhead costs incurred at the project level and associated with performing under the contract. These include engineering, managerial and secretarial support, office and office supplies, timekeepers, business agents, superintendents, copying machines, and utilities to the offices, including power and telephone. These are the costs of keeping a project going that must be borne by the contract. Recovery of these costs through a change order is generally covered by a percentage markup of the direct costs of the change. However, the Armed Services Board of Contract Appeals denied the contractor any percentage field overhead markup on changes absent specific proof establishing the elements of the field overhead expenses that were increased by the change in *M.A. Mortenson Co.*[56] The decision in *Mortenson* examined the long-standing practice that added field office overhead costs as a percentage markup on the direct costs of change-order work, regardless of whether the contract performance time is extended.

Sometimes the contract limits the items that are entitled to a markup. In such situations, the contract is enforced even though additional costs are incurred that are not marked up.[57]

However, a change may also delay performance so that these overhead costs now must be incurred over a longer period of performance, and these project office overhead costs must be recovered as part of the change. The use of a percentage markup to recover these extended costs is inappropriate because the delay is not

---

[53] Raley, *The Eichleay Bandwagon: Should We Pause Before Jumping Aboard?*, 31 Procurement Law. 3 (No. 2, Winter 1996).

[54] M. Kauffman & C. Holman, *The Eichleay Formula: A Resilient Means for Recovering Unabsorbed Overhead*, 24 Pub. Cont. L.J. 319 (No. 2, Winter 1995).

[55] 44 Fed. Cl. 406, 1999 U.S. Claims LEXIS 178 (1999).

[56] ASBCA No. 40,750, 97-1 BCA (CCH) ¶ 28,263 (1996).

[57] Bunkers v. Jacobson, 653 N.W.2d 732 (S.D. 2003).

necessarily a function of the direct cost of the change. For example, there could be a no-cost or low-cost change that could delay the project, and a percentage markup on such a low number would yield no or little compensation for the extended field office overhead costs incurred.

Typically, extended field office overhead is calculated by combining all time-related costs incurred (that is, those costs that continue as a function of time) and dividing by the number of days the project has been active, to determine a daily rate.[58]

[G] Labor Inefficiency Costs

Often, changes affect the cost of labor by disrupting planned performance, by causing work to be performed in less productive periods, and by overcrowding a site. This effect may be felt on parts of the work that are not directly changed, but yet are adversely affected by the impact of the change.

The equitable adjustment granted under the changes clause is not limited to the increased costs of the specific changed work.[59]

> It is well established that the increased cost of disrupted unchanged work flow-
> ing directly from a change . . . is compensable under the changes clause; the
> *Rice* Doctrine is long dead. *See Luria Brothers & Co. v. United States,* 177 Ct.
> Cl. 676, 369 F.2d 701 (1966); *Paul Hardeman, Inc. v. United States,* 186 Ct.
> Cl. 743, 406 F.2d 1357 (1969); *Merritt-Chapman & Scott Corp. v. United
> States,* 192 Ct. Cl. 851, 429 F.2d 431 (1970). Claims for the costs of cumula-
> tive impact, "the impact on unchanged work which is not attributable to any
> one change but flows from the synergy of the number and scope of changes
> issued on a project" are well recognized by the courts and boards of contract
> appeals.[60]

The Armed Services Board of Contract Appeals (ASBCA) has recognized that a contractor can experience a loss of efficiency due to repeated mobilization and demobilization of its crews.[61] The ASBCA has also held that a contractor's inability to plan in advance and to follow an efficient sequence of operations

---

[58] See Harrison W. Corp. & Franki-Denys, Inc., (JV), ENGBCA Nos. 5556, 5576, 93-1 BCA (CCH) ¶ 25,382 at 126,430 (1992); Shirley Contracting Corp., ASBCA No. 29,848, 85-1 BCA (CCH) ¶ 17,858 at 89,406 (1984).

[59] *See* Coastal Dry Dock & Repair Corp., ASBCA No. 36,754, 91-1 BCA (CCH) ¶ 23,324 at 117,002 (1990).

[60] McMillin Bros. Constructors, Inc., EBCA No. 328-10-84, 91-1 BCA (CCH) ¶ 23,351 at 117,102 (1990) (citing Fruehauf Corp., PSBCA No. 477, 74-1 BCA (CCH) ¶ 10,596 (1974); Bechtel Nat'l, Inc., NASABCA No. 1186-7, 90-1 BCA (CCH) ¶ 22,549 (1989)). *See also* Coastal Dry Dock, ASBCA No. 36,754, 91-1 BCA (CCH) ¶ 23,324 (1991); Freeman-Darling, Inc., GSBCA No. 7112, 89-2 BCA (CCH) ¶ 21,882 at 110,101 (1989).

[61] Sovereign Constr. Co., ASBCA No. 17,792, 75-1 BCA (CCH) ¶ 11,251 (1975).

known to its workers and supervisory personnel adversely affect efficiency and productivity.[62] The necessity for overtime to perform additional, or changed, work has also been widely accepted to have a detrimental effect on labor productivity.[63]

Extended scheduled overtime is also recognized as a factor that reduces overall efficiency. Overtime indirectly affects productivity by disrupting the work environment. In extreme cases, overtime can contribute to ripple effects. Overtime itself does not lead to productivity losses but causes other variables to be activated. Variables such as the lack of materials, lack of equipment, lack of supervision, out-of-sequence work, and other similar disruptions cause the reduced productivity rather than the overtime. If project management decides to go from a work week of four ten-hour days to six ten-hour days, labor is increased by 50 percent. In addition, the entire system must respond to the increase in work hours. Materials must be made available 50 percent faster; equipment will be used 50 percent more; and the project staff must respond to 50 percent more questions. Everything is accelerated. If a project is behind schedule because of disruptions, an overtime schedule will only make matters worse.[64]

It is believed that as more days per week are worked, the more difficult it is to provide resources such as material, labor, equipment, tools, and information. Research has showed that the number of disruptions caused by changes and rework varied according to the days worked per week, with no consistent pattern. Management-related disruptions (congestion, out-of-sequence work, supervision, and miscellaneous) were more for the five-day-per-week schedule than for the other schedules. Disruptions caused by lack of resources (materials, equipment, tools, and information) increased consistently with the number of days worked per week. Rework had the greatest impact on performance.[65]

There are several methods available to quantify its impact. The most persuasive methods utilize historical productivity comparisons on the same or comparable jobs—examining performance under normal, unimpacted schedules and under extended overtime operations. In practice, however, these data are seldom available, and generic findings of prior studies are often used. Most notable among these are the findings of the Department of the Army Corps of Engineers and those of the Business Roundtable.

Figure 18-1 is a replication of a chart by the Department of Army, Office of the Chief Engineers that depicts the effect of overtime on worker productivity. As shown by the chart, the adverse impact on work efficiency increases along with the amount of overtime and the duration of the overtime work. The cost of overtime is the difference between standard and premium rates, plus the percentage of inefficiency on all hours worked resulting from extended hours.

---

[62] Paccon, Inc., ASBCA No. 7890, 1963 BCA (CCH) ¶ 3659 (1963).

[63] *See* J.W. Bateson Co., ASBCA No. 6069, 1962 BCA (CCH) ¶ 3529 at 17,943 (1962).

[64] H. Thomas & K. Raynar, *Scheduled Overtime and Labor Productivity: Quantitative Analysis*, 122 J. Constr. Eng'g & Mgmt. 181-82 (June 1997).

[65] Thomas & Raynar at 186.

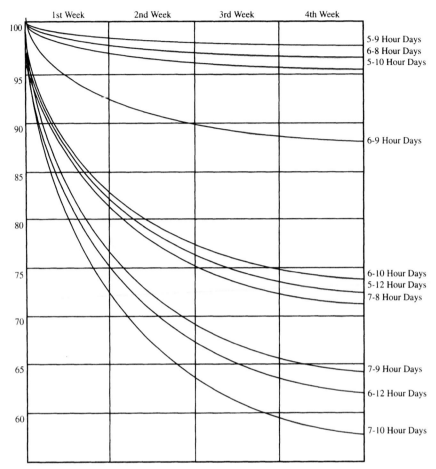

FIGURE 18-1.   EFFECT OF WORK SCHEDULE ON EFFICIENCY.

Studies of the Business Roundtable's Construction Industry Cost Effectiveness Task Force produced similar findings.[66] The task force found that extended overtime reduced productivity because of fatigue, absenteeism, injury, and reduced ability of the workers. It reported that, as a general rule, for overtime above 8 hours a day and 48 hours a week, three hours were required for two additional hours of output when work was light, and two hours were needed for one additional hour of output when work was heavy. The Roundtable report provides data on overtime inefficiencies for only a 50-hour schedule and a 60-hour schedule and cautions readers that study data relate only to operations where the entire job is placed on overtime for an extended period of time.[67] Nevertheless, the findings

---

[66] *Scheduled Overtime Effect on Construction Projects* (The Business Roundtable, New York, N.Y.), Nov. 1980.

[67] See **Table 18-4**.

of the report can be appropriate to interpolate different overtime schedules and periodic overtime as well.

Table 18-4 is a reproduction of the cost chart for overtime under 50-hour schedules provided in the Roundtable report. Coupled with appropriate labor cost information and premium pay rates, the data can easily be converted to computer processing and can provide fairly comprehensive cost reporting. Total cost overtime (expressed in hours) is calculated in column 8 of the chart. The calculation includes the premium hours and the hours lost to inefficiencies (column 6). Premium hour costs are only those costs in excess of standard hourly rates. In **Table 18-4**, for example, a full 10 hours of overtime cost has been added to 3.7 hours of inefficiency because the premium rate was double time. Had the premium rate been time and one-half, only five overtime hours (10 x .5) would have been added as premium costs, providing a revised cost of overtime operation of 8.7 hours, to be calculated at prevailing hourly rates.

Thomas and Raynar reported that they found efficiency on days when disruptions occurred reduced to an average of 73 percent of what it would have been had there been no disruption. It is the authors' theory in this article that there is a causal link between overtime and disruptions. Thomas and Raynar note that few articles or publications have reliably studied the effect of scheduled overtime on labor productivity. Those graphs and data that have been published suggest an upper bound on the loss of efficiency, but the studies from which they come offer no guidance as to what leads to the losses.[68] To determine the effect that overtime may have on efficiency, Thomas and Raynar studied several industrial projects and focused on an average crew of electricians and pipefitters. The projects selected reflected tranquil labor environments and did not have an inordinate number of changes. None of the projects studied had labor problems, jurisdictional disputes, or labor shortages. The projects were studied long enough to include a straight-time and an overtime schedule, and the crew performances were compared. The straight-time schedule was 40 hours a week.[69] The initial investigation, based on 120 weeks of work, showed that there was, on average, about a 10 to 15 percent loss of productivity when the crews worked longer than a normal 40-hour or 4-day work week. The loss of efficiency for five- and six-day work weeks was about the same.[70]

Based on their study, Thomas and Raynar concluded that the efficiency of 50- and 60-hour work weeks followed the same downward trend as established in the Business Roundtable (BRT) study of 1980. That is, after three weeks of overtime, the crews were approximately 85 percent as efficient as they were when working straight time. After seven weeks of overtime, the efficiency dropped to 68 percent. The authors conclude that the BRT curve is a reasonable estimate of

---

[68] Thomas & Raynar at 181.
[69] Thomas & Raynar at 182.
[70] Thomas & Raynar at 185.

TABLE 18-4
Relationship of Hours Worked, Productivity and Costs
(40 hours vs. 50 hours)

1	2	3	4	5	6	7	8
50 Hour Overtime Work Weeks	*Productivity Rate 40 Hour Week*	*Productivity Rate 50 Hour Week*	*Actual Hour Output for 50 40 Hour Week*	*Hour Gain Over 40 Hour Week*	*Hour Loss Due to Productivity Drop*	*Premium Hours*	*Hour Cost of Overtime Operation (at 2x)*
0-12	1.00	.926	46.3	6.3	3.7	10.0	13.7
2-3-4		.900	45.0	5.0	5.0	10.0	15.0
4-5-6		.870	43.5	3.5	6.5	10.0	16.5
6-7-8		.800	40.0	0.0	10.0	10.0	20.0
8-9-10		.752	37.6	-2.4	12.4	10.0	22.4
10-11-12 & up		.750	37.5	-2.5	12.5	10.0	22.5

the minimum loss of productivity. On projects where there are resource problems, incomplete design, numerous changes, or other problems, the productivity losses may approximate those of earlier studies that indicate much greater losses.[71]

Research by the Construction Industry Institute has measured the effect of overtime on productivity. They found lower inefficiency factors and that inefficiency is not the inevitable result of overtime over a three- to four-week period unless the project was behind schedule before the overtime was initiated.[72] The Construction Industry Institute's research on the effect of changes and change orders on productivity showed an average 30-percent loss of efficiency when working on changed work, although it is possible to perform changed work without any loss of efficiency.[73]

A study by A. Hanna, J. Russell, E. Nordheim, and M. Bruggink, "Impact of Change Orders on Labor Efficiency for Electrical Construction,"[74] suggested that:

---

[71] Thomas & Raynar at 185.

[72] *The Effects of Scheduled Overtime and Shift Schedule on Construction Craft Productivity*, Source Doc. 43 (Dec. 1988); Thomas & Raynar, *Effects of Scheduled Overtime on Labor Productivity: A Quantitative Analysis*, Source Doc. 98 (Aug. 1994).

[73] *The Impact of Changes on Construction Cost and Schedule*, Publication 6-10 (Apr. 1990); *Construction Changes and Change Orders: Their Magnitude and Impact*, Source Doc. 66 (Oct. 1991); H. Thomas & C. Napolitan, *The Effects of Changes on Labor Productivity: Why and How Much*, Source Doc. 99 (Aug. 1994).

[74] 125 J. Constr. Eng'g & Mgmt. 224, 225 (No. 4, Jul./Aug. 1999).

- A productivity study at the time of the change would not account for the effects of the change on later activities.

- Survey showed that there were direct relationships between change orders and schedule compression, trade stacking, and sequence of work.

- Research confirmed that larger projects have a higher capacity for absorbing loss of efficiency caused by change order work.

The Hanna, Russell, Nordheim, and Bruggink study also found that the amount of time available between instructing the contractor to make changes and the actual execution of the changes by the contractor also affected labor inefficiency. If the lead time was small, loss of efficiency tended to be much higher than when the lead time was adequate. The study concluded that the factors that affect or increase loss of efficiency due to change orders are:

- Effects of the Amount of Change. The estimated change order hours as a percentage of the original project estimate were more than two times larger for impacted projects than for unimpacted projects. As a result, as the amount of change order hours increased, so did a contractor's chance of experiencing losses in labor efficiency. The finding supported the theory that contractors did not make more money as the amount of change order hours increased.

- Effects on Schedule Extension. Projects impacted by change orders experienced an average increase in duration of nearly 40 percent. Projects not impacted by change orders experienced schedule extensions of less than 10 percent, four times less than that of impacted projects.

- Effects of Timing of Changes. Changes have more impact when projects are between 50 and 75 percent complete.[75] The study also developed a formula that may assist owners and contractors in determining an equitable adjustment to the original contract when the model is used within the set parameters.[76]

According to the study, the following requirements must be fulfilled for the model to be applicable to a project:

1. Projects are contracted in a fixed-price/lump-sum manner.

2. Change orders must be the greatest cause of loss of labor efficiency on candidate projects considered to be impacted.

---

[75] Hanna, Russell, Nordheim & Bruggink at 229.

[76] Hanna, Russell, Nordheim & Bruggink at 229-30 (the formula is: Delta%Tot = −22.00 − 0.14 MgrYears + 6.47 ln(EstCO%Est) + 9.66 ln(EstCO) − 0.90[ln(EstCO)]^2 + random error. Where Delta%Tot = (actual total hours − estimated change order hours − original estimate hours/actual total hours) x 100; MgrYears = total years worked in construction industry by project manager; ln = natural log; ln(EstCO%Est) = ln(estimate of change order hours/original estimate of hours) x 100; and ln(EstCO) = ln(estimate of change order hours)).

3. The range of true values for Delta%Tot for candidate projects must be between + 40 and − 40 percent.

4. The range of the estimate of change order hours as a percentage divided by the original estimate of hours must be between 1.4 and 155 percent.

5. The range of the estimate of change order hours for candidate projects must be between 100 and 26,500 hours.[77]

Sanders and Thomas found that of the 564 days included in the data set, 104 were classified as disrupted. Among the identified disruptions were weather, congestion/interference, sequencing/reassignment, material storage, material availability, rework, improper or insufficient tools, accidents, improper or insufficient equipment, lack of supervision, overstaffing, and remobilization.[78] A *disruption* was defined as an event occurring on site that adversely affected the masonry crew's productivity for most of the workday. Work continues during a disrupted period but at a less productive rate.

Sanders and Thomas also measured the "learning curve effect." Their analysis indicated that masonry productivity improved with each repetitive floor until the last floor. An improvement of over 15 percent was seen between the first and second groups, and an improvement of 12 percent between the second and third groups.[79] *Finish work* includes the final dismantling of scaffolding, removal of excess materials, patching, and cleanup. Sanders and Thomas also found that productivity worsened during this phase because much of the work is support work. Finish-related work showed one-half the productivity of normal masonry activities.

Previous research had shown productivity for labor-intensive activities to be best at moderate temperatures and for productivity to worsen as the temperature deviates to either extreme. Sanders and Thomas's analysis showed just the opposite effect. The average productivity when the temperature was below 41 degrees was almost 20 percent better than for higher temperatures. Work in temperatures above 79 degrees also showed better productivity, but was not significantly different. The improvement of productivity at colder temperatures was not expected and should be examined in more detail.[80]

The results of the analysis of the effect of humidity also were contradictory to what would be expected. It was assumed that productivity would get worse at higher humidities. However, productivity actually improved as the humidity increased. Worst productivity is seen when temperature is medium and humidity is low; the best productivity is when temperature is low and humidity high.[81]

A study by H. Thomas, D. Riley, and V. Sanvido detailed the impact of adverse winter weather conditions on structural steel erection activities on three

---

[77] Hanna, Russell, Nordheim & Bruggink at 230.

[78] S. Sanders & H. Thomas, *Factors Affecting Masonry-Labor Productivity*, 117 J. Constr. Eng'g & Mgmt. 631 (No. 4, Dec. 1991).

[79] Sanders & Thomas at 633.

[80] Sanders & Thomas at 640.

[81] Sanders & Thomas at 642.

similar projects. The original schedule called for a four-week erection period in November 1991. Because of delays in the shop drawings, and other factors related to completion of other buildings at the site, the erection did not begin until January 26, 1992. Erection took place in harsh winter conditions.[82]

The daily and baseline productivity showed the best that the contractor could do based on actual performances. Once the effect of repetition dissipated on work-day 7, the baseline productivity was about 1.25 wh/pc. In the absence of the disruptions, the contractor should have performed at this baseline rate. The contractor worked at or near this baseline for 11 of the 21 workdays.

The most significant factor affecting the construction plan was the complexity of the steel. This meant that considerable time was spent shaking out steel as it arrived. Instead of setting the steel directly from the delivery trucks, all the steel was off-loaded and sorted prior to resuming the erection process. This practice resulted in double-handling of the steel.[83] It appeared that an orderly sequence of the work was not maintained. For instance, although all 579 pieces of steel were erected, only a few pieces were aligned, bolted, and tightened. Also, all 304 joists were in place, but no welding was done. No decking was installed. The absence of joist welding and decking was caused by fabrication errors in some joint connection plates. Access to these joints had to be maintained until the errors were corrected. The completion of several other connections was delayed because pieces of steel were lost in the snow. The remaining work on the connections resulted in a delay to the welding of metal joists and the erection of metal decking. Once these connections were completed, the joists and decking were completed.[84]

The work was affected by weather events, such as high wind, snow, and cold temperatures. On three weather days, the crew worked less than a full day. Interestingly, on each of these days, productivity was near or better than the baseline. Overall, weather affected 12 of the 21 workdays. Of these days, the productivity was near or better than the baseline on three days. These were the only days when the crew worked less than a full day.

The most significant weather event was snow, which reduced crew efficiency by 35 percent. This value is less severe than losses reported in an earlier publication by the same authors on weather events (losses of 65 percent). Those events were principally rain. Cold temperatures also had an effect, resulting in a loss of efficiency of about 30 percent. This value was greater than losses estimated by the National Electrical Contractors Association, which estimated that for a relative humidity of 3 to 5 percent and temperatures of -12°C, the loss of efficiency was in the range of 12 to 14 percent. The loss of efficiency (about 30 percent) due to temperatures less than −7°C was greater than that stated in other literature sources. The workdays on which material deliveries were made showed the largest reduction in efficiency, by almost 40 percent.

---

[82] *Loss of Labor Productivity Due to Delivery Methods and Weather*, 125 J. Constr. Eng'g & Mgmt. 39, 40 (No. 1, Jan./Feb. 1999).

[83] Thomas, Riley & Sanvido at 40.

[84] Thomas, Riley & Sanvido at 42.

In evaluating labor inefficiency, it is helpful to identify and isolate a period when similar work was being performed that was unimpacted by the change. This period can serve as a "measured mile" to which actual costs of performing after the change occurred can be contrasted. This approach has been widely accepted.[85]

The term *disruption* as used in evaluating inefficiency costs can refer to a multitude of activities that prevent workers from developing a productive job rhythm, including such conditions as frequent stops and starts, performing work out of sequence, unscheduled movement, and access problems. Proof of disruption requires identification of specific events that caused interruption of work; identification of the time, place, and activities affected; and quantification of the individual and collective impact of these acts. There are three major strategies to establish proof:

1. Comparison of productivity under normal, unimpacted, or undisrupted conditions (that is, "a measured mile") versus disrupted periods is the preferred approach. Proof strategies of this type include a comparison of actual performance to the initial budget estimate, comparisons to undisrupted performance on prior projects, or comparisons to undisrupted performance on similar functions on the disrupted job.

2. Comparisons to the initial budget estimate require that it be established that budget estimates are reasonable and representative of reasonable productivity. This burden can be difficult to bear, particularly in the absence of actual job history.

3. Comparisons to undisrupted periods of productivity are generally considered superior evidence, but they should be used with caution. The key concern in using this approach is to assure that the periods being compared involved comparable and representative work, that the period is truly undisrupted, and that the methods used actually measure what they purport to measure.

In the absence of a "measured mile," it may be possible to locate industry studies that have calculated the productivity that should be expected under certain conditions. Associations for electrical contractors, mechanical contractors, and the previously mentioned U.S. Army Corps of Engineers and Business Roundtable have all published studies that can be used to measure inefficiency of labor and loss of productivity.

Quite often, disruption costs in a major claim are based entirely on estimates derived from the experience of experts in construction management. In fact, some consultants have developed ranges of impact and average levels of impact based on years of study that reasonably should be expected for various types of disruption and other job problems. Their findings and the foundations are susceptible to detailed examination and contradiction by other experts and opposing counsel,

---

[85] *See, e.g.,* United States Indus., Inc. v. Blake Constr. Co., 671 F.2d 539 (D.C. Cir. 1982); Flex-Y-Plan Indus., Inc., GSBCA No. 4117, 76-1 BCA (CCH) ¶ 11,713 (1976).

but they may be valuable depending on the weight given to their testimony by the triers of fact.

[H] Claim Preparation Costs

Often on a government contracts project, the contractor will involve legal counsel, experts, and other consultants in the identification, preparation, and presentation of claims. The question arises whether a contractor can recover the costs of claim preparation as part of an equitable adjustment.

Generally, a contractor can recover claim preparation costs so long as it can demonstrate that they were not incurred in prosecuting "a claim against the Government."[86] The courts and boards have, however, broadly defined what constitutes prosecuting a claim against the government. For example, in a recent case, the Armed Services Board of Contract Appeals held that even if a contractor's claim did not constitute a dispute under the Contract Disputes Act (CDA), it could still constitute a claim prosecuted against the government that disallowed the recovery of consultant fees.[87] The board reasoned that the definition of "claim" under the FAR cost principles was not the same as a "dispute" under the CDA. Thus, contractors may be left in the intolerable and inexplicable position of being advised that activities that do not constitute a CDA dispute or claim under federal law (thus preventing the commencement of interest) could equal a sufficient "claim" against the government under other interpretation of federal law, to disallow consultant fees incurred in connection with the negotiations.[88] Two judges dissented and argued that if a claim is not a dispute under the CDA, then it cannot equal a claim prosecuted against the government.

The contractor subsequently appealed the decision of the Armed Services Board of Contract Appeals. In *Bill Strong Enterprises, Inc. v. Shannon*,[89] the court of appeals reversed the ASBCA, allowing recovery of reasonable consultant fees, and remanded the case to the ASBCA for determination of quantum. The court found a strong legal presumption that consultant costs incurred *before* a CDA claim are *not* incurred in connection with the prosecution of a claim against the government. The court stated that consultant costs are not automatically allowable just because those costs were incurred before a CDA claim came into existence. The government must receive some benefit from the services of the contractor's consultant for the consultant's costs to be allowable.

Costs incurred in connection with contract performance or contract administration should ordinarily be recoverable because they normally benefit the contract

---

[86] FAR 31.205-47.

[87] Bill Strong Enter., Inc., ASBCA Nos. 42,946, 43,896, 93-3 BCA (CCH) ¶ 25,961 (June 28, 1993); *see also* Barfield Indus., ASBCA No. 18,057, 77-1 BCA (CCH) ¶ 12,348 (1977); Erickson Crane Co., EBCA No. 50-6-79, 83-1 BCA (CCH) ¶ 16,145 (1982), *aff'd*, 731 F.2d 810 (Fed. Cir. 1984); Excavation Constr., Inc., ENGBCA 3858, 82-1 BCA (CCH) ¶ 15,770, *reconsideration denied*, 83-1 BCA (CCH) ¶ 16,338 (1982).

[88] Bill Strong Enter., Inc., ASBCA Nos. 42,946, 43,896, 93-3 BCA (CCH) ¶ 25,961 (June 28, 1993).

[89] 49 F.3d 1541 (Fed. Cir. 1995).

purpose, and reimbursement of those costs is in the best interest of the United States. Benefit to the contract purpose or administration is therefore a prerequisite for allowability of recovery of any contract cost. The court of appeals permitted recovery of the contractor's consultant fees because the court found benefit in the consultant's efforts to resolve the contractor's claim through the contractor's negotiations with the government. Efforts to resolve differences amicably reflect a mutual desire to achieve a result acceptable to both. This negotiation process often involves requests for information by the contracting parties or auditors, and this exchange of information involves costs for the contractor. These costs are contract administration costs, which should be allowable because the negotiation process benefits the government, regardless of whether a settlement is finally reached or whether litigation eventually occurs; the availability of the process increases the likelihood of settlement without litigation. Note that the court of appeals decision in *Bill Strong Enterprises* was made under the 1987 version of FAR 31.205-33(d) and not the current revision.

However, in *Reflectone, Inc. v. Dalton*,[90] the court, *in a footnote*, purported to overrule its decision in *Bill Strong Enterprises v. Shannon*. The government refused to continue the hearings with the ASBCA concerning the value of the consultant fees that should be reimbursed to Bill Strong Enterprises and filed motions to dismiss the contractor's claim based on *Reflectone*. Despite the footnote and the government's refusal to continue negotiations with Bill Strong Enterprises, the case, with its overarching focus on recoverability of claim preparation costs, may be alive and well. Several cases subsequent to both *Reflectone* and *Bill Strong Enterprises* have adhered to the latter's inquiry into the purpose for which a contractor incurred legal and other consulting costs. The presumptions adopted are based on the "bright line" of when a claim is deemed submitted, but are rebuttable with evidence establishing that the contractor's purpose in incurring the consulting costs was to administer or perform the contract.[91]

The *Bill Strong Enterprises* position for the recovery of claim administration costs also appears to have been adopted by the DCAA in a recently issued

---

[90] 60 F.3d 1572 (Fed. Cir. 1995).

[91] See Betancourt & Gonzales, S.E., DOTCAB Nos. 2785, 2789, 2799, 96-1 BCA (CCH) ¶ 28,033 at 139,985 (although post-claim consultant costs may be reimbursable, professional fees incurred after negotiations initially broke down, after an impasse, were not allowable because they were related to preparation and filing claim, despite statement that submission sought negotiations, upon an objective analysis of the purpose of the costs); Beckman Constr. Co., ASBCA No. 48,141, 96-1 BCA (CCH) ¶ 28,205 (1996) (consultant services to quantify and present comprehensive impact analysis to facilitate negotiated settlement and discussions for equitable resolution were not sufficient to provide benefit to government and make consultant costs part of contract administration); Pearl Properties, HUDBCA No. 95-C-118-C4, 96-1 BCA (CCH) ¶ 28,219 (1996) (legal and accounting costs incurred in connection with routine submission, prior to certified close-out claim, permitted because incurred to provide contracting officer additional information and clarification of legal basis for request); Southwest Marine, Inc., DOTCAB No. 1665, 96-1 BCA (CCH) ¶ 28,168 (1996) (contractor's request for equitable adjustment was claim under Contract Disputes Act; recovery of preparation costs denied because incurred prior to submission of request and not incidental to contract administration or performance, but incident to prosecution of claim).

memorandum to its regional directors providing guidance on *Reflectone*.[92] The revised DCAA *Contract Audit Manual*'s Chapter 12, "Terminations, Delay/Disruption and Claims," included changes concerning recoverability of legal costs on claims. Although there is a presumption that costs incurred prior to filing a Contract Disputes Act claim are allowable prosecution costs, the auditor is required to determine in fact that the costs do not relate to the costs for filing a Disputes Act claim. Claim prosecution costs incurred after submission of the claim to the contracting officer are not allowable. The manual encourages preparation of a chronology of events by the auditor to help determine allowability of consultant costs.[93]

In *Plano Builders Corp. v. United States*,[94] the U.S. Court of Federal Claims decided that consultant costs incurred in preparing a claim for presentation to the contracting office are part of the prosecution of the claim and cannot be recovered. The contractor argued that under *Bill Strong Enterprises,* new fees were incurred as part of contract administration and not in connection with the prosecution of a claim. The *Bill Strong Enterprises* court concluded that because neither the initial nor the revised claim was a valid CDA claim because no existing dispute existed, the consultant's fees were incurred as part of the contract administration, not claim prosecution, and were recoverable. The *Plano* court determined that the definition of a claim in *Bill Strong Enterprises* was implicitly modified by *Reflectone*. In *Reflectone*, the court held that a valid CDA claim existed as soon as the contractor submitted a written demand seeking the payment of money regardless of whether there was an existing dispute between the parties. In *Plano*, the court decided that a consultant's fees for the resubmitted claims were costs incurred in connection with the prosecution of claims, and any analyses or negotiations supporting or forming the claim were parts of the entire claim prosecution process regardless of whether the fees were incurred before the claim was submitted to the contracting officer. The function, and not the timing, of the consultant's work determined whether it was a part of the prosecution process.

The point at which a contractor loses its ability to recover its consultant fees should not be the time at which the contractor submits its claim to the contracting officer. A contractor does not prosecute its claim against the government, for the purpose of FAR,[95] until the contracting officer renders its final decision. The demarcation line should be at the contracting officer's final decision. Costs related to preparation and presentation of the claim incurred prior to the contracting officer's decision should be presumptively allowable. However, costs should be allowed regardless of when they are incurred if there is a connection between the costs and the contract purpose, such as contributing to a negotiated resolution of the claim, and the costs are reasonable and allocable. Moreover, disqualifying

---

[92] *See DCAA Issues Guidance on Reflectone Definition of Claim and Allowability of Costs*, 65 Fed. Cont. Rep. 239 (Mar. 1996).

[93] *DCAA Issues Changes to Its Audit Manual*, 4 GCA Report 2 (No. 2, Mar.-Apr. 1998).

[94] 40 Fed. Cl. 635 (1998).

[95] FAR 31.205-47(f)(1).

requests for equitable adjustments as claims should be unnecessary if the demarcation line lies at the contracting officer's final decision and the emphasis is on "why the costs were incurred and not when."[96]

The government's and contractor's interests are best served if the demarcation line for the presumption of allowability is at the point when the contracting officer renders an adverse final decision. Not only would this allow for a brighter-line test as to when a claim is being prosecuted, but the government's policy to resolve controversies at the lowest level would also be served. Although the FAR states that these controversies should be resolved prior to the submission of a claim, the government policy is equally furthered as long as the controversy is resolved without litigation. A contractor can litigate only if the contracting officer renders an adverse decision.[97]

[I] Interest

The cost principles in the FAR are direct and precise: "Interest on borrowings (however represented) . . . are unallowable."[98] Despite earlier rulings by boards and courts interpreting federal contracts, the mandatory application of the cost principles in FAR 31.2 to construction precludes the payment in current change order pricing.

Contractors should be alert, however, to the allowability of facilities capital cost of money.[99] This cost is "an imputed cost determined by applying a cost-of-money rate to facilities capital employed in contract performance." The regulation explicitly states that the "resulting cost of money is not a form of interest on borrowings." The calculation of this "cost," as set forth in the FAR, is complex, and there are certain restrictions on allowability spelled out in the FAR.

On nonfederal projects, the allowability of interest, either as an element of cost in a change or as a statutory pre- or post-judgment interest, needs to be examined on a state-by-state basis in pricing a change. In some instances, the interest, unallowable as a direct cost, can be included as an element of profit.

With the passage of the Contract Disputes Act of 1978, the federal government agreed to pay interest on a claim against the government from the date the contracting officer received the claim until the date of payment.[100] Considerable litigation has occurred recently over exactly what constitutes a "claim" for these purposes, but this interest should certainly be considered as part of an equitable adjustment if the change order becomes a claim.

---

[96] E. Farber, *The Allowability of Costs Incurred in the Preparation of Request for Equitable Adjustments After Reflectone*, 25 Pub. Cont. L.J. 781, 800 (No. 4, Summer 1996).

[97] Farber at 801-02 (citing FAR 33.204).

[98] FAR 31.205-20.

[99] *See* FAR 31.205-10.

[100] 41 U.S.C. § 611 (1988).

TABLE OF CASES

References are to sections.

A

B

C

25 A.D.2d 707-08 (N.Y. App. Div. 1965), 15.02[A][5]
224 N.E.2d 866 (N.Y. 1967), 15.02[A][5], 15.02[A][6]
245 N.E.2d 800 (N.Y. 1969), 15.02[A][5]
Dermott v. Jones, 7.02[D][1]
Design & Prods., Inc. v. United States
   18 Cl. Ct. 168 (1989), 3.06[B]
   21 Cl. Ct. 145 (1990), 3.06[B]
DeSombre v. Bichel, 9.05
D.E.W., Inc. & D.E. Wurzbach, A Joint Venture
   ASBCA No. 50,796, 98-2 BCA (CCH) ¶ 29,385 (1998), 12.02[D][1][e]
   ASBCA No. 50,796, 2000-2 BCA (CCH) ¶ 31,104 (2000), 12.02[D][1][c]
D.F.K. Enters., Inc. v. United States, 2.04[D][3][a]
Diagle v. Donald M. Clement Contractor, Inc., 13.04[A]
Diamond B. Constr. Co. v. City of Plaquemine, 3.03[A]
Dick Corp. v. State Pub. Sch. Bldg. Auth., 3.05[A], 4.07
Dickerson Florida, Inc. v. McPeek, 14.09[B][1]
Dick v. Geiger, 9.05[B]
Diedrich v. Northern Illinois Publ'g Co., 5.03[A][1][b]
Dillingham NA, Inc. v. United States, 6.01[A][2][d]
Dillon v. United States, 4.06[C]
District of Columbia et al. v. Kora & Williams Corp., 12.03[A][6][b]
District of Columbia v. Organization for Envtl. Growth, Inc., 12.02[A], 12.02[B][2],
   12.02[C][2]
D.K. Meyer Corp. v. Breveo, 4.04
D.L. Muns Eng'g & Bldg. Contractors, 9.08[A]
Dodge v. Harbor Boat Bldg. Co., 11.06[A]
Donald B. Murphy Contractors, Inc. v. State, 15.04[B][3]
Donald R. Stewart Assocs., 9.08[D]
Dondevold v. Blaine Sch. Dist. No. 503, 4.01
D'Onofrio Bros. Constr. Corp. v. New York City Bd. of Educ., 3.05[B]
Dougherty Overseas, Inc., 4.06[C]
Douglas Northwest, Inc. v. Bill O'Brien & Sons Constr., Inc., 7.03[B][1]
Drillmation Co., 4.06[C]
Ducote v. Arnold, 9.05
Dudley v. St. Regis Corp., 10.02
Duncan v. Cannon, 2.02
Dusenka v. Dusenka, 2.04

E

E. Paul Kovacs & Co. v. Alpert, 3.03[B]
Eastern Air Lines, Inc. v. Gulf Oil Corp., 10.02
Eastern Air Lines, Inc. v. McDonnell Douglas Corp., 10.02, 10.03[B]
Eastman Kodak Co. v. Southern Photo Co., 18.04
East West Research, Inc., 8.06
E.C. Ernst, Inc. v. Koppers Co., 11.06[C]
Edward Hines Lumber Co., 3.04[A]
Edward L. Bledsoe, 9.04[A][2]
Edward M. Crough, Inc. v. Department of Gen. Servs. of the Dist. of Columbia, 7.02[C][2]
Edward R. Marden Corp., 13.03[B]
Edward R. Marden Corp. v. United States
   442 F.2d 364, 369-70, 194 Ct. Cl. 799 (1971), 9.06, 11.01, 11.04[A]
   803 F.2d 701, 705 (Fed. Cir. 1986), 8.02, 8.05[B]

F

First Sav. & Trust Co. v. Milwaukee County, 9.05[A]
Fischbach & Moore Int'l Corp., 4.06, 4.06[B]
Fisher Skylights, Inc. v. CFC Constr. Ltd. P'ship, 16.11
Fizzell v. Meeker, 5.03[B][3]
Fleisher Eng'g & Constr. Co. v. United States ex rel. Hallenbeck, 13.04[E]
Fleming v. United States, 6.02[A][6]
Fletcher v. Laguna Vista Corp., 3.06[B]
Fley-Y-Plan Indus., Inc., 18.05[G]
Flinchbaugh Prod. Corp., 3.04[D]
Flooring Sys. v. Staat Constr. Co., 4.04
Flores Drilling & Pump Co., 7.05[A]
Florida Power & Light Co. v. Westinghouse Elec. Corp., 10.03[B]
Foster Constr. C.A. & Williams Bros. Co. v. United States, 2.04[D][3][a], 7.02[D][1],
    10.02, 10.03[B]
Foster Constr. Co., 18.05[A], 18.05[B]
Foster Wheeler Corp. v. United States, 10.03[C]
Foundation Co. v. State, 15.02[A][5]
Foundation Int'l Inc. v. E.T. Ige Constr., Inc., 2.04[D][4][b]
Fox v. Mountain W. Elec., Inc., 4.06
Frank Coluccio Constr. Co. v. City of Springfield, 14.10[B]
Franklin E. Penny Co. v. United States, 7.02[B][1]
Franklin Pavkov Constr. Co. v. Ultra Roof, Inc., 9.04[A][1]
Frank Sullivan Co. v. Midwest Sheet Metal Works, 3.03[B], 3.06[B]
Frederick Snare Corp. v. Maine-New Hampshire Interstate Bridge Auth., 7.02[D][1],
    7.05[A]
Freeman-Darling, Inc., 18.05[G]
Fritz-Rumer-Cooke Co. v. United States, 9.04[A][1]
Froeschle Sons, Inc. v. United States, 8.02, 8.05[B]
Frontier-Kemper Constructors, Inc. v. American Rock Salt Co., 7.03[B][3]
Fru-Con Constr. Corp. v. United States, 2.04[D][1], 2.04[D][3], 2.04[D][3][d], 2.04[D][5]
Fruehauf Corp., 18.05[G]
Fruehauf Corp. v. United States, 10.03[B]
Fruin-Colnon Corp. v. Niagara Frontier Transp. Auth., 7.01[A]
Fruin-Colnon Corp. v. United States, 8.05[B]
Fuller Co. v. Brown Minneapolis Tank & Fabricating Co., 11.06[C]
F.W. Sims, Inc. v. Federal Ins. Co., 16.11

G

Gainesville-Alachua County Reg'l Airport Auth. v. R. Hyden Constr., Inc., 5.02[B],
    9.05[B]
Galloway Corp. v. S.B. Ballard Constr. Co., 14.09[B][1]
Gasparini Excavating Co. v. Pennsylvania Turnpike Comm'n, 9.04[A][1]
General Contracting & Constr. Co. v. United States, 11.03, 11.04[A]
General Dynamics Corp. v. United States, 15.04[B][3], 16.06
General Federal Constr., Inc. v. D.R. Thomas, Inc., 16.11
General Motors Corp. v. Northrop Corp., 10.03[D]
General Ship Corp. v. United States, 7.02[C][2]
George F. Marshall & Gordon F. Blackwell, 4.07
George Hyman Constr. Co., 15.04[B][2]
George Sollitt Constr. Co. v. United States, 9.05
German v. United States, 6.02[A][3]
Gillet & Assoc., 3.03[A]

H

H.L.C. & Assocs., 13.03[E]

H&M Moving, Inc. v. United States, 7.02[F][2]

Hoel-Steffen Constr. Co. v. United States, 13.03[A], 13.03[C]

Hoffman v. United States, 9.04[A][1]

Hol-Gar Mfg. Corp. v. United States, 4.06, 10.03[A], 10.03[C]

Holland v. Tandem Computers, Inc., 2.06[B][1]

Hollerbach v. United States, 7.02[D][1], 7.03[A][2]

Holloway Constr. Co. and Holloway Sand & Gravel Co., 13.03[B]

Holmer v. General Dynamics Corp., 6.02[A][1]

Home Indemnity v. United R.R. Co., 16.09

Horton Indus., Inc. v. Village of Moweaqua, 7.04[B], 9.06

Housing Auth. of Texarkana v. E.W. Johnson Constr. Co.
    264 Ark. 523 (1978), 11.06[B]
    573 S.W.2d 316 (1978), 2.06[B][2]

Howard Contracting, Inc. v. G.A. MacDonald Constr. Co., 9.04[A][1]

Howard J. White, Inc. v. Varian Assocs., 2.04[C]

HPI/GSA-3C, LLC v. Perry, 7.02[F][2]

HRE, Inc. v. United States, 8.02

H&S Oil Co., 4.06[C]

H&S Torrington Assocs. v. Lutz Eng'g Co., 13.06[B][2]

H.T.C. Corp. v. Olds, 4.04, 11.01, 11.04[A], 11.05[A], 11.06[C]

Huffines v. Swor Sand & Gravel Co., 10.02

Hughes v. United States, 6.02[A][1]

Hunydee v. United States, 14.10[E]

Hurd v. Wildman, Harrold, Allen & Dixon, 5.03[B][3]

Husar Indus., Inc. v. A.L. Huber & Sons, 9.05

Hutchinson v. Cullum, 11.06[C]

Hydromar Corp. of Delaware & E. Seaboard Pile Driving, Inc., JV v. United States,
    7.04[B]

I

Iannuccillo v. Material Sand & Stone Corp., 10.03[D]

Idaho Power Co. v. Cogeneration, Inc., 1.08

Ideker, Inc., 12.02[D][1][a]

ILM Sys., Inc. v. Suffolk Constr. Co., 9.05[A], 9.05[B]

Indiana & Michigan Elec. Co. v. Terre Haute Indus., 9.04[A][1]

Industrial Research Assocs., Inc.
    DCAB No. WB-5, 71-1 BCA (CCH) ¶ 8680, 13 Gov't Cont. Rep. (CCH) ¶ 405 (1971),
        15.02[E][1]
    DCAB No. WB-5, 68-1 BCA (CCH) ¶ 7069 at 32,686 (1968), 4.06

Inland-Ryerson Constr. Prods. Co. v. Brazier Constr. Co., 16.09

INTASA, Inc., 3.07

Intermountain Rural Elec. Ass'n v. Colorado Cent. Power Co., 18.01

International Fabricators, Inc. v. Losco Group, Inc., 12.03[B][1]

International Hardwood Co., 3.04[D]

Interstate Contracting Corp. v. City of Dallas, Tex., 14.10[A], 14.10[B]

Interstate Gen. Gov't Contractors, Inc. v. Stone, 8.02, 8.04, 8.05

Interstate Gen. Gov't Contractors, Inc. v. West, 15.02[E][1]

Irwin & Leighton v. United States, 6.01[A][2]

Iversen Constr. Co., 4.06[B]

I.W. Matteson, Inc. v. United States, 10.02

Iwen v. U.S. W. Direct, 14.09[A][4]

J

K

L

V

W

INDEX

References are to sections.

T

Termination for convenience, 12.02
  bad faith, 12.02[C][2]
  contract clauses, 2.08, 12.02
    federal clause, 12.02[C][1][b]
    standard form clause, 12.02[C][1][a]
  costs
    federal principles, 12.02[B][1][a]
    claims preparation expenses,
      12.02[B][1][f]
    completed work, costs of,
      12.02[B][1][c]
    fair compensation, 12.02[B][1][a]
    lost labor productivity,
      12.02[B][1][d]
    pre-award costs, 12.02[B][1][b]
    profits, 12.02[B][1][e]
    settlement expenses,
      12.02[B][1][f]
    standard form clauses,
      12.02[B][1][a]
    local principles, 12.02[B][2]
    state principles, 12.02[B][2]
    subcontractor costs, 12.02[B][3]
  deductive changes, *versus*, 12.02[B]
  default termination, change of,
    12.03[A][4]
  exercising the election to terminate
    administrative procedure,
      12.02[C][1]
    bad faith, 12.02[C][2]
  subcontractor costs, 12.02[B][3]
Termination for default
  costs, recovery of
    party who is improperly terminated,
      12.03[C][2]
    party who terminates
      additional performance costs,
        12.03[C][1][a]
      terminated contractor's set-offs,
        12.03[C][1][b]
  "cure" period, 12.03[A][2]
  improper default termination,
    12.03[A][4]
  notice of termination, 12.03[A][2]
  progress of work untimely
    assurance of timely completion,
      12.03[B][1]
    excusable delay, consideration of,
      12.03[B][2]

  standard contract clauses,
    12.03[A][1]
  subcontractor's contract, effect on,
    12.03[A][5]
  termination for convenience, change
    to, 12.03[A][4]
  third-party certification, 12.03[A][3]
  waiver of right to terminate
    defective work, 12.03[A][6][a]
    interference, by, 12.03[A][6][c]
    timely performance, waiver of,
      12.03[A][6][b]
Termination of contract
  contract clauses, 12.01
    termination for default,
      12.03[A][1]
    termination-for-convenience
      clauses, 2.08, 12.02
      federal clause, 12.02[C][1][b]
      standard form clause,
        12.02[C][1][a]
  convenience termination. *See*
    Termination for convenience
  default termination. *See* Termination
    for default
Time. *See* Contract sum/time

U

Unexpected events, 1.02[C]
Unit pricing. *See* Pricing change orders

V

Variation-in-quantities clauses, 15.02[B]

W

Waiver
  default termination, right of,
    12.03[A][6]
  notice(s), 13.04[B]
  release contained in executed change
    order, challenging, 5.03[B][5]
Warranties. *See* Implied warranties
Whistleblower protection
  False Claims Act. *See* Qui tam actions
    under False Claims Act